IAA Reports, No. 34/1

MW00683217

EXCAVATIONS AT KADESH BARNEA (TELL EL-QUDEIRAT) 1976–1982

PART 1

TEXT

RUDOLPH COHEN AND HANNAH BERNICK-GREENBERG

With contributions by

Daniella E. Bar-Yosef Mayer, Israel Carmi, Michal Druk, Iris Eldar-Nir, Avivit Gera, Mordechai Haiman, Dalia Hakker-Orion, Yshayahu Lender, Stefan Münger, Dov Nahlieli, Dror Segal, Orit Shamir and Pnina Shor

ISRAEL ANTIQUITIES AUTHORITY
JERUSALEM 2007

IAA Reports
Publications of the Israel Antiquities Authority

Editor-in-Chief: Zvi Gal

Series Editor: Ann Roshwalb Hurowitz

Volume Editor: Ayelet Gilboa

Front Cover: Tel Kadesh Barnea, looking north; a group of Negebite Ware vessels (photographer, N. Sneh)
Back Cover: Wadi el-Qudeirat, looking west; a group of pottery vessels (left to right): Edomite, Cypro-Phoenician, Midianite and Black-Painted Wares (photographer, N. Sneh)

Typesetting, Layout and Production: Margalit Hayosh, Ann Abuhav, Hagar Maimon
Cover Design: Margalit Hayosh
Illustrations: Natalia Zak, Elizabeth Belashov, Irina Berin
Printing: Keterpress Enterprises, Jerusalem

In Memoriam

Dr. Rudolph Cohen

Southern District Archaeologist, 1966–1989
Deputy Director, Israel Antiquities Authority, 1989–1999

CONTENTS

PART 1: TEXT

PART 2: PLATES, PLANS AND SECTONS

PLATES

CHAPTER 11: THE CERAMIC ASSEMBLAGES AND THE WHEEL-MADE POTTERY TYPOLOGY

CHAPTER 12: THE NEGEBITE WARE TYPOLOGY

CHAPTER 13: THE SMALL FINDS

PLANS

SECTIONS

ABBREVIATIONS

AASOR	Annual of the American Schools of Oriental Research
ADAJ	*Annual of the Department of Antiquities of Jordan*
'Atiqot (ES)	English Series
'Atiqot (HS)	Hebrew Series
BA	*Biblical Archaeologist*
BAR	*Biblical Archaeology Review*
BAR Int. S.	BAR International Series
BASOR	*Bulletin of the American Schools of Oriental Research*
BIES	*Bulletin of the Israel Exploration Society*
BN	*Biblische Notizen*
BSAE	Publications of the Egyptian Research Account and British School of Archaeology in Egypt
ESI	*Excavations and Surveys in Israel*
HA	*Hadashot Arkheologiyot* (Hebrew)
HUCA	*Annual of the Hebrew Union College Biblical and Archaeological School in Jerusalem*
IEJ	*Israel Exploration Journal*
JAS	*Journal of Archaeological Science*
JBL	*Journal of Biblical Literature*
JFA	*Journal of Field Archaeology*
JNES	*Journal of Near Eastern Studies*
MSSMNIA	Monograph Series of the Sonia and Marco Nadler Institute of Archaeology, Tel Aviv University
NEAEHL	E. Stern and A. Lewinson-Gilboa eds. *New Encyclopedia of Archaeological Excavations in the Holy Land.* Jerusalem 1993
OBO	Orbis Biblicus et Orientalis
OBO SA	Orbis Biblicus et Orientalis Series Archaeologica
OIP	Oriental Institute Publications
PEFA	*Palestine Exploration Fund Annual*
PEFQSt	*Palestine Exploration Fund Quarterly Statement*
QDAP	*Quarterly of the Department of Antiquities of Palestine*
RB	*Revue Biblique*
ZDPF	*Zeitschrift des Deutschen Palästina-Vereins*

FOREWORD

This report summarizes the Kadesh Barnea (Tell el-Qudeirat) excavations, conducted under Rudolph Cohen's directorship between 1976 and 1982, on behalf of the Israel Department of Antiquities (now the Israel Antiquities Authority). Preliminary general overviews and presentations of the main discoveries have been published in Hebrew (primarily Cohen 1976b, 1981b, 1982, 1983a, 1983b), in English (Cohen 1981a, 1983b), and in French (Cohen 1985).

THE EXPEDITION

Due to the site's remote location, logistics were complex, and most excavation seasons lasted for a few weeks of concentrated work only, with many excavators (staff and volunteers). A tent camp was erected north of the tell, administered by Nahshon Sneh and Yigal Israel, ensuring reasonable living conditions for the personnel. Sneh, whose main task was that of the expedition's photographer, was in attendance during all the excavation seasons.

Most of the work was conducted during the winter, and we worked for very long hours. Pottery washing and registration were carried out in camp under the supervision of Lori Lender and Nellie Steltzer, but orderly pottery sorting was not conducted on site; all the material, including all ceramics, was packed and transferred to Jerusalem for restoration. This eventually turned out to be advantageous. It enabled us, for example, to assess the relative amount of Negebite vs. wheel-made wares, and it was possible, after preliminary processing, to re-examine the material at leisure, discern previously unnoticed inscriptions, impressions on pottery, etc.

The surveyors' team was headed by the late Michael Feist and also included Israel Vatkin, Wolf Shleicher and Valentin Shorr. Aharon van Lepen and Benny Peleg assisted voluntarily in recording elevations in the field during most of the seasons.

Geologist Prof. Hendrik Bruins accompanied the excavations for a number of seasons and studied the morphology of the site and its environs. His conclusions were summarized in his doctoral dissertation (Bruins 1986).

Numerous volunteers, from Israel and from abroad, took part in the dig, as did students of the Denmark High School in Jerusalem, under the supervision of Shulamit Cohen.

Staff Members

General

Director:	Rudolph Cohen
Assistant director:	Pnina Shor
Chief surveyor:	Michael Feist
Assistant surveyors:	Igor Palepa, Benny Peleg, Wolf Shleicher, Valentin Shorr, Aharon van Lepen, Israel Vatkin
Photographer:	Nahshon Sneh
Registration:	Sari Arad, Yehudit Ben-Michael, Rachel Graf, Lori Lender, Nellie Steltzer
Camp directors:	Yigal Israel (1981–1982), Nahshon Sneh
Assistants to camp directors:	Amiram Arbeli, Avi Arbeli, Gideon Avni, Yair Kamaisky, Stella Varnik
Kitchen:	Pnina Ben Hanania, Shula Hayosh, Malka Kraus, Stella Varnik

Field Supervisors and Assistants:

Area A1. Supervisor: Rudolph Cohen; assistants: Uzi Avner, Esther Bezem, Alon De Groot, Dani Dothan, Carl Ebert, Yaakov Majar, Dov Nahlieli, Pnina Shor, Orli Venezia.

Area A2. Supervisor: Rudolph Cohen; assistants: Esther Bezem, Alon De Groot, Carl Ebert, Mordechai Haiman, Yshayahu Lender, Dov Nahlieli, Pnina Shor

Area B. Supervisor: Mordechai Haiman

Area C. Supervisors: Pnina Shor, Avivit Gera; assistants: Alon De Groot, Carl Ebert, Dov Nahlieli, Ben Steltzer.

Area D. Supervisor: Hannah Bernick-Greenberg; assistant: Raphael Greenberg.

Area E. Supervisors: Iris Eldar-Nir, Erel Gilboa, Yshayahu Lender, Dov Nahlieli.

Area F. Supervisor: Yshayahu Lender; assistant: Gideon Avni.

Area G. Supervisors: Yshayahu Lender, Ben Steltzer.

Area H. Supervisor: Dov Nahlieli; assistant: Ornit Ilan

Members of the 'Ein el-Qudeirat and 'Ein Qadis Survey

Survey Team: Gideon Avni, Roy Dwimes, Sima Goldschmidt, Malka Kraus, Yizhar Noyman, Haya Schwartz, Yaron Uzan.

Surveyors: Sue Dave, Michael Gibbons, Alexander Ichilov, Ben Steltzer, Nellie Steltzer, Alexander Yafeh.

Field Work and Registration

Grid, Elevations, Numbering of Loci, Walls and Baskets

A grid of 5 × 5 m squares, oriented to the north, was established at the beginning of the excavation over the entire fortress area. Initially, the schematic plan of the upper fortress (Stratum 2), drafted by Immanuel Dunayevsky and Asher Hiram, and published by Moshe Dothan (1965), was used as a rough estimate of the fortresses' outlines. Subsequently, the lines of the walls were redrawn and the original sketch corrected.

As a rule, 1 m wide balks were left between excavation units. However, in many cases these were eventually removed so as not to obscure architectural elements, especially when dug into deeper levels. Some of the balk sections were drawn and most of these section drawings are presented in this report (see Part 2).

The elevation of the site as indicated on topographical maps of the region is 385 m asl. The elevations marked on the plans do not indicate absolute levels. All of them were measured from a benchmark established on the fortification wall of the Stratum 2 fortress during Dothan's excavation at the site in 1965; this measurement has since been lost. Thus, at present, absolute levels cannot be reconstructed precisely, unless the extant remains of the fortress are re-surveyed, a task that we could not undertake.

During the first four seasons, locus and basket numbers for the entire excavation were allotted from one 'bank'. From the fifth season and on, after excavation areas have been defined, each area was assigned a separate 'bank' of numbers (Appendix 2).

Excavation Strategy

Excavation was conducted manually, and selected contexts (mainly floor deposits) were sifted. The cistern (in Area D) was only partially uncovered and its western half, about 2 m wide, was left intact. The earthen glacis surrounding the rectangular fortresses was first excavated manually, but in the final seasons earth was bulldozed, mainly in search of the fortresses' gates. The northwestern external side of the fortresses, however, has not been excavated, and the glacis there remains untouched. On the east soundings were dug to uncover the retaining walls and the moat.

The debris and stones removed from the excavation were piled mainly in the northern part of the site to protect this area, which is today worked by the Beduin, and to prevent the blockage of Wadi el-Qudeirat, which runs south of the fortress. The stones were laid out and marked in a way that will not cause confusion between them and the actual ancient architectural elements. The stones that lined the four large silos in Area F were dismantled and later re-assembled in the exhibition 'Man through the Ages' at the Hecht Museum in Haifa in 1981, supervised by Rivka Gonen.

The huge mass of soil and debris that had to be removed caused severe logistical problems. This, and our efforts to prevent the undermining of wall foundations, led to the decision to backfill the casemates of Stratum 2 to a height of 0.5 to 1.0 m above their floor levels. Similarly, some of the deeper excavation units, mainly in the southeastern part of the courtyard, were backfilled. We placed objects of obvious modern date at the bottom of these fills.

PROCESSING AND THE PREPARATION OF THE SITE REPORT

Until 1990, processing of the material for publication was coordinated by Pnina Shor, and under her supervision most of the drawings, photographs, and descriptions of ceramics and other 'small finds' were completed. She was assisted by Avivit Gera, Rika

Itzhaki, Mimi Lavi, Leea Puraneh-Porat and Dalit Regev (who were then also processing the material from other sites in the Negev), and by Hannah Bernick-Greenberg and Michal Druk, who concentrated on the Kadesh Barnea finds alone. Subsequently, between 1990 and 1998, Hannah Bernick-Greenberg coordinated publication work; during this time the chapters on the stratigraphy/architecture and the pottery were written. Itzhaki assisted with the documentation of the finds prior to their transfer to Egypt in December 1994.

Michael Feist, the chief surveyor of the site during excavation, also prepared the many plans for publication. For many years, he invested intensive work in summarizing the stratigraphy, but to our great sorrow he passed away in September 1996 and did not see his work published. The plans presented in this report were redrawn by Valentin Shor, based on those prepared by Feist, and prepared for final publication by Natalia Zak.

Restoration of the pottery was initially (1976–1978) carried out by Nira Kopilov, Freida Raskin and Miriam Shemayin, and later by Sari Arad and Olga Shorr. Artifacts were drawn over the years by Michal Ben-Gal, Rachel Graf, Marina Keller, Tanya Kornfeld and Lori Lender. The bones (Chapter 19) were drawn by Graf. The pottery from the survey was drawn by Graf and Lender and the flint artifacts by Druk. Before the finds were transferred to Egypt (see below) we re-checked all the drawings. Some items indeed had to be redrawn, and in this we were greatly assisted by Graf and Keller. The finds were photographed in the laboratories of the Department of Antiquities by Clara Amit and Tsila Sagiv. The plates of illustrations (line drawings) were prepared by Carmen Hersch.

In 1994, Avital Zintroblat recorded the relative quantities of wheel-made vs. Negebite ceramic wares. Her database is stored in the IAA archives. In addition, the Kadesh Barnea file in those archives contains many photographs, illustrations of finds and other records that we decided not to include in this publication.

EXHIBITIONS AND THE CURRENT STORAGE OF FINDS

In 1982, an exhibition of Kadesh Barnea finds was held at the Rockefeller Museum, Jerusalem and a catalogue was prepared by the Israel Museum (Cohen 1983c). This exhibit was then moved to the Be'er Sheva' Museum, where it remained until the late 1980s.

In 1994 all the portable finds unearthed during the excavations were transferred to Egypt, following the peace treaty between Israel and Egypt.

THE PUBLICATION

Organization of the Publication

This volume is divided into two parts. Part 1 contains the text, schematic plans, photographs and selected line drawings. Part 2 contains the top plans, sections and the plates of the line drawings of the pottery and major small finds. Chapter 1, as well as presenting the introduction to the site, also includes the summary that usually appears at the end of a site report, i.e., an overview of the main architectural, artifactual, chronological and other aspects of the Kadesh Barnea sequence. The stratigraphy/architecture chapters (Chapters 2–10) are arranged in the following order: Chapter 2 begins the exposition with the area dubbed 'A2', the fortifications of the Strata 3–2 fortresses (and some elements above them); then Chapters 3–6, the areas inside the fortification, roughly from west to east; and finally, Chapters 7–10, the areas outside these fortifications, counter-clockwise, starting on the east. Chapters 11–20 deal with the various artifacts and ecofacts, and Chapter 21 presents the archaeological survey conducted in conjunction with the excavations.

The illustrations are arranged as follows (with some exceptions): photographs (of stratigraphy/architecture and finds), labeled 'Figures', are incorporated in the text, in Part 1. The photographs of the artifacts and other finds are generally not to scale, unless so indicated, and their dimensions may be deduced from their line drawings. The line drawings of pottery and other small finds (Chapters 11–13) are presented as 'Plates' and appear in Part 2. The line drawings of Chapters 14–19 and 21 are incorporated into their respective chapters in Part 1.

Two types of plans appear in this publication. Schematic plans, of Strata 4, 3 and 2, are incorporated into Chapter 1 in Part 1. The detailed top plans and sections appear in Part 2, where Plans 1 and 2 are bound into the volume, and Plans 3–9 can be found in the pocket at its back. Though the architecture is discussed by area (Chapters 2–10), the plans and sections were not similarly divided and are numbered sequentially (i.e., Plan 1 to Plan 9, and Section 1-1 to Section 28-28), as they relate to the entire site.

Site Name

A short note is in order here regarding the spelling of the site's biblical identification as employed here—Kadesh Barnea. This is neither the biblical spelling (the commonest one in English versions of the Bible is 'Kadesh-barnea'), nor is it a modern transliteration of the Hebrew. As the name figures prominently in the report, we opted for a simple form, which is also that employed in most preliminary reports of the excavation, as well as in major archaeological textbooks. For this reason also, we chose to employ throughout the text the simpler (and short) conventional biblical identification of the site, and not its Arab name.

ACKNOWLEDGEMENTS

The late Prof. Benjamin Mazar, a friend and mentor, continuously assisted us in our efforts to understand the Kadesh Barnea finds and their implications. He displayed constant interest in our work and visited the site regularly during the ten seasons of excavations. For this support we shall ever remain grateful.

Prof. Ruth Amiran, who passed away while this report was being prepared for publication, was ever willing to comment on our pottery; Prof. Itzhaq Beit-Arieh examined the Edomite material, in particular the Edomite cooking pots; and Alon De Groot put at our disposal the unpublished late Iron Age and Persian-period pottery assemblages from the City of David, and advised us on dating the Stratum 3 assemblage.

We acknowledge with gratitude the financial and logistical assistance we received during the excavation from the Staff Officer of Archaeology in Sinai. Further financial assistance was provided by the Reuven and Edith Hecht Foundation. Most of the preparation of the material for publication was carried out under the auspices of the IAA as part of 'Past Publication Debts' project and was partially financed by the government of Israel in accordance with the 1954 Hague Convention and the 1979 peace treaty with Egypt, as a result of which, in December 1994, all the finds were handed over to the Egyptian Supreme Council of Antiquities. The survey finds were partially processed with the aid of a research grant from the Sinai Research Foundation in 1987.

Special thanks are due to the volunteers who joined us for many seasons; it is they who made this excavation possible. To all who were involved in preparing this report and to the many who stood by us throughout this long period, we wish to express our gratitude, for without their help we would not have overcome.

We would also like to thank Shelly Sadeh, who translated the manuscript from Hebrew, and the editorial staff of the IAA, especially Ayelet Gilboa, whose dogged and excellent work made this publication possible. During the editing process, especially in its final stages, we were greatly assisted by the following people: As part of the editorial process, Ben Gordon reviewed all the stratigraphic material. Nehama Marguelis and Edna Oxman helped in editing tables and catalogues in the various chapters and in cross-checking the stratigraphy of finds vs. the locus list, and Natalia Zak consulted us on the format of the plans. Lori Lender edited Chapter 21 and assisted with the editing of the reference list. We wholeheartedly thank them all.

* * *

Editor's Note

To our deepest regret, while this report was being prepared for publication, Rudolph Cohen fell ill and could not be consulted. Consequently, he did not have the opportunity to introduce any changes he might have felt necessary, to update the text, or to address current relevant debates. He passed away on December 13, 2006.

This situation created numerous dilemmas during the editing process, the major question being whether to leave his text untouched, or to update it, especially by referring to new site reports and other publications. We do not know, for example, what his stance would have been regarding the current debate on the absolute chronology of the early Iron Age in Israel, in which the Kadesh Barnea sequence holds center stage. We decided to introduce as few changes and updates as possible, in order to honor his intentions.

Hannah Bernick-Greenberg and I would like to devote these two volumes to the director of this outstanding, indeed, by now, nearly mythological, excavation.

Ayelet Gilboa
Volume Editor
December, 2007

CHAPTER 1

INTRODUCTION

THE SITE AND ITS SETTING

Tell el-Qudeirat (map ref. 0949/0064; 385 m asl), identified with biblical Kadesh Barnea, is situated in an oasis in the eastern part of the northern Sinai desert, southeast of the Egyptian village of Quseima, about 35 km west of the town of Mizpe Ramon in Israel (Fig. 1.1). The region is bordered on the east by the Negev Highlands. On the west, Wadi el-Qudeirat, in

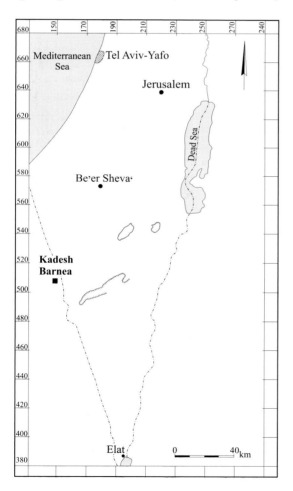

Fig. 1.1. Location map.

which the site is located, drains into the drainage basin of Wadi el-'Arish.

The tell is situated on the northern bank of Wadi el-Qudeirat at an elevation of 385 m asl (Figs. 1.2–1.4). North of the tell, the mountainous ridge of Jebel el-Qudeirat rises to a height of 500 m asl, and to the south, stretches another ridge, at 400–500 m asl.

Wadi el-Qudeirat, surrounded by mountains, is one of the most opulent water sources in this wilderness. It is fed by a small perennial spring, 'Ein el-Qudeirat, which is still used by the Beduin to water their fields and orchards, mainly olive groves. Today the spring sprouts about 1.6 km east of the fortress, but, at least in the Byzantine period, it was probably even farther to the east, where remains of an ancient dam and water channels dated to that period were found in the narrow part of the wadi (Porath 1985:144–155; see also Chapter 21). We assume that in the Iron Age the spring also was located east of the fortress. During the British Mandate over Egypt, Major C.S. Jarvis, Governor of the Sinai Peninsula (1922–1937), constructed a dam and a water reservoir over the wadi, as well as irrigation channels to provide water to the orchards and small plots that he encouraged the Beduin to cultivate (Jarvis 1938).

The Sinai desert is characterized by short winters and long summers and suffers from unstable precipitation. The average annual rainfall is 100–200 mm, but years with no rain, or with very little precipitation (less than 100 mm), are frequent. Usually there is one major annual rainfall event, causing sudden floods, with water rapidly filling up wadi beds and also running down the mountain cliffs into the wadis. Trees are found only in streambeds and oases.

Despite its remote location and great distance from the Mediterranean Sea, Kadesh Barnea was relatively easily accessible, as it was situated in proximity to what was later named *Darb el-Ghazzal*—the road leading from the Red Sea to Gaza. In addition to its perennial

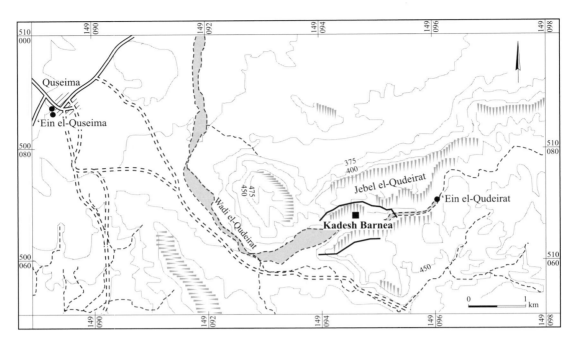

Fig. 1.2. Topographic map of the Kadesh Barnea area.

Fig. 1.3. General view of Tel Kadesh Barnea and Wadi el-Qudeirat; looking east.

Fig. 1.4. Kadesh Barnea at the beginning of the excavation, 1976; looking southeast.

spring, it is this that dictated the construction of the fortresses here during the Iron Age.

Two enigmatic constructions dominate the landscape around the oasis: Two fieldstone walls/fences, about 1 m wide and standing about 1.5 m high, run for a few kilometers above and parallel to both banks of the wadi (Fig. 1.2). The southern 'fence' runs on the crest of the cliff overlooking the wadi, and the northern wall runs along the slope (for some suggestions regarding the purpose of these walls, see, e.g., Aharoni 1958a:108–110; 1961 and cf. Chapter 21). We did not conduct any new examinations of these walls.

KADESH BARNEA IN BIBLICAL TRADITION

Kadesh Barnea is mentioned several times in the Bible, facilitating its identification and location. It is first cited in the context of the war between the Canaanite kings in the Valley of Siddim (Gen 14:1–11), where it is also called 'En Mishpat (Gen 14:7). From this description it is clear that it was a center for nomads and semi-nomads (see Cohen 1981a:93–94), a cultic focus for the tribes that wandered in the Negev and Sinai deserts. The role of Abraham in this episode and the fact that he is described as dwelling in the Negev "between Kadesh and Shur" (Gen 20:1) establishes an association between the beginning of the Patriarchal epoch and Kadesh Barnea and its vicinity.

The site, however, figures most prominently in the Exodus narratives describing the wanderings of the tribes of Israel in the wilderness (Num 33:36–37). Kadesh Barnea is also mentioned in Deuteronomy, as the place where the tribes of Israel lingered for many days (Deut 1:2, 19, 46). It was the first religious center around which the tribes of Israel united under the leadership of Moses, and whence Moses sent out spies to explore the land (Num 13:26) and emissaries to the kings of Edom and Moab to request safe passage through their territories (Num 20:14).

Kadesh Barnea's location in southern Canaan, in the Wilderness of Zin (Num 20:1; 27:14; 33:36) corresponds to the description of the southern border of Canaan and the Promised Land (Num 34:4; Ezekiel 47:19; 48:28), and also to the description of the southern border of the tribe of Judah (Josh15:3). In Num 13:26 it is described as located in the Wilderness of Paran.

IDENTIFICATION AND PREVIOUS ARCHAEOLOGICAL RESEARCH

Scholars first looked for Kadesh Barnea in the 'Aravah Valley. For example, in the nineteenth century, K. Von Raumer (1935:480) suggested identifying it with 'Ein el-Hosb ('En Ḥazeva), and E. Robinson (1860:175, 194), with 'Ein el-Wabeh ('En Yahav).

Other scholars, however, located Kadesh Barnea in Sinai. In the late nineteenth century, H.C. Trumbull (1894) suggested identifying it with 'Ein Kadis, situated *c.* 8 km southeast of 'Ein el-Qudeirat. This was based on the similarity of the Arabic name to Hebrew 'Kadesh'. Somewhat later, N. Schmidt proposed 'Ein el-Qudeirat; he was apparently the first to discern the mound near the spring (Schmidt 1910:61–76). A similar identification was offered by T. Kühtreiber (1914).

Today the identification with Tell el-Qudeirat is widely accepted, especially following the investigations of C.L. Woolley and T.E. Lawrence (1914–1915:69–71), who were the first to discern here the remains of a rectangular fortress with eight towers. They were apparently also the first to pay attention to the 'Negebite' pottery. The importance of Tell el-Qudeirat and the nearby spring were also pointed out by N. Glueck (1935:118–121), R. de Vaux and R. Savignac (1938) and Y. Aharoni (1958a:101–110; 1961).

The first excavations at Kadesh Barnea were conducted in 1956 by M. Dothan on behalf of the Israel Department of Antiquities (Dothan 1965). Dothan conducted a few soundings alongside the perimeter of the rectangular fortresses (of Strata 3 and 2, see below) and near the northeastern tower. He further exposed part of the glacis on the north (Stratum 2 in our sequence), some of the (Stratum 2) casemate walls, mainly on the north and west, part of the floor of the middle tower on the west, and some Persian-period remains over the fortress (our Stratum 1). Dothan's excavations were the first to provide concrete data regarding the plan of the fortresses and the chronology of the site. He concluded that "the fortress" was built at the end of the Iron Age. He also discerned a phase preceding the construction of the single fortress he defined, which contained Negebite pottery.

THE 1976–1982 EXCAVATIONS

From 1976 to 1982, ten seasons of excavations took place under the supervision of Rudolph Cohen, on behalf of the Israel Department of Antiquities (now the Israel Antiquities Authority). The aims of the renewed excavations were to conduct an extensive and in-depth study of the stratigraphy and to establish the sequence and dates of the occupations. As work progressed, the elucidation of this long sequence, spanning the tenth century BCE to the end of the Iron Age, was also meant to enable a better understanding of contemporaneous settlements in the Negev, particularly in the Negev Highlands. Another goal was an extensive study of the Negebite pottery, which was then known only from single-period sites.

The first two seasons (in 1976) were considered exploratory. One row of squares was dug in the eastern part of the fortress (Area A1; Chapter 6), which created a 10 m wide north–south section/trench. A depth of 4 to 5 m was reached in these squares, probing all occupation horizons.

The following two seasons (1978) had two primary goals: (1) to uncover the casemates of the upper, Stratum 2, fortress (Area A2; Chapter 2) and to retrieve ceramic assemblages from its destruction layer; and (2) to open new squares both within the courtyard of this fortress (Areas B and C; respectively, Chapters 3 and 5), and east of it (Area E; Chapter 7), where remains of an earlier fortress were uncovered (Stratum 4).

From the fifth season onward (1980–1982), after we realized the extent of the remains and the importance of the site, we decided to divide the excavation (arbitrarily) into distinct excavation areas, each with its own field supervisor. The aim was to reveal as much as possible of the various strata, including the deeper ones. In these seasons, in addition to the areas mentioned above, we worked in the western part of the site and started to uncover the cistern situated there (Area D; Chapter 4), as well as the retaining walls outside the fortress (Areas E, F, G, H; Chapters 7–10). *Inter alia*, these areas were opened in order to locate the gate(s) to the Strata 3–2 fortresses (see below).

THE KADESH BARNEA OCCUPATIONAL SEQUENCE, CULTURAL AFFINITIES AND CHRONOLOGY

Three superimposed Iron Age fortresses were revealed at Kadesh Barnea (Figs. 1.5–1.7; Plans 1, 2). The earliest fortress (Stratum 4) was erected on the natural deposits of the northern bank of Wadi el-Qudeirat. Over part of this fortress and the settlement dispersed around it,

*Fig. 1.5. The rectangular fortresses of Strata 3–2 above the Stratum 4 oval
fortress on the northern bank of Wadi el-Qudeirat; looking west.*

*Fig. 1.6. The site during the 1979 excavation season. Note the depression in the
southwestern corner of the fortress, formed by the cistern; looking north.*

Fig. 1.7. The site during the last excavation season, 1982. In the foreground, the retaining wall of the moat; looking south.

a second, larger fortress (Stratum 3) was constructed, its foundations laid directly on Stratum 4 remains, and fortified with solid walls. The third, uppermost fortress (Stratum 2) in many respects continues the Stratum 3 plan, but sports casemate walls. It also differs in the buildings constructed within it.

In turn, Stratum 2 is superimposed by an ephemeral Babylonian(?)/Persian-period occupation and by some later remains (Stratum 1).

In previous publications these fortresses were named, respectively: the lower fortress (or Fortress III), the middle fortress (or Fortress II) and the upper fortress (or Fortress I). In order not to employ confusing alternative terminologies, the definition of

the fortresses employed in this report is that of *strata* (Strata 4 through 2 for the three fortresses and Stratum 1 for the overlying Persian-period occupation).

In Chapters 2 to 10, the stratigraphy and architecture of each excavation area are presented separately (despite the fact that divisions between the areas were arbitrary). In order to render coherence to these disparate stratigraphical summaries, we present below an overall synthesis of the site's stratigraphy and architecture (Table 1.1), augmented by summaries and discussions of principal finds, cultural characteristics and chronology. Illustrations referred to in this summary are only those of the major architectural element.

Table 1.1. Stratigraphy and Chronology of Kadesh Barnea

Stratum	Substratum	Occupation	Period	Date (BCE)
4	4c	Settlement?	?	?
	4b, 4a	Oval fortress and unfortified settlement	Iron IIA	10th c.
3	3c	Rectangular fortress with solid wall (construction)	Iron IIB	Second half of 8th c.
	3b, 3a	Rectangular fortress with solid wall (occupation)		
2	–	Rectangular fortress with casemates	Iron IIC	Late 7th/early 6th c.
1	–	Unfortified settlement?	Babylonian(?)/ Persian	6th(?)–4th c.

STRATUM 4 (C–A): IRON IIA, THE TENTH CENTURY BCE (Plans 1.1, 3, 4)

Stratigraphy and Architecture

Substratum 4c: The Pre-Fortress Occupation
The earliest occupation at the site (Substratum 4c) was barely excavated and is ill defined. It is represented by a very thin layer of ashes alongside narrow walls preserved only one course high, under the Substratum 4b constructions (see below). These were located in Areas B and E (Chapters 3 and 7; Plan 3). No chronologically diagnostic artifacts were associated with this occupation; its date is thus unclear.

Substrata 4b–a: The Oval Fortress
Substratum 4b (Plans 1.1, 3) comprises a roughly oval casemate fortress and nearby, mainly to the west, an unfortified settlement. The fortress is of moderate size, *c.* 27 m in diameter, and consists of a wide (*c.* 1.5–1.7 m) outer wall and a narrower (1.0 m) inner wall, both built of large fieldstones, preserved at places 2 m high. All the casemates on the east were uncovered (at least partially), as well as some on the south and west (see Areas A1, C and E; Chapters 6, 5 and 7; Figs. 5.3, 7.3). The fortress' courtyard, or at least some of it, was divided into sub-spaces. Floors in the casemates and in other units were mostly earthen and rarely stone.

Both in the casemates and in the courtyard only one clear floor level was usually observed. Upon it obvious signs of destruction were discerned; in several cases these included *in situ* broken pottery vessels.

An additional building stage, identified above this destruction level and termed 'Substratum 4a' (Plan 4) was found only in the southern part of the fortress (in Area E). It is unclear whether this substratum postdates the fortress (and thus constitutes an intermediary occupation between it and the Stratum 3 fortress) or represents a phase of reconstruction still associated with the Stratum 4 fortress, which went unnoticed in other areas. Some of the Substratum 4b walls continued to be used in Substratum 4a; it is apparent that there was no significant temporal gap between the two occupations.

Although the Stratum 4 fortress was reached in non-contiguous excavation areas and some parts of the fortress were poorly preserved, the stratigraphical correlations between the remains in the various areas is quite straightforward: they are all buried deep beneath the constructional fill of Stratum 3 (see below) and are of similar construction. Also, the general layout—an oval casemate fortress—is clear. Specific details of its plan, however, may be reconstructed in more than one way (see, for example, the discussion of the western casemates in Area C, Chapter 5). Plans 1.1 and 4 represent the reconstruction we deemed preferable.

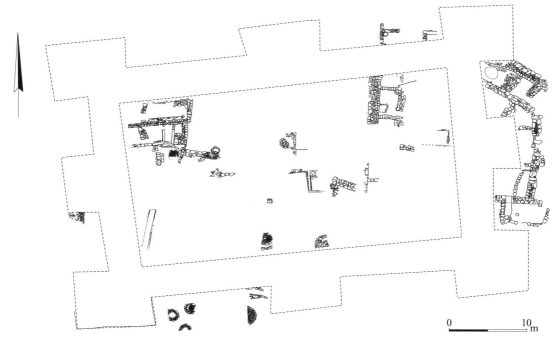

0 10 m

Plan 1.1. Schematic plan of Substratum 4b.

The gate of this fortress may have been situated on the south, obscured by the Stratum 3 solid wall (see discussions in Areas A1 and E; Chapters 7, 6).

Substrata 4b–a: The Unfortified Settlement

The settlement associated with the Stratum 4 fortress (Plans 1.1, 3, 4) was traced mainly to its west, but portions of it were also uncovered north of the fortress (see Areas B, D, C, F, G, H; respectively Chapters 3–5, 8–10 and e.g., Figs. 3.1, 5.5). In some excavation areas, two phases were discerned (designated 'Substrata 4b' and '4a'). The buildings were built of mud bricks on stone socles, some very wide, others narrow (one or two rows of stones, occasionally incorporating dressed stones and columns). A characteristic feature of this settlement is the many silos in the courtyards of the houses (for example in Areas B; Chapter 3; Figs. 3.6, 3.9). Six additional silos were excavated in the open area in the southwestern part of the site (Areas D, C, H; Chapters 4, 5, 10; e.g., Figs. 10.1, 10.2).

Direct correlation between the two sub-phases in the fortress and the two in the settlement was impossible, a problem that could not be resolved by the pottery either, as there is no clear distinction between the assemblages of the various Stratum 4 substrata (see Chapter 11). Thus, Substrata 4b and 4a in the fortress on the one hand and in the settlement on the other do not necessarily correspond. One possibility is that Substratum 4b in the settlement correlates to Substratum 4b in the fortress and that similarly Substrata 4a in both are stratigraphically equal. However, it is also possible that both phases of the settlement relate only to the fortress phase (Substratum 4b), and that if indeed Substratum 4a in the fortress is a post-fortress phase, no settlement existed then (Plans 1.1 and 4 reflect the former option).

Pottery and Other Finds

More than half of the pottery in the Stratum 4 assemblages is wheel made, and although some types are unique to the site, others are similar to those found in other Negev sites, such as Tel Masos, 'Arad, Be'er Sheva', and the Negev Highland sites (see Chapter 11), indicating that Kadesh Barnea was part of the same cultural sphere and political entity.

In addition, however, the significant percentage of handmade Negebite pottery (Chapter 12) points to an interaction with the local Negev population. This crude handmade pottery had a long tradition in the Negev

and 'Aravah, where it was used mainly in domestic contexts, and its distribution, confined to the Negev only, indicates that it was not transported over any significant distances.

Other than pottery, Stratum 4 produced some weaponry, bone objects, jewelry, among which two faience 'Horus Eye' pendants are worthy of note (Chapter 13), and one seal (Chapter 14: No. 1). One inscription, engraved on a lamp, may also come from this stratum (Chapter 15: No. 14). Most of the finds uncovered in the Substratum 3c constructional fills probably originated in Stratum 4.

Chronology

In previous publications (e.g., Cohen 1981a; 1981b), the Stratum 4 occupation was dated to the tenth century BCE, the days of King Solomon. This was based on similarities between the ceramic assemblages of the Substratum 4b destruction layer and those of Iron IIA sites, both in the north, such as Megiddo, Strata Vb and Va–IVb and Hazor, Strata X–IX, as well as in the south, chiefly Lachish, Stratum V, Be'er Sheva', Strata VII–VI, Tel Esdar, Strata III–II and 'Arad, Strata XII–XI.

In recent years, the dating of all these assemblages to the tenth century BCE has been questioned and a lower chronology proposed, assigning most of them to the ninth century BCE (Finkelstein 1996; for the conventional chronology, see, e.g., Mazar 1997). To date, this debate concerns mainly sites in Judah, the Shephelah and the north, and at this stage it is yet unclear how it reflects on assemblages such as those of Kadesh Barnea (for a recent treatment of this subject, see Herzog and Singer-Avitz 2004).

In this report, the traditional chronology is maintained, and the Iron IIA Stratum 4 fortress is dated to the tenth century BCE. This notwithstanding, some of the ceramic types have long life-spans, and could also be dated to the eleventh century BCE (and some may continue into the ninth; see Chapter 11). Consequently, the dating of the Midianite pottery, occurring in this stratum, should be considered. Usually, this ceramic group is dated to the eleventh century BCE at the latest, but it is definitely possible that it continued into the tenth century; only new data from the 'Aravah Valley and Transjordan may aid in clarifying this issue.

As opposed, however, to this 'early' material, there are in this stratum red-slipped and burnished vessels, a few 'Black Juglets' and, most importantly, a few fragments of Cypriot Black-on-Red Ware. These, and the rest of the pottery, corroborate the Iron IIA, tenth-century BCE date for Stratum 4 (see Chapter 11).

Discussion and Summary

In its layout, the Stratum 4 fortress at Kadesh Barnea resembles the numerous Iron IIA oval/elliptical fortresses known in the Negev Highlands (Cohen and Cohen-Amin 2004), which are characterized by well-planned fortifications. Architecturally, the main difference is that at Kadesh Barnea the outer wall is very wide (about 1.5 m) and the inner one is narrower, while in most others cases the two walls are of equal width, and built of one row of large stones. The only similar fortress in this respect is Meẓudat Naḥal Ḥorsha (Cohen and Cohen-Amin 2004:67). Contrary to Z. Herzog's suggestion (e.g., Herzog 1983; Herzog and Singer-Avitz 2004:226), we would not cluster Kadesh Barnea with his proposed 'enclosed settlements', as at Kadesh Barnea both outer and inner walls of the casemates are continuous, and were clearly constructed simultaneously. This is in contrast to such sites as Be'er Sheva', Stratum VII, 'Arad, Stratum XII and Tel Masos, Stratum II, where the external walls are staggered, indicating a consecutive construction of the units (cf. Herzog 1994: Figs. 5, 6, 8).

We thus consider Stratum 4 at Kadesh Barnea part of the network of fortresses constructed in the Negev under the aegis of the United Monarchy (for further discussion, see Cohen and Cohen-Amin 2004:154–158). We attribute the violent destruction of Stratum 4 to Shishak's campaign in 925 BCE, concurrently with the destruction of the Negev fortresses (Cohen 1981a:103; Cohen and Cohen-Amin 2004:155–157 and references therein).

Subsistence at Kadesh Barnea during the tenth century BCE was based on agriculture, as evidenced by the flint sickles (Chapter 17) and the numerous limestone and basalt groundstone tools (Chapter 13). Animal husbandry comprised the usual domesticates, but the fortress' inhabitants also practiced some hunting, mainly of gazelles (Chapter 19). A major phenomenon emerging from the faunal analysis is the abundance of camels at this early date. This might prove the key to assessing the role of the 'Negev sites'. Kadesh Barnea's regional contacts are evidenced mainly by shells, originating in the Red Sea, the Nile River and the Mediterranean Sea (Chapter 18). The few Cypriot vessels in this stratum probably also arrived via some Mediterranean coastal site. Spindle whorls and loom weights (Chapter 16) attest to some of the domestic activities.

THE STRATUM 3 (C–A) FORTRESS: IRON IIB, THE SECOND HALF OF THE EIGHTH CENTURY BCE
(Plans 1.2, 5–7)

Stratigraphy and Architecture

Stratum 3 has been subdivided as follows: Substratum 3c is the construction stage, which comprises mainly the fortress itself (walls and towers), the constructional fills inside the perimeter of these walls, the ramparts supporting them externally, the moat surrounding the fortress, and a large cistern and a granary within the fortress (Plan 5). All these were apparently parts of a single planning and building operation, which clearly lasted for a relatively long period, involving extensive excavation into natural deposits and Stratum 4. As both the cistern and granary were built simultaneously with the fortress itself, the above-mentioned earthen constructional fills also functioned as supporting fills for these two installations.

Substrata 3b and 3a (Plans 1.2, 6, 7) comprise structures built within the perimeter of the fortress walls and outside them. These two distinct phases were discernible mainly inside the fortress, chiefly in Area B. Constructions that could not be assigned with certainty to either substratum (some of them very plausibly pertaining to both), were designated 'Substrata 3a-b'. All the 'Substratum 3c' elements continue to exist concurrently with Substrata 3a-b. No destruction events were discerned within the Stratum 3 sequence.

The Fortress, Constructional Fills and the Moat
The Stratum 3 fortress is rectangular, with solid walls *c.* 4 m wide, and towers in the corners and in the midpoint of each wall—eight towers in all. It is 33 × 50 m (external dimensions, excluding the towers) and thus, both in plan and size, it differs completely from the previous fortress. The walls and towers (e.g., Figs. 1.7, 3.2, 8.1) were built of large, roughly hewn limestones on their inner and outer faces, with a solid fill of stones and rubble in between, and transversal wooden beams. The towers were preserved 2–4 m high (they are better preserved in the segments adjoining the solid wall). Only their outlines are clear, as the

towers themselves were not excavated. The walls were usually preserved *c.* 1 m above the floors of the internal buildings and their foundations, established on the ruins of the Stratum 4 fortress and settlement (and only slightly cutting through them) were more than 2 m deep. (For a detailed description of the fortress walls and towers, see Area A2; Chapter 2.)

The courtyard of the fortress (24.0 × 40.5 m) comprised a 1.5–2.0 m deep constructional fill of earth and debris, stabilized by some flimsy stone constructions (see Area B; Chapter 3). The walls and floors of the structures in the courtyard were built on top of this fill (Substrata 3a-b).

Externally, the solid walls of the fortress were preserved 3–4 m above the Stratum 4 remains, and certainly rose higher than that. A stone-lined moat surrounded the fortress at a distance of 8 m from the line of the walls and 4 m from the towers (see Areas E, F, G; Chapters 7–9; Figs. 7.12, 7.13); it apparently did not extend to the southern perimeter of the fortress. The space between the moat and the walls of the fortress was filled with earthen ramparts, retained by a stone wall. They were 1.5–2.0 m high, above the remains of Stratum 4 (Areas E–H; Chapters 7–10). These ramparts provided support for the lower parts of the solid fortress walls, countering the heavy mass pressing them from inside.

A major lacuna in our understanding of the way the fortress functioned is the position of its gate, which remains elusive despite the fact that most of the external perimeter of the fortification walls was traced (except for the northwestern corner). Similarly, the inner face of the fortifications was exposed in many places down to foundation level, including the northwestern corner. Thus we are forced to reconstruct an entrance by way of a ramp that either climbed to the top of the wall or passed through an opening in it, but still at least one meter above the level of the buildings in the courtyard. This would require a descent into the courtyard, probably by way of stairs (possibly constructed of wooden beams and mud bricks). The implication of such a reconstruction is that animals and carts could not enter the courtyard, but had to be accommodated outside it, in the strips between the moat and the wall. Some stone platforms uncovered outside the fortress on the east, north and west (in Areas E, F and G; Chapters 7–9; e.g., Fig. 9.8) may belong to such access ramps.

Constructions in the Courtyard, the Cistern and the Granary

Houses, alleys and working areas were built in the space enclosed by the fortress walls (Areas B, D, C, A1; described in detail in Chapters 3–6).

Substratum 3b. The fortress' area was built up according to a pre-conceived plan (Plan 6). A cistern was constructed in the southwestern quadrant (Area D); and east of it (Area C) was a granary, surrounded by small structures, possibly workshops of sorts (for the cistern and granary, see below). It appears that in this phase the area around the cistern was open rather than built-up. North of these two installations, a street crossed the fortress from east to west. North of this street, dwellings, comprising several rooms, were erected, and between them were alleys leading from the street to the fortification wall (Areas B, C; Chapters 3, 5; e.g., Fig. 3.16). In some of the narrow alleys stairwells could be reconstructed; they led up to the top of the fortress walls. A large structure, albeit of unclear plan (Area A1; Chapter 6; Fig. 6.7), occupied the southeastern corner of the courtyard. In most cases the walls of all these buildings comprised a stone socle of one or two rows of stones; some walls still retained remnants of their mud-brick superstructure.

Substratum 3a. This substratum (Plan 7) exhibits mainly a continuous accumulation of occupation layers. In some areas, such as Area A1 on the east (Chapter 6), considerable architectural continuity is attested vs. Substratum 3b, but there are also some constructional changes. For example, in the northwestern area (Area B, Chapter 3), above the Substratum 3b dwellings, a new large tripartite building was constructed, apparently of a public nature, perhaps a storage facility. Additional changes were introduced on the east (Area A1; Chapter 6) and around the granary (Area C; Chapter 5) and new structures were erected around the cistern (Area D; Chapter 4), in places that had previously been empty. The elimination, on the northwest, of some of the Substratum 3b houses may have necessitated the construction of new dwellings in their stead.

The Cistern. The nearly square cistern was dug and constructed in Substratum 3c in the southwestern corner of the fortress (Area D, Chapter 4; Figs. 4.4, 4.5). It remained in use until some point during

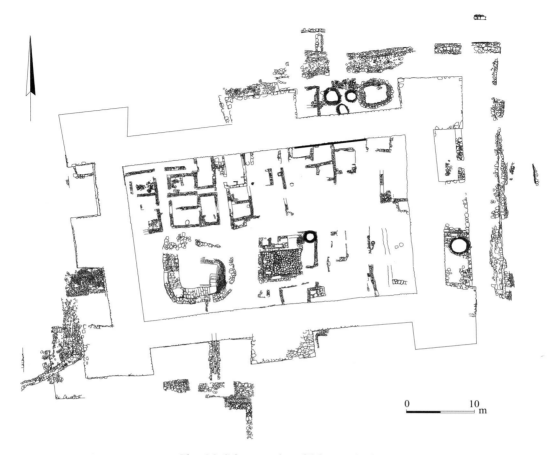

Plan 1.2. Schematic plan of Substrata 3a–b.

Stratum 2. It was apparently open, *c.* 10 × 10 m at its preserved top, and at least 7 m deep, constructed of large stones coated with thick plaster. Its maximum capacity is about 120 cu m. The bottom could be reached via a well-constructed stairway (Figs. 4.7, 4.8). A plastered water channel runs into the cistern through the southern wall of the fortress, from an unclear point south of the fortress (Area H; Chapter 10; Figs. 4.10, 10.7).

The Granary. East of the cistern, a sunken rectangular granary was established (*c.* 4 × 5 m), its walls and floor built of medium-sized fieldstones. The walls were preserved 2.5 m high (Area C; Chapter 5; Figs. 5.23, 5.24). The granary continued to function in Stratum 2, but not until its end.

Silos outside the Fortress and Related Constructions
In a few locations outside the fortress, between the towers and over the earthen ramparts, silos were sunken into the latter (Areas E–H: Chapters 7–10; e.g., Figs.

7.17, 8.6, 9.3). They were apparently built during the initial construction phase of the fortress. Near the silos were walls and occupation layers associated with the solid fortress wall (Fig. 8.7), indicating that some sort of activity took place outside the fortress, perhaps as the courtyard itself was very crowded. It is unclear to which sub-phases these external constructions belong and thus they are designated 'Substrata 3a-b'.

Pottery and Other Finds

The pottery in the Substratum 3c constructional fills chiefly originates in the Stratum 4 debris, and thus the only ceramics that can be directly associated with the Stratum 3 fortress are those of Substrata 3a-b. The most conspicuous aspect of those assemblages is the dominance of the Negebite ware, comprising about 80% of the pottery (Chapter 12). This is the peak of its occurrence. In addition, other wares, especially that which we termed 'Black-Painted Ware' (see Chapter

11), are unparalleled elsewhere and seem to be of Negev, perhaps local, production. The rest of the pottery comprises (a specific selection of) Judahite types.

Other finds comprise, for example, a few zoomorphic figurines and vessels (not all of them are attributed with certainty to this stratum), bone tools, metal artifacts including arrowheads, and scant jewelry (Chapter 13). Substrata 3a-b produced no inscriptions. A few finds, such as a small stone altar (Chapter 13), may attest to cultic activities. A cluster of textiles (Chapter 16), uncovered under the Stratum 3 glacis in Area G, probably belongs to Stratum 3, but this could not be ascertained.

Chronology

It is difficult to offer a precise date for the Stratum 3 fortress, both because no pottery in primary deposition was encountered, and there is no real chronological anchor for the Negebite pottery that abounds there. However, based both on the fact that some wheel-made pottery types are similar to those found in late eighth-century contexts in Judah (chiefly Lachish, Stratum III, Be'er Sheva', Stratum II and 'Arad, Stratum VIII) and that our impression is that the Kuntillet 'Ajrud assemblage (*c.* 800 BCE) is earlier than that of Stratum 3, we suggest a date in the second half of the eighth century BCE for Stratum 3. Neither its beginning nor its end can be dated with better precision.

This proposed date leaves an extensive temporal gap between Strata 4 and 3, which is plausible, considering the total change in architecture and the very nature of the site. On the other hand, it is difficult to reconcile this postulated gap with the marked similarities between the ceramic assemblages of the two strata, not only as regards the Negebite pottery, but also in some of the wheel-made types, which hints at cultural continuity.

Discussion and Summary

The Stratum 3 fortress is extremely difficult to interpret, not only in regard to its date, but also vis-à-vis regarding its function and the identity of its builders and occupants. As mentioned, no violent destruction was discerned in the Stratum 3 sequence, though in certain places layers of ash covered the floors. It seems that occupation was continuous, with gradual architectural changes within Stratum 3, and also, to a certain extent, from Stratum 3 to Stratum 2 (see below).

The plan of the fortress is unique, though certain elements of it are comparable to some sites in Judah. The plan, for example, has been compared by Y. Aharoni (1958b:35) to the fortress at Ḥorbat 'Uza and by D. Ussishkin (1983:136) to that of the Stratum II gate at Lachish. Other scholars, on the other hand, have suggested that the plan is a 'foreign' one, possibly Assyrian (e.g., Rothenberg 1967:94), but there is no real evidence of any foreign architectural influence. The only site that somewhat resembles the Kadesh Barnea fortress is that of Kuntillet 'Ajrud (Meshel 1976), situated about 50 km south of Kadesh Barnea. It is a rectangular fortress (although with casemates), equipped with four corner towers.

The moat and the retaining walls as found at Kadesh Barnea are not a typical feature of Iron Age Israel or Judah. Thus they should be regarded as an innovative creation, meant to protect this remote and isolated outpost.

Cisterns attributed to the Iron Age are known from other Negev sites (e.g., Haiman 1991:18, Cohen and Cohen Amin 2004:151–153) and have been divided into two types: (1) pits hewn in bedrock and usually roofed; and (2) stone-lined pits dug into the ground and probably open or partially covered, apparently with branches. Most of these cisterns have not been excavated, and it is unknown whether they were plastered (it should, however, be borne in mind that the attribution of these cisterns to the Iron Age is problematic, as they are usually located in open areas). The cisterns at Ḥorbat Ḥaluqim (Cohen 1976a), Bor Ḥemet (Haiman 1991:333), Mishor Ha-Ruḥot and Borot/Ma'agorat Loẓ (Evenari et al. 1958:241–242, 246–247, Figs. 11, 22, 24, Pl. 47c) are similar in general shape and technique to the Kadesh Barnea cistern (open pits, dug rather than hewn). At Bor Ḥemet and in the large cistern at Borot Luẓ there is also evidence of stairs.

However, all these installations differ in overall concept from that of the Kadesh Barnea cistern. They were not situated within settlements, were primarily fed by runoff water, and mostly served agricultural purposes. The Kadesh Barnea cistern, dug within a walled system and possibly not covered (see p. 55), on the other hand, is closer in concept to water systems within towns (and fortresses), which were destined to function in an emergency.

An outstanding feature at Kadesh Barnea is the plastered water channel, which directed water into the cistern from the wadi, through the fortress wall. There was clearly a great investment both in its planning and construction. A similar concept—a water channel passing through the fortress wall and leading to a plastered cistern—is evidenced at the Judahite fortress at 'Arad. It was constructed there in Stratum X, dated by Herzog to the mid-eighth century BCE (and continued to be used until Stratum VI; Herzog 2002:72–76). The 'Arad cistern itself is different in that it is part of a subterranean reservoir consisting of three cisterns (and the channel is also cut in bedrock).

At Kadesh Barnea the water channel is wide and high enough for a person to walk in (and pass through the fortress wall). It could have been used as a postern, similarly to the 'Arad channel.

Who built this fortress? Initially, based on the date suggested above, it was suggested that its construction be attributed to the days of King Uzziah of Judah (Cohen 1981a:103), but, in fact, there is no definite evidence that it was built by a king of Judah at all (nor evidence to the contrary). The artifactual assemblages in the fortress do not provide any decisive indication regarding the identity of the fortress builders.

Nevertheless, it is our conviction that the planning and construction of such a fortress, at this location, which certainly demanded complex logistics and a large, organized workforce, could only have been carried out by the Judahite kingdom. Under this scenario, the fact that not all the eighth-century BCE Judahite wheel-made ceramic assemblage is represented in Stratum 3 (see Chapter 11) is perhaps a result of the distance from the pottery-producing centers of Judah. Part of these 'missing' types had local, Negebite, substitutes.

The elaborate fortification, and similarly the plastered cistern (50–120 cu m in capacity), whose construction seems superfluous considering the nearby perennial water source, indicate that trouble was anticipated, perhaps on the part of the local population, the producers of the Negebite pottery, who were probably exploited by the occupants of the fortress. Indeed, the only possible explanation for its construction is a concern for water supply during turmoil.

However, on the whole, archaeological evidence seems to indicate that life was peaceful, and that close relations were forged between the inhabitants of the fortress and their neighbors.

Though we consider Kadesh Barnea a Judahite fortress, it does not, in our opinion, mark the border of the kingdom. Similarly to other (not necessarily contemporaneous) desert locales such as Kuntillet 'Ajrud and Tell el-Kheleifeh, it was an administrative center located at a strategic point along the trade route from the Red Sea to the Mediterranean, probably intended to control the local population.

As mentioned, there was no destruction layer between this fortress and the one above it, but there is a clear distinction between the ceramic repertoires of the two fortresses. In Stratum 2, Negebite pottery is barely represented, the Black-Painted Ware has disappeared, and the assemblage becomes a standard Judahite one.

Subsistence of the fortress seems to have been very similar to the previous stratum, with similar evidence of agriculture, agricultural industries and animal husbandry (Chapters 13, 17, 19), with lesser evidence of hunting (mainly ibexes and gazelles) and some fish consumption. Similarly to Stratum 4, a significant quantity of camel bones was unearthed. Spinning and weaving are attested by spindle whorls and loom weights (Chapter 16). Shells, as in the previous stratum, arrived at the site mainly from the Red Sea, but also from the Mediterranean Sea and the Nile River.

THE STRATUM 2 FORTRESS: IRON IIC, THE LATE SEVENTH/EARLY SIXTH CENTURIES BCE (Plans 1.3, 8)

Stratum 2 is the best understood occupation at the site. Nearly all the fortress was excavated, and as it met a sudden end, it was well sealed by destruction debris. However, the areas surrounding the cistern were badly preserved, as remains were apparently washed into it, and some other locations, mainly on the east, were disturbed by Stratum 1 pits.

Stratigraphy and Architecture

The Fortress
The Stratum 2 fortress, carefully planned, was built as a direct continuation of the Stratum 3 fortress, but its character changed considerably. Above the Stratum 3 solid fortification wall, on the exact same lines (or nearly so; see below), casemates were built. New construction is also evident above the Stratum 3 towers (see Area A2; Chapter 2). The fortress thus created is rectangular in shape, its outer dimensions 33.0 × 50.0 m, and its eight towers protrude another 4.0–4.5 m on each side (Fig. 1.6). In most cases the top of the Stratum 3 solid wall was leveled and in a few places there is evidence of an earthen fill above the stones, which was

apparently laid in order to create a horizontal surface for the Stratum 2 floors. In a few cases the casemates are somewhat narrower than the solid wall, but in no case do they protrude beyond its faces. Thus, although the casemates were not always clearly preserved, their outlines can be reconstructed with certainty. In most places, a clear seam is evident between the stones of the casemates and those of the underlying solid wall (Fig. 3.16, in background; Fig. 5.19, on right; Fig. 6.16), and sometimes a gap about 5 cm wide is evident between the two, on the inner face.

The Problem of the Gate

As was the case in Stratum 3, the entrance to the Stratum 2 fortress has not been located. One possibility is that access to the courtyard was via one of the casemates, which was reached from the outside by the earthen glacis surrounding the walls. Dothan (1965:137) suggested two possibilities, both of them unsatisfactory. One is that the entrance was via Casemate 423 on the north, where the middle parts of both the inner and outer walls were missing. However, the slope of the glacis at this spot is too steep. His second option was that access was on the southwest, through the north–south fortress wall (Area E), where he uncovered part of a pavement outside the walls and where he postulated an opening in the outer wall of the casemate.

Another possibility is that the fortress was entered through one of the towers. An attractive possibility (for Stratum 2) is the northeastern tower, as the northeastern part of the courtyard seems to have been an open space, perhaps an entrance 'piazza' (see Areas C, A1; Chapters 5, 6).

Casemates

The preservation of the casemates (e.g., Figs. 2.1, 2.11) was good on the east, north and west and poor on the south, apparently due to the proximity of the wadi on that side. On average, the casemate rooms are 2.0–2.5 m wide and 5.0–8.0 m long (inner dimensions), except those situated near the middle towers on the north and south (Casemates 501, 404), which are smaller than the rest.

All the excavated casemates, except for one (903 on the southwest) could be entered directly from the courtyard. It seems that the location of the entrances was carefully considered. As a rule, the entrances are located in one of the inner corners. In the eastern and western casemates, the entrance is in the southern corner and in the northern and southern casemates, on the west. Thus it seems that care was taken to keep a distance between the entrances. Only in cases where this would have placed entrances too close to the entrances to the towers (for example, in Casemate 553 on the west), were the openings located in the *middle* of the casemates' walls.

The outer and inner walls of the casemates were constructed of two rows of large and smaller fieldstones, with a fill of smaller stones in between. Their width is quite consistent, *c.* 1 m. The cross walls between the casemates, 0.6–0.8 m thick, were also usually built of two rows of fieldstones (with stones in between), though in some walls only one row of large stones is evident (whether this is due to partial preservation is unclear). Many burnt wooden beams were uncovered in the destruction debris within the casemates, apparently fallen from their roofs.

No casemate had more than one floor level. In most of them a layer of burnt and collapsed debris, about half a meter deep, covered the floors, burying large assemblages of pottery vessels and other finds. Some of the casemates were obviously used as storage spaces, as indicated by the numerous storage jars found in them (e.g., Casemate 553; Fig. 2.9). Others yielded pottery assemblages of a domestic nature, but no cooking installations were uncovered in any of the casemates.

Towers

As the upper parts of the towers were badly preserved, it is difficult to assess the changes they underwent in the transition from Stratum 3 to Stratum 2. Only in a few places (in Towers 422 and 516) is there evidence of new Stratum 2 walls. The towers were accessed via their adjoining casemates, but the entrances leading to them were never situated on the same axes as the entrances leading into the casemates themselves, and thus they were not visible from the courtyard. The entrances to the four corner towers were via L-shaped corridors or entrance rooms (L218, L427, L542; the situation in the southeastern tower is unclear), which perhaps included stairwells leading to the top of the towers.

Tower 516 produced a significant assemblage of pottery, including two *in situ* pithoi. (Chapter 11). This indicates that at least some of the towers also functioned (at least ad hoc) as storerooms.

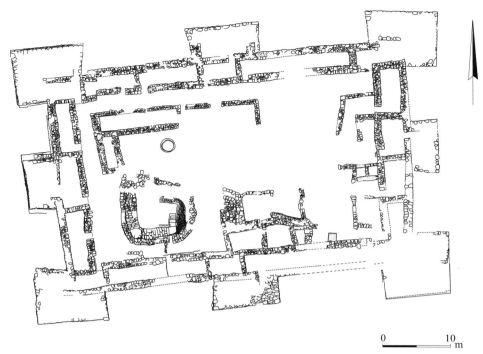

Plan 1.3. Schematic plan of Stratum 2.

Constructions in the Courtyard

Inside the courtyard as well, the plan changed almost completely. The cistern, however, continued to be used, at least for a while, and it probably ceased to function before the destruction of Stratum 2 (see Area D; Chapter 4). If there were any buildings around the cistern in this period, they have washed into it.

The granary also functioned at least during part of the life span of Stratum 2, but was subsequently abandoned, probably because its eastern wall had collapsed, and it was sealed by new constructions (Area C; Chapter 5).

On the east, some of the Stratum 3 walls were re-used, and rooms were built adjoining the casemates along the entire eastern and southeastern sides (Area A1; Chapter 6; Fig. 6.15). In the northwestern part of the fortress, a large public building with a wide stone-paved court was constructed (Building 485; Area B; Chapter 3; Fig. 3.31), and in an inner court of the same building a large installation built of mud bricks was uncovered (Installation 721; Fig. 3.30). The finds in this building were few and its function is unclear.

In general, it appears that the structures in the fortress were not crowded and included only a few dwellings. In nearly all the Stratum 2 buildings only one floor level was discerned, except for a few isolated places (in Area C) where there were some superimposed floors.

The Area outside the Fortress and the Glacis

A significant change took place outside the fortress as well. In the areas between the moat and the fortification wall (Areas E–H; Chapters 7–10), over the Stratum 3 living surfaces and silos, layers of earth and pebbles were dumped, creating an earthen glacis. It sloped down from the fortress wall to the retaining wall of the moat. It appears that initially these layers did not extend into the moat; however, toward the end of the Stratum 2 period, the eroded fills of the glacis were the main cause for the blocking of the moat.

Pottery and Other Finds

The pottery assemblage of Stratum 2 is very different from that of the preceding Stratum 3. While in Stratum 3 the percentage of Negebite pottery was very high (in relation to wheel-made wares), in Stratum 2 most of the pottery was wheel made and Negebite pottery was scarce. Thus, the Stratum 2 assemblage (Chapter 11) is essentially Judahite. This Judahite assemblage, moreover, is extremely variegated, as opposed to that of Stratum 3, and incorporates most of the known types of the era (with some regional variations). Indeed, the typological variability stands out also when compared to contemporaneous sites in the Negev.

In addition to the Judahite types, Edomite pottery (decorated and unadorned) is represented in restricted numbers (and unstratified Edomite pottery apparently all relates to Stratum 2), and there are also some Assyrianized types. However, most of the latter are in fact best paralleled in Jordan and thus they probably do not indicate direct Assyrian 'influence'. A hitherto unknown ware group is the one we termed 'Red Sandy Ware' (mainly jars), whose significance is not yet understood. Other pottery vessels, mainly jars, originate in Phoenicia and Philistia.

Other portable finds in Stratum 2 were quite scarce, notably a few figurines, groundstone tools and vessels, some bone tools (including a delicately carved handle in the shape of a deer head), some beads and pendants, two fibulae, arrowheads (Chapter 13), very few spindle whorls and loom weights (Chapter 16) and two seals (Chapter 14: Nos. 2, 3).

In addition, however, Stratum 2 produced an important body of inscriptions (Nos. 1, 3–8, 10, 11 in Chapter 15 belong, with various degrees of confidence, to this stratum, as well as probably some of the unstratified items). Most are Hebrew inscriptions, oftentimes accompanied by Egyptian hieratic numerals. Some are of administrative function, and others are probably scribal exercises.

Chronology

The destruction date of the Stratum 2 fortress can quite easily be dated by the abundant primary pottery sealed by its destruction, especially by the Judahite types in the assemblage. These are paralleled in Judah in such contexts as Lachish, Stratum II, Tel Baṭash, Stratum II, 'Arad, Strata VII–VI, 'Aro'er, Strata II–I and more, pointing to a destruction date in the late seventh/early sixth centuries BCE. There are no real data, however, regarding the construction date.

Discussion and Summary

An alternative interpretation of the Strata 3–2 sequence has been offered by D. Ussishkin (1995). He hypothesized that the two rectangular fortification systems (solid wall and superimposed casemates) are not two systems but one. He suggested that the fortress, starting with Stratum 3, was protected by a casemate wall, the casemates constructed on a massive foundation, and that this single fortification served all architectural levels of the Strata 3–2 range within the fortress.

There is no unequivocal stratigraphical or architectural evidence to prove this claim or to refute it. There are two main points in favor of Ussishkin's suggestion. The first is that the width of the solid wall (c. 4 m) may hint that it meant to serve as a base for casemates.

Second, assuming the obvious—that the casemates needed to be entered from the courtyard of the fortress—a major consideration is the location of the openings of the casemates vs. the layout of the Substrata 3b and 3a structures in the courtyard (see especially Plan 2). Indeed, except for one wall in Area A1 (W124 of Substratum 3a), which interferes with the passage into Casemate 39 on the east, all other known openings of the casemates could co-exist with the Substrata 3a-b walls and are not blocked by them. This, if accidental, would be remarkable. It is definitely possible that all the Strata 3b and 3a spaces adjoining the openings of the various casemates were unroofed spaces. The casemates, in this case, in Stratum 3, would have been accessed by stairs or ramps.

On the other hand, the Stratum 2 floor levels of the buildings inside the courtyard (elevations c. 25.00) coincide almost perfectly with the level of the casemate floors. This would be a strange coincidence if they represent just the raising of floors in the casemate fortress.

Another consideration is the stratigraphical sequence outside the fortress(es) walls. There it is clear that there are two 'events'. One is the construction of the silos and related structures, clearly relating to the solid wall (Stratum 3) and then their replacement with the glacis, which abuts the bottom of the Stratum 2 casemate walls.

Thus, we prefer the two-different-systems/strata interpretation, as initially suggested.

As evidenced by the Hebrew inscriptions and its ceramic assemblage, the Stratum 2 fortress, similarly to its predecessor, was a fortified Judahite administrative center, most probably constructed under Josiah (Cohen 1981a:103) and maintaining close contact with Judah.

The drastic decrease in the occurrence of Negebite pottery may indicate that contacts with the local population were not as close as they had previously been, and may even have been hostile. Indeed, the construction of the glacis at a certain stage during the lifespan of Stratum 2 (not in the very beginning of this stratum; see Areas E–H; Chapters 7–10), as well as the elimination of the silos and related activity areas outside the confines of the fortress walls, indicate a deterioration in security. Alternatively, it is possible that the production of Negebite pottery slowly died out as wheel-made pottery became more accessible. We still do not know enough about the occurrences of this pottery in the late Iron Age to decide on this point.

It is also not exactly clear how the (scant) Edomite pottery should be interpreted. Some scholars suggested that ostraca found at 'Arad and Ḥorbat 'Uza from the end of the Iron Age indicate Edomite penetration into this region and Edomite control over some of the desert settlements, prior to the final destruction of Judah (see discussion in Beit-Arieh 1995:311–316). Could it attest to Edomite involvement in the destruction of the fortress? Alternatively, these items could have arrived at Kadesh Barnea through trade with the Negev sites or with Transjordan.

Some connection with Mediterranean coastal areas (Philistia and Phoenicia), probably trade relations, is attested by storage jars originating in these regions and by the shells (most of which, however, are from the Red Sea; Chapter 18).

The violent destruction of the Stratum 2 fortress, well dated to the late seventh/early sixth centuries BCE, indicates that the fortress was destroyed with the annihilation of Judah by the Babylonians in the year 587/6 BCE, alongside other Judahite sites in the south, such as in the Be'er Sheva' Valley. An alternative was offered by Lemaire and Vernus (1983:302)—that the fortress was destroyed by Pharaoh Necho.

STRATUM 1: THE BABYLONIAN(?)/PERSIAN-PERIOD OCCUPATION, SIXTH(?)–FOURTH CENTURIES BCE
(Plan 9)

Stratigraphy and Architecture

Above the ruins of the Stratum 2 fortress, in a few places within the courtyard and the casemates (mainly in Areas A1, B, A2; Chapters 6, 3, 2), some walls and occupation levels dateable to the Persian period were uncovered. The walls were encountered directly below the surface and some even protruded above ground (some of these remains, mainly on the east, had already been excavated by Dothan's expedition in 1956; see Dothan 1965). Correlating between walls and nearby floors in these cases was not always straightforward.

Only at one spot, in Casemate 52 on the east (Area A2), did the occupants of Stratum 1 alter the casemates. A wall (W53) was erected across this casemate, obliterating its entrance. Above the walls of Casemate 402 on the north, as well as inside it (Area A2), shallow hearths were uncovered. In addition, small and large pits, excavated in Areas B, C, and A1 (Chapters 3, 5, 6), had penetrated the earlier strata and contained Persian-period pottery.

In Area B, in the western part of the fortress, a number of small pits that disturbed the earlier deposits were discerned, alongside some floors. These, however, did not produce any diagnostic Persian-period pottery and therefore could not be attributed with certainty to the Persian period, as could the remains mentioned above. The supervisor of this area, M. Haiman, was inclined to view these remains as earlier than the Persian period, attributing them to the Babylonian period (see Chapter 11). The pottery assemblages from these contexts (Chapter 11; Pls. 11.129, 11.130) were too scant to resolve the question. Thus in Plan 9 these remains are amalgamated with Stratum 1 of the Persian period. Nowhere were these remains and those attributed to the Persian period found in superposition; from a stratigraphic point of view, there is no distinction between them.

Pottery and Other Finds, Chronology and Summary

The Persian-period ceramic repertoire of Kadesh Barnea is very similar to those in the Levantine regions to its north, especially of the coasts and lowlands. Open vessels are mainly thick *mortaria*, and the primary jar types are the prolific basked-handled jars, straight-shouldered jars and 'torpedo' jars. Noteworthy, however, in this unimpressive occupation, are the frequent occurrences of Aegean pottery, both 'East Greek' transport amphorae and table amphorae, and four Attic *lekythoi*. These, the jars, and the shells originating in the Red Sea and the Mediterranean Sea (Chapter 18) indicate that in the Persian period Kadesh Barnea was involved in supra-regional contacts, possibly in association with the Persian-period fortresses in the Negev Highlands (Cohen and Cohen-Amin 2004: Map 2 on p. 159).

The *lekythoi* are also the only vessels that allow a more precise dating. They indicate that the Persian-period occupation at the site must have encompassed the mid-fifth century BCE.

Two outstanding finds relating to Stratum 1 are the two jar handles with *yhd* sealings (Chapter 15). This is the southernmost occurrence of such stamps. In addition, an engraving on a jug fragment (Fig. 11.98; Pl. 11.130:6) may be part of an inscription.

LATER REMAINS

Long after the abandonment of Stratum 1, and after the moat and the cistern had filled with alluvium, graves were dug into the area of the fortress, which at that time stood as a conspicuous mound in Wadi el-Qudeirat. About 32 graves were encountered, most of them dug into the casemates and the blocked cistern, probably because the soil there was softer and easy to dig into (additional graves were visible only in the sections). The grave pits reached a depth of 1.0–1.5 m below the surface and no markings of any sort were placed above them. In all cases where complete interments were encountered they were oriented east–west, with the head facing south. Only a few pieces of jewelry accompanied some of the burials. All the bones were re-buried at the foot of the tell. These are apparently modern graves, probably of the Beduin who inhabit the area to this day.

CHAPTER 2

AREA A2: THE WALLS OF THE STRATA 3–2 FORTRESSES

RUDOLPH COHEN

INTRODUCTION

Area A2 comprises the four solid walls and accompanying towers of the Stratum 3 fortress, the Stratum 2 casemates constructed on top of them and the Stratum 1 remains above and in the casemates (see Plans 1.2, 1.3, 1, 2, 5–9). This 'area' was defined post-excavation, in order to facilitate its presentation. In fact, in many cases, the different parts of the fortifications were exposed during the excavations of the units adjacent to them, in different areas, and were excavated under different supervisors.

THE STRATUM 3 SOLID WALL AND TOWERS

Superstructure

The Stratum 3 fortress (Plans 1.2, 5–7) is a rectangular construction, consisting of thick solid walls 4.2–4.8 m wide. The northern and southern walls (respectively W200, W202) are about 50 m long, and the eastern and western walls (W201, W203), about 32 m long. The fortress has eight solidly built external rectangular towers projecting 4.0–4.5 m from its walls.

The four corner towers (W400 on the northeast, W402 on the southeast, W404 on the southwest and W406 on the northwest) measure approximately 8 × 10 m. The four lateral towers (W401 on the east, W403 on the south, W405 on the west, and W407 on the north) are about 7.6 × 10.0 m in size.

The walls and towers (see, e.g., Figs. 1.5, 1.7, 3.2, 8.3) were constructed of courses of large roughly hewn stones with small stones embedded in between them. No evidence of a mud-brick superstructure was recorded. Wooden beams (found unburned) were incorporated in the construction of the walls. This was most clearly indicated in Area B, where several beams in W200 were found below the Substratum 3b floor level (see Section 1-1). According to their levels these beams could not

have formed part of the Substrata 3a-b buildings in the courtyard; we assume that they were part of the Stratum 3 fortress wall. In Area D, while excavating alongside the inner face of the southern wall (W202), a wooden fragment with an iron nail was found in the wall. Other nails encountered while cleaning the face of the wall were recorded in Areas B and F. In Area B, some larger gaps between stones in the southern face of the northern segment of the wall probably indicate the locations of beams inserted perpendicularly to the wall, at about 23.50, i.e., below the level of the Substrata 3a-b floors (see Fig. 3.2; Section 1-1). The walls were preserved to a maximum height of *c*. 4 m.

The Towers

The towers were preserved to the same elevations as the wall itself, but only in the parts that are adjacent to the wall. Their external parts stand 1–2 m lower.

Tower 400. The northeastern tower was exposed on its eastern side, down to its foundations, during Dothan's excavations in 1956. No floors of Stratum 3 were found below that of Stratum 2 (L218).

Tower 401. Only the external outline of this tower, the middle tower on the east, is known, as it was not excavated (other than by a small probe in its center).

Tower 402. The southeastern corner tower has not been excavated. The outer faces of its walls were poorly preserved, having been damaged by erosion and floods.

Tower 403. The middle tower on the south has not been excavated. It is evident, however, that it was not preserved to its full height.

Tower 404. The walls of the southwestern corner tower of the fortress were hardly preserved; only their outer faces were discernible.

Tower 405. The middle tower of the fortress on the west was previously excavated by Dothan in 1956. The walls were ill-preserved and low.

Tower 406. The northwestern tower was preserved below floor level and only its outer faces were exposed.

Tower 407. The middle tower on the north was excavated by Dothan in 1956. The northern wall of the tower was only partially preserved and no clear remains of a floor or of any floor deposit were discerned.

Foundations and Constructional Fills

The earliest floor levels relating to the fortress walls (floors of Substratum 3b) reach them about 1 m below their preserved tops. Thus it may be concluded that the lower 2–3 m of the walls comprise (buried) foundations.

In some cases, the entire extent of the fortification wall, foundation part included, was constructed fully vertically (for example in Area B, Sq F/9; Area C, Sqs L–M/10; Area E, Sqs O/9–10; Area H, Sq F/4). In other places the lower part of the foundations was somewhat wider, projecting 0.2–0.3 cm (both externally and internally; e.g., in Area B, Sqs E/8–9; Area D, Sqs G–H/5; Area E, Sqs O/6–7; Area F, Sq L/11; Area G, Sq D/6, Area H, Sq H/4; see, e.g., Figs. 3.5, 4.2). Externally, the projection was usually between 0.3 and 0.6 m above the base of the wall, and internally, about 1 m.

These wider parts of the walls led M. Feist, the head of the excavation's surveying team, to consider the possibility that an earlier rectangular fortress predated that of Stratum 3 (intermediate between it and Stratum 4). However, taking into consideration all the information regarding the Stratum 3 fortress construction, the possibility of two such fortresses (or constructional stages) within the currently defined Stratum 3 must be dismissed.

Deep earthen fills (designated Substratum 3c) supported these foundations internally (see Chapters 3–5) and earthen ramparts were piled against the lower parts of the walls externally as high as 2.0–2.5 m (Chapters 7–10). The reason for this deep foundation fill may have been the need to raise the level of the fortress in order to protect it from winter floods.

In most places the foundations of the Stratum 3 fortress walls were laid directly above Stratum 4 remains, and only on the east do they cut slightly into them.

The Problem of the Gate

The entire circumference of the Stratum 3 fortress walls was exposed, either externally, internally, or from both sides; neither a gate, nor a possible blocked entrance or even a seam in the stone construction could be located. It is thus postulated that the entrance to the fortress was from above the walls and not through them, though it could have been situated high up the wall, in parts that have not been preserved (see discussion in Chapter 6). The opening of the channel leading from the south to the cistern (see Chapter 10) could have served as a postern, but as it drops into the cistern this could not have been very convenient; in any case, surely this was not the main entrance to the fortress.

THE STRATUM 2 CASEMATES AND TOWERS

In Stratum 2, a rectangular casemate structure was built on top of the Stratum 3 walls and probably atop all the towers (see Plans 1.3, 2, 8). A gap, about 5 cm high, is apparent at the seam between the solid Stratum 3 wall and the bottom of the casemates, both externally and internally (see, e.g., Figs. 3.16, 5.19). Though no section was cut through the fortresses' walls, some indication regarding the manner in which the Stratum 2 casemates were founded is provided by probes dug in several places below the floors of the casemates.

In all these probes, a fill comprising small stones and gravel was encountered; it was understood to be part of the core of the Stratum 3 solid wall. The casemates are described below.

The Eastern Casemates and Eastern Towers

There were four casemates on the eastern side, of similar dimensions (Casemates 186, 39, 52 and an unexcavated and unnumbered casemate on the south; Fig. 2.1).

Fig. 2.1. Area A2, Stratum 2. Casemates 39 and 186; looking north.

Casemate 186. This room (L186, L157) is 7.5 m long and 2.7 m wide, preserved 1 m high (Fig. 2.2). The opening leading from the courtyard is in the southwestern corner, 0.9 m wide. The beaten-earth floor was located at elevation 25.25; above it was a rich assemblage of pottery (mainly in the southern part of the room), which had been crushed under a 0.35 m thick destruction debris (Fig. 2.3; for the pottery see Pls. 11.81–11.83), as well as Hebrew ostraca inscribed with hieratic numerals (Chapter 15, Nos. 3, 4), a figurine, an arrowhead and a bead (Tables 13.1:9, 13.6:25, 13.7:28).

Casemate 39. This casemate (L39, L229b) is 5.2 m long and 3.0 m wide; its walls were well preserved, *c.* 1 m high. The entrance is in the southwestern corner and an additional opening, 0.6 m wide, leads eastward into Tower 65. The floor here is at elevation 25.24–25.35, and the accumulation on it is 0.2 m deep. The finds here included pottery (Pls. 11.84, 11.85), as well as a fragment of a basalt bowl and a bead (Tables 13.3:112, 13.7:34). They were sealed by earth and stone debris

that blocked the room (and above which a Stratum 1 floor was uncovered; see below).

Casemate 52. The size of this casemate (L52, L60; 5.2 × 2.7 m) is similar to that of Casemate 39 to its north (the eastern wall was poorly preserved). The entrance, 1 m wide, is in the southwestern corner. The beaten-earth floor, at elevation 25.40, was founded on a fill of stones. In this case it is unclear if these stones are part of the inner stone fill of the Stratum 3 solid wall, or alternatively indicate some leveling operations prior to the construction of the casemate floor (Fig. 2.4). The floor was covered by a thick burnt layer of collapsed material, 0.4 m thick, which sealed a meager pottery assemblage (Pls. 11.97–11.100), as well as an ostracon (Chapter 15, No. 1), and was superimposed by a Stratum 1 occupation level (see below).

The Southern Casemate. Similarly to the entire southeastern part of the fortress, this casemate was damaged by erosion and was badly preserved; it was not excavated and is thus unnumbered. The opening leading to it was apparently in the middle of its inner wall, similar to the location of the entrance in the southwestern casemate, 553. It is unclear whether this casemate gave access to the southeastern tower, but in analogy to the layout in the southwestern corner of the fortress, that tower was probably entered from the west.

Tower 218. Wall 630, which was uncovered over this tower, probably belongs to Stratum 2. This is deduced from the fact that similar walls exposed over Towers 427 and 542 (below) are aligned with outer walls of the casemate system. This wall apparently delineated an entrance chamber leading to the tower. A destruction layer was encountered at elevation 25.15; it was attributed to Stratum 2, as it is at about the same level as the floors of the casemates. It was disturbed by a Stratum 1 pit.

Tower 65. In a probe excavated in this tower, an earthen floor was encountered at elevation 25.15, founded on a 0.45 m deep beaten-earth fill, apparently a leveling fill above the stones of the tower. Its elevation indicates it should be attributed to Stratum 2. Only a scant assemblage of pottery was found here.

Fig. 2.2. Area A2, Stratum 2. Casemate 186; looking north.

Fig. 2.3. Area A2, Stratum 2. In situ pottery on Casemate 186 floor; looking north.

*Fig. 2.4. Area A2, Stratum 2. Floor of Casemate 52 founded
on the stone fill(?) of the Stratum 3 solid wall; looking west.*

The Northern Casemates and the Northern Middle Tower

The northern part of the casemate system comprises four or five casemates (from east to west—Casemates 423, 501, 402, 459; Fig. 2.5). The larger, eastern casemate (423) was damaged and thus it is unclear if originally this was indeed one casemate, or two. Tower 422 is located centrally along the norhern line of casemates.

Casemate 423. This area (L423, L409, L400, L37, L58) was already partially excavated by Dothan in 1956. The casemate is *c.* 15 m long and 2 m wide, but originally there may have been a partitioning wall in its center, forming two casemates, each about 7 m long, similarly to other casemates of the fortress. In the center of this long casemate the outer and inner walls are also missing. The remaining parts of the walls stand to a height of one meter. One opening was found, in the southwestern corner.

In its eastern part, this casemate was excavated down to floor level (on the west it is unclear whether floor level has been reached). The floor, at elevation 25.30, was founded on a fill of earth and stones 0.35 m thick and covered by a thick layer of burnt debris, 0.2–0.4 m deep, sealed by a sizeable stone collapse. Only scant pottery was found here (Pls. 11.97–11.101), as well one arrowhead (Table 13.6:24).

Casemate 501. The short casemate (L501, L424; 4.5 m long; Fig. 2.5) served as an entrance to the middle tower on the north. A possible opening leading from the courtyard was located in the southwestern corner, but this was not very clear. The entrance to the tower, on the other hand, was clearly located in the northeastern corner of the casemate. The western wall, W141, was not fully preserved and it seems that there was another opening here, connecting Casemates 501 and 402. If indeed there were no opening to Casemate 501 from the courtyard, this would have been the only way to enter this space. The earthen floor was apparently at elevation 25.30, covered by a thick burnt layer, but the room had been disturbed and the pottery was mixed with Persian-period material (Pls. 11.97–11.101, 11.131–11.134). Other than the pottery there were bone spatulae, a fibula and a bead

(Tables 13.5:38, 13.6:29, 13.7:29). Above that was an accumulation of collapsed stones to elevation 26.40.

Casemate 402. This casemate (Figs. 2.5, 2.6) is 8.5 m long and its walls were preserved 1 m high. In the southwestern corner, a 1.4 m wide opening connects it to the courtyard. The earthen floor of the room, at elevation 25.00, was covered by a layer of burnt debris, 0.3 m thick, containing many pottery vessels (Pls. 11.86–11.89), as well as groundstone tools and fragments of faience vessels (not illustrated), all sealed by an accumulation of collapsed stones 0.5 m thick. This, in turn, was superimposed by Stratum 1 remains (see below). The floor was founded over an earthen and stone fill laid over the solid wall of Stratum 3, which in several places was 0.8 m deep.

Casemate 459. This casemate (L401, L414, L413, L456, L459) was 7 m long and was preserved 1 m high (Figs. 2.5, 2.7). The entrance, 1 m wide, is situated close to the center of the southern wall, rather than being located at a corner. This placement was apparently chosen as it is distant enough both from the entrance to Casemate 402 on the east and from that to Room 427, leading to the northwestern tower, on the west. The floor of this casemate is at elevation 25.06 and above it a layer of ash, 0.25 m thick, contained many ceramic vessels, including a Black-on-Red juglet (Pls. 11.90–11.92), and also produced bronze fibulae (Table 13.6:28, 36) and an ostracon (Chapter 15, No. 8). These artifacts were sealed by a layer of collapses debris, 0.6 m thick.

In the eastern part of the room the floor was founded directly on the stone fill of the solid Stratum 3 wall, but on the west it lay over an earthen fill (L482), 0.2 m thick. The only explanation for the existence of this fill is that it served to level the uneven top of the Stratum 3 solid wall, indicating that the construction of that wall and the construction of the casemates are two separate events. This room was disturbed by Beduin graves (see Plan 9; Section 3-3).

Tower 422. In Stratum 2 this tower was entered via Casemate 501 to its south. Two north–south walls (W138, W139), dovetailed with the northern casemate wall, partially delineate a chamber within the tower.

Fig. 2.5. Area A2, Stratum 2. Casemates 459, 402 and 501; looking east.

Fig. 2.6. Area A2, Stratum 2. Casemate 402; looking west.

Fig. 2.7. Area A2, Stratum 2. Casemate 459; looking west.

The Western Casemates and Towers

On the western side of the fortress there were three casemates—425, 491, 553—as opposed to the four on the east; all were excavated. The northwestern and southwestern towers, and the middle western tower are described here.

Casemate 425. This northernmost casemate (L425, L408, L405; 2.0 × 7.7 m) was well preserved (Fig. 2.8). On the earthen floor, at elevation 25.23, were a few concentrations of ash, but it is unclear whether these are remains of hearths or indicate destruction by fire. Above the floor was an accumulation of collapsed material to elevation 26.00. Few potsherds were uncovered here, one of them of a cooking pot apparently dating to the Persian period (Pl. 11.99:11), which probably indicates that this casemate had been disturbed. In addition to pottery, there were some beads (Table 13.7:24, 32, 33).

Casemate 491. The central casemate here (L479, L508, L491; 2.6 × *c.* 7.0 m; preserved *c.* 1 m high) also served as an entrance to the middle tower on the west, Tower 516. The opening from the courtyard to the casemate is in the southeastern corner of the room and is 1 m wide. The casemate's western wall was not well preserved and the exact size of the opening leading to the tower is unknown. Clearly, however, it was not situated on the same axis as the entrance from the courtyard to the casemate.

On the earthen floor of the room (elevation 24.80) was a layer of burnt material 0.4 m deep and in it was a small ceramic assemblage comprising mainly jars (Pl. 11.93), accompanied by stone tools and a clay stopper or stamp (Table 3.2:20).

Casemate 553. This casemate (L523, L535, L553, L637; 2.3 × 8.4 m) was well preserved, to a height of *c.* 1 m (Fig. 2.9). The entrance was located approximately in the center of the eastern wall. The earthen floor (at elevation 25.25) was laid over a fill that leveled the top of the solid fortification wall of Stratum 3. On it was a 0.4 m deep accumulation of many pottery vessels, including numerous store jars, one of them

Fig. 2.9. Area A2, Stratum 2. Casemate 553 with jars on floor; looking north.

Fig. 2.8. Area A2, Stratum 2. Casemate 425; looking north.

full of wheat (see Pls. 11.94–11.96). Also found were a spatula and a bone handle (Table 13.5:40, 41). This deposit was sealed by destruction debris that accumulated up to elevation 26.00.

Tower 427. The northwestern corner tower of the fortress was reached by way of an opening in the northwestern corner of the fortress, between Casemates 401 and 425. Through this opening one would reach an entrance space (L427), which was clearly delineated by W624 that continues the line of W140 of Casemate 401. It is reasonable to assume that this was part of a stairwell leading up to the tower. The exact floor level of this space could not be defined. For the pottery found here, see Pls. 11.97–11.101; there were no other finds.

Tower 516. The middle, western tower was partly excavated by Dothan in 1956. In it, above the Stratum 3 remains, were two east–west walls (W151, W152, preserved only at foundation level), which were bonded with the casemate wall here. Inside the tower, adjoining the nearby casemate, two large crushed pithoi (see Pl. 11.100:17, 18) were uncovered at elevation 25.03 (Fig. 2.10).

Tower 542. In Stratum 2, over the Stratum 3 solid tower, W627 was constructed, which is the continuation of W170 of Casemate 903. It was preserved only at foundation level. This wall probably served as a support

for a stairwell that could be reached either from the courtyard to the north, or by an opening in the western wall of Casemate 903. The floor of this space has not been detected, and only a few potsherds and a glass bead (Table 13.7:26) were found here.

The Southern Casemates and Tower

Along the southern side of the fortress there were at least four casemates (from west to east—903, 901, 404, 412). The eastern casemates were almost completely destroyed by erosion and flooding. It is reasonable to assume that the very long Casemate 412 actually comprises two casemates, but no partition wall was preserved here.

The western part of this row of casemates was also not as well preserved as the casemates on the other sides of the fortress. The floors were not always detectable and were not covered by accumulations of burnt debris and artifacts, as was the case elsewhere. Either the casemates here were not damaged by the fire that had consumed the rest of the fortress, or alternatively, floor materials and overlying debris had been completely washed away into the wadi or into the cistern in the courtyard. The southern, middle tower is also poorly preserved.

Casemate 903. The western casemate here (Fig. 2.11) is 2.3 × 7.2 m in size. Its eastern wall was very poorly

Fig. 2.10. Area A2, Stratum 2. Tower 516 with crushed pithoi on floor; looking east.

preserved (only its eastern face was uncovered). The entrance to this room (1.1 m wide) is different from those of the other casemates: it does not lead directly from the courtyard, but rather is an indirect entrance, through the entrance to the southwestern tower.

Floor level here is unclear and there was no evidence of destruction. Under the casemate walls, the stone fill of the solid fortification wall of Stratum 3 was reached. The entire room was full of earth and stones to elevation 25.40. In the eastern part of the room there was a 'Black Juglet' (Pl. 11.99:14), and other finds comprise a bone spatula, an arrowhead and a bead (Tables 13.5:37, 13.6:23, 13.7:25).

Casemate 901. This casemate (Fig. 2.12) measures *c.* 2.0 × 5.30 m and was preserved to a maximum height

Fig 2.11. Area A2, Stratum 2. Casemate 903 and the opening connecting it with Tower 542; looking west.

Fig. 2.12. Area A2, Stratum 2. Casemate 901; looking east.

of 0.5 m. It has an opening in its northwestern corner, 0.6 m wide.

Casemate 404. This small casemate (L404, L419) is 2.3 × *c.* 4.4 m in size. Where the walls still stand, they are about one meter high. The entrance from the courtyard, 0.9 m wide, is in the northeastern corner. The southern wall was preserved to a maximum height of only 0.56 m, and not for its entire length; it is therefore difficult to determine where the entrance to the tower was located. As opposed to the other side towers, in this particular case it is possible that the entrance was situated opposite the entrance to the casemate itself.

The floor of the casemate (at elevation 25.02) had a layer of burnt debris overlying it, with a cooking pot in the northwestern corner (see Pl. 11.99:7); above that was an accumulation of stones and earth (the floor itself was not detected). This room was damaged by later graves.

Casemate 412. The eastern casemate here (L412, L600) appears to be very long (*c.* 20 m), even longer than the eastern casemate on the north. However, as mentioned above, although walls were not preserved here above floor level, apparently there originally were two casemates here. The only entrance encountered, 0.9 m wide, is situated *c.* 6 m from the northwestern corner of the room, and thus presumably near the northeastern corner of the more westerly room. As the openings to the casemates were usually not situated in close proximity to each other, nor to the entrances to the towers, it is reasonable to deduce that the entrance to the more easterly casemate was in the eastern half of its northern wall (at the spot where the wall is missing). The southern wall of this casemate has not been preserved. Possibly, the entrance to the side tower was by way of the postulated western casemate, 412.

The floor in the eastern part of the room, L600, was unclear (excavating to elevation 24.90 did not reveal any floor). On the west (L412), a floor was found at elevation 24.95 with a thin layer of burnt debris and potsherds on it and above that a stone collapse. The floor was founded on the stone fill (L420) of the solid fortification wall of Stratum 3.

The Middle Tower. Over the Stratum 3 solid tower, a few stones protrude southward from the face of W170 in Casemate 412, perhaps indicating the position of an entrance to the tower.

STRATUM 1 OCCUPATIONS ABOVE THE CASEMATES

Remains that can be demonstrated to be later than Stratum 2 (Plan 9) were uncovered over the casemates at three spots only—above the eastern casemates, and in one casemate on the north.

On the east, above the destruction layer of Casemate 186 (see Section 2-2) was an occupation level (L98) and a pit (L111, L122) that penetrated into the casemate and contained Persian-period pottery (Pls. 11.131–11.134). A similar occupation layer (L31, L229a; Fig. 2.13) was uncovered south of these remains, in Casemate 39, at elevation 25.85 (for the pottery, see Pl. 11.131:2).

Above the destruction layer of Casemate 52 was an occupation level (L60) associated with one wall (W53), which was built across the casemate and indicates its re-use in Stratum 1. This is the only place where post-Stratum 2 construction is evident inside the casemates.

In the northwestern part of the fortress, above the debris of Casemate 402, a shallow ash pit (L416) was uncovered, and another shallow pit (L410) cut into the northern wall of the casemate (W140). Both pits were attributed to Stratum 1.

In modern times, about sixteen graves were dug into the fill of Casemates 402 and 459 in the north and two into Casemates 404 and 412 in the south (see Chapter 1 and Plan 9).

Fig. 2.13. Area A2, Stratum 1. Persian-period mortarium in L229a above Casemate 39.

CHAPTER 3

AREA B: THE WESTERN PART OF THE STRATA 3–2 COURTYARD

MORDECHAI HAIMAN

INTRODUCTION

Area B comprises approximately the western half of the courtyard of the Strata 3–2 fortresses, excluding the cistern and its vicinity (designated Area D). Excavation in this area, which began in the third excavation season (1978) and continued in all subsequent ones, revealed extensive architectural remains of Strata 4–2, as well as some remains of Stratum 1.

STRATUM 4

The structures in Area B assigned to this stratum (Plans 1.1, 3, 4) are apparently part of an unfortified settlement associated with the oval casemate fortress located further to the east. Stratum 4 was exposed over a relatively wide area, and thus in many places it is possible to reconstruct the layout of buildings, courtyards and alleyways. Preservation was best near the walls of the Stratum 3 fortress, while the buildings below the courtyard of that fortress, and those near the cistern, had been razed to foundation level.

Although there is no evidence of major architectural changes in these buildings, two constructional phases can be defined. Most of the rooms had a single floor level, but the courtyards and alleys between the buildings usually had two (designated Substrata '4b' and '4a'); a few repairs and changes were also discerned in some walls. Floors underlying the walls, uncovered in very few places, are designated 'Substratum 4c'.

Although the Stratum 4 remains here were uncovered in four non-contiguous areas, the stratigraphical association between them is clear, as they were all buried below 2.0–2.5 m deep constructional fills of Stratum 3 (Substratum 3c; see Sections 4-4–7-7). The various buildings are described below from north to south.

Building 3199

Under the northwestern corner of the Stratum 3 courtyard, a complex of rooms was uncovered whose complete plan has not been clarified (Figs. 3.1–3.3). The main elements are Rooms 3199 and 3212 on the north, and four small spaces abutting them on the south; in two of these spaces two constructional phases were clearly discerned (see below). For the pottery of this building, see Pls. 11.20:1–13; 11.21:1, 2.

Room 3199. This large room (2 × 6 m) could be entered from two directions. On the east, an opening in W308, 0.8 m wide, was equipped with a stone threshold set slightly lower than the level of the earthen floor of the room. On the west, in W362, was a 1.25 wide opening, without a stone threshold. The southern wall (W307), 0.8 cm wide and preserved *c.* 1 m high, was constructed of two rows of stones *c.* 0.5 m long, with smaller stones in between. Along the entire northern face of this wall was a 0.3 m high plastered stone wall (W634), whose top was at floor level. This could be either a bench or, more probably, an earlier wall (Substratum 4c?), whose top was used as a platform of sorts. Wall 365, uncovered directly below the northern fortress wall of Stratum 3 (Fig. 3.2) may be the northern wall of the room. In the northeastern corner, adjacent to W308, there is a small segment of a wall or some other unclear construction, which had been damaged by the Stratum 3 solid wall.

The floor of the room, at elevation 21.00, was composed of beaten earth and must have reached the stone socles of the walls. Under the floor and walls, at elevation 20.70, natural deposits were encountered.

Room 3199 was full of collapsed debris and signs of conflagration, but only scant pottery was retrieved here.

Room 3212. The room, to the west of Room 3199, was only partially exposed, as it continues westward below the solid wall of the Stratum 3 fortress. An ash floor was uncovered here at elevation 20.89–21.00 (Fig. 3.1).

Fig. 3.1. Area B, Stratum 4. Building 3199; looking east.

Fig. 3.2. Area B, Stratum 4. Building 3199; looking north.

Room 3206. This is the westernmost room in the row of rooms south of Rooms 3199 and 3212. The eastern wall (W551) is 0.8–1.0 m wide and constructed of three rows of large and medium stones. The southern wall (W346) is constructed differently, of one row of large stones. This wall clearly had a brick superstructure (bricks have been preserved above its eastern part). A beaten-earth floor was encountered at elevation 21.10, where it abutted the socles of W307 on the north and W551 on the east.

Room 3204. This room measures *c.* 2 × 3 m and its beaten-earth floor (greenish-gray in color) reached the walls at elevation 21.06. Below this floor, another beaten-earth floor (L3207; elevation 20.84) passes below all the walls except W307 and thus may be defined as belonging to Substratum 4c.

Room 3205. This is a small space (*c.* 1.0 × 2.50 m) with walls 0.5 m wide, constructed of single rows of bricks founded on small stones. The beaten-earth floor (elevation 21.20) reaches the stone socle. In the brick wall separating this room from Room 3204 an opening, *c.* 5 cm above floor level and 0.4 m wide (Fig. 3.3), was discerned. About 0.4 m above the threshold some pink substance was encountered, possibly evidence of a decayed wooden beam.

A similar opening was detected (but not excavated) in W345, between Room 3205 and Room 3160 to the east, where part of a staircase was revealed (see below). It thus seems that the opening in W345 led to some space under that staircase.

Below the floor of Room 3205 was another floor (L3208; elevation 20.65), which underlies all the walls here. This floor should be attributed to Substratum 4c.

Room 3160. This space is similar in size to Room 3205. Three large stone steps have survived here, which are probably the lowermost steps of a staircase that was approached from the south, from Courtyard 3195. The eastern wall (W309) was constructed of large stones and its southern end was built of roughly hewn stones in a header-and-stretcher configuration.

As mentioned above, the western wall of this space (W345) apparently had a small square opening similar to that in W552 (Fig. 3.4; not excavated). As suggested above, this opening apparently led to a

Fig. 3.3. Area B, Stratum 4. Building 3199; looking west.

Fig. 3.4. Area B, Stratum 4. Blocked opening in W552; looking east.

small compartment (L3160) below the stairs; it probably served for storage (but produced very few artifacts).

Room 3209. Only the northern part of this room has been excavated, with W346 on the north and W550 on the east. This room is situated south of Room 3206 and is either a continuation of Building 3199 or part of a separate building or courtyard extending south and west of the excavated area. An ash floor was uncovered at elevation 20.97, at the level of the socles of the walls; below it was a layer of gravel.

Space 3162. This space, east of Room 3209, is connected by a passageway to its east (L3211) to Building 3200 (Fig. 3.5; see below). A beaten-earth floor was uncovered here at elevation 21.60 (probably to be attributed to Substratum 4a) and another, similar one (L3210) below it at elevation 20.92 (Substratum 4b). On the east, a flimsy wall seems to have blocked the passageway in the lower phase. It is also possible, however, that this is a step leading up to the courtyard on the east.

In the eastern part of this space, a stone-lined silo, *c.* 2 m in diameter and about 0.6 m deep, was

uncovered (L3213; Fig. 3.6). It was most probably dug from Floor 3210, but this could not be ascertained. Benches were attached to the eastern face of W550

Fig. 3.6. Area B, Stratum 4. Silo 3213 in Floor 3210; looking east.

Fig. 3.5. Area B, Stratum 4. Passage 3211 between Courtyard 3185 and Room 3162; looking west.

and to the southern face of W346, constructed of a combination of stones and brick material. They were abutted by Floor 3210.

Building 3200

The remains of this building (Fig. 3.7) comprise two walls in Sqs F–G/8, which form a corner, and another wall in Sq G/7 (W335), in which columns were apparently incorporated (see below). The east–west wall in Sqs F–G/8 (W358), 5 m long and preserved *c.* 1 m high, was constructed in its eastern part of two rows of small stones and in its western part of a single row of large stones. It is unclear whether these different constructions represent different building phases. The north–south wall, W357, is 1.5 m long, constructed of small stones and still stands one course high. In addition, a few stones (W553) at the junction between the two parts of W358 may represent a north–

south wall, parallel to W357. A gray floor (L3200), at elevation 21.25, was encountered between the three walls; it was devoid of finds. Below it were boulders and natural deposits

About 2 m south of W358 stood W335, 3 m long, probably comprising four, or possibly five, stone columns. These were made of two to four courses of un-hewn stones *c.* 0.5 m in diameter, preserved 1 m high (Fig. 3.8). Three of the columns were abutted by a fill of earth and small stones (perhaps evidence of some blocking) and two others were perhaps freestanding.

On the south, the columns were abutted by a beaten-earth floor (L1237), at elevation 21.00 (no artifacts were found here) and on the north, Floor 782 (probably the continuation of L3200), was discerned north of W335 at elevation 21.28.

For the pottery of Building 3200, see Pl. 11.20: 14–20.

Fig. 3.7. Area B, Stratum 4. Building 3200; in center, W358; on its left, Floor 3200; in background, southern part of Building 3199 and behind it the Stratum 3 fortress wall; looking west.

Fig. 3.8. Area B, Stratum 4. Wall 335 with columns and above it W237 of Substratum 3b; looking north.

Courtyard 3195

Between Buildings 3200 and 3199 were clear occupation levels; however, they presented no traces of construction other than a possible stone bench, 0.3 m wide, built against the northern face of W358 (but for another possibility, see below). This apparently was an open space. Two superimposed floor levels were discerned here; they extend over the entire area excavated between the two buildings. The lower floor (L3195), at elevation 21.20, abuts the base of what seems to be a stone bench, W633, built alongside W358. Against the eastern end of the bench was an open silo, L3201, lined with small stones, *c.* 1 m in diameter and 0.4 m deep (Fig. 3.9).

The higher floor, L3185 (= L3096), at elevation 21.30–21.40, abuts W358 and W309 and covers the bench.

It is, however, possible that the 'bench' (W633) is actually what remains of a wall that is constructionally earlier than W358. In this case this wall, Floor 3195 and the silo should be attributed to Substratum 4b, while W358 and Courtyard 3185 belong only to Substratum 4a.

As is evident, reconstructing the different constructional phases here is quite difficult. One possible reconstruc-tion views Substratum 4b as comprising the northern part of Building 3199 alone, with no rooms attached to it on the south. In their place is an open courtyard (with Floors 3207, 3208, 3210, possibly different parts of the same floor) and Silo 3213 with some walls or installations (benches?). In Substratum 4a, the southern rooms were added, the floors were raised, but it is unclear what happened to the silo. The 'blocking' of L3211 could reflect the raising of the floor level and thus is not actually a blocking.

The second possibility is that what we have here is a pre-fortress phase (Substratum 4c, as in other areas), which includes the floors that underlie the walls and perhaps some of the so-called 'benches'. The rest of the architectural remains, in this case, are either Substratum 4b, 4a or both.

Building 3194

All that remains of this structure is one wall running approximately north–south (W300) and a segment of a floor (L3194 = L3191) abutting it from the east. The wall is *c.* 5 m long, about 1 m wide at its base, and was constructed of mud bricks on a foundation of small stones. The floor was composed of a layer of black ash 0.3 m thick, and abutted this stone socle at elevation

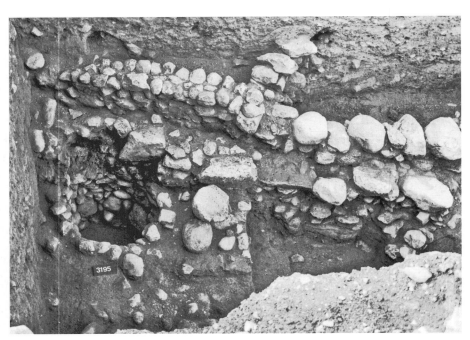

Fig. 3.9. Area B, Stratum 4. Courtyard and Silo 3201 abutting the bench (W633) north of W358; looking south.

21.0–21.2 (Fig. 3.10). Below this floor (L3192) were boulders and natural stream deposits. For the pottery see Pl. 11.22.

Building 3071

In Sq J/8, a possible corner between two walls and a silo were uncovered (Fig. 3.11). In fact, the only clear wall is the north–south wall (W356), which is 3 m long and preserved to a height of *c*. 0.3 m. It consists of one row of large fieldstones, each about 0.5 m long. It is unclear whether this row comprises the entire width of the wall, or if the wall was originally wider. A floor, L3071, composed of ash mixed with gravel, abuts W356 on the west at elevation 20.92–21.05, from which Silo 3072 was dug. The silo is *c*. 1 m in diameter, 1.2 m deep and widens slightly towards the bottom. It was lined with small stones that were coated with a layer of light colored mud and was sealed with a stone slab and a layer of mud similar to the mud employed to line it. The silo was found empty.

On the east, the base of W356 is abutted by Floor 3068, comprising an ash layer 0.2 m thick, at elevation 21.18. Below this floor there was a layer of gravel and natural sand, excavated to a depth of 0.35 m (L3077).

Fig. 3.10. Area B, Stratum 4. Mud-brick wall on stone foundation (W300) and Floor 3194 adjoining it, with in situ vessels; looking south.

Fig. 3.11. Area B, Stratum 4. Building 3071; Silo 3072 in Floor 3071 after removal of covering stone; looking west.

STRATUM 3 (C–A)

Area B is the main area in which the three phases of Stratum 3 were discerned: Substratum 3c, the constructional phase, and Substrata 3b and 3a, the occupation horizons (Plans 1.2, 5–7).

The solid fortification walls of the Stratum 3 fortress were founded here on the remains of Stratum 4. In contrast, the Stratum 3 buildings inside the courtyard were constructed c. 2 m higher. In order to create this higher level, the builders dumped layers of earthen fill over the Stratum 4 remains and stabilized these fills with layers of gravel and with narrow stone walls. This phenomenon was discerned throughout the fortress (see below, Areas D and C; Chapters 4 and 5).

Above this fill, well-planned buildings of mud bricks on stone socles were constructed, separated by alleys (Substratum 3b). Subsequently (Substratum 3a) the plan was changed and a large public building was erected above part of the Substratum 3b buildings. The walls of both substrata abut the solid fortification wall. No violent destructions mark the end of either substratum and therefore no extensive artifactual assemblages were recovered. Part of the Substratum 3a constructions in this area were, however, well sealed by the stone floor of Building 485 of Stratum 2 (see below).

SUBSTRATUM 3C

The lowest part of the large constructional fill (1–2 m deep) comprises black, gray and yellow layers, which originated from the Stratum 4 debris (Sections 4-4–7-7). The top of this fill was at an average elevation of 23.50, c. 1.5 m above the top preservation of the Stratum 4 walls. A significant part of this fill must have originated from the excavation of the cistern and the moat, which *inter alia* damaged Stratum 4 remains (sea also Areas E, F and H; Chapters 7, 8 and 10).

The fill contained very large quantities of both hand-made and wheel-made pottery, and other artifacts, most of which probably antedates the construction of the Stratum 3 fortress. However, as the construction of the wall, the cistern, the retaining walls and the moat, all achieved at this stage, must have been a lengthy process, some of the material in the fill probably represents the period of construction.

In the upper part of the constructional fill, above the deposits described above, a layer of gravel, c. 0.5 m deep, was laid. In most cases it reached elevation 24.00, but at some points, such as in Sq F/8, it reached elevation 24.35.

On the gravel, narrow walls were constructed (see Fig. 3.13, on right). These could not have been freestanding walls, as each usually comprised only one row of small stones, which could not have supported the weight of a wall. Indeed, they never exceeded one or two courses. No real floors were uncovered adjoining these walls. A few ash layers associated with them are perhaps to be related to the period of construction.

SUBSTRATUM 3B

In this substratum, the northwestern part of the fortress was occupied by three buildings separated by alleys, situated between the northern wall of the fortress (W200) and the cistern. (The area around the cistern itself was coated with thick white plaster, intended to drain water into it and protect it; see below, Area D, Chapter 4.) The buildings, of mud bricks on stone socles, were erected on the fill layers of Substratum 3c. In many cases, their plans could be reconstructed in their entirety and the overall impression is that they are all part of some pre-conceived plan.

Building 3173
This building, in the northwestern corner of the fortress, was very badly preserved. Its walls probably had bricks above the stone socles, but no bricks survived. The building abuts the Stratum 3 solid wall on the west only; on the north it was separated from it by a blind alley (see below). The plan of this building is not entirely clear but three rooms could be discerned. For pottery from this building, see Pl. 11.37.

Room 3172. The northern room of the building (L3172, L1210, L1228, L1212) has a stone paving in its southern part, at about elevation 24.10. In the southeastern corner, an installation comprising a stone bowl was incorporated into it (left on site). North of the pavement was an earthen floor. The relation between W635 on the west and this room is unclear, and likewise the location of the entrance(s).

Room 3173. This room is situated south of Room 3172. It had an earthen floor at elevation 24.24 in its northern part, and a stone pavement (L1213) in its southern. Only the northern (W567) and the eastern wall (W272) were well preserved; the southern wall (W566) survived only partially. About the middle of the room, there was one course of a few stones, slightly above the level of the earthen floor. It is unclear if this is part of Pavement 1213, part of an installation, or a corner formed by two walls. If the latter is the case, it is possible that Room 3173 was in fact divided into three spaces: the northern room with the earthen floor, a southern stone-paved room or courtyard, and a corridor (L1225; 1.75 m wide) between these and the fortress wall. As the walls of this complex are only partially preserved, it is unclear where the entrances were located.

Alley 3179

East of Building 3173, an alley, 1.4 m wide, leads from Street 723 on the south (see below) to the fortress wall. It allowed access to Building 733 and possibly also to Building 3173. Its beaten-earth floor was at elevation 24.10 on the north and at 24.45 on the south. At its northern end, toward the west, the alley opens unto an east–west narrow space (L1202), which stretches between Building 3173 and the fortress wall and leads to the northwestern corner of the fortress.

Building 733

This building has five rectangular rooms of nearly identical size—4–5 m long and approximately 2.5 m wide. It was very well preserved (0.4–0.5 m high), having been sealed by Building 713 of Substratum 3a. The walls apparently had mud bricks on their stone socles, but no bricks survived. It is perhaps possible to distinguish here two separate, annexed units of similar plan, the northern one comprising Rooms 1214, 3052, 720 and 751, and the southern one Rooms 750, 3004 and 733. Pottery from this building is illustrated in Pls. 11.38 and 11.39.

Rooms 1214 and 3052.

These two rooms, in the northwestern part of the building, are very narrow (c. 0.75 m wide), and the wall separating them (W256; see Section 8-8) does not reach W268 on the east. Both had floors at about elevation 24.00, upon which collapsed bricks and very little pottery were found. These two 'rooms' seem to have been parts of a stairwell, leading from Alley 3179 to the roof of Building 733 and to the fortress wall.

Room 720. This room, south of the possible stairwell and sharing one wall with it, is situated 2 m from the fortification wall (Fig. 3.12). The eastern part of the room (L785) had an earthen floor at elevation 24.05, while the western part (L720) was equipped with a stone pavement, at elevation 24.10. An installation (L730), consisting of a circle of 0.4 m high upright stones with a shallow stone bowl at its bottom, was incorporated into the floor. At the eastern margins of the stone paving was a row of large flat stones (W641), which could be either part of this floor, or a remnant of a partition wall separating the stone-paved and beaten-earth floor parts of the room. The relation between this wall and W632 on the south was obscured by a Stratum 2 disturbance.

Understanding the layout of the southern part of the room is problematic. Wall 565 and W268 did not reach the southern wall of this room (W632), and it is unclear if originally they did reach it, or if there was an opening at least in one of these corners (no other opening into the room was located). North of W632,

Fig. 3.12. Area B, Substratum 3b. Room 720 in Building 733; looking west.

roughly parallel to it, is a very small wall segment (W642), which is either a foundation for a wall that ran alongside W632 (this then, would have been the wall closing Room 720 on the south), or alternatively, a bench or part a pavement.

Room 751. This room abuts the fortification wall. In its eastern wall (W269) was an opening leading from Alley 748. Its earthen floor (L751 = L728) was uncovered here at elevation 24.10.

Room 750. This room, south of Room 720, may have had an opening in its incompletely preserved western wall (W267), leading to Alley 3179. It seems that the room was also connected to Room 3004 to its south via W563 (the western part of this wall was not well preserved). The floor here was of dark beaten earth, at elevation 24.38.

Room 3004. The southern room (L3004, L738) had a black ash floor 0.1 m thick, which contained a large amount of bones. In the southern part of the room was Ṭabun 739, lined with potsherds.

Room 733. This room (Figs. 3.13, 3.14) is situated east of Rooms 750 and 3004. Its northern wall (W561) was built at a distance of 0.7 m from W560 to its north, forming a narrow space between these two rooms, whose purpose is difficult to understand. The entrance to the room was apparently from Room 3004 on the west, through W238. Room 733 was damaged when a

Fig. 3.14. Area B, Strata 3 and 2. Brick Installation 721 of Stratum 2 penetrating into Room 733 of Stratum 3 and cutting W239; looking southwest.

Fig. 3.13. Area B, Substratum 3b. Room 733 of Building 733 cut by Installation 721 of Stratum 2. On right, Alley 791 and below it, the narrow walls incorporated in the Substratum 3c constructional fill; looking north.

large brick installation (L721) of Stratum 2 penetrated down to its floor level and slightly cut into the eastern wall (W239). It was thus difficult to determine the floor level, but traces of a beaten-earth floor were detected at elevation 24.28 on the north (L733) and at elevation 24.18 on the south (L1223).

Alley 748

This is another long and narrow space (L494b, L748)—an alley or a corridor, 1.1–1.4 m wide. It leads from Street 723 northward, between Buildings 3014 and 733, toward their entrances. Against W231 of Building 3014, near the opening to Room 3014 (see below), was a staircase constructed of a rectangular block of mud bricks (W249), on which the stone stairs were founded (Fig. 3.15; see Section 9-9; only three stairs were uncovered). The staircase apparently led to the roof of Building 3014 and from there to the fortification wall (the building does not seem to have had a second story as its walls were not wide enough).

The alley, however, did not lead right up to the fortification wall. Passage to the wall was hindered by a short wall (W270), which projected into the alley and may have been intended to enclose a small area at the end of the alley, against the fortification wall and behind Staircase W249. In this small enclosed space a floor (L531, L727) was exposed at elevation 24.10, on which were many potsherds.

The floor of the alley was uncovered at elevation 24.10–24.25 and on it were the remains of two ṭabuns: one against W270 and the other between W269 and W239.

Building 3014

This partially preserved building, 5.85 × 11.00 m, occupies the eastern sector of Area B and abuts the Stratum 3 fortress wall (W200). The walls comprise one row of mud bricks, 0.6 m wide, constructed on a socle of fieldstones 0.5 m high. The earthen floors abut the base of the stone socle. The plan of the rooms on the east could only be partially reconstructed, while on the west there are three well-defined rooms, preserved in their entirety (Fig. 3.16). For pottery of this building, see Pls. 11.40, 11.41.

Room 3014. This room (inner dimensions 2.00 × 5.45 m), in the northwestern part of the building (Fig. 3.17), is the best preserved. It was built against the solid fortification wall. There was an opening in the western wall, with heavy stone door jambs that were incorporated into the brick walls (see Fig. 3.17). This entrance, from Alley 748, is the only entrance to this room.

The floor, at elevation 24.15, was of beaten-earth and upon it was a heavy layer of ash with other signs of conflagration. Installations built of bricks laid on

Fig. 3.15. Area B, Substratum 3b. Alley 748 and the stairwell (W249)
abutting Building 3014; looking northeast.

*Fig. 3.16. Area B, Substratum 3b. The western part of Building 3014
against the fortification wall (W200); looking north.*

*Fig. 3.17. Area B, Substratum 3b. Room 3014 of Building 3014; in foreground,
Staircase W249 and the entrance to the room; in background, brick installations
and W229, constructed of mud bricks on stone foundations; looking east.*

*Fig. 3.18. Area B, Substrata 3b and 3a. Room 3007 of Building 3014; Installation 3075
in the northwestern corner of the room belongs to Substratum 3a; looking north.*

their sides stood against W295 and W229. This room
continued in use in the following substratum, when its
floor was raised.

Room 3007. This room (Fig. 3.18), situated south of
Room 3014, had a floor of beaten-earth and ash, which
reached the stone socle of the walls at elevation 24.20.
The eastern wall, W288 (which is also the eastern
wall of Room 792 to the south) is peculiar as it is not
in line with the eastern wall of Room 3014 (W229),
Its western face, however, seems to have reached
the external southeastern corner of Room 3014 (see
Figs. 3.18, 3.19). In the southwestern corner of the
room were a number of flat stones, which apparently
formed a bench or working surface. It is unclear where
the entrance to this room was located, perhaps in the
incompletely preserved southern wall (W558).

Room 792. Only the stone foundation, 0.5 m high, and
a dark earthen floor at elevation 24.10 remain of this
small square room. Its northwestern corner had been
damaged, apparently when Installation 717 of Stratum 2
was constructed (see below). The outer face of the
southern wall (W289) was abutted by a small cell or
installation (L3090).

Room/Space 778. This is the northern room in the
eastern part of the building (L526, L778). It abuts the
fortification wall and was apparently delineated on the
south by W555, which was only partially exposed. On

*Fig. 3.19. Area B, Substratum 3b. Building 3014: in foreground,
Floor 3013 of Room 3025, with rounded installation; in
background, juncture of W288 and W229; looking west.*

the east it may have been bounded by an (unexcavated)
continuation of W554. The earthen floor was at
elevation 24.30–24.35, and, in its western part, a *ṭabun*
was constructed, at elevation 24.25. This may have
been an open space.

Room 3025. Very partially preserved, this room (Figs.
3.19, 3.20) was enclosed by W555 on the north and by
W556 on the south, but it is not clear how far it extends

Fig. 3.20. Area B, Substratum 3b. Building 3014: on left, Alley(?) 3026 with
ṭabun; in center, Corridor 3061(?) of Building 3014 with stone installation;
on right, western part of Room 3025 of the same building; looking south.

to the west as this part is obscured by unexcavated balks. Near the eastern wall (W554), an earthen floor, encountered at elevation 24.20, reached the stone socles of W555 and W556. In the postulated western part of the room (L3013) there was a floor at elevation 24.35, with a rounded installation of small stones (see Fig. 3.19).

Courtyard 794. The entire southeastern part of Building 3014 (L794, L1229, L3009) seems to have been a large open space. Its floor, at elevation 24.00–24.20, was of beaten earth.

Corridor(?) 3061. A long and narrow space (L3021, L3061; 1.3 m wide; see Fig. 3.20), this may have been a corridor, which led from the southern part of the building to the rooms adjacent to the fortress wall and to the wall itself. The earthen floor was at elevation 24.11, and on it, against the eastern wall (W287), was an installation built of small stones.

Alley(?) 3026
This is the easternmost part excavated in Area B and it is unclear if it was an alley similar to other alleys uncovered in this area, or part of the Substratum 3b building excavated in Area C (see Chapter 5). A beaten-earth floor was exposed here (L3060, L3026). It abuts W287 of Building 3014 to its east at elevation

24.09–24.18, and a fragmentary *ṭabun* was uncovered on it (see Fig. 3.20).

Street 723
This east–west street is clear in the western half of the fortress and may have stretched further to the east (but not all the way to the eastern wall of the fortress; see Area A1, Chapter 6). On the west it separated the houses situated in the northwestern part of the fortress from the cistern to their south. A surface containing lime and remains of plaster was uncovered in Sqs F–G/7 (L709, L723) slanting southward from elevation 24.26–24.11 to elevation 23.11 on the southeast, near the northern wall of the cistern (W293). This surface was apparently designed to drain run-off water into the cistern.

The Southwestern Quadrant

Surface 3053
A thick white plaster surface in the southwestern corner of the fortress (L1216, 3042, L3053) stretches between its western and southern walls and the cistern. It slopes sharply toward the cistern, starting at elevation 24.00 by the fortification wall, and descending to elevation 23.20 at the rim of the cistern. This surface obviously aided in draining run-off water to the cistern. In Substratum 3b, no buildings were erected in the immediate vicinity of the cistern (see also Area D, Chapter 4).

SUBSTRATUM 3A

In Substratum 3a, the western half of the fortress comprised some new architectural elements, while some of the Substratum 3b constructions remained in use. In the south, the cistern continued to function (see Area D, Chapter 4), but some new poorly built structures were erected to its west and south. In the northwest, a new, large building (713) was erected over the buildings of Substratum 3b and Alley 3179. East of that, parts of the Substratum 3b structures in Sqs H/8–9 continued to function and their floors were raised. These remains are described below from west to east.

Building 713

This is a rectangular tripartite structure, whose plan suggests a storage facility. It measures 10.0 × 13.5 m and each hall is about 2.2 m wide. Its walls were built of two rows of un-hewn stones, up to 0.4 m long. They are *c.* 0.7 m wide, preserved to a maximum height of 0.45 m. The northern wall (W226) also had a mud-brick superstructure (Fig. 3.21), the bricks being 0.3 × 0.5 × 0.6 m in size, some laid on their narrow faces.

The plan of the building can be reconstructed almost in its entirety, apart from the southern stretch of the eastern wall (which was cut by Installation 721 of Stratum 2, see below) and the southeastern corner

(which had probably collapsed into the cistern). Thus, the eastern wall of the building (W220) survived only at its northern end.

In the southern wall of the building (W265), facing the cistern, some peculiar construction details were revealed. Four cylindrical, crudely hewn column bases were incorporated into the wall. Each column, *c.* 0.7 m in diameter, is surrounded by a square frame of four long, flat stones (Fig. 3.22). Since all that survived of this wall were foundations, it is difficult to know if these were freestanding columns, and thus whether the entire southern hall was a porch of sorts, or if the columns were incorporated into a solid wall.

The location of the entrance to the building is unclear. The northern wall (W226) ends *c.* 1.5 m west of W220 so there might have been an entrance here. On

Fig. 3.21. Area B, Substratum 3a. The northern wall of Building 713 (W226), built of mud bricks on a stone socle running parallel to the northern fortress wall (W200). The tops of W256 and W266, W565 of Substratum 3b are visible under Building 713; looking west.

Fig. 3.22. Area B, Substratum 3a. Wall 265, the southern wall of Building 713, with column bases; north (right) of it are W562 and W267 of Substratum 3b; looking west.

the other hand, it is logical to assume that the entrance to the building was located in the middle of its eastern wall (W220), where the wall is now missing, and led to Hall 713 from Alley 494a. Pottery from this building is illustrated in Pl. 11.42.

Northern Hall 712. This long space was partly stone paved. The pavement, at elevation 24.45, was uncovered mainly in its center, along W257 (see Fig. 3.21 and Section 8-8), and it is slightly lower than the floor of the central hall. An opening at the eastern end of the southern wall (W257), 0.7 m wide, allowed passage to this hall from Hall 713 (Fig. 3.23).

Fig. 3.23. Area B, Substratum 3a and Stratum 2. In center, eastern end of Hall 712 of Building 713 (Substratum 3a) with opening; on right, W146 of Stratum 2. On extreme right, in the balk, the Stratum 2 destruction debris may be seen between W146 and the fortress wall; looking west.

Central Hall 713. The beaten-earth floor of this hall was encountered at elevation 24.60. As the walls of Hall 713 were damaged by Building 485 of Stratum 2 (see below), it is difficult to assess where the doorways might have been. The eastern wall did not survive here, but we assume that the entrance to the building was on this side. At the eastern preserved end of W225 there were a few stones, possibly part of a wall, but as the remains were found immediately below surface and were also damaged by Installation 721, their relation to the hall is unclear. At the western end of the wall, there was a 1 m wide opening, leading to the southern hall.

The Southern Hall. The southern part of the building was apparently divided into two rooms (L1204, L714),

which could be entered from the central hall. The north–south wall separating them (W267) is a Substratum 3b wall which remained in use. It is unclear whether at this stage it stood to a regular height or was just a low partition wall. The space west of this wall (L1204) could be reached by an opening in the northern wall (W225), situated very close to the fortress wall.

This space had a beaten-earth floor at elevation 24.70 and a stone paving, probably a foundation for that floor, on the southeast. The paving partially reused tops of Substratum 3b walls. In the northeastern corner of the room a child was buried in a pit, which cut into the floor (Fig. 3.24). It could not be determined whether the burial belongs to this substratum or to Stratum 2.

In the eastern space (L714), the northern part of room was paved with wadi pebbles. The walls were preserved only slightly above floor level and thus it is unclear how this room was entered. The eastern part of this room had been damaged, probably by the construction of Installation 721 in Stratum 2, and thus the extent of this room on the east is unknown.

Fig. 3.24. Area B, Substratum 3a or Stratum 2. Child burial, cut from or into Floor 1204; looking south.

The Southwestern Quadrant

South of Building 713, along the western wall of the fortress, a row of rooms was uncovered. They were of very poor construction compared to the buildings on the north. The rooms were built over the thick lime-plaster surface that in Substratum 3b functioned as a drainage basin directing rainwater into the cistern. The attribution of this row of rooms to Substratum 3a is also based on the observation that the floor of the northernmost room (L741) abuts Building 713. The eastern walls of these rooms, facing the cistern, had washed away. It is very difficult to reconstruct the exact plans of these structures.

South of Building 713 are the remains of a stone paving (L741) at elevation 24.70, and south of the latter an earthen floor (L798 = L742) at elevation 24.50. The wall separating these floors (W578) incorporated at least two column bases and seems to have been similar in character to that of W265 north of it. South of W578, another wall (W577) runs perpendicularly to it. This wall has no clear faces and its relation to the surrounding walls has not been elucidated.

South of W578, the small rooms were built against the fortification wall, but we do not know if they also abutted the cistern. Wall 576, W575 and W574 form a narrow room (L1216a) with a beaten-earth floor at elevation 24.30. South of this room was a small open space (L1208) with an earthen floor at elevation 24.30. To its south, at the corner of the fortress, W573, W572, W571, W579 and W569 form two or three very small rooms, but a floor was detected only in the corner room (L1207), at elevation 24.22.

The area south of the cistern appears too narrow for any real construction; despite this, a fragment of a wide wall (W569) was uncovered here. It abuts the solid wall of the fortress, and next to it was a floor (L1221) at elevation 24.30.

Remains North and West of Building 713

Space 514
North of Building 713 there is a long and narrow space (Fig. 3.25), stretching between it and the northern wall of the fortress. It is nearly 1.5 m wide; no clear Substratum 3a floor levels were discerned in it, only accumulations of bricks and potsherds. It seems that this space remained purposefully blocked in Substratum 3a, but perhaps, like the northern part of Alley 494b (see below), it allowed access to the fortress walls.

Fig. 3.25. Area B, Substratum 3a. Space 514 between Building 713 and the northern fortification wall. On right, the northwestern corner of Building 485 of Stratum 2; looking east.

Alley 494a

This alley, *c.* 2 m wide, separated Building 713 from Building 3005 to its east, and essentially continues Alley 494b of Substratum 3b. A beaten-earth floor was located at elevation 24.54. At the northern end of the alley, the Substratum 3b staircase remained in use. The area behind the staircase was found full of mud-brick material and seems to have been blocked.

Building 3005

The northern part of Building 3014 of Substratum 3b continued to function (designated in Substratum 3a as 'Building 3005'), and its floor was raised. (Later, part of this building was sealed under the large stone pavement, L485, of Stratum 2.) The building apparently had two rooms but only the northern one survived. As opposed to the earlier phase of the building, when the floors reached the stone socles of the walls, the Substratum 3a floors met their mud-brick superstructures (which were preserved about 0.2–0.3 m above the floors).

Room 3005. This room remained the same as in Substratum 3b (Room 3014, see above), with a higher earthen floor at elevation 24.60 and upon it a layer of burnt material (see Section 10-10). The Substratum 3b brick installation, however, ceased to exist.

Room 3049. South of Room 3005, the northern part of another room was preserved. Abutting W295 was an earthen floor, at elevation 24.60. An installation constructed of mud bricks (L3075) was constructed in the northwestern corner of the room. As the bottom level of the installation was above Floor 3059 of Substratum 3b, we assigned it to Substratum 3a. Any architecture that may have existed further to the south was apparently washed into the cistern.

Alley 3006

West of Building 3005 there was apparently a narrow, north–south alley (L3006, L526b; Figs. 3.26, 3.27) with an earthen floor at elevation 24.60 abutting a brick wall, W229. On the north, in L526b, the floor of the alley abuts W228, W229 and the fortress wall.

The Easternmost Remains

In the easternmost part of Area B, remains of walls running parallel to the fortification wall were uncovered (W228, W580, W232 and W218) and fragments of associated earthen floors (L497 = L773, L536 and L537). They probably belonged to rooms built along the fortification wall, of which only the northern parts survived (contrary to what might be deduced from the plans, the walls are *not* cut by the fortress wall). South

Fig. 3.26. Area B, Substratum 3a. Alley 3006 between W228, and W229 of Building 3005, both abutting the northern fortification wall (W200). The ṭabun belongs to Substratum 3b (Room 778); looking west.

Fig. 3.27. Area B, Substrata 3b and 3a. On left, corner of W229 and W295 of Buildings 3014 (3b) and 3005 (3a); on right, Alley 3006; looking north.

and southwest of these walls, in Sqs H/8 and J/9, at elevation 24.50–24.60, a layer of either lime or beaten earth (L1217, L504, L3047 and L790) may represent an open area. Alternatively, there may have been walls here, which have completely eroded.

STRATUM 2

The Stratum 2 remains in Area B (see Plans 1.3, 8) comprise one large building (Building 485), which extended over the entire northwestern quarter of the courtyard and seems to have been of public nature. Its thick walls and the stone pavement of its courtyard sealed the Stratum 3 remains below it. The building was erected at a distance of 2 m from the fortification walls on the north and west. This created alleys/passageways that enabled access to the casemates.

Stratum 2 terminated in a violent destruction, but the conflagration was observable mainly in the area between the building and the northern fortification wall (see below), differing in this from the rooms of the building itself, which were found almost completely empty, and where the burnt layers were not as thick.

After the destruction of the large building, its remains were damaged (mainly in its northern part) by Stratum 1 constructions and pits, but in two places repairs to the walls could be discerned (Building 485, Phase a; see below).

In the southwestern part of the fortress, between the cistern and the western fortress wall, only scant architectural remains were uncovered; apparently, there was no substantial construction here.

Alley 486

This alley runs east–west between Building 485 and the northern casemate wall. In its western part, on the floor, a *ṭabun* was constructed adjacent to W221 of Building 485 (but the face of the wall was not entirely clear here). The beaten-earth surface of the alley (L490, L460, L486, L524 and L769; at elevation 25.00) was covered by a *c.* 0.8 m deep accumulation of collapsed and burnt substances (Section 11-11). This destruction debris is similar to that in Casemate 402 to the north. Its upper layer comprises large collapsed stones blackened by intensive fire and between them broken bricks that the fire had baked; below this debris was a layer of smaller stones mixed with black ash. The walls on either side of the alley were blackened by the fire. On the floor, especially near Casemate 402, a

Fig. 3.28. Area B, Stratum 2. Segment of Floor 486 with vessels in destruction debris; looking south.

rich assemblage of pottery was found, including many jars and a miniature clay altar (Fig. 3.28; Pls. 11.102–11.105; Table 13.2:29). This indicates that this area was used for storage and not only as a passageway.

The floor was *c.* 0.2 m thick and below it, at elevation 24.75, the solid fortification wall of Stratum 3 was discerned below the casemate wall (the southern wall of the casemate here is about 0.2 m offset to the north). On the floor, near W221, was a *ṭabun*.

The burnt bricks, stones and wooden beams all stand witness to the severe destruction here and to the intensive fire, which apparently consumed the contents of the jars. All these are similar to the evidence of destruction encountered in the casemates themselves (in which many jars were stored; see Area A2), as opposed to Building 485, which was empty of finds and where there was significantly lesser evidence of destruction.

Alley 746

This north–south alleyway runs between Building 485 and the western casemate wall. Its beaten-earth surface (L492, L746 and L480; at about elevation 25.00–25.24) was irregular and difficult to locate. In the northern part (L492), near the corner of the fortress, the level was lower by 0.5 m than its continuation to the south. Apparently this was purposely done, as this spot also functioned as a storage place for jars (see Pls. 11.106, 11.107). The floor was overlaid with a layer of intensive destruction and conflagration debris, *c.* 0.6 m thick, which dwindled to the south, where there were only occasional signs of burning and significantly fewer finds.

Building 485
This is a large, rectangular building, 9 × 24 m, of which apparently only the northern part survived. It seems that the southern part had eroded into the cistern. The remaining portion of the building includes the following: on the west are two rectangular rooms, L461 and L515, situated at right angles to each other; and a courtyard between them (L708 = L702; whose floor had mostly washed away), with a round brick installation (L721). East of the latter was a paved court (L485), enclosed on the east by W181.

Room 461, Phase b. This is a long and narrow room (inner dimensions *c.* 2.5 × 11.0 m), whose walls still stand, apart from the southeastern corner, where the entrance may have been located. The walls, 0.6–0.9 m wide, preserved two–three courses high, were constructed of two rows of medium and small stones. The beaten-earth floor of the room (L493) abutted the walls and was covered by a *c.* 0.3 m deep layer of burnt material. Artifacts were scarce on this floor—only a few complete juglets and lamps (see Pl. 11.109) were discovered below W146 of Phase a of this room (L523; for the interpretation of this wall, see below).

The western wall of the room (W222) was coated on its inner face with a thick layer of white plaster, as were the western ends of W221 and W223, to a point

c. 2.5 m east of the western wall (Fig. 3.29). It seems that there was a plastered installation in the corner of the room, whose closure to the east has not survived.

Room 461, Phase a. The northeastern corner of this room underwent some repairs, evidenced by the addition of two walls, W146 (Section 11-11) and W147. The typical Stratum 2 burnt layers north of Room 461 (in L486), as well as those in the room itself, abutted these walls and therefore they can safely be attributed to the destruction phase of Stratum 2 (see also Pl. 11:108). This attribution, however, is somewhat problematic as both these walls are fragmentary and are not in line with the other walls of this room. In comparison, the original (Phase b) walls below these (W227 and W248), although preserved only one course high, are well defined and straight. Perhaps W146 and W147 are not walls at all, but parts of the collapsed upper parts of W227 and W248.

Room 515. This room is 1.5 × 4.5 m (internal measurements) and its floor, which adjoins the stone socles of the walls, was of beaten earth. Over it was a layer of ash *c.* 0.3 m thick. The eastern and southern walls (W236 and W177) were badly preserved as they partially collapsed into the cistern.

Fig. 3.29. Area B, Stratum 2. The western end of Room 461 (W223, W222, W221) coated with white plaster; looking west.

Courtyard 708 and Installation 721. The extent of this southern courtyard (L708 = L702) is mostly conjectured. The southern wall and most of the floor had apparently washed away over the years into the cistern, which stood partially empty (as indicated by the fact that Persian-period pottery of Stratum 1 was found deep in it). The floor could be observed only at a few spots in the western part of the courtyard. In L702, part of a miniature altar was discovered (Table 13.2:30; Pl. 11.110:19). It is similar to the one from Alley 486 (see above), but its attribution to this stratum is not entirely obvious.

Installation 721 (Fig. 3.30) was uncovered in the eastern part of the courtyard, in the Stratum 2 debris, but had no demonstrable relation to any wall or floor of this stratum; its preserved top is not higher than that of the (postulated) Stratum 2 floor here. It is a rounded brick installation, *c.* 1.9 m in diameter and preserved *c.* 0.75 m high; by the curvature of its walls, it had a domed upper part. By the shape and size of the dome the maximum height of this installation may be determined to have been *c.* 1.2 m. The installation was found unsealed, full of white ash, bone fragments (see Chapter 19) and fragments of its upper parts. Over these was some pottery, which apparently penetrated the installation after it ceased to be used.

As mentioned above, the stratigraphic association of this installation is unclear. Its top was exposed immediately below the surface, and thus an attribution to Stratum 1 was considered, but eventually dismissed, as this would mean that its bottom (at about elevation 24.10) would have been *c.* 2 m lower than the Stratum 1 floors.

Another possibility would be to attribute this installation to Substratum 3b, as the level of its base could correspond to that of the occupation levels of this substratum. The main argument against this attribution is that the installation seems to cut W225 of Room 733 of Substratum 3b (see Fig. 3.14). However, this relationship is not entirely clear and it can equally be postulated that the installation was built in conjunction with the wall. The installation is indeed well accommodated in Room 733, but on the other hand it is hard to envisage how it could have functioned in this room. Thus, the installation is tentatively attributed here to Stratum 2. As the courtyard floor was apparently at about elevation 25.00, the installation would have been dug to a depth of about one meter.

The pottery within the installation includes pottery typical of Stratum 2, as well as a fragment of a Persian-

Fig. 3.30. Area B, Stratum 2. Brick Installation 721 with collapsed roof inside; looking north.

period *mortarium*, which must belong to Stratum 1. It seems then that the installation went out of use during the lifetime of Stratum 2, and perhaps remained at least partially empty later as well.

The function of Installation 721 is unclear. There is no evidence in its vicinity of pottery production, and no kiln wastes were found. Examination of the very rich assemblage of bones (Chapter 19) revealed no evidence of cultic practices, though such a function was considered by the excavators.

Paved Courtyard 485. The courtyard's estimated extent is *c.* 9 × 9 m (the line of its missing southern wall may possibly be reconstructed if we assume that W177 extended eastward to form a corner with W181, but this is only conjecture). The northern wall of the courtyard survived nearly in its entire length, two courses high. It is *c.* 0.7 m wide and up to *c.* 0.3 m long, and built of two rows of stones originating from the nearby wadi. A 1.6 m wide gap was located in the wall, probably a result of a later pit cutting through the wall (and not an opening, as previously suggested). The eastern wall was similarly constructed. The courtyard was densely paved with wadi stones of various sizes (Fig. 3.31). The floor was uncovered very close to the surface, covered by a 5 cm thick layer of ash, but devoid of finds.

Below the paving, its bedding comprised a layer of black earth (Section 7-7). In Sq J/8, where some of the paving stones had been washed away and only the black layer survived, was a square (1.2 × 1.2 m) construction of small stones, whose upper surface was slightly higher than that of the pavement—perhaps a base or a pedestal for a now missing feature.

Fig. 3.31. Area B, Stratum 2. Stone-paved floor of Courtyard 485; looking west.

Fig. 3.32. Area B, Strata 3 and 2. Installation 717 of Stratum 2 is seen in the
balk in the middle and behind it Installation 721, probably also of Stratum 2.
In background on right is part of Courtyard 485 of Stratum 2. In foreground,
W289,W288 and W558 of Substratum 3b; looking northwest.

In Sq H/8, in its southwestern corner and immediately below the surface (where the paving stones had washed away), Installation 717 was uncovered, near-rounded in shape, 0.8 m in diameter, and constructed of mud-brick material (Fig. 3.32). It was found full of ash, but no other finds indicate its function. No strict stratigraphic association between the installation and the floor was observed, other than the fact that it was embedded in the black foundation layer of the floor of the courtyard,

and may have been sunken into it. Another possibility is that the installation cut the courtyard's floor and belongs to Stratum 1.

The Southwestern Part of the Fortress

In the southwestern corner of the fortress, Floor 774 was preserved at elevation 24.80 and a *tabun* was found there, adjacent to Casemate 553 (Fig. 3.33). On

Fig. 3.33. Area B, Stratum 2. Floor 774 with ṭabun against the casemate wall; looking west.

the south, segments of two walls (W636 and W581) adjoined Casemate 903. These are the only clear surviving remains here and it seems that this area too had been damaged by runoff into the cistern.

STRATUM 1

Walls, Floors and Pits 706 and 705

Above the ruins of Stratum 2 in Area B, a few segments of walls, as well as some pits, were discerned (Plan 9). The pottery associated with them is typical of the end of the Iron Age (see Pls. 11.129, 11.130) and there is no diagnostic Persian-period material. Thus the possibility has been raised that this occupation dates to the Babylonian period (see Chapter 1).

In the northwestern corner of the fortress, in Sq E/9, W148 was uncovered, 5 m long, 0.75 m wide and preserved two courses high. The wall abuts the inner wall of Casemate 459 of Stratum 2 but overlies W222 of that stratum. Floor 426 overlies the destruction debris of Stratum 2 and reaches W148 and W127 (of Stratum 2). It was composed of beaten-earth mixed with ash and on it was a ṭabun, *c.* 0.4 m in diameter and 0.3 m high.

Parallel to W148 is another one, W55 in Sq H/9, uncovered in Dothan's 1956 excavations (Dothan 1965: Fig. 1). It is 1.5 m long and built over the destruction

layer of Stratum 2. It is possible that both these walls, alongside the inner faces of the casemates, here formed a structure, *c.* 5 × 15 m in size, to which Floor 426 belonged. The southern wall of this structure, alongside most of its floor, had apparently washed into the cistern to the south.

It thus appears that during Stratum 1 at least some of the walls of the fortress were protruding above the destruction debris, and were high enough to provide shelter.

In the area between the two above-mentioned walls, two pits were uncovered. They have no obvious stratigraphic association, other than the fact that they cut through the destruction layers of Stratum 2 (Section 11-11). Pit 706 is *c.* 1.2 m in diameter and 0.7 m deep, and Pit 705 is 2 m in diameter and 1 m deep. In both pits, the pottery was similar to that of Stratum 2, with no clear Persian-period material (see Pls. 11.129, 11.130).

Pit 3084

This pit (*c.* 0.8 m in diameter, 0.4 m deep) was clearly discerned. It is considerably deeper than the other elements attributed to Stratum 1 and situated just north of the area where most of the remains had eroded into the cistern. It has no demonstrable stratigraphic association with other Stratum 1 elements, and seems to cut into debris and fills associated with the cistern. The pottery found in it is also similar to Stratum 2 pottery, with no clear Persian-period material.

Beduin Graves

In addition to these remains, six Beduin graves were uncovered in Area B at elevation 25.00–25.80, dug to a depth of 0.4–0.5 m into the destruction debris of Stratum 2 and later occupation levels. No grave, however, disturbed the floor level of the Stratum 2 fortress.

The Stratum 1 occupation in this area, alongside earlier remains, was damaged by erosion and had mostly washed into the cistern. The eroded debris is in the form of a funnel, which narrows toward the bottom. In this way, the higher the remains, the more damage they underwent. In addition, in Sqs J/7–9, for example, rainwater flowed in a northeast–southwest direction, from the wall of the fortress into the cistern. This also determined the extent of preservation of the buildings in the strata below.

CHAPTER 4

AREA D: THE SOUTHWESTERN PART OF THE STRATA 3–2 COURTYARD AND THE CISTERN

HANNAH BERNICK-GREENBERG

INTRODUCTION

Area D is located in the southwestern part of the courtyard of Strata 3 and 2. Excavation here began in the fifth season (1979–1980), but most of the work took place during the sixth, eighth and ninth excavation seasons (1980–1981). In this area, the initial surface level was one–two meters lower than in other parts of the fortress courtyard, and therefore from the very beginning the possibility that a cistern is located here was considered. This indeed proved to be the case, and a large cistern, constructed in Stratum 3 and continuing in use in Stratum 2, was excavated in four squares (G–H/5–6).

STRATUM 4

In Area D, Stratum 4 remains were uncovered only in a few isolated places and they do not contribute much to our understanding of this stratum (Plans 1.1, 3, 4). Very little pottery attributable to this occupation has been recovered here, none of which was diagnostic.

Excavating along the external perimeter of the cistern down to Stratum 4 deposits proved to be too dangerous, and would also have weakened the cistern or caused it to collapse. Thus, although it is clear that the bottom of the cistern is much lower than the Stratum 4 floors, the direct stratigraphical relationship could not be examined. *Inter alia*, the possible existence of an earlier cistern, associated with Stratum 4, remains a moot point.

In Sq H/6, east of the sloping W280 of Substratum 3c (see below), a segment of an east–west wall (W598) preserved one course high (Fig. 4.1) was uncovered. To the south of the wall, an earthen floor (L1502 at elevation 21.23) is associated with it. Below this floor was a fill containing pottery (L1511), perhaps indicative of at least two occupation levels here.

South of these remains, in Sq H/5, a stone-lined silo was exposed (L1417; Fig. 4.2, see Section 12-12). Its

floor, at elevation 19.88, was paved with small stones and above it was a thin, well-packed layer of yellowish material. Along the walls of the silo and in its bottom was preserved a gray fill, 0.35 cm thick, which is associated with the silo (it is not part of the later fills that filled it up). Immediately south of the silo ran a curved wall (W599), but the space between the two was too narrow to examine their relationship. The southern wall of the Stratum 3 fortress was built above the level of these remains.

South of the cistern earlier deposits were excavated in two places. West of W274 (see below, Substratum 3c), a floor (L1412; Fig. 4.3), partially constructed of white lime, was reached at elevation 21.14 below the bases of

Fig. 4.1. Area D, Stratum 4. Wall 598 deep below Substratum 3c fills; looking north.

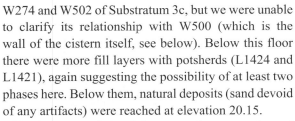

Fig. 4.2. Area D, Stratum 4. Silo 1417 and W599 below
the Stratum 3 solid fortification wall; looking south.

Fig. 4.3. Area D, Stratum 4. Floor 1412 below the
retaining walls of the Stratum 3 cistern; looking south.

W274 and W502 of Substratum 3c, but we were unable to clarify its relationship with W500 (which is the wall of the cistern itself, see below). Below this floor there were more fill layers with potsherds (L1424 and L1421), again suggesting the possibility of at least two phases here. Below them, natural deposits (sand devoid of any artifacts) were reached at elevation 20.15.

To the west of the Substratum 3c water channel (described below) we excavated down to a fill layer that could belong to Stratum 4 (L1405), but no floors were discerned here and below this layer sand and pebbles (L1423) were reached at elevation 19.90.

STRATUM 3 (C–A)

SUBSTRATUM 3C: THE CONSTRUCTIONAL PHASE OF THE CISTERN

The Stratum 3 cistern was uncovered in the western part of Area D, surrounded by a system of fills and supports (see Plan 5; Sections 12-12, 13-13). By definition, these

belong to Substratum 3c—the constructional phase of the fortress (see Chapter 1). Substrata 3b and 3a are the occupation phases associated with the cistern, excavated around it.

The Cistern

Cistern 1514 was constructed in the southwestern corner of the fortress, c. 2 m north of the southern fortress wall and c. 4 m from the western wall. Its wall(s) were uncovered nearly along its entire circumference. It is almost square in shape, measuring externally about 10 × 10 m at the top. The external southeastern and southwestern corners are rounded (the other two were not exposed).

The cistern was not completely excavated: its eastern part was dug all the way to the bottom, while on the west a 2 m wide balk was left intact. Still, taking into consideration the inward slope of the walls (see below) it is possible to determine that its lower part is rectangular in shape, about 5.0 × 3.5 m, or 17.5 sq m.

The cistern's capacity can be calculated based on the following considerations: The water channel that passes through the southern fortress wall (Plans 5–7 and see below) opens into the cistern 3.5 m above its floor. Thus, if its bottom was indeed *c.* 17.5 sq m and the cistern held water only to the level of the channel, its maximal capacity can be roughly estimated at about 60 cu m or slightly more. The walls of the cistern were preserved *c.* 7 m high. If the channel's opening could be sealed off, the maximum capacity of the cistern would be at least twice as much—at least 122 cu m.

It is unclear if and how the cistern might have been roofed (an open cistern in such a hot and dry climate would have resulted in extensive evaporation, especially in summer). No evidence of a stone roof was revealed.

As mentioned, the upper part of the cistern is about 10 × 10 m, which would require long wooden beams (wooden beams this length were probably available, as beams were used in the construction of the fortress itself). Such a wooden construction would have been supplemented by branches, and perhaps textiles and mats.

It is possible, however, that the cistern was only partially roofed. In such a case it may have been provided with a central support pillar (concealed in its unexcavated part?), similar to some of the cisterns known in the Negev sites (see Chapter 1; but the pillars in the latter, like the cisterns themselves, are rock-hewn).

One cannot, of course, dismiss the possibility that the cistern was not roofed at all, but this would be illogical, even if it did not function as the fortress' main water source (as water for daily use was available from the nearby stream).

Walls

The inner face of the cistern wall(s) (W278 = W500 = W501 = W570 = W293) was completely exposed on three sides: on the north (in the lower part only; the upper part is hidden in a balk), east and south (Figs. 4.4, 4.5). The upper parts of the outer faces of the wall were

Fig. 4.4. Area D, Substratum 3. Southern and eastern walls of the cistern with staircase and water channel; looking south.

Fig. 4.5. Area D, Substratum 3. Eastern and northern walls of the cistern. In foreground, the water channel; looking north.

exposed on the east, south and west and only partially on the north. The wall descended to a great depth but as it sloped inward we could not follow it down due to safety considerations. Only on the south and west, where the staircase to the cistern stabilized the wall, was it possible to expose its external face, to a depth of one meter. On the north and east the wall sloped very steeply and was supported mainly by the layers of the constructional fill and supporting walls. Excavating these, as mentioned, would have endangered the cistern.

The wall was constructed of two rows of medium to large fieldstones, some of them roughly hewn, with small stones laid between them and between the courses (similarly to the construction of the walls of the Strata 3 and 2 fortresses). Its maximum preservation (on the west and east) was to about elevation 23.80. It is approximately 6.7 m high (Fig. 4.6; the plaster bottom of the cistern was encountered at elevation 17.18–17.10). The inner faces of the walls were plastered. Plaster survived in a number of places, up to about one meter above the bottom, see below).

In the inner faces of the walls, especially on the east, a horizontal 'seam' is visible at the level of the bottom of the water channel incorporated in the southern segment of the wall (e.g., Fig. 4.6). It thus appears that the wall was constructed in two stages: first it was built to

elevation 20.60 (i.e., to the elevation of the walls of the channel, W340 and W341), and then the upper parts of the walls were added. These are technical stages only, and bear no chronological significance.

Stairs

A staircase descends to the bottom of the cistern, starting in the northwestern corner. This upper part is not well preserved and it is therefore difficult to determine how the entrance level may have looked. Likewise, the relationship between the staircase and the northern wall segment is unknown. The stairs were well preserved only from elevation 22.84 downward. Above this point only the wide foundation ramp of the staircase survived, but no stairs (Fig. 4.7).

The ramp is built of the same medium–large fieldstones as the walls. It is unclear whether it was structurally a later abutment to the cistern wall, or if it forms an integral part of it. As the cistern continued in use in Stratum 2 as well (see below), when occupation levels were higher, it is possible that additional stairs were added here then.

The western part of the staircase was 1.9 m wide. Ten steps were preserved here, leading down to a plastered landing at the southwestern corner of the cistern, at elevation 21.20. The stairs here were composed of flat, medium-sized stones, two to four stones per step.

Fig. 4.6. Area D, Stratum 3. The cistern, looking east. Visible at bottom, the plaster floor of the cistern and the lower part of the staircase. Note plaster adhering to the walls.

Fig. 4.7. Area D, Stratum 3. The western part of the
stairs leading into the cistern. In background, where
the stones are missing, the stone ramp supporting
the staircase is visible; looking north.

Fig. 4.8. Area D, Stratum 3. The southern part of
the stairwell of the cistern; looking west.

From the southwestern landing, the staircase
descends alongside the southern segment of the cistern
wall to another plastered landing at elevation 18.61
(Figs. 4.4, 4.6, 4.8). Here, all the stairs were preserved,
twelve in number. This part of the stairwell is 1.2–1.5 m
wide (wider at the upper part, narrower at the bottom).
The opening of the water channel is exactly aligned
with the end of this part of the stairwell, 2 m above
the landing in the southeastern corner (see Fig. 4.4 and
Section 12-12).

In the eastern part of the stairwell (see Figs. 4.4, 4.6)
there are six steps, *c.* 0.8 m wide. In general, the rise is
quite low (*c.* 0.1–0.2 m) and only in the lower stairs is
the rise higher (*c.* 0.25–0.3 m).

The Water Channel
Water Channel 1304, which conducted water from
the area south of the fortress, passed through the

Stratum 3 fortress wall to the southeastern corner
of the cistern (Figs. 4.4, 4.5, 4.6, 4.9, 4.10; Sections
12-12, 13-13). The walls of the channel were
incorporated both into the fortress wall and into the
cistern itself. Its southern, external part was excavated
in Area H (see Chapter 10, Channel 5075).

The channel slopes in an almost negligible
gradient—from 20.60 in the south, next to the fortress
wall, to 20.58 in the north. As mentioned, the opening
of the channel is located *c.* 2 m above the southeastern
landing of the cistern's stairwell. Apparently, the flow
of water in the channel was not always intensive and
when the cistern was not full one could pass below the
channel to the lower stairwell.

The channel is *c.* 0.6 m wide (it narrows in the north,
where it was incorporated into the cistern) and 0.9 m
deep. Its plaster floor is at elevation 20.60, 3.5 m above
the floor of the cistern (see above).

The two walls of the channel (W340, W341) were
constructed in a similar manner to the fortress walls
and the cistern: large, roughly hewn stones with small

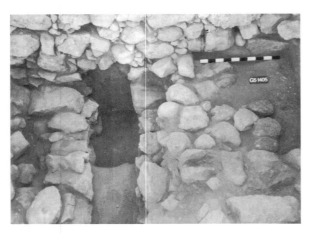

Fig. 4.9. Area D, Stratum 3. Channel 1304 between the fortress wall and the cistern; looking south.

Fig. 4.10. Area D, Stratum 3. Channel 1304 passing through the Stratum 3 fortress wall; looking south.

stones between them. The stones at the southern end of the channel are incorporated into the fortress wall, at the level of the protruding course of the fortification wall (for which see Chapter 2).

These were not freestanding walls: their outer faces are uneven, indicating that they were abutted by

earthen fills. A sounding near W341 revealed its base at approximately elevation 21.50 and demonstrated that it had been built on Stratum 4 occupation remains.

The channel must have been covered, as it was incorporated in the Substratum 3c constructional fill. However, as no capstones were encountered, it seems that the roof was constructed of a material that has not survived, possibly wood. When excavating through the Substratum 3c fills directly above the channel (and only there) a layer of medium-sized stones was encountered (L1100, L1305, L1405; see Fig. 4.9 and p. 65 below), above which the Substratum 3c fills were dumped. These stones thus seem to relate to the channel. Probably the channel was covered with a wooden construction, which was, in turn, covered and protected by these stones.

The situation in this respect further to the south, outside the fortress wall, is unclear (see Chapter 10, Area H). There the channel may have remained open at least until Stratum 2, when the glacis was constructed. If indeed the glacis on the south extended along the entire fortress wall, the channel could not have functioned any longer. Alternatively, some measure must have been devised to keep the glacis fills from filling it up.

The inner faces of the channel walls were plastered with gray-white plaster, which coated the floor and curved upward to cover the lower parts of the walls (for an analysis of the plaster, see below).

The channel was found full with very fine silt, similar to that encountered in the upper part of the fill in the cistern (see below), with only a few potsherds, alongside a carved bone spatula (Table 13.5:49).

As mentioned, the external part of the channel is at elevation 20.55. If water in Wadi el-Qudeirat did not reach this level (at the time of excavation water here was at elevation 14.80), water could not flow directly from the stream into the channel. One theory that could overcome this problem would assume that outside the fortress, the channel would have extended to the southern retaining wall (it was preserved nearly to that point), turned to the east, over this wall, and continued eastward to collect water upstream. No evidence, however, of such an extension was discovered.

Another possibility is that water would have been brought from the stream manually (in jars), as was suggested, for example, for 'Arad (Herzog 2002:74–75). The external part of the channel is further discussed in Chapter 10 (Area H) and the operation of the cistern and channel in Chapter 1.

Plaster

The floor of the cistern was completely coated with a grayish-white plaster with an uneven surface (see Figs. 4.6, 4.11). The maximum difference between the highest and lowest points on the surface is 8 cm. A sounding into the makeup of the floor (L1516) revealed several layers of plaster (see below). The same plaster was also discerned on the wall of the cistern (it was especially well preserved on the northern segment of the wall, and on the south, on the wall of the staircase), as well as on the stairs themselves, in the eastern part of the staircase and on the lowermost stairs on the south.

While excavating, two different layers of plaster could be discerned. A dark gray plaster covers the walls to a height of 1 m above the floor (this plaster was also observed on the south, above the stairs and below the water channel). This plaster penetrates in between the stones. Over this plaster is a gray-white plaster, which is excellently preserved up to 0.4–0.5 m above floor level, for example on the southern part of the staircase (Fig. 4.11) and in the northeastern corner (Fig. 4.12).

In order to check the number of layers comprising the plaster (possibly indicating repairs), the plaster was probed at the bottom of the cistern, in the northern, inner part of the channel, and at its southern end.

Plaster at the Bottom of the Cistern (L1516). This probe (0.8 × 1.1 m; Fig. 4.13; Section 12-12) was excavated through the plaster in the southeastern corner of the cistern. Examination of the floor plaster

Fig. 4.11. Area D, Stratum 3. Plaster on the southern wall of the staircase; looking south.

Fig. 4.12. Area D, Stratum 3. Plaster on northeastern corner of the cistern; looking northeast.

Fig. 4.13. Area D, Stratum 3. Sounding 1516 in the plaster floor of the cistern; looking south.

revealed a number of layers, as follows (starting from the lowermost layer): (1) A surface of small and medium-sized stones, spread over the natural deposits at elevation 16.92. (2) A gray layer of plaster *c.* 0.15 m thick. (3) A thin gray layer of sediments. (4) A 5–8 cm thick compacted layer, hard as cement, composed of brown soil mixed with pebbles and sherds, at elevation 17.12. (5) A surface of very hard brown plaster 1.5–3.0 cm thick, at elevation 17.15. (6) At the juncture between the floor and the walls (only) a 0.1 m thick layer of plaster, forming a step of sorts, apparently intended to seal and smooth the angle between the floor and the wall. (7) A compact layer of white plaster 2–7 cm thick.

The fact that the different layers of plaster are separated by layers of sediments indicates that these layers are not part of one plastering episode (for a similar conclusion regarding the outer part of the channel, see below).

Plaster on the Walls of the Cistern. This plaster was examined by a small probe on the wall of the eastern segment of the staircase. Here, indeed, only two layers were revealed, the lower one being a thick (over 5 cm) layer of black-gray plaster, and the upper one white-gray.

Plaster in the Northern Part of the Channel (L1521). The opening of the channel (into the water cistern) was also coated with a layer of white plaster 1–2 cm thick, covering the sides and bottom of the channel. At the bottom of the channel, this upper layer of plaster (elevation 20.58; Section 13-13) was spread over a layer of small and medium-sized stones and fragments of gray and brown plaster (no deeper probes were made here). On the sides of the channel, however, under the white plaster there was also a thick gray plaster similar to the plaster of L1517 outside, and very hard brown plaster, similar to that on the bottom of the cistern (L1516).

Plaster in the Southern Part of the Channel (see Chapter 10: Area H, L5074). At a distance of 2.8 m outside the fortress wall, a 1.2 m long segment of the channel was probed. Four layers of plaster were revealed here (Fig. 4.14), over a layer of clay with loess (L1522), which incorporated medium-sized stones. On its eastern side patches of ash and charcoal were observed, as well as Stratum 4 potsherds. (1) The earliest layer of plaster (L1520; elevation 20.41–20.46), was black-gray,

Fig. 4.14. Area H, Stratum 3. Probe in Channel 5074 (= 1304) showing four layers of plaster; looking north.

crumbly, 3–6 cm thick, and founded on medium-sized stones. It covered the walls and floor of the channel continuously, creating a trough-like configuration. Its surface sloped slightly northward, but it is impossible to determine whether this was the original gradient. (2) A very hard, light gray layer of plaster (L1518; elevation 20.55) was applied as a uniform horizontal surface *c.* 4 cm thick over the entire bottom of the channel and at least the lower part of the channel walls. This plaster was founded on medium-sized stones and penetrated between the stones. When exposed, this layer was cracked and segments of it appear to have shifted slightly (Fig. 4.15). (3) Over a layer of loess, above which were small stones and potsherds, was a *c.* 2.5 cm thick layer of hard gray plaster (L1517; elevation 20.59), coating the side walls and parts of the bottom of the channel. (4) The upper layer of plaster (L5074; elevation 20.60) coated only the bottom of the channel and not the side walls, and was not homogeneous along the channel. On the north it consisted of two layers (1.5–3.0 cm thick) of crumbly white plaster, containing small stone grits and founded upon a layer (8 cm) of clay and loess. On the south, the upper white plaster was 1 cm thick, and founded directly upon the gray plaster of L1517.

Plaster at the Southern (Preserved) End of the Channel (L1519). An additional sounding was sunk at the southern end of the channel (in Area H; see Chapter 10). (1) The lowermost layer here, at elevation 19.82, was composed of clay and ash containing bones and potsherds, similar to L1522 described above. (2) Above it were disintegrating remains of crumbly gray plaster

Fig. 4.15. Area H, Stratum 3. The second (L1518) plaster
layer in Channel 5074 (= 1304); looking north.

Fig. 4.16. Area D, Stratum 3. Potsherds on the
floor of the cistern; looking northwest.

(L1520), hard gray plaster (L1518) and stones. (3) At elevation 20.60 was another layer of gray plaster (similar to that in L1517, see above), which was applied in a thick mass (0.15 m) over a fill of gravel, sand and brick material. It seems that all the plaster layers identified in the northern part of the channel were present here as well.

The Fill within the Cistern

Excavation of the deep fill in the cistern was both extremely difficult and dangerous. At a certain point a mechanical pulley was employed to remove the stones and buckets of earth. As mentioned, we left the western part of this fill (*c.* 2 m wide) unexcavated (Section 13-13).

At the bottom of the cistern, on the plaster floor, was a 10 cm thick layer of muddy clay. In and on this layer were a number of potsherds attributed to the seventh century BCE (Fig. 4.16; Pl. 11.122). It is reasonable to assume that this deposit accumulated when the cistern

was full of water, and thus these potsherds provide a *terminus post quem* for the destruction of the cistern, or at least for the period in which it went out of use.

In the fill that accumulated in the cistern after it ceased to function as such, various layers could be discerned: on the layer of clay at the bottom was a 0.10–0.15 cm thick layer of loose brown earth; close to the walls it was mixed with crumbled plaster that detached from the walls. This layer covered the entire bottom and the eastern part of the staircase.

The next layer was a 2 m thick accumulation of large collapsed stones and bricks, some of which were almost completely preserved. In the eastern and southern part was a larger concentration of collapsed stones, and it appears that the walls of the cistern collapsed inwards and subsequently the earthen fills surrounding the cistern poured in (Fig. 4.17). Only scant pottery was found in this layer.

Above the collapsed stones and bricks was a layer of dark brown earth containing numerous potsherds

*Fig. 4.17. Area D, Stratum 3. Collapsed
stones inside the cistern; looking east.*

*Fig. 4.18. Area D, Stratum 3. Silt deposits
in the cistern; looking west.*

dating to the end of the Iron Age and the Persian period
(see Pls. 11.123, 11.124), as well as bones and ash. The
thickness of this fill is not uniform; in places, it reaches
one meter. It may represent the use of the cistern as a
dump.

The next layer, *c.* 2 m deep, comprises large collapsed
stones oriented southeast–northwest, between which

was a fill of silty clay that seeped in over a long period
of time and sank into thin dark brown to light brown
laminations, and deposits of small stones (Fig. 4.18).
These stones collapsed into the cistern long after the
cistern went out of use and had already filled up with
the above-mentioned deposits. This probably happened
after the fortress had already been abandoned.

The uppermost fill in the cistern was composed of
a layer of alluvium and loess 1.0–1.5 m thick. Within
this material were a number of Beduin graves and a
few Byzantine potsherds. This fill certainly belongs to
a period when the site was deserted.

Fills and Retaining Walls Surrounding the Cistern

East of the cistern was a long retaining wall running
north–south (W280 = W274), which abutted the
southern wall of the fortress (Fig. 4.19; Section 12-12).
The top of this wall is between elevations 23.45–24.07
(its highest point is on the south and its base on the
south was about elevation 21.60). The wall was
constructed of stones and pebbles of small to medium
size and sloped from east to west, retaining the fills
east of the cistern. In the upper course of the wall large
stones were incorporated. Possibly the western face of
this course formed a terrace wall of sorts.

To the east of this sloping wall, below ash Floor
1057 = Floor 1058 of Substratum 3b (see below) was
a deep accumulation of multi-colored fills, their upper
part coinciding with the top of the wall (23.62–23.82).
It was clear that they were dumped from southeast
to northwest. In Sq H/5, in the upper part of the fill
(between elevations *c.* 23.00 and 23.80), there was a
gray fill containing collapsed bricks (L1059, L1060,
L1070, L1081, L1071 and L1083). Below it was a
loose fill (L1406 and L1413) mixed with collapsed
bricks, and from elevation 22.20 and down it contained
much loess, sand and stream pebbles, down to the top
of Stratum 4 deposits at elevation 21.18. Wall 273,
built within the fill, was probably intended to stabilize
the dumped fill layers.

In Sq H/6 as well, a fill of various colors containing
collapsed bricks (L1079, L1082, L1085 and L1302)
was uncovered under an ash floor of Substratum 3b
(L1065, L1076 and L1091) to approximately elevation
23.25. Within this fill the continuations of W273
and W274 = W280 were uncovered (Fig. 4.20). The
foundations of W273 were deeper on the north (22.60)
than on the south (23.50–23.70). Further down, the fills
(L1401, L1402, L1414, L1415 and L1501) contained

*Fig. 4.19. Area D, Stratum 3. Retaining walls east of the cistern, abutting the
fortress wall (on left W273, on right W274 = W280); looking south.*

Fig. 4.20. Area D, Stratum 3. Sloping retaining W280 (= W274); looking south.

mainly collapsed blocks of nearly intact bricks, as well as gray layers, down to the top of Stratum 4 at elevation 21.30.

In the area west of W274 = W280, between it and the cistern, were collapsed bricks whose origin is unclear (Fig. 4.21). If indeed W274 = W280 also functioned as a terrace wall, these bricks may have fallen here from the higher area east of that wall (in contrast to the other side of the walls, no floor was discerned above these fills). The observation that the fills west of W274 = W280 were lower here than on its east is further corroborated by W252 of Substratum 3a that overlies them (see Plan 7). The foundations of this wall on the west are c. 0.4 m deeper than on the east.

Under the collapsed bricks was gray-brown fill material, slanting from east to west, indicating the direction from which these fills were dumped (L1056, L1075, L1077, L1078 and L1092). A Hebrew ostracon was found in L1075 (Chapter 15, No. 13).

At about elevation 23.00, the top of an east–west wall (W511), built of bricks and rows of pebbles, was uncovered (see Fig. 4.20). On the east this wall abuts the sloping retaining wall, W274 = W280, and on the west it abuts W278, which is part of the wall surrounding the cistern (its upper part was not well preserved here). The fill south of W511 was composed of dark collapsed material, which was crumbly at first and became more packed as we descended. Here the excavation reached

elevation 21.75 but did not continue down to Stratum 4 remains.

North of W511, at elevation 22.70, a layer of rounded stones (L1099) was uncovered; it abuts W511, W280 and W278 around it (see Fig. 4.20, foreground). Above the stones, dark brown clayey material had accumulated, c. 0.15 m thick. The significance of this 'installation' is unclear. It may have functioned as a small settling basin intended to separate clay from runoff water directed to the cistern.

Near the southern wall of the fortress, a wall running northwest–southeast was exposed (W502; elevation at base c. 21.80, top c. 22.30). Its southeastern end adjoins the point where W274 = W280 abuts the fortress wall and its northwestern end abuts W500 of the cistern (Fig. 4.22). This wall seems to have functioned as a retaining wall for the fills immediately adjacent to the cistern. East of W502 were collapsed bricks and a dark brown fill with many potsherds (L1408); these fills reached down to elevation 21.44, where the remains of Stratum 4 were encountered.

Fig. 4.21. Area D, Stratum 3. In the section at the far end, collapsed mud bricks on both sides of W274 = W280 are visible; looking south.

Fig. 4.22. Area D, Stratum 3. Retaining walls east of the cistern. In foreground, W274; in center, W502 abuts the fortress wall on the south and the cistern on north; looking west.

South of the cistern, in the small area between W502, the fortress wall and the eastern wall of the water channel (W341), the excavation went through brick material down to approximately elevation 21.30. It was difficult to determine if this matrix comprised Stratum 4 remains, or was a deliberate, constructional fill.

West of the latter, the area between the cistern and the fortification wall west of the water channel (L1072, L1086, L1088, L1087 and L1403, not on plan) was composed of multi-colored fill material with numerous potsherds and bones. At about elevation 23.00, collapsed stones and isolated broken bricks began to appear, and below them, at elevation 22.70, was a gray-brown fill, which ended on a surface of smooth, closely packed stones, *c.* 0.6 m thick (L1100, L1305 and L1405) at elevation 22.06–22.18. This layer overlay the walls of the channel (W341, W340). The level of the stone layer coincides here with the level of the protruding course in the Stratum 3 solid wall. Directly above the channel, the layer of stones must have rested on some support, probably of wood, which has not survived (see the discussion above).

Below the layer of stones, west of the channel, was a 0.5–0.6 m thick layer of brown soil with gravel and occasional stones, apparently still associated with the structure of the channel. Below this fill appeared layers of brick material and a gray layer 0.4 m thick, which apparently belongs to Stratum 4.

The volume of earth employed in the constructional fill of the cistern was tremendous. Pebbles and loess originated in the immediate vicinity, possibly from the hewing of the cistern. The earthen fills, with abundant potsherds, must have originated from earlier occupation levels.

SUBSTRATA 3B, 3A: THE OCCUPATION LEVELS

The area around the cistern was very sparsely built. Considering the entire layout of the construction in the fortress (Plans 1.2, 6, 7), an east–west street, separating the cistern area from the row of houses to its north, can be reconstructed. During Stratum 3 the area immediately adjacent to the cistern (a strip about 5 m wide) was somewhat lower than its surroundings. In Substratum 3b, this was an open area, other than possibly some ephemeral architecture, while in Substratum 3a a few

brick walls, which enclosed small spaces, were built here.

The attribution of these remains to Stratum 3 is not based solely on stratigraphic grounds. Other than the fact that they are obviously later than Stratum 4, there are no direct links between them and any other architecture. The pottery, however, is definitely not of Stratum 2 and thus the only possible attribution is to Stratum 3.

Substratum 3b

Only a few segments of floors may be attributed to this substratum. In the eastern part of Sq H/6, a thin ash floor at elevation 23.75–23.86 survived in small patches only and not at a uniform level (L1065, L1076 and L1091; in the western part of the square the floor surface could not be located). The floor passes below the foundations of W281 and W279 (of Substratum 3a) at elevation 23.64, and their stones could be seen to have been embedded into the floor. Very little pottery was retrieved from this ash surface.

In Sq H/5 the situation was similar. A thin ash floor (L1058, L1068, L1057 and L1063) passes below W252 of Substratum 3a and slopes from east to west (elevation 23.40–23.84). Here too the foundation stones of W252 were sunk into the floor.

In Sq G/5, a very small segment of an ash floor (L1094; elevation 23.46–23.52) was preserved to the west of a short north–south wall (W282, see below). The floor did not pass under the wall and thus possibly reached it. It is unclear, however, if the wall and floor belong to Substratum 3b or to 3a.

Substratum 3a

Only a few wall and floor segments in this area can be associated with Substratum 3a. In Sq H/6, two perpendicular but unconnected walls (W281 and W279), built of stone foundations with a brick superstructure, form part of some ramshackle structure. Wall 279 abuts W278 (the eastern wall of the cistern; Fig. 4.23).

In Sq H/5, W252, about 4.5 m long, runs east–west. It is constructed of a stepped stone socle (it is higher east of W274 = W280 of Substratum 3c and lower to its west) and a brick superstructure. For W282 and Floor 1094, see above.

*Fig. 4.23. Area D, Substratum 3a. Wall 281 and W279 over
Substratum 3c retaining walls; looking south.*

STRATUM 2

The cistern apparently continued to function in
Stratum 2 (Plans 1.3, 8), but otherwise no other
occupational remains of this stratum were preserved
here. It seems that the area around the cistern was never
built up to any significant extent, and constructions
that would have been here were washed into the open
cistern over the years.

No evidence was found of any construction above
the cistern. The pottery recovered at the bottom of
the cistern and within the layer of mud on its plaster
floor (see above), which must belong to its last period
of use, dates to the late seventh/early sixth centuries
BCE (see Pl. 11.122). This is a clear indication that
the cistern was used by the Stratum 2 inhabitants. The
fill blocking the cistern contained pottery typologically
attributable to Stratum 2, mixed throughout with
Persian-period material (see Pls. 11.123, 11.124). The
cistern thus ceased to function either during the lifetime
of Stratum 2, or subsequently.

CHAPTER 5

AREA C: THE EAST-CENTRAL PART OF THE STRATA 3–2 COURTYARD

PNINA SHOR AND HANNAH BERNICK-GREENBERG

INTRODUCTION

Area C is located in the east-central half of the courtyard of the Strata 3–2 fortresses, between Areas B and D on the west and Area A1 on the east. As the division into areas was completely arbitrary, there is architectural continuity between this area and the adjacent ones (except with Area D, the cistern, which is an architecturally independent unit). The architecture and stratigraphy of these areas must then be considered when discussing Area C. This area, more than others, had been damaged both by erosion (in the upper layers), and by Persian-period pits.

STRATUM 4 (B, A)

Stratum 4 (Plans 1.1, 3, 4) was reached in a number of places, but these are not contiguous and thus it is very difficult to reconstruct an overall plan. The remains include both the western part of the oval fortress and part of the settlement west of it. The stratigraphic correlation between these two units is crucial for understanding the chronological relation between them, but unfortunately this issue has not been clarified as there are no direct stratigraphic links in the excavated units.

Regarding the overall plan of the fortress, the most problematic remains are those in Sq L/7. They can either be attributed to the fortress or to the settlement (see more below). In the fortress itself, only one substratum was defined, while in the settlement two clear phases were discerned.

THE OVAL FORTRESS

In the northern part of Area C (Sqs L–M/9–10), under the Substratum 3c constructional fill and passing under the Stratum 3 solid wall, segments of the casemates of the oval fortress were uncovered. One casemate room was completely excavated, as well as parts of two others.

The external north–south wall of the fortress (W363) runs below the northern solid fortification wall of Stratum 3 (Figs. 5.1, 5.2). It is 1.5–1.7 m wide and constructed of large and medium-sized roughly

Fig. 5.1. Area C, Stratum 4. Wall 363, the external, western north–south wall of the oval fortress, running below the solid fortification wall of Stratum 3 (W200); looking north.

Fig. 5.2. Area C, Stratum 4, Casemate 6300. In foreground, Probe 6293 and the external wall of the fortress (W363); in background, the entrance to the casemate, in W604. On right, part of Casemate 6292 is visible; looking east.

hewn stones. A probe west of this wall (L6293; Fig. 5.2) indicates that the remains of the wall here were preserved at least 1.3 m high (the bottom of the wall has not been reached). The fortress' inner wall is about 1 m wide, also built of medium to large roughly hewn stones, and was preserved about 2 m high.

Casemate 6300

In Sqs L–M/9–10 (see also Area A1; Chapter 6), a casemate room was excavated, 2.5 wide and 3.5 m long. The western (outer) wall of the room is W363 and the eastern (inner) wall is W604. In the southern part of this latter wall an opening, about one meter wide, connected the casemate with the fortress' courtyard (Fig. 5.2). The northern and southern walls of this casemate (W603, W364), built of a single row of large stones, were 0.5 m wide. All these walls were preserved 1–2 m high.

The beaten-earth floor of Casemate 6300 (L6300 = L6294; Fig. 5.3) was uncovered at elevation 21.50–21.60. In the southwestern part of the room an installation built of a row of small stones contained a pithos (see Pl. 11.8:7). Another, smaller installation constructed of bricks was situated in the northeastern corner of the room.

On the floor was a layer of ash and many pottery vessels, both wheel made and Negebite (see Pls. 11.8,

Fig. 5.3. Area C, Stratum 4, Casemate 6300. On right, the inner wall of the fortress, W604; looking north.

11.9:1–11). Also found were an arrowhead, two 'Horus Eye' pendants and an ivory amulet (Tables 13.6:2, 13.7:1–3).

Casemate 6304

To the north of Casemate 6300, a small part of another casemate was exposed. (Part of this room had been unearthed in the first excavation seasons and was included then in Area A1; most of it remains unexcavated as it lies below the Stratum 3 solid fortification wall.) This casemate apparently forms the northwestern corner of the oval fortress. This is evident by the fact that W363 curves here eastward, and by the sharp angle between W604 and W320 that turns to the east (the latter was partly excavated in Area A1). This casemate was apparently closed on the east by W321 (excavated in Area A1), in which a 0.9 m wide opening was situated, connecting this small room to another one further east (see Area A1; Chapter 6).

Casemate 6292

To the south of Casemate 6300 the northern part of another casemate was excavated (see Fig. 5.2), with an earthen floor at elevation 21.45. Only a small part of the eastern wall (W637) was exposed, and its probable continuation is in Area A1 (see Chapter 6). On the floor were Negebite vessels (Pl. 11.9:12–14).

Wall 359 and Associated Constructions

In Sq L/7, Stratum 4 was exposed very minimally (only in the western part of the square), and in this confined area the eastern face of W359 was uncovered (Fig. 5.4), with its top at elevation 22.17 and its base at elevation 21.12. (The width of this wall is unknown as most of it remains below the western balk of this square) Abutting this wall is W360, whose top is at elevation 22.27 and its base at 21.17.

Two floor levels were uncovered on either side of this latter wall. The lower floors, L6235 on the south and L6236 on the north, are beaten earth and ash floors and appear to abut the socle of the wall at elevation 21.37. They were thus attributed to Substratum 4b. The upper floors, L6226 and L6227 (Substratum 4a) were earthen/ashy floors 0.1–0.2 m thick, and reached the wall at about elevation 21.65. On Floor 6226 were found a few pottery vessels (Pl. 11.24:9–13).

It is possible that W359 was abutted on the west by W355 (Substratum 4b), but the corner is obscured by the western balk of Sq L/7.

The correlation of these walls with the rest of the Stratum 4 plan is not straightforward. The eastern face of W359 is not in line with that of W363, but slightly west of it. Still, it is possible that it is indeed the continuation of the outer wall of the oval fortress; if so, it should be reconstructed as c. 1.5 m wide. In such a case, the floors and the perpendicular wall (W360) are located within the fortress and are part of the casemate system (this is the option presented in Plan 3).

Another possibility is to assume that W363, south of its exposed part, curved in a southeasterly direction and that W359 and W360 were situated outside the fortress, with W360 abutting the fortress from outside. In this case all the elements in Sq L/7 belong to the adjacent settlement and not to the oval fortress.

Fig. 5.4. Area C, Stratum 4. Wall 359 abutted by W360 (seen on the right); looking west.

The correlation of the remains in Sq L/7 with
either the fortress or the settlement has important
consequences for understanding the Stratum 4
occupational sequence. In other parts of the fortress,
only one floor level was discerned. In contrast, two
floor levels were distinguished, both here and in
Area B. If we attribute the elements in Sq L/7 to the
fortress, this becomes the only place in the casemates
that exhibits two substrata (but it is not clear how they
relate to the substrata defined in Area E; see Chapter 7).

THE UNFORTIFIED SETTLEMENT

In addition to Area B, Area C is the place where remains
of the Stratum 4 settlement were most extensively
exposed. Nevertheless, it is difficult to reconstruct
a clear plan of the buildings here. In most cases two
phases can be discerned, defined as Substrata 4b and
4a. Usually they were represented only by the raising
of floors, but occasionally, in particular in Sq K/7,
also by more substantial changes to the architecture.
The rectangular granary attributed to Stratum 3 (see
below) penetrates down to Substratum 4a remains and
it is unclear if it cut the walls or re-used some of them.
(The walls of the granary are mostly situated below
balks and the few points of contact we examined did
not present an unequivocal picture.)

Substratum 4b

Three architectural units associated with this substratum
were uncovered (Plan 3): House 6117 on the west,
House 6120 on the east (both near the fortress' wall)
and Silo 643 south of these.

House 6117

In Sq J/7, a 0.5 wide wall (W354) runs east–west (partly
in the northern balk of this square), and perpendicular
to it is another wall (W353; Fig. 5.5), which divides
the building into two rooms, 6117 and 6109. The walls
are constructed of mud bricks on stone socles. The
floors of both rooms, composed of earth with a thick
(c. 0.15 m) layer of ash and founded on a layer of small
stones, abut the socles of the walls. In Room 6117 the
floor is at elevation 21.13–21.30 and in the northwest
corner was a ṭabun. On the floor were found fragments
of a Negebite krater, a jug and a Midianite body sherd
(Pl. 11.24:1–3).

Fig. 5.5. Area C, Substratum 4b, Building 6117. In foreground,
Room 6117 with ṭabun and behind it, Room 6109; looking west.

The floor in Room 6109 was at elevation 21.24–
21.04 and on it Negebite vessels and a Midianite jug
were unearthed (Pl. 11.24:5–7). The wall closing this
room on the east is probably hidden in the eastern balk
of Sq J/7.

Remains of Stratum 4 were also encountered north
of these rooms, in Sq J/8 (see Area B; Chapter 3): Wall
356 runs there north–south and perhaps abutted W354
from the north (at a right angle) and thus apparently
belongs to the same building. Likewise, a segment of
an east–west wall (W589), uncovered in Sq H/6 in Area
D, can also perhaps be attributed to the same series of
rooms (see Chapter 4).

House 6120

In Sq K/7, part of a building was uncovered whose
orientation and relationship to House 6117 to its west
is problematic. Wall 355, 1 m wide, runs southeast–

northwest and its orientation vis-à-vis House 6117 is strange (Fig. 5.6). At its western end the wall may have been cut by Installation 638 of Substratum 4a (Plan 4; see Fig. 5.20). Otherwise, one may postulate an opening there. As mentioned above, at its eastern end a corner with W359 can be reconstructed in the balk.

On the north, W355 is abutted by earthen Floor 6120 = Floor 6112, at elevation 21.30–21.40. On it were a Negebite krater, three cooking pots, four juglets, a krater and a jug (Fig. 5.7; Pl. 11.23). To the south, Floor 6126 = Floor 6118, c. 0.3 m thick, was located at elevation 21.48–21.35.

Fig. 5.6. Area C, Stratum 4. Wall 355 (Substratum 4b) cut at its western end by Installation 638 and overlain by W350 of Substratum 4a. In background, Ṭabun 6088 of Substratum 3c; looking south.

Fig. 5.7. Area C, Stratum 4. Floor 6120 (Substratum 4b) with in situ vessels, under W350 and W605 of Substratum 4a; looking northeast.

Silo 643

In Sq J/5, exposure of Stratum 4 was minimal and confined to a stone-lined silo (Section 16-16), located partly below the solid fortification wall of Stratum 3. The top of the silo was at elevation 21.38 and its floor at 20.80. There may have been living horizons here, at elevation 21.20–21.30 (L687 and L644). The silo is apparently part of the series of silos uncovered in Areas D and H (see Chapter 4, 10).

Substratum 4a

The only place where a clear constructional change is evident in this substratum (Plan 4) is Sq K/7, where a new room, Room 6104, was constructed. The eastern wall of this room (W350) runs northeast–southwest above W355 of Substratum 4b and Floors 6120 and 6126 (see Fig. 5.6), indicating a major change in plan in this area. On the north, W350 is abutted, at a right angle, by W605 and on the south by W351. This latter wall is somewhat enigmatic, as it also appears to reach W352 of the Stratum 3 granary (Section 15-15). Possibly the eastern wall of the granary was founded over an undetected Stratum 4 wall (and in any case, assigning the granary to Stratum 4 is impossible).

Room 6104 had an earthen floor at elevation 21.60 (with a Negebite cup on it; Pl. 12.4:30). An oval installation (W638), constructed of a row of stones, which apparently belongs to this substratum, cut W355 of Substratum 4b (see Fig. 5.6). To the east of W350 was an earthen floor (L6110), with concentrations of ash.

West of this room, in the southwestern corner of Sq J/7, a short segment of a north–south wall (W606) was exposed above Floor 6109 of Substratum 3b. It is unclear whether W353 and W354 continued to be used alongside this wall. No higher floors were encountered, but the fill west of W353 (L6090) produced wheel-made and Negebite vessels (Pl. 11.25).

In Sq L/7 to the east, W359 and W360 are abutted by Floors 6227 and 6226, at elevation 21.50, and belong to Substratum 4a.

As in Sqs J–K/5 only one phase of construction is evident, it cannot be determined if Silo 643 indeed belongs to Substratum 4a and not to 4b.

STRATUM 3

As in other areas, we were able to distinguish in Area C between the constructional phase of the fortress (Substratum 3c), and the two subsequent occupation phases, which could be differentiated in a few places (Substrata 3b, 3a).

Substratum 3c

As in other excavation areas, the deep constructional fill of Substratum 3c was encountered here. It comprises not only natural deposits but also anthropogenic residues, such as earth mixed with ash, mud-brick material and many potsherds, and overlies Stratum 4 architecture (Plan 5; Sections 14-14–16-16, 18-18). Here too the solid fortress wall was founded directly on the ruins of Stratum 4 with hardly any foundation trenches.

The Construction of Granary 6291

The floor of the granary, in Sq J/6, was slightly higher than the lowermost Substratum 4b floor (about elevation 21.40). The granary either cut through Stratum 4 remains or otherwise incorporated in its walls segments of existing walls. It was enclosed by four slightly slanting walls, each comprising one row of medium-sized stones supported externally by the earthen fill. This kind of construction required coordination between the erection of the walls and the dumping of the fill around them (see description of the granary below).

North of the granary, in Sq J/7, a north–south narrow wall (W286) was built of a single row of stones and was preserved about 0.15 m high (Fig. 5.8; see Section 18-18). This could not have been a freestanding wall, but should be viewed as a constructional element within the Substratum 3c fill. Likewise, in the balk between Sqs L/10 and M/10, two perpendicular narrow walls (W611 and W607), constructed of one row of stones, run immediately under Substratum 3b walls. A similar phenomenon was revealed in Area D, where sloping walls were encountered around the cistern, and in Area B (see Chapters 3, 4).

An unusual discovery associated with the constructional phase of the fortress was *Ṭabun* 6088, exposed east of the granary, next to (and slightly lower than) a layer of small stones (L6082), seemingly *in situ* (Fig. 5.9). A possible explanation is that these remains belong to the construction phase of the fortress. Another possibility, proposed during the excavation by M. Feist, is that they represent an intermediate occupation, later than the Stratum 4 fortress but prior to Stratum 3 (in his opinion, the slightly protruding lower parts of the solid walls may belong to this stage, see Chapter 2).

Fig. 5.8. Area C, Substratum 3c. Wall 286
in constructional fill; looking north.

Substrata 3a–b

Adjacent to the northern wall of the fortress (Plans 6, 7), a series of buildings was constructed, extending through the northern parts of Areas B (Chapter 3), C (in Sqs L–K/9–10) and A1 (Chapter 6). In Area B, these structures were replaced in Substratum 3a by the large building erected there and thus in that area the two substrata could be clearly differentiated. In Area C (and A1) no such change occurred and the Substratum 3b structures continued in use. Additional structures were erected in the southeastern part of the fortress around the granary (extending to Area A1). In Area C, stages within Stratum 3 are evidenced mainly by the raising of floors.

The Stratum 3 buildings did not undergo any violent destruction and were not burnt. Most of the floors were made of beaten earth, and often had no overlying layer of ash, nor vessels in primary deposition. Therefore it was difficult to locate the floors and even more so to associate them with any walls. As no typological differences were discerned between the pottery assemblages of Substrata 3b and 3a, no distinction is possible based on ceramic data.

Building 6135

Built against the solid fortification wall on the north was a series of rooms, which belong to a building that

Fig. 5.9. Area C, Substratum 3c. Ṭabun 6088 near layer of stones,
L6082; on right, W352 of the Stratum 3 granary; looking south.

Fig. 5.10. Area C, Substrata 3a-b. Building 6135, looking east.

Fig. 5.11. Area C, Substrata 3a-b. Building 6135, looking south.

was only partially excavated and whose plan cannot be completely reconstructed (Figs. 5.10, 5.11). The eastern part of the building was founded conspicuously higher than its western part and it is unclear whether this is indeed how it was originally constructed, or if this is evidence of different constructional phases in Stratum 3. It is possible that originally the house comprised the western part only, and subsequently, after the construction of Building 713 in Area B above the Substratum 3b smaller constructions (see Chapter 3), there was a need to extend Building 6135 to the east, at a higher level.

Wall 503, perpendicular to and abutting the fortress wall, separates the western part of the building (Rooms 6135 = 6121 + 6105, and 6101 and probably another room to their south and the rooms to their west) from the eastern rooms (Rooms 6133, 6134 and 3024). It is 0.5 m wide and constructed of two rows of medium and small fieldstones. The wall's foundations on the south are lower than on the north.

The Western Rooms. Room 6135, built against the fortification wall, had a small stone installation in its northwestern corner. The room was entered via an opening in its southwestern corner, through Corridor 6278. On its floor, at elevation 24.44–24.23, were some Negebite bowls and fragments of a Negebite krater (Pls. 11.47, 11.48). West of Room 6135 was a smaller room (6136), also abutting the fortification wall. Wall 218 in Sq J/10 (Area B) is perhaps the western wall of this room (see Chapter 3).

South of Corridor 6278 are two rooms separated by W507, which is built of one row of large stones and is perpendicular to and abuts W506 from the south. The southern parts of these rooms were damaged by Pit 6093 of Stratum 1 (see Figs. 5.10, 5.11). Although W510, the southern wall of Room 6101, seems to have been cut by the pit, it is probable that the entrance to this room was from the south. South of Room 6101 there was another room, as indicated by the fact that W503 continues southward (under the balk).

The floors of the western rooms were composed of beaten earth with very small stones and lime, and covered with a thin layer of ash; they abut the socles of the walls.

The Eastern Rooms. As mentioned, the rooms east of W503 are higher than those on the west. The main room here is Room 6134 (= L3027), the only one excavated in its entirety (about 3 × 3 m; Fig. 5.12). Its northern

Fig. 5.12. Area C, Substrata 3a-b. Southern part of Room 6134, with two ṭabuns in corners; looking west.

wall (W505; 0.8 m wide) is located 1.2 m from the fortress wall. Above the western face of the eastern wall (W610; located below W52 of Stratum 1), traces of mud bricks were preserved above the stone socle (Section 17-17). The entrance to the room was from the south, through an opening in W504. The floor, of beaten earth and small stones, is at the level of the base of the walls, at elevation 24.65–24.80. Above it was a layer of collapsed bricks and burnt material. Two ṭabuns were constructed in the southern corners of the room.

Room 3024, south of Room 6134, was only partially excavated. It was damaged by Pit 3023 of Stratum 1 and thus it is unclear where it was bounded on the east. The eastern wall was either obliterated by the pit, or the room was wider than Room 6134 and its eastern wall was located further to the east. The earthen floor reaches the bases of the walls at elevation 24.77. In this room were found a spatula and a bone spoon (Table 3.5:22, 26).

North of Room 6134, between it and the wall of the fortress, a very narrow space was left, which most plausibly was not a room *per se*, but a stairwell (the stairs, of bricks or wood would not have survived), which would have been entered from the east. It probably led to the top of the fortification wall and the roofs of the houses (for similar stairwells see Area B).

Installations around the Granary

The area excavated around the granary was limited and on the north also damaged by erosion and by Stratum 1 pits. North and south of the granary were only small spaces and installations, perhaps some working areas. East of the granary there are stubs of walls that might relate to the structure assigned to Stratum 3 in Area A1 (see Chapter 6). Here too, two phases of occupation were discerned.

Structures North and East of the Granary. Abutting Granary 6291 on the north are two or three small (1 × 1 m) rooms or installations, their stone walls preserved only 5–15 cm high. Only in the easternmost room (Fig. 5.13) was there an earthen floor (L657), at elevation 24.36. Wall 285, which is the southern boundary of these rooms, seems to be the upper, slanting part of the northern wall of the granary (W516). To the north of these spaces, there was a beaten-earth floor (L658) at elevation 24.35.

To the east of the installations and east of the granary, an L-shaped room, Room 629, was uncovered. Its walls (W275, W261 and W262; 0.4 m wide) were built of small stones and on its beaten-earth floor (L629 = L6002) was a thick accumulation of occupation debris, perhaps indicating that it was used for a long time. Above the floor, other than potsherds, there was a complete decorated strainer cup (Pl. 11.50:7), an arrowhead and a bronze bracelet (Table 13.6:11, 18).

In the northeastern corner of the room, at the corner of W261 and W275, was a stone-lined silo (L675), *c.* 2 m in diameter and 0.75 m deep (Fig. 5.14; Section 18-18). It seems to be dovetailed into these walls. To the west of the silo, between it and the northern wall of Granary 6291, was a stone pavement (L662), *c.* 0.4 m higher than the floor to the south—probably a bench or work surface.

Overlying these remains in Sq K/7 there was a thick burnt layer (L655), a large ash pit (L670; above Silo 675) and additional ash pits or small hearths (see Fig. 5.14; Section 18-18). These remains may be assigned to Substratum 3a.

To the east of Room 629 a number of additional walls were uncovered (W258, W512, W609, W514 and W513). Most of them are located in balks or in partially excavated units and thus only a very general outline of the structure they formed can be reconstructed and they cannot be related to specific substrata (Figs. 5.15, 5.16). These walls probably connected to the remains found east of here, in Area A1 (Chapter 6). A few clear segments of earthen floors were discerned here: Locus 635, east of W261, at elevation 24.07; L6073, north of W512, at elevation 24.04–24.29 with part of a *tabun* (L6024) that might belong to it; and L1108, south of W512. The latter two were probably cut by Pit 6029.

Structures South of the Granary. Between the granary and the southern wall of the fortress there were apparently a number of small rooms and an installation. Wall 246 on the west perhaps connects with the system of walls uncovered in Area D, east of the cistern (attributed to Substratum 3a).

The western room (L464) is a small room with an earthen floor at elevation 24.21, with *in situ* pottery vessels on it (Fig. 5.17; Pl. 11.51:10–16), including *inter alia* two Negebite bowls and a Negebite krater, as well as a metal pin (Pl. 13.7:14). The room was apparently entered from the west, from the vicinity of the cistern. No wall was uncovered delimiting this room on the north. Possibly such a wall was situated slightly below W132 of Stratum 2. Alternatively, Room 464 may have abutted the southern wall of the granary, as is the case in Room 629 east of the granary, and in the small rooms on the north.

East of Room 464, Room 606 (= L613 = L609; Fig. 5.18) was built against the fortress wall, with an earthen floor at elevation 24.00–24.07. In the eastern part of the room two constructional phases were discerned. In the lower phase (Substratum 3b), W255 closed the room on the east and the room was *c.* 2.5 × 5.0 m in size (the only floor discerned here is to be associated with this phase). Wall 255 did not reach the fortress wall, but turned eastward, forming a passage (L612), 0.7 m wide.

At a later date, in Substratum 3a, a few changes were introduced to this room. The opening on the east went out of use and a small, 1.0 × 1.5 m cubicle (W253, W254, W639 and W263) was built over W255. Wall

Fig. 5.13. Area C, Substrata 3a-b. Room 657 with layer of potsherds; looking east.

Fig. 5.14. Area C, Substrata 3a-b. Silo 675 in the corner of W275 and W261 (Substratum 3b) and a layer of ash above them (Substratum 3a); looking south.

*Fig. 5.15. Area C, Substrata 3a-b, Sq L/7.
On left, W514 is in the balk; looking south.*

*Fig. 5.16. Area C, Substrata 3a-b, Sq L/7.
On right, W514 of Substrata 3a-b; on left,
W614 of Stratum 2 and below it, Ṭabun 6024
of Substrata 3a-b. At the bottom, L6085
belongs to the Substratum 3c
constructional fill; looking east.*

*Fig. 5.17. Area C, Substrata 3a-b, Room
464, with in situ pottery. In background,
W132 of Stratum 2; looking north.*

253 abuts the fortification wall on the south (Fig. 5.19). In the eastern part of this 'cubicle', at the level of the top of its walls, a layer of flat stones was encountered (not on plan; see Fig. 5.19). It is unclear whether they relate to this installation, or were part of the Stratum 2 floor above it. In the former case, it is possible that the 'cubicle' was a small foundation structure for a work area composed of these stones. No other floors attributable to Substratum 3a were uncovered south of the granary.

Fig. 5.18. Area C, Substrata 3a-b, Room 606. On left, W264 below W159 of Stratum 2; looking east.

Fig. 5.19. Area C, Substrata 3a-b. Small cubicle (Substratum 3a) against the southern fortress wall (W202), built over Room 606 of Substratum 3b. Also visible are Stratum 2 walls: on left, W159; in background, W167; and on right, W166 above W202 of Stratum 3; looking east.

Granary 6291

The granary (Figs. 5.20–5.24; see Section 16-16) was constructed concurrently with the Stratum 3 fortress and is retained by the Substratum 3c constructional fills into which it is sunk. The function of this structure is conjectured, as no remains of grain were found. It is rectangular, *c.* 4 × 5 m in size. The granary's floor, paved with flat, medium-sized stones at elevation 21.40, is higher than the floors of Substratum 4b here but may have cut through the remains of Substratum 4a, Floor 6104 and W350 (Fig. 5.20).

The walls were 1.5–2.5 m high, built of one row of medium to large stones. The upper parts of the walls

Fig. 5.20. Area C. The northeastern corner of Granary 6291 (Stratum 3) cutting(?) W351 of Substratum 4a; to the north is W355 (Substratum 4b); looking west.

tilt outward. It is unclear how high the walls originally stood, as their upper parts are almost entirely obscured in balks.

On the north, W285, which was (only partially) uncovered in the southern balk of Sq J/7, is apparently the upper part of the northern wall of the granary (labeled W516 in its lower part); its width is unknown. Judging by this wall, it seems that the walls of the granary were purposely inclined outward (a similar phenomenon was observed in the cistern). Another possibility is that the upper parts of the walls were purposely thickened externally, protruding above the level of the surrounding surface, and functioning as freestanding walls. In such a case only the lower parts of the walls held the earthen fill around the granary.

Likewise, on the south it seems that W259 is the upper part of W515. Unfortunately, however, when the lower parts of the granary walls were uncovered, most of the upper segments of these walls had already been removed and it was not clear if there was any gap between them. On the west the situation is unclear. Wall 608 was preserved to a height of 1.6 m but here it is possible that W131, built here in Stratum 2 (Plan 8), incorporated the upper part of this wall (which was removed when the Stratum 2 architecture was dismantled during excavation).

On the east only the lower part of the granary wall was preserved (W352), surviving 1.3 m above its floor. This is the only wall whose outer face was exposed. Here it was evident that the wall was constructed of one row of medium to large stones. It is not entirely unclear why the upper part of this wall was not encountered, but

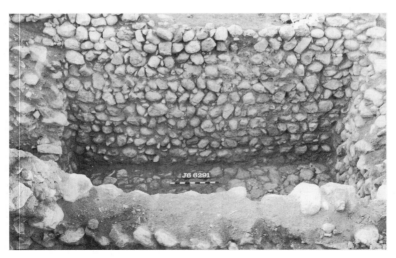

Fig. 5.21. Area C, Stratum 3. Granary 6291; looking south.

Fig. 5.22. Area C, Stratum 3. Granary 6291; looking north.

Fig. 5.23. Area C, Stratum 3. Granary 6291; looking east.

Fig. 5.24. Area C, Stratum 3. Granary 6291; looking west.

it seems that the wall had collapsed inward, alongside the earthen fills behind it. Perhaps this is the reason the granary ceased to function.

In Stratum 2, W131 and W169 were built above the granary, indicating that at this stage the granary had already been blocked by earth and debris and was no longer in use. It was sealed by floor of Courtyard 607 = L274 at elevation 25.00 (see Plan 8). (The foundations of the Stratum 2 reach down to elevation 24.75.) No other walls or floor levels were found above the granary and thus it seems to have functioned at least to the end of Stratum 3.

The pottery retrieved from the fill that blocked the granary (Pls. 11.54–11.57) is more typical of Stratum 2 than of Stratum 3. However, it does not include vessels typical of the destruction contexts of Stratum 2. Therefore it can be assumed that the granary filled up at an early stage of Stratum 2 and the walls and floor built over it were constructed later within that stratum (the granary, however, does not appear on the Stratum 2 plan).

STRATUM 2

There was an open area in Stratum 2 (Plan 8) in the northern part of Area C, between the rooms built against the eastern casemates (Area A1) and the large building in Area B. No Stratum 2 architecture whatsoever was uncovered here. South of this area, W131 and W169 were built over Granary 6291, with associated earthen floors. No substantial constructional changes occur within this stratum, but in some places two phases are represented by two floor levels.

The Stratum 2 remains here suffered many disturbances: Stratum 1 walls penetrated deeply and many pits cut through the walls and floors. Other later disturbances were caused by Beduin graves that penetrated into this occupation (see Plan 9).

The Open Area on the North

In the northern squares of Area C (east of Building 485 in Area B), below the Stratum 1 building, no architectural remains were found that could be attributed to Stratum 2. Layers of ash at elevation 24.15–25.40 are evidence of an open area (L6113, L1351, L6122, L1350 and L3015), a square or piazza of sorts.

This open area also extends to the east, to Area A1 (see Chapter 6). As both the inner and outer walls of the casemates did not survive in this area (see Area A2, Chapter 2), it was postulated by Dothan and both Cohen and Feist that the entrance to the fortress may have been located here, through one of the casemates. The existence of an open area here corroborates this suggestion.

'Courtyard' 607 and Space 616 above the Granary

Over the granary there was a 4 × 4 m, probably open space (L607 = L274; Fig. 5.25, see Section 16-16).

Fig. 5.25. Area C, Stratum 2. Courtyard 607 and W159; looking east.

On the north, W169 is 0.5 m wide, built of one row of large roughly hewn stones. On the west is a very wide wall (W131), but it is not clear whether its entire width (3.3 m) indeed reflects one construction. As its western part is in line with W158 to the south, it is possible that this mass of stone comprises two 'original' walls, one continuing W158, another narrow wall bounding Courtyard 607, and a fill of stones in between them, which could either still belong to Stratum 2 or may have been added in Stratum 1.

On the south, Courtyard 607 is bounded by an eastern extension of W132 and by the western part of W159 (see below) and between the two is an opening connecting this courtyard to Room 421. No wall closed this courtyard on the east; it opened unto Space 616.

Two superimposed beaten-earth floors were discerned in the courtyard, the lower one (L607) at elevation 25.00, and the upper (L603) at elevation 25.40. Of the artifacts uncovered on the upper floor, at least one—a *yhd* seal impression on a jar handle (Pls. 11.112:13, 11.134:14; Fig. 15.16)—must be associated with Stratum 1.

East of Courtyard 607 there is an ill-defined space, L616, bounded on the south by a wide irregular wall (W159). Here too there were two floors: a low earthen floor (L616), at elevation 24.90, which produced an extensive and peculiar assemblage of animal bones (see Chapter 19) and above it Floor 608, at elevation

25.37–25.45. The latter floor produced a fragment of a *lekythos* (Pl. 11.112:8).

The Southern Rooms

Built against the southern casemates was a series of rooms, through which the southern casemates were accessed. The western room, 421 (= L602; 3 × 4 m), had an earthen floor at elevation 25.00. The room had three openings: an opening in the southwestern corner led to Casemate 419; a narrow opening (0.4 m wide) in the eastern wall led into Room 601; and another narrow opening on the north (0.5 m wide), led into Courtyard 607.

To the east of Room 421 was Room 601 (L601, L520, L528) with an earthen floor at elevation 25.05 (Fig. 5.26). In addition to the opening connecting this room to Room 421 west of it, an opening on the south led into Casemate 420. In a pit in the floor of this room, fragments of an ostracon bearing hieratic numbers were found (Chapter 15, No. 5).

To the east of Room 601, two additional small rooms were uncovered. Room 624, measuring 1.2 × 2.1 m, connects to Room 633 east of it by way of an opening in its wide eastern wall (W612). It is unclear how the northern wall of Room 624 (W640) relates to W159. Both rooms had beaten-earth floors, that in Room 624 at elevation 25.38 and that of Room 633 at elevation

Fig. 5.26. Area C, Strata 3 and 2. Room 601 of Stratum 2 above tops of W253, W254, W255, W639 and W263 of Substratum 3a used as foundations for its floor; looking south.

25.45. These floors are higher than floor levels west of them. It is unclear whether this was indeed the situation here, or if lower floors existed below the ones discerned in the eastern rooms (excavation did not continue under these floors).

A (Postulated) Building on the East

In Sqs L/6–7 some badly preserved walls were uncovered; only their foundations survived. Wall 260, running north–south, had at its southern end a wide opening with a threshold constructed of flat stones (Fig. 5.27; see Section 14-14). The door jamb is constructed of ashlars. This wall is probably part of the large building that can be reconstructed in the southeastern corner of the fortress (see Area A1, Chapter 6); it is unclear how it relates to W159. On the north, a wall segment that seems to belong to W260 creates a corner with a segment of another wall (W297), which is perpendicular to it and extends to the east. This latter wall is probably the continuation of W122 in Area A1. Floors here were very patchy (the area was disturbed by pits): Floor 1105 at elevation 25.04 (with a concentration of burnt bones; see Chapter 19) and Floor 696 at elevation 25.20. North of W297 is another short segment of an east–west wall (W614).

The strange configurations of W131 and W159, the fact that they were preserved relatively high, and the Persian-period pottery uncovered in their vicinity may indicate that these walls were modified in Stratum 1 (and W260 may have been cut by W159).

STRATUM 1

Structures and Installations

In the eastern part of Area C there are a few architectural remains attributed to Stratum 1 (Plan 9), which are part of structures that were mostly excavated in Area A1 to the east.

In Sqs L/9–10, W52 (running north–south) is the western wall of Room 20 of Area A1. To the south, in Sq L/6, wall segments W615 and W613 (which run east–west), are probably the continuations, respectively, of W56 and W57 in Area A1.

As mentioned above, W131 and W159 of Stratum 2 may have still served in this stratum, with some alterations. Thus at least part of the Stratum 2 fortress seems to have been reused.

In Sq L/7, part of a round stone installation (L690) was uncovered. Its inner stone paving at elevation 25.40 cuts W297 of Stratum 2.

No floors that could be attributed with certainty to Stratum 1 were found in Area C, probably due to the proximity to the surface.

Pits

At least four large ash pits attributable to Stratum 1 that cut into the earlier strata were clearly discerned in Area C. Pit 6064 was traced in the balk between Sqs J/7 and J/8 and its reconstructed diameter is 3 m (it has not been unexcavated). Pit 6062 was

Fig. 5.27. Area C, Stratum 2. Wall 260 with flat threshold stone and ashlar door jamb; in foreground, W513 of Stratum 3; looking west.

discerned in the balk between Sqs K/7 and K/8. Its reconstructed diameter is 3.75 m and it cuts earlier strata to a minimum depth of 1.75 m. To the north of these pits were two additional ones: Pit 6093 in Sq K/9, *c.* 4 m in diameter and *c.* 1 m deep, cutting as deep as Stratum 3 (Fig. 5.28). In the section this pit is clearly seen to have been partially cut by another (unnumbered) pit, but the two were not differentiated during excavation. East of these, another pit (L3023) was excavated in its entirety in Sq L/9; it is *c.* 1.75 m in diameter, 1 m deep and cuts Stratum 3 remains. The pits produced scant pottery (and thus it does not seem that they were refuse pits). Ceramics recovered from them date to the Persian period and to earlier periods (Pls. 11.131–11.134).

Persian-period material was also retrieved from other loci in the southern part of Area C, such as L499,

Fig. 5.28. Pit 6093 of Stratum 1 cutting into Strata 3 and 2 deposits; looking southeast.

situated above Room 421 of Stratum 2. It is possible that there were additional small pits here, which were not discerned during the excavation.

CHAPTER 6

AREA A1: THE EASTERN PART OF THE STRATA 3–2 COURTYARD

RUDOLPH COHEN AND HANNAH BERNICK-GREENBERG

INTRODUCTION

Area A1 includes the eastern part of the fortresses' courtyard, adjoining the eastern fortification line. This area was excavated mainly during the first three seasons (1976, 1978), when the general stratigraphy of the site had not yet been deciphered. It was the first area to be excavated inside the courtyard. This, the relative limited exposure here, and the fact that many balks and walls were not removed when earlier levels were excavated, make it the stratigraphically least understood excavation area at Kadesh Barnea. During the last three excavation seasons (1981–1982), concurrently with the excavation of Area C, excavation continued here, in Sqs M–N/9. The division between Area A1 and Area C to the west is arbitrary and therefore most of the architectural elements in the former continue into the latter.

Generally speaking, in the Strata 3–2 range there is much more continuity here than in other excavation areas (both within Stratum 3 and between Strata 3 and 2). This adds further complexity to the stratigraphy and its interpretation.

According to the interpretation offered below, quite a few walls continue from Stratum 3 to Stratum 2. This phenomenon, if true, is very important in understanding the relationship between these two strata. It should however be borne in mind that the following reconstruction is indeed tentative.

STRATUM 4

Remains of Stratum 4 (Plans 1.1, 3, 4) were unearthed here in several, but relatively small, probes. They include structures inside the courtyard of the oval fortress, part of a casemate on the south and part of another one on the north. The limited exposure renders the understanding of the substrata within Stratum 4 rather difficult, but the general character of the stratum is nonetheless clear. In a few places, two substrata could be defined, mainly

based on the existence of superimposed floors, and only rarely by more substantial architectural changes. The correlation between these phases in the non-contiguous squares, and between them and the casemates, is extremely difficult. For these reasons, we chose to describe the remains of all substrata as one and relate to the different substrata only in the relevant places.

THE CASEMATES OF THE OVAL FORTRESS

In the northern part of Area A1 (Sq M/10), a small part of the northwestern casemate, 298, was uncovered. Wall 320 (Fig. 6.1) is its inner wall, which, at its western end, forms a corner with W604 (see Area C, Chapter 5).

Fig. 6.1. Area A1, Substratum 4b. Wall 320 and Casemate 298 below the solid fortification wall of Stratum 3; looking east.

Only the northern face of the wall was exposed, but we may assume it was between 0.8 and 1.0 m wide. About 0.9 m north of the wall and perpendicular to it is W321, which separates this casemate from Casemate 6304 to the west (in Area C). This wall continuous to the north under the solid wall of Stratum 3; only a small segment of it was exposed. The floor of Casemate 298 was of beaten earth, covered by ashes at about elevation 21.50–21.60. In the accumulation above the floor (L291) were broken vessels (Pl. 11.15:1–5), including a Midianite cup (Pl. 11.15:5), a complete pyxis (Pl. 11.15:6) and a grinding stone (Table 13.3:7). A burnt wooden beam lay on the floor in the doorway between the two casemates. Excavation below this floor revealed natural sediments.

In the southern part of Area A1 (Sqs M–N/5–6), several segments of walls, located immediately below the Stratum 3 fortress wall, were uncovered. As those walls were unearthed in very small probes, the reconstruction of a possible casemate here, as suggested below, is tentative.

In Sqs N/5–6, the western face of W302 was exposed beneath W201 of Stratum 3. It runs north–south and abuts W301 on the south. One cannot rule out the possibility that W302 does not in fact belong to Stratum 4 and is actually the protruding, lower part of the Stratum 3 solid wall (W201; see Chapter 2), but as this phenomenon became known to us only during later excavation seasons (in other parts of the fortress), this possibility was not further investigated here.

Wall 301, built of two faces of large stones, is about 0.9 m wide and was only partially uncovered; its continuation to the west is not clear. Its width might indicate that it is an inner wall of a casemate.

About 0.4 m west of the corner of those walls, another wall (W316; Figs. 6.2, 6.3) abuts W301 from the north. Wall 316 is 0.7 wide, and constructed of small and medium stones. It curves towards the west and its continuation was uncovered in Sqs M/5–6, where it is wider (about 0.8–0.9 m). A floor (L267), consisting

Fig. 6.2. Area A1, Stratum 4. Wall 316 adjoining W301 below the solid Stratum 3 wall; on left, W302, either of Substratum 4a or part of the Stratum 3 solid wall; looking south.

Fig. 6.3. Area A1, Substrata 4a, 4b; in background, W631 of Substratum 4b below W202 of Stratum 3. In foreground, W316 of Substratum 4a; looking south.

of earth and ash, was exposed south of this wall, at elevation 22.10 m. At floor level, a round construction of small stones, built against W316, could be part of a paved floor or an installation A floor (L278; elevation 21.97) was reached inside this 'installation'.

In Sqs M/5–6, below Floor 267, another (ash) floor was detected (L290; elevation 21.60–21.50), and near it a possible segment of a wall relating to it (W613; Fig. 6.3).

There are two possible stratigraphic attributions for these lowermost remains. One is that they belong to a pre-oval fortress phase and they then should be designated Substratum 4c (their flimsy and segmented character would suit such an attribution). Alternatively, considering the fact that the levels of these remains correlate to walls and floors designated Substratum 4b in Areas C and E (see Chapters 5 and 7), they may be attributed here to Substratum 4b.

Concomitantly, the upper phase, with W316, W301 and W302 and the stone installation or pavement, are either Substratum 4b or Substratum 4a. The latter possibility is more compatible with Substratum 4a elevations in Area E (see Plan 4).

Attempting to reconstruct the course of the oval fortress in this area depends on our understanding of the remains in Sqs M–N/5–6. If they belong to Substratum 4b, they can either be part of a casemate, part of some construction within the courtyard of the fortress, or some building outside it, i.e., part of the settlement. The right angles of the southwestern corner of Casemate 938 in Area E and between W302 and W301 may indicate that an entrance to the fortress is located here (that may explain the irregularity of the structure), but unfortunately it is situated below the solid wall of Stratum 3. Another possibility altogether is that these remains belong to a settlement postdating the oval fortress (Substratum 4a). It is this latter option that is reflected in Plans 1.1, 4, but a decisive verdict is impossible.

The Courtyard of the Oval Fortress

In the probes dug here below the constructional fill of Substratum 3c, two phases of structures and/or floor levels were defined. Walls uncovered in Sq N/8 indicate that units were constructed not only adjacent to the inner walls of the casemate system, but also within the courtyard itself. Here too, however, the stratigraphic correlation of the remains in the different probes, as well as their relationship to the subdivision of Stratum 4 as best defined in Area E (Chapter 7), remains tentative.

In Sq M/9, two floor levels were defined. The upper floor is a burnt layer (L88) at elevation 21.98– 21.89, probably belonging to Substratum 4a. The lower floor (L114) is a beaten-earth layer at elevation 21.60–21.45, with a destruction accumulation above it (L100), which produced complete pottery vessels (Pl. 11.15:7– 15). Floor 114 could thus relate to the Substratum 4b fortress.

In Sq N/8, the faces of four walls were uncovered, all in sections of this probe. In the northern section is W311, and parallel to it, at a distance of 2 m to the south, is W312, which continues westward in Sq M/8 (= W314). Below this wall is an earlier one, W313.

Another wall, W310, was discovered directly below the solid wall of Stratum 3, in the eastern section of the probe. However, though it was defined as an independent wall, it is possible that it actually constitutes the protruding lower courses of that Stratum 3 solid wall (W201; see Chapter 2). It was unclear whether W311 and W313 abut W310, or were cut by it. Wall 312 seems to have been cut by the solid wall of Stratum 3.

Two floor levels were exposed here. The lower floor (L280; elevation 21.57–21.45; Fig. 6.4) abutted W311 and W313 and is thus attributed to Substratum 4b. It was of beaten earth and had on it an accumulation of fallen stones (including grinding stones), ash, earth, and pottery (Pl. 11.16:4–8). The upper floor (L265; elevation 22.00–21.85) abutted W311 and W312 and had ash and mud-brick debris on it. The relations of both floors to W310 is unclear (no foundation trench has been detected here).

In Sq M/8, W314 was uncovered, 0.6 m wide, constructed of medium-sized stones; it is the continuation of W312 to the east (Fig. 6.5). The western end of W314 seems to abut a north–south wall seen in the western balk of the unit. This latter wall is probably the inner wall of the western casemates of the oval fortress—the continuation of W637 in Sq M/9 (Area C; see Chapter 5).

In the western balk, another segment of a possible wall was visible; it seemed to abut W314 from the north, and could have been part of W637. This wall does not appear on the plans.

Abutting W314 from the south is W315 (see Fig. 6.5), constructed of one row of medium-sized stones.

Fig. 6.4. Area A1, Substratum 4b. In background, W313 and L280. Above W313 is W312 of Substratum 4a and on left, W201 of the Stratum 3 fortress; looking south.

Fig. 6.5. Area A1, Substratum 4a; W315 and W314, looking south.

Two floor levels were traced here. The lower floor (L285; elevation 21.42) abuts W314 and passes under W315; it is attributed to Substratum 4b. It consisted of beaten earth with little ash and had a few vessels above it (see Pl. 11.16:1, 2). An upper set of floors includes L271, north of W314 at elevation 22.30, covered by a burnt layer; and L276 east of W315 at elevation 21.93. As W315 was built over the lower floor (L285), it was attributed to Substratum 4a only, alongside Floors 271 and 276.

In Sq M/7 no architecture was encountered, other than a beaten-earth floor (L302) at elevation 21.40, with a juglet on it (Pl. 11.16:3). Considering the level of the floor, we assume it belongs to Substratum 4b.

STRATUM 3 (C–A)

As in other areas, the solid wall of the Stratum 3 fortress was founded directly on Stratum 4 architecture, but the structures within the fortress' courtyard and the occupation levels associated with them were located *c.* 1.5 m above the tops of the earlier walls. As in other excavation areas, Substratum 3c is defined as the constructional stage of Stratum 3, and Substrata 3b and 3a are the two occupational horizons.

In general, the remains here resemble the architecture encountered in the other excavation areas within the fortress (Areas B, C; see Chapters 3, 5). Structures were built in an orderly fashion against and parallel (*grosso modo*) to the fortress walls.

Throughout most of Area A1 two substrata (3b and 3a) could be detected. In some places there was a clear architectural change between them and in others minor ones, in floor level and installations. As opposed to all other areas within the fortress, it seems that here some of the Stratum 3 walls were reused in Stratum 2.

SUBSTRATUM 3C

As mentioned, a 1.5 m deep earthen fill separated the tops of Stratum 4 walls and the bases of Stratum 3 walls (Plan 5). In Area A1, hardly any architectural remains or clear surfaces were discerned within this fill, below the Stratum 3 floors, except for one location. In the balk between Sqs M10 and L10, under Stratum 1 (Persian-period) remains, two narrow walls (W611, W607) were discovered below the floor levels of Stratum 3b, which in this vicinity are at elevation 24.70. All that remains of these walls is a single course of small stones, with no adjoining floors. Very similar narrow walls were unearthed in Areas B, C and D, attributed there to Substratum 3c (see Chapters 3–5).

SUBSTRATUM 3B

Room 194

In the northern part of the area (Square M/10), close to the northeastern corner of the courtyard, segments of three walls were uncovered (W617, W618 and W619; Fig. 6.6; Plans 1.2, 6), forming a room (194), apparently a continuation of Building 6134 to the west (Area C). The walls, constructed of small fieldstones, were preserved 0.2–0.3 m high. As their tops are very even, it seems that they used to support a mud-brick superstructure. The earthen floor associated with these walls (L194; elevation 24.70) was laid over a layer of pebbles (L195). Although the stratigraphic relationships between this room and the Stratum 3 fortress wall (as deduced from the photographs), are not entirely clear, the attribution of this structure to Stratum 3 is the only possible option. Both the floor and the walls were founded on the Substratum 3c constructional fill and are lower than the Stratum 2 architecture. It was impossible, however, to ascertain if they belong to Substratum 3b or 3a. They may have been in use during both these phases (as reflected in Plans 1.2, 6, 7), or, alternatively, were constructed only in Substratum 3a alongside the eastern part of Building 6134 of Area C (in which case this particular spot was an open area in Substratum 3b).

Fig. 6.6. Area A1, Substrata 3a-b. Room 194 (W618, W617)
built against the solid fortification wall, looking east.

East of W617, in the space between Room 194 and the corner of the fortress, only a packed earth surface (L263) was discerned, at elevation 24.46. This area could possibly have been part of an alley, similar to those found in Area B (See Chapter 3).

Room 174

This room, situated south of Room 194, abuts W201— the eastern wall of the Stratum 3 fortress. Only its southern and western walls survived. They are built of small fieldstones and preserved only slightly above floor level (respectively W230 and W213; Fig. 6.7). The northern wall of the room was not uncovered and it is also unclear where the entrance was situated. In the southwestern part of the room, a stone pavement was revealed at elevation 24.24–24.38 (see Fig. 6.7). The pottery here was very meager.

Abutting the southern wall of Room 174 is a quarter circle of one row of small stones, apparently some installation. No floor was encountered around it (L211, L213) .

Building 206

Further to the south, parallel to the eastern wall of the fortress, two parallel walls were uncovered. They are over 10 m long (W215 = W245 and W216) and delineate a long narrow space between them, or alternatively an alley separating two structures. Wall 215 = W245 is constructed of small fieldstones and above them one to two courses of boulders survived, laid in a single row (Fig. 6.8). It is unclear whether these comprise foundations and superstructure, or two building stages of chronological significance (the level of the interface between the two 'stages' is unclear). Plans 1.2, 6 and 7 reflect the latter possibility: the small fieldstone stage is attributed to Substratum 3b and the courses of large stones, to Substratum 3a. As the courses of large stones have not been dismantled, the lower stage of W215 = W245 is indicated in Plan 6 in outline only. According to the photographs (Fig. 6.8, and Fig. 6.10 below) it is clear that the lower stage extended at least through Sqs M/6–7, but it is unclear if it extended north to Sq M/8, under the larger stones. In this square only the large stones were clearly discerned and, as in levels and construction technique they correspond to the upper stage of the wall in its southern part, they were attributed to Substratum 3a; this attribution, however, has its own problems (see below). On the south, the lower stage stops about 1.5 m short of the southern fortress wall. Wall 216, by its leveled top, seems to have carried a brick superstructure.

*Fig. 6.7. Area A1, Substratum 3b. In left foreground, W213 and the stone pavement of Room 174
below W621 of Substratum 3a. In background, W124 of Substratum 3a against
W201, the eastern wall of the Stratum 3 fortress; looking east.*

Fig. 6.8. Area A1, Substrata 3a-b. The two stages of W215; looking east.

Fig. 6.9. Area A1, Substratum 3b. Floor 206 of Building 206, looking east.

'Building' 206 was only partially excavated and its division into rooms/subspaces is not entirely clear. East of W215 = W245 only a small segment of an earthen floor, L206, was uncovered, in the northern part of this building (Fig. 6.9). This floor relates to W215.

The southern preserved end of the lower stage of W215 = W245 is abutted by W244, which delineates a narrow space (L202) in the southeastern corner of the fortress, possibly a passage to an ascent onto the fortress wall.

Alley(?) 197

In the space between W215 = W245 and W216 (L197; Fig. 6.10, see Section 19-19) an earthen floor was uncovered; it abuts both walls, with a burnt surface over its entire extent (L198, L197 and L187; elevation 24.20–24.30). Near W216, a stone bowl (L193), supported by a circle of small stones, was sunk into the floor (Fig. 6.11). In the northern part of this space (L119), below an accumulation of collapsed material, an earthen floor was revealed (elevation 24.35); it

Fig. 6.10. Area A1, Substratum 3b, Alley(?) 197. On left, W216 and on right,
W215 = W245; in background, W217 of Substratum 3a; looking north.

Fig. 6.11. Area A1, Substratum 3b. Stone bowl
sunk in the floor near W216; looking west.

produced a relatively rich pottery assemblage (Pl. 11.59).

The Area West of W216

On the west, W216 is abutted by W620, of which only a short segment was uncovered. South of W620

there are indications of an (unnumbered) north–south wall slightly protruding under a north–south balk. These walls apparently belong to a building whose continuation was excavated in Area C, but there remains an unexcavated strip between these areas and direct connections could not be established (furthermore, in Area C, Sqs L/5–6 have not been excavated down to Stratum 3 [see Chapter 5]).

SUBSTRATUM 3A

In Substratum 3a (Plans 1.2, 7), there were constructional changes vs. the previous buildings, but due to the problematic stratigraphy here it is unclear whether the general layout of the buildings was maintained or changed altogether.

As mentioned, in the northern part of the area, near the northeastern corner of the fortress, only one occupation level that could be attributed to Stratum 3 was defined, and it is unclear if Building 194 was in use in one phase or in both. This issue cannot be settled even when artifacts are considered, as typologically, the ceramic assemblages of Substrata 3b and 3a cannot be differentiated (see Chapter 11).

Room 182

This room, in Sqs M–N/8, was built above the remains of Room 174 of Substratum 3b, abutting the fortress' eastern wall. Wall 124, the southern wall of this room (see Fig. 6.7) was well preserved (about 1.2 m high, up to Stratum 2 floor levels), but the western wall (W621) was badly preserved (and its eastern face is unclear) and the northern wall of the room has not been located. Likewise, no floor has been discerned here, though much pottery was found in the fill (Pls. 11.60, 11.61).

To the west of W621 two sub-stages apparently need to be defined. In the lower one, W215 (the large stones) runs here parallel to W621 (for the attribution of the large stones of W215 to Substratum 3a, see above). In turn, W215 is superimposed by a floor at elevation 24.70–24.80 (L92 and L84), which was partly stone paved and comprised a very large stone—perhaps some kind of installation.

South of Room 182 is a very narrow space, L128, with no observable floor. Possibly this was an alley which led to the fortress wall between Room 182 and Building 79 to the south.

Building 79

This large building, in the southeastern part of the fortress' courtyard, reuses some of the Substratum 3b walls, but nonetheless it signifies a change in the architectural layout of this area. The northern wall of the building is W217, the eastern end of which abuts the solid fortress wall. In Sq M/7 there is an opening in this wall, 0.9 m wide, beyond which the wall continues to the west. This wall appears on the plans in outline only, as W122, constructed exactly above it in Stratum 2, has not been dismantled.

The construction of W217 is significant, as it crosses over Alley(?) 197 of Substratum 3b. A crucial question is the relationship between this wall and the upper (large stones) part of W215 = W245 south of it. This relationship can be deduced, for example, from Fig. 6.10; see also Fig. 6.14 below. There it seems that the W215 = W245 abuts W217.

Wall 215 = W245 divides the space south of W217 into two rooms. Parallel to W217, *c.* 1.3 m south of it, a new east–west wall (W211) was built of mud bricks on a stone socle. It abuts the fortress wall on the east and stops 0.2 m short of W215 = W245 on the west. In between these three walls an earthen floor was detected (L106; elevation 24.70).

To the south of W211 is another room, Room 107, partially stone paved, at elevation 24.70–24.80. This area was heavily disturbed by a Stratum 1 pit (Fig. 6.12). This room was apparently bounded on the south by a mud-brick wall (W125), preserved in the balk between Sqs N7 and N6 (Fig. 6.13). (The attribution of this wall to Substratum 3a is based on the level of its foundations, as seen in the balk.) In the large room west of W215 = W245, Room 79, an earthen floor was

Fig. 6.12. Area A1. In background, Stratum 1 pit in balk between Sqs M–N/7; on its left, projecting from the balk, is a stub of W211 of Strata 3a, 2. In foreground, W215 of Substrata 3a-b; looking east.

Fig. 6.13. Area A1, Strata 3a, 2. Northern face of mud-brick W125 in the balk between Sqs N/6–7; on left, the opening of Casemate 52 of Stratum 2; looking south.

Fig. 6.14. Area A1, Substratum 3a. Wall 215 = W245 and adjacent ṭabun; looking east.

found (L79; elevation 24.55) and near the wall was a clay *ṭabun* (Fig. 6.14). This floor related only to the upper stage of W215 = W245, and covered W216 of Substratum 3b and Stone Installation 193.

In the southern and western balks of Sq M/7, two additional wall segments were discovered (W622, which is in line with W125, and W623); by their levels they could belong to Substratum 3a and if so they enclose a small room here.

It is unclear whether in this phase, too, W215 = W245 extends south, beyond W125 and W622. No clear floors that could be associated with Substratum 3a were discerned here.

STRATUM 2

In the northern part of Area A1, Stratum 2 (Plans 1.3, 8) marks a new building operation (as was the case in other excavation areas). In the southern part of the area, however, it seems that some of the Substratum 3a walls were reused, but internal divisions of the structure there were changed. Most of the changes here in Stratum 2 were apparently dictated by the need to regulate access to the casemates.

An accumulation of conflagration and destruction debris was discerned in most places, in some of them as deep as 0.4–0.6 m. The Stratum 2 remains were damaged by Stratum 1 (Persian-period) constructions, mainly in the south, and by small pits of that stratum, which were not always discerned during excavation.

In the northeastern corner of the fortress there were no buildings and the area was apparently open, a courtyard of sorts, which continued also to the west, in Area C. This fact corroborates the assumption that the entrance to the casemate fortress was in this vicinity. Floor 38 here was at elevation 25.18.

Building 97

The northern building in this area, built against the casemate wall, has a rather peculiar plan. Its northern wall (W183), abuts Casemate 186 (Fig. 6.15) and in turn, at its western end, W183 is abutted by W120, which runs north–south and forms an L-shaped passage/corridor (L34) enabling (indirect) access to the casemate. Both walls were built of two rows of stones and incorporate large, flat stones. In L34, a beaten-earth floor was uncovered at elevation 25.10, its level clearly indicated by a door socket or a mortar found *in situ* on it. On the floor was an accumulation of destruction debris, *c.* 0.33 m deep. The western face of W120 was abutted by a stone bench, which probably served those passing west of the building.

South of Passageway 34, opposite the opening of Casemate 39, a floor (L45) was uncovered, with segments of stone paving at elevation 25.30, and upon it an accumulation of burnt and collapsed material *c.* 0.5 m deep (and including an ostracon; see Chapter 15, No. 10). This seems to have been an open space; a stone bench built along the western face of W121 (see below), probably served passersby.

Passageway 34 enclosed Room 97, which was constructed against Casemate 39 (Fig. 6.16). The room is enclosed on the north by W184, and on the west by

Fig. 6.15. Area A1, Stratum 2. Wall 183 abutting Casemate 186; in foreground, W120 with a bench on its western face; looking east.

Fig. 6.16. Area A1, Stratum 2. Wall 184 abutting Casemate 39, and the entrance in W103 to Casemate 186; looking east.

*Fig. 6.17. Area A1, Substratum 2. Stone Pavement 117
against top of W124 of Subtratum 3a; looking south.*

W121. Is seems to have been purposely left open on the south and southwest and linked to the passage to Casemate 39. In it, a pavement of large stones (L117) was uncovered approximately at elevation 25.30 (Fig. 6.17), and the top of W124 of Substratum 3a was incorporated into the floor at the level of the threshold of Casemate 39. As W124 slightly blocks the opening of this casemate, its top in Stratum 2 could not have been much higher than the actual top as uncovered. Burnt destruction debris and pottery (Pl. 11.115:10–17) accumulated in this room to a height of *c.* 0.5 m above floor level, and a seal was uncovered here (Chapter 14, No. 3).

Building 40

This building, in the southern half of the area, largely continues the building that stood here in Substratum 3a. It is possible that the remains termed here Building 40 are in fact part of a much larger building—which extends westward to Area C and was enclosed on the west by

W260 and entered from the west through the opening in that wall (see Chapter 5).

The northern wall of the building is W122, built over W217 of Substratum 3a. On the west there is an opening in it (1.2 m wide), flanked by two large stone doorjambs (an opening here was also discerned in Substratum 3a, but in Stratum 2 it has been narrowed). Beyond this opening the wall continues westward into Area C.

South of W122, a north–south wall (W210), 2 m long and constructed of large boulders, extends to the south. It is unclear where its southern end was located, and if W240 in Sq M/6 is the continuation of this wall. Wall 210 was constructed above, and in about the same line as W215 of Substratum 3a. It divides Building 40 into two. East of W210 is east–west W211, constructed of mud bricks on stone foundations and preserved *c.* 0.5 m high; this wall continues in existence from Substratum 3a. It delineates a narrow room in the northeastern corner of the building, which is further subdivided, by W212, into two small rooms or cells: L76 (which produced a figurine; Chapter 13: Pl. 13.1:8) and L71. South of these is an open space or short alleyway (L72), which allows access to Casemate 52. On the hard-packed earthen floor of this space (at elevation 25.22) was a 0.2 m deep layer of burnt debris (L57), including collapsed mud bricks, pottery (Pls. 11.118, 11.119:1–10), burnt bones and burnt wooden beams, which was disturbed by a Persian-period pit (of Stratum 1). East of this floor, adjoining the solid wall under Casemate 52, was a pedestal or bench (W214), whose top coincides with the level of the earthen floor (Fig. 6.18); it too was covered with burnt debris.

West of Space 72 was a room or courtyard (L40) with a beaten-earth floor (elevation 25.10) and an accumulation of destruction debris 0.5 m thick.

Spaces 40 and 72 are bounded on the south by W125 = W622, whose northern face was observed in the balk (this wall may have already been constructed in Substratum 3a, see above). From this wall, W240, built of large stones, extends to the south (regarding its relationship to W210, see above). Wall 240 is constructed above W245 of Stratum 3 (for this problematic wall, see also above). Its exact stratigraphic relationship with W125 = W622 is unclear.

Wall 240 divides the southeastern corner of the courtyard into two. In the eastern space (L183) no floor was encountered. Abutting W240 here were two

Fig. 6.18. Area A1, Stratum 2, Alley(?) 72. On right, the western wall of Casemate 52 with a bench against it, adjoined by burnt Floor 72; looking north.

Fig. 6.19. Area A1, Stratum 2. Intact mud bricks in the destruction level on the floor of Room 175, perhaps belonging to an installation; looking north.

walls, W241 and W243, which alongside W242 that connects them, form a small cubicle of sorts (L199). No clear floors were found adjoining these walls. It is possible that at least one of the narrow spaces between this cubicle and the corner of the fortress was used as a stairwell leading to the top of the fortress wall, similarly to those found in other areas.

West of W240, Room 175 had a floor at elevation 25.15–25.05 (for the pottery, see Pl. 11.121), covered by an ash layer and many collapsed mud bricks, some of them nearly intact (Fig. 6.19, see Section 19-19). The latter may have belonged to some installations, but this was not ascertained. In the southern part of Room 175, abutting the southern wall of the fortress, a plastered

area (L130) was partially revealed at elevation 25.00, surrounded by remains of mud bricks. Room 175 was severely damaged by W54 of Stratum 1, whose foundations were dug deep.

STRATUM 1

Area A1, as Area 2, revealed the clearest architectural remains and ceramic assemblages of Stratum 1, overlying the destruction layer of the Stratum 2 (Plan 9). These, however, were poorly preserved as they lay exposed for centuries. As specified below, it appears that some of the eastern casemates continued in use and most of the area to their west was apparently open grounds. Living surfaces were encountered immediately below the surface, accompanied by a few small and shallow pits.

Only in the northeastern corner of the courtyard was there evidence of more substantial construction. Adjoining the northeastern casemate, where some of the walls still stood to a reasonable height, Building 20 was constructed (see also Dothan 1965: Fig. 1), with stone walls (W50, W51, and W52, the latter in Area C) 0.7–0.8 m wide and preserved 0.4–1.0 m high. Wall 51 continues eastward but does not reach W103 of the eastern casemate here. Thus a corridor of sorts is formed (L99), leading towards the northeastern tower, which was also still in use (see Chapter 2, Area A2). In Room 20, a floor composed of earth and ash

Fig. 6.20. Area A1, Stratum 1. Living surface and stone installation in Sq M/8 below topsoil; looking west.

was uncovered at elevation 26.35–26.40, with stones scattered about it but no datable pottery.

Adjoining the room on the south, Floor 21 was uncovered at elevation 26.07. There were only meager remains other than this floor, in the entire area south of Building 20. Floors here were located at surface level and were characterized by thin layers of ash and many scattered stones. In Sq M/8 was a small pit (L26; 0.6 m deep) that contained typical Persian-period pottery (Pl. 11.134:1) and near it, a partially preserved circular

stone installation (L23; Fig. 6.20). In Sqs M/7 were a deep pit (which disturbed earlier remains here), a possible wall (W58) and possibly another wall or part of an installation.

In the south, in Sqs M/5–6, a structure consisting of W54, W56 and W57 was erected, adjoining the southern casemate (these walls had already been exposed by Dothan in 1956). The walls were preserved 0.3–0.6 m high and in places their foundations reached down to Stratum 2. No floors survived here.

CHAPTER 7

AREA E: THE AREA EAST OF THE STRATA 3–2 FORTRESSES AND THE EASTERN PART OF THE STRATUM 4 FORTRESS

YSHAYAHU LENDER, DOV NAHLIELI, IRIS ELDAR-NIR AND HANNAH BERNICK-GREENBERG

INTRODUCTION

Area E includes all the remains uncovered east of the rectangular fortresses of Strata 3–2. It was excavated from the first season onward. During the first seasons (1978–1981), remains belonging to the entire occupational sequence were uncovered here; later on (1981–1982), some soundings were dug, which uncovered, *inter alia*, the moat that surrounded the fortification in Strata 3–2. In a few cases, re-examination of the stratigraphy here led us to different conclusions than those hitherto published. In particular, activity areas outside the fortress (including the silos described below) are now attributed to Stratum 3 rather than 2 (cf. Cohen 1983: figure on p. 14).

As the Stratum 3 fortress was built only over the western part of the oval Stratum 4 fortress, the eastern part of the oval fortress was easily reached outside the confines of the Strata 3–2 fortresses. This is the only area where an occupational phase predating the oval fortress was defined ('Substratum 4c') and possibly also a phase postdating Stratum 4 and predating the Stratum 3c constructional fill.

STRATUM 4 (C–A)

SUBSTRATUM 4C: THE PRE-FORTRESS OCCUPATION

Excavation below the floors of the oval fortress (Substratum 4b) was carried out in a number of places, revealing significant differences between the northern and southern parts of the area (Plan 3). In the north, the fortress was founded on natural stream deposits, including a fill of pebbles, while on the south a thin gray layer (L1012, L5058) was encountered at elevation 21.09–21.24 below the foundations of W325 and W334 of Substratum 4b. This layer is apparently associated with a corner of two narrow walls (W600 and W643; Figs. 7.1, 7.8, see Section 21-21) and probably also W644 and W645, which were constructed north of and

parallel to the latter. This level produced only a few non-diagnostic potsherds. Though it is attributed here to the pre-fortress occupation (Substratum 4c), it cannot be ruled out that these remains are in fact the earliest phase of the fortress itself. Meager remains antedating Substratum 4b were encountered in other areas as well (Areas C, F; see Chapters 5, 8), and it is difficult to determine their nature. There are no means, artifactual or other, to date this occupation.

Below this layer there was a fill of pebbles and yellowish material (Fig. 7.2), apparently natural stream

Fig. 7.1. Area E, Substratum 4c. Wall 600 (on right) below walls of the Substratum 4b oval fortress; looking north.

Fig. 7.2. Area E, Substratum 4c. Pebbles and silt below W337 of Substratum 4b; looking west.

deposits similar to those in the northern part of the area.

SUBSTRATUM 4B: THE OVAL FORTRESS

East of the eastern fortification of the rectangular fortresses of Strata 3 and 2, remains of the Stratum 4 oval casemate fortress were uncovered. Substratum 4b (Plan 3; see Sections 20-20, 21-21) is the main, and perhaps only constructional phase of this fortress in Area E. As mentioned, in the north it was clear that the floors of the fortress were founded directly on stream deposits.

The deep foundations of the Stratum 3 fortress were laid directly on the earlier fortress, their foundation trenches causing only slight damage. The main damage to Stratum 4 was caused by the digging of the moat in Stratum 3 and by the construction of its retaining walls. As a result, the outer wall of the Stratum 4 fortress and a few casemates were destroyed. Based on the number of openings along the inner wall of the eastern casemates, it is possible to reconstruct at least five rooms. One of

the casemates in the north is divided into two (Room 823 and Room 811).

The Stratum 4 fortress was violently destroyed. In all the rooms and in the courtyard a layer of ash was found, and in some rooms there was evidence of intensive fire.

The Northern Casemates

South of the northern tower of the Stratum 3 fortress (W400), remains of the northeastern casemates were uncovered (both inner and outer walls), preserved 0.5–0.1 m high (Fig. 7.3). The outer wall (W318; 1.5 m wide) is constructed of a row of medium-sized stones on its inner face, a row of large stones on its outer face, and between them small and medium-sized stones. The inner wall (W329; *c.* 1 m wide) was built of two rows of medium-sized stones.

Casemate 816/811. The northernmost casemate (Fig 7.4) was at least 5 m long, and was divided by W327 into two small rooms—816 and 811. An opening

Fig. 7.3. The northeastern casemates; looking northwest.

Fig. 7.4. Area E, Substratum 4b. Casemate 816 with stone paving. On right, pithos sunk into floor; looking south.

Fig. 7.5. Area E, Substratum 4b. Pithoi in Pit 2005 in Casemate 816; looking west.

leading to Room 816 from the courtyard was located at the northern end of the inner wall, where a flat stone, probably a threshold, was unearthed. There was a stone floor in the southwestern part of Room 816 (elevation 21.75) and beaten-earth floors in its northwestern part (elevation 21.63) and in Room 811 (21.70). On the northwest, a pit (L2005) was dug; it contained the bottom parts of pithoi that had apparently been sunk into the floor (Fig. 7.5; the contours of the pit were not clearly discerned). There may have been a low stone bench against the eastern wall of Room 816.

The partition wall (W327), one course wide, was founded about floor level, and delineated the southern margins of the paved part of the casemate. Room 811 (1.5 × 2.7 m) was entered from the south through Casemate 823.

Above the floors was a layer of ash and over it an accumulation of collapsed bricks and stones, attesting to violent destruction. Other than the pithoi (not illustrated) and many potsherds, there were a lamp and a Negebite bowl (Pl. 11.10).

A probe below the floor of Room 811 revealed that the walls and the floor were founded upon a layer of *kurkar* containing numerous stream pebbles and no pottery, i.e., natural deposits.

Casemate 823. Casemate 816/811 was separated from the next casemate by W328, 1 m wide, with an opening 0.8 m wide. Casemate 823 was largely destroyed by the construction of the Stratum 3 moat. A small segment of an earthen floor was uncovered at elevation 21.65 and on it was an accumulation of ash and collapsed stones (see Fig. 7.3, in foreground).

The Eastern Casemates

The casemates south of Room 823 were destroyed by the construction of the moat and only their inner walls survived (Figs. 7.6, 7.7). Segments of floors in Casemates 956 and 957 were uncovered about elevation 21.70. No clear partition walls were discerned between the casemates, but it can be assumed, based on the openings in W337 (the inner wall of the casemates),

*Fig. 7.6. Stratum 4 casemates (in foreground) cut by W206 of the Stratum 3 moat;
looking southeast.*

*Fig. 7.7. Area E, Substratum 4b. In foreground, corner between W337, W325
and W344. Above them are later elements; in background, W317
of Substratum 4a; looking south.*

that there were at least two more spaces between Room 823 and Room 938 on the south.

The Southern Casemates
As mentioned, the southern part of the oval fortress was founded on earlier architectural remains. The original ground surface here was probably lower than on the north and both foundation levels of walls and floor levels here are about 0.25–0.3 m lower than they are on the north. This is the area in which the destruction was fiercest and destruction debris very deep and burnt.

Fig. 7.8. Area E, Substratum 4b. Casemate 938. In foreground, W600 of Substratum 4c; in background, W334 below W317 of Substratum 4a; looking west.

Fig. 7.9. Area E, Substratum 4b. Pottery in Casemate 938.

Casemate 938. The walls of Casemate 938 (Fig. 7.8) were damaged on the east by the Stratum 3 moat and on the south by Tower 402 of Stratum 3. Its western wall (W334) was uncovered below W317 of Substratum 4a. Despite the poor preservation of this casemate's walls, a floor (L938 = L926) was encountered at elevation 21.40, with a layer of ash, and 0.3 m deep destruction debris with numerous pottery vessels (Fig. 7.9; Pls. 11.11–11.14).

Casemate 506. West of Casemate 938 the beginning of another casemate was traced. This spot, overlooking Wadi el-Qudeirat, would be a logical location for the gate leading to the courtyard. This supposition may be corroborated by the fact that the overall layout of the walls here is rectilinear, as opposed to other parts of the fortress.

The Courtyard of the Oval Fortress

Within the courtyard, small spaces/rooms were built against the casemates, through which the casemates were entered. The northernmost room exposed (Room 820) had a beaten-earth floor at elevation 21.70, covered by a layer of burnt destruction debris in which many pottery vessels were found (Pls. 11.17, 11.18), including jars whose contents may have caused the intense fire. Large quantities of carbonized seeds were also uncovered here.

The southern wall (W330) of Room 820 was 1 m wide; a 0.6 m wide opening connected it to Room 807 to its south. The opening was found blocked, providing evidence that some repairs or changes had been made in the Stratum 4 fortress. This room too, as well as Room 952/953 further south, had a beaten-earth floor (elevation 21.70), and over it an accumulation of destruction debris, ash and pottery (Pl. 11.16:16–19).

The two rooms are separated by a narrow wall (W342; 0.5 m wide). A very poorly preserved wall on the south (W601), of which only one course survived, may be a remnant of the southern wall of this casemate. About 0.3 m south of W601 was a line of small stones (W645), which may have been part of the same wall (which then was originally wider, *c.* 1 m, similar to W330). Alternatively, this row of stones may be attributed to Substratum 4c, as is shown on Plan 3.

A narrow wall, one course wide (W344), runs north–south about one meter west of W337, the western wall of the casemates. Its northern end is located below Tower 401 of the Stratum 3 fortress, but it may have originally formed a corner with W601. The stratigraphic attribution of this wall is unclear. If it indeed belongs to Substratum 4b, it would mean that access to the nearby casemate would have been blocked. However, attributing this wall to Substratum 4c would imply that it was left protruding above the Substratum 4b floor here (L5051; this latter locus produced an unusual concentration of dog bones, see Chapter 19).

West of W344, a beaten-earth floor (L940, L507a and L944) was uncovered at elevation 21.40, and over it, a layer of destruction debris (L930, L933 and L941). It is unclear whether it occupied a closed or open space. There were no signs of burning here, but many collapsed stones and bricks and some pottery vessels (Pl. 11.19:1–10). Some of the vessels were found higher than floor level and may have fallen from shelves, or from an upper floor.

SUBSTRATUM 4A: THE POST-FORTRESS PHASE

In the southern part of Area E, a constructional phase was defined that was not discerned in other excavation areas (Plan 4). It comprises walls overlying the oval fortress (Substratum 4b) and covered by the Substratum 3c constructional fill. In places, it is clear that these remains were cut by the Stratum 3 fortress walls, but in other instances no clear foundation trenches were distinguished. As only walls (and no floors) could be attributed to this phase, it is not datable.

Above the western wall of Casemate 938 of Substratum 4b (W334) and above W325 of that substratum, a 1 m wide wall was constructed (W317; top elevation at 22.68), with a stone bench (W322) along its western face (Fig. 7.10; see also Fig. 7.7 and Section 21-21). The wall is well built of two rows of medium-sized stones and a fill of smaller stones in between them. On the north, the wall ends in a straight line and on the south it is cut by Tower 402 of Stratum 3 (as is the bench).

East of W317 no clear floor was encountered, only a number of flat stones adjacent to it. The entire area east of the wall was covered by mud-brick material. On the west, the top of the extant part of Bench W322 is abutted by a possible floor (L488), above which were horizontal levels of earth and ash that reached W317. This fill (also L488) was cut by the Stratum 3 fortress wall.

Fig. 7.10. Area E, Stratum 4. Wall 317 and Bench W322 (Substratum 4a) above W325 (Substratum 4b); looking south.

North of W317, remains of three walls were uncovered (W323, W324 and W602); the southern end of W323 abuts W317. Although W323 is not clearly cut by Tower 401 of Stratum 3 it evidently predates it, as it is superimposed by the Substratum 3c constructional fill. As was observed in other excavation areas, especially in Area C, there were places were the Stratum 3 fortress walls were founded directly on the earlier architectural remains.

Between W317, W323 and W324 were collapsed stones and a layer of burnt material (L217) at elevation 21.90.

STRATUM 3

With the construction of the Stratum 3 rectangular fortress, large earthworks were undertaken. The fortress walls and towers were built over the Stratum 4 remains with deep foundations, which, on the eastern side the fortress, cut the earlier remains to a depth of one meter. Inside the fortress the floors were laid on a constructional fill 1.5–2.0 m deep (see, for example, Areas B, C and A1; respectively Chapters 3, 5 and 6) while outside it, in the spaces between the towers, the area was filled with a rampart of earth and pebbles to a level of c. 1.5–2 m above the Stratum 4 remains. A moat was dug at a distance of about 4 m from the fortress walls. In Area E, nearly the entire length of the eastern part of the moat was uncovered.

The earthen rampart created by the fills dumped against the fortress walls was retained on the outside by the inner retaining walls of the moat (W206, W207), and they created an elevated surface above the moat. The spaces between the towers were enclosed in this area by walls, creating rooms that were entered from the east (see Sections 20-20, 21-21).

The Moat

The moat (Plans 1.2, 6, 7) was dug about 4 m east of the fortress into terrain that sloped from west to east. It cut through Stratum 4 occupational remains and, from elevation 21.00 and down, into natural stream deposits comprising many pebbles. It destroyed all the eastern casemates of the Stratum 4 oval fortress (Fig. 7.11; see Sections 20-20, 21-21). The enormous amount of material extracted from the moat, both anthropogenic and natural, was undoubtedly used as part of the constructional fills of Stratum 3.

Fig. 7.11. Area E. In foreground, the retaining walls of the Stratum 3 moat (W206 and W207). Behind them is Casemate 823 of Stratum 4, which is cut by them; looking west.

The inner, eastern retaining wall of the moat (W206; see Fig. 7.6), is about 40 m long and 1.5–1.8 m high, constructed of large, medium and small fieldstones. Against the eastern face of W206 another retaining wall, 0.75–1.00 m wide, was constructed, sloping inward, preserved over 1.5 m high (W207; Fig. 7.12). Its top is about 1 m lower than the top of W206. It is unclear if this wall is part of the original construction of the moat, intended to buttress W206, or a later addition.

Eight probes were excavated adjacent to the eastern faces of these two walls, to a depth of *c.* 1.5 m below present surface. In most of them, between elevations 18.85–19.40, one or two layers of ash, occasionally sloping, were revealed inside the moat. At a few spots,

for example in Sq Q/9, horizontal surfaces of stones were encountered. All these elements indicate that some sort of activity took place within the moat. Above these layers were collapsed stones, loess and stream deposits.

Most of the pottery found in the moat (Pls. 11.125, 11.126) is typologically and chronologically comparable to that of Stratum 2. Significantly, no Persian-period material was recorded here.

In Sq Q/9 the probe was expanded towards the east and deepened until the foundations of W206 and W207 were reached. This is the only place in Area E where the outer retaining wall of the moat (W408) was uncovered, slightly below surface level (Fig. 7.13). This wall is similar to the other retaining walls of the moat, built of medium-sized fieldstones, preserved to a maximum height of 1.9 m and only slightly sloping. The moat can thus be determined to have been *c.* 4.5 m wide. Its bottom was encountered about 3 m below surface level, about 4.5 m below the top of the Stratum 3 rampart.

Inside the moat there was a fill of stones (Fig. 7.12). Under it were a burnt layer and a stone surface, and below them, layers of fill and a surface of earth mixed with ash at the level of the bases of W207 and W408.

In Sq Q/13 on the north, the inner northeastern corner of the moat was revealed (formed by W206 and W205; Fig. 7.14). The southeastern corner, similar to the remains of the fortress itself in that area, was destroyed by erosion and flooding.

Fig. 7.12. Area E, Stratum 3, Sq Q/9. The eastern retaining wall of the moat, W206 and against it W207; the stones in the foreground on the right are part of the uppermost fill within the moat; in the background are the Stratum 4 casemates and above them the eastern walls of the fortresses of Strata 3 and 2; looking west.

Fig. 7.13. Area E, Stratum 3, Sq Q/9. Locus 2159 in the moat and the two retaining walls of the moat (W207 on right, and W408 on left); adjacent to W207 are the remains of L2012; looking south.

Fig. 7.14. Area E, Stratum 3. The inner northeastern corner of the moat, formed by W206 on the east and W205 on the north; looking southwest.

The Rampart

The rampart was built as part of the construction operation of Stratum 3, and thus is defined as Substratum 3c. The fill layers of the eastern rampart were laid against the fortress wall (W201) and between its towers, over the remains of the Stratum 4 fortress. They comprised earth and many small stones and were preserved to a maximum height of 1.5 m above Stratum 4. On the east they probably reached the western wall of the moat, but the area east of the line of the towers was not well preserved, and more often than

not it was impossible to separate there the rampart's fills from natural accumulations over the slope.

Belonging to the rampart fill are L805, L812 (Sq O/10); L803, L806 (Sq P/10); L240, L810 (Sq O/9); L808 (Sq P/9); L204, L1008 (Sq O/7); L924, L929 (Sq P/6); and L188, L471 (Sq O/6) (not on plans).

Rooms between the Towers

Floors and a silo were constructed above and into the rampart. They were assigned to Substrata 3a-b.

Room 801

This room was enclosed between Towers 400 and 401 by W175 = W176 on the east. This wall, 1 m wide, was preserved to a height of 0.70 to 0.85 m, and had an opening 1.2 m wide (Fig. 7.15). Its northern end was missing, as this area was dug as a sounding both in Dothan's excavations (Dothan 1965: Pls. 27a, 28a) and in the 1976 season. (This part of the wall does not appear on any plan.) There was a stone floor in the southern half of the room at elevation 24.35 and above it a thin accumulation of ash with hardly any potsherds.

Both below this floor and east of Room 801 a layer of burnt material was encountered (L804), at elevation 24.00. It is unclear whether this is part of the Substratum 3c rampart/constructional fill or perhaps indicates the existence of two occupation phases within

Fig. 7.15. Area E, Stratum 3. Room 801; looking north.

Stratum 3 here (the erection of the walls between the towers would thus belong to the later phase). East of Room 801, at elevation 23.00, the constructional fills also incorporated a layer of stones.

Room 181

This room, constructed between Towers 401 and 402, was enclosed on the east by W150, 0.5 m wide, preserved 0.6 m high (Fig. 7.16). It was built of a row of medium and small stones and only its outer face was

clearly discerned. Two narrow walls (W164, W165) were constructed alongside the towers to the north and south; their relation to W150 has not been determined. The only explanation for the existence of these walls is that Room 181 had a roof that was lower than the tops of the towers.

In the northern part of the room a stone-lined silo (Silo 109), 3 m in diameter and 1 m deep, was dug into the rampart (Fig. 7.17). On the east, the silo was incorporated into W150. As two floor levels seem to

Fig. 7.16. Area E, Stratum 3. Room 181 with stone floor and Silo 109; looking south.

Fig. 7.17. Area E, Stratum 3. Silo 109 and Pavement 116 to its north; looking west.

have been encountered (L109 over L203), it is possible that there were two constructional stages in the silo. The area between the silo and the fortress wall on the west and north (L116), was paved with stones at elevation 24.13 (see Fig. 7.17).

In the southern half of the room, a stone floor (L181), almost devoid of finds, was uncovered at elevation 24.34 (see Fig. 7.16). (This area had already been excavated by Dothan in 1956; see Dothan 1965: Fig. 1.) Below this floor was a layer of ash (L453) and below that another layer of stones, apparently an earlier floor. This, again, testifies to some activity here associated with the Stratum 3 fortress, perhaps in an open area, as on the northern and western sides of the fortress (Areas F and G). At some later phase (but still within Stratum 3) the spaces between the towers were closed.

The floors of Rooms 801 and 181 (at about elevation 24.34) are 1.5 higher than the topmost preservation of the retaining walls of the moat (c. 22.86). This difference results from the fact that while the rooms were protected by the towers and were also covered by the earth and stones that are part of the Stratum 2 glacis (see below), all the remains east of the towers were exposed to the ravages of nature.

A Possible Entryway to the Fortress

Dothan discussed the possibility of a gate to the fortress, located in its southeastern corner. At that spot, outside the fortress wall, he encountered a pavement, but noted that though there were some traces for an opening in the fortress' wall, it was too narrow to indicate a gate (Dothan 1965:137).

We are unable to say whether the pavement in question is associated somehow with the stone pavement we excavated north of the southeastern tower (L181, see above), or whether Dothan's description relates to a stone surface that appears on the plan he published, east of that tower, with no elevation indicated. Indeed, a stone feature of unknown date can be seen on early photos of this area, but was never studied. Considering the fact that in Areas F and G as well (Chapters 8 and 9), some stone platforms that may have formed part of entryways to the fortress were unearthed, this may have also been the function of Dothan's pavement. It is impossible, however, to deduce the stratigraphical associations of this feature.

STRATUM 2

The Glacis

In Stratum 2, the area outside the fortress walls was apparently occupied by an earthen defensive glacis (L53, L108 in Sq O/7; L55, L163 in Sq O/6; L180 in Sq O/9). It abutted the Stratum 2 casemates and the upper parts of the Stratum 3 solid wall (see Sections 20-20, 21-21). In this area some of Dothan's soundings in 1956 were conducted, e.g., around the northeastern tower and near the southeastern tower (Dothan 1965: Fig. 1; Pl. 27). It is unclear whether during the renewed excavations the actual glacis was successfully separated from other debris over the slope and the backfill of Dothan's excavations. No coating layers of stones were noted, though such a coating was uncovered by Dothan in a section on the northern side of the fortress (Dothan 1965: Pl. 29a). The glacis as we uncovered it was comprised of earth and large stones only (a somewhat different composition was reported by Dothan [1965:138]).

In Area E, this glacis/earthen fill covered the Stratum 3 rooms constructed between the towers (see Sections 20-20, 21-21). It is unclear by what means these fills were supported on the east.

The Fill in the Moat

The moat was excavated to its full depth and width only in the probe in Sq Q/9 (see Plans 6, 7; Section 20-20), which enables the following reconstruction. The lower part of the fill in the moat, about 0.5 m deep, seems to have been composed of earth and stones that had gradually and naturally eroded into it (L2159, L2029 and L2150). This fill contained bones and numerous potsherds attributable to Stratum 2 typological considerations, including Edomite pottery (see Pls. 11.125, 11.126).

Above that fill was a thick sloping layer of ash, between elevations 18.90 and 18.62 (L2012, L2022 and L2028), above which was a fill of earth and large stones with scant pottery (L2025, L2157). Most of the pottery is attributable to Stratum 2, but here there were also some Persian-period fragments. The ash layer seems to represent the surface of the former moat after it had filled up in Stratum 2, a surface that remained unchanged in Stratum 1.

Some of the other probes along the moat also revealed a layer of ash and small stones, reached at elevations between 19.45 and 18.90 (L2026 in Sq Q/11; L2021 in Sq Q/10; L2013, L2023 in Sq Q/8; L2014 in Sq Q/6, L2016 in Sq Q/5). In these squares, however, excavation did not continue below the ash layer.

It seems that the moat, as mentioned, started to fill up naturally during the lifetime of Stratum 2, and from a certain moment and on, still in Stratum 2, it was converted into a refuse dump.

CHAPTER 8

AREA F: THE AREA NORTH OF THE STRATA 3–2 FORTRESSES

YSHAYAHU LENDER

INTRODUCTION

Area F is located north of the walls of the fortresses of Strata 3–2. Excavation here was conducted during the sixth to ninth seasons (1980–1981), and was concentrated in the area between the eastern and the middle towers. It revealed remains relating to the Stratum 4 oval fortress, parts of the Stratum 3 moat and other Stratum 3 remains.

STRATUM 4 (C, B)

The remains of this stratum (Plans 1.1, 3, 4) were uncovered below the Stratum 3 external constructional fill /rampart. They were badly damaged by the Stratum 3 constructions here—the northern fortress wall, a deep silo (861), the moat and the retaining wall. Still, two clear substrata could be defined here within Stratum 4.

SUBSTRATUM 4C: THE PRE-FORTRESS OCCUPATION

The earliest remains here (Plan 3) were attributed to Substratum 4c, the pre-fortress occupation, as this seems the preferable attribution, based on the flimsy nature of the remains. However, the possibility that they belong either to Substratum 4b or 4a cannot be disproved.

These remains were encountered only in a few spots. Below Floor 7002 of Substratum 4b (see below) was a fill of soft earth and ash with a few potsherds (L7021; see Section 22-22), apparently an earlier living surface; and below Floor 7004 of that same substratum, an earthen layer containing collapsed bricks and ash (L7007) reached as deep as elevation 21.44. This too seems to indicate occupation here prior to Substratum 4b.

North of these loci, in L7003 and L7006, remains of seemingly the same living horizon were unearthed, at elevation 21.41. They are associated with a curved line of stones (W646). All these 'floors' are at the same

level as, or somewhat below, the foundations of the Substratum 4b walls.

All these remains are reminiscent of those of Substratum 4c in Area E. The pottery was meager and not diagnostic.

To the west, in Sq K/11, a few probes revealed layers of pebbles intermingled with pockets of earth, ash and potsherds (L7028, L7029 and L7030; see Sections 20-20, 23-23). Under the pebbles was a layer of sand (L7031, L7034), which, alongside the pebbles, forms part of the natural stream deposits in the area.

SUBSTRATUM 4B

This is the main occupation of Stratum 4 here (Plan 3), of which parts of at least three rooms were uncovered:

Fig. 8.1. Area F, Stratum 4. Remains north of the rectangular fortresses; the narrow, one-course-wide rounded wall is the bottom course of Silo 854 of Stratum 3 after most of it had been dismantled; looking east.

*Fig. 8.2. Area F, Substratum 4b. Room
7002 with ṭabun; looking south.*

*Fig. 8.3. Area F. In foreground, W303 of Substratum 4b and
abutting it W304, cut by Silo 854 of Stratum 3; looking east.*

Loci 7002, 7003 and 7004 (Figs. 8.1, 8.2). The walls,
preserved only 0.15–0.40 m high, comprise foundations
of small stones upon which were brick superstructures
(brick remains were preserved on W304 and W305 and
collapsed bricks were uncovered in Rooms 7003 and
7004 (Fig. 8.2).

Only the northwestern corner of Room 7004 was
excavated, as most of the room is concealed below
the Stratum 3 fortification (Fig. 8.3). The earthen floor
here had traces of ash at elevation 21.76. Only the
northwestern corner of Room 7002 survived (on the
east this room was damaged by the construction of Silo
861 in Stratum 3). Wall 304 is probably the continuation
of W305. On the earthen floor, at elevation 21.78, were
ashes and a few potsherds, and in the northwestern
corner was a ṭabun (see Fig. 8.2).

West of this structure, in Sq K/11, no architectural
remains attributable to Stratum 4 were discerned, apart
from a living surface (L7022) at elevation 21.80.

As the remains described above were defined as
Substrata 4c and 4b, there are no remains here definitely
attributable to Substratum 4a (cf. Area E; Chapter 7).

STRATUM 3

Fortifications

Excavations in Area F revealed the remains of the
outer fortification system of Stratum 3. As described
in Chapter 1, this system surrounded the fortress on
the three sides that lacked natural protection (north,
east and west; for the latter two see respectively Areas
E and G). As discussed above (Area E, Chapter 7) it
seems that this system continued to be used, as such,
till a certain point within the lifetime of Stratum 2. This
assertion, however, is based on typological rather than
stratigraphical considerations.

The outer fortification here comprised an earthen
rampart, which was horizontal in the intervals between
the towers (and thus could be used for various activities
and for construction, see below) and then descended
in a moderate incline northward to a retaining wall
(W205), beyond which was the moat.

Silos and Associated Occupation Levels

Silos and Surrounding Surfaces
Between Towers 407 and 400, four large silos—858,
862, 864, and 854—were built (Fig. 8.4; Plans 1.2,

*Fig. 8.4. Area F, Stratum 3. General view of the northern wall of the
Strata 3–2 fortresses and the Stratum 3 silos to the north; looking east.*

6, 7). It is unclear whether the silos were erected as part of the initial layout/construction phase of Stratum 3 (which seems to be the more plausible explanation) or were a later addition (though still within Stratum 3). We could not determine whether they cut the fills of the ramparts or were constructed with them, but they certainly do not cut any other Stratum 3 feature.

Silo 854 (= 861) on the east is the largest one. It is oval, measuring 4.5 × 5.5 m at the top and 2.5 × 3.0 m at the bottom, and *c.* 1.9 m deep (Fig. 8.5). Its walls, constructed of wadi pebbles alongside larger stones, slant toward the bottom, which was also made from the same kind of pebbles. The fill inside the silo included large amounts of potsherds (mostly Negebite ware; see Pls. 11.67–11.69), two clay cones (Table 13.2:18, 19) and bones. On the floor there was a hearth (L861), constructed of pebbles detached from the silo's floor. It must have been constructed after the silo no longer served for storage.

Fig. 8.5. Area F, Stratum 3. Silo 854, looking west.

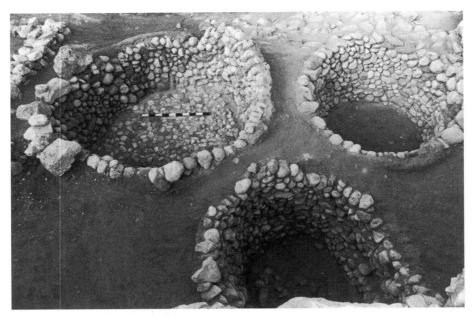

Fig. 8.6. Area F, Stratum 3. Silos 858, 862 and 864; looking north.

West of Silo 854 there is another, much smaller silo (Silo 864; 1.2 m in diameter and *c.* 0.9 m deep; Fig. 8.6). Its slightly slanting walls were lined with wadi pebbles and its floor was composed of packed stream deposits. West of the latter is Silo 858 (2.4 m in diameter, *c.* 0.8 m deep), whose walls and floor were lined with wadi pebbles.

The fourth silo (Silo 862) abuts the Stratum 3 fortress wall (W200), which served as its southern wall. It is 1.5–1.7 m in size, 1.2 m in depth, and is lined with wadi pebbles; its floor is of earth. Large stones were found in it.

Towards the end of Stratum 3 the silos ceased to function as such and were turned into waste pits: large quantities of potsherds, bones, ashes and organic mattter were found in them, typical of refuse dumps. The latest pottery recovered here (Pls. 11.67–11.70) can be associated with Stratum 3 (and not with 2). This means that during Stratum 2 the silos were already filled up and covered.

Between Silos 862, 858 and W290 to their west, a floor was uncovered (L857, at elevation 23.24), on which was *Ṭabun* 859, largely destroyed.

North of Silo 864 was a surface paved with pebbles (L863; see Fig. 8.4 and Section 22-22), which slopes down toward the north, at elevations 23.15–22.90. It indicates that some sort of activity was being carried out between the silos. Generally, however, the area

immediately north of the silos, to the retaining wall (see below), was destroyed over the years, as unlike the area between the towers it was not protected by the Stratum 2 glacis.

Room 853

On the leveled surface between the towers, west of the silos, two walls (W290, W291), which enclosed the corner between Tower 407 and the fortress wall, were constructed. They formed a 3.75 × 5.00 m rectangular room (Room 853; Fig. 8.7; see Section 23-23), whose entrance was apparently on the north.

The walls, *c.* 0.3 m wide and preserved 0.15–0.30 m high, are built of two rows of small stones and apparently served as foundations for a brick superstructure. The floor of the room, at elevation 23.15, was of beaten earth. On it were layers of ash, many intact pottery vessels, among them Negebite items (Pls. 11.65, 11.66), a game piece and some beads (Tables 13.4:6, 13.7:9, 15, 16).

West of W290, *Ṭabun* 856 was built, flanked by two small wall-like stone constructions: north of it is a bench, built against W290, and south of it is W292. This seems to have been a cooking corner. Inside the *ṭabun* an intact Negebite cooking krater was *in situ* (Pl. 11.66:11) and in between the *ṭabun* and the wall was a shell pendant (Table 13.7:17).

*Fig. 8.7. Area F, Stratum 3. Room 853 with Ṭabun 856 and
Negebite krater inside it; looking east.*

Platform 865

During cleaning operations next to the central tower on
the north (Tower 407), a stone wall or platform about
1.5 m wide and 7–8 m long, was uncovered (see Fig.
8.5, in background). It is attributed to Stratum 3, as a
probe dug north of the tower (L7035; Section 24-24)
revealed that this 'platform' was clearly built over the
earthen fill of the Stratum 3 rampart and abutted the
Stratum 3 tower; also, it is too low to be associated
with Stratum 2.

There are two possibilities for the interpretation of
this structure. It could simply be part of the Stratum 3
occupation levels outside the fortress; on the other hand,
it may belong to some construction that provided access
into the fortress.

Similar paved areas were also uncovered in Area G
(see Chapter 9), abutting the southwestern tower of the
fortress. An external paved area was also encountered
by Dothan east of the southeastern tower, but both its
function and stratigraphic relations are unclear (see
Area E, Chapter 7).

The Rampart

The rampart was constructed over the Stratum 4 remains
and extended between W205, the inner, southern wall
of the moat here, and the wall of the Stratum 3 fortress.
It projected to a distance of 6 m north of the wall,
c. 1.5 m north of the towers, and was at least 1 m high
(L7000, L7001 in Section 22-22; and L7022 in Section
23-23).

The rampart consisted of alternating layers of earth,
wadi pebbles and other deposits. Its upper part, between
the towers, is horizontal and was clearly intended
to serve as a surface on which daily activities could
take place outside the fortress. Beyond this line, it is
obvious that both the rampart and the retaining wall
of the moat (W205) did not survive to their full height
and thus there is no telling what the incline might have
been here. As mentioned, W205 must have been at
least 1.5 m higher than preserved in order to support
the rampart's fills.

The Moat and the Retaining Wall

The moat was uncovered here at a distance of about
8 m north of the fortress wall, for a length of *c.* 30 m,
and was delineated by two retaining walls. The top
of the inner retaining wall (W205), constructed of
large fieldstones, was exposed immediately below
the surface at elevations 21.60–20.60 on the west and
19.30 on the east (Fig. 8.8). In a sounding in Sq K/13
the base of the moat was discovered at elevation 17.86.
It is reasonable to assume that the wall originally stood
at least to elevation 23.00, and most probably higher,
as it was intended to support the earthen rampart that
surrounded the walls of the fortress. This is also the
reason for the need to buttress it with another sloping
wall within the moat (W647), which rendered it
trapezoidal in section (Fig. 8.9; Section 23-23).

Fig. 8.8. Area F, Stratum 3. Top of retaining W205 when exposed; looking east.

The outer, northern retaining wall of the moat, also of large fieldstones, was only uncovered in two short segments below the surface, at elevation 19.58 (W204 in Sqs K/13 and P/14; Fig. 8.10). North of this wall, only layers of loess and pebbles were encountered.

The moat as exposed was about 4 m deep. If the top of W205 is reconstructed to have stood to elevation 23.00 (and not higher), the moat must have been at least 6 m deep. It was *c.* 4.5 m wide in its upper preserved part and *c.* 2.75 m at the bottom.

At the bottom of the moat, there was a layer of large boulders, part of bedrock here. In the sounding in Sq K/13, a 0.5 × 2.5 m rectangular installation(?), constructed of small stones, and exposed over these boulders (L7050; see Figs. 8.9, 8.10), provides evidence that some use was made of the bottom of the moat before it filled up.

The moat was found full of earth and large stones (L7025, L7026, L7036, L7038, L7039, L7051 and L7052) along with potsherds (not illustrated) and bones. Typologically most of the pottery here belongs to Stratum 2, but there were also some Persian-period potsherds and a complete cooking pot, attributable to Stratum 1 (Pl. 11.131:8). The latter, however, originated in one locus only (L7026), which may have been a pit dug into the largely filled-up moat, which was already nearly full by the end of Stratum 2.

Fig. 8.9. Area F, Stratum 3. Retaining W205 abutted by revetment W647; north of them is Installation 7050 and the boulders underlying it; looking south.

Fig. 8.10. Area F, Stratum 3. The outer retaining wall of the moat, W204, Installation 7050 and the boulders underlying it; looking north.

STRATUM 2

The filled-up silos of Stratum 3 were overlain by a fill (L852), which abutted the Stratum 2 casemates and the upper part of the Stratum 3 solid wall. Its maximum preserved height (near the fortress wall) was about 1.5 m. It consists of the following: a slightly sloping layer, about 1 m thick, of wadi pebbles of various sizes, with pockets of earth in it (see Fig. 8.7, in background); on top of that was a thin dark layer of earth, 5 cm thick; and above that a top layer (L850) of earth and large stones (apparently fallen stones) with some pockets of burnt material (see Sections 22-22, 23-23). Locus 852 contained pottery attributed to the eighth–seventh centuries BCE, and included no Persian-period material (see Pls. 11.127, 11.128).

Dothan's excavations in 1956 revealed here a sloping surface of stones, which he interpreted as part of a glacis (Dothan 1965:138, Pl. 29a; according to him,

the glacis was also composed of *pisé*, brick fragments and gravel). It is unclear whether the above-mentioned stones we uncovered are related in any way to Dothan's glacis.

If indeed this was a glacis, it could only have been retained by W205. It provided support to the casemates and also had a defensive function, as it increased the angle of the slope between the fortress wall and the moat and rendered the former less accessible. It is possible that eventually the fills of the glacis were the main cause for the blocking of the moat.

STRATUM 1

One complete cooking pot and a few Persian-period potsherds, attributable on typological grounds to Stratum 1, were recovered from the upper part of the fill inside the moat (Pl. 11.131:8).

CHAPTER 9

AREA G: THE AREA WEST OF THE STRATA 3–2 FORTRESSES

YSHAYAHU LENDER AND HANNAH BERNICK-GREENBERG

INTRODUCTION

Area G is located west of the Strata 3–2 rectangular fortresses. Excavation here began in the third season (1978) and continued for five seasons, during which remains underlying the Stratum 2 glacis were uncovered. Work was concentrated in the spaces between the towers and also in the southern corner of the area, where many stones were visible prior to excavation.

STRATUM 4

Remains of Stratum 4 (see Plans 1.1, 3, 4; Section 25-25) were unearthed in one 1.5 m wide sounding only, in Sqs D–C/6, south of Tower 405, perpendicular to the fortress wall. This probe started at elevation 22.79, below stone Floor 8000 attributed to Stratum 3 (see below), into a yellow loess fill, which is part of the Substratum 3c constructional fill/rampart (L8007, L8008; 2 m thick).

Under these, in the western part of the probe, a stone pavement (L8012; elevation 20.80), which slopes to the west, was uncovered. East of that, at elevation 20.71, was a layer of ash (L8011; *c.* 0.15 m thick), on which were *ṭabun* fragments and some pottery. The floor continued to the east and north below the base of the Stratum 3 fortification and was not cut by it.

STRATUM 3

Stratum 3 remains west of the fortresses (Plans 1.2, 6, 7) were preserved mainly between the Stratum 3 towers, where they were protected by the Stratum 2 glacis constructed over them. West of the line of the towers the remains were just below surface level and were severely damaged by later activities. *Inter alia*, walls were probably dismantled and the stones burnt in the lime kiln situated *c.* 25 m west of the fortress (Fig. 9.1). The pottery was mixed and useless for dating purposes. Only between the towers, below the Stratum 2 glacis,

Fig. 9.1. General view of the fortress with lime kiln to its west (on the right); looking east.

did we uncover well-preserved remains. To Stratum 3 are attributed here further segments of the moat, the earthen rampart supported by a retaining wall, and above it floors and a sunken silo.

Living Horizons between the Towers and a Possible Entryway to the Fortress

Between the northern and middle towers, in Sq C/9, a surface (L475) was uncovered at elevations 22.70–22.65. North of it, in the corner between the fortress wall and the northern tower (W406), a rectangular stone-lined silo (Silo 473) had been sunk into the Substratum 3c fill (L510, L511; see Section 26-26) to a depth of about one meter (Figs. 9.2, 9.3). The top of the silo on the west was at elevation 22.78 and on the south at elevation 23.20 (the lining of the silo on the north and east is provided by the fortress wall and tower). Above the southern wall of the silo large stones were found, preserved to elevation 23.60. They formed a wall or partition (W233), which separated the silo from the living surface to its south. Many potsherds were recovered from the silo (Pl. 11.71); three of the sherds mended with pottery from the lower part of the glacis.

Southeast of the silo is a segment of another wall (W235), constructed above the fill of the Substratum 3c rampart.

In the area between the middle and southern tower only the northern part has been excavated. A beaten-earth floor was exposed here (L6504; elevation 22.86), with a layer of ash on it and remains of a *ṭabun* built against the fortress wall (L6502; Fig. 9.4, Section 25-25). This layer produced a bundle containing numerous textile fragments (Chapter 16).

Below this floor was a stone floor (L8000; elevation 22.58–22.78), which apparently formed the foundation for the earthen floor (Fig. 9.5). The floor slopes south and west (L8006), and west of the southern tower (W404) it forms a series of shallow steps or platforms (L8009, L8003; Figs. 9.6–9.8, Section 27-27), which

Fig. 9.3. Area G, Stratum 3. Silo 473 against the fortress wall and Tower 406; looking east.

Fig. 9.2. Area G, Stratum 3. Locus 475 and the top of Silo 473 against the fortress wall; looking east.

Fig. 9.4. Area G, Stratum 3. Earthen Floor 6504 and tabun against the fortress wall; looking east.

Fig. 9.5. Area G, Stratum 3. Stone Floor 8000
abutting the fortress wall; looking south.

Fig. 9.6. Area G, Stratum 3. Stone Pavements
8003, 8009; looking east.

Fig. 9.7. Area G, Stratum 3. Pavements 8003, 8009; looking south.

Fig. 9.8. Area G. Wall 180 of Stratum 2(?) passing over the moat and the stone
pavements of Stratum 3 and reaching Tower 404; looking east.

finally seem to be bonded with the retaining wall of the moat (W208; see below). External stone 'platforms' were also uncovered in Area F north of the central tower (Chapter 8), and possibly also in Area E in the vicinity of the southeastern tower (Chapter 7). All of them may have been connected to some sort of access to the fortress.

The Retaining Wall, the Rampart and the Moat

Only a small segment of the inner retaining wall of the moat (W208) was uncovered in this area (in Sq B/3)— 5 m long and at least five courses high (its bottom was not reached). Its preserved top was at elevation 19.77–19.89 and it slopes to the west. At its southern end this wall must have joined W409, the inner wall of the moat in its southern stretch. As in Areas E and F, W208 supported the earthen rampart constructed east of it over the Stratum 4 remains.

The outer wall of the moat (W209) was revealed in Probe 8002 in Sq B/3 and four courses of it were uncovered. The top of the wall was at elevation 19.25, which is very low compared to the other sides of the moat. This is probably due to the scavenging of stones here for the lime kiln (see above).

STRATUM 2

In Stratum 2 (Plan 8), as in Areas E and F, a glacis was constructed abutting the Stratum 2 casemates and the top of the Stratum 3 solid wall. Part of it was excavated

stratigraphically—between the northern and middle towers (L428, L429 and L430) and between the middle and southern towers (L6501) (see Sections 25-25, 26-26), and other parts were removed by heavy equipment. The fills here were composed of a layer of earth (over 1 m thick), a few large stones alongside pockets of ash with many potsherds (L430, L429), and above that a layer of light colored soil with little pottery (L428). Only at the top was there a layer of large stones, which could be part of the Stratum 2 destruction debris. Ceramics in these fills seemed to relate to Stratum 2 (see Pls. 11.127, 11.128); there was no Persian-period pottery. It thus seems that the glacis was constructed early in Stratum 2 or somewhat later during its lifetime and most of the material in it originated from the leveling of earlier strata within the fortress. It is also clear that concomitantly the Stratum 3 paved areas and silo went out of use.

In the southern part of the area, a diagonal wall (W180) climbs up the stone-lined slope of Stratum 3 from the southwest and abuts Tower W404 (see Fig. 9.8). The wall passes over the moat and it is clear that when it was constructed the moat had already filled up. It may thus belong either to Stratum 3 or to Stratum 2. It is unclear what the function of this wall might have been, one possibility being that it formed part of an entryway into the fortress, alongside the stepped surfaces of Stratum 3. Another possibility is that it dates to a much later period, possibly associated with the lime kiln. As it lies immediately under the surface, it was not datable.

CHAPTER 10

AREA H: THE AREA SOUTH OF THE STRATA 3–2 FORTRESSES

DOV NAHLIELI AND HANNAH BERNICK-GREENBERG

INTRODUCTION

Area H is located immediately south of the Strata 3–2 rectangular fortresses. A small-scale excavation was conducted here east of the middle tower during the fourth season (1978). The main area here, between the middle and western towers, was excavated during the fifth to eighth seasons (1979–1981) and the entire face of the Stratum 3 fortress wall was cleaned and exposed in the last seasons (1981–1982).

STRATUM 4

Stratum 4 remains (Plans 1.1, 3, 4) were reached between the middle and western towers, on either side of, and about one meter deeper than, the Stratum 3 water channel (for which, see below). They were founded at

elevation 19.71 on natural deposits containing wadi pebbles, and superimposed over sand and clay, which was excavated down to elevation 19.28 (L918, L919, L5084, L5087 and L5089).

Four silos and a living surface were uncovered at about elevation 20.10. Three of the silos were situated in Sq F/3 (Silos 5080, 5081 and 5085), each 1.5 m in diameter and 0.6–0.8 m deep (Fig. 10.1). The largest silo (Silo 5090) was unearthed in Sq H/3. It is 2.5 m in diameter and about 1 m deep (Fig. 10.2, see Section 28-28). All the silos were lined and paved with stones and dug into natural deposits. The scant pottery found in them was not diagnostic, but nevertheless their attribution to Stratum 4 is unequivocal: Silo 5085 is superimposed by the Stratum 3 retaining wall (W409; see below and Fig. 10.1).

Fig. 10.1. Area H, Stratum 4. Silos in Sq F/3; the southern silo, 5085, is cut by W409; looking east.

Fig. 10.2. Area H, Stratum 4. Silo 5090; looking south.

Fig. 10.3. Area H, Stratum 4. Pebble Floor 5082 and silos; looking west.

*Fig. 10.4. Area H, Stratum 4. Floor 917 (in section) and below it W648, W649 and W650
at the base of the solid Stratum 3 wall. In the background, at a higher elevation, are
the Stratum 3 water channel (5074) and the retaining wall (W409); looking west.*

In Sq F/3, below the Stratum 3 constructional fill, a 0.3 m thick layer of ash (L5079) was discerned. Below it, at elevation 20.10, were patches of a pebble floor (L5082; Fig. 10.3; the pebbles are not indicated on the plans), whose relation to the silos and to the Stratum 3 wall could not be determined. In Sq H/3 was another, ashy, living surface (L917 at elevations 20.33–20.38), which was associated with Silo 5090 (Fig. 10.4; in the balk the silo was preserved somewhat higher than in the unit itself). Below this surface two to three flimsy walls (W648, W649 and W650) are located at the base of the Stratum 3 fortification (Fig. 10.4). These may represent an earlier phase within Stratum 4 (but no associated floor was encountered).

STRATUM 3

The fortification system on the southern side of the fortress (Plans 1.2, 6, 7) differs from that on the other three sides. At least in the one excavated strip (Sq H/1), no moat was uncovered. The reason, of course, is the proximity to Wadi el-Qudeirat, which provides a certain measure of protection. Other than the fortifications, excavations in this area revealed the water channel,

which passes through the fortress wall into the cistern. Living surfaces, like those found east, north and west of the fortress, were not clearly discerned here, but as evidenced by the remains of at least one silo, some activity did take place here.

Silo 618

East of the middle tower (Tower 403), a fragmentary rectangular silo (Silo 618) was uncovered close to the corner between the tower and the fortress wall (Fig. 10.5). The top of the silo was at elevation 22.60–23.20 and it was 2 m deep. The sides were lined with pebbles, preserved only next to the wall and the tower, the entire southern and eastern walls having been destroyed.

No living surface could be attributed to the silo, and as it was found unsealed, the material inside it cannot be used to date it. Based on the elevations only it is difficult to decide whether the silo belongs to Stratum 3 or is later. Also, the silo was uncovered very close to the surface and the deposits overlying it were disturbed. As on the other sides of the fortress silos outside the fortresses belong to Stratum 3, this is the attribution we prefer here as well.

Fig. 10.5. Area H, Stratum 4. Silo 618 east of Tower 403; looking north.

The Fill of the Rampart

As on the other sides of the fortress, the rampart/
constructional fill (L910, L911, L914, L915, L920a,
L5070, L5071, L5073, L5076) covered the remains of
Stratum 4 and was supported by a retaining wall. In Sqs
H/3–4 the fill was preserved to a maximum elevation
of 22.60–22.90 m. This is significantly higher than the
top preservation of the walls of the water channel in
Sqs G/3–4. If the channel was unroofed (see discussion
in Area D, Chapter 4), the fill near it must have been
lower (its top not higher than *c.* 21.50), which would
mean that the fill sloped here, probably retained by
the walls of the channel. Another possibility is that
the walls were originally higher, at least up to 22.60,
coinciding with the top level of the opening through
the fortress wall (described below).

The composition of the constructional fill was
revealed west of Tower 403: a layer of crushed lime
plaster (L902; elevation 22.90; Section 28-28) on a
foundation of gravel (elevation 22.60), and below that
a fill of earth and ash (L907). Unfortunately, the fill
was removed in later seasons by mechanical means and
thus it was not possible to ascertain if this plaster layer
was indeed continuous throughout the area and what
its relation to the water channel might have been. One
possibility is that it was devised to direct runoff water
into the channel (assuming that the channel was not
roofed).

The Retaining Wall

The wall retaining the constructional fill (W409), which
also protected the fill from the stream, was exposed
between the middle and western towers for a length of
13.5 m. It was preserved to a maximum height of 2.2 to
2.6 m and cut the underlying Stratum 4 remains.

In the eastern part of the area (Sqs H/1–2) a narrow
probe (L1523), 1 m wide, was excavated to the bottom
of the wall (Fig. 10.6, Section 28-28). Here the top
preservation of the wall was at elevation 19.50 and the
upper part of the wall widened on its inner face, the
face resting against the Stratum 4 deposits. It would be
logical to assume that originally W409 stood about one
meter higher, to *c.* elevation 20.50–20.60, coinciding
with the bottom level of the water channel, but this
could not be demonstrated.

In Probe 1523 the base of the retaining wall was
uncovered at elevation 17.00, and from there to elevation
15.00 were boulders (Fig. 10.6); whether they occurred
there naturally or not could not be determined. At the
western end of Area H, the top course of the retaining
wall can be observed to create a corner with W208,
the retaining wall west of the fortress (see Area G,
Chapter 9).

Probe 1523 was excavated for a length of 6.5 m south
of W409 and no parallel wall was found that would
have served as an external wall for a moat. This attests

Fig. 10.6. Area H, Stratum 3. Probe 1523 and the retaining
wall (W409), resting on boulders; looking north.

Fig. 10.7. Area H, Stratum 3. Water Channel 5074
incorporated in the Stratum 3 wall (W202, in
background); in foreground, W409; looking north.

that this side, as indicated above, was apparently not
protected.

The Water Channel

Channel 5074 was uncovered between the southern
and middle towers (Fig. 10.7). Its northern
extent, inside the fortress, was exposed in Area D
(Channel 1304; Chapter 4). The channel was founded
on the Substratum 3c constructional fill (Fig. 10.8) and
was planned and built concurrently with the Stratum 3
fortress and constructional fills. Its incline (from south
to north) is very moderate. The channel walls (W596,
W597) are constructed of medium-sized stones, and

Fig. 10.8. Area H, Stratum 3. Water Channel 5074 built on
the earthen rampart; looking west.

were preserved 0.8 m high in the north and *c.* 0.45 m high in the south. The channel was *c.* 0.6 m wide and plastered on the bottom and probably on the walls as well. The plaster layers were uncovered at elevation 20.58 on the south and at elevation 20.54 on the north (see the discussion of the plaster in Chapter 4 and Figs. 4.14, 4.15, Section 13-13). Some of the layers of plaster found here are clearly repairs, indicating maintenance and prolonged use.

No covering stones were discovered to indicate that the channel was roofed and in the earthen fill around it no significant quantities of stones were encountered.

The channel is well preserved to a distance of 5 m from the fortress wall, but remains of its various plaster coatings (see discussion in Chapter 4), as well as the foundations for its walls, can be still seen at a distance of 6 m from the wall, *c.* 0.8 m north of the retaining wall (W409). Exactly how the channel was incorporated into the retaining wall is unknown. It may have continued southward in a straight course, over the wall towards the stream (today at a distance of 12 m from the retaining wall) or alternatively turned east and ran along the top of the wall.

At its northern end, the channel was incorporated into the lower courses of the Stratum 3 fortress wall (see Fig. 10.7); narrow opening, 0.5 m wide and 2.0 m high, allowed water to flow into the cistern (see discussion of the inner part of the channel in Chapter 4, Area D). As the fortress wall is over 4 m wide, we were unable to examine the middle part of the channel. Only a one-meter-long stretch was excavated, from which we learned that the channel was blocked by stones.

There are two main problematic points regarding the construction of the channel. The first is the manner of its roofing. As mentioned, no covering stones were found and therefore the only possibility is that the channel was roofed with wooden planks, which did not survive, or that it was haphazardly covered with branches and other light materials (some sort of covering was important to prevent earth and stones from falling in and blocking the channel and silting the cistern itself).

The second problem is the discrepancy between the height of the opening through which the channel passed the fortress wall, which is as high as elevation 22.60, and the height of the channel walls, which were preserved to elevation 21.66 only. This means that the opening through the wall was visible from outside (even if the channel was covered by wooden planks, etc.). As discussed above, it might be postulated that originally the walls where higher (to elevation 22.60) and the channel was indeed roofed with planks and covered with branches to camouflage it.

STRATUM 2

Prior to the excavation, Area H (similarly to the other excavation areas around the fortress' perimeter) was covered entirely with earth to the top of the Stratum 3 walls (elevation 25.00). The external walls of the Stratum 2 casemates were very poorly preserved (see Area A2, Chapter 2). In a probe west of the middle tower (Tower 403), a fill composed of soft soil and medium-sized stones (L411) was found to abut the Stratum 3 wall (W202). It was just below the level of W170, the Stratum 2 external casemate wall here. It rests on the plastered surface discussed above (L902; elevation 22.90, see Section 28-28). If this surface is indeed an occupational surface of Stratum 3, then L411 may be part of the Stratum 2 glacis, but it is also possible that it actually comprises post-occupational debris. Thus, no clear evidence for the existence of a glacis attributable to Stratum 2 was unearthed here (no orderly, packed or stone-lined surfaces), and most of the material here was removed by mechanical means.

Constructing a glacis here in Stratum 2 would have created difficulty vis-à-vis the water channel. Assuming that the channel continued to serve in Stratum 2, the channel must have been covered in one way or another. Alternatively, it is possible that the channel ceased to function then and the cistern was fed only by runoff water collected within the fortress.

CHAPTER 11

THE CERAMIC ASSEMBLAGES AND
THE WHEEL-MADE POTTERY TYPOLOGY

HANNAH BERNICK-GREENBERG

INTRODUCTION AND METHOD OF PRESENTATION

This chapter deals with all the ceramic ware groups attested at Kadesh Barnea, other than the Negebite 'family', which is presented and discussed in Chapter 12. Most of the material published here originates in 'good' contexts, i.e., stratigraphically secure loci, apparently undisturbed. Only rarely did we include material of dubious provenance. This selection means that the illustrations in the pottery plates represent *c.* 85% of all the ceramics drawn. The pottery presented here comprises about two thirds of all diagnostics excavated.

The pottery is presented stratigraphically, from early to late. Within each stratum, the first plates are arranged by typology, followed by plates arranged by context (i.e., assemblages). Although this has resulted in some repetition of drawings, this method was deemed crucial in order to obtain easily both typological and contextual vistas.

The typological plates do not include all the types represented in any given stratum, but only the most frequent ones, and occasionally 'special' or otherwise important vessels/fragments. Additional ceramic forms may be found in the contextual plates. Similarly, only the most typical and significant (chronologically or otherwise) types are discussed. The typological designations (type numbers) are random. As the ceramics were studied starting with the later strata, the sequential numbering of types usually started with the later types.

Comparanda for the various types are usually cited in the framework of the stratum where the types were most common.

The contextual plates include both the wheel-made ceramics discussed here and the Negebite vessels discussed in Chapter 12. The presentation of any given context usually includes all complete and near complete vessels uncovered, and a representative selection of the remainder. Therefore, the typological spectrum of each context is presented, and when relevant, a correct ratio between wheel-made and Negebite vessels has been maintained.

At the end of the chapter we present and discuss the pot-marks found on the wheel-made pottery. Incisions and impressions on Negebite vessels appear in Chapter 12.

Fabric descriptions of the vessels usually accompany the plates illustrating the assemblages. Only in cases where special ware families are presented in a typological plate, e.g. Midianite Ware, Edomite Ware, etc., were the fabric descriptions presented there.

POTTERY OF STRATUM 4
(Figs. 11.1–11.23; Pls. 11.1–11.26)

In the casemates of the oval fortress, in its courtyard and in the rooms of the adjacent settlement, relatively rich ceramic assemblages were unearthed. Many of the assemblages were found in primary deposition, having been sealed under the destruction debris of this stratum.

The most conspicuous characteristic of the Stratum 4 ceramic assemblage is the abundance of hand-formed Negebite pottery alongside the wheel-made wares (nearly half the assemblage). The Negebite assemblage comprises mostly cooking vessels, kraters and bowls. On the other hand, containers, such as jugs and jars, are rare in this fabric and most of these classes of vessels were wheel made.

While processing the material we attempted to differentiate chronologically between the assemblages of the fortress and those of the settlement, but concluded that they are chronologically homogeneous. Thus, in the following typological discussion the types of both settlement and fortress are presented together (but see the contextual analysis below).

TYPOLOGY OF WHEEL-MADE SHAPES

Bowls

The bowl repertoire of Stratum 4 differs from that of other Iron II assemblages in Judah in the scarcity of red slipped and burnished surfaces, and of bar or knob handles. The bowls are classified below based on shape, size and production technique.

Type B1 (Pl. 11.1:1, 2). These are small rounded or slightly carinated bowls characterized by very thin walls and a simple rim. They can be further subdivided into three main groups according to their surface treatment. The largest group comprises 19 bowls with a black-brown band (Pl. 11.1:2), usually on both sides of the rim, but on several bowls on its external face only. Occasionally the band of color was not applied on the rim itself, but somewhat below it. These bowls are neither slipped nor burnished. Of this group, three are from Stratum 4, eleven from Substratum 3c and five from Substrata 3a-b.

The second group (11 examples) includes bowls that were red slipped inside (Pl.11.1:1) and only occasionally outside as well, or may bear a red band on the upper part of their external face. Most of the bowls in this group are also (irregularly) burnished. Of this group, a single example was found in Stratum 4, four in Substratum 3c and six in Substrata 3a-b.

To a third group belong nine bowls without any surface treatment. This subgroup was not represented in Stratum 4. Two specimens are from Substratum 3c and seven from Substrata 3a-b. Stratum 2 produced ten small rounded bowls that are slightly different in shape and have no surface treatment (see below).

In addition, there were in Stratum 4 thirteen other bowls, which were generally similar to Type B1 both in shape and surface treatment, but were not designated as such when the pottery was processed. As they could not be re-examined, we are unable to determine whether they indeed are of the same type.

Similar small rounded bowls were found at Be'er Sheva', Stratum VI (Herzog 1984: Fig. 26:18), 'Arad, Stratum XI (M. Aharoni 1981: Fig. 6:1–6) and Lachish, Stratum IV (Type B2; Zimhoni 1997: Fig. 3.5), and later on at Be'er Sheva', Stratum II (Y. Aharoni 1973: Pl. 59:37) and 'En Gedi, Stratum V (Mazar, Dothan and Dunayevsky 1966: Fig. 15:10). Parallels to the decorated bowls are known from Kuntillet 'Ajrud (Ayalon 1995: Fig. 3:17) and, in the far north, from Hazor Area A, Stratum VII (Yadin et al. 1958: Pl. XLIX:9).

Type B2 (Pl. 11.1:3, 4). These small carinated bowls have everted rims and rounded lower parts. The bowl in Pl. 11.1:3 is similar, in the shape and stance of its rim, to Iron Age chalices, but these, however, are usually of larger diameter (e.g., at Be'er Sheva' V, Y. Aharoni 1973: Pl. 54:7). At Kadesh Barnea, however, nothing indicates that these bowls were part of chalices. Some of these bowls (e.g., Pl. 11.1:4) are coated with red slip inside and outside. Type B2 bowls also appear in Substratum 3c. Parallels to the slipped carinated bowls are found in Be'er Sheva', Strata VII and VI (Herzog 1984: Figs. 21:3; 26:2, 3) and in Lachish Stratum IV (Type B16; Zimhoni 1997: Fig. 3.21:15, 19, 21).

Type B3 (Pl. 11.1:5, 6). These small rounded bowls differ from Type B1 in that the walls are thicker and the tip of the rim is thickened inside and out. Very few specimens of this type were registered. Similar bowls occur at 'Arad, Strata XII and XI (M. Aharoni 1981: Figs. 1:10; 6:10–12) and Lachish, Strata V–IV (Zimhoni 1997: Figs. 3.13:3; 3.14:5; 3.17:5).

Type B4 (Fig. 11.1; Pl. 11.1:7, 8). This designation refers to bowls of various sizes with rounded or slightly carinated walls and an everted rim. The base is usually a low ring base but disc bases also occur. Surface treatment varies between irregular burnish, slip and burnish and no treatment at all. This large group of about 230 bowls was divided into subtypes (4.1– 4.5) according to rim shape and size. Some of these subtypes occur throughout the Strata 4–2 range and others first appear in either Substratum 3c or Substrata 3a-b.

In general, about 8% of the Type B4 bowls were found in Stratum 4, 20% in Substratum 3c, about 46% in Substrata 3a-b, and nearly 20% in Stratum 2. This

Fig. 11.1. Stratum 4. Bowl Type B4 (Pls. 11.1:7; 11.16:17).

wide range renders these bowls unreliable for exact dating purposes. As both in absolute numbers and the range of subtypes these bowls are most significant in Stratum 3, what follows is only a description of the Stratum 4 occurrences.

Subtype B4.1 (Pl. 11.1:8) represents medium-sized bowls with a flaring rim, neither slipped nor burnished. This subtype occurs throughout Strata 4–2.

Subtype B4.5 (Pl.11.1:7) represents medium-sized bowls with hammer-shaped rims projecting and thickened both inward and outward. These too are neither slipped nor burnished and also continue until Stratum 2. As they are most common in Subtrata 3a-b, their parallels are discussed below.

Type B12 (Fig. 11.2; Pl. 11.1:9). These bowls are similar morphologically, and to some extent also in their decoration, to Type B4 bowls. In addition, however, they bear a very typical decoration on the rim; it consists of short strokes in black paint. The parallel strokes are spaced around the rim in groups of five to nine. Usually there is no other surface treatment, but six examples were irregularly burnished inside and out. A few bowls of this type from Substrata 3c and 3a-b bear incisions, executed after firing, on their rims or walls (see below).

Type B12 bowls were very common at Kadesh Barnea—about 100 such vessels and fragments were registered, which constitute about 10% of all the wheel-made bowls at the site. Twelve are from Stratum 4, 36 from Substratum 3c, 33 from Substratum 3a-b, nine from Stratum 2, and the rest are from unstratified loci. It should also be taken into consideration that some of the bowl fragments defined as (different variants of) Type B4 may in fact belong to B12 bowls, but happened to retain only the undecorated parts of the rims' circumference. This, we assume, will not affect much the relative distribution of Type B12 in the different strata.

It is very difficult to establish a chronological framework and regional associations for these bowls, as

Fig. 11.2. Stratum 4. Bowl Type B12 (Pls. 11.1:9; 11.8:2).

very few parallels are known from Judah, and similarly from more distant regions such as Transjordan. In Iron IIA, black strokes are known mainly on red-slipped kraters from Ashdod, Strata IX–VIII ('Ashdod Ware'; for example in Area D, Strata 4 and 3, Dothan and Freedman 1967: Figs. 36:13, 17; 42:3, 5, 6). At Be'er Sheva', a bowl of different shape but bearing similar decoration was retrieved from Stratum VI (Herzog 1984: Fig. 26:4). Later on, similar black strokes on rims are attested on Edomite goblets and kraters dated to the seventh century BCE (Bennett 1974: Fig. 15:13, Oakeshott 1983: Figs. 1:7, 8, 3:5).

Type B5 (Pl. 11.1:10). This is a bowl with a low carination and two pierced handles attached to the carination point, near the base. Additional fragments of such bowls were found in Substratum 3c. No real parallels could be located, but a body sherd of a bowl with a pierced handle was published from Hazor, Strata X–IX (Yadin et al. 1961: Pl. CCXIII:11).

Type B6 (Pl. 11.1:11). This is a very small fragment, but its thin wall and diameter permit its definition as a bowl, probably with slight carination at mid-body. The upper part of the wall is upright with a few delicate ridges, and the rim is thickened. Similar bowls are known from Be'er Sheva', Stratum VI (Herzog 1984: Fig. 26:11), Ḥorbat Ḥaluqim (Cohen 1976a: Fig. 9:2) and Lachish, Stratum IV (Type B5; Zimhoni 1997: Fig. 3.9:7).

Type B7 (Pl. 11.1:12). This sherd belongs either to a bowl or to a krater (it is unclear whether it had handles). The walls are carinated, their upper part is upright, and the rim is thickened inside and out. Parallels may be found in Be'er Sheva', Strata VII and VI (Herzog 1984: Figs. 21:12; 27:6), Lachish, Stratum V (Zimhoni 1997: Fig. 3.26:7), Meẓad Sirpad (Cohen and Cohen-Amin 2004: Fig. 72:5) and Ḥorbat Ḥaluqim (Cohen 1976a: Fig. 9:11, 14).

Type B8 (Pl. 11.1:13, 14). These are open shallow bowls with simple rims. Specimen No. 13 has a slightly wavy wall and a rounded base, while No. 14 has straight flaring walls and a disc base. These bowls continue at Kadesh Barnea until Stratum 2, in similar small quantities. In Stratum 4 the bowls have no surface treatment, but in Strata 3 and 2 a few are red slipped or burnished. Substratum 3c and later contexts also produced similar shallow bowls with cut rims (Type B9; see below).

Type B8 bowls are not very common in the Negev sites, but were found at Kuntillet 'Ajrud (Ayalon 1995: Fig. 3:1–5), Lachish, Stratum IV (Type B1; Zimhoni 1997: Fig. 3.4:2), and in the eighth century and even later at Lachish, Stratum III (Y. Aharoni 1975: Pls. 44:11; 46:3), Be'er Sheva', Stratum II (Y. Aharoni 1973: Pls. 66:9; 74:3), Ashdod, Stratum VI (M. Dothan 1971: Fig. 93:25, 28) and 'En Gedi, Stratum V (Mazar, Dothan and Dunayevsky 1966: Fig. 15:3).

Other Bowls
A fragment of a black-slipped and burnished bowl and a fragmentary three-legged bowl were found on the upper floor level in the settlement (Pl. 11.21:12, 13). Such vessels were also encountered in Substratum 3c. The three-legged bowl is of Type B13, which was very common in Strata 3 and 2 and is discussed below. Two small fragments of small rounded bowls of Type B25 were also encountered (not illustrated; for a discussion of this type, see below, Substratum 3c).

One bowl in Substratum 4b (Pl. 11.11:3) is probably of Cypriot Bichrome III Ware.

Kraters

Type K1 (Pl. 11.1:15–17). This type is represented here mostly by rim sherds and thus it is very difficult to determine the exact shape or define parallels. Fragment No. 15 belongs to an open vessel with vertical walls that curve only towards the base. It has a folded-out rim, to which the handles were attached. These kraters are usually slipped and burnished. Similar vessels are known at Lachish, Stratum V (Zimhoni 1997: Fig. 3.30:11) and Be'er Sheva', Stratum VI (Herzog 1984: Fig. 27:13).

Kraters Nos. 16 and 17 are deep open vessels with slightly rounded walls and no pronounced neck. The rim is thickened or folded outward, and two handles extend from the edge of the rim to the wall. Those kraters are occasionally red slipped. They are typical of Stratum 4, but are also present in Substrata 3c and 3a-b (rim sherds only, without handles). Similar rims appear as late as Stratum 2.

No meaningful parallels to these kraters can be cited from Iron Age contexts in the Negev sites, but they do

have corollaries at Lachish, Stratum V (Zimhoni 1997: Fig. 3.30:7–10) and at Tell Qasile, Strata IX and VIII (A. Mazar 1985: Figs. 53:8, 12; 54:9–11).

Holemouth Krater (Fig. 11.3; Pl. 11.1:18). This is a unique shape. The body is rounded, the rim is cut inward and the vessel has a ring base. There are possible traces of a handle attached below the rim. No parallels to this vessel were found.

Fig. 11.3. Stratum 4. Holemouth krater (Pls. 11.1:18; 11.23:1).

Cooking Pots

The cooking pots are discussed below in the probable chronological order of their typological evolution.

Type CP3 (Figs. 11.4, 11.5; Pl. 11.2:1, 2). These pots are wide and squat, with a sharp carination at mid-body. Two handles extend from the rim to the shoulder and are attached above the carination point. The rim is usually thickened or folded.

Two subtypes were defined: Subtype CP3.1 (Fig. 11.4; Pl. 11.2:1) has a folded rim that forms an inner groove. Many parallels may be cited from sites in Judah and the southern coastal plain, such as Atar Ha-Ro'a (Cohen 1970: Fig. 8:1–5), Naḥal Boqer and Naḥal La'ana (Cohen and Cohen-Amin 2004: Figs. 16:10; 48:4, 5), Be'er Sheva', Strata VII (Herzog 1984: Fig. 22:1, 2) and VI (Y. Aharoni 1973: Pl. 55:10, 11), 'Arad, Stratum XIIb (M. Aharoni 1981: Fig. 2:14), Ashdod, Stratum IX (Dothan and Freedman 1967: Fig. 36:14), Lachish, Stratum IV (Zimhoni 1997: Fig.

Fig. 11.4. Stratum 4. Cooking pot Subtype CP3.1 (Pls. 11.2:1; 11.23:4).

*Fig. 11.5. Stratum 4.
Cooking pot Subtype CP3.2
(Pls. 11.2:2; 11.23:3).*

3.43:1–3) and Tell Qasile, Stratum VIII (A. Mazar 1985: Fig. 55:8).

Subtype CP3.2 (Fig. 11.5; Pl.11.2:2) has a folded and ridged rim whose angle continues that of the walls. Similar cooking pots occur in the Negev sites, such as at the Naḥal Ela fortress (Cohen and Cohen-Amin 2004: Fig. 64:1, 3), ʿArad, Stratum XI (M. Aharoni 1981: Fig. 7:1, 2) and Lachish, Stratum IV (Zimhoni 1997: Fig. 3.38:14).

Both subtypes are thus especially typical of Iron IIA contexts in Judah.

Type CP4 (Fig. 11.6; Pl. 11.2:3). These wide and squat cooking pots resemble Type CP3 but have a thickened, everted rim with hardly any neck. An example of this type is attested at Beʾer Shevaʿ, Stratum VII (Herzog 1984: Fig. 22:4).

*Fig. 11.6. Stratum 4.
Cooking pot Type CP4
(Pls. 11.2:3; 11.23:2).*

Type CP5 (Pl. 11.2:4). This is a large, wide cooking pot typified by a vertical neck and simple rim. It is quite rare at Kadesh Barnea. A few similar vessels are known from the following southern sites: Beʾer Shevaʿ, Stratum VI (Herzog 1984: Fig. 28:4); ʿArad, Stratum XII (M. Aharoni 1981: Fig. 5:16, 17); Tel Esdar, Stratum II (Kochavi 1969: Fig. 5:6); and Lachish, Stratum IV (Zimhoni 1997: Fig. 3.37:13).

Type CP1. Only Subtype CP1.1 (Pl. 11.2:5) appears in this stratum.

On the cooking pots of this subtype the neck is not pronounced, and the rim is ridged (for other CP1 subtypes, see below). There were only a few fragments in Strata 4 and Substratum 3c, and subsequently, in the Strata 3a-b–2 range, the type becomes very common and more varied in rim shape.

Such cooking pots are known in the Negev (and the Shephelah) in Iron IIA, for example at Meẓudat Naḥal

Sirpad (Cohen and Cohen-Amin 2004: Fig. 58:6) and Beʾer Shevaʿ, Stratum VII (Herzog 1984: Fig. 22:5, 7).

Type CP2 (Pl. 11.2:6). This is a rounded cooking pot with a short ridged rim. The main difference between Types CP2 and CP1 is that CP2 is thinner and its rim is upright. This type was represented in Strata 4–3c by a few sherds only, but it is common in Substrata 3a-b (see discussion there), and less so in Stratum 2.

Juglets

Juglets (including many complete examples) were the most common class of vessel in the destruction assemblages of Stratum 4. Most are dipper juglets, a few are 'Black Juglets' and the rest are singular shapes.

Type JT1 (Pl Figs. 11.7, 11.8; 11.2:7–12). These are oval dipper juglets with pronounced shoulders, and are either red-slipped and burnished or undecorated. The neck is relatively long, upright or flaring, and the top of the (usually pinched) rim is thickened and inverted or upright. A handle extends from the rim to the shoulder. This a common type in Judah, including the Negev sites, throughout the Iron Age. Iron IIA examples are from Naḥal Boqer, Meẓudat Naḥal Sirpad and Meẓudat 'Ein Qedeis (Cohen and Cohen-Amin 2004: Figs. 16:12; 58:12; 78:2, 3), ʿArad, Stratum XI (M. Aharoni 1981: Fig. 7:16, 17) and Beʾer Shevaʿ, Stratum IV (Y. Aharoni 1973: Pl. 55:14). Beʾer Shevaʿ, Stratum II (Y. Aharoni 1973: Pl. 62:116–118) and ʿArad, Stratum VIII (Herzog 1984: Fig. 3:15) may be cited for the eighth century BCE, and 'En Gedi, Stratum V (Mazar, Dothan and Dunayevsky 1966: Fig. 19:8, 9) and ʿArad, Stratum VI (Herzog 1984: Fig. 29:9), for the seventh century BCE.

The juglet in Pl. 11.2:13 is morphologically similar to the dipper juglets, with the addition of a small spout

*Fig. 11.7. Stratum 4.
Juglet Type JT1 (Pls.
11.2:7; 11.22:5).*

*Fig. 11.8. Stratum 4.
Juglet Type JT1 (Pls.
11.2:8; 11.23:8).*

at about mid-vessel. One possible parallel is a juglet with a similar spout at Kuntillet 'Ajrud (Ayalon 1995: Fig. 18:3).

Type JT2 (Fig. 11:9; Pl. 11.2:14–16). These are the so-called 'Black Juglets'. In Stratum 4 they are characterized by a globular body, occasionally squat, with a long, narrow neck and a handle extending from mid-neck to shoulder. The fabric is usually gray-black and the vessels are burnished externally. Juglet No. 16 is made of brown rather than black fabric but is associated with the 'Black Juglets' in all other attributes.

'Black Juglets' are common at the Negev sites, for example at 'Arad, Strata XII and XI (M. Aharoni 1981: Figs. 4:5, 6; 7:15) and Be'er Sheva', Stratum VI (Herzog 1984: Fig. 30:5–7). Juglets of this type that are not of black fabric were found, for example, at 'Arad, Stratum XII (M. Aharoni 1981: Fig. 4:4) and Tel Esdar, Stratum II (Kochavi 1969: Fig. 5:6) and possibly also at Ḥorbat Raḥaba (Cohen and Cohen-Amin 2004: Fig. 4:16).

Fig. 11.9. Stratum 4. Juglet Type JT2 (Pls. 11.2:16; 11.17:2).

Other Juglets
The juglet in Fig. 11.10, Pl.11.2:17, is a large globular juglet with a long, narrow neck and a handle apparently attached to its middle. Decoration consists of four horizontal lines in red paint. No exact parallels to this juglet can be cited.

A tiny rounded juglet (Fig. 11.11; Pl. 11.2:18) is a singular vessel at the site. The neck is wide relative to the body and everted. No parallels are known to us.

A Black-on-Red juglet (Fig. 11.12; Pl. 11.2:19) was found in the destruction layer of Casemate 938 and thus has important chronological implications for the entire Stratum 4 assemblage. It has a wide globular body and a flat base, and is adorned with red slip, horizontal black lines and concentric black circles on

Fig. 11.10. Stratum 4. Juglet (Pls. 11.2:17; 11.17:3).

Fig. 11.11. Stratum 4. Juglet Type JT4 (Pls. 11.2:18; 11.23:6).

Fig. 11.12. Stratum 4. Black-on-Red juglet (Pls. 11.2:19; 11.11:13).

the shoulder. In both Judah and Israel these juglets appear for the first time in Iron IIA (conventionally the tenth century BCE) and continue to the end of the Iron Age (for another such fragment, see Pl. 11.19:4). In the Negev, Black-on-Red juglets are known from Be'er Sheva', Strata VII and VI (Herzog 1984: Figs. 24:7; 30:8).

Pyxis (Fig. 11.13; Pl. 11.2:20). This vessel is small, squat and unadorned. Although pyxides in the Levant are especially frequent in the Late Bronze and Early Iron Ages, they do occur in the south as well, as late as Iron IIA. Examples in the south appear, for example, at Tel Masos, Stratum II (Area H, House 314; Fritz and Kempinski 1983: Pl. 143:6) and Tel Esdar, Stratum III (Kochavi 1969: Fig. 13:11). Larger pyxides with disc bases, red slipped and bearing black decorations, are known from Tel Masos, Stratum II (Fritz and Kempinski 1983: Pl. 143:5) and Naḥal Boqer (Cohen and Cohen-Amin 2004: Fig. 16:5).

Fig. 11.13. Stratum 4. Pyxis (Pls. 11.2:20; 11.15:6).

Jugs

The Stratum 4 assemblage includes a large number of complete jugs, many of which are red slipped and burnished.

Type J1 (Pl. 11.3:1–4). These jugs are globular in shape, with a rounded base, a wide and tall neck and a simple rim, from which a handle extends to the shoulder (No. 1 is an unusually small example). They are neither slipped nor burnished.

Jugs of this type are known, for example, from 'Arad, Strata XII and XI (M. Aharoni 1981: Fig. 3:5; 7:3–6), Be'er Sheva', Strata VII–V (Y. Aharoni 1973: Pl. 54:12–18, defined as cooking jugs; Herzog 1984: Figs. 22:11–16; 28:7–12) and Lachish, Stratum V (Y. Aharoni 1975: Pl. 42:2–5).

Type J2 (Pl. 11.3:5). This is a rather unusual jug, similar in shape to Type J1 but with a flaring neck and no handles. A similar jug, with a pronounced ridge at the junction of the neck and body, was uncovered at Tel Esdar, Stratum II (Kochavi 1969: Fig. 5:10).

Type J3 (Fig. 11.14; Pl. 11.3:6). This is a unique shape at Kadesh Barnea. It is a relatively large oval jug, with a rounded base, a tall narrow neck (the rim is missing) and a handle apparently extending from mid-neck to shoulder. An upper part of a seemingly similar jug was published from 'Arad, Stratum XI (M. Aharoni 1981: Fig. 7:9).

Fig. 11.14. Stratum 4. Jug Type J3 (Pls. 11.3:6; 11.11:17).

Type J4 (Fig. 11.15; Pl. 11.3:7–9). These are large pear-shaped jugs on a ring base. The neck is tall and wide, the rim is thickened, creating an inner gutter of sorts, and pinched (occasionally there is a slight ridge under the rim). The handle extends from rim to shoulder.

Similar jugs are known in the Negev from Ḥorbat Mesura and Naḥal Ela (Cohen and Cohen-Amin 2004: Figs. 11:1; 64:6, 7), 'Arad, Stratum XII (M. Aharoni

Fig. 11.15. Stratum 4. Jug Type J4 (Pl. 11.3:8; 11.12:1).

1981: Figs. 3:1, 7, 5, 11 and Tel Esdar, Stratum II (Kochavi 1969: Fig. 5:9), as well as from Lachish, Stratum V (Y. Aharoni 1975: Pl. 42:1).

Type J5 (Figs. 11.16, 11.17; Pl. 11.3:10, 11). These jugs are either rounded or slightly oval and have a ring base. As opposed to jugs of Type J4, the neck is tall and relatively narrow, and has a slight ridge at mid-height, from which a handle extends to the shoulder. The rims, on the other hand, are quite similar to those of Type J4, thickened at the top and inverted. All the (few) jugs uncovered were red slipped and vertically hand burnished.

Comparanda may be cited from 'Arad, Stratum XI (M. Aharoni 1981: Fig. 3:3) and Ashdod, Stratum Xa (Area M, Stratum 10; Dothan and Porath 1982: Fig. 8:4).

Fig. 11.16. Stratum 4. Jug Type J5 (Pls. 11.3:10; 11.15:12).

Fig. 11.17. Stratum 4. Jug Type J5 (Pls. 11.3:11; 11.12:2).

Type J6 (Fig. 11.18; Pl. 11.3:12). This is a red-slipped and burnished pear-shaped strainer jug with a tall neck and a narrow disc base (the rim is broken and probably the handle as well). The spout and strainer are located at mid-body.

No exact parallels for this vessel were found. In general, strainer jugs in the south are known, e.g., from 'Arad, Stratum XII (M. Aharoni 1981: Fig. 3:2; unslipped), Naḥal Boqer (Cohen and Cohen-Amin

2004: Fig. 16:6; red slipped on its upper half), Ḥorbat Mesura (Cohen and Cohen-Amin 2004: Fig. 10:7; with a basket handle, unslipped) and from Tel Masos Stratum II, in Area H, House 314 (Fritz and Kempinski 1983: Pl. 145:2; burnished; the shape of the jug is more angular).

Fig. 11.18. Stratum 4. Strainer jug Type J6 (Pls. 11.3:12; 11.12:3).

Other Jugs

The small jug in Pl. 11.19:5 has a squat globular shape, a tall wide neck, a thickened, pinched and ridged rim, a handle extending from rim to shoulder and a low disc base. It is vertically burnished.

Flasks

Only one complete flask was found in Stratum 4, as well as fragments of two others, of different shape. The flask (Fig. 11.19; Pl. 11.4:1) has two symmetric bulging sides, and is rhomboid in section. The neck is tall and narrow with a simple everted rim, and thin handles extend from mid-neck to the shoulders. Both sides are painted with red and white circles, one handle bears a red-painted double cross on its lower part, with a red-painted vegetal motif rendered under it.

There are no parallels for this shape, but a flask fragment decorated with concentric circles was retrieved from ʻArad, Stratum XI (Y. Aharoni 1981: Fig. 10:13). Generally, in the Iron Age, flasks painted with concentric circles and additional decorations on the handles and below them are typical of the Phoenician Bichrome flasks and jugs; they are common in the north.

Fig. 11.19. Decorated flask (before complete restoration) (Pls. 11.4:1; 11.17:5).

The fragment in Pl. 11.4:2 belongs to a small thin-walled flask decorated with three circles of dark brown-black paint on each side (but there may have been more circles in the center). This most probably is a barrel-shaped flask of Cypriot type, though by its fabric it is difficult to judge whether it is an actual Cypriot import. The Negev sites yielded one other similar barrel-shaped flask (Naḥal Laʻana; Cohen and Cohen-Amin 2004: Fig. 48:11).

Another, thin walled and finely burnished barrel shaped-flask (or jug) was uncovered in Substratum 4b (see Pl. 11.10:11). This, too, is of apparent Cypriot shape, but it is uncertain whether it is of Cypriot manufacture.

Jars

Type SJ2 (Fig. 11.20; Pl. 11.4:3). This is a very small jar/amphoriskos, with a pointed base and two handles that extend from the shoulder downward. The rim is upright and thickened, and there are three grooves around the shoulder. Generally speaking, similar small jars (some of them decorated) are typical of the Iron Age in the north, but usually these jars are more than twice this size and the neck is higher; see, for example, Hazor, Stratum XI (Yadin et al. 1961: Pl. CCIII:16) and Ḥorbat Rosh Zayit (Gal and Alexandre 2000: Figs. III.74:21; III.87:8). No parallels, however, are known in the south.

Fig. 11.20. Stratum 4. Jar Type SJ2 (Pls. 11.4:3; 11.12:5).

Type SJ1 (Fig. 11.21; Pl. 11.4:4–6). These relatively common jars are long, narrow and cylindrical in shape, with sloping shoulders, moderate carination between shoulder and body, and pointed bases. The rims are short and upright, thickened at their top, and handles extend down from the shoulder. These jars are also common at other sites in the south, for example at Ḥorbat Mesura, Har Eldad (Meẓudat Naḥal Ẓin), Naḥal Ela (Cohen and Cohen-Amin 2004: Figs. 11:3; 35:4; 64:8) and ʻArad, Strata XII and XI (M. Aharoni 1981: Figs. 4:1, 2; 8:5), and further to the north, e.g., at Ashdod, Stratum Xa (Area M, Stratum 10; Dothan and Porath 1982: Fig. 9:1–3).

Short upright rims of jars were also found in Strata 3 and 2. This long time span renders them quite useless as a chronological tool (for eighth-century BCE jars with such rims, see, for example, Be'er Sheva', Y. Aharoni 1973: Pls. 66:7; 73:4).

Fig. 11.21. Stratum 4. Jar Type SJ1 (Pl. 11.12:4).

Egyptian Jar. In Area D, a fragment of an Egyptian jar was uncovered (Pl. 11.26:3). It is the only such fragment recognized at Kadesh Barnea.

Pithoi

Type P1 (Fig. 11.22; Pl. 11.5:1). This pithos is very wide at the shoulders and then narrows toward the base, which was apparently flat. Four handles extend from the shoulder downward. The rim is thickened and folded outward. Only one complete such vessel was encountered (in L820 part of another vessel of the same type was found but not illustrated).

Rim fragments that may belong to such pithoi were published, for example, from the Negev sites of Naḥal Ẓin (Meẓudat Har Sa'ad) and Meẓudat Naḥal 'Aqrav (Cohen and Cohen-Amin 2004: Figs. 51:9; 70:4, 5).

Fig. 11.22. Stratum 4. Pithos Type P1 (Pls. 11.5:1; 11.17:5).

Type P2 (Pl. 11.5:2). This is a large pithos with a long pear-shaped body, conspicuously rounded shoulders and a pointed base. There is no neck and the rim is low and thickened outward. No handles were preserved on the one fragmentary example recovered.

A similar, handle-less pithos was uncovered at Tel Masos, Stratum II (in Area H, House 314; Fritz and Kempinski 1983: Pl. 143:9).

Other Pithoi
Other rim fragments apparently belonging to pithoi are illustrated in Pl. 11.5:3–5. Their shoulders appear to be rounded, they barely have necks and the rims are externally thickened. Pithos No. 3 has a ridged rim; No. 4, a folded-out rim (and no neck); and No. 5, a thickened rim with a ridge below it.

A single fragment of a collared-rim pithos was found in the settlement in Area B (see Pl. 11.20:16). This is an Iron IIA successor of the popular Iron I Hill Country pithos, as, for example, at Khirbet ed-Dawwara (Finkelstein 1990: Fig. 16:6–12) and in the Negev at Tel Masos, Stratum II (Area H, House 314; Fritz and Kempinski 1983: Pl. 140:12).

Lamps

The rounded lamps (Fig. 11.23; Pl. 11.5:6, 7) are the dominant type throughout the occupational sequence at Kadesh Barnea and the sole type encountered in Stratum 4. For similar lamps in Judah, see, e.g., Lachish, Stratum V (Y. Aharoni 1975: Pl. 42:11–13) and Be'er Sheva', Stratum VI (Herzog 1984: Fig. 30:10–12).

Fig. 11.23. Stratum 4. Lamp Type L1 (Pl. 11.10:6).

Varia

Kernos Bowl (Pl. 11.5:8). This fragment, found during the cleaning of a section within Stratum 4 (L6111) is similar to three others, from Substratum 3c (see below).

MIDIANITE POTTERY, MAINLY OF STRATA 4
AND 3 (Figs. 11.24, 11.25; Pls. 11.6, 11.7)

In order not to break up the small Midianite assemblage, Pls. 11.6 and 11.7 illustrate all the Midianite pottery uncovered at Kadesh Barnea by type and decorative motifs, disregarding stratigraphical attributions.

Midianite pottery was first explicitly identified at Timna' in the southern Aravah Valley and dated there, mainly by accompanying Egyptian finds, to the XIXth and XXth Dynasties of Egypt. Stylistic and petrographic analyses established that it originated at Qurayyah in the Hijaz. Further to the north, Midianite pottery has been identified at Tell el-Kheleifeh, Meẓudat Yoṭvata, Ḥaẓeva, Tel Masos, Tell el-Farʻah (S) and Tell Judūr, as well as in Transjordan (e.g., Rothenberg and Glass 1981; Rothenberg 1988; the Ḥaẓeva finds are unpublished). Most of these examples were dated to the thirteenth/twelfth centuries BCE, occasionally, at the latest, to the eleventh century. In a few cases the Midianite pottery was used to established the date of the entire assemblage, for example at Yoṭvata, first dated to the beginning of the tenth century BCE (see Meshel and Sass 1974; Rothenberg and Glass 1983:74) or at Barqa el-Ḥetiye in the Feinan region (Fritz 1994).

Two near-complete vessels of Midianite ware were unearthed at Kadesh Barnea, as well as 18 additional body fragments (of which only 16 could be examined and illustrated). Five items (Pl. 11.6:1, 3; 11.7:1, 9, 13), including the near-complete vessels, originate in Stratum 4, of Iron IIA. Two of these vessels (Pl. 11.6: 1; 11.7:1) are composed of two fragments (in both cases one fragment was found in Stratum 4 and the other in the Substratum 3c constructional fill, which apparently comprises mainly Stratum 4 pottery). Six sherds (Pl. 11.7:5, 6, 8, 10–12) originate in Substratum 3c. Five other sherds came from disturbed contexts or are intrusive in Stratum 3 (Pls. 11.6:2; 11.7:2, 3, 4, 7).

All the Midianite specimens from Kadesh Barnea in regard to fabric, inclusions, slip and the paint, seem very similar, at least to the naked eye. The clay is light brown-pink, with black and red shale fragments. The vessels are usually coated with thick cream-white slip over which are red- and black-painted designs. According to the fabric descriptions in Rothenberg and Glass 1983:102–107 and Rothenberg 1988: Figs. 4–10,

it seems that in these respects the Midianite pottery of Timna' was very similar.

At Kadesh Barnea, the differences between the Midianite ware and Edomite pottery (see below, Stratum 2) are very clear, both typologically and stratigraphically/chronologically, as opposed, for example, to Tell el-Kheleifeh, where these two fabrics were not separated (Glueck 1967: Figs. 4, 5).

Most of the sherds here are small body sherds of closed vessels, probably jugs, and only two belong to bowls.

Bowls

The fragmentary bowl in Fig. 11.24, Pl. 11.6:1 (two joining sherds) is of rather small diameter and has high walls, resembling a cup. It is coated with a thin white (kaolin) slip inside and out, a slip that differs from the thick slip on the other Midianite sherds. Similarly, the black decoration inside the bowl is different from the decorations attested on other bowls and resembles patterns appearing in the lower register of some of the jugs at Timna' (Rothenberg and Glass 1981: Fig. 9:4). Externally, the bowl is adorned by a band of crosses or zigzag motifs. The red and black bands of paint are wide and sloppily executed.

The fact that this vessel is different from the rest of the Midianite group at Kadesh Barnea (both in shape and in its surface treatment) is reminiscent of the situation at Qurayyah. There, too the Midianite assemblage comprised a number of subgroups, differing in all aspects other than their fabric (matrix and temper; see Rothenberg and Glass 1983:69–72).

The body fragment in Pl. 11.6:2 apparently also belongs to a bowl, as it is painted on both faces. Inside is a wide red band bounded by narrow black ones, with a group of vertical black lines above them. Part of a red zigzag motif remains on the exterior. A two-handled bowl at Timna' is decorated with a similar pattern (Rothenberg 1988: Fig. 4:9 and see also the motifs in Rothenberg and Glass 1981: Figs. 10:2; 12, 13).

Fig. 11.24. Stratum 4. Midianite bowl (Pls. 11.6:1; 11.15:5).

Jugs

The sole near-complete jug (Fig. 11.25; Pl. 11.6:3) has a rounded body, a wide flat base, a tall wide neck and a handle that extends from below the (missing) rim to the shoulder. The fabric is light colored with many medium-sized red shale inclusions. The slip is light red, thin inside and thick outside, and it tends to peel.

The vessel is divided into horizontal decorative friezes by groups of three lines and a row of black dots (see Rothenberg and Glass 1983: Fig. 11:1, Motif K). In the lower register are groups of four vertical lines; in the middle frieze, which extends over the upper part of the vessel and the shoulder, groups of diagonal lines form triangle-like shapes; and a similar motif occupies the upper frieze on the neck. Flanking the handle are two vertical bands, and two lines were drawn on the handle itself.

In both shape and fabric, this jug resembles the Midianite jugs at Timna' (Rothenberg and Glass 1983: Fig. 6:8, 9; 1988: Fig. 6:20), and a jug from Tell el-Kheleifeh (Glueck 1967: Fig. 5:1). The decoration resembles that of the above-mentioned Tell el-Kheleifeh jug (which is red slipped and has geometric patterns in black only).

Fig. 11.25. Stratum 4. Midianite jug (Pls. 11.6:3; 11.24:5).

All the other fragments (Pl. 11.7) belong to closed vessels, probably jugs, on which the following geometric motifs in red and black may be noted:
1. Plate 11.7:1. On the neck of the jug is a frieze with an hourglass motif in a frame. The decoration is in black and red on a light colored slip (for the decoration, see Timna', Rothenberg and Glass 1981: Fig. 10:23, 24).
2. Pl. 11.7:2. This fragment is red slipped and retains a partial black net pattern. The decoration is similar in nature to that on the complete jug (and see also Pattern C.2 at Timna', Rothenberg and Glass 1983: Fig. 9).
3. Plate 11.7:3–6. The decoration on the upper part of the jugs comprises friezes within which are isolated motifs in a double-line frame. The filling motif is a black dot surrounded by a red circle, in turn surrounded by a circle made up of black dots (for similar designs without the central continuous circle; cf. Motif M at Timna', Rothenberg and Glass 1983: Fig. 11:2, 3).
4. Plate 11.7:7–10. Remains of zigzags with dots incorporated between the 'triangles' decorate these sherds. This pattern is most common on bowls at Timna' (Rothenberg and Glass 1981: Figs. 2:9; 3:3).
5. Plate 11.7:10. Above the zigzag, between the shoulder and the neck, is a band of short vertical strokes alternating with dots in black (at Timna', see Rothenberg and Glass 1983: Figs. 5:3; 6:6).
6. Plate 11.7:11–13. The surviving decoration consists of groups of two to three black vertical lines and between them arched designs in red (parallels for these designs are known at Timna', Rothenberg and Glass 1981: Figs. 9:2, 3; and the motifs in Fig. 10:34).

STRATUM 4 CERAMIC ASSEMBLAGES
(Pls. 11.8–11.26)

The Stratum 4 pottery is presented here according to its two main architectural components: the fortress and the settlement (and where possible, by further architectural subdivision). Within each unit, where possible, the contexts are arranged according to stratigraphical order, from early to late.

Pre-Fortress Occupation, Substratum 4c

Floors underlying the walls of the oval fortress were uncovered only in the southern part of Area E and in a few places below the settlement layer (Areas B, F). The material from this level is not diagnostic, it has not been illustrated and there is too little to date this substratum.

The Oval Fortress Occupation, Substratum 4b
(Pls. 11.8–11.19:1–10)

Ceramic assemblages on the floors sealed by the destruction of the casemates were uncovered mainly in Areas C (Pls. 11.8, 11.9), E (Pls. 11.10–11.14) and A1 (Pl. 11.15:1–6). These include a relatively large number of complete vessels. In Area E (near the southern casemate), there was an exceptionally deep accumulation of destruction debris, which perhaps resulted from the collapse of shelves or of an upper story.

In all the assemblages two distinct ware groups are present: most of the bowls, the kraters and the cooking pots belong to the handmade Negebite family (discussed in Chapter 12), while juglets, jugs and jars are wheel made.

The pottery that originates in the courtyard of the fortress (Pls. 11.15:7–15, 11.16–11.19:1–10) is contextually more problematic. In the areas adjacent to the casemates, where artifacts were sealed by destruction debris, associating finds with Substratum 4b was straightforward, but in areas where living surfaces had no relation to architecture it was difficult to distinguish between pottery belonging to the various substrata within Stratum 4 and similarly, to distinguish between Stratum 4 floor deposits and the Substratum 3c fills overlying them.

The Oval Fortress, Substratum 4a (Pl. 11.19:11–16)

In the southern part of Area E, above the walls of the oval fortress and its destruction layer, a wall and remains of floors were discovered that apparently were cut by the constructions of Substrata 3a-b (see Chapter 7). Only a few sherds were uncovered here; they are not enough to date this context.

The Settlement, Substrata 4a-b (Pls. 11.20–11.26)

Buildings belonging to the Stratum 4 settlement were located mainly in Areas B and C. In a few places in Area B, mainly in courtyards, two phases were discerned and their ceramic assemblages are presented separately in Pls. 11.20–11.22. There are very few complete vessels in these contexts. Negebite vessels were very common, accompanied by a much smaller quantity of wheel-made pottery.

Area C is the main area in which two substrata could be clearly differentiated, but the pottery seems to be very close chronologically. Substratum 4b produced a somewhat more extensive collection (Pls. 11.23, 11.24:1–8), including cooking pots, a jug and some juglets, a few Negebite bowls and kraters, and a Midianite jug. The relatively restricted assemblage of Substratum 4a is presented in Pls. 11.24:9–13, 11.25.

In Areas D, F, G and H (Pl. 11.26), exposures of Stratum 4 were limited, and consequently ceramics are few and no segregation was possible between substrata.

SUMMARY AND CHRONOLOGY

General Characteristics

As detailed below, the Stratum 4 ceramic assemblages comprise two major groups: the Negebite group (for which see Chapter 12) and wheel-made vessels of Judahite types. In fact, the abundance of Negebite pottery is perhaps one of the most conspicuous phenomena in this stratum.

Ceramics originating from farther regions are not many. Some Midianite vessels probably came from the southeast, originating in the Hijaz, and one jar (fragment) is of clear Egyptian morphology. In addition, some vessels are either Cypriot imports or imitate Cypriot prototypes (such as the Black-on-Red juglet and some of the flasks). Though few, these attest that the inhabitants of Stratum 4 participated in some inter-regional, probably commercial, contacts.

Chronology

Initially, during the excavation, the Stratum 4 fortress and the settlement alongside it were dated by Cohen to the tenth century BCE, based on comparisons with other sites dating to this period, and especially taking into account the presence of red-slipped vessels and the absence of collared-rim jars and Philistine wares. Other scholars, mainly weighing historical considerations, suggested a date in the eleventh century BCE (see discussions in Herzog 1983; Finkelstein 1985). These dates were based on the then unanimously embraced Iron Age chronology (today dubbed the 'High Chronology').

We are now able to offer a date for Stratum 4 that takes into account the entire ceramic assemblage. This is based primarily on comparison with the now fully published pottery of the Negev Highlands, of other sites in Judah, of sites in the Shephelah outside Judah, and occasionally with sites further to the north, in Israel.

The Stratum 4 assemblage is closely associated with those of the Negev Highland sites. Similarly to these sites, 45–50% of the ceramics are Negebite handmade vessels, whose distribution does not even reach the Be'er Sheva' Valley (for a full discussion of the Negebite ware, see Chapter 12).

In contrast, the wheel-made pottery comprises typical Judahite types (a short list: Cooking Pots CP3 and CP5; Juglets JT1 and JT2; Jugs J1, J4 and J6; Jars SJ1; Pithoi

P1, P2), alongside types that are more characteristic of the Negev (Bowl B4; Cooking Pot CP4; the pyxis). Another group comprises pottery that apparently originates from other, as yet undefined regions outside Judah (e.g., Bowl B1 with the black band, and Bowl B12 with the short black strokes of paint).

Generally speaking, the assemblages of Stratum 4 are strongly linked to those of 'Arad, Strata XII–XI, Be'er Sheva', Strata VI–IV, Tel Esdar, Stratum II, Lachish, Strata V– IV, and Tel Masos, Stratum II.

Some of the pottery types are common in the Negev both in Iron I and Iron IIA. However, there are in the assemblage many types that do not occur before Iron IIA, such as the 'Black Juglets' and Black-on-Red Ware. Most probably, the Stratum 4 fortress and settlement were constructed in Iron IIA, the tenth century BCE.

The issue of a possible slightly later date for this stratum will apparently remain an open question, as Iron IIB assemblages are barely known in the Negev, and new studies are still in process and/or controversial.

Examination of the pottery assemblages of the various subphases, both in the oval fortress and the unfortified settlement nearby, did not reveal any chronological differences, and the two seem to have been occupied side by side. We thus conclude that both fortress and settlement date to Iron IIA. By the conventional, high chronology, this is the tenth century BCE.

In light of this date, the chronology of the Midianite ware needs to be re-evaluated. As mentioned, current dates would allow this group a range between the thirteenth and eleventh centuries BCE. At Kadesh Barnea, however, as far as we can judge, there is no occupation dating to these periods. There are, thus, two possibilities. Either the Midianite specimens (most of them not found in primary deposition), originated in such a yet-undetected earlier settlement (either at Kadesh Barnea itself or nearby), or, which is much more plausible, that the chronology of this group should be extended to encompass the tenth century BCE as well.

POTTERY OF SUBSTRATUM 3C
(Fig. 11.26; Pls. 11.27–11.29)

Substratum 3c is the construction phase of the Stratum 3 fortress. Pottery attributed to this substratum comes from the deep fill within the walls of the fortress, underlying the Substrata 3a-b buildings, as well as from within the earthen ramparts surrounding the fortress' walls. Most of the material within all these fills probably originates in the Stratum 4 occupation layers, which in all likelihood were taken from those parts of Stratum 4 that were left outside the confines of the Stratum 3 fortress.

The Substratum 3c fills produced very large amounts of ceramics. The material illustrated in Pls. 11.27–11.29 is only a representative sample, intended to illustrate the typological variety in these fills; it originates from loci that clearly belong to them.

All this notwithstanding, it is very likely that the fills also include a certain, indeterminable amount of pottery belonging to the period of construction of Stratum 3. Thus, the value of these ceramics is mainly for establishing a *terminus post quem* for Substrata 3a-b.

TYPOLOGY OF WHEEL-MADE SHAPES
Bowls

A wide range of bowl types exists here, most of which appear also in both Stratum 4 and Subtrata 3a-b.

Type B1 (Pl. 11.27:1–3). In Substratum 3c, some of these small rounded or slightly carinated bowls are red slipped and burnished, and others bear a black band of paint on the rim or below it, on the exterior. These bowls were already attested in restricted quantity in Stratum 4; they are more numerous in Substrata 3a-b (see parallels above, Stratum 4).

Type B25 (Pl. 11.27:4, 5). These are small rounded bowls with no surface treatment other than one or two shallow incisions on the external side of the vessel, below the rim (they are very similar to Type B1 bowls). Generally speaking, thin rounded bowls with grooves on the exterior are known in Judah and the Shephelah in the Iron Age, but only a few examples closely resemble those from Kadesh Barnea. They occur, e.g., at Lachish, Strata V–IV (Zimhoni 1997: Fig. 3.10; Type B), Tel Baṭash, Stratum IV (Mazar and Panitz-Cohen 2001: Pl.82:3) and the the City of David, Stratum 15 (De Groot and Ariel 2000: Fig. 11:6).

Twelve fragments of such bowls were encountered, of which two were found in Stratum 4, eight in Substratum 3c and two in Substrata 3a-b. It seems therefore that these bowls are mostly typical of Stratum 4, but they also continue later, in diminished quantities.

Type B2 (Pl. 11.27:6, 7). These are small, slightly carinated bowls with an everted rim, which were already attested from Stratum 4 (see parallels above).

Type B5 (Pl. 11.27:8). A lower part of this small carinated bowl had one small pierced handle (out of two) preserved at the carination point near its rounded base. This type is attested in Substratum 3c by one other fragment (in addition to the one from Stratum 4).

Type B13 (Pl. 11.27:9, 10). These rounded bowls/cups have a single handle extending from the rim. This category also includes strainer bowls and three-legged bowls, although such vessels were not clearly attested in Substratum 3c. Bowl No. 9 is a closed vessel with a vertical rim, while No. 10 is more open. Such vessels were already attested in Stratum 4 (by one example); they are mostly typical of Substrata 3a-b and Stratum 2 (see discussion below, Substrata 3a-b).

Type B4 (Pl. 11.27:11–15). These rounded or slightly carinated bowls with everted rims vary in size and were divided into subtypes according to rim shape. Some of the subtypes were already evident in Stratum 4, but mostly these bowls are later, being most common in Substrata 3a-b. Most of the subtypes also continue to Stratum 2 (see discussion and parallels below).

Subtype B4.1 (Pl. 11.27:11) represents small–medium bowls with an everted rim, attested from Stratum 4 to Stratum 2. Subtype B4.2 (Pl. 11.27:12) is a small bowl with a ledge-like rim. It first occurs in the Substratum 3c fills and continues to be present in Substrata 3a-b, but reaches the peak of its distribution in Stratum 2 (see parallels below). Subtype B4.3 (Pl. 11.27:13, 14) represents small and medium bowls with an externally thickened rim. There are a few in Substratum 3c contexts, possibly even in Stratum 4 (Pl. 11.26:11), but they are most typical of Substrata 3a-b, continuing to Stratum 2 (see below). Subtype B4.4 bowls (Pl. 11.27:15) have a diagonal rim, folded inward. A flat, elongated ear-shaped handle is attached on the exterior. Another such fragment was found in Substrata 3a-b (Pl. 11.30:13). Such appendages are usually part of bar handles and are common on Iron

IIA bowls, though later examples are also known (cf. 'Arad, Stratum XI—M. Aharoni 1981: Fig. 9.9; Be'er Sheva', Stratum IV—Y. Aharoni 1973: Pl. 55:6; and Tel 'Eton, Stratum I—Zimhoni 1997: Fig. 4.8:7).

Type B12 (Pl. 11.27:16–18). These are the bowls that are similar in size and shape to Type B4, but with a decoration of black strokes on the rim. They already appear, in restricted quantities in Stratum 4 (see above, discussion and parallels), but they are mostly typical of Substrata 3a-b.

Type B9 (Pl. 11.27:19, 20). These are shallow, nearly flat bowls, quite similar to Type B8 bowls (see above, Stratum 4), but with a diagonally-cut everted rim that sometimes slopes sharply downward. Similar bowls already occur in Stratum 4, see Pl. 11.11:2, but the type is mostly typical of Substrata 3a-b (see discussion below) and of Stratum 2.

Other Bowls
Black-Painted Ware Bowl, Type B2 (Pl. 11.27:21). The Black-Painted Ware vessels are typical of Substrata 3a-b at Kadesh Barnea (and are discussed below), but a significant quantity has also been uncovered in Substratum 3c; only a few fragments were attested in Strata 2 and 1 and may be considered re-depositions.

Black-Slipped and Burnished Bowl (Pl. 11.27:22). This (fragmentary) vessel is a deep, thick-walled bowl, made of black clay and closely wheel burnished. The bowl is equipped with a bar handle and a ring base. Fragments of two other such bowls were found at Kadesh Barnea, one in Substratum 3c (not illustrated) and the other in Stratum 4 (Pl. 11.21:12). Bowls of this type are known, for example, from Hazor, Strata IX, VIII and VI (Yadin et al. 1960: Pls. LII:10; LIV:24; LXIII:23; LXVII:7; defined as Samarian bowls).

Petalled Bowl (Fig. 11.26; Pl. 11.27:23). This unique, tiny rounded bowl was found broken into several

Fig. 11.26. Substratum 3c. Bowl with plastic rosette decoration (Pl. 11.27:23).

(non-joining) fragments. It was apparently wheel made and inside it bears a finger-impressed decoration forming a rosette; the rim is simple. No meaningful parallels to this vessel are known to us.

Fine Ware Bowl (Pl. 11.27:24). Among the unique occurrences at Kadesh Barnea, one fragment belongs to a very thin, red-slipped and burnished so-called 'Samarian' bowl. At Tyre, for example, carinated Fine Ware plates of similar shapes do not occur before Stratum IV of the eighth century BCE (Bikai 1978: FWP 1–3).

Kraters

Similarly to the bowls, there are many forms of kraters in Substratum 3c, more so than in Stratum 4. Most of the types appear here for the first time.

Type K1 (Pl. 11.28:1, 2). These deep and open kraters usually have upright or slanting upper walls; the rim is folded or thickened and everted. On No. 1 it appears that handles extended from the rim; however, this type is primarily represented by sherds and it is difficult to establish where the handles were attached. Kraters of this type begin to appear in Stratum 4 (see above) and continue throughout the entire occupation at Kadesh Barnea.

Type K3 (Pl. 11.28:3, 4). These are open kraters with a rounded body and a slight S-shaped carination that emphasizes the outward-thickened rim; two handles extend from the rim to the walls. These kraters are first attested in Substratum 3c and they become common in Strata 3a-b (see below).

Type K2 (Pl. 11.28:5, 6). These kraters have a rounded lower part and a neck. The rim is folded and inverted. Only a few fragments of this type were found in Substratum 3c, as well as a few in Substrata 3a-b. Kraters of this type are known from Iron IIA contexts in the Negev, such as Ḥorbat Ḥaluqim (Cohen 1976a: Fig. 9:14) and Tel Masos, Area H, House 314 (Fritz and Kempinski 1983: Pls. 139:1; 142:3). Later, in the late ninth century BCE, they are found, for example at Tel Sera' (Oren 1992: Fig. 11:21), and in the eighth century, at Be'er Sheva', Stratum II (Y. Aharoni 1973: Pl.72:14).

Other Kraters
Black-Painted Ware Kraters, Types K1, K2 (Pl. 11.28:7, 8). The Black-Painted Ware at the site is mostly typical of Substrata 3a-b and is discussed below, but kraters of this ware occur in about equal numbers in Substrata 3c and 3a-b. Plate 11.28:7 illustrates a thickened and slightly emphasized rim and Pl. 11.28:7, a simple rim. The kraters are decorated with geometric and floral patterns in black.

Cooking Pots

Three types of cooking pots are represented in Subtratum 3c, of which two (CP1 and CP2) were also in evidence in Stratum 4 and continue into Stratum 2; the third (CP 10) appears solely in Substratum 3c (and is only represented by fragments).

Type CP1. Only Subtype CP1.1 appears in these substrata.

Subtype CP1.1 (Pl. 11.28:9) represents those cooking pots whose molded rims comprise a direct continuation of the shoulder (there is no neck) and both the walls and the rim itself are thicker. A few fragments of this type were found in Stratum 4; subsequently, in Strata 3 and 2, other variations of the molded ridged rim become common (the fragment in Pl. 11.28:10 is more similar to CP1.2; see below).

Type CP2 (Pl. 11.28:11, 12). These are the cooking pots with upright, molded rims that form a neck. They appear at Kadesh Barnea throughout its occupation (see discussion above, Stratum 4), but are especially typical of the Substrata 3a-b–Stratum 2 range.

Type CP10 (Pl. 11.28:13, 14). These cooking pots have a narrow aperture and a folded-out rim with a triangular section attached to the walls of the vessels. Only a few such fragments were encountered. Though this type is not attested in Stratum 4, it is known from other Judahite Iron I–IIA contexts, such as Lachish, Strata V–IV (Zimhoni 1997: Fig. 3.38:6; Type CP2) and Be'er Sheva', Stratum VIII (Herzog 1984: Fig. 20:11).

Juglets, Amphoriskos and a Jug

Type JT1 (Pl. 11.29:1, 2). These dipper juglets with a long upright neck and a simple rim were found in

Substratum 3c only in fragmentary form, but probably had an oval lower part, similar to those of Stratum 4 (see above).

Type JT2 (Pl. 11.29:3). Four upper parts of relatively large 'Black Juglets' were found. The handle extends from below the rim (as opposed to the Stratum 4 examples, where the handle extends from mid-body; see above). 'Black Juglets' continue to appear at the site until Stratum 2.

Small Amphoriskos (Pl. 11.29:4). The vessel has a piriform body and a flat base. The neck is missing but it was apparently very narrow, and the handles were thin and apparently stretched far from the body. No exact parallels to this combination are known to us, but amphoriskoi of other shapes were found in Substrata 3a-b and in Stratum 2 (see below).

Red-Slipped Jug (Pl. 11.29:5). This ring-based fragment belongs to a red-slipped and vertically burnished jug. Similar jugs are very typical of Stratum 4 (Type J5).

Jars and Pithoi

Type SJ1 (Pl. 11.29:6–9). These short jar necks/rims belong to cylindrical jars that are mainly typical of Stratum 4 (see above), but they continue, in small percentages, throughout the Iron Age.

Type SJ3. Two subtypes of this storage jar appear here.

Subtype SJ3.1 (Pl. 11.29:10, 11) has a short upright neck with a shallow ridge below the rim. This subtype is typical mainly of Substrata 3a-b, where the examples were somewhat less fragmentary (Pl. 11.34:1–3). In Substratum 3c, only a few were encountered. Jars of this type are common in the northern part of the country, for example at Hazor, Strata IX–V (Yadin et al. 1958: Pls. XLVIII:12, 13; L:33, 34; LXII:3, 4; Yadin et al. 1960: Pls. LII:23, 24; LX:4, 5, 8; LXXI:13–16). Although in Substratum 3c only rims were found, it is clear that they belong to the 'Hippo' jar type. Similar jar rims were also found at Lachish, Strata V–IV (Zimhoni 1997: Fig. 3.53; Group SJ8).

Subtype SJ3.2 (Pl. 11.29:12) has a low vertical neck and a ridge below the rim, similarly to Subtype SJ3.1, but there is also a groove on top of the rim, perhaps to support a lid. Only a few examples of this rim type were found at Kadesh Barnea, in Substrata 3c and 3a-b (Pls. 11.40:6; 11.41:23).

Pithoi (Pl. 11.29:13–17). No attempt was made to cluster the pithos rims into types, as they all differ from each other in small details. Rim No. 17 seems to belong to a neck-less wide-shouldered pithos, similar to Type P2 found in Stratum 4 (Pl. 11.5:2).

Varia

Lamps (Pl. 11.29:18, 19). The Substratum 3c lamps have either a flattened or rounded base and an everted or ledge rim. Such lamps occur throughout Iron II in Judah.

Bowl Kernoi (Pl. 11.29:20–22). Four fragments of (different) bowl *kernoi* were encountered at Kadesh Barnea, three in Substratum 3c and one in Stratum 4 (Pl. 11.5:8). None was decorated in any way. The fragment in Pl. 11.29:20 apparently did not have many apertures/appendages above the ring. In Iron II, bowl *kernoi* are known, for example at Ashdod, Stratum VII (red slipped; an eighth–seventh-century BCE context; M. Dothan 1971: Fig. 29:58) and from the 'Israelite Shrine' E207 of Samaria, Periods III–IV (Crowfoot 1957: Fig. 26:10).

NEGEBITE, MIDIANITE AND 'BLACK-PAINTED WARE' VESSELS

Substratum 3c produced abundant Negebite pottery, which will be presented and discussed in Chapter 12.

Midianite pottery was represented in the Substratum 3c fills by six fragments only (see Pl. 11.7:5, 6, 8, 10, 11, 12), which probably originated from the Stratum 4 debris (for a discussion, see above, Stratum 4).

Black-Painted Ware in these contexts comprises 18 fragments, about 37% of all the occurrences of this ware group at Kadesh Barnea (for illustrations of Substratum 3c examples, see Pl. 11.27:21; 11.28:7, 8; the group is discussed below with Substrata 3a-b).

SUMMARY AND CHRONOLOGY

As explained above (see also the summary in Chapter 1) the Substratum 3c constructional fills probably chiefly come from the underlying Stratum 4 debris. This is indeed borne out by the pottery, as most of the types in Substratum 3c are similar to those of Stratum 4 and seem to represent an Iron IIA horizon. It should be noted, however, that some of the Stratum 4 types that were one of the means for dating that assemblage to Iron IIA (for example, cooking-pot Types CP 3, CP4, CP5) are curiously missing here. In addition, some of the Substratum 3c types indeed first appear in Stratum 4 but are more common in Subtrata 3a-b (for instance, Bowls B12 and B13 and CP1).

Other pottery types (though not many, for example, kraters Types K2, K3, storage jar Type SJ3 and the Black-Painted Ware fragments), are unknown before Substratum 3c. As, on the other hand, they are attested in Substrata 3a-b, they probably represent the construction period of the Stratum 3 fortress.

The single exemplar of Fine Ware, the so-called 'Samarian' bowl, of the carinated variety (Pl. 11.27:24) is a rare occurrence in the Negev. In Israelite and Phoenician sites, such bowls are generally not attested before the eighth century BCE. This bowl, and other fragments, such as the late type of 'Black Juglets' (JT2; Pl. 11.29:3), the cooking pot in Pl. 11.28:10 and storage jar Subtype 3.1 (Pl. 11.29:10, 11) provide a *terminus post quem* around 800 BCE for the construction of the Stratum 3 fortress, most probably around the mid-eighth century BCE.

POTTERY OF SUBSTRATA 3A-B
(Figs. 11.27–11.43; Pls. 11.30–11.71)

A major difficulty in studying the Substrata 3a-b pottery is the fact that, in contrast to Strata 4 and 2, Stratum 3 did not end in destruction and thus produced neither extensive pottery assemblages nor complete vessels. In addition, most of the pottery (about 80%) belongs to the handmade Negebite ware, which is currently useless as a chronological index (see Chapter 12).

The following typological list comprises the most common and otherwise important types of these substrata, from among the loci we considered 'cleanest', originating in the contexts presented in Pls. 11.37–11.71.

In these latter plates the pottery of the best contexts of the Substrata 3a-b occupations is presented by areas and architectural units within them, separating Substratum 3b from Substratum 3a where possible.

One note of caution is in order here: in presenting the Substrata 3a-b material we took into consideration the pottery found in the Stratum 3 silos both within and outside the fortress. These silos were not always sealed, and theoretically could either have been filled in after the Stratum 3 occupation, or contain Stratum 2 intrusive material. However, the abundant pottery in them is very similar to that of other Stratum 3 contexts and does not contain typical Stratum 2 types. We are thus confident that this material indeed belongs to Stratum 3.

TYPOLOGY OF WHEEL-MADE SHAPES

Bowls

Type B1 (Pl. 11.30:1–3). These are the thin, small, rounded or slightly carinated bowls with a simple rim, which were already attested in Strata 4/3c. They can be further subdivided by their surface treatment. In Substrata 3a-b, five bowls have a black band on the rim, six are red slipped and/or burnished, and seven are plain. Taken together, these bowls from Substrata 3a-b comprise about half the Type B1 bowls from the entire Kadesh Barnea sequence. This specific type does not continue to Stratum 2.

Type B4 (Fig. 11.27; Pl. 11.30:4–15). As described above (Stratum 4), bowls of this type share the same rounded to slightly carinated walls and have everted rims, but otherwise this designation agglomerates a relatively large group of bowls differing in size, finish and specific shape of rim.

Subtype B4.1 (Pl. 11.30:4–6) comprises bowls with flaring rims, occasionally diagonally cut, and slanting inwards. This subtype comprises about 30% of the Type B4 bowls at Kadesh Barnea, and has a very long time span. Starting in Stratum 4, it becomes very common in Substrata 3a-b and continues in Stratum 2. Parallels in the tenth–ninth century range are from Kuntillet 'Ajrud (Ayalon 1995: Fig. 3:10), 'Arad, Stratum XII (M. Aharoni 1981: Figs. 1:18; 5:1) and Lachish, Strata V–IV (Zimhoni 1997: Fig. 3.15:1, 2). In the eighth century such bowls are known, for example, at Be'er Sheva', Stratum II (Y. Aharoni 1973: Pl. 74:8),

Lachish, Stratum III (Zimhoni 1997: Fig. 5.4:22), Tell Beit Mirsim, Stratum A (Albright 1943: Pls. 65:20b; 21; 66:3) and Tel 'Eṭon, Stratum I (Zimhoni 1997: Fig. 4.4:6). For seventh–sixth-century parallels, see 'En Gedi, Stratum V (Mazar, Dothan and Dunayevsky 1966: Fig. 14:12), 'Aro'er, Strata II–I (Biran and Cohen 1981: Fig. 15:6), Ramat Raḥel, Stratum Va (Y. Aharoni 1964: Fig. 16:29–34) and Meṣad Ḥashevyahu (Naveh 1962: Fig. 4:3) (some of the bowls from the two latter sites are smaller).

Subtype B4.2 (Pl. 11.30:7) represents small bowls (c. 9 cm in diameter) with a ledge-like rim. They are first encountered in the Substratum 3c fills but are more common in Substrata 3a-b and in Stratum 2. Parallels may be found, for example, at Tell Beit Mirsim, Stratum A (Albright 1932: Pl. 65:23, 26).

Subtype B4.3 (Pl. 11.30:8–12) is the most common, comprising 35% of the Type B4 bowls. These are the small and medium-sized bowls with thickened rims projecting outward. They start in Substratum 3c (possibly even in Stratum 4), but they are noticeably more numerous in Substrata 3a-b (twice as many as in Substratum 3c or in Sratum 2). Parallels occur mainly in eighth-century Judahite sites, such as Be'er Sheva', Stratum II (Y. Aharoni 1973: Pl. 74:9), Tell Beit Mirsim, Stratum A (Albright 1932: Pl. 65:24, 25; 1943: Pl. 21:8, 10–12, 15) and Lachish, Stratum III (Zimhoni 1997: Fig. 5.4:15).

Subtype B4.4 (Pl. 11.30:13), with a folded-in diagonal rim and the peculiar flat, elongated ear-shaped knob handle, is represented here by one example, as was the case in Substratum 3c (Pl. 11.27:15, and see parallels there).

Subtype B4.5 is represented by medium-sized bowls whose rims have inner and outer thickened projections, creating a hammer-shaped rim (Fig. 11.27; Pl. 11.30:14, 15). Bowls of this subtype were found in all Iron Age strata, but they are mainly typical of Substrata 3a-b. Similar bowls are known from the entire span of Iron II, for example at 'Arad, Stratum XI (M. Aharoni 1981: Fig. 6:14), Kuntillet 'Ajrud (Ayalon 1995: Fig.3:9); Be'er Sheva', Strata IV and II (Y. Aharoni 1973: Pls. 55:8, 9; 59:58) and Tell Beit Mirsim, Stratum A (Albright 1932: Pls. 65:22; 66:4; 1943: Pl. 26:5).

Type B12 (Pl. 11.30:16–20). These are the bowls decorated with the black strokes on their rims, which morphologically (including their morphological variants) and in their dimensions, are similar to Type B4 bowls. This type was first attested in Stratum 4 (see discussion there), but it was mostly encountered in Substrata 3c and 3a-b.

Type B11 (Pl. 11.31:1–3). These are slightly carinated open bowls with low carination and uniformly thick walls. The rims are simple and rounded at the top. The bowls are also quite distinct in their fabric: most of them are of light brown-reddish clay with a gray core and gray and white inclusions; some are red slipped. These bowls are characteristic of Strata 3 and 2 alike. They are known at other sites in the south, in the eighth century, for example at Tell Beit Mirsim, Stratum A, (Albright 1932: Pl. 65:3), Tel 'Eṭon (Zimhoni 1997: Fig. 4.1:1, 2, 6) and Kuntillet 'Ajrud (Ayalon 1995: Fig. 3:7; possibly also 19, 20).

Type B8 (Pl. 11.31:4–6). The shallow bowls with straight, flaring walls and simple rims are attested in equally small numbers throughout Strata 4–2 (see parallels above, Stratum 4).

Type B9 (Figs. 11.28, 11.29; Pl. 11.30:7–9). These are the flat bowls with straight, flaring walls, which are very similar to Type B8, but the tips of the rims are sharply cut. On some of them (Fig. 11.29, Pl. 11.31:7, 8) the tip of the cut rim is also grooved and on others the rims are sharply inclined outward and downward (Pl. 11.31:9). The bowls with the cut rims were already encountered in Stratum 4, but they are common only in Strata 3a-b and 2. Those with the inclined rim first appear in Substratum 3c and they continue until Stratum 2. Some of these bowls bear incisions executed both before and after firing (see below).

Fig. 11.28. Substrata 3a-b. Bowl Type B9 Pls. 11.31:7; 11.65:2).

Fig. 11.27. Substrata 3a-b. Bowl Subtype B4.5 (Pls. 11.30:15; 11.51:17).

Fig. 11.29. Substrata 3a-b. Bowl Type B9 (Pls. 11.31:8; 11.41:5).

Eighth-century parallels to the variety with a cut rim are known from Tell Beit Mirsim, Stratum A (Albright 1943: Pl. 21:4, 5; No. 5 has a groove along the rim), and from Kuntillet 'Ajrud (with a grooved rim; Ayalon 1995: Fig 3:6). Bowls with inclined rims were found at Ashdod, Strata VIII (Dothan and Freedman 1967: Fig. 37:5) and VII (M. Dothan 1971: Fig. 93:26). Parallels from contexts of the end of the Iron Age appear, for example, at 'En Gedi, Stratum V (Mazar, Dothan and Dunayevsky 1966: Fig. 15:4) and Ramat Raḥel Stratum Va (Y. Aharoni 1964: Fig. 16:1–13, 24 with cut rims; Fig. 16:14 with a grooved rim; Fig. 16:20–23, 25–28 with inclined rims).

Type B10 (Pl. 11.31:10). These are rounded bowls, some of them with a slight carination below the rim, and a folded-out rim. Two subtypes were defined.

Type B10.1 is represented by small and medium bowls (Pl. 11.31:10), and B10.2, by large bowls with handles (Pl. 11.55:2–5). In Substrata 3a-b both subtypes are present, but not numerous. Also, most of them originate in fills inside the granary and the silos, and it is possible that they actually belong to Stratum 2, where these shapes are very common (see discussion and parallels below, Stratum 2).

Type B13 (Fig. 11.30; Pl. 11.31:11–16). These carinated bowls/cups, already attested in restricted numbers from Stratum 4, were frequently encountered in Stratum 3, and they continue in restricted numbers in Stratum 2. All have rounded walls, are carinated at mid-body and have one handle. Some of the bowls are wide and shallow with an everted rim (Pl. 11.31:13), while others are closed and cup-like, where the upper part of the wall and the rim are upright or everted (Pl. 11.31:11, 12). Some of these bowls/cups are in fact strainers and others are three-legged bowls.

Fig. 11.30. Substrata 3a-b. Bowl Type B13 (Pls. 11.31:16; 11.45:3).

In Substrata 3a-b, this category also includes some unusual vessels. The bowl/cup in Pl. 11.31:14 is slightly carinated, and has a handle, but in size and thickness of its walls it differs from all other B13 bowls. The complete, three-legged strainer bowl in

Pl. 11.31:15 is adorned with a pattern of black- and red-painted bands, a decoration typical of Transjordanian sites in the eighth–seventh centuries BCE, for example at Saḥab (Harding 1948: Figs. 6.54, 55, 61, 62), though not on cup/bowls. The bowl in Pl. 11.31:16 is a near-complete handle-less carinated bowl with a spout. It has a counterpart in a seventh-century context at Buṣeirah (Bennett 1975: Fig. 7:16).

In Iron II, such bowls/cups are known from sites in the Negev, such as 'Arad, Stratum XI (M. Aharoni 1981: Fig. 10:10) and Tel Sera', Stratum D-6 (Oren 1992: Fig. 10:7). They are common at Tell el-Kheleifeh (Glueck 1967:32, Fig. 3; Pratico 1993: Pls. 25:1–18, 29:1–7), and especially in Transjordan in the eighth century until the end of the Iron Age, e.g., as at Saḥab (Harding 1948: Fig. 4:22–30), 'Amman (Harding 1945: Nos. 10–13), Umm el-Biyara (Bennett 1966: Figs. 2:1, 3; 3:7, 8) and Buṣeirah (Bennett 1974: Fig. 15:1; 1975: Fig. 5:16, 17; 7:18). Similar bowls, however, are also common in the north, for example at Hazor, Strata VIII–V (Yadin et al. 1958: Pls. XLIX:31, LIV:18, LXXXIII:2, 3; 1960: Pls. LI:17, LIV:20–22, LV:43–44). The presence of this type at Kadesh Barnea provides evidence of some Transjordanian influence.

Other Bowls and a Basin

The following unique shapes are not included in the typological plates.

The bowls in Pls. 11.54:8 and 11.58:7 are rounded open bowls with an out-turned rim, under which, externally, there are two slight grooves. The only meaningful parallels for these bowls are from Lachish, Stratum V (Zimhoni 1997: Type B-5, Fig. 3.8:17, 19).

The bowls in Pls. 11.54:11, 12 and 11.67:6–8 are thin-walled carinated bowls of Type B19, which is common in Stratum 2 (see below). In Substrata 3a-b they were only found in the fill of a silo and in the fill of the granary, and thus they may in fact belong to Stratum 2.

The interior of the bowl fragment in Pl. 11.54:28 bears a wedge-shaped decoration, known mainly in the late Iron Age in the Samaria hills (Zertal 1989).

The small deep bowl in Fig. 11.31; Pl. 11.67:2 has a narrow rounded base. No exact parallels are known to

Fig. 11.31. Substrata 3a-b. Miscellaneous bowl (Pl. 11.67:2).

us, but the shape resembles some of the so-called 'rice bowls', typical of Iron II in Judah (cf., at Ramat Raḥel, Stratum V (Y. Aharoni 1962: Pl. 11:5).

Plate 11.57:8 represents a wide, shallow basin with a ledge rim. Basins are common in the Iron Age but there are no exact parallels for this particular shape.

Kraters

Fragments of wheel-made kraters associated with Substrata 3a-b were very few, and the variety of types limited. Apparently, one of the reasons for this phenomenon is the high frequency of Negebite kraters, which probably fulfilled the same functions.

Type K1 (Pl. 11.32:1–3). These are deep open kraters with walls slanting inward, lacking any pronounced neck, and having a rim that is either folded or out-turned and thickened. This type was already attested in Stratum 4 (see parallels there), but it also occurs throughout Strata 3–2. In Substrata 3a-b, this type is represented only by rim sherds, but we assume that handles were attached to the rim, as in Stratum 4 (Pl. 11.1:15, 16).

Type K3 (Pl. 11.32:4, 5). These are the rounded kraters with a slight S-shaped carination, an outward-thickened rim and handles attached to the rim. Example No. 4 is a relatively large sherd indicating that such kraters had a ring base. Kraters of this type were common in Substrata 3a-b, but they were already represented in Substratum 3c. A similar krater was found at Be'er Sheva', Stratum II (Y. Aharoni 1973: Pl. 60:77).

Type K2 (Pl. 11.32:6). These necked kraters were already attested by a few fragments in Substratum 3c (see parallels above). In Substrata 3a-b they were not frequent.

Other Kraters
The closed krater in Pl. 11.55:7 has a well-defined upright neck and two horizontal handles on the shoulder. Closed kraters with horizontal handles, but with folded upright rims are known from Be'er Sheva', Stratum II (Y. Aharoni 1973: Pls. 69:2, 75:1, 2).

The rim fragment in Pl. 11.70:3 belongs to a krater bearing red slip and black paint, similar to the slipped and painted 'Ashdod Ware' kraters (Dothan and Freedman 1967: Fig. 42:3–6).

Cooking Pots

Only a few cooking-pot fragments were found in the assemblages of Substrata 3a-b, and most of them belong to a single type. This is probably explained by the fact that mainly Negebite vessels were used for cooking.

Type CP1 (Pl. 11.32:7, 8). These are the globular cooking pots with ridged rims, already attested in Stratum 4 and Substratum 3c (see above, discussion in Stratum 4). In Substrata 3a-b, this type is represented by Subtype CP1.2, typified mainly by a more pronounced neck and its relatively thickened and molded rim. Parallels are known, for example, at Be'er Sheva', Stratum II (Y. Aharoni 1973: Pl. 60:81, 82), 'Arad, Stratum VIII (Herzog 1984: Fig. 22:7), Tell Beit Mirsim, Stratum A (Albright 1943: Pl. 19:1–4) and Tell Qasile, Stratum VIII (A. Mazar 1985: Fig. 54:18).

Type CP2 (Pl. 11.32:9). This cooking pot is similar to CP1 but squatter, and with a short neck and a molded rim that is thinner and more upright. A few examples of this type already occur in Stratum 4 and in the Substratum 3c fills (see discussion and parallels above, Stratum 4). Parallels in Iron IIA contexts in the south may be cited, for example, from Be'er Sheva', Stratum VII (Herzog 1984: Fig. 22:8) and Lachish, Stratum IV (Zimhoni 1997: Fig. 3.38:11); and in the eighth century, from Be'er Sheva', Stratum II (Y. Aharoni 1973: Pls. 60:83; 61:88; 66:11; 69:4; 73:11, 12). Seventh-century examples occur, e.g., at 'Aro'er, Stratum II (Biran and Cohen 1981: Fig. 10:6).

Type CP6 (Pl. 11.32:10). These are the closed globular cooking pots with narrow upright necks bearing a number of ridges (cf. Pl. 11.55:9). Only two examples were recorded at Kadesh Barnea. This is the cooking-pot type that typifies Judah in the eighth century BCE, for example at Be'er Sheva', Stratum II (Y. Aharoni 1973: Pl. 61:89–97), 'Arad, Stratum VIII (Herzog 1984: Fig. 22:6, 8) and Lachish, Stratum III (Zimhoni 1997: Fig. 5.6:4–9).

Other Cooking Pots
The vessel in Pl. 11.55:13 is a wheel-made cooking pot with an unusually shaped rim and splotches of black paint on its walls. The cooking-pot fragment in Pl. 11.67:23 has an inverted, elongated rim. This shape of

the rim (but not of the vessel) is reminiscent of Type CP3. No parallels are known to this shape.

Juglets

As opposed to the assemblages of Strata 4 and 2, those of Substrata 3a-b produced only a few juglets, and hardly any complete shapes.

Type JT1 (Pl. 11.33:1, 2). The dipper juglets here have upright or slightly everted necks/rims. Such juglets were found throughout Strata 4–2 (see discussion above, Stratum 4).

Type JT2 (Pl. 11.33:3, 4). As in the other Iron Age strata at Kadesh Barnea, only rare examples of 'Black Juglets' were recorded from Substrata 3a-b. Only one juglet (Pl. 11.33:4) retains its neck, and on that juglet the handle extends from the rim, a feature which is indicative of the later development of this group (see discussion above, Stratum 4).

Other Juglets and an Amphoriskos
The unusual juglet in Pl. 11.33:5 is small and rounded with a narrow upright neck and a flat base; this vessel is unparalleled. The intact, flat-based juglet in Fig. 11.32, Pl. 11.65:12 is also unique at Kadesh Barnea and without parallels.

The fragmentary amphoriskos in Fig 11.33, Pl. 11.56:1 has thick handles close to the body and bears traces of red paint or slip. Only two sherds of such vessels were found, though they are common in Iron Age Judahite sites, for example at Tell Beit Mirsim, Stratum A (Albright 1932: Pl. 66:17–20) and Be'er Sheva', Stratum II (Y. Aharoni 1973: Pls. 69:18; 71:5).

Jugs

Substrata 3a-b did not produce many jugs and each type is represented by a few examples only. Therefore, relative frequencies cannot be established.

Type J14 (Pl. 11.33:6). This is a small and squat barrel-shaped jug with a wide and tall neck. The jug has a simple upright rim and one handle attached to it. There is a slight carination towards the base, which is rounded. This is the only jug of this type found at Kadesh Barnea. In Iron II in Judah, on the other hand, this is a very common shape, appearing in different sizes, shapes of necks and occasionally red slipped (for example at Lachish, Stratum III (Y. Aharoni 1975: Pls. 44:16; 45:1, 3), Be'er Sheva', Stratum II (Y. Aharoni 1973: Pls. 62:105–107; 64:12, 13) and Tell Beit Mirsim, Stratum A (Albright 1932: Pl. 57:1, 4, 5, 8).

Type J7 (Fig. 11.34; Pl. 11.33:7). This globular jug has a narrow neck, similarly to Type J8 (below), but it differs in its thin walls, its funnel-shaped rim with an inner gutter, and the protruding ridge at mid-neck. The vessel is red slipped, and on the neck and body are a series of thin black lines. No exact parallels were found for it, but comparable vessels are a jug from Kuntillet 'Ajrud (with a different rim; Ayalon 1995: Fig. 14:10) and one from Buseirah, from the end of the Iron Age (Bennet 1975: Fig. 6:4). Both shape and treatment of rim may indicate a Cypriot origin for this vessel.

Type J8 (Fig. 11.35; Pl. 11.33:8–10). These are globular jugs with a narrow ridged neck and an everted rim. A single handle extends from the ridge to the shoulder.

Fig. 11.32. Substrata 3a-b. Flat-based juglet (Pl. 11.65:12).

Fig. 11.33. Substrata 3a-b. Red-slipped amphoriskos (Pl. 11.56:1).

Fig. 11.34. Substrata 3a-b. Jug Type J7 (Pls. 11.33:7; 11.71:8).

Fig. 11.35. Substrata 3a-b. Jug Type J8 (Pls. 11.33:10; 11.68:3).

Jug No. 8 has no surface treatment, while Nos. 9 and 10 are red slipped and vertically burnished.

Type J9 (Pl. 11.33:11). This is a large (but fragmentary) pillar-handled jug (it is unknown how many handles it may have had). The vessel was defined as a jug as it is thinner than the usual pillared jars and the vessel is vertically burnished in the manner of jugs. The neck of the jug is not high but is very wide, and a small ridge encircles it below the rim. Another sherd of a similar vessel, with a protruding knob below the handle, was also found in Substrata 3a-b (Pl. 11.37:8).

Other Jugs

A fragmentary cooking jug (Pl. 11.64:19) was stamped on its handle (see below).

The fragment in Pl. 11.64:22 is the bottom part of a flat-based and red-slipped and burnished jug, perhaps of Type J14.

Flasks

A few flask fragments were retrieved, including a few near-complete shapes (Pl. 11.33:12, 13), and no two are alike. The barrel-shaped No. 12 is made of greenish clay. A few other small fragments of flasks, jugs and perforated spouts made of similar greenish-white or of light brown clay with a greenish surface were encountered in all Iron Age strata (mostly not illustrated, but see Pls. 11.56:2; 11.90:12; 11.96:4). Parallels to these vessels, seemingly of the same fabric, may be cited from Kuntillet 'Ajrud (Ayalon 1995: Fig. 18:6), Be'er Sheva', Stratum II (Y. Aharoni 1973: Pl. 63:132), Lachish Tomb 120 (Tufnell 1953: Pl. 92:429) and Hazor, Stratum Va (Yadin et al. 1960: Pl. LXXXVIII:8).

The smaller flask, Pl. 11.33:13, is nearly globular, red slipped and burnished. Also found were a few other fragments of flasks, some of them burnished, which apparently belong to similar shapes.

Jars

As Stratum 3 was not violently destroyed, no complete jars were preserved, only fragments, and even they were not numerous.

Type SJ3 (Pl. 11.33:1–3). Both subtypes of SJ3 were relatively frequent in Substrata 3a-b: SJ3.1, with a short, ridged upright rim, and SJ3.2, with a rim with a groove at the top (for which see Pls. 11.40:6; 11.41:23). Both subtypes were already encountered in Substratum 3c.

Type SJ1 (Pl. 11.34:4, 5). These fragments probably belong to jars of Type SJ1 with short upright necks, already encountered in Stratum 4 and Substratum 3c (see above, discussion in Stratum 4).

Type SJ4 (Pl. 11.34:6, 7). These are jars with no necks, and an externally thickened rim. As only rim sherds were encountered, there is no information regarding the general shape and handles. Rims of this type first occur in Substrata 3a-b, but apparently similar vessels are primarily typical of Stratum 2 (see below, SJ11).

Type SJ8 (Pl. 11.34:8). Such fragments probably belong to jars with pronounced shoulders, no neck and with a very short upright rim, defined in Stratum 2 as Type SJ8. As they were common in this latter stratum, they are discussed below. We are unable to tell to which of the SJ8 subtypes these fragments belong.

Pithoi

Only a few pithos sherds were found in Substrata 3a-b.

Type P3 (Pl. 11.34:9, 10). This is an externally thickened rim with a triangular section, projecting outward, similar to that of pithoi found in Stratum 4 (Type P1). However, No. 9 has handles extending from the rim to the shoulder.

Lamps

Very few lamp fragments were recovered from the Substrata 3a-b contexts. All of them are shallow, rounded to flat, with a clear ledge rim (Pl. 11.34:11, 12). No lamps with raised bases, such as are common as from the eighth century BCE in Judah, are known here.

Varia

Stands(?)/Pithoi(?)

The tall grooved flaring rims in Pls. 11.56:14 and 11.70:21 may belong to jars or pithoi, but as no jars with such necks/rims are known, it stands to reason that they are fragments of stands (cf. at Lachish, Tufnell 1953: Pl. 30:396). Three similar rims were recorded from Stratum 2 (see Pl. 11.78:10). The two rims in Pl. 11.68:11, 12 though different in shape, probably also belong to stands with upright walls. In addition, four fragments with rims resembling that of Pl. 11.68:12 were registered, all from Substrata 3a-b.

Incense Stand
The fragment in Pl. 11.42:10 is part of an incense stand with thin upright walls and apertures (cf. such stands at Ashdod—M. Dothan 1971: Fig. 44:14–16, 18). The coarse fragment in Pl. 11.39:23 probably also belongs to a stand.

Ring Kernos and Petalled Incense Burner
The fill of Granary 6291 produced a fragmentary ring kernos (Pl. 11.57:4) and part of a petalled incense burner (Fig. 11.36; Pl. 11.57:5). However, because of the mixed nature of this deposit (see below) these vessels cannot be attributed with certainty to Substrata 3a-b.

Fig. 11.36. Substrata 3a-b. Petalled stand (Pl. 11.57:5).

BLACK-PAINTED WARE (BPW)

This wheel-made group, defined here for the first time (Figs. 11.37–11.42; Pls. 11.35; 11.36) includes bowls, kraters and jars, characterized by black-painted geometric and floral patterns. The clay is usually of conspicuously reddish-brown color, occasionally with a gray core, and with numerous white inclusions. The surface of the vessels is greenish, bears no additional slip and is not burnished.

In all, 53 vessels/fragments of this ware were registered, among them about 18 body sherds. This notwithstanding, in most cases it was possible to attribute the fragments to a specific class of vessels—18 bowls, 25 kraters and 10 jars.

The stratigraphical distribution is as follows: two fragments in Stratum 4 (the first from the upper part of L1237, the other from L3206; Pl. 11.20:13); 18 in Substratum 3c (of which 12 are illustrated in Pls. 11.35:1, 3, 7, 12, 14, 16, 18, 23; 11.36:2, 5, 11, 12);

23 in Substrata 3a-b (of which 16 are illustrated in Pls. 11.35:4–6, 8–11, 17, 19, 20, 22; 11.36:1, 6–8, 10), four in Stratum 2 (Pls. 11.35:15, 21; 11.36:3; 11.113:18) and a single example in Stratum 1 (Pl.11.36:4). The five remaining fragments (three are illustrated in Pl. 11.35:2, 13; 11.36:9) are from unclear contexts.

It thus seems that this ware is particularly typical of Substrata 3a-b. However, as it is fairly well represented in Substratum 3c, and a few are also present in Stratum 4, one cannot rule out the possibility that this ware group was indeed already in use in Stratum 4 (a similar distribution was recorded for other black-painted vessels, such as B1 and B12, see above). The fragments in Strata 2 and 1 are probably residual.

As this ware is unknown at other sites in the Negev, nor in any other region in the vicinity, there are no chronological anchors for this group elsewhere, and the chronology, for the time being at least, will have to be based on the chronological framework of Kadesh Barnea.

Bowls

Eighteen bowl fragment were registered, and three bowl types were defined based on decoration and shape.

Type BPW B1 (Fig. 11.37; Pl. 11.35:1, 2;). These are carinated/S-shaped bowls with a simple rim. The inner part of the rim, above the carination, bears a decoration consisting of a horizontal black stripe/band, and above it, around the rim's circumference, a frieze of 'weed' patterns. These bowls are represented by two fragments, one from the Substratum 3c fills and the other from a mixed locus.

Fig. 11.37. Substratum 3c and Stratum 1. Black-Painted Ware bowl Type BPW B1 (Pl. 11.35:1).

Type BPW B2 (Pl. 11.35:3, 4). Morphologically, these bowls resemble the previous type, but they are larger and also differ in their decorative pattern and its location. The decoration here was applied only externally. The patterns were applied with a free hand, and in one example (Pl. 11.35:3), there seems to be some division into metopes of sorts. Three such sherds were found, in Substrata 3c and 3a-b.

Type BPW B3 (Figs. 11.38–11.40; Pl. 11.35:5–13). This type differs from the above two in both shape and decoration. These are small and deep closed bowls with a rounded base. Some of the bowls are slightly S-shaped while others have straight walls. Two of the bowls of the former shape are equipped with spouts below the rim (now broken; Pl. 11.35:5, 6). On one of the latter and on an additional bowl fragment there is evidence of a handle extending from the rim.

The decorations on these bowls vary. On No. 5 the decoration is freely rendered, similarly to that on Type BPW B2 bowls, and the horizontal lines form a frieze, which is further subdivided by vertical dividers (branches?). On Nos. 8 and 9 the pattern is more composite, but also seems to be some vegetal design (see Fig. 11.39). On Nos. 6 and 10 there are metopes with lattice or net patterns. The other patterns (especially Fig. 11.40; Pl. 11.35:12, 13) seem to be simple vegetal ones, possibly representing roots and shrubs.

This group of bowls consists of nine fragments, of which six originate from Substrata 3a-b, two from Substratum 3c and one from an unclear context. Four additional body sherds from mixed loci apparently belong to this group, but this could not be ascertained.

Fig. 11.38. Substratum 3a.
Black-Painted Ware bowl Type
BPW B3 (Pls. 11.35:5; 11.46:9).

Fig. 11.39. Substrata 3a-b.
Black-Painted Ware bowl
Type BPW B3
(Pls. 11.35:9; 11.70:12).

Fig. 11.40. Substratum 3c.
Black-Painted Ware bowl
Type BPW B3 (Pl. 11.35:12).

Kraters

Twenty-five krater fragments were registered, nine of which are body sherds (Pl. 11.36:9–11). The 16 rim fragments were divided into two main types

differentiated by their shape or, more specifically, rim shape.

Type BPW K1 (Figs. 11.41, 42; Pl. 11.35:14–19). These are holemouth kraters with simple rims (for the decorations, see below). About seven such rim fragments were found; one is from Stratum 2 and the rest are equally divided between Substrata 3a-b and 3c.

Fig. 11.41. Substratum 3c.
Black-Painted Ware krater
Type BPW K1
(Pls. 11.35:14; 11.28:8).

Fig. 11.42. Stratum 2.
Black-Painted Ware krater
Type BPW K1
(Pl. 11.35:15).

Type BPW K2 (Fig. 11.43; Pls. 11.35:20–23, 11.36:1–4). These kraters are similar in general shape to the previous type, but the rim is somewhat emphasized by a slight concavity below it, such as on Pl. 11.35:20, 21, or by an external thickening, such as on Pl. 11.35:22, 23. The krater in Pl. 11.36:4 has a more elaborate rim. Among the eight rim fragments assigned to this type, two are from Substratum 3c, three from Substrata 3a-b, two from Stratum 2, and one from Stratum 1. The krater in Pl. 11.36:5 (Substratum 3c) differs from these kraters in that it has a protruding ridge below the slightly everted rim (in decoration, however, it is similar to some of them).

All the kraters bear external black-painted decoration, among which the following patterns can be discerned. The most common patterns are the crosshatched panels and the hatched and/or crosshatched 'hour-glass' motifs. These patterns either occupy the entire surface of the vessel (Pl. 11.35:14), or, more often, are placed in intermittent metopes between which are empty spaces (as no complete vessels were preserved, the overall composition cannot be reconstructed).

Fig. 11.43. Substrata 3a-b.
Black-Painted Ware krater
Type BPW K2.2 (Pl. 11.35:20).

The pattern seen in Pl. 11.35:17 resembles that on some of the bowls (Pl. 11.35:8, 9).

On the kraters in Pl. 11.36:1, 2 the decorative designs consist of vertical lines crossed by shorter horizontal ones. This design is somewhat reminiscent of the incised decoration occurring on some Negebite vessels (e.g., Pl. 12.27:11–18).

On Pl. 11.36:3, 4 only horizontal lines are attested but it is possible that the rest of the pattern is missing. It should be noted that these two kraters are stratigraphically the latest (Strata 2 and 1).

Jars

Type BWP SJ1 (Pl. 11.36:6–8). Jars are relatively scarce in this ware group. The only characteristic of these jar fragments is the sharp carination between the shoulder and the body. The decoration consists of horizontal lines on the shoulder, and below them, on the body, crosshatched metopes and other designs. The three larger (and illustrated) shoulder fragments are from Substrata 3a-b. Seven other body sherds are probably of storage jars with similar decoration (one of which is illustrated in Pl. 11.36:12), of which four are from Substratum 3c and three from Substrata 3a-b.

NEGEBITE WARE

Negebite wares dominate the Substrata 3a-b assemblages. In Pls. 11.37–11.71 the Negebite pottery of these substrata is illustrated in the context of the loci that were selected to be presented. A detailed typological presentation and discussion of this pottery appears in Chapter 12.

SUBSTRATA 3A-B CERAMIC ASSEMBLAGES
(Pls. 11.37–11.71)

In Pls. 11.37–11.71 the Substrata 3a-b assemblages are presented by area, and where possible, by substrata within the areas. Segregation between assemblages of Substrata 3b and 3a was possible only in some places in Areas A1 and B.

The first assemblages to be presented (Pls. 11.37–11.63) are those from the architectural units within the courtyard of the fortress, in the same order as the stratigraphical/architectural chapters: Area B, Area D, Area C and finally Area A1. Following these are the living horizons and silos surrounding the fortress'

walls (Pls. 11.64–11.71): Areas E, F and G. Of all the assemblages presented here, that from Granary 6219 in Area C (Pls. 11:54–11.57) is the least secure, as it seems to have been disturbed during Stratum 2. Also, it is possible that it contains pottery that was originally part of the Substratum 3c constructional fill, which became mixed with the pottery in the granary fill when some of the granary walls collapsed.

Occasionally other pottery typical of Stratum 2 was traced in Substrata 3a-b contexts, which must be regarded as belonging to intrusions that were not discerned during excavation. These fragments were not omitted from the respective pottery plates. Such are, for example, ceramics from Silo 675 (see below, Pl. 11.52); the 'Edomite' jar fragment in L1108 in Area C (Pl. 11.51:9); and jar fragments from Alley 197 in Area A1 (Pl. 11.59:11, 12, 16, 17).

Architectural Units in the Fortress Courtyard

Area B (Pls. 11.37–11.45)
As mentioned, in this area it was possible to differentiate between Substrata 3b and 3a assemblages. The Substratum 3b pottery presented here is from Building 3173 (Pl. 11.37), Building 733 and Alley 3179 (Pls. 11.38, 11.39) and Building 3014 (Pl. 11.40), as well as various floors of buildings, and an alley in the eastern part of the area (Pl. 11.41).

The Substratum 3a pottery originates from Building 713 (Pl. 11.42), from floors in the southwestern part of the area (Pl. 11.43), and from floors of Building 3005, Space 514, Alleys 494a and 3006 and some other units in the eastern part of area (Pls. 11.44, 11.45).

Area D (Pl. 11.46)
The pottery here originates from Substratum 3b floors in the area east of the cistern (Pl. 11.46:1–7) and from Substratum 3a fills in the same area (Pl. 11.46:8–18).

Area C (Pls. 11.47–11.57)
Structures in the Central Part of the Fortress Courtyard. This includes pottery found in the eastern part of Building 6135 in the north (Pls. 11.47–11.49) and from the structures around Granary 6291 (Pls. 11.50, 11.51, 11.53).

Silo 675 (Pl. 11.52). Part of the material from this silo, both from the lower phase (L675) and the ash pit in the upper phase (L670) is typologically later than the rest of the Substrata 3a-b pottery, for example, the bowl in Pl. 11.52:2 (Type B10.1); the thin-walled bowl and the cooking pot in Pl. 11.52:4, 6; and the jars in Pl. 11.52:7 (SJ12) and 9–11(SJ8[?]), which are common in Stratum 2. This impression is corroborated by the Edomite stand (Pl. 11.52:15), as this ware is typical of Stratum 2, and by the jar in Pl. 11.52:14, which may even date to the Persian period. It is thus clear that the fill in the silo incorporates Stratum 2 pottery. Apparently a disturbance here was not noticed.

The Fill of Granary 6291 (Pls. 11.54–11.57). Granary 6291 was found full of earth, stones and abundant pottery. It was not sealed, but a beaten-earth floor attributed to Stratum 2 was traced above it.

Part of the pottery in the granary is well at home in Stratum 3, but some of these types were also recorded in Strata 4 and 3c. Such are bowl of Types B1, B4, B9 and B12 (Pl. 11.54:1, 3, 15, 16, 18–21), cooking pots of Types CP1.2 and CP2 (Pl. 11.55:10–12) and jars of Type SJ3 (Pl. 11.56:7, 8). Also compatible with the Stratum 3 chronological horizon (for which see below) are the krater in Pl. 11.55:7; the Type CP6 rounded cooking-pot fragment (Pl. 11.55:9; a rare shape at Kadesh Barnea, clearly dateable to the eighth century BCE); and the pithos rim in Pl. 11.56:12, with eighth-century BCE parallels at Kuntillet 'Ajrud (Ayalon 1995: Fig. 8:1, 2), Be'er Sheva', Stratum II (Y. Aharoni 1973: Pl. 65:120), 'Arad, Stratum IX (Herzog 1984: Fig. 19:5) and Tel 'Eton, Stratum I (Zimhoni 1997: Figs. 4.4:14; 4.8:3, 11).

On the other hand, much of the material here is more typical of Stratum 2. Such are the carinated bowls, Type B19 in Pl. 11.54:11, 12; the bowls with folded rims, Type B10.1 (Pl. 11.54:23–27; though a few such bowls were already present in Substrata 3a-b) and B10.2 (Pl. 11.55:2–4); the bowl fragment with wedge-shaped decoration (Pl. 11.54:28), probably of the seventh century BCE; bowl Type B21 (Pl. 11.54:13); and jar Type SJ8 Pl. 11.56:9, 10) and Subtype SJ12.3 (Pl.11.56:11).

It is thus reasonable to conclude that the chronologically mixed pottery in the granary represents at least Substrata 3a-b and Stratum 2 (it is unclear whether Substratum 3c is represented here as well, though this is possible, as it is evident that at least the eastern wall collapse and the Substratum 3c fill spilled in). The granary ceased to function either at the end of Stratum 3 or within Stratum 2 (as at a certain point within this stratum the granary was built over). A more decisive verdict is hampered by the fact that there are undetected intrusions.

However, it is notable that some of the ceramic types that are most typical of the Stratum 2 destruction assemblages are missing here, such as juglets of Type JT3, cooking pots of Types CP7, CP8 and CP9 and the 'Red Sandy Ware' jars (see below). This indicates that if the granary still functioned in Stratum 2, this must have ended early within this stratum. Likewise, the relative abundance of Negebite ware in the granary points to the fact that it was probably blocked early during Stratum 2, or earlier.

The fill of the granary also produced some unique artifacts: a ring kernos (Pl. Pl. 11.57:4), which is the only such vessel recovered from Kadesh Barnea (four sherds of kernos bowls were found in Substratum 3c); a fragmentary petalled incense burner (Pl. 11.57:5), of which one fragment was uncovered in Substratum 3a in Area B, about 18 m northwest of the granary); three zoomorphic figurines and a stone cosmetic bowl (Pls. 13.1:5–7; 13.4:2), the latter probably dating to the eighth century BCE.

Area A1 (Pls. 11.58–11.63)
In this area too, pottery from Substratum 3b (Pls. 11.58, 11.59) could be separated from that of Substratum 3a (Pls. 11.60–11.63). The pottery assemblages presented are mainly from the two phases—Rooms 174 and 206 and Alley 157 from Substratum 3b; and Room 182, Surface 33 and Building 79 from Substratum 3a.

The Areas around the Fortress

Area E (Pl. 11.64)
The Area E assemblages originate in Rooms 181 and 804 situated between the eastern towers, and in Silo 109.

Area F (Pls. 11.65–11.70)
The assemblages presented from this area comprise those found in Room 853 and Silos 854 (which produced an abundant ceramic assemblage), 861, 862 and 858.

Generally, most of the pottery is characteristic of Substrata 3a-b, both in the high percentage of Negebite pottery, as well as in wheel-made types such as the black-painted bowls of Type B12 (e.g., Pls. 11.67:11, 12; 11.70:19), and those of Type B13 (Pl. 11.67:16–19). On the other hand there are a few vessels that are more characteristic of Stratum 2, such as the carinated bowls of Type B19 (Pl. 11.67:6–8). However, the quantity of 'late' pottery is meager and typical Stratum 2 types are missing. It thus seems that the silos had already been filled in before the Stratum 2 glacis was constructed over them.

Area G (Pl. 11.71)

Silo 473. The fill inside this silo (Pl. 11.71) produced the only substantial ceramic assemblage from this area. The pottery in it resembles that uncovered in Substrata 3a-b within the courtyard, despite our expectation that it would contain later material, accumulating after it went out of use, and from the construction of the Stratum 2 glacis. No types in it could be clearly associated with Stratum 2; on the other hand, the pottery includes much Negebite ware, which is characteristic of Stratum 3. It seems that either the silo went out of use and gradually filled up during the lifetime of Substrata 3a-b or that it was deliberately filled with Substrata 3a-b debris when the Stratum 2 glacis was built, early in Stratum 2.

SUMMARY AND CHRONOLOGY

The Substrata 3a-b ceramic assemblage is difficult to characterize in all respects—chronologically, spatially and culturally. The wheel-made pottery, in all the assemblages of these substrata, is accompanied by a large amount (*c.* 80% of the material recorded) of Negebite ware, testifying to a flourishing local pottery industry, the products of which were used by the occupants of the fortress alongside the wheel-made pottery. Negebite ware was indeed already present in Stratum 4 (and in Substratum 3c), but in lesser quantities. As the Negebite pottery is difficult to date (see Chapter 12), the chronology of Substrata 3a-b has to rely on a relatively restricted assemblage.

Dating is also hampered by the fact that the wheel-made vessels comprise quite a few types that are unparalleled elsewhere, such as bowls of Types B1, B12, and the Black-Painted Ware vessels (bowls of Types B1 and B12 were already present in Stratum 4).

The rest of the wheel-made pottery is generally at home in the Judahite horizon of the eighth/seventh centuries BCE, for example bowls of Types B4, B8, B9, B10.1, B13; 'Black Juglets' (Type JT2); red-burnished jugs of Type J8 ; and storage jars of Types SJ1, SJ3 and SJ8, the latter with parallels in such contexts as Lachish, Stratum III, Be'er Sheva', Stratum II and 'Arad,

Stratum VIII. However, no type should *necessarily* be dated to the seventh century and thus, a general date in the eighth century is the best approximation for Stratum 3, probably in its second half.

In contrast, however, some of the most typical shapes of eighth-century Judah are nearly or completely missing at Kadesh Barnea, for example the so-called 'rice bowls' (B15), the large bowls with folded rims and four handles (B10.2); the ridged globular cooking pot (CP6); the decanter and the squat jug (J14); the holemouth jar and the pillar-handled jar (see Aharoni and Aharoni 1976: Nos. 1, 2, 4, 8, 10 ,12). This may be due to the site's distance from Judahite production centers. The various functions of these vessels must have been fulfilled by the local, Negebite vessels. As at other sites in the Negev, red-slipped vessels at Kadesh Barnea are relatively scarce.

It is unclear whether some substantial chronological gap should be postulated between Strata 4 and 3, perhaps paralleling the existence of Kuntillet 'Ajrud (dated by its excavators and by radiometric dating to the late ninth–early eighth centuries BCE).

Some cultural proximity between Strata 4 and 3 is indicated by the Negebite pottery and the Black-Painted Ware in both, but the chronological spans of these groups are unknown.

Regarding the regional associations of the pottery: As mentioned, some of the pottery types here are definitely Judahite. Other ware groups, such as the Negebite pottery and the Black-Painted Ware, by their main distribution, were probably produced in the Negev, possibly also in Transjordan (but this needs to be corroborated by petrographic analysis). The Transjordanian connection is also exemplified by the various variants of Bowl B13.

POTTERY OF STRATUM 2
(Figs. 11.44–11.81; Pls. 11.72–11.128)

The Stratum 2 fortress was destroyed by fire and many complete vessels, fragmentary ones and sherds were preserved on its floors. The ceramic assemblages include mostly jars, juglets, cooking pots and bowls. Most of the material is wheel made and resembles types common in Judah and the coastal plain at the end of the Iron Age. Indeed, as opposed to the earlier strata, the association of the Stratum 2 pottery assemblage with those of Judah is very conspicuous.

Similarly to other contemporaneous sites in the Negev (for the chronology, see below), the assemblage is augmented by the local Negebite ware, by some Edomite pottery, and by imitations of Assyrian/Transjordanian types.

TYPOLOGY OF WHEEL-MADE SHAPES

The large assemblages preserved in the casemate rooms and in several other 'clean' loci in the courtyard served to determine the typological spectrum of Stratum 2. Some of these types were already recorded in Substrata 3a-b, but most make their initial appearance in this stratum. The parallels below are cited mainly from well-dated sites in Judah, especially southern Judah, and in Philistia. The Edomite pottery is compared to that known at other Negev sites and in Transjordan.

Bowls

Bowls are the most common vessels in Stratum 2, and the most variegated group.

Type B1 (Pl. 11.72:1). These are the small rounded bowls with thin walls and a simple rim, which were already attested in Strata 4 and 3. In Stratum 2, bowls of this type seem to be slightly different. Their walls are thicker and more rounded, and the tip of the rim is not as thin. Most of the bowls in Stratum 2 are plain and only a few are not slipped or burnished (none bears black decoration), in contrast to those in the earlier contexts.

Type B4 (Pl. 11.72:2–4). These rounded or slightly carinated bowls with everted rims first appear in Stratum 4 but they are most common in Substrata 3a-b (for discussion and parallels, see above, Strata 4 and Substrata 3a-b). They were divided into subtypes according to rim shape. In Stratum 2 the subtypes encountered are B4.1 with the diagonally cut rim (Pl. 11.72:2); B4.2 with a ledge-like rim ((Pl. 11.72:3; these rims are very similar to those of Type B18 bowls); and B4.3 with thickened rims projecting outward (Pl. 11.72:4).

Type B11 (Pl. 11.72:5). These are the carinated bowls with uniformly thick walls and a simple rim. They were already attested in Substrata 3a-b (see discussion above).

Type B8 (Fig. 11.44; Pl. 11.72:6). The shallow bowls with straight, flaring walls and a simple rim are attested at Kadesh Barnea from Stratum 4 onward (see discussion above, Stratum 4).

Fig. 11.44. Stratum 2. Bowl Type B8 (Pls. 11.72:6; 11.94:2).

Type B9 (Pl. 11.72:7). These flat bowls are similar to Type B8, but with a cut rim (some of which inclined outward and downward). They first appear in Substratum 3c, but are more common in Substrata 3a-b (see above).

Type B10. This type comprises bowls with thickened and folded-out rims. They are either rounded or have a slight carination below the rim. The bases are always ring bases. As discussed above (Substrata 3a-b), there are two subtypes.

Subtype B10.1 (Fig. 11.45; Pl. 11.72:8–10) is represented by small or medium bowls; most of them are about 20 cm in diameter. Occasionally these bowls are wheel burnished inside and on the external face of the rim. These are the most common bowls in Stratum 2, but a few examples also occur in Stratum 3 (see above).

In Judah, these bowls first appear in the eighth century BCE, but they are more typical of the end of the Iron Age. Selected examples from the eighth century come from Lachish, Stratum III (Zimhoni 1997: Fig. 5.4:16–21) and Be'er Sheva', Stratum II (Aharoni 1973: Pl. 59:63–71); and in the seventh/early sixth centuries—Ramat Raḥel, Stratum Va (Y. Aharoni 1964: Figs. 16:35–60; 17:1–48), 'En Gedi, Stratum V (Mazar, Dothan and Dunayevsky 1966: Fig. 14:1–11), Lachish, Stratum II (Y. Aharoni 1975: Fig. 47:11–16), Meṣad Ḥashavyahu (Naveh 1962: Fig. 4:10–13) and 'Aro'er, Strata II–I (Biran and Cohen 1981: Fig. 14:1, 2, 15:1–4). Their abundance and uniform size led M. and Y. Aharoni to suggest that they were mass produced (1976:86).

It is interesting to note that the very small and thin-walled bowls with a flattened folded rim, which are typical of the very end of the Iron Age in Judah (cf. 'En Gedi, Stratum V, Mazar, Dothan and Dunayevsky

Fig. 11.45. Stratum 2. Bowl Subtype B10.1 (Pls. 11.72:8; 11.86:4).

1966: Fig. 14:1–11; and 'Aro'er, Stratum II, Biran and Cohen 1981: Fig. 10:4, 11) are completely absent at Kadesh Barnea.

Subtype B10.2 (Fig. 11:46; Pl. 11.72:11). In general shape these bowls are similar to Subtype B10.1, but they are considerably larger. They are deep and rounded, with slightly inverted walls, a folded rim, a ring base and two or four handles extending from the rim. Most have a very characteristic fabric—well-fired red-brown clay with a gray core and inclusions. At Kadesh Barnea these bowls appear mainly in Stratum 2, and only a restricted number are attested in Substrata 3a-b.

Fig. 11.46. Stratum 2.
Bowl Subtype B10.2
(Pls. 11:72:11; 11.102:11).

In Judah, such bowls are typical of the eighth century BCE and continue until the end of the Iron Age. For parallels in the eighth century see Lachish, Stratum III (Zimhoni 1997: Fig. 5.5:3) and Be'er Sheva', Stratum II (Aharoni 1973: Pl. 60:73–76). For seventh/sixth centuries contexts, see 'En Gedi, Stratum V (Mazar, Dothan and Dunayevsky 1966: Fig. 16:3–6), Lachish, Stratum II (Y. Aharoni 1975: Pl. 47:18), 'Arad, Stratum VII (Herzog 1984: Fig. 25:6), Meṣad Ḥashavyahu (Naveh 1962: Fig. 4:14, 15), Ramat Raḥel, Stratum Va (Aharoni 1964: Fig. 18:1–6) and 'Aro'er, Stratum II (Biran and Cohen 1981: Fig. 5:3).

Type B13 (Pl. 11.72:12, 13). These are the small rounded or carinated bowls/cups with one handle; some of them are strainer bowls and some are three legged. They first appear in Stratum 4, they are mainly attested in Substrata 3a-b (see discussion and parallels above) and there are only a few fragments Stratum 2.

Type B15 (Fig. 11.47; Pl. 11.72:14). This, the so-called 'rice bowl', is the most typical bowl of the eighth century BCE in Judah, continuing into the seventh century, for example at Lachish, Stratum III (Zimhoni 1997: Fig. 5.4:2–5), Be'er Sheva', Stratum II (Y. Aharoni 1973: Pl. 59:39–43), Ramat Raḥel, Stratum Va (Y. Aharoni 1964: Fig. 17:53–56) and 'En Gedi, Stratum V (Mazar, Dothan and Dunayevsky 1966: Fig. 15:6, 7). These bowls have thin, straight, slightly flaring walls and a simple rim. There is a carination in the lower wall near the base. Occasionally these bowls

Fig. 11.47. Stratum 2.
Bowl Type B15 (L299).

are red slipped. Only a few fragments of this type were uncovered at Kadesh Barnea, all in Stratum 2.

Type B16 (Pl. 11.72:15). These are rounded bowls with incurving walls/rims. Very few fragments of this type were encountered, some of them red slipped (Pl. 11.84:1). This is not a common type and meaningful parallels occur only in eighth-century contexts, such as Be'er Sheva', Stratum II (Aharoni 1973: Pl. 59:37) and Tell Beit Mirsim, Stratum A (Albright 1932: Pl. 67:17, 18; 1943: Pl. 15:13).

Type B17 (Pl. 11.72:16). These rounded bowls are typified by a slight carination, or groove, below their rims. Only few fragments of this type were recorded. In Judah, such bowls are characteristic of the end of the Iron Age, for example at 'En Gedi, Stratum V (Mazar, Dothan and Dunayevsky 1966: Fig. 14:16), 'Arad, Stratum VI (Herzog 1984: Pl. 29:2), 'Aro'er (Biran and Cohen 1981: Fig. 10:3) and Meṣad Ḥashavyahu (Naveh 1962: Fig. 4:4, 7).

Type B18 (Pl. 11.72:17, 18). These are shallow bowls with an everted or ledge rim, typified by their ridged walls. The bowl in Pl. 11.72:18 is red slipped and its rim projects inside and out. Parallels to these bowls may be cited from Tel Baṭash, Stratum II (Kelm and Mazar 1985: Fig. 16:4) and 'Arad, Stratum VI (Herzog 1984: Pl. 25:5).

Type B19 (Fig. 11.48; Pl. 11.73:1–3). These are carinated bowls with very thin walls and a simple everted rim; the sharp carination is between the shoulder and the rim. These bowls differ from Type B2 and B13 bowls, whose walls are thicker and where the carination is at mid-body and not as accentuated. The bowl in Pl. 11.73:1 is unusual as it has a second slight carination down the wall.

In the late Iron Age, similar carinated bowls, apparently imitating Assyrian shapes, are quite rare, but they occur, e.g., at 'Aro'er, Stratum II (Biran and Cohen 1981: Fig. 15:12–20), Qiṭmit (Beit-Arieh 1995: Figs. 4.1:40; 4.9:17; 4.11:9) and Tell el-Kheleifeh (Glueck 1967:35, Fig. 4:2).

The carinated bowl in Fig. 11.48, Pl. 11.73:3, is small and thin, with a sharp carination at mid-body. The rim is sharply everted, and below the carination are a number of indentations forming a rosette pattern, apparently in imitation of metal vessels (cf. bowls at 'Aro'er Strata II–I, Biran and Cohen 1981: Fig. 15:13; and at Tawilan, Bennett and Bienkowski 1995: Fig. 6.8:9, 10).

Fig. 11.48. Stratum 2. Bowl Type B19 (Pls. 11.73:3; 11.90:3).

Type B20 (Fig. 11.49; Pl. 11.73:4, 5). These deep necked bowls are either rounded or slightly carinated, with a ring or disc base. Only few bowls of this type were encountered in Stratum 2; two rim fragments from Substrata 3a-b might also belong to this type, but this is uncertain (Pls. 11.45:15; 11.47:4). In their shape these bowls resemble Edomite kraters, but they are unadorned. Morphological parallels occur at 'Aro'er, Strata II–I (Biran and Cohen 1981: Fig. 15:19), Buṣeirah (Bennett 1974: Fig. 15:4) and Umm el-Biyara (Bennett 1966: Fig. 2:10).

Fig. 11.49. Stratum 2. Bowl Type B20 (Pls. 11.73:4; 11.102:12).

Type B21 (Pl. 11.73:6, 7). These are open carinated bowls with the carination in the middle of the wall. The rims are everted and the bowls are provided with disc bases. There are two size categories: small bowls, about 17.5 cm in diameter (Pl. 11.73:6) and larger and deeper ones, about 30 cm in diameter (Pl. 11.73:7). They are not common. One parallel may be cited, from Ramat Raḥel, Stratum V (Y. Aharoni 1962: Pl. 11:11).

Type B22 (Pl. 11.73:8). These rounded bowls have simple inverted rims with a ridge below them, under which is a slight carination. This type is represented by two fragments only (see Pl. 11.102:14), and the only parallels in the Negev are from Ḥorbat Qiṭmit (Beit-Arieh 1995: Figs. 4.2:21; 4.16:9). Similar bowls were

found at Dor and were recognized as Assyrianized types (Gilboa 1996: Fig. 1:1–8).

Type B23 (Pl. 11.73:9). These are large, thick bowls with straight, flaring walls, an everted, folded rim forming a triangular section and a ring base. No parallels were found for this type, but in both shape and size they recall the late Iron Age *mortaria*, Type B24.

Type B24 (Pl. 11.73:10). These are *mortaria* with thick flat bases. (The Persian-period *mortaria* have high ring bases; when only the rims are preserved it is difficult to determine to which period the fragments belong.) In Judah in the late Iron Age *mortaria* are known from such contexts as 'Arad, Stratum VI (Herzog 1984: Fig. 29:4), 'En Gedi, Stratum V (Mazar, Dothan and Dunayevsky 1966: Fig. 16:1), Meṣad Hashevyahu (Naveh 1962: Fig. 4:16, 17) and 'Aro'er, Stratum II (Biran and Cohen 1981: Fig. 6:1).

Other Bowls

The complete bowl in Fig. 11.50, Pl. 11.81:5 has very thick vertical walls and a simple rim. It is crudely made, but it was not clear if it was made by hand and consequently whether it relates to the Negebite ware.

Fig. 11.50. Stratum 2. Thick, flat-based wheel-made bowl (Pl. 11.81:5).

The Type B12 bowl in Pl. 11.92:12, with black lines on the rim, is typical mainly of Substrata 3a-b and seems to be re-deposited here .

The fragmentary large bowl/krater in Pl. 11.98:17 has a ring base and three loop handles/feet extending from the lower part of the walls to the base. An additional similar fragment was encountered in Substratum 3c (not illustrated). It is possible that the Stratum 2 example is re-deposited, as such bowls are known in southern Judah in Iron IIA, for example at Be'er Sheva', Stratum VII (Herzog 1984: Fig. 21:10). However, later examples are also known, for example at Tel 'Eton, Stratum I (Zimhoni 1997: Fig. 4.8:4).

Kraters

The variety of krater types in Stratum 2 is quite limited. (The open bowls/kraters with folded rims and handles extending from the rim to shoulder were included in bowls, Type B10.2, and the large holemouth vessels are discussed below under jars, Type SJ12.)

Type K1 (Pl. 11.73:11). These are the neck-less kraters with a nearly vertical and thickened rim, which is occasionally hammer shaped. In Stratum 2, as only rims were encountered, it is unclear whether they are really the same as kraters defined as Type K1 in earlier strata (occurring as early as Stratum 4). It was difficult to find parallels for this type in assemblages that parallel Stratum 2 (for the date, see below).

Type K5 (Pl. 11.73:12, 13). These are small, thin-walled, closed rounded kraters, with pronounced shoulders and a well-defined neck. The rim is slightly everted and cut obliquely inwards. Plate 11.73:12 is in fact the only example at Kadesh Barnea that unequivocally belongs to this well-known type.

Such kraters, occasionally red slipped, are known at Judahite sites toward the end of the Iron Age, for example at Lachish, Stratum II (Zimhoni 1997: Fig: 5.32:1), 'En Gedi, Stratum V (Mazar, Dothan and Dunayevsky 1966: Fig. 15:12, 13), Ramat Raḥel, Stratum V (Aharoni 1962: Fig.12:3) and 'Aro'er, Stratum IV (Biran 1987:31). At the City of David (Shiloh 1985: Fig. 6:1, 2) kraters that are similar in shape also have a high foot, creating a goblet of sorts. It is unclear if No. 13 is related to this type (in shape it resembles the bowls defined above as Type B20).

Other Kraters
The handle-less krater in Fig. 11.51, Pl. 11.73:14, is unique at Kadesh Barnea, and no meaningful parallels for it are known. It is wheel made, with a rounded base, upright walls and a flat grooved rim.

Fig. 11.51. Stratum 2. Krater (Pls. 11.73:14; 11.103:3).

Cooking Pots

Cooking pots are very common in Stratum 2. They comprise mostly four types that are typical of the end of the Iron Age in Judah and are augmented by a few

Edomite cooking pots, as well as by numerous Negebite examples (for which see Chapter 12).

Type CP1 (Pl. 11.74:1). These are globular cooking pots with a molded ridged rim; the neck is not pronounced. Cooking pots of this type were first attested in Stratum 4 (CP1.1), and then they became popular in Substrata 3a-b (CP1.2) (see discussions in those strata). In Stratum 2, only a few examples were encountered, of which some belong to Subtype CP1.2 (Pls. 11.99:1; 11.120:8). Others belong to a third subtype, CP1.3 (Pl. 11.74:1), characterized by relatively thin walls.

Cooking pots of similar shape but different fabric have been classified as Edomite, both at Kadesh Barnea (below, Type ECP 1) and at 'Aro'er, Strata II and I (Biran and Cohen 1981: Fig. 16:2).

Type CP2 (Fig. 11.52; Pl. 11.74:2). These are the rounded cooking pots with a short upright neck and a thin molded rim, present in all Iron Age strata at Kadesh Barnea (see discussion above, Stratum 4).

Fig. 11.52. Stratum 2. Cooking pot Type CP2 (L6113).

Type CP7 (Fig. 11.53; Pl. 11.74:3–5). Cooking pots of this type are wide, rounded and usually squat, with no neck and with an everted rim grooved at its top. This is a very common Judahite type, dated exclusively to the late seventh/early sixth centuries BCE, and it thus constitutes an important chronological peg. These cooking pots typify such contexts as 'En Gedi, Stratum V (Mazar, Dothan and Dunayevsky 1966: Fig. 18:1–8), Lachish, Stratum II (Y. Aharoni 1975: Pls. 47:19, 20; 49:4; 50:12), 'Arad, Strata VII and VI (Herzog 1984: Figs. 25:8; 29:5), Ramat Raḥel, Stratum Va (Y. Aharoni 1964: Fig. 18:7–12), Meṣad Ḥashavyahu (Naveh 1962: Fig. 5:1–3) and 'Aro'er, Stratum II (Biran and Cohen 1981: Figs. 6:2; 16:1).

Fig. 11.53. Stratum 2. Cooking pot Type CP7 (Pls. 11.74:3; 11.94:9).

Type CP8 (Fig. 11.54; Pl. 11.74:6–8). A closed globular cooking pot with a tall, slightly everted neck and a ridge at mid-neck. The vessels are relatively thin and well fired. The handles are usually strap-like, but some have a rounded section. These cooking pots appear at Kadesh Barnea in Stratum 2 only, and are fairly common. They are a Judahite type, to be found in all sites in Judah in the seventh and early sixth centuries BCE, having developed from the closed cooking pots with a high neck and multiple ridges; however, only two rim fragments of this latter type were encountered. Parallels occur, for example, at 'En Gedi, Stratum V (Mazar, Dothan and Dunayevsky 1966: Fig. 17:1–5); Lachish, Stratum II (Y. Aharoni 1975: Fig. 47:21), 'Arad, Stratum VI (Herzog 1984: Fig. 29:6) and Ramat Raḥel, Stratum V (Y. Aharoni 1962: Fig. 11:22).

Fig. 11.54. Stratum 2. Cooking pot Type CP8 (Pls. 11:74:6; 11.87:5).

Type CP9 (Fig. 11.55; Pl. 11.74:9, 10). These thin-walled, squat cooking pots have a high neck, usually slightly everted. The rim, on the other hand, is slightly inverted with a protruding ridge below it. Very often the rim is grooved externally. The reddish clay usually contains many small quartz grits.

These cooking pots are not common in Judah. They are typical to the coastal plain, but are also attested in the Shephelah, and also occasionally in the Negev (cf., for example, at Meṣad Ḥashavyahu (Naveh 1962: Fig. 5:4), Lachish, Stratum Ib (Tufnell 1953: Pl. 51:13), Tel Baṭash, Stratum II (Mazar and Panitz-Cohen 2001: Pl. 43:3, 5–7), Tel Miqne-'Eqron, Stratum Ib (Gitin 1989: Fig. 2.13:13) and Tel Masos (in an Iron II context in Area G; Fritz and Kempinski 1983: Pl. 165:10–12).

Fig. 11.55. Stratum 2. Cooking pot Type CP9 (Pls. 11.74:10; 11.103:8).

Juglets and Small Bottles/Amphoriskoi

Stratum 2 produced a wide variety of juglets, among which the most common are the rounded juglets (JT3). The dipper juglets (JT1) are less common here, as opposed to Judah, where dipper juglets seem to dominate. In the ceramic assemblages within the casemates, juglets comprise the second largest group, outnumbered only by jars.

Type JT1 (Fig. 11.56; Pl. 11.75:1). These are the oval dipper juglets, widening slightly toward the base, with a slightly everted neck/rim. Some of the juglets were vertically burnished. In Stratum 2, such juglets are not numerous, and mostly fragmentary examples were found. Similar juglets occur at Kadesh Barnea from

 the beginning of the Iron Age sequence (see above, Stratum 4). In Stratum 2, some of these juglets are thin walled and elongated, features that are typical of these vessels in the late Iron Age.

Fig. 11.56. Stratum 2. Juglet Type JT1 (Pls. 11.75:1; 11.82:12).

Type JT2 (Fig. 11.57; Pl. 11.75:2). The so-called 'Black Juglets' are uncommon in the Negev at the end of the Iron Age. In Stratum 2, there were three complete specimens, all small and rounded at the base, with a short everted rim, a handle extending from the rim, and vertical burnish.

Fig. 11.57. Stratum 2. Juglet Type JT2 (Pl. 11.99:14).

JT3 (Fig. 11.58; Pl. 11.75:3–5). These are the commonest juglets in Stratum 2, having a wide variety of sub-shapes. Most are rounded, with a rounded base that occasionally has a protruding point. The neck is tall and narrow, sometimes wider in its lower part and then tapering. The handle extends from the rim to the shoulder. A few juglets bear traces of burnishing. These juglets begin to appear in the eighth century BCE and continue to the end of the Iron Age. Similar vessels are known, for example, from Be'er Sheva', Strata III and II (Y. Aharoni 1973: Pls. 56:2, 4, 11; 62:120–122; 66:14–18), 'En Gedi, Stratum V (Mazar, Dothan and Dunayevsky 1966: Fig. 9:1–3; 19:1–7), Tel Batash, Stratum II (Kelm and Mazar 1985: Fig. 17:7), Lachish, Stratum II (Y. Aharoni 1975: Fig. 47:28) and Tel Masos (in Iron Age II; Fritz and Kempinski 1983: Pl. 165:19, 20).

Fig. 11.58. Stratum 2. Juglet Type JT3 (Pl. 11.95:4).

Type JT4 (Pl. 11.75:6, 7). This type designation amalgamates a wide variety of juglets, but with the following common characteristics: They are rounded or pear-shaped with a flat or disc base, in which they are akin to jugs. The neck is tall, occasionally slightly everted, and the rim is simple. The handle extends from the rim to the shoulder. Some of those vessels have red slip and burnish (e.g., pear-shaped No. 7).

Type JT5 (Pl. 11.75:8). This type is similar to JT4, but the handle is drawn from below the neck to the shoulder (the rim is missing). No Iron Age parallels for this shape could be found. Such handles are characteristic of perfume juglets of the Persian period.

Type JT6 (Fig. 11.59; Pl. 11.75:9). This type represents a rounded bottle with no handles. The neck is short and the rim is folded outward and has a triangular section. Rounded bottles, apparently imitating Assyrian shapes, are typical of the end of the Iron Age, and (with some variations) continue into the Persian period (Stern 1982: Bottle Types E and F; Figs. 199, 200). The balloon-

Fig. 11.59. Stratum 2. Juglet Type JT6 (Pls. 11:75:9; 11.91:10).

shaped bottles from Tel Batash, Stratum II (Mazar and Panitz-Cohen 2001:Pl. 37:8–11; 69:1–3; 75:1) and Tel Miqne-'Eqron, Stratum Ib (Gitin 1989: Fig. 2.13:11) are most similar in body shape, but they have a ridge below the rim. Rims that are externally smooth are usually associated with 'carrot-shaped' bottles, for example at Tel Batash, Stratum II (Mazar and Panitz-Cohen 2001: Pl. 49:10), Sahab (Harding 1948: Fig. 4:31–33), and 'Amman (Harding 1945: Pls. XVII:22; XVIII:55, 56, 60).

Type JT7 (Fig. 11.60; Pl. 11.75:10). Two examples of elongated *alabastra* with two degenerated knob handles—one complete and one fragmentary—were found. The complete specimen is made of greenish clay and vertically burnished. Such shapes in clay are common from the end of the seventh century to the fifth century BCE, peaking in the sixth century, in Judah and Transjordan (Stern 1982:127, Type B, Fig. 196).

Fig. 11.60. Stratum 2. Alabastron Type JT7 (Pls. 11:75:10; 11.95:13).

Other Juglets

Green-Glazed Juglet (Pl. 11.75:11). Based on a similar (unpublished) late Iron Age juglet uncovered at Hazeva, this vessel apparently had one handle. This unusual juglet was crudely manufactured of green-gray clay and coated with a greenish glaze. The rim is missing. Glazed vessels are known in the Assyrian world but no meaningful parallels for this juglet could be found. Stratum 2 produced body sherds of at least one additional juglet with similar glaze.

Black-on-Red Amphoriskos (Fig. 11.61; Pl. 11.75:12). The body is rounded, the base flat, and the tall neck terminates in an everted rim. A protruding ridge is located on the lower half of the neck, and two small handles extend from it to the connection point of the

Fig. 11.61. Stratum 2. Cypro-Phoenician amphoriskos (Pls. 11.75:12; 11.90:10).

neck and shoulders. The vessel is made of brown clay with some white inclusions. The body and the upper part of the neck are red slipped and discontinuously horizontally burnished. The body is decorated with concentric circles in black, on the upper neck there are three red bands, in addition to one black band between the shoulder and neck.

Black-on-Red amphoriskoi (and similar vessels of related wares), also equipped with two small handles, are known from Judah and Transjordan in the eighth–seventh centuries BCE (however, they have a longer neck and a pear-shaped body, and the decoration consists of black bands only). Examples are known, for example, at Saḥab (Harding 1948: Fig. 7:64, 65, 68, 69), Be'er Sheva', Stratum II (Y. Aharoni 1973:62:110); 'Arad, Stratum VIII (Herzog 1984: Fig. 22:16) and Tell Beit Mirsim, Stratum A (Albright 1932: Pl. 66:17–20). For an undecorated amphoriskos of this type, see Pl. Pl.11.117:12.

Greek Lekythos. Locus 608 produced a fragment of a *lekythos* (Pl. 11.112:8), which must be considered a Stratum 1 intrusion.

Jugs and a Large Bottle

Stratum 2 produced only a very limited number of jugs, though in contemporaneous contexts in Judah these are always very common vessels. In addition, the burnished jugs with the tall wide neck with a protruding ridge and a pinched rim, common in Judahite sites of the late Iron Age, are completely absent here (for these jugs in Judah, see, e.g., 'Aro'er, Stratum II [Biran and Cohen 1981: Fig. 5:4], 'En Gedi, Stratum V [Mazar, Dothan and Dunayevsky 1966: Fig. 9:11] and Lachish, Stratum II [Y. Aharoni 1975: Pls. 47:23; 50:13]).

Type J10 (Pl. 11.75:13). This small, narrow jug has a disc base and a narrow ridged neck. The handle

extends from the ridge to the shoulder. Only one, near-complete jug clearly belongs to this type. In general shape this jug is reminiscent of the small decanters typical of Judah in the late Iron Age, for example, at Lachish, Stratum II (Zimhoni 1997: Fig. 5.35), but it is less carinated.

Type J11 (Fig. 11.62; Pl. 11.75:14). The so-called decanters, most typical of the late Iron Age in Judah, were represented in Stratum 2 (only) by very few examples. They are wide, have a pronounced carination between the body and shoulder, and a ring base. There is a small ridge at mid-neck, the rim is thickened and everted and the handle extends from the ridge to the shoulder. For parallels cf. decanters at Lachish, Stratum II (Zimhoni 1990: Fig. 33:4), Meṣad Ḥashavyahu (Naveh 1962: Fig. 5:14–17), 'En Gedi, Stratum V (Mazar, Dothan and Dunayevsky 1966: Fig. 20:1–5) and Tel Masos (Iron II; Fritz and Kempinski 1983: Pl. 165:15, 16). One small decanter (Pl. 11.87:16) bears red- and black-painted bands.

Fig. 11.62. Stratum 2. Jug Type J11 (Pls. 11.75:14; 11.87:15).

Type J12 (Pl. 11.75:15–18). This type includes various jugs with rounded shoulders and a short, rather wide neck. There are many variations to the rims, but usually there are one or two ridges below them. The handles extend from the rim to the shoulder, sometimes close to the pinched rim. All the examples are fragmentary and thus the following *comparanda* are based on the upper parts of the vessels only. They occur in the late Iron Age, for example at 'Aro'er, Stratum II (Biran and Cohen 1981: Fig. 6:4), but also earlier, e.g., at Be'er Sheva', Stratum II (Y. Aharoni 1973: Pls. 64:11, 68:13) and Lachish, Stratum III (Y. Aharoni 1975: Pl. 44:15). Jug No. 18 is unusual in that the neck is very wide and the joint between the body and neck is not pronounced.

Elongated Bottle (Fig. 11.63; Pl. 11.75:19). This well-fired, elongated bottle ends in a narrow rounded base (rather than with the more common pointed base, such as at Tel Baṭash, Stratum II (Mazar and Panitz-Cohen 2001: Pls. 37:12, 49:8, 9) and in the Meqabelein tomb (Harding 1950: Pl. 16:2, 5). The neck is tall, wide and S-shaped, topped by a slightly everted rim. The joint between the shoulder and the neck is emphasized.

Such bottles are apparently imitations of Assyrian vessels. A similar bottle, also from Stratum 2, is made of coarse reddish material and is discussed below with the Red Sandy Ware (see Fig. 11.80; Pl. 11.80:9).

Fig. 11.63. Stratum 2. Elongated bottle Type J14 (Pls. 11.75:19; 11.122:5).

Flasks

There are only a few flasks in Stratum 2, a situation similar to that in the Negev sites at the end of the Iron Age.

Grooved Lentoid Flasks (Fig. 11.64; Pl. 11.76:1, 2). These small lentoid flasks have a short wide neck, on which a ridge or two are situated below the rim; small handles extend from ridge to body. Both sides of the flasks bear a series of incised concentric circles. No meaningful parallels for this type can be cited.

Fig. 11.64. Stratum 2. Grooved lentoid flask (Pls. 11.76:2; 11.105:7).

Funnel-Necked Flask (Pl. 11.76:3). This large, probably asymmetric flask has a high funnel-shaped neck, a simple rim and two large handles extending from below it to the body. There are no traces of decoration. There are no late Iron Age parallels for this flask in the Negev, but in the eighth century BCE a similar flask is known from Be'er Sheva', Stratum II (Aharoni 1973: Pl. 63:129).

Basket-Handled Flask (Fig. 11.65; Pl. 11.76:4). This is an unusual small, lentoid flask (the neck is missing), with two basket handles. No parallels are known.

Fig. 11.65. Stratum 2. Basket-handled flask (Pls. 11.76:4; 11.83:4).

Large Delicate Flask (Pl. 11.76:5). The large and relatively wide flask has very thin walls; it is manufactured of red clay and regularly wheel burnished. In Judah, this clay and surface treatment are typical of vessels such as bowls and decanters at the end of the Iron Age; a similar flask was found at Vered Yeriḥo (unpublished).

Jars

Type SJ6 (Fig. 11.66; Pl. 11.77:1). These jars are very similar to Type SJ1 with the short upright rim and narrow body (see above, discussion in Stratum 4), except that Type SJ6 jars have wider and more rounded shoulders, and their bases are narrow and pointed. Rims of these two types cannot be differentiated. For parallels, cf., for example, Lachish, Stratum II (Zimhoni 1997: Group IIc; Fig. 5.24).

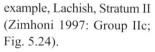

Fig. 11.66. Stratum 2. Jar Type SJ6 (Pls. 11.77:1; 11.93:8).

Type SJ7 (Pl. 11.77:2). This is a sack-like jar with a wide rounded lower part and base, and a tall wide neck with an outward-thickened rim. There is a slight 'waist' below the handles. The clay is well fired. Only one such complete vessel was encountered in Stratum 2, alongside a few fragments.

This jar type is typical of the end of the Iron Age in Judah, for example at 'Arad, Strata VII and VI (Herzog 1984: Figs. 25:15; 29:11), 'En Gedi, Stratum V (Mazar, Dothan and Dunayevsky 1966: Fig. 22:3, 4), 'Aro'er, Stratum II (Biran and Cohen 1981: Fig. 5:1) and Tel Masos (Iron Age II; Fritz and Kempinski 1983: Pl. 166:14).

Type SJ8 (Figs. 11.67, 11.68; Pl. 11.77:3–6). This is the commonest jar type in Stratum 2 (as mentioned above, a few fragments of such jars already occur in Substrata 3b-a). The jars are 50–60 cm high, very wide at mid-body, with very pronounced shoulders and a carination between the shoulders and body. Two protruding handles extend from the carination point to the body. There is no real neck, and at the join between the rim and the shoulder there is occasionally a depression in the shoulder. There are many variations to the rim shape, but most of the rims are thickened in their lower, inner part, where they connect to the shoulder. Many of these jars have a potter's mark on the shoulder or on the handles (see below).

Two subtypes were defined, dictated by the shape of the base (Zimhoni (1997:211–262): SJ8a with a rounded base and SJ8b with a narrow and truncated base (based on rims alone these two types cannot be differentiated). The Kadesh Barnea jars of Subtypes SJ8a and SJ8b most resemble, respectively, Zimhoni's Groups IID and IIE, of Stratum II at Lachish (Zimhoni 1997: Figs. 5.26, 5.28, 5.29:1–5).

Fig. 11.67. Stratum 2.
Jar Type SJ8a
(Pls. 11.77:4; 11.88:2).

Fig. 11.68. Stratum 2.
Jar Type SJ8b
(Pls. 11.77:6; 11.88:3).

Type SJ9 (Figs. 11.69, 11.70; Pls. 11.77:7, 8, 11.119:1). Type SJ9 is a general category, comprising all commercial Phoenician jars. The jar in Pl. 11.77:7 has a sharp carination between the shoulder and rim,

a slightly 'waisted' body and a low, folded-out rim. Stratum 2 produced one nearly complete jar and eight additional rim and shoulder fragments. Such jars are, naturally, especially common along the Phoenician coast, starting in the late eighth century BCE (for Tyre see, for example, Bikai 1978: Pl. III:8, from Stratum II). There are, however, also some examples from the Shephelah, in eighth- and seventh-century contexts, for example at Tel Miqne-'Eqron, Stratum Ib (Gitin 1989: Fig. 2.12:4), as well as from the northwestern Negev, as in Be'er Sheva', Stratum II (Aharoni 1973: Pl. 57:7). Similar jars, but with dfferent rim shape are known from Tel Baṭash, Stratum II (Mazar and Panitz-Cohen 2001: Pls. 36:2; 47:4).

Fig. 11.69. Stratum 2. Jar Type SJ9 (Pl. 11.119:1).

The jar in Fig. 11.70, Pl. 11.77:8, is a small triangular and pointed jar with a very sharp carination between the shoulder and neck and an obliquely cut rim. Only one such example was found. Outside Phoenicia these jars are attested, for example, at Ashdod, Stratum VII (Dothan and Porath 1982: Fig. 22:2) and Tel Baṭash, Stratum II (Mazar and Panitz-Cohen 2001: Pls. 36:1: 47:1–3).

Fig. 11.70. Stratum 2.
Jar Type SJ9
(Pls. 11.77:8; 11.105:6).

Jar/Jug (Fig. 11.71; Pl. 11.77:9). This unique jar/jug has a wide cylindrical body, a small ring base, and a high and wide neck. The rim is missing but it is clear that there was a ridge below it. There are three vertical handles; one extends from the rim to the shoulder and the other two extend from the shoulder to the wall of

*Fig. 11.71. Stratum 2.
Jar Type SJ10
(Pls. 11.77.9; 11.96:3).*

the vessel. A similar vessel was found at Tel Baṭash in Stratum II (Kelm and Mazar 1985: Fig. 7:4).

Type SJ11 (Pl. 11.78:1). This category comprises small holemouth jars. They were very common in Stratum 2 but no complete example was unearthed. Still, it is clear that they had rounded shoulders. The thick rounded rims are folded out over the wall of the vessel. The jars are made of reddish-brown or light brown clay and the surface is white-brown or greenish. There are no clear parallels in the Negev, other than a surface find at Qiṭmit (Beit-Arieh 1995: Fig. 4.14:42, 45).

Type SJ12 (Fig. 11.72; Pl. 11.78:2–7). These are holemouth jars/kraters with an elongated folded rim and multiple handles, of Judahite type. As mainly rims were found, it is difficult to reconstruct the complete shape and to determine whether the base was rounded or a ring base. Subtypes were defined based on rim shape and the location of the handles.

Subtype SJ12.1 (Pl. 11.78:2) is apparently a very large vessel with a flat folded rim and handles extending from it. Below the rim is a bar handle. No clear parallels were found.

Subtype SJ12.2 (Pl. 11.78:3) is characterized by a ridged rim and multiple handles extending from the rim to the shoulder. There are horizontal grooves on the shoulders. Parallels are known, for example, at Qiṭmit (Beit-Arieh 1995: Fig. 4.6:39).

Subtype SJ12.3 (Pl. 11.78:4) is similar to SJ12.2, but the handles are located on the shoulder. Here, too, the shoulders are horizontally grooved. A complete jar of this type, with a rounded base, was unearthed at 'Aro'er, Stratum II (Biran and Cohen 1981: Fig. 6:5), and cf. also a jar at Qiṭmit (Beit-Arieh 1995: Fig. 4.6:36).

Subtype SJ12.4 (Pl. 11.78:5–7) jars have smooth folded-over rims, either protruding outwards or hammer-shaped, and four or more handles extending from below the rim to the shoulder. Parallels are known from 'En Gedi, Stratum V (Mazar, Dothan and Dunayevsky 1966: Fig. 9:15) and Qiṭmit (Beit-Arieh 1995: Fig. 4.3:16). Jar/krater No. 5, with the small ring base, is the only complete such vessel unearthed at Kadesh Barnea. The jar in Pl. 11.78:7 has a small knob protruding below the rim, paralleled on a jar with a different rim at Qiṭmit (Beit-Arieh 1995: Fig. 4.3:15). Though holemouth jars with inverted, smooth, flat folded rims are common in eighth-century contexts in Judah, for example at Be'er Sheva', Stratum II (Aharoni 1973: Pl. 65:1–4, 7), the Kadesh Barnea Stratum 2 examples are different, having a more protruding rim. They are more akin to the seventh/sixth century examples.

*Fig. 11.72. Stratum 2.
Jar Subtype SJ12.4
(Pls. 11.78:5; 11.90:11).*

Pithoi

Only a few pithoi were uncovered in Stratum 2— apparently jars were used for storage. Only two complete pithoi (Type P3) were unearthed, side by side in the middle tower on the west (Tower 516).

Type P3 (Fig. 11.73; Pls. 11.78:8; 11.100:17, 18). These are large, barrel-shaped pithoi with very thick walls, round shoulders, a wide flat base and four handles attached to the shoulder. The neck is short and upright, with a simple rim. No parallels to this shape are known. Both pithoi were very crudely made, and it is unclear whether they were fashioned on the wheel or not. They may, in fact, belong to the Negebite group. The base of one pithos was coated, externally, with a thick layer of hard plaster.

Type P4 (Pl. 11.78:9). Only fragments of this type, characterized by very thick walls, a very short neck,

Fig. 11.73. Stratum 2. Pithos Type P3 (Pl. 11.100:17).

and an externally thickened rim, were found. No parallels are known.

Stands(?)/Pithoi(?) (Pl. 11.78:10). Several rim fragments, which either belong to pithoi or alternatively to stands (see also Pls. 11.84:17, 11.117:4), were retrieved. The 'necks' are tall and flaring, with a grooved rim. Such fragments were already attested in Substrata 3a-b (see above).

Lamps

Of the 65 wheel-made lamps encountered in all Iron Age strata at the site, 35 were from Stratum 2; amongst these, two main shapes are attested. They are supplemented by lamps in Negebite ware, presented in Chapter 12. The two wheel-made types are typical of the late Iron Age in Judah.

Rounded Shallow Lamps with a Rounded or Flat Base (Pl. 11.78:11). In Stratum 2, 17 such lamps have a rounded base and five have a slightly thickened flat base (five others were missing their bases). The rims are usually wide and everted. For similar lamps, cf. 'En Gedi, Stratum V (Mazar, Dothan and Dunayevsky 1966: Fig. 23:1–4) and Meṣad Ḥashavyahu (Naveh 1962: Fig. 5:19, 20).

Lamps with a Thick Base (Pl. 11.78:12). Eight lamps in Stratum 2 have a high, thick and solid base and an everted rim. Such bases are diagnostic of the end of the Iron Age in Judah. Similar lamps were uncovered, for example, at 'Arad, Stratum VI (Herzog 1984: Pls. 25:14; 29:10), Meṣad Ḥashavyahu (Naveh 1962: Fig. 5:18, 21), 'Aroʿer, Stratum II (Biran and Cohen 1981: Fig. 5:5, 6) and Tel Masos (Fritz and Kempinski 1983: Pl. 166:16–19).

EDOMITE POTTERY

In all, some 45 Edomite sherds and fragmentary vessels, both decorated and undecorated, were uncovered at Kadesh Barnea. About four sherds originate in loci that were disturbed by Stratum 1, and the bulk, 41 examples, are from Stratum 2. We can thus safely assert that Edomite pottery is associated with this stratum only. About 30 fragments were found in the Stratum 2 casemates and within buildings in the courtyard of the fortress (those from 'clean' contexts are illustrated in Pls. 11.51:9; 11.52:15; 11.79:6, 9, 11; 11.80:3, 4; 11.85:7; 11.98:5, 19, 20; 11.110:6; 11.115:16; 11.119:13). The rest are from the fill of the moat in Area E (Pls. 11.79:3, 14; 11.125:21–24; 11.126:3, 7) or are unstratified (Pl. 11.79:8).

Similar Edomite pottery is known in Transjordan and in the Negev/Aravah Valley. Of the major Edomite sites, Tawilan (Bennett and Bienkowski 1995), and Buṣeirah (Bennett 1974; 1975) produced the main assemblages of decorated Edomite pottery, while at Umm el-Biyara, for example (Bennett 1966) there were no decorated wares in the late Iron Age. Thus, our acquaintance with the typology and chronology of this pottery is still incomplete. However, M. Oakeshott (1978) presented a large collection of pottery from several Edomite sites, classified into types based on method of production, decoration and shape.

In the Negev/Aravah, Edomite pottery is known from Tell el-Kheleifeh (Glueck 1967; Pratico 1993), Ḥaẓeva (unpublished), 'Aroʿer (Biran and Cohen 1981) and Qiṭmit (Beit-Arieh 1995); see also E. Mazar 1985.

The repertoire at Kadesh Barnea, however, includes a wider range of types. The typology constructed below is based on the types/classes of vessels and on their shape, rather than on technology of production or decoration.

Bowls

Type EB1 (Fig. 11.74; Pl. 11.79:1, 2). These are large, shallow, thick-walled bowls, with either a disc or a low ring base. The fabric is coarse, reddish or greenish. The bowls are decorated inside with black concentric circles, usually flanking red ones. At the top of the rim, which is turned down, there are indentations made with a sharp instrument, at regular intervals (the bowl in Pl. 11.79:1 apparently also had similar indentations, but the rim is very worn). Six examples were uncovered. This is Oakeshott's (1978) Type A1, of which examples are known at Buṣeirah (Bennett 1975: Fig. 6:13, 16), Tawilan (Bennett and Bienkowski 1995: Figs. 6.1; 6.2), Tell el-Kheleifeh (Glueck 1967:37; Fig. 5:6; Pratico 1993: Pl. 37:11), Qiṭmit (Beit-Arieh 1995: Fig. 4.1:4) and Aroʻer, Strata II–I (Biran and Cohen 1981: Fig. 14:8–10).

Fig. 11.74. Stratum 2. Edomite bowl Type EB1 (Pls. 11.79:1; 11.110:6).

Type EB2 (Pl. 11.79:3, 4). The small deep bowls with very thin walls are represented by three examples. The walls are either slightly concave or flaring and the rim is simple. The painted decoration is applied externally, featuring horizontal black bands bordering red ones and short vertical black strokes in the reserved bands in between. The bowl in Pl. 11.79:3 has additional black strokes below the horizontal bands, an unparalleled feature. The bowl in Pl. 11.79:4 may also have been red slipped inside.

There are no exact parallels to these bowls; in general shape they resemble bowls adorned with impressions in the shape of deer, known from Buṣeirah (Bennett 1975: Fig. 8:9, 10).

Type EB3 (Fig. 11.75; Pl. 11.79:5–7). These are open, delicate carinated bowls with a simple rim and apparently a rounded base. Two subtypes where defined: on Subtype EB3a (Pl. 11.79:5, 6) the carination is located at the middle of the vessel or in its lower part. Four examples of this subtype were recorded. The bowls are decorated similarly to Type EB2, but there are more reserved bands with short strokes, and on one or two examples, the upper inner part is also decorated. This is Oakeshott's 'Assyrian' beaker Type K3 (1978: Pl. 16:21–23, 27, 31). Similar bowls are known from Buṣeirah (Bennett 1975: Fig. 8:6), Tell el-Kheleifeh (Glueck 1967:35, Fig. 4:6–8) and Aroʻer, Strata II–I (Biran and Cohen 1981: Fig. 14:4).

Fig. 11.75. Stratum 2. Edomite bowl Type EB3 (Pl. 11.79:6).

Subtype EB3b bowls (Pl. 11.79:7) are characterized by a more accentuated carination, below the rim. Two

such examples were found. The decoration comprises mostly a number of horizontal black lines, occasionally also red. This is Oakeshott's Type J1 (1978: Pl. 15:7–10, 24–35), occurring at Buṣeirah (Bennett 1975: Fig. 5:9), Tawilan (Bennett and Bienkowski 1995: Fig. 6.8:1–5) and Qiṭmit (Beit-Arieh 1995: Fig. 4.11:7).

Type EB4 (Fig. 11.76; Pl. 11.79:8, 9). These rounded bowls have a simple, slightly inverted rim and slightly protruding ridges under them, to which knob handles are attached. Two such bowls were recorded. Bowl No. 8 is decorated with the same pattern as Types EB2 and EB3. Bowl No. 9 is unadorned.

There are no exact parallels to these bowls, but Buṣeirah yielded a decorated bowl of similar shape with a bar handle forming a ridge of sorts (Bennett 1974: Fig. 15:12), equaling Oakshott's Type J2a (1978: Fig. 15:14).

Fig. 11.76. Unstratified. Edomite bowl Type EB4 (Pl. 11.79:8).

Type EB5 (Pl. 11.79:10, 11). These bowls are similar to Type EB4, but the rim above the ridge is either upright (No. 10) or slightly flaring (No. 11). Plate 11.79:10 has small bar handles under the carination. Externally, these bowls are decorated with the pattern that is typical of Types EB2–4.

A bowl that is similar in shape to No. 11 was found at Ghrareh in Edom (Hart 1988:95, No. 4) and a bar handle is attested on an open bowl from Buṣeirah (Bennett 1975: Fig. 6:1).

Kraters

Type EK1 (Fig. 11:77; Pl. 11.79:12, 13). These large spherical kraters have a short upright rim (the bases are missing). Two such fragmentary vessels, as well as small fragments of another, were found. On the lower part there is an applied plastic band of clay. It was cut with a sharp instrument to form a series of protruding triangular indentations at regular intervals. The upper part of the vessel, above this band, is painted. There is a central, wide horizontal decorative zone, divided into metopes containing net patterns and hourglass motifs. This band, in turn, is flanked by patterns identical to those adorning bowls of Types EB2–5, with the addition of bands of alternating red and black triangles.

These kraters are known at other sites. 'Aro'er, Strata II–I produced an upper part of a krater, similar in shape and decoration (Biran and Cohen 1981: Fig. 14:1). At Tell el-Kheleifeh there is an undecorated upper part of a krater, with a band of indentations on its shoulder (Pratico 1993: Pl. 37:7). At Qiṭmit, small fragments with indentations on them also seem to belong to this type (Beit-Arieh 1995: Figs. 4.10:13; 4.12:32–35). Plastic bands with indentations are common on Edomite open bowls and incense burners at Ḥazeva (unpublished)

and Tell el-Kheleifeh (Glueck 1967:37; Fig. 5:1–5; Pratico 1993: Pl. 37:7).

Fig. 11.77. Stratum 2. Edomite krater Type EK1 (Pls. 11.79:12; 11.126:3).

Type EK2 (Pl. 11.79:14). A single sherd was found of a possibly plain krater (only its upper part survives), with a short upright neck and a thickened rim. On the rounded shoulder, below the joint of the neck and body, a band with indentations is attached, similar to those on Type EK1 kraters, but the apexes of the indentations point up.

Cooking Pots

Type ECP1 (Pl. 11.80:1, 2). These are rounded, deep cooking pots with no neck, and with a ridged rim, in direct continuation of the walls. Two handles extend from the rim to the sloping shoulders. The vessel resembles in shape the cooking pots of Subtype CP1.2 that are most common in Stratum 3, but even more so, Subtype CP1.3 with thin walls, attested in Stratum 2. There is, however, a significant difference in fabric. The fabric of the Edomite cooking pots comprises many sandy inclusions that create a very rough surface, and their walls are thinner. Stratum 2 produced five such sherds and another eight might belong to this type.

In Edom in the late Iron Age this type comprises the most common cooking pot, for example at Buṣeirah (Bennett 1975: Fig. 5:7, 14) and Tawilan (Bennett and Bienkowski 1995: Figs. 6.33:1, 3; 6.35:1–3, 5), also

occurring at Tell el-Kheleifeh (Pratico 1985:24; Fig. 14:1–3), and in the Negev, as at Qiṭmit (Beit-Arieh 1995: Figs. 4.5:21; 4.6:22–25; 4.9:33–34; 4.11:25).

Jars

Type ESJ1 (Pl. 11.80:3, 4). These jars are of well-fired clay with a greenish surface, and adorned on the shoulder with horizontal incisions flanking a row of thumb-impressed depressions. Only three such sherds were encountered and it is unclear what form the complete shapes might have taken. No parallels for these fragments are known from Jordan; it is possible that these are in fact Assyrian-influenced rather than actual Edomite ware. In the Aravah Valley and in the Negev such jars have been found at sites that also produced Edomite pottery, such as at Tell el-Kheleifeh (Glueck 1967:19; Fig. 5:5, 1969:4, Fig. 1:3, 4, 6), 'Aro'er (Biran and Cohen 1981: Fig. 16:6) and Qiṭmit (Beit-Arieh 1995: Fig. 4.17:41).

Stand

Type ES1 (Pl. 11.80:5). A fragmentary stand with thick walls was manufactured of coarse clay with a greenish surface, similar to the fabric of Type EB1 bowls. It is decorated externally with horizontal black lines bordering red-painted bands, a decoration that also recalls that on Type EB1 bowls. Parallels are known from Buṣeirah (Oakeshott 1978: Pl. 23:3) and 'Aro'er, Strata II–I (Biran and Cohen 1981: Fig. 11:14).

'RED SANDY WARE'

This is a well-defined group of wheel-made vessels, characterized by common fabric, technology and surface treatment. They are manufactured of red sandy-gritty fabric with a gray core and were fired at a low temperature. The surface of the vessels has a self slip, some of which took on a greenish hue after firing. Petrographic analysis conducted by Y. Goren (pers. comm.) indicates that the source of the clay was the Judean Shephelah.

The group comprises two bowls (Fig. 11.78; Pl. 11.80:6, 7), one cooking pot (Fig. 11.79; Pl. 11.80:8;

Fig. 11.78. Stratum 2. 'Red Sandy Ware' bowl (Pls. 11.80:7; 11.81:3).

Fig. 11.79. Stratum 2. 'Red Sandy Ware' cooking pot (Pls. 11.80:8; 11.81:13).

Fig. 11.80. Stratum 2. 'Red Sandy Ware' bottle (Pls. 11.80:9; 11.82:15).

Fig. 11.81. Stratum 2. 'Red Sandy Ware' jar.

similar in shape to Type CP7), one bottle (Fig. 11.80; Pl. 11.11.80:9; resembling the elongated bottle in Pl. 11.75:19), and mainly numerous jars of identical shape (Fig. 11.81; Pl. 11.80:10). The rims of most of these vessels are diagonally cut.

The hallmark of this ware—the jars—are relatively narrow vessels, sack-shaped and about 50 cm high. There are numerous rim variants, but as a rule the rims are everted and there are no necks. Bases are narrow and rounded and two handles are attached at carination point.

Six of the jars, alongside the open bowl, the cooking pot and the bottle were unearthed in one assemblage in Casemate 186 (Pls. 11.81:3, 13; 11.82:15, 17, 18, 19; 11.83:1, 2, 3; alongside other vessels).

No parallels to this group are known, but the body and rim shapes of the jars, and the sandy clay are reminiscent of some handle-less storage jars in Judah (Zimhoni 1997:250–251, Figs. 5.31:1–4; 5.33:1).

NEGEBITE WARE

Like its predecessors, Stratum 2 also produced Negebite ware, but here it constitutes a very low percentage of the ceramic assemblage, a conspicuous phenomenon in contrast to the underlying Stratum 3. The Negebite vessels are presented according to their contexts in Pls. 11.81– 11.128 and are discussed in Chapter 12.

BLACK-PAINTED WARE

Two (different) bowls of this ware were retrieved from L402 (Pl. 11.86:17, 18). They should probably be considered as re-depositions from Stratum 3, where this ware was well attested.

STRATUM 2 CERAMIC ASSEMBLAGES
(Pls. 11.81–11.128)

Plates 11.81–11.101 present the ceramic assemblages from the casemates. Pottery from floor deposits in the courtyard is illustrated in Pls. 11.102–11.121, following the order of the stratigraphical discussion (Area B, Area C, Area A1). For each assemblage, the illustrated material includes all the complete and near-complete vessels and a complete typological representation of the fragments.

In addition to these, we chose to present the pottery found on the floor of Cistern 1514 in Area D (Pl. 11.122), which represents its last period of use, and a sample of the material from the fill in the cistern (Pls. 11.123, 11.124), in order to indicate when the cistern started to fill up.

Plates 11.125 and 11.126 include a typologically representative assemblage of the material uncovered in the moat in Area E, and Pls. 11.127, 11.128 present a typological selection of the material embedded in the Stratum 2 glacis in Areas E, F, and G.

The Casemates, Area A2 (Pls. 11.81–11.101)

All the casemate assemblages that were preserved to a certain degree have been illustrated. The casemates that produced rich ceramic assemblages are 186 on the east (Pls. 11.81–11.83), 402 on the north (Pls. 11.86–11.89) and 553 on the west (Pls. 11.94–11.96). In addition to assemblages from individual casemates,

Pls. 11.97–11.101 present pottery retrieved from the poorly preserved casemates and towers.

Some casemates are characterized by a large percentage of containers (Casemates 186, 553, 491; Pl. 11.93). The numerous jars and juglets indicate that they were used for storage, but these were also accompanied by relatively numerous cooking pots. In other casemates, such as Casemate 39 (Pls. 11.84, 11.85) and Casemate 459 (Pls. 11.90–11.92), a wide variety of vessels, comprising mainly small vessels, was encountered.

In certain casemates, the distribution of certain *types* of vessels is of interest. For example, in Casemate 402 on the north, six complete jars of Type SJ8 were uncovered alongside cooking pots of Type CP8 (respectively Pls. 11.88:1–6; 11.87:5–7). Nine other complete jars of the same type were retrieved from Alleys 486 and 746 in Area B, which are adjacent to this casemate, and were accompanied by Type CP9 cooking pots (respectively, Pls. 11.105:1–5; 11.107:1–4; 11.103:7, 8). On the other hand, in Casemates 186 on the east, and 553 on the west, some nine near-complete 'Sandy Ware' jars were found, alongside about 14 spherical juglets of Type JT3 and at least ten complete cooking pots of Type CP7 (Pls. 11.81:11–14; 11.82:4–10, 17–19; 11.83:1–3; 11.94:7–12; 11.95:1–4, 10–12, 18; 11.96:1, 2).

No doubt, these differences indicate functional variability; *inter alia*, different casemates (and types of jars) must have been used to store different commodities.

The Structures in the Courtyard in Areas B, C, A1
(Pls. 11.102–11.121)

Only floor deposits that contained relatively substantial assemblages have been illustrated here. Other than those parts of Alleys 486 and 746 that were adjacent to the casemates, the floors of the structures did not produce extensive assemblages of complete vessels, probably due to erosion in this area. Occasionally, Persian-period pottery that must belong to Stratum 1 is included in these assemblages, testifying to undetected intrusions.

The Floor and the Fill of Cistern 1514 in Area D
(Pls. 11.122–11.24)

Locus 1514 (Pl. 11.122) produced vessels that were embedded in the thin clay layer that covered the plaster floor of the cistern. These represent the last use of the cistern and are datable to the late seventh/early sixth centuries BCE. The Type J11 decanter, the elongated bottle and the Type SJ7 jar (Pl. 11.122:4, 5, 6) are very typical of Judah at the end of the Iron Age. They indicate that the cistern was in use until a certain stage within Stratum 2.

Above that floor were fill layers of earth and numerous stones that produced large amounts of pottery, of which a representative typological selection is presented (Pls. 11.123, 11.124). Examination of the entire body of this assemblage revealed that throughout the fill there was an admixture of (scant) pottery typical of Substrata 3a-b (e.g., Pls. 11.123:10; 11.124:1), as well as large amounts of ceramics typical of Stratum 2 (e.g., Pls. 11.123:12, 13; 11.124:3, 5) and of Stratum 1 (e.g., Pls. 11.123:9, 17, 18; 11.124:13–15; for Stratum 1 pottery, see below). Other types cannot be attributed unequivocally to either stratum (for example Pl. 11.123:7, 8).

It thus appears that the cistern went out of use with the destruction of the Stratum 2 fortress. The uppermost layer of the fill, which constituted fine-grained silt from the period of abandonment, also included a few potsherds attributable to the Roman/Byzantine period (Pl. 11.124:10, 17).

The Fill of the Moat (Pls. 11.125, 11.126)

The moat was dug as part of the Stratum 3 fortification system and there are no stratigraphical grounds to assess when it went out of use. The attribution of the fill in it to Stratum 2 is typological.

Plates 11.125 and 11.126 present the pottery originating from the best context of the lower part of the fill in the moat. It produced abundant wheel-made pottery typical of the eighth–seventh centuries BCE (e.g., Type B10 bowls, Pl. 11.125:9–16), but lacks types characteristic of the final stage of the Iron Age (late seventh/early sixth centuries BCE), such as Types CP7 and CP8 and the high-footed lamps, but this could be accidental. Decorated Edomite pottery is fairly well represented here (Pls. 11.125:21–24; 11.126:3), as well as carinated bowls influenced by Neo-Assyrian types, datable to the seventh century BCE (Type B19; Pl. 11.125:17–20). Chronologically, then, this material can only be associated with Stratum 2.

The fact that all the different fills in the moat produced abundant pottery that is typical of Stratum 2 corroborates our impression that the moat continued to be used during Stratum 2, most probably as a dump.

Only after the destruction and abandonment of the Stratum 2 fortress did the moat fill up completely with debris and stones. The latest pottery in that fill was of the Persian period.

The Makeup of the Glacis (Pls. 11.127, 11.128)

Stratigraphically, all that can be stated regarding the glacis is that it is constructionally later than the Stratum 2 fortress wall. As, however, it is inconceivable that it was constructed in Stratum 1, Stratum 2 is its only possible attribution. The material presented in Pls. 11.127 and 11.128 originates in a few selected loci that produced abundant pottery.

Most of the pottery is wheel made, comprising chiefly eighth–seventh-century types, but there is also abundant Negebite ware, mainly bowls and kraters.

Some of the wheel-made vessels are of types that were common in Stratum 3 only, such as Types B11 and SJ3 (Pls. 11.127:15; 11.128:2), and many are of types that were common to both Strata 3 and 2, for example bowls of Type B4 and B10 (Pl. 11.127:7–10, 12). The latest types are those found in Stratum 2 only, such as the holemouth jars of Types SJ12.3 and SJ12.4 (Pl. 11.127:18, 20) and the jars of Type SJ11 (Pl. 11.128:5).

However, many ceramic types that are typical of the *end* of Stratum 2 and of the end of the Judahite Iron Age are missing here. These are, for example, the carinated bowls of Type B19, cooking pots of Types CP7 and CP8, juglets of Type JT3, decanters of Type J11, jars of Type SJ8 and lamps with a high base. It thus seems that the glacis was constructed during the life span of Stratum 2, probably at its beginning. Naturally, it consisted mostly of earlier debris and artifacts. No material that is necessarily later than Stratum 2 was uncovered in any of the loci within the glacis.

SUMMARY AND CHRONOLOGY

The ceramic assemblage of Stratum 2 is very different in nature from the assemblages of Strata 4 and 3 and is characterized mainly by a very high percentage of wheel-made pottery in relation to the Negebite ware, as opposed to the earlier strata. In addition, there is evidence of a much stronger association with Judah. The latter phenomenon allows us to establish a fairly secure chronological framework for this stratum.

The 'Judahite connection' is not only exemplified by the dominance of these wares in general, but also by the *variety* of Judahite types represented in the assemblage (mainly Types B8, B9, B10, B15, K5, CP7, CP8, JT1, JT3, J10, J11, SJ7, SJ10). Some types, though, are represented by single vessels only.

In addition to the association with Judah, the pottery also attests to links with other regions and ceramic traditions, mainly those of the coastal plain (Types CP9 and SJ9) and Transjordan (Type B13 and Edomite Ware); Neo-Assyrian impact is embodied by Types B19, JT6, JT7, the glazed juglet and the elongated bottle. In the late Iron Age this variety of traditions is also attested in southern parts of Judah, such as the Be'er Sheva' Valley. However, at Kadesh Barnea, both Assyrian/Tranjordanian impact on one hand, and Philistine/coastal on the other are much more prominent. This repertoire is augmented by the Negebite pottery and the 'Red Sandy Ware', rendering the ceramic blend of Stratum 2 at Kadesh Barnea unique.

The occasional Persian-period pottery uncovered in Stratum 2 contexts (regarding which see further below) is clearly intrusive, mostly due to undetected pits.

Pinpointing the beginning of Stratum 2 is not easy, mainly because dating the end of the previous stratum is difficult, and also because there is some architectural and ceramic continuity between the two strata.

In contrast, the abundant ceramic assemblages relating to the destruction of Stratum 2 can safely be dated to a late seventh–early sixth-century BCE range, roughly contemporary with the end of such occupations as Lachish (Stratum II), Tel Baṭash (Stratum III), 'Arad (Strata VII–VI), 'Aro'er (Strata II–I), Ramat Raḥel (Stratum VA) and 'En Gedi (Stratum V). The uniqueness of the Stratum 2 ceramic composition does not allow a resolution beyond that and a more exact date will have to rely on historical considerations.

POTTERY OF STRATUM 1
LOCI 426, 705, 706 IN AREA B
(Pls. 11.129, 11.130)

As explained in Chapter 1, Stratum 1, stratigraphically, is an amalgamation of all the elements encountered above the ruins of the Stratum 2 fortress, mainly segments of floors and pits. The pottery of Stratum 1 is generally datable to the Persian period (see below), but in a few contexts in Area B that postdate the Stratum 2 destruction (Loci 426, 705, 706), the ceramic vista, albeit scant, seemed to be closely related to the late Iron Age, and no clear Persian-period material was associated with them. It could be claimed that the absence of Persian-period material is accidental and that the Iron Age fragments are re-deposited, but it cannot be ruled out that these assemblages are in fact earlier than the bulk of Stratum 1.

The bowl in Pl. 11.129:1 is an Edomite bowl of Type EB1. Most of the other bowl shapes are of Subtype B10.1 with a folded rim (Pls. 11.129:6–11, 11.130:4), which were very typical of Stratum 2. The cooking pots (Pl. 11.129:16–18) are of clear Iron Age types. Plate 11.129:17 in particular is very similar to the coastal cooking pot (Type CP9), well attested in Stratum 2. The cooking-pot fragment in Pl. 11.130:5, with a molded rim and no neck, is an Edomite cooking pot of Type ECP1. The holemouth jar/pithos rim in Pl. 11.129:22, with an inverted rim and a protruding ridge separating the rim and the body, is typical of the end of the Iron Age (cf. at 'En Gedi, Stratum V—Mazar, Dothan and Dunayevsky 1966: Fig. 21:8; but no such examples were found in loci securely attributed to Stratum 2).

It has been suggested by Morderchai Haiman, the supervisor of Area B, that these few contexts may represent a distinct chronological phase, datable to the Babylonian period. From the ceramic point of view this suggestion can neither be corroborated nor refuted, as pottery of the Babylonian period in this region (similarly to the situation in Judah) is very poorly known.

POTTERY OF STRATUM 1
THE REST OF THE ASSEMBLAGE
(Figs. 11.82–11.92; Pls. 11.131–11.134)

Stratum 1 contexts, mainly the pits, produced chiefly Persian-period pottery, but there were hardly any 'clean' assemblages and thus this pottery is presented typologically and not by context. In addition, in order to augment the 'assemblage' we also present in these plates Persian-period pottery found in earlier strata (where it is clearly intrusive). Such pottery was especially abundant in the fill of the cistern in Area D, which comprised debris that had been washed in after the cistern ceased to function, and also, though much less so, in the very upper part of the fill of the moat in Area E. There was, however, not enough Persian-period pottery to construct a meaningful typology.

Bowls

Mortaria (Fig. 11.82; Pl. 11.131:1, 2). The ring-based *mortaria* are one of the clearest chronological markers of the Persian period (see Stern 1982:98; Fig. 121, Type B5b). At Kadesh Barnea, two complete examples, as well as bases of additional vessels, were found. When only rims are preserved it is difficult to attribute them either to such vessels or to flat-based *mortaria*, which are known from both the late Iron Age and the Persian period. Persian-period *mortaria* were also recovered during Dothan's early excavations at the site (Dothan 1965: Fig. 7:5, 6), and in the Negev they are known from Ḥorbat Rogem, Ḥorbat Mesura, Ḥorbat Ha-Ro'a, Be'erotayim (Cohen and Cohen-Amin 2004: Figs. 101:2, 4, 6; 106:3–5; 109:4–8; 118:1, 2), and Ḥorbat Ritma (Meshel 1977: Fig. 8:12, 13).

Fig. 11.82. Stratum 1. Mortarium (Pl. 11.131:1).

Rounded Bowls (Pl. 11.131:3–5). The open bowl in Pl. 11.131:3 has a simple rim and an external groove below it. Wheel marks are very conspicuous on its exterior and the base is a disc base. The bowl in Pl. 11.131:4 is closed, with thin walls and a simple rim. A slight groove below the rim emphasizes the tip. Persian-period parallels may be cited from Qadum (Stern and Magen 1982: Fig. 2:1) and Tell Jemmeh (Petrie 1928: Pl. L:22e). The thick bowl in Pl. 11.131:5 has a folded thickened rim and external ridges that are reminiscent of those on the Persian-period *mortaria*.

Kraters

The kraters in Pl. 11.131:6, 7 are characterized by a tall wide neck, almost as wide as the vessel itself, but clearly differentiated from the narrow shoulders. The tip of the rim is thickened and out-turned and the handles extend from it to the top of the shoulders. Such kraters are known from Dothan's excavations at Kadesh Barnea (Dothan 1965: Fig. 7:8). They are common throughout the Persian period (Stern 1982:99, Fig. 124; Type 2a; also Stern 1978: Fig. 5:7, from Tel Mevorakh; Stern and Magen 1982: Fig. 3:1–3, from Qadum; and Stern et al. 1995: Fig. 2.3:1, from Dor).

Cooking Pots

All the Persian-period cooking pots at Kadesh Barnea (Fig. 11.83; Pl 11.131:8–12) belong to a single type. They are large and 'swollen' and the base is nearly flat. The tall neck tends to flare and the tip of the rim is everted and is triangular in section. This is Stern's Type B (1982:100; Figs. 129, 130), which he dates mainly to the fifth–fourth centuries BCE. In the Negev, such a cooking pot is known from Ḥorbat Ha-Roʻa (Cohen and Cohen-Amin 2004: Fig. 110:1).

Fig. 11.83. Stratum 1.
Cooking pot (Pl. 11.131:12).

Juglets, Jugs and a Flask

Only a few juglet fragments were encountered in Stratum 1, which is anomalous, as in most Persian-period assemblages these are common shapes (and thus comprise a good chronological indicator). Dipper juglets are altogether missing.

The juglets in Pl. 11.131:13, 14 have folded-out rims, and a handle extends from below the rim to the shoulder, a feature typical of perfume juglets (Stern 1982:121, Fig. 186; Type C3).

In its morphology, the jug in Fig. 11.84, Pl. 11.131:15 resembles the perfume juglets of Stern's Type C5a, but it is larger (see Stern 1982:122, Fig. 188 and a similar vessel from Shiqmona, Elgavish 1968: Pl. XXXII:7).

The large lentoid flask (Fig. 11.85; Pl. 11.131:16) has a short, swollen neck and a folded rim. Two handles extend from the wider part of the neck to the shoulder. Thin burnishing marks in concentric circles are evident on either side, cf. Stern's Type A (1982:114, Fig. 166). On the upper part of the flask there is an incision, added after firing.

Fig. 11.84. Substratum 3c.
Jug (Pl. 11.131:15).

Fig. 11.85. Stratum 1.
Flask (Pl. 11.131:16).

Flasks of this type are known in the sixth–fourth centuries BCE, for example at Tel Michal (Singer-Avitz 1989: Fig. 9.13:16), ʻEn Gedi (Mazar, Dothan and Dunayevsky 1963: Fig. 32:1), Sheikh Zuweid in Sinai (Petrie and Ellis 1937: Pl. XXXVIII:85p) and Ḥorbat Rogem in the Negev (Cohen And Cohen-Amin 2004: Fig. 103:1, 2 one of which bears a similar incision).

Attic *Lekythoi*

Four fragmentary cylindrical Attic *lekythoi* (Figs. 11.86, 11.87; Pl. 11.132:1–4) were unearthed. The near-complete No. 1 is decorated in red over a white slip, the decoration consisting of an ivy stem flanked by geometric motifs. *Lekythos* No. 2 is adorned with a similar design in black, also over a white slip. The small fragment, No. 3, is a red-slipped shoulder fragment and retains a pattern of black tongues. The area immediately below the shoulder was undecorated. *Lekythos* No. 4 is decorated with black and red bands. Two other fragments of a *lekythos*, whose bottom part seems similar to that of our No. 2, were uncovered by Dothan (1965: Fig. 7:16, 17).

These so-called Pattern *Lekythoi* date to the fifth century BCE, most probably to its second or third quarter.[2] They are our only means of assigning a somewhat more narrow chronological range to Stratum 1.

Fig. 11.86. Stratum 1.
Attic lekythos
(Pl. 11.132:1).

Fig. 11.87. Stratum 2.
Attic lekythos
(Pl. 11.132:2).

Jars and Amphorae

The fragments in Pl. 11.132:5–7 are either jar or jug rims. They are characterized by thin rims folded outward and downward (for thin ledge-like rims of sack-shaped jugs, see Stern 1982:116–117, Figs. 169, 172).

Cylindrical Jars (Fig. 11.88; Pl. 11.132:8–10). These are narrow elongated jars with narrow, slanting shoulders. The rims preserved on Nos. 8 and 10 are thickened and everted. Below the shoulder are one or two handles. These so-called 'torpedo' jars are mainly known in the coastal area, but also occur in other regions. They are, however not common. This is Stern's Type G (Stern 1982:105–107, Fig. 146), dated to the sixth–fourth centuries BCE (see additional examples at Tel Mevorakh, Stern 1978: Fig. 7:5–11; Dor, Stern 1995: Fig. 2.23:12; and Qadum, Stern and Magen 1982: Fig. 5:3). In the Negev, such jars were encountered at Ḥorbat Rogem, Ḥorbat Mesura and Ḥorbat Ha-Roʻa (Cohen and Cohen-Amin 2004: Figs. 102:5; 106:9; 112:1–4).

Fig. 11.88. Stratum 1. 'Torpedo' jar (Pl. 11.132:8).

Straight-Shouldered Jars (Fig. 11.89; Pl. 11.133:1–4). These jars, with the twisted handle, evolve from the straight-shouldered jars of the late Iron Age. In the sixth–fourth centuries BCE such jars were common mainly at sites on the coast (see Stern 1982: 107–110, Figs. 148–155, Type H). Among the Negev sites, one such jar was found at Ḥorbat Rogem (Cohen and Cohen-Amin 2004: Fig. 102:2). The base in Pl.11.133:8 probably belongs to a jar of this type.

Fig. 11.89. Stratum 1. Straight-shouldered jar (Pl. 11.133:1).

Basket-Handled Jars (Fig. 11.90; Pl. 11.133:5–7). These jars are very typical of the Persian period and are known mainly from coastal sites (Stern 1982:110–111, Figs. 156–158; Type I). No complete vessels were found in Stratum 1; based on rim fragments only, it is difficult to differentiate subtypes within this general category. It seems, however, that Pl. 11.133:5 (Fig. 11.90), which has somewhat wide shoulders and high handles, is a relatively late type, datable to the fifth–fourth centuries BCE only (Stern 1982: Fig. 157; Type I 2). The bases in Pl. 11.133:9, 10 probably belong to jars of this sort. Basket-handled jars were also encountered in Dothan's excavations (1965: Fig. 7:12, 13, 14, 15).

Fig. 11.90. Stratum 1. Basket-handled jar (Pl. 11.133:5).

Amphorae (Figs. 11.91, 11.92; Pl. 11.134:1–13). At Kadesh Barnea, these so-called 'East Greek' amphorae, which generally start to appear in our region in considerable numbers in the sixth century BCE, are represented by quite a large variety of shapes, and two size categories. The small table amphorae (Pl. 11.134:1–6) have very rounded shoulders, a tall wide neck and a rim that is either folded out or thickened outward. The handles extend from high up the neck to the shoulders. The fragment in Pl.11.134:7 is the ring base of such an amphora.

The large amphorae (Pl. 11.134:8–13) are manufactured of well-levigated clay with few inclusions and are well fired. The neck in Pl. 11.134:10 is unusual in that the neck is slipped (red-brown) inside and the rim is a wide gutter rim. For another amphora in the Negev sites, see Cohen and Cohen-Amin 2004: Fig. 102:7, from Ḥorbat Rogem.

Fig. 11.91. Stratum 1. East Greek amphora (Pl. 11.134:1).   *Fig. 11.92. Stratum 1. East Greek amphora (Pl. 11.134:4).*

Jars with YHD Impressions. (Pl. 11.134:14, 15) These two fragments are the southernmost examples of *yhd* jars ever uncovered in the Levant (see discussion in Chapter 15).

Lamp

Only one Persian-period lamp (Pl. 11.134:16) has been clearly identified. It is relatively large and shallow, and the rim is wide and sharply everted, forming a ledge. The base is flat and scraped. For a discussion of these common lamps, see Stern 1982:127–129, Figs. 202, 203; he dates them to the sixth–fourth centuries BCE). Such lamps were also uncovered by Dothan (1965: Fig. 7:19). Among the Negev sites, such lamps are known, for example, from Ḥorbat Rogem and from Be'erotayim (Cohen and Cohen-Amin 2004: Figs. 103:5, 6; 117:10).

SUMMARY AND CHRONOLOGY

Most of the Persian-period ceramics found at Kadesh Barnea are similar to those known from regions further to the north, and most of the types are characteristic of the Mediterranean coastal area. This is also true regarding the contemporaneous pottery published by Dothan from his 1956 excavations (Dothan 1965). The Pattern *Lekythoi* indicate that the Stratum 1 occupation encompassed at least some period of time around the mid-fifth century BCE, but the entire chronological scope, within the sixth- to fourth-century range, is currently impossible to establish.

INCISIONS AND IMPRESSIONS ON WHEEL-MADE POTTERY

The following discussion presents the corpus of incisions and simple impressions on the wheel-made pottery of Kadesh Barnea (some more elaborate impressions are discussed in Chapter 14). About 193 of these 214 incisions and impressions originate in well-stratified contexts, of which 43% are of Substrata 3a-b and 24% of Stratum 2. Strata 4, Substratum 3c and Stratum 1 each produced less than 10%. Contrary to our impression at the beginning of this study, it turned out that most of the incisions (179) were made after firing and only 15 were incised prior to firing. To the latter one must add the 20 impressions, which were, of course, introduced before firing the vessels.

Distinguishing between incisions executed before and after firing was based on the following observations:

1. The best indication for pre-firing incisions are remains of small clay chunks that remained from the clay that was displaced when incising the vessel; they are visible along the margins of the incisions and inside them. This phenomenon, naturally, does not occur with incisions made after firing.

2. The quality of the incisions themselves is also indicative. Single strokes (albeit not necessarily straight) and precise junctions between strokes are typical of incisions made before firing. In contrast, in post-firing marks, lines were often created by more than one stroke, and traces of sawing back and forth are often visible. The strokes tend to be linear and the junctions between them are not precise.

3. Another criterion is the color of the surface of the incision in relation to that of the rest of the vessel's surface. Incisions that were of a different color were taken to be post-firing marks, while incisions whose color was identical were usually interpreted as introduced before firing.

4. Additional information is provided by the mineral inclusions in the clay. Incising a vessel before firing occasionally displaces the smaller inclusions in the incised portion, leaving their 'negatives' or, occasionally, delicate scratches. In incisions made after firing the non-plastic inclusions are sawn away with the clay.

PRE-FIRING

Incisions

Among these 15 incisions, only three were complete. Only one type of incision repeats itself (five times) and the rest are singular occurrences.

'Shin-Shaped' Incisions (Figs. 11.93–11.95; Pl. 11.135: 1–5). This common incised symbol resembles the Hebrew letter *shin*, with two diagonal strokes emanating laterally from its top to the left and right. The incision occurs twice in full, on two bowls, and on three other bowls the incisions are fragmentary. It appears on three types of bowls: the flat and shallow bowls of Type B9 (Pl. 11.135:1–3), the slightly carinated bowls of Subtype B4.3 (Pl. 11.135:4; this one also bears another,

Fig. 11.93. Incision before firing on a Type B9 bowl, Substrata 3a-b (Pls. 11.135:1; 11.65:2).

Fig. 11.94. Incision before firing on a Type B9 bowl, Substrata 3a-b, 2 (Pls. 11.135:2; 11.127:2).

Fig. 11.95. Incision before firing on a Subtype B4.3 bowl, Substrata 3a-b (Pls. 11.135:4; 11.67:14).

Fig. 11.96. Ankh incised before firing on a cooking pot, Stratum 2 (Pl. 11.135:6).

Fig. 11.97. Incision before firing on a jar, Stratum 1 (Pl. 11.135:9).

Fig. 11.98. Incision (inscription?) before firing on a jug, Stratum 1 (Pls. 11.135:13; 11.130:6).

Fig. 11.99. Punctured marks introduced before firing on a jar handle, Stratum 2 (Pl. 11:135:14).

post-firing incision), and the bowl with black-painted rims of Type B12 (Pl. 11.135:5). All these bowls originate in Area F, from Stratum 3–Stratum 2.

Interestingly, similar incisions were also added *after* firing to bowls of the same types, and to some jars (see Figs. 11.102–11.105; Pl. 11.137:1–18). No exact parallels to this type of incision are known to us.

The remainder of the pre-firing incisions were found on walls or shoulders of large and small closed vessels (jars or juglets; Pl. 11.135:6–13) and also on jar handles (Pl. 11.135:14–18). Most of them are incomplete. The following incisions are noteworthy:

The fragment in Fig. 11.96, Pl. 11.135:6 is a shoulder of a vessel produced of cooking-pot fabric, from Stratum 2. The incision on it is in the shape of an Egyptian *ankh*. An *ankh* accompanying an inscription in Hebrew and a hieratic numeral were incised on a jar from Tel Haror (Oren 1993: photograph on p. 583).

The incomplete incision on a closed vessel from Stratum 1 (Fig. 11:97, Pl. 11.135:9) differs from all the others in that it was made with a double-edged tool. The very fine incision on a jug (Fig. 11.98; Pl. 11.135:13), also from Stratum 1, may be part of a more elaborate decoration or even an inscription, but is too fragmentary to tell.

The (fragmentary) jar handle Fig. 11.99, Pl. 11.135:14 (Stratum 2) bears a punctured pattern. It was unclear if this particular piece belongs to a wheel-made or Negebite vessel.

A handle from Stratum 4, probably of a jar (Pl. 11.135:15), bears an incision comprising a vertical line and horizontal strokes, a pattern also known to have been introduced after firing (see below). It is combined with either an impression or an additional incision.

Impressions

Kadesh Barnea produced 20 simple impressions on handles of jars and cooking pots, which were divided as follows.

Elliptic Impressions (Fig. 11.100; Pls. 11.135:15–18). The four handles are of very crude fabric and it was impossible to determine if they belong to wheel-made pithoi or rather to Negebite vessels. The impressions

Fig. 11.100. Elliptic incision before firing, or impression on a jar or pithos handle, Stratum 3b (Pl. 11.135:17).

themselves were also unclear and they could in fact be incisions (but introduced before firing). All are elliptical in outline and probably were made with a multi-toothed tool; they differ only slightly from each other. They come from fill loci of Strata 4, 3 and 2, and all of them may have originated in Stratum 4. No parallels to them are known.

Reed Impressions (Pl. 11.136:1–4). The jar and pithoi handles with these impressions are all from Substrata 3a-b.

Round Impressions with Cross Shapes (Fig. 11:101; Pl. 11.136:5–8). These cooking-pot handles bear round impressions within which are protruding cross-shaped designs. The pot in Pl. 11.136:5 was retrieved from the fill of the granary and Nos. 6 and 7 from Stratum 2 floors, so we may assume these impressions date to the end of the Iron Age. The impression in Fig. 11.101, Pl. 11.136:8 found in Area E above a floor of Strata 3a-b, is unusual as it is diamond shaped and not rounded, and between the arms of the cross are small rounded protrusions.

For impressions with crosses and *ṭet*-symbols, see Type XIII in the City of David (Ariel and Shoham 2000:156–159; L101–L108). In Judah, mostly in the eighth century BCE, cross-shaped incisions (not impressions) were commonly added before firing to handles of cooking pots (usually of the globular, ridged-neck type), for example at Lachish, Stratum III (Zimhoni 1997: Fig. 5.6:4, 6), Tell Beit Mirsim, Stratum A (Albright 1932: Pl. 55:3, 6, 10), Be'er Sheva', Stratum II (Aharoni 1973: Pls. 61:96, 97; 66:13; 67:7, 11; 68:4; 71:14), 'Arad, Strata X–IX (Herzog 1984: Figs. 12:9; 18:6) and the City of David (Shoham 2000: IH A1–A163; Figs. 17, 18–20:1–12). At Kadesh Barnea, such incisions on cooking pots were not encountered, probably as cooking pots of that type (CP6) were not common in Stratum 3. There are, however, two such incisions made after firing (see below).

Fig. 11.101. Cross-shaped impression on a cooking-pot handle, Substrata 3a-b (Pls. 11.136:8; 11.64:19).

Finger Impressions (Pl. 11.136:9–16) survived on four cooking pots, a jug and three jars, of which cooking pot No. 12 comes from a Stratum 2 fill, the jar handle No. 14, from a Stratum 4 fill and the other items, from Substrata 3a-b. Finger impressions on clay vessels are not very common in Iron Age Judah, but cf. Be'er Sheva', Stratum II (Aharoni 1973: Pl.70:19) and at Tel 'Ira (Beit-Arieh 1999: Fig. 6.153:1) .

POST-FIRING

Incisions

Most of these incisions occur on jars (about 60%) and bowls (about 24%), but also on jugs (about 14%), kraters and cooking pots.

When considering bowls only, an equal number of incisions appear on the rims and on the walls. The case is different with jars, as most of the incisions are situated below the shoulder or on it (60%), and only half this number appear on the handles (30%); the rest are on rims.

The incisions that occurred more than once are divided below into twelve groups. The division was based mainly on the type/shape of the incision itself, and also on its location and on the type of vessel it was incised on. These groups include both complete designs and incomplete ones whose overall shape can be reconstructed with certainty. In addition to these 'groups' there are five complete singular incisions. About 15 more were incomplete, and their original form cannot be deduced.

'Shin-Shaped' Incisions (Figs. 11.102–11.105; Pl. 11.137:1–18). These vessels are incised with a symbol resembling a Hebrew *shin*, with two vertical or diagonal strokes emanating laterally left and right from its top (diagonal strokes may be drawn upward or downward).

Incisions of this type appear on bowls (on their walls, externally), on a jug handle and on shoulders of jars of indeterminable types. Many of the incisions attributed to this group are incomplete, and though their reconstruction as the symbol in question is very plausible, this cannot, of course, be established with certainty. The variations of this symbol differ mainly in the angles of the lateral strokes and are perhaps merely a result of the skills of the engravers. The

*Fig. 102. 'Shin-shaped'
incision after firing on a
Type B9 bowl, Strata 3a, 2
(Pls. 11.137:1; 11.102:1).*

*Fig. 11.103. 'Shin-shaped' incision
after firing on a Type B4 bowl,
Stratum 2 (Pls. 11.137:4; 11.113:3).*

*Fig. 11.104. 'Shin-shaped'
incision after firing
on a Type B13 bowl,
Substratum 3b
(Pls. 11.137:6; 11.58:12).*

*Fig. 11.105. 'Shin-shaped'
incision after firing on a
jug, Substratum 3a
(Pl. 11.137:7).*

Of the 18 fragments in this group, three are from Strata 4 and Substratum 3c (Nos. 3, 5 and 13), ten from Substrata 3a–b (Nos. 2, 6 – 9, 11, 12, 14, 16, 18), three from Stratum 2 (Nos. 4, 10, 17) and two are unstratified. There are no known parallels at other sites.

'Hourglass Designs' (Figs. 11.106, 11.107; Pl. 11.137:19–22). One bowl and three jars bear 'hourglass' designs (double triangles joined at their apexes), but they differ greatly in the quality, depth and accuracy of execution. Examples Nos. 19 and 22 are from the Stratum 2 glacis; Nos. 20 and 21 were found, respectively in a Substratum 3a installation and floor, the latter in Area G, below the glacis. Therefore it is difficult to determine whether they belong to Stratum 3 or 2, or to both.

Similar incised designs are known from eighth-century Judah on jars of Zimhoni's 'coastal' Type IIIE (1997:235–239), at Lachish, Stratum III (Tufnell 1953: Pl. 94:472) and Be'er Sheva', Stratum II (Aharoni

*Fig. 11.106. 'Hourglass'
incision after firing on a
bowl, Stratum 2
(Pl. 11.137:19).*

*Fig. 11.107. 'Hourglass'
incision after firing on a jar,
Stratum 2 (Pl. 11.137:22).*

incision on the rim of Pl. 11.137:5 is different from the rest. It comprises four instead of three 'vertical' strokes and the bottom 'horizontal' stroke is missing. The location of this incision is also unusual as is the fact that it was engraved over a painted design.

Exactly the same symbol, but incised before firing (and with all examples having their diagonal side strokes pointing downward), is attested on some bowls (see Fig. 11.93; Pl. 11.135:1–5). Interestingly, as was the case with the latter, the bowls to which these symbols were added after firing belong to types that are most common in Substrata 3a–b: B9 (Pl. 11.137:1, 2), B4.3 (Pl. 11.137:4) and B12 (Pl. 11.137:5). In addition it appears on a Type B13 cup/bowl with a handle (Pl. 11.137:6), on a jug (Pl. 11.137:7; the only example on a handle) and on jars of morphologically undetermined types (Pl. 11.137:8–18), though by their clay and the high quality of firing, most probably are jars of Type SJ8, typical of Stratum 2.

1973: Pl. 57:3), and on a pithoi at Tel 'Ira, Stratum VII (Kletter 1999: Fig. 6.153:2, 11).

Stars (Figs. 11.108–11.110; Pl. 11.138:1–8). Eight vessels were incised with this design. The Type B9 bowl in Fig. 11.108, Pl. 11.138:1 is unique as it has two incisions: a seven-pointed star on the inner wall and a nine-pointed star outside. It is also the only occurrence of a star in Substrata 3a–b. The fragment in Pl. 11.138:2 apparently also belongs to a bowl, found in the fill of the moat, which contained pottery of Strata 2 and 1. It is incised, like the rest of the examples, with a five-pointed star. The incisions in Figs. 11.109, 1.110, Pl. 11.138:3–8 are very similar in their (relatively shallow) execution and all of them were incised on shoulders of Type SJ8 jars made of reddish clay, whose surfaces are worn. These incisions should probably be attributed to Stratum 2.

In the late Iron Age, star-shaped incisions on jars and pithoi are known, for example, from Tell el-Umeiri in Jordan (London 1991:394; Fig. 21.10:10), Tel 'Ira, Stratum VII (Kletter 1999: Fig. 6.153:4, 16), Tell Beit Mirsim (Albright 1932:88, Fig. 15:1), Tel Haror (Oren and Morrison 1986: Fig. 19:2; on a Type SJ8 jar) and further to the north at Tell Keisan (Briend and Humber 1980: Pl. 93:54).

Fig. 11.108. Star incised after firing on a Type B9 bowl, Substratum 3b (Pls. 11.138:1; 11.41:5).

Fig. 11.109. Star incised after firing on a Type SJ8 jar; Strata 3, 2 (Pls. 11.138:7; 11.57:6).

Fig. 11.110. Star incised after firing on a Type SJ8 jar(?), Stratum 2 (Pl. 11.138:8).

Vertical 'Arrow'-Shaped Incisions Pointing Up (Pl. 11.138:9–12) appear on jar handles and, as a rule, are deep and wide. The example in Pl. 11.138:9 is from a Substrata 3a-b fill; Nos. 10 and 12 are from the Substratum 3c constructional fill; and No. 11 is unstratified. For a possible parallel, cf. Be'er Sheva', Stratum VII (Herzog 1984: Fig. 25:15).

Vertical 'Arrow'-Shaped Incisions Pointing Down (Pl. 11.138:13, 14). These are similar to the previous category. They appear on a handle from Substrata 3a-b and on one of either Stratum 3 or 2. In these cases it is difficult to determine whether the handles belong to jugs or jars. For a possible parallel, see above, the incision from Be'er Sheva', Stratum VII.

Trident-Shaped Incisions (Pl. 11.139:1–9) appear on bowl rims, handles and shoulders of jars. The two fragments in Pl. 11.139:1, 2, found together in the Substratum 3c fill but not joining, may belong to a single Type B12 bowl. The bowl in Pl.11.139:3, from Substratum 3b, is very similar and may also be of Type B12 (or B4.3). The incisions on them are very clear, and appear alongside black-painted strokes. (Type B12 bowls also bear other types of incisions, see below.)

The incision in Pl.11.139:4 is the only one of its kind on a jar handle, from the fill of the glacis (Stratum 2).

The incisions in Pl. 11.139:5–9 are probably the same as those described above, but they are incomplete. The 'tridents' in these cases are engraved below the carination point of jar shoulders, pointing upward in Nos. 5 and 6 (both from Substrata 3a-b floors) and downward in Nos. 7–9 (of which No. 8 is from the same Substratum 3b locus as No. 6, and Nos. 7 and 9 are from fills above floors in Stratum 2 casemates).

Parallel Strokes (Fig. 11.111; Pls. 11.139:10–16; 11.140; 11.141:1–11). The most common incisions consist predominantly of series of three or four parallel strokes They are grouped below according to the type of vessel on which they appear, and on their locations. Of the 30 incisions of this group, 19 were incised on rims of bowls (7), jars (10), a krater and a cooking pot. Other than these there are seven examples of strokes on shoulders of jars and four examples on handles of bowls and jugs.

Fig. 11.111. Three parallel strokes incised after firing on a Type B13 bowl handle, Substrata 3a-b (Pls. 11.141:11; 11.67:18).

The bowls in Pl. 11.139:10–16 are mostly Types B4 and B12 bowls, four of them from Stratum 2, and two from Substrata 3a-b (outside the walls of the fortress). Bowl No. 13, on the other hand, is of Subtype B10.1, from a Stratum 1 pit. Most of the incisions on them are clear. On Nos. 14–16 there is in fact only one incised line and thus they may not belong to the 'group' (but originally there may have been more incised strokes).

Plate 11.140:1 is one of the few cases of an incision on the rim of a krater, from Substrata 3a-b. The incised strokes do not extend over the entire width of the rim. The example in Pl. 11.140:2 (Substratum 3c) is a unique case where a ridged cooking pot rim was incised, externally; the pot is of a type that is uncommon at Kadesh Barnea. The vessel in Pl. 11.140:3 is a holemouth jar/krater (SJ12.2), from a Stratum 2 casemate. The jar in Plate 11.140:4 is of a type rarely encountered at Kadesh Barnea (and originates from a mixed locus). The eight jar rims in Pl. 11.140:5–12 were found in contexts ranging from Substratum 3c to Stratum 1.

Plate 11.141:1–7 are jars/fragments of jar shoulders with series of vertically incised strokes, all wide and deep (Nos. 2 and 3 may belong to the same vessel, as may Nos. 4 and 5, but the pieces do not join). Rims were preserved on two examples: No. 1 is a Type SJ8 jar of Stratum 2 (this jar type was typical of Stratum 2, from which Nos. 4 and 5 also originate). Jar No. 2 (Substratum 3b) is of Subtype SJ3.1, typical of Substrata 3c and 3a-b (from which Nos. 3, 6 and 7 also originate).

Plate 11.141:8, 9 represent incisions comprising short parallel strokes across jar handles. The complete No. 8 is from a Stratum 2 casemate, and handle No. 9 is from the fill of the granary (and cf. the discussion of the incisions of Group E in the City of David (Shoham 2000:111–112; Fig. 24:2, 4–7). The handles in Fig. 11.111, Pl. 11.141:10, 11 (a jug and a Type B13 bowl) were incised with three parallel strokes; both are from Substrata 3a-b (for other incisions on B13 bowls see above and below).

Three Parallel Strokes Crossed by a Perpendicular Stroke (Figs. 11.112–11.115; Pl. 11.141:12–20). This design occurs on various vessels, and in various locations on them, from Substratum 3c to Stratum 2.

Fig. 11.112. Incision after firing on a jug handle, Substratum 3b (Pls. 11.141:13; 11.39:20).

Fig. 11.113. Incisions after firing on a krater handle, Substratum 3c (Pl. 11.141:14).

Fig. 11.114. Crossed strokes incised after firing on a Type B4 bowl rim, Substratum 3a (Pl. 11.141:15).

Fig. 11.115. Crossed strokes incised after firing on a jar, Substrata 3a-b (Pls. 11.141:18; 11.51:24).

Fig. 11.116. Hatch-shaped design incised after firing on a bowl, Stratum 3c (Pl. 11.142:2).

Fig. 11.117. Hatch-shaped design incised after firing on a jar, Substratum 3c (Pl. 11.142:5).

Fig. 11.118. Hatch-shaped design incised after firing on a krater, Substratum 3c (Pl. 11.142:21).

Hatch-Shaped and Other Similar Incisions (Figs. 11.116–11.118; Pl. 11.142). This quite varied group includes mainly designs composed of pairs of perpendicular short stokes (Pl. 142:1–12) and other similar, but somewhat more composite designs (Pl. 142:13–24). These incisions are attested in all Iron Age strata at Kadesh Barnea. In some cases the incision is clear and deep and in others it is shallow and sawing lines can be discerned.

Incisions of two pairs of perpendicular strokes appear on three bowls of three different types (Pl. 11.142:1–3), two of which are from Substrata 3a-b. Each appears at a different location on the vessel. The example in Pl. 11.142:1 is a rim of a Type B12 bowl (another bowl of this type, Pl. 11.142:13, bears a similar but more composite design). Bowl No. 3 is of Type B13. In two cases, such incisions appear on kraters (No. 14, on a rim of Type K1, Stratum 2; and No. 15, on the handle of Type K3, Substratum 3c).

Of the other incisions, 12 are on jars (Pl. 11.142:4–7, 9, 11, 12, 16, 19–21, 23), two on kraters (Pl. 11.142:14, 15), one is on a bowl (Pl. 11.142:13) and the rest (five) are on unidentified potsherds.

The two jars that retained their rims are of Type SJ8, and both are from Stratum 2. The jar in Pl. 11.142:4 is the only (albeit incomplete) example of an incision on the inner part of a jar rim. On No. 12 the incision is on the handle.

On the other jars the incisions are located on the shoulders or just below them. Some of them are shallow, and sawing marks are clearly visible (Pl. 11.142:5, 7, 9, 10). In contrast, the jar in Pl. 11.142:6, bears a deep and wide incision.

Cross-Shaped Symbols (Fig. 11.119; Pls. 11.143, 11.144, 11.145:1, 2) are generally among the commonest engravings on ceramics in the Iron Age. At Kadesh Barnea they appear on walls, handles and rims of bowls, cooking pots, jugs and jars in Stratum 4 (5), Substratum 3c (2), Substrata 3a-b (12), Stratum 2 (13) and Stratum 1 (1); others (4) are from unclear contexts. These incisions are grouped below according to the location of the incision and the type of vessel.

Fig. 11.119. Cross incised after firing on a jar handle, Stratum 2 (Pls. 11.144:14; 11.111:17).

In four cases (Pl. 11.143:1–4) such symbols were incised on rims of carinated bowls of Types B4 and B12 (No. 4 has an X-shaped incision rather than a cross). Bowl No. 3 has an additional incision down the wall, similarly to the bowls in Pl. 11.143:7–10, of Types B1, B8, B4 and B12. Of these eight bowls, six are from Substrata 3a-b, one is from Stratum 2, and one is from Strata 2–1. Only in two cases were cross designs engraved on rims of jars (Pl. 11.143:5, 6). The complete jar, No. 5, is of Type SJ8 (jars of this type also bear other incisions).

Many of the cross-shaped incisions appear on handles of various closed vessels: cooking pots (2), jugs (3) and storage jars (about 14). Cooking pot No. 11, an unusual form, is from Stratum 2, and No. 12 is from Substrata 3a-b (Pl. 11.143:11, 12). In eighth-century Judah, crosses engraved on cooking pots *prior* to firing are common, but incisions introduced after firing are less so. This is the case, e.g., at the City of David (see the many incisions of Group A, as opposed to those of Group D; in contrast, cross-shaped incisions there on jar handles where mostly made after firing [Group E]—see Shoham 2000).

Of the three to four jugs (Pl. 11.143:13–16), No. 13 is a complete cooking jug from a Stratum 4 casemate. No incisions on this type of vessel are known elsewhere.

Fourteen cross-shaped incisions are on handles of storage jars/pithoi (Pl. 11.144:1–14). They are attested in all strata. Of these, only three retained their rims, allowing for a more accurate identification of the vessels. Example No. 10 is probably a pithos (found in Stratum 1 debris), No. 11 is a store jar of Type SJ12, from Stratum 2; and No. 12 is of Type SJ1, from Stratum 4.

Five cross-shaped incisions are on body fragments of jars (Pl. 11.144:15–19), three of them on the carinated shoulders. The three jars that had their rims preserved (Nos. 15, 16, 19) are of Type SJ8, two of which are from Stratum 2. Jar No. 16 bears on its other side a 'bow and arrow' incision (see below and Pl. 11.145:11).

In two cases (Pl. 11.145:1, 2; Substrata 4a and 3b), jar handles were incised with pairs of cross symbols.

Crosses with Two Crossbars Figs. 11.120, 11.121; (Pl. 11.145:3–7). These designs are present in all strata. On Nos. 5–7 the two parallel strokes are not of equal length. These incisions occur mostly on jar handles, of which No. 3 belongs to a Type SJ8 jar, from Stratum 2. Only No. 7 was incised on a handle of a juglet.

Fig. 11.120. Cross with two cross-bars incised after firing on a jar handle, Substratum 4a (Pl. 11:145:5).

Fig. 11.121. Cross with two cross-bars incised after firing on a jar handle, Stratum 1 (Pl. 11:145:6).

'Bow and Arrow' Incisions (Figs. 11.122–11.124; Pl. 11.145:8–11). Three jars of Type SJ8 from Stratum 2 and an additional unstratified jar fragment carry, on their shoulder below the carination point, a symbol comprising a semicircular or trapezoidal engraving,

Fig. 11.122. 'Bow and arrow' incised after firing on a Type SJ10b jar, Stratum 2 (Pls. 11:145:9; 11.107:4).

Fig. 11.123. 'Bow and arrow' incised after firing on a
Type SJ10a jar, Stratum 2 (Pls. 11:145:10; 11.107:3).

Fig. 11.124. 'Bow and arrow' incised after firing on a
Type SJ10 jar, Stratum 2 (Pls. 11:145:11; 11.107:4).

crossed by a vertical stroke. There is some variation
in this type of incision. Incisions in Pl. 11.45:8 and 9
are quite similar to each other, though on No. 8 the
semicircle is more symmetric: Nos. 10 and 11 are also
similar to each other (the 'bow' is trapezoidal rather
than rounded), but on No. 11 the vertical stroke is
shorter.

Two of these jars exhibit additional incisions: on
No. 9 there is an asterisk-shaped incision on the one
preserved handle and No. 11 has an X-shaped incision
on the shoulder of the vessel, on the opposite side (Pl.
11.144:16).

Gazelles (Pl. 11.145:12, 13). Two bowls from Substrata
3a-b, of Types B12 and B4, bear on their external sides
shallow incisions that seem to be schematic renderings
of gazelles. These are the only figurative designs among
the Kadesh Barnea incisions on wheel-made pottery
(for figurative designs on Negebite ware, see Chapter
12).

Various Incisions (Pl. 11.146). In addition to the
incisions presented above, which to various extents
seem to be recurring symbols, other incisions are
mostly singular occurrences.

On a handle of a jug with a pinched rim and a ridge
below the rim (Type J8; Pl. 11.146:1; Stratum 2) a
unique symbol appears, though possibly it should have
been classified with the more elaborate cross-shaped
symbols presented above.

On the jug handle in Pl. 11.146:2 (Substratum 3c)
there is a deep, clear incision (but still executed after
firing), which somewhat resembles the Hebrew letter
yod. A very similar incision appears on a rounded lamp
from Stratum 2 (Pl. 11.101:4), which is the only lamp
at Kadesh Barnea bearing an incision.

The incisions in Pl. 11.146:3–5 are incomplete,
but could perhaps be defined as a 'group'. They
survived on small body sherds of jars, from Strata 3
and 2. If the original form indeed comprised only two
consecutive triangles, the sign may be compared to the
South Arabian *mem* (Naveh 1982:43–51, Fig. 42), but
whether this letter is indeed what was meant here is
impossible to establish.

Various other symbols were incised on Type B8 and
B4.1 bowls, on a jug and on jars (Figs. 11.125, 11.126; Pl.
11.146:6–13), as well as on body sherds of vessels, the
exact types of which cannot be determined (Pl. 11.146:
14–23). Other than No. 9, all of them are incomplete.

Two incisions (Figs. 11.125, 11.126; Pl. 11.146:6,
7) are in the shape of a palm branch or herringbone
design. Of these, No. 6 is on a bowl from Stratum 1
and is very shallow and worn. That on No. 7, a
fragment of a jug or juglet from Substratum 3a, is
a similar, but upright design, accompanied by an
X-shaped incision.

Fig. 11.125. Palm motif   Fig. 11.126. Vegetal and
incised on a bowl,   x-shaped incisions on a jug,
Stratum 1 (Pl. 11:146:6).   Substratum 3a (Pl. 11:146:7).

Plate 11.146:8, from Stratum 2, is the only mark at
Kadesh Barnea excuted by chiseling, a technique that
was common in Judah in Iron II, for example at the
City of David, Strata 12–10 (Shoham 2000: Figs. 21,
22; mostly on handles of jars). The Kadesh Barnea
example is similarly on a jar, but below the shoulder.

NOTES

[1] This report was finalized in 1998. Studying the pottery was not easy, as a significant portion of the material is still unparalleled, both in the southern regions of Judah, and in Transjordan. Since then quite a few site reports and other studies have been published, regarding sites in Judah, Philistia and Transjordan, which are highly relevant for the Kadesh Barnea ceramic assemblage. However, we decided not to refer to these studies in order not to delay publication further. The only 'new' publication we could absolutely not ignore is the final report of the Iron Age Negev sites (Cohen and Cohen-Amin 2004).

[2] We thank Rebecca Martin for these comments.

CHAPTER 12

THE NEGEBITE WARE TYPOLOGY

HANNAH BERNICK-GREENBERG

INTRODUCTION

A very conspicuous group of handmade pottery, found alongside the wheel-made wares, was in use in the Negev during the Iron Age. It was first recognized by Woolley and Lawrence (1914–1915:67) at Kadesh Barnea and then 'rediscovered' in Nelson Glueck's excavations at Tell el-Kheleifeh (Glueck 1938:14). Later on, similar handmade vessels were uncovered at other sites in the Negev (Evenari et al. 1958:241; Aharoni et al. 1960:97–102), and were termed by Ruth Amiran (1969:300–301) 'Negebite-Edomite'. Subsequently, the term 'Negebite' became the common appellation for this ware.

To date, Kadesh Barnea is the only site where this ware appears in a stratified sequence, in more than one subperiod of the Iron Age. This, as well as the fact that quantities here by far surpass any other known site, renders Kadesh Barnea a key site for the study of this pottery.

The Negebite vessels are mostly of very basic shapes, which probably would have been produced by any inexperienced individual forming pots by hand. Only very few vessels exhibit a real effort invested in shape or decoration; some vessels echo in their morphology wheel-made forms (for example, three-legged strainers, spouted jars, bowls with bar handles and thin-walled cooking pots), which they seemingly 'imitate'.

At present, the production centers of the Negebite pottery of Kadesh Barnea are unknown. Preliminary results of petrographic analyses indicate that most of the vessels were produced from northern Negev clay, other than the thin-walled cooking pots, which apparently originate in central Transjordan.[1]

STRATIGRAPHICAL DISTRIBUTION, QUANTITIES AND METHOD OF PRESENTATION

The Negebite vessels are primarily prolific in Strata 4 and 3a-b, where they comprise, respectively, about 45% and 80% of the ceramic assemblages. They continue to appear in Stratum 2, but then they are much fewer (about 10%). These estimates are based on a count of all handmade vs. wheel-made items recorded (and drawn), comprising rims and other diagnostics.[2] This count was also the basis for the relative assessment of the distribution of the types defined in the Negebite assemblage (below).

In contrast to Kadesh Barnea, at other sites in the Negev, Negebite pottery is known only from Iron IIA contexts, which indeed provide parallels for the Kadesh Barnea types, but no other published site reveals a continuity of this ware into the eighth and seventh centuries BCE.

Being handmade, very coarse and evidencing very little care in forming and finishing, the Negebite vessels are extremely difficult to classify. Likewise, temporal changes within this group are very hard to trace. Indeed, at first glance, this seemed an impossible task; no two vessels were really similar. Still, a study of the entire body of Negebite vessels from the site revealed that the assemblage may be divided into general morphological groups, and further subdivided according to size. Similarly, occasionally, certain shapes could be demonstrated to have a more restricted time span.

The abundance of Negebite vessels is reflected in the pottery plates. The graphic presentation of the contexts (i.e., the Chapter 11 plates of assemblages; see Part 2) attempts to mirror their relative frequency.

The Negebite pottery is presented typologically in Pls. 12.1–12.24; within each type the illustrations are arranged stratigraphically (vessels from Substratum 3c are grouped with Stratum 4 and pottery from the fill of the granary is grouped into Substrata 3a-b). Most (though not all) of the pottery in these plates originates from secure contexts. Occasionally, in order to present as wide a typological vista as possible of this unique corpus, we also took into consideration vessels from dubious loci.

Specific fabric descriptions of the Negebite vessels are provided only for those illustrated in the plates of the assemblages, in Chapter 11 (see Part 2). This is supplemented by a general characterization of the technology and fabric in the current chapter, further below.

TYPOLOGY

In general, the Negebite assemblage comprises mainly open shapes. About 58% are bowls. Strata 4/3c and Substrata 3a-b each produced about 40% of the Negebite bowls, and Stratum 2, less then 9%. The next frequent category are cooking kraters (for this term, see below), comprising 22% of the Negebite specimens. Out of these, 49% are from Strata 4/3c, 36% from Substrata 3a-b and 8.7% from Stratum 2.

Containers/closed vessels and cooking pots are less common, probably due to difficulties in the production process, and the functions of such forms were filled mostly by wheel-made products. The thin-walled cooking pots (see below) are about 6% of the Negebite assemblage; juglets and jugs about 6.5%; and various other shapes, such as lamps, trays and goblets, 6.7%.

Bowls

Open vessels/bowls are the best attested group of vessels among this ware, and concomitantly are dividable into different type groups. The following three-fold division is based on size: tiny bowls (diam. 3–20 cm), small bowls (diam. 10–25 cm), and medium–large bowls (diam. 25–35 cm). Each group is further subdivided by morphology and other attributes such as handles and decoration.

Tiny Bowls
Type NB1 (Figs. 12.1–12.7; Pls. 12.1, 12.2). These are tiny bowls/cups, of indeterminate function. They are very different from each other and are subdivided according to size.

Subtype NB1.1 represents bowls with a diameter of 3–9 cm only. They are attested in Strata 4/3c (Fig. 12.1; Pl. 12.1:1–7), Substrata 3a-b (Pl. 12.1:8–14) and Stratum 2 (Fig. 12.2; Pl. 12.1:15–20).

Subtype NB1.2 represents slightly larger bowls, up to 12 cm in diameter, most of them having vertical walls and a flat base. They occur in Strata 4/3c (Fig. 12.3; Pl. 12.1:21–26) and in Substrata 3a-b (Pl. 12.1:27–32).

Bowls of Subtype NB1.3 are slightly rounded with a diameter up to 12 cm. They have knob/ledge handles

(and rarely a loop handle), which convert them into a cup of sorts. A few complete examples with one handle only indicate that this may have been the rule, but the possibility that some of them had two cannot be excluded. These bowls occur in Strata 4/3c (Fig. 12.4; Pl. 12.1:33–38), 3a-b (Fig. 12.5; Pls. 12.1:39–42, 12.2:1–4) and 2 (Pl. 12.2:5).

Subtype NB1.4 bowls are 10–13 cm in diameter. They usually have nearly upright walls and a rounded to flat base, and some are equipped with handles. In no case can the existence of more than one handle be demonstrated. These bowls were encountered in Strata 4/3c (Fig. 12.6; Pl. 12.2:6–11), 3a-b (Fig. 12.7; Pl. 12.2:12–16) and 2 (Pl. 12.2:17–19).

Fig. 12.1. Negebite bowl Type NB1.1, Substratum 3c (Pl. 12.1:3).

Fig. 12.2. Negebite bowl Type NB1.1, Stratum 2 (Pl. 12.1:20).

Fig. 12.3. Negebite bowl Type NB1.2, Substratum 4b (Pl. 12.1:22).

Fig. 12.4. Negebite bowl Type NB1.3, Substratum 4b (Pl. 12.1:35).

Fig. 12.5. Negebite bowl Type NB1.3, Substratum 3a (Pl. 12.2:2).

Fig. 12.6. Negebite bowl Type NB1.4, Substratum 4b (Pl. 12.2:10).

Fig. 12.7. Negebite bowl Type NB1.4, Substrata 3a-b (Pl. 12.2:13).

Type NB2 (Pl. 12.3). These small shallow bowls have a flat base and upright or flaring walls, further divided into subtypes according to size.

Subtype NB2.1 bowls are 8–9 cm in diameter. They occur in Strata 4/3c (Pl. 12.3:1–3), 3a-b (Pl. 12.3:4, 5) and 2 (Pl. 12.3:6, 7).

Subtype NB2.2 bowls, with slightly incurving or straight walls, are 12–15 cm in diameter. They appear in Strata 4/3c (Pl. 12.3:8–11), 3a-b (Pl. 12.3:12) and 2 (Pl. 12.3:13).

Subtype NB2.3 represents small and shallow, but wider bowls, with splayed walls and a diameter between 10 and 16 cm. They were found in Strata 4/3c (Pl. 12.3:14, 15), 3a-b (Pl. 12.3:16–19) and 2 (Pl. 12.3:20).

Type NB3 (Fig. 12.8; Pl. 12.4:1–10). These are small bowls of different shapes, but have in common rounded walls, a rounded or flat base, and a diameter of 8 to 19 cm. They are common in Strata 4/3c (Fig. 12.8; Pl. 12.4:1–4), 3a-b (Pl. 12.4:5–8) and 2 (Pl. 12.4:9, 10).

Fig. 12.8. Negebite bowl Type NB3, Substratum 4b (Pl. 12.4:2).

Type NB4 (Fig. 12.9; Pl. 12.4:11–13). These shallow bowls have rounded walls and a pierced base (the perforation is not always complete). The bowls resemble baking trays, but they are very small. Only a few such fragments were found, in Stratum 4 (Pl. 12.4:11, 12) and in mixed contexts (Pl. 12.4:13).

Fig. 12.9. Negebite bowl Type NB4, Substratum 4b (Pl. 12.4:12).

Type NB5 (Fig. 12.10; Pl. 12.4:14–16). These are small, nearly flat, plate-like bowls with a very slightly incurving rim. The base is either flat or a disc base. It is unclear if Pl. 12.4:14 has a raised base. Only three examples were encountered, all in Substrata 3a-b.

Fig. 12.10. Negebite bowl Type NB5, Substrata 3a-b (Pl. 12.4:16).

Type NB6 (Figs. 12.11–12.13; Pl. 12.4:17–23). This category includes small bowls whose common denominator is the treatment of the rim, either by finger impressions or incision. Otherwise they differ, in both shape and size.

Such bowls were found in Strata 4/3c (Figs. 12.11, 12.12; Pl. 12.4:17–20), 3a-b (Fig. 12.13; Pl. 12.4:21, 22) and 2 (Pl. 12.4:23).

Fig. 12.11. Negebite bowl Type NB6, Substratum 4a (Pl. 12.4:18).

Fig. 12.12. Negebite bowl Type NB6, Substratum 3c (Pl. 12.4:20).

Fig. 12.13. Negebite bowl Type NB6, Substratum 3a (Pl. 12.4:22).

Type NB7 (Pl. 12.4:24–26). These are small, cone-shaped bowls, 7.5–10.0 cm in diameter. As all of them had been broken at the base, it is possible that they are in fact parts of larger vessels. There are only three examples: the unadorned No. 24 from Stratum 4, and Nos. 25 and 26 in Substrata 3a-b (decorated with protrusions and knobs around the rim and body or on the rim only).

Type NB8 (Pl. 12.4:27–29). These small pierced bowls, 7–9 cm in diameter, are probably strainers, each of a different shape. The three examples are from Substrata 3a-b.

Type NB9 (Fig. 12.14; Pl. 12.4:30–33). These small deep and narrow tubular bowls or cups are 4–5 cm in diameter and 5–8 cm deep. All examples are very simple and undecorated. They were found in Strata 4/3c (Pl. 12.4:30, 31) and 3a-b (Pl. 12.4:32, 33).

Fig. 12.14. Negebite bowl Type NB9, Substratum 4a (Pl. 12.4:30).

Small Bowls

Type NB10 (Figs. 12.15, 12.16; Pl. 12.5:1–7). These are small deep bowls (most of them about 7 cm in diameter), decorated with protruding knobs around the rim. The shapes of the bowls vary. Those from Strata 4/3c (Fig. 12.15; Pl. 12.5:1–4) have a continuous series of knobs around the rim, while on the bowls from Substrata 3a-b (Fig. 12.16; Pl. 12.5:5–7), the knobs are spaced.

Fig. 12.15. Negebite bowl Type NB10, Stratum 4/3c (Pl. 12.5:2).

Fig. 12.16. Negebite bowl Type NB10, Substratum 3b (Pl. 12.5:7).

Type NB11 (Pl. 12.5:8–11; see Figs. 12.73–12.76). These small rounded bowls, 14 cm in diameter, have bar handles/protruding ridges under the rim. The handles are decorated with punctures, incised herringbone patterns, or a series of U-shaped impressions. Only a few examples were found, from all strata. For the incised decorations, see below.

Type NB12 (Fig. 12.17; Pl. 12.5:12–24). These are deep rounded bowls with a rounded base, 13–23 in diameter. Some of them have a knob handle. They occur in Strata 4/3c (Fig. 12.17; Pl. 12.5:12–16), 3a-b (Pl. 12.5:17–22) and 2 (Pl. 12.5:23, 24). For the sign engraved on the bowl depicted in Pl. 12.5:21, see below.

Fig. 12.17. Negebite bowl Type NB12, Stratum 4 (Pl. 12.5:12).

Medium and Large Bowls

Type NB13 (Pl. 12.6:1–5). These medium-sized deep bowls, 13–30 cm in diameter, have straight flaring walls. They are known from Stratum 4/3c (Pl. 12.6:1, 2) and Substrata 3a-b (Pl. 12.6:3–5).

Type NB14 (Pl. 12.6:6–8). These medium-sized bowls have an S-shaped profile. This is a very unusual shape in the Negebite repertoire; one example is known from Stratum 4 (Pl. 12.6:6) and two from Substrata 3a-b (Pl. 12.6:7, 8).

Type NB15 (Pls. 12.6:9–17, 12.25:1–7, 12.26:3, 4; see Figs. 12.57, 12.58, 12.61, 12.62, 12.64). These bowls differ in their morphology, their common characteristic being the technology of their manufacture. The lower parts of the bowls were cast in a mold and the upper part freely formed by hand (on some examples it was evident that they were coil made). This creates a distinct difference in wall thickness between the upper and lower parts of the vessel. On some of these bowls traces of mat impressions remain (see discussion below).

Type NB16 (Fig. 12.18; Pls. 12.7, 12.8:1–9). These are medium-sized wide and shallow bowls with either slightly flaring straight or rounded walls. They were divided into subtypes according to size and shape.

Subtype NB16.1 bowls are 20–25 cm wide, with straight, upright or everted walls. They were encountered in Strata 4/3c (Pl. 12.7:1–3) and Substrata 3a-b (Pl. 12.7:4, 5).

Subtype NB16.2 bowls are 20–25 cm wide, with rounded walls. Some of them have a bar or knob handle. They are known from Strata 4/3c (Pl. 12.7:6–11) and Substrata 3a-b (Fig. 12.18; Pl. 12.7:12–16).

Fig. 12.18. Negebite bowl Type NB16.2, Substratum 3b (Pl. 12.7:15).

Subtype NB16.3 bowls are large, rounded and shallow, 25–35 cm in diameter, with knob or bar handles. Examples are from Strata 4/3c (Pl. 12.7:17–19), 3a-b (Pl. 12.7:20, 21) and 3/2 (Pl. 12.7:22). The latter two are very shallow and the walls are everted.

Subtype NB16.4 bowls are very wide (30–40 cm) and shallow. The walls are slightly rounded or straight and the base is flat. Some of them have knob handles. They are known from Strata 4/3c (Pl. 12.8:1–6) and Substrata 3a-b (Pl. 12.8:7–9).

Type NB17 (Pls. 12.8:10–13, 12.9:1–7). These are deep bowls/kraters with straight, flaring walls. The tip of the rim is usually flat and knob or bar handles are attached to the walls. This type appears in a wide range of sizes, but is only known in fragmentary form. Examples are from Strata 4/3c (Pl. 12.8:10–13), 3a-b (Pl. 12.9:1–5) and 2 (Pl. 12.9:6, 7).

Type NB18 (Pl. 12.9:8–13). These are bowls/kraters of uncertain shapes, as they are few and represented by fragments only. The walls are not very thick, upright and terminate in simple rims. Such fragments were encountered in Strata 4/3c (Pl. 12.9:8–10), 3a-b (Pl. 12.9:11, 12) and 2 (Pl. 12.9:13).

Cooking Kraters

These are the best known vessels in the Negebite group. They are often referred to as cooking pots, which indeed seems to have been their function. At Kadesh Barnea many bear traces of soot and one was found *in situ* in a *ṭabun*. The term 'cooking kraters' is employed here in order to differentiate this group from the 'cooking pots' discussed below, which are made of a different fabric.

The cooking kraters were manufactured of the same clay as the other Negebite vessels and the walls were built up from coils. The bases are rounded or flat, the walls either upright or inverted and the rims are simple. Most of the kraters apparently had two or four knob handles and there is a wide variety in their shapes: simple, wide, split, bar and more.

Most of the kraters were clustered into two main types, based on shape: Type NK1, with upright walls; and Type NK2, with inverted walls. Other shapes are represented by a few examples only.

Type NK1 (Figs. 12.19–12.21; Pls. 12.10, 12.11). These kraters are typical mainly of Stratum 4. The common characteristic of this type are the upright walls; thus, the apertures of the vessels are as wide as the vessel themselves, which attain a barrel shape. Otherwise they vary in size and shape of base, which is either flat

Fig. 12.19. Negebite cooking krater Type NK1, Substratum 4b (Pl. 12.10:1).

Fig. 12.20. Negebite cooking krater Type NK1, Substratum 4b (Pl. 12.10:5).

Fig. 12.21. Negebite cooking krater Type NK1, Substratum 4b (Pl. 11.18:3).

or rounded. Some of the kraters have two or four knob handles. Of the 62 kraters of this type encountered at Kadesh Barnea, 67% originate from Strata 4/3c (Pl. 12.10), many of them complete or near complete, and 24% were found in Substrata 3a-b (Pl. 12.11).

Type NK2 (Figs. 12.22, 12.23; Pls. 12.12, 12.13). This is the most common Negebite vessel at the site (over 100 items were recorded) and the dominant krater shape in Substrata 3a-b. It is a holemouth krater, whose widest circumference is usually at its lower part. The rims are simple and various kinds of handles are attached under them: bar handles, single, double and triple knob handles, and horizontal loop handles. Occasionally, there are traces of scraping on the lower part of the vessels and mat impressions on their bases, indicative

Fig. 12.22. Negebite cooking krater Type NK2.1, Substratum 4b (Pl. 12.12:3).

Fig. 12.23. Negebite cooking krater Type NK2.1, Substratum 3a (Pl. 12.12:7).

of the method of production (see the discussion on technology, below). The following subtypes were defined based on size.

Subtype NK2.1 (Figs. 12.22, 12.23) comprises medium-sized kraters, about 15–20 cm high and with rim diameters between 15 and 20 cm. They are known from Strata 4/3c (Pl. 12.12:1–6), 3a-b (Pls. 12.12:7–9, 12.13:1–5) and 2 (Pl. 12.13:6, 7). There is no significant difference in the relative quantities of these kraters between Strata 4/3c and Substrata 3a-b, but in Stratum 2 they are much scarcer.

Subtype NK2.2 represents smaller kraters, about 12 cm high and with a rim diameter of about 13 cm. They are known from Strata 4/3c (Pl. 12.13:8–10), 3a-b (Pl. 12.13:11, 12) and 2 (Pl. 12.13:13), but they are especially typical of Substrata 3a-b.

Type NK3 (Pl. 12.14:1–6). These are kraters with upright or inverted walls and loop handles extending down from the rim (as they were attested by fragments only it is unclear whether there was one handle or more). On some examples the handle is very large and wide relative to the vessel's size. Nineteen sherds of such large and small kraters were recorded, of which nine were from Strata 4/3c (Pl. 12.14:1–3), four from Substrata 3a-b (Pl. 12.14:4–6) and three from Stratum 2.

Type NK4 (Figs. 12.24, 12.25; Pl. 12.14:7–13). These are spouted kraters, most of them quite small. Although no two vessels are really similar, there is some consistency in their general shape and in the shape of the spouts (other than in Pl. 12.14:10, where the spout is more tubular). About 24 sherds of this type

Fig. 12.24. Negebite krater Type NK4, Substratum 4a (Pl. 12.14:7).

Fig. 12.25. Negebite krater Type NK4, Substratum 4b (Pl. 12.14:8).

were recorded, equally distributed between Strata 4/3c and Substrata 3a-b.

Type NK5 (Pl. 12.14:14–17). These are kraters of different sizes, with very short, slightly molded and flaring rims, usually with a pointed tip. The few examples are from Strata 4–2.

Type NK6 (Pl. 12.15:1–4). These kraters/deep bowls have straight or everted walls. Knobs or handles are attached below the rim. They are few and appear in Strata 4/3c (Pl. 12.15:1, 2) and Substrata 3a-b (Pl. 12.15:3, 4).

Type NK7 (Pl. 12.15:5, 6). These are deep and narrow kraters. As only a few fragments were found, the complete shape cannot be determined. These vessels come from Stratum 4 and Substratum 3c only.

Various Kraters
The kraters in Pl. 12.15:7–10 are morphologically similar to some cooking-pot types (see below), but, as mentioned above, they differ in their fabric. The vessel in Pl. 12:15:7, from Substratum 4b, resembles in shape the wheel-made cooking pots with the molded rim (Type CP1), but is handmade and has a knob handle typical of Negebite ware. The krater in Pl. 12:15:8, from Substratum 3b, is a small vessel with a thick flattened rim, and a horizontal handle below it. That in Pl. 12:15:9, from Substratum 3c, also resembles some of the wheel-made cooking pots; it has a straight upright rim and a handle. The small vessel in Pl. 12:15:10, from Stratum 2, has an everted rim and one or two loop handles; in general shape it resembles late Iron Age wheel-made cooking pots, of Type CP7.

Cooking Pots

The vessels termed here 'Negebite cooking pots' are handmade vessels, and thus were included here, but in fact, in their fabric they resemble contemporary wheel-made cooking pots. They are manufactured of red-brown clay, some of them having a dark core, and white or quartz inclusions. The surface of the vessels is usually dark gray.

Preliminary results of the petrographic analyses conducted by Y. Goren on six fragments from Strata 4–2 indicate a provenience in central Transjordan. Indeed, other thin-walled cooking pots, very similar in their fabric, are known as Edomite cooking pots (see Chapter 11), but they were formed on a wheel and differ in rim shape. If it indeed turns out that these vessels were produced in Transjordan, this will necessitate a reconsideration of this group.

The cooking pots are typified by a holemouth shape and very thin walls. Only the rims seem to have been formed using a rotary motion; they occasionally seem to have been cut. In many cases, degenerated handles, made from tiny lumps of clay, adhere to the upper walls of the vessels; in fact, this seems to have been the rule. These 'handles' are too small to have served for holding the pots, but they may have had some role when placing and removing them from the oven.

About 65 such vessels and sherds were recorded; relative to the Negebite cooking kraters, this was not a very common vessel. No significant difference was observed between their frequencies in Strata 4/3c and Substrata 3a-b, but in Stratum 2 only three such sherds were encountered.

The thin-walled cooking pots were divided into types based on the shape of the rim, as otherwise they vary little. All subtypes appear in Strata 4–2.

Type NCP1 (Figs. 12.26, 12.27; Pls. 12.16:1–6). Holemouth cooking pots where the tip of the rim is only slightly everted. The rims vary in their thickness.

Fig. 12.26. Negebite cooking pot Type NCP1, Substratum 4 (Pl. 12.16:4).

Fig. 12.27. Negebite cooking pot Type NCP1, Substrata 4a/3c (Pl. 12.16:3).

Type NCP2 (Pl. 12.16:7–13). These cooking pots are similar to the above in all aspects other than their everted rims. Occasionally, as in Pl. 12.16:13, this tendency is stronger and the everted rim more accentuated.

Type NCP3 (Fig. 12.28; Pl. 12.17). On these cooking pots the rims have a vertical stance, and the angle

between shoulder and rim is thus emphasized. In some instances, as in Pl. 12.17:2, the tip of the rim has an inner thickening.

Fig. 12.28. Negebite cooking pot Type NCP3, Substratum 4c (Pl. 12.17:1).

Juglets

The vessels defined as juglets are small containers, ranging in height from 6 to 13 cm. Similarly to the jugs (below) the necks are hardly narrower than the body. The juglets differ in their specific morphologies. Nearly all of them can be clustered into three morphological types, and others are singular shapes.

Type NJT1 (Figs. 12.29, 12.30; Pl. 12.18:1–6). These juglets are provided with a loop handle (a rare feature in the Negebite group), which must be related to their function. The vessels vary in shape. Some have more clearly defined necks than others, but the 'neck' may have actually been created by pressing the vessel when the handle was attached. These juglets are attested in Strata 4/3c and Substrata 3a-b, but they are not frequent.

Fig. 12.29. Negebite juglet Type NJT1, Stratum 4 (Pl. 12.18:1).

Fig. 12.30. Negebite juglet Type NJT1, Stratum 4 (Pl. 12.18:2).

Type NJT2 (Fig. 12.31; Pl. 12.18:7, 8). These are miniature juglets with narrow, well-defined shoulders and necks. Only very few and fragmentary examples are known, from Strata 4–2.

Fig. 12.31. Negebite juglet Type NJT2, Substratum 4a (Pl. 12.18:7).

Type NJT3 (Pl. 12.18:9, 10). These miniature holemouth juglets, very rarely attested, appear in Substrata 3a-b and Stratum 2.

Jugs

The vessels of this category are classified as jugs, though rarely were complete vessels found to indicate clearly that they had only one handle. (When attested, however, the handle could not have been used to lift these heavy vessels.) The jugs range in height from 17.5 to 35 cm. All of them are crudely made and irregular, the walls varying in thickness. Complete and near complete examples are known mainly from the destruction assemblages of Stratum 4; the jugs in Substrata 3a-b and Stratum 2 are fragmentary. It thus seems that they were used in the entire Strata 4–2 range, but this cannot be ascertained.

Type NJ1 (Figs. 12.32, 12.33; Pls. 12.18:11–15, 12.19:1–3). These jugs echo in their shape the juglets of Type NJT1. They have one handle and either straight, or slightly tapering walls (the lower part of the body is slightly wider than the upper part), with a more or less defined 'neck' and a simple rim (the example in Fig. 12.32, Pl. 12.18:11 has a pinched rim). These jugs are known throughout Strata 4–2. One such jug (Pls. 12.19:1, 12.30:11) bears an incised mark, executed after firing.

Fig. 12.32. Negebite jug Type NJ1, Stratum 4 (Pl. 12.18:11).

Fig. 12.33. Negebite jug Type NJ1, Stratum 4 (Pl. 12.18:13).

Type NJ2 (Pl. 12.19:4–6). A few jug fragments, though generally resembling the previous type in shape, have no 'shoulders' to speak of. There is, however, a well-defined angle between the body and neck, and the rims are short and either upright or slightly everted. The few examples of this type occur in Strata 4–2.

Type NJ3 (Pl. 12.19:7–9). These jugs are of different shapes, the common attribute being a cup-shaped appendage, which, in most cases, has a single-hole perforation. They were probably meant to support a miniature vessel holding a liquid, and the hole would have enabled the draining of this liquid into the jug, similarly to the wheel-made 'pillar-handle' jars/jugs.

Various Jugs

There is one jug with a strainer (Fig. 12.34; Pl. 12.19:10). It possibly imitates contemporaneous wheel-made shapes.

Fig. 12.34. Miscellaneous Negebite jug, Substratum 4b (Pl. 12.19:10).

Flasks

The vessel in Pl. 12.19:11, from Substratum 4a, can be defined either as a flask or a small jar; its exact shape cannot be determined (it is not clearly lentoid). It has a relatively tall narrow neck and two handles that extend from the neck to the shoulders. On the neck there is a cross-shaped incision, introduced after firing (see below).

The crude and badly-proportioned flask in Fig. 12.35, Pl. 12.19:12, from the fill of Granary 6291, is very small and heavy, with a very minimal capacity; perhaps it was a votive vessel. It bears an engraving executed after firing, possibly depicting a chariot (see below, Fig. 12.86; Pl. 12.29:1).

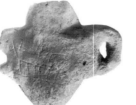

Fig. 12.35. Negebite flask, Strata 3/2 (Pls. 12.19:12, 12.29:1; Fig. 12.86).

Jar(?) and Pithoi

The rim in Pl. 12.20:1 apparently belongs to a larger container, but its walls are relatively thin. It is unclear what the complete shape might have been.

The rims in Pl. 12.20:2–4 belong to handmade pithoi, but it is unclear if their fabric is related to that of the Negebite group. They were not many, and their association with this group is tentative.

Lamps

Some 14 fragments of handmade lamps were found, of which one (Pl. 12.20:5) belongs to Substratum 4c; seven (Pl. 12.20:6–10) are from Substrata 3a-b; and six (Pl. 12.20:11–13) from Stratum 2. They all have pinched spouts, which often bore traces of soot. They can be clustered into two major 'types', though the significance of this grouping is unclear.

Type NL1 (Fig. 12.36; Pl. 12.20:5–7). These lamps have a flat base, upright walls and a relatively long and wide spout. They are present in Strata 4, 3a-b, and absent in Stratum 2, but as they are generally quite rare, this is hardly significant.

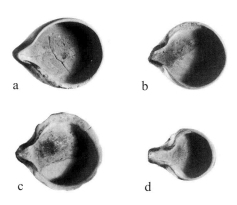

Fig. 12.36. Negebite lamps Type NL1.
(a) Stratum 4 (Pl. 12.20:5); (b–d) Substrata 3a-b
(b: Pls. 12.20:6, 11.57:17; d: Pl. 12.20:7).

Type NL2 (Pl. 12.20:8–11). These lamps, as opposed to the previous ones, are rounded, but they have a similar long and wide spout.

Type NL3 (Fig. 12.37; Pl. 12.20:12, 13). These lamps were manufactured from deeper bowls. They have

Fig. 12.37. Negebite lamp Type NL3, Stratum 2 (Pl. 12.20:13).

a rather narrow and short pinched spout. The few examples originate in Stratum 2.

Three-Legged Strainers

A single near-complete strainer and two that are fragmentary (Fig. 12.38; Pl. 12.21:1–3) were found in loci attributed to Substrata 3a-b. Though these vessels are crudely handmade, they resemble the wheel-made strainers (Type B13) found in Substrata 3a-b and in Stratum 2. The vessel in Pl. 12.21:1 is a goblet- or cup-like strainer with a handle from the rim to the body. The three legs extend from the center of its narrow base. The examples in Pl. 12.21:2, 3 are vessels with upright walls, a wide and flat base, and legs extending from the external circumference of the base. No traces of handles remain on them and apparently there were none.

Fig. 12.38. Negebite three-legged strainer, Substrata 3a-b (Pl. 12.21:2).

Goblets/Chalices

Strata 4/3c produced four complete goblets/chalices, each of them different (Figs. 12.39–12.41: b, c; Pl. 12.21:4–7). The vessel in Fig. 12.39, Pl. 12.21:4, from Substratum 4a, is more 'goblet-shaped'—narrow and relatively deep, with a tall solid foot that widens at its base. The goblet in Fig. 12.40, Pl.12.21:5 is deep and relatively wide and quite carefully made. It has a short foot, divided into four 'petals'. This goblet was found above a Stratum 4 floor, and could in fact belong to the material incorporated in the Substratum 3c constructional fill. The example in Fig. 12.41b, Pl. 12.21:6, from Substratum 3c, is smaller than the previous vessel and crudely made. The bowl itself is hemispherical, the foot short, and its underside not quite flat. Under the rim, protruding knobs were

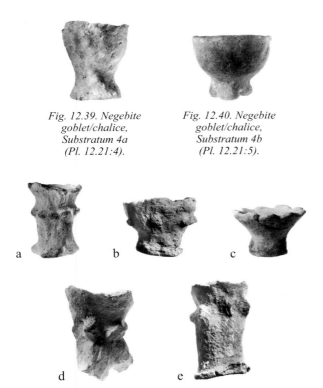

Fig. 12.39. Negebite
goblet/chalice,
Substratum 4a
(Pl. 12.21:4).

Fig. 12.40. Negebite
goblet/chalice,
Substratum 4b
(Pl. 12.21:5).

Fig. 12.41. Negebite goblets/chalices. (a–c) Substratum 3c;
(d) Substratum 3b; (e) Strata 2/1 (Pls. 12.21:6, 7, 9, 10, 12).

attached, a typical decoration on Negebite chalice feet
and on small bowls. The shallow chalice-like vessel
in Fig. 12.41:c, Pl.12.21:7, from Substratum 3c, has a
wavy rim, its base tall and solid.

The tall bases in Fig. 12.41:a, d, e, Pl. 12.21:8–12
belong either to chalices or to goblets. They are of
varying lengths and shapes. Those in Pl. 12.21:8, 9,
from Strata 4/3c, are solid, with flat bases, triangular
or square in cross section; No. 9 (Fig. 12.41:a) has a
series of protruding knobs. The bases of Fig. 12.41:d,
Pl. 12.21:10; (Substratum 3b) and 12.21:11 (Substratum
3a) are split in their lower part into three feet, and
may be parts of strainer vessels; the former also bears
the common knob decoration, as does Fig. 12.41:e,
Pl. 12.21:12 from the fill of the cistern in Area D.

Although most of the goblets/chalices (including all
the complete specimens) originate in Strata 4/3c, the
two fragments in Substrata 3a-b indicate that these
vessels may have had a longer existence.

Stand

The fragment in Pl. 12.21:13, from Substratum 3b, is
part of a fenestrated stand, whose exact shape cannot

be determined. It was manufactured by hand of typical
Negebite fabric.

Basins

The vessels in Pl. 12.22:1–3 are very wide and open,
with thick walls. Based on these attributes they were
determined to be basins, but their shapes are unknown.
They are not numerous and morphologically differ
from each other. Fragment No. 2 is from Strata 3/2 and
Nos. 1 and 3 are from Stratum 2.

Trays

Two types of trays were defined. Their purpose is
unclear, likely possibilities being the processing of
dough or baking. The tray in Pl. 12.23:1 was burnt, but
this could be a result of the conflagration it underwent.

Type NT1 (Fig. 12.42; Pl. 12:22:4–12). These are wide,
rounded and flat trays with thick short upright walls.
They are of light brown fabric with large amounts of
organic temper and are very crudely handmade. Of the
32 examples recorded, 9 originate in Strata 4/3c (Pl.
12.22:4–6), 4 in Substrata 3a-b (Pl. 12.22:7–9) and 15
are from Stratum 2 (Pl. 12.22:10–12). This latter figure
is significant, as generally in Stratum 2 Negebite ware
was scarce. In Strata 4/3c most of the trays were larger
and thicker than the later examples.

Fig. 12.42. Negebite tray Type NT1,
Substratum 4a (Pl. 12.22:4).

Similar vessels are common over a long period of
time, in various regions, and are usually interpreted
as basins or kneading troughs. Examples are known
from Late Bronze Age Deir el-Balaḥ (unpublished);
Ashdod, Strata XIIIa (Dothan and Porath 1993: Fig.
23:13), VIII and VII–VI (Dothan and Freedman 1976:
Figs. 39:21, 41:20, 21); and Tell Qasile, Stratum X
(A. Mazar 1985:80, Photo 84). This means that the
inclusion of these vessels in the Negebite group may
be misleading.

Type NT2 (Figs. 12.43, 12.44; Pl. 12.23:1–4). These are
nearly flat trays with curving walls, and either one or
two knob or loop handles (none was found complete).

Fig. 12.43. Negebite tray Type NT2.1, Substratum 4b (Pl. 12.23:1).

Fig. 12.44. Negebite tray Type NT2.1, Substratum 4b (Pl. 12.23:2).

Subtype NT2.1 (Figs. 12.43, 12.44; Pl. 12.23:1, 2) is represented by these two near-complete examples, from Substratum 4b. That in Pl. 12.23:1, with a slightly concave base, has a raised rim to which the loop handle was attached. A similar small fragment with a knob handle was encountered in L702 of Stratum 2 (+1) (not illustrated). The tray in Pl. 12.23:2 is slightly convex and has no rim.

Trays of Subtype NT2.2 (Pl. 12.23:3, 4) are totally flat, perforated, with a slightly raised rim and loop or knob handles. Only some of the perforations were pierced all the way through and it seems that they were intended to roughen the surface of the vessel, or, perhaps more likely, to allow hot air to reach the vessel's surface. The tray in Pl. 12.23:3 originates from Stratum 2, and Pl. 12.23:4 is unstratified.

Various Trays

The fragment in Pl. 12.23:5, from Substratum 3a, is a base of a very wide and flat vessel of unclear shape, presumably a tray. It has three interconnected feet. The fragment in Pl. 12.23:6 is part of a flat, apparently oval ceramic tray/plate, from Substratum 3c. There are traces of some red substance (perhaps ocher) on its upper side; its function is unclear.

Shallow Receptacles with Compartments

The unique vessel in Fig. 12.45, Pl. 12:24:1 was found on a Stratum 4 floor. It is shaped like a rounded bowl, with a flat base, and is divided into a central rounded compartment surrounded by four others. As it is unique, it probably had a special use.

Fig. 12.45. Negebite receptacle, Stratum 4 (Pl. 12.24:1).

Such a small vessel may have contained cosmetic or spices.

Two rectangular receptacles (Fig. 12.46; Pl. 12.24:2, 3) were incorporated in the Substratum 3c constructional fill and thus probably belong to Stratum 4. The one in Pl. 12.24:2, nearly intact, is divided into two square compartments; attached to the partition between them is a socket, which may have been used to accommodate the hinge of a lid, or perhaps a brush or stick, indicating that the box may have been used for cosmetics.

One compartment of the box in Pl. 12.24:3 has survived, but clearly there were at least two. This object is larger than the former and there is no evidence here of a socket.

Fig. 12.46. Negebite receptacle, Substratum 3c (Pl. 12.24:2).

Lids

The objects in Figs. 12.47–12.49, Pl. 12.24:4–13 probably served as lids for containers. They are associated here with the Negebite group due to their fabric (and they are, of course, also handmade). Most of the examples that originate in clear contexts are attributable to Stratum 4.

Two major groups may be defined here. The lids in Figs. 12.47, 12.48, Pl. 12.24:4–7 have two pierced 'lug handles', which render the vessel's outline oval in shape. Their perforations were probably intended to string the lids in place. On some items (e.g., Fig. 12.47; Pl. 12.24:4, 5) one side of the lid (probably the bottom) is thick and convex in the middle, to fit the rounded apertures of selected vessels. The four complete lids are undecorated and apparently originate in Stratum 4, other than Pl. 12.24:7, which was found during cleaning.

Fig. 12.47. Negebite lid, Substratum 4a (Pl. 12.24:4).

Fig. 12.48. Negebite lid from the fill of the granary (Pl. 12.24:7).

The fragmentary objects in Fig. 12.49, Pl. 12.24:8–10 retained only one pierced handle and their margins are accentuated; they also seem to have been lids. Those in Pl. 12.24:8, 9 (from Strata 4/3c) are decorated with incised patterns, a phenomenon typical of small Negebite bowls. The upper part of the lid in Pl. 12.24:10 (from a mixed locus) bears small reed impressions.

Fig. 12.49. Negebite lid(?), Stratum 4 (Pl. 12.24:8).

The objects in Pl. 12.24:11–13 are probably also lids (but rounded, and lacking handles). The only complete example is No. 11, from the fill of the Stratum 2 glacis. It is slightly concave below, and its upper face is slightly convex. The objects in Pl. 12.24:12 (a surface find) and Pl. 12.24:13 (Stratum 4) bear incised decorations; their shapes are unclear, either rounded or elliptical, and they may, in fact, be fragments of pendants and not lids (see below).

Pendants(?)

The objects in Figs. 12.50, 12.51, Pl. 12.24:14–16 are oval in shape and have one perforation. The only complete example is that in Fig. 12.50, Pl. 12:24:14 (from Substratum 3c), which is undecorated. As it is rather large and heavy, its interpretation as a pendant is tentative. Alternatively it may have functioned as a lid for a vessel with a similarly shaped aperture.

Fig. 12.50. Negebite pendant(?), Substratum 3c (Pl. 12.24:14).

The object in Pl. 12:24:15 (from Substratum 4b) is either round or elliptical, completely flat, and has at least one perforated edge. Here, too, it cannot be determined decisively whether it was a pendant or a lid. Figure 12.51, Pl. 12:24:16 (from Substratum 3c) is unusual as it is thicker than the other objects of this

'group' (but of uneven thickness), and on one side it bears a punctured decoration (the holes are not pierced all the way through). Presumably there was a hole for suspension at its presently broken end.

Fig. 12.51. Negebite pendant(?), Substratum 3c (Pl. 12.24:16).

Other Objects

As there is no evidence of a pottery production locale in the excavated parts of Kadesh Barnea, it is reasonable to assume that the following (fired) objects are not some industrial waste, but de facto objects. The fragmentary item in Pl. 12.24:17 is a cylindrical lump of clay from Substrata 3a-b. It is of irregular shape and pierced at one end; it may have been a pendant. The object in Fig. 12.52, Pl. 12.24:18 is a small fired lump of clay (of Negebite fabric), from Substratum 3c, into which four depressions were finger-pressed. These, judging by their size, must have been made by a young child.

Fig. 12.52. Undefined Negebite object, Substratum 3c (Pl. 12.24:18).

NOTES ON PRODUCTION TECHNOLOGY

As mentioned above, most of the Negebite vessels seem to have been manufactured in the northern Negev. At Kadesh Barnea, no definite pottery workshops, kilns, tools, or wastes that could be associated with pottery production were encountered. Nor was there any evidence of pits, etc. in which the vessels could have been fired.

THE FABRIC

All the Negebite forms of Strata 4–2, except the thin-walled cooking pots, were produced of similar fabric. The clay, as indicated by the petrography, includes loess, and is usually of brown or light brown color. The temper is varied, including mainly limestone, grog and organic matter, attested by the voids remaining after the vessels had been fired. In some cases, the long and narrow shapes of these voids seem to indicate the use of chaff.

The low quality of production is also indicated by the fact that various substances were included in the clay seemingly unintentionally: in one instance (Fig. 12.53), a complete date pit became embedded in the clay and was fired with the vessel. Occasionally, plants that stuck to the vessels while wet seem not to have been removed, but were fired with the vessel.

Fig. 12.53. Outer face of a Negebite cooking krater fragment, with a date pit embedded in clay; Reg. No. 736, L425, Stratum 2.

FORMING TECHNIQUES

Negebite pottery, generally speaking, is handmade; there are definitely no signs of the vessels having being worked on a fast wheel.

Various production techniques can be discerned, usually in accordance with the type of vessel. Kraters and jars were built up with coils, while small bowls, for example, were made by the pinched-pot method. Some of the large bowls are partially made in molds Whatever the basic forming process, it is obvious that vessels were rotated by hand during the manufacturing process, in order to produce more-or-less uniform walls and smooth surfaces (see below).

In general, the external finish of the vessels, although attesting to some effort invested in smoothing the traces of coiling (for which see below), nearly always manifests fingerprints and the smoothing marks. On most vessels these are irregular, probably executed with a cloth.

Coil-Made Vessels

Most of the large vessels, such as pithoi, basins, jugs and cooking kraters, were built up with coils of clay (Fig. 12.54; see also, for example, Fig. 12.32). The

bases of these vessels were, however, slabs, flattened from a clay lump, and not coil formed, and in many instances it is clear that the base, along with the lower part of the vessels, were formed in a 'mold' (see below). Vessels in which individual coils could be discerned indicate that these were about 1.5 cm in diameter. It is impossible to establish whether the vessels were built from a single long coil or a series of rings.

Internally, the vessels were usually carelessly smoothed (fingerprints, often diagonal, were usually noticeable). The inner joints between bases and lower coils received some attention, and were occasionally smoothed. All these marks, however, are part of the manufacturing process and do not exemplify any aesthetic considerations. Only seldom was there evidence of treatment of the exterior of the vessel, beyond careless smoothing (Fig. 12.55; see also Fig. 12.21). Similarly, when handles or other plastic appendages were attached to the vessels, rarely was there any effort invested in eradicating the marks left by the potters' fingers.

Fig. 12.55. Smoothing marks on outer face of a Type NK1 Negebite cooking-krater fragment, Substratum 3a (Pl. 12.11:4).

Pinched Vessels

Most of the small and tiny vessels such as the small bowls, juglets, lamps, etc., were probably produced by the basic method of pinching (Fig. 12.56). These vessels, naturally, are more regular and better finished than the larger, coil-made ones. On some examples the finger impressions around the vessel are still visible, but in most cases the walls were well finished, and except for irregularities in thickness and symmetry, no traces of the manufacturing method remain.

Fig. 12.54. Outer face of a Negebite fragment formed with coils; Reg. No. 93, L70, Substratum 3a.

Fig. 12.56. Pinched Negebite bowl Type NB12; Reg. No. 5338, L3198, Substratum 3c.

Partially Mold-Made Vessels

Some of the large Negebite bowls of Type NB15 presented clear evidence that they were partially constructed in some form of mold. Such is indicated by the facts that the lower part of these bowls is significantly thinner than the upper part, and that it seems to have been pressed against some object (Figs. 12.57, 12.58; Pl. 12.25:1–7; see also, for example, Pl. 12.6:10–16). The molds may have been ceramic vessels or fragments thereof, possibly wooden containers, and certainly plaited baskets (for which see below).

Fig. 12.57. Rim and part of lower wall of a Type NB15 Negebite bowl, partially formed in a mold, Substrata 3a-b (Pl. 12.6:14).

Fig. 12.58. Rim and part of lower wall of a Type NB15 Negebite bowl, partially formed in a mold, Substratum 4b (Pl. 12.6:10).

Occasionally the vessels provide other hints that they were, at least partially, formed in a mold: some bowls exhibit signs of scraping, apparently caused when the vessels were detached from the mold with a sharp tool (Fig. 12.59). Similar signs of scraping were also found on the lower parts of some kraters (Pl. 12.25:8), implying that these too were partially mold made.

However, one cannot rule out an alternative possibility for these scrape marks, i.e., that at a certain stage, while leather hard, the vessels were scraped in order to smooth the lower part of the walls, or even to shape the base.

Fig. 12.59. Lower wall of a Type NB16.2 Negebite bowl, with scraping marks, Substratum 4b (Pl. 12.7:11).

The Production of Cooking Pots

As mentioned, the handmade 'Negebite' cooking pots (Types NCP1–NCP3; Figs. 12.26–12.28; Pls. 12.16, 12.17) are distinct from the other Negebite vessels in their fabric. Whether this implies a different region of manufacture remains to be determined. Their very thin walls also imply that they were manufactured differently—probably by flattening the clay over some sort of mold. One coil (probably not more than one) was added then to form the slightly thickened rim, whose tip was subsequently cut. (Due to their thinness these cooking pots were usually fragmentary, but from the few near-intact examples it can be determined that they were produced by the same technique.)

The outer surfaces of these pots are irregular, resulting from the impressions of the potters' hands, which were not eliminated.

Basketry and Textile Impressions

In the Southern Levant, mat impressions on the bases of clay vessels are known mainly from the Neolithic and Chalcolithic periods and it is commonly assumed that mats were used as turntables on which the vessels remained throughout the production stages. Subsequently, the mats were either removed before firing, or fired with the vessels. Crowfoot (1956:419) noted that when vessels are placed on mats throughout the consecutive production stages, the mat impressions tend to be smeared, and when vessels are placed on mats only for drying, impressions are clearer. However, it is difficult to accept that vessels placed on mats for drying only would retain conspicuous impressions at all (Elisheva Kamaisky, pers. comm.).

Iron Age Negebite vessels with basket and textile impressions have been recorded at other sites, such as at Tell el-Kheleifeh (two body sherds with mat or basket impressions; Glueck 1938: Fig. 3:5); Tel Masos, Stratum II (a textile impression on the base of a cooking pot; Sheffer 1976: Fig. 1); and Timna' (a textile impression on a potsherd; Sheffer and Tidhar 1988: Pl. 129:1, 2). Iron Age textiles and baskets have been published from a number of Negev sites, such as Kuntillet 'Ajrud (Meshel 1976: No. 18; Sheffer and Tidhar 1991:1–26), Be'er Sheva' (apparently a sieve;

Table 12.1. Basketry Impressions on Walls of Negebite Vessels

No.	Basket	Locus	Stratum/ Substratum	Vessel	Type of Impression	Location of Impression	Technique	Width of Coil Impression (mm)	Width of Wrapping Impression (mm)	Illustrations
1	8194/4 8216/3	6090	4a	Bowl NB15	Basket	Wall	Coils	5.0	2.0	Fig. 12.61; Pls. 11.25:13, 14, 12.26:3
2	2653/15	854	3a-b	Bowl NB1.2	Basket	Wall	Coils	1.5–2.0	1.5	Fig. 12.60; Pls. 11.68:19, 12.1:29
3	5016/2	3001	3a	Bowl	Basket	Wall	Coils	4.0	1.5–2.0	Pl. 12.26:2
4	5104/1	3058	3c	Bowl NB15	Basket	Wall	Coils	2.5	1.5	Pl. 12.6:9
5	2758/3	1072	3c	Bowl/ basin	Basket	Base + wall	Coils	6.0	2.5	Fig. 12.62
6	2623/5	852	2	Krater	Basket(?)	Lower wall	Coils(?)	-	-	

Sheffer 1973: Pl. 31) and Timna' (textiles and basketry; Sheffer and Tidhar 1988: Pl. 133:1–5).

At Kadesh Barnea, 45 fragments of Negebite vessels bear basket or textile impressions. They indicate that some of the vessels were manufactured on mats or even within baskets, while others were apparently only placed on mats or textiles to dry. Eighteen of these impressed fragments originate in Substrata 3a-b, 12 in the Substratum 3c fill, and only two examples can be attributed with certainty to Stratum 4.

They are divided below into five groups based on the type of weave/basketry and on the location of the impression on the vessel (the terminology employed is that of Crowfoot 1956).

Basket Impressions on Vessel Walls
Six such impressions were recorded (Table 12.1; Figs. 12.60–12.62; Pl. 12.26:2, 3; see also Pls. 12.1:29, 12.6:9), mostly on small bowls with upright walls. In some cases the impression extends over the entire wall up to the rim (Fig. 12.60; Pl. 12.1:29) and in others only over the lower part of the vessel (Pl. 12.6:9). The example in Fig. 12.62, a wide flat vessel, is unusual in that the impression covers both walls and base. Examination of all the specimens in this group indicates that they were manufactured within baskets—during construction the walls were pressed against the baskets, which served as molds. (The fact that some Negebite vessels were

produced in molds was also deduced in regard to other vessels, which did not retain basket impressions; see above.) Occasionally, the impressions on these vessels are smudged, which probably occurred when the vessel was removed from the 'mold', before firing.

As the vessels were manufactured within baskets, one should expect impressions on the base as well. This, however, apart from the one exception mentioned above,

Fig. 12.60. Basket impression on wall of a small Type NB1.2 Negebite bowl, Substrata 3a-b (Pl. 12.1:29).

Fig. 12.61. Basket impression on wall of a small Type NB15 bowl, Substratum 4a (Pl. 12.26:3).

Fig. 12.62. Basket impression on wall and base of a small Negebite bowl (Pl. 12.26:3).

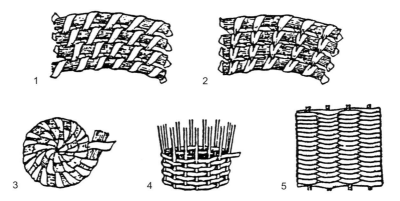

Fig. 12.63. Selected basketry techniques, after Crowfoot 1956: Figs. 258: a, b, e; 260d; 262b. (1) Coiled basketry, wrapping piercing underlying coil; (2) coiled basketry, wrapping piercing underlying wrapping stitches; (3) snail-centered base; (4) stake-frame; (5) plain weave basketry, reeds on cord warp.

is not the case. Two explanations may be offered here: either the impressions were purposefully eradicated after the vessels were removed from the baskets, or there may have been a layer of a substance (sand?) separating the bottom of the basket from the clay.

The impressions also attest to the basketwork techniques of the molds. In all of them the coiled technique was employed, with very tight wrapping (for the coiling technique, see Fig. 12.63:1, 2). The impressions, however, do not indicate exactly how the coils were attached to each other. There are two main possibilities: the wrapping stitches either penetrated the coil below them ('strip piercing coil'; Fig. 12.63:1) or the stitches below them ('strip piercing stitch–split stitches'; Fig. 12.63:2).

Basket-Tray(?) Impressions on Bases and Lower Part of Walls

Five such examples have been recorded, on bases and lower walls of large open bowls with everted walls (Table 12.2; Fig. 12.64; Pl. 12.26:4; see also Pl. 12.6:16). It seems that these bowls were constructed while positioned in wide, tray-like baskets. The impressions indicate that here too the baskets were constructed of coils. The coils were wider than those attested by most other impressions encountered at

Fig. 12.64. Basket-tray(?) impression on wall of a Type NB15 bowl, Substratum 3c (Pl. 12.26:4).

Table 12.2. Basket-Tray Impressions on Bases and Walls of Negebite Vessels

No.	Basket	Locus	Stratum/ Substratum	Vessel	Type of Impression	Location of Impression	Technique	Width of Coil Impression (mm)	Width of Wrapping Impression (mm)	Illustrations
1	2488/1	793	3c	Bowl NB15	Basket-tray	Lower wall	Coils	15.0	4.0–5.0	Fig. 12.64; Pl. 12.26:4
2	5165/1	3082	3b	Bowl NB15	Basket-tray	Lower wall	Coils	15.0	4.0	Pl. 12.6:16
3	2268	W263	3a-b	Krater(?)	Basket-tray	Lower wall	Coils	15.0	4.0–5.0	
4	3070/2	1408	3c	Krater(?)	Basket	Base	Coils	15.0	4.0	
5	-	486	2		Basket	Base	Coils	15.0	4.0–5.0	

Kadesh Barnea on bases of bowls or kraters (15 mm as opposed to 7–10 mm).

Typically, the joints between the clay coils that formed the vessels' walls can be discerned on their external faces, while the interiors were apparently smoothed.

Basket or Mat Impressions on Bases

Twenty-three such examples were recorded (Table 12.3; Figs. 12.65–12.68; Pl. 12.26:5–8; see also Pls. 12.3:19, 12.12:9, 12.13:10). This group comprises nearly half the impressions recorded on Negebite vessels, most of them bowls or kraters. The impressions never extend beyond the bases. Only three examples are of near-complete bases and on those three the central part of the mat/basket correlates with the centers of the bases of the pots (Figs. 12.65, 12.66). Thus it is reasonable to assume that these vessels were formed on small round mats/baskets that functioned as turntables. The alternative possibility—that the vessels were only placed on the mats/baskets to dry—is less likely, as then there would not always be a perfect correspondence between the center of the vessels and that of the mat/basket. In some cases (Table 12.3:1, 7–9, 12, 13, 21; Fig. 12.67), the impressions are blurred or doubled, and it appears that the vessel shifted on the mat.

Alternatively, it is possible that these vessels were actually made within closed baskets, but that subsequently the surface of the walls was smoothed, which left only the impression on the base; such a scenario cannot be proved or disproved. In one case (Pl. 12.26:7) there might be some trace of an impression also on the lower part of the vessel, c. 2.5 cm above the base, but shaving or scraping with a sharp tool here removed those marks.

All the impressions in this group indicate a coil technique with tight wrapping, but the diameters of the coils vary. In five or six examples, the diameter of coils is 10 mm and that of the wrapping stitches, 4 mm. In all the others, the average diameter of the coils is 7 mm, and for the wrapping stitches, 2 mm. In one example the basketry is more delicate, the coils being 3–4 mm in diameter. In the few examples that retained a near-complete base it can be determined that the technique employed for the base is that of 'snail center' (Fig. 12.63:3).

Fig. 12.65. Mat or basket impression on base of a Negebite bowl or krater; Reg. No. 1305/4, L604, Stratum 2.

Fig. 12.66. Mat or basket impression on base of a Negebite vessel; Reg. No. 1050/2, L531, Substrata 3a-b.

Fig. 12.67. Mat or basket impression on base of a Negebite bowl or krater; Reg. No. 5064, L3063, Strata 2, 1.

Fig. 12.68. Mat or basket impression on base of a Negebite bowl; Reg. No. 9009, L7001, Substratum 3c.

Table 12.3. Mat and Basketry Impressions on Bases of Negebite Vessels

No.	Basket	Locus	Stratum/ Substratum	Vessel	Type of Impression	Location of Impression	Technique	Width of Coil Impression (mm)	Width of Wrapping Stitches (mm)	Illustration
1	2721	1050	2, 1	Bowl/ krater	Mat or basket	Base	Coiled	10.0	4.0	
2	1305/4	604	2	Bowl/ krater	Mat or basket	Base	Coiled, snail centered	10.0	3.0	Fig. 12.65
3	8030	6019	3a-b	Krater	Mat or basket	Base	Coiled	10.0	4.0	

Table 12.3 (cont.)

No.	Basket	Locus	Stratum/ Substratum	Vessel	Type of Impression	Location of Impression	Technique	Width of Coil Impression (mm)	Width of Wrapping Stitches (mm)	Illustration
4	9009	7001	3c	Bowl	Mat or basket	Base	Coiled	10.0	4.0	Fig. 12.68
5	-	-	-	Body sherd	Mat or basket		Coiled	10.0	4.0	
6	8402	474	3a-b	Body sherd	Mat or basket	Lower wall	Coiled	8.0–9.0	3.0	
7	5023	3007	3b	Bowl/ krater	Mat or basket	Base	Coiled snail center	6.0	2.0–3.0	
8	5150	3076	3c	Bowl/ krater	Mat or basket	Base	Coiled	4.0–7.0	2.0	
9	5064	3063	2, 1	Bowl/ krater	Mat or basket	Base	Coiled	3.0–6.0	2.0	Fig. 12.67
10	586	294	2	Bowl/ krater	Mat or basket	Base	Coiled	6.0–7.0	2.0	Pl. 12.26:8
11	1050/2	531	3a-b	Body sherd	Mat or basket	Base	Coiled snail center	7.0–9.0	2.0	Fig. 12.66
12	456	222	3c	Body sherd	Mat or basket	Base	Coiled	4.0–6.0	3.0	
13	5056/2	3021	3b	Bowl NB16.1	Mat or basket	Base	Coiled	4.0–7.0	2.0–3.0	Pl. 12.26:5
14	-	-	-	Bowl/ krater	Mat or basket	Base	Coiled	8.0	2.0–3.0	
15	2646/2	854	3a-b	Bowl NB16.4	Mat or basket	Base	Coiled	6.0–7.0	2.0	Pls. 11.69:1, 12.26:7
16	5015	3010		Bowl	Mat or basket	Base	Coiled	7.0	2.0	Pl. 12.26:6
17	2589/1	1230	3c	Krater NK2.2	Mat or basket	Base	Coiled	7.0	2.0–3.0	Pl. 12.13:10
18	2593	1230	3c	Bowl	Mat or basket	Base	Coiled snail center	3.0–4.0	1.0–2.0	
19	1334/6	612	3a-b	Krater NK2.1	Mat or basket	Base				Pls. 11.53:9, 12.12:9
20	2771	1053	3a	Bowl NB2.3	Mat or basket	Base	Coiled	6.0	2.0–3.0	
21	5030/1	3014	3b	Bowl NB16.2	Mat or basket	Base	Coiled	7.0–9.0	2.0–3.0	
22	2779	1058	3b	Bowl	Mat or basket	Base	Coiled			Pl. 12.3:19
23	-	-	-	Bowl/ krater	Unclear	Base	Coiled	7.0	2.0	

Impressions of Strand Basketry (of Mats or Baskets)
Four such examples are recorded (Table 12.4; see Figs. 12.69, 12.70; Pl. 12.8:9), on which only the impressions of the weft strands are preserved. These passed above and below the strands of the warp frame, in the plain weave technique (see Fig. 12.63:4, 5). No example retains the central part of the impression, and thus the technique used for the bases is unclear. From the extant impressions it can be established that the weft strands were 2–4 mm in diameter and that the distance between the strands in the warp frame ranged between 15 and 20 mm.

One example, of a fragment apparently belonging to the base of a vessel, bears a complex weave pattern, apparently resembling a twill weave pattern. As the fragment is small and the pattern cannot be discerned in its entirety, the exact type of weave cannot be positively ascertained.

The few specimens of this group did not exhibit impressions on their walls and therefore we cannot determine whether baskets or mats were employed.

Textile Impressions on Bases
Seven such impressions are recorded, produced by textiles (probably woven mats/carpets, or garments; Table 12.5; Figs. 12.71, 12.72; Pl. 12.26:1). They were all impressed on thick bases of large and heavy vessels such as kraters or jars.

Fig. 12.69. Impression of strand basketry (of mat or basket) on base of a Negebite krater; Reg. No. 8594, L6298, Substratum 3c.

Fig. 12.70. Impression of strand basketry (of mat or basket) on base of a Negebite krater; Reg. No. 2652/8, L854, Substrata 3a-b.

Fig. 12.71. Textile impression on base of a Negebite vessel; Reg. No. 8537/2, L6267, Substratum 3c.

Fig. 12.72. Textile impression on base of Negebite krater; Reg. No. 5105/2, L3049, Substratum 3a.

Table 12.4. Strand Basketry Impressions on Bases of Negebite Vessels

No.	Basket	Locus	Stratum/ Substratum	Vessel	Impressions of Weft Segments (mm)		Illustration
					Width	Length	
1	1605/1	733	3b	Bowl NB16.4	2.0	18.0	Pls. 11.38:17, 12.8:9
2	5008	3008	3c	Unclear	-	-	
3	8594	6298	3c	Krater	3.0	15.0	Fig. 12.69
4	2652/8	854	3a-b	Krater	4.0	20.0	Fig. 12.70

Table 12.5. Weave Impressions on Bases of Negebite Vessels

No.	Basket	Locus	Stratum/ Substratum	Vessel	Location of Impression	Number of Visible Impressions (Threads) per cm		Illustration
						Warp	Weft	
1	579	223	4a	Jar/krater	Base	4	8	Pl. 12.26:1
2	8537/2	6267	3c	?	Base	4	8	Fig. 12.71
3	5178/3	3080	3c	Krater	Base	3	8–9	
4	485	231	-	Krater	Base	3	7–8	
5	5105/2	3049	3a	Krater	Base	5	8+	Fig. 12.72
6	1955	915	3c	Krater	Base	4	8+	
7	1721	708	2	Krater	Base	9	34	Fig. 16.19

The fact that the impressions point to textiles and not to basketry was indicated by the following considerations. (1) Faint marks, observed on the weft threads, indicate that they were z-spun. (2) The impressions are straight rather than curved. (3) In all the examples the impressions are not continuous and it even seems that the surface was not stretched and blocked.

Thus, it appears that the vessels were made or placed to dry on a woven mat/carpet. The following observations could be made in regard to the specific materials and the weaving technique, (1) On most of the examples (Table 12.5:1–6) the impressions are very similar, both in the type of weave employed and also in the size of the warp and weft threads. Thus it is possible that mats/carpets of the same type were utilized. (2) The technique seems to be plain weave. Only the weft threads can be discerned in the impressions; therefore, the weft count must be doubled since the threads passing over the warp do not show in them. The average number of actual threads would have been 4 warp threads and 16 wefts per centimeter. As the wefts predominate and cover the warps, this probably indicates tapestry weave. (3) The fact that the warps are much smaller in number than the wefts may indicate that in all these cases the material employed was wool (in linen the numbers are usually equal). Since wool threads tend to tangle, the warp threads were usually widely spaced when strung on the loom and the weft threads were woven significantly closer (Sheffer 1976:86).

One impression (Table 12.5:7) was formed by a much more delicate textile and is discussed in Chapter 16.

DECORATION

As mentioned above, most of the Negebite pottery is very crudely finished and usually no effort was invested in smoothing the walls or removing vegetal matter (thorns, seeds, etc.) that adhered to the vessels while wet. Most of the pottery is undecorated and when decorations do occur, they are almost exclusively incisions; only two fragments bear painted decoration, in black. Most of the decorated fragments recorded have been illustrated in Pls. 12.27 and 12.28.

The differentiation between 'decorations' and 'potters' marks' (discussed below) was quite arbitrary. Incisions dubbed 'decorations' are those which extend over substantial parts of the vessels, while 'potters' marks' are singular, localized marks.

Incised or Punctured Decorations on Rims

This sort of decoration usually appears on bowls which, with few exceptions, have a bar handle (or a protruding ridge) below the rim (Type NB11). This group has been divided into the following subgroups.

Floral or Herringbone Patterns (Fig. 12.73; Pl. 12.27:1, 2)
This sort of decoration appears either on thickened rims or on bar handles under rims. Similar, but less delicate decorations appear on the walls of kraters (see below).

Fig. 12.73. Herringbone or floral incision on rim of a Type NB11 Negebite bowl, Stratum 2 (Pls. 12.5:11, 12.27:2).

Crescent Patterns (Figs. 12.74, 12.75; Pl. 12.27:3, 4)
A series of crescents, of inconsistent thickness and shape, is stamped on bowls, on the protruding ridge/ bar handle under the rim. It appears that the crescents were impressed with a flexible object, such as a folded leaf, reed or rind—hence the non-uniform impressions. There was no attempt to create a regular pattern.

Fig. 12.74. Crescent-shaped incisions on rim of a Type NB11 Negebite bowl, Substrata 3a-b (Pls. 12.5:9, 12.27:3).

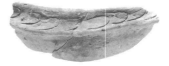

Fig. 12.75. Crescent-shaped incisions on rim of a Type NB11 Negebite bowl, Substrata 3a-b (Pls. 12.5:10, 12.27:4).

Punctured Decoration (Figs. 12.76, 12.77; Pl. 12.27:5–7)
This decoration comprises one or two rows of carelessly made punctures on the rim or the bar handle/ridge below it. In Fig. 12.76, Pl. 12.27:5, the punctures were

Fig. 12.76. Punctured decoration on bar handle of a Type NB11 Negebite bowl, Substratum 3c (Pls. 12.5:8, 12.27:5).

Fig. 12.77. Punctured decoration on bar handle of a Type NB1.1 Negebite bowl, Substrata 3a-b (Pls. 12.27:7, 11.70:25).

made with a sharp object 2–3 mm in diameter. In Pl. 12.27:6 they are arranged more or less in a circle, but this configuration is neither regular nor continuous; the holes are 2 mm wide, and some are very shallow. The small bowl in Fig. 12.77, Pl. 12.27:7 bears a combined pattern. On the rim, one or two rows of punctures (diam. 1 mm) were carelessly impressed and two shallow zigzag bands were incised below them.

Zigzags (see Fig. 12.77; Pl. 12.27:7, 8)
The zigzags are incised under the rims, around the entire circumference.

Simple Groove on Rims (Pl. 12.27:9)
On the one example illustrated here a groove is incised on top of the rim and crossed by short perpendicular strokes. A few other bowl rims, with flat tops or with a ridge just below the top, bear a similar incised groove, without the cross-strokes.

Incised Decoration on Walls

Palm Branches(?) (Figs. 12.78–12.80; Pl. 12.27:10–18)
These are the most common incised decorations, appearing mainly on kraters of various sizes (the fragments in Pl. 12.27:10, 18 also exhibit other decorations). The designs are formed by a vertical line that extends down from the rim or along the handle, and emanating from it are diagonal strokes, either straight or curved. Occasionally the incisions are deep and seem to have been incised with a sharp object, but in other cases they are shallow and careless. The fragment in Pl. 12.28:11 probably bears on the right a short segment of such a decoration, alongside the wavy lines.

Fig. 12.78. Palm branch(?) on a Type NB13 Negebite bowl, Substratum 3b (Pl. 12.27:11).

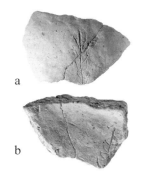

Fig. 12.79. Palm branch(?) on a Negebite bowl, Substratum 4a (Pl. 12.27:13). (a) Outer surface; (b) inner surface.

Fig. 12.80. Palm branch(?) on a Negebite bowl or krater, Substratum 3a (Pls. 12.27:15, 11.46:16).

Figurative Representations (Figs. 12.81, 12.82; Pl. 12.28:1, 2)
Two such instances were recorded, on kraters of Subtype NK2.1. On Pl. 12.28:1 the decoration is set in a horizontal panel, the upper border of which is formed by two parallel incisions, probably executed with a reed; the lower border incision is thin. Within the panel thus formed, two horned animals, possibly ibexes, were partially preserved. On Pl. 12.28:2 the decorative panel seems to have been divided into metopes, but the incised patterns are incomprehensible and seem to be no more than random scribbles. The incisions here, however, are very delicate, achieved with a sharp object. For another figurative composition on a flask, see below (Fig. 12.86; Pl. 12.29:1).

Fig. 12.81. Ibexes incised on a Type NB18 bowl or Negebite krater, Substratum 3a (Pls. 12.28:1, 11.42:19).

Fig. 12.82. Unclear designs on a Negebite krater, Substratum 3c (Pl. 12.28:2).

Various Vertical and Horizontal Lines (Fig. 12.83; Pl. 12.28:3–7)

In this group one may differentiate between simple and composite patterns. The incisions in Pl. 12.28:3, 4 are simple patterns. They comprise one or more thin lines, occasionally wavy, engraved around the vessels' circumference below the rim, probably with a reed. In the more composite patterns this horizontal line (or lines) is further augmented by series of vertical lines/ strokes (Pl. 12.28:5–7). In Fig. 12.83, Pl. 12.28:6, it seems that the vertical lines extend over the entire surface of the vessel. These patterns apparently appear primarily on bowls, of Type NB13.

Fig. 12.83. Vertical incisions on a Type NB13 Negebite bowl, Substrata 3a-b (Pls. 12.28: 6, 11.70:8).

Wavy Lines (Fig. 12.84; Pl. 12.28:8–11)

This pattern appears on deep wide bowls or kraters with upright walls. Those in Fig. 12.84, Pl. 12.28:8, 9, 11 bear shallow incisions, while Pl. 12.28:10 exhibits a wide, deep incision, probably executed with a small stick or reed; this latter fragment apparently belongs to a bowl or a krater.

Fig. 12.84. Wavy incisions on a Type NB18 Negebite bowl, Stratum 2 (Pls. 12.9:13, 12.28:9).

Others Incisions (Pl. 12.28:12–15; see also Pl. 12.27: 10, 18)

The designs on all these examples seem to be incomplete. Some may in fact be part of one of the 'groups' defined above, and others might be potters' marks (see below).

Painted Decoration

As mentioned, black-painted decoration is attested on two Negebite sherds only. In Fig. 12.85, Pl. 12.28:16 (a bowl of Type NB14), the decoration is clear. Between two sloppy horizontal zigzag bands is a horizontal chain. The partial design on Pl. 12.28:17 is indistinct.

Fig. 12.85. Black-painted decoration on a Type NB14 Negebite bowl, Substratum 4a (Pl. 12.28:16).

Chariot Scene on a Flask

The incision on the tiny crude flask in Fig. 12.86, Pl. 12.29:1 is unique in the Kadesh Barnea Negebite repertoire. It is thin, shallow and very worn, and thus it was difficult to assess whether it was incised before or after firing. However, the fact that such a small design was rendered quite accurately (as seen, for example, at the junctions between strokes) indicates that it was most probably executed before firing.

The surface of the vessel is very uneven and many scratches and imprints of vegetal matter remain; they are not always easy to tell apart from deliberate incisions. The scene seems to include the schematic figure of a horse pulling a cart, of which only a large wheel with eight spokes can be discerned, and a driver, possibly wearing a headdress.

Fig. 12.86. Chariot scene incised on a Negebite flask, Strata 3/2 (Pls. 12.19:12, 12.29:1).

Incised Decorations on Various Objects

As mentioned above, small clay lids and pendants bear incised decoration (Pl. 12.29:2–6; see Figs. 12.49, 12.51). Figure 12.51, Pl. 12.29:2 exhibits a simple punctured decoration. The design on Pl. 12.29:3 is linear, possibly concentric. Figure 12.49, Pl. 12.29:4 has a combination of a floral/herringbone design and zigzag patterns, as well as a punctured design along the object's circumference. The object in Pl. 12.29:6 shows a very shallow net pattern incised with a thin sharp tool.

IMPRESSIONS AND SIMPLE INCISIONS

Four impressions and fifteen simple incisions were recorded on Negebite vessels. As mentioned, we distinguished between incisions on Negebite vessels that were defined as 'decorations' (above) and incisions that were apparently meant to convey some specific information. This separation, however, was quite arbitrary. Some of the simple designs may have been potters' marks. Seven of the incisions were made before firing and eight were incised after firing. The almost equal numbers of specimens in these two categories is different from the phenomenon on wheel-made pottery at Kadesh Barnea, where most of the incisions were executed after firing.

What was the purpose of all these marks? The Negebite pottery seems to have been manufactured mostly for local, domestic use, and was probably produced in a domestic context. Also, most of the vessels bearing the incisions/impressions are open vessels (and not containers). Thus it is likely that these marks are neither potters' marks, nor indicate contents; instead, the most plausible interpretation seems to be that they designate ownership, whether executed either before or after the vessels were fired.

Impressions

In three cases (Fig. 12.87; Pl. 12.29:7–9) there are indentations on handles, which seem to have been executed with an implement (they do not seem to be thumb impressed).

Fig. 12.87. Impressions on handle of a Type NB12 Negebite bowl, unstratified (Pl. 12.29:7).

The impression in Fig. 12.88, Pl. 12.29:10 appears next to the knob handle of a krater of Subtype NK2.1. It consists of a rectangular frame enclosing two X-shaped signs. Above the frame

Fig. 12.88. Impression near handle of a Type NK2.1 Negebite krater, Substratum 3b (Pls. 12.29: 10, 11.41:19).

there is a floral design of three petals (a lotus?), which has no parallels—either on Negebite pottery, or on any other Iron Age vessel in the region.

Another impression on a Negebite krater is discussed in Chapter 15 (No. 5).

Incisions before Firing

Most of the incisions in this group (Figs. 12.89, 12.90; Pl. 12.30:1–7) are complete and thus it is obvious that they are not part of some larger designs. They usually consist of a single geometric shape and are deep and clear.

Fig. 12.89. Incision executed before firing on a Type NB12 Negebite bowl, Substratum 3a (Pls. 12.5:21, 12.30:4).

Two similar square marks, Pl. 12.30:1, 2, appear on two (different) bowls of the same type (NB17). Another bowl, of Type 16.4 (Pl. 12.30:3) has three incised strokes on the handle.

Two bowl fragments (NB12) and one krater (NK2.1), each carry a single mark, which in each case is different (Figs. 12.89, 12.90; Pl. 12.30:4–6). These marks bear some resemblance to characters of the South Arabian script (but they could also simply be potters' marks). South Arabian letters appear on pottery at other sites, for example at Tell el-Kheleifeh (on a jar; Glueck 1967: Fig. 5; Naveh 1982: Fig. 38), and in the City of David (Hofner 2000:26–28). At both these sites the incisions were introduced after firing, by chiseling.

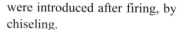

Fig. 12.90. Incision executed before firing on a Type NB12 Negebite bowl, Substratum 3c (Pl. 12.30:5).

Incisions after Firing

Simple X-shaped marks were incised on the neck of a flask and on the base of a tiny bowl (Pl. 12.30:8, 9). Cross-culturally, these are the most common marks on pottery. Two similar designs, on a Type NK2.1 krater and a Type NJ1 jug (Fig. 12.91; Pl. 12.30:10, 11), are ladder-shaped, and in three cases (Pl. 12.30:12–14) the geometric designs are more composite, but incomplete.

In one case (Pl. 12.30:15), a handle of a small bowl (Type NB1.3) was marked with a floral pattern, which is similar to some of the floral designs incised before firing (Pl. 12.27:14), but shorter.

Fig. 12.91. Incision executed after firing on a Type NJ1 Negebite jug, Stratum 2 (Pls. 12.19:1, 12.30:11)

DISCUSSION: THE PHENOMENON OF THE NEGEBITE POTTERY

Kadesh Barnea stands out in regard to Negebite pottery, which is clearly represented from Iron IIA (Stratum 4) through the late seventh/early sixth centuries BCE (Stratum 2). The exceptionally large assemblage, as well as the longevity of the ware, when compared to other sites in the Negev, raises, of course, the question of the producers and users of this pottery.

As noted above, the fabric of these vessels indicate a probable northern Negev provenance; they were most plausibly locally produced (other than in the case of the thin-walled cooking pots, where either the vessels or the raw materials were brought from Transjordan).

The Negebite pottery reveals extremely humble technological skills with very little effort invested in quality or aesthetics. This suggests a household production with a very restricted distribution area. The fact that no production facilities or tools were uncovered does not negate this assumption, as these were probably very simple and may not have been recognized.

Was this pottery associated with a specific group of people, perhaps desert nomads living in the Negev and active around Kadesh Barnea, whose dwellings remain undetected? (It should be borne in mind that the association of handmade wares with the arid regions in and south of Canaan/Israel is not confined to Iron II, e.g., at Timna'.) Were these people distinct from the inhabitants of the fortresses, and if this ware indeed represents a distinct group of people, does the intensive use of this pottery in the fortresses indicate their *presence* within the walls, among the other occupants, or does the pottery just indicate that these 'Negebites' supplied the fortresses with simple household vessels? Did they eventually assimilate into the Judean matrix of the fortresses? Can this be demonstrated by the fact that some of the Negebite pottery imitates wheel-made types? These answers to all these questions, at present, are very difficult to ascertain (see also Chapter 1).

NOTES

[1] The petrographic analyses were performed by Yuval Goren.

[2] Counts of ceramics were conducted by Avital Zintroblat in 1994.

CHAPTER 13

THE SMALL FINDS

AVIVIT GERA

INTRODUCTION

The Kadesh Barnea 'small finds' are listed below in catalogue/table form, with occasional comments. They are presented according to medium/material, except the jewelry items of all categories that are clustered at the end. The order of presentation is as follows: clay figurines; other clay objects; simple groundstone tools and vessels; other stone objects; bone objects; metal objects (including some jewelry items); jewelry. Within each category (except those that include very few items), the objects are presented more-or-less stratigraphically, from early to late, and they are arranged in the same order in the plates. Catalogue numbers have been assigned

for each category separately. Occasional comments on individual objects also appear in stratigraphical order.[1]

Artifacts not included here are objects considered part of the Negebite ceramic group, which are presented and discussed in Chapter 12; glyptics and inscriptions (Chapters 14, 15); textiles, spindle whorls and loom weights (Chapter 16) and flints (Chapter 17). Additional artifacts made of shell and bone are discussed in Chapters 18 and 19, respectively.

CLAY FIGURINES AND ZOOMOPHORIC VESSELS

This category encompasses human and animal figurines, as well as fragments of zoomorphic vessels.

Table 13.1. Catalogue of Clay Figurines and Zoomorphic Vessels

Cat. No.	Object	Reg. No.	Locus	Locus Description	Area	Stratum	Plate
1	Human female figurine	8091	6053	Fills	C	3c	Pl. 13.1:1
2	Fragment of zoomorphic vessel	513/11	243	Fills	A1	3c	Pl. 13.1:2
3	Figurine fragment	2771/2	1077	Fills	D	3c	Pl. 13.1:3
4	Spout of zoomorphic vessel	1559/5	713	Floor	B	3a	Pl. 13.1:4
5	Zoomorphic figurine	8054	6026	Fill of granary	C	3, 2	Pl. 13.1:5
6	Fragmentary zoomorphic figurine	8031/1	6016	Fill of granary	C	3, 2	Pl. 13.1:6
7	Fragmentary zoomorphic vessel	8506	6257	Fill of granary	C	3, 2	Pl. 13.1:7
8	Human male figurine	140	76	Floor	A1	2	Pl. 13.1:8
9	Head of horse figurine	365/2	157	Floor	A2	2	Pl. 13.1:9
10	Figurine fragment	4130/3	2159	Floor in moat	E	2	Pl. 13.1:10
11	Figurine fragment	3027/1	1404	Fill in cistern	D	2, 1	Pl. 13.1:11
12	Zoomorphic figurine fragment	772/5	457	Fill	B	1	Pl. 13.1:12

Fig. 13.1. Clay figurines and zoomorphic vessels (Cat. Nos. 1, 4, 5, 7–9).

Stratum 3c

Female Figurine No. 1 (Fig. 13.1:1; Pl. 13.1:1)
The figurine is handmade, 8 cm high. It was attached at its bottom to a curved ring, now broken. The body is flattened, and the head elongated, narrow, tapering and round at the top. The eyes are made of two balls of clay, pierced at their center. The nose extends from the forehead and the nostrils are emphasized and large. The chin is short and rounded. The neck widens toward the (broken) arms, which are turned inward and apparently held something. The breasts are indicated by two rounded lumps of clay.

This is an uncommon type for Iron II, though the following quite similar figurines may be quoted: a human clay figurine sitting in a wheeled vehicle, from Tell Jemmeh, Stratum GH of the tenth–ninth centuries BCE (Petrie 1928: Pl. XXXIX:14); and a figurine from the City of David, of the eighth–seventh centuries BCE (Gilbert-Peretz 1996: Fig. 10:13). In its general shape, the stance of the arms, and the fact that it was attached to an object, the figurine also resembles figurine No. 8 of Stratum 2.

Strata 3–2

Horse Figurine No. 5 (Fig. 13.1:5; Pl. 13.1:5)
The (broken) figurine is handmade, 4 cm high, 3 cm wide at the back and 5.5 cm long. The rounded, slightly elongated head lacks any facial details. The ears are pulled backward, thick and rounded. The neck is long and cylindrical, the body cylindrical and short, and the legs thick, short and rounded (only one front leg has survived).

This type of horse figurine is common in Iron Age Israelite sites, for example at Lachish III, of the eighth century BCE (Aharoni 1975: respectively Pls. 13:3, 33:7; 13:4, 33:8) and in Stratum II there, of the seventh/early sixth centuries BCE (Tufnell 1953: Pl. 32:5); in Jerusalem (Holland 1975: Figs. 23:3, 7; 26:5; 28:4; 33:3; 44:11), including Burial Cave No. 1 on the eastern slope of the Ophel (Holland 1977: Figs. 8:18; 9:2), and at the City of David (Gilbert-Peretz 1996: Fig. 16:9, 11).

Fragmentary Zoomorphic Vessel No. 7 (Fig. 13.1:7; Pl. 13.1:7)
The vessel was made on the wheel; it is now about 6 cm high and 7 cm long. This is the back half of a vessel in the shape of a four-legged animal with short,

thick rounded legs. The body/container is cylindrical. For similar complete wheel-made zoomorphic vessels cf., for example, Lachish Tomb 1002, dated to the ninth–eighth centuries BCE (Tufnell 1953: Pl. 30:23, 24).

Stratum 2

Human Male Figurine No. 8 (Fig. 13.1:8; Pl. 13.1:8)
The figurine is handmade, 8 cm high. The head is pointed at its upper end. The face is pinched and pointed; the nose is narrow and curves downward and the eyes are represented by two shallow depressions. The neck is wide and the body lacks any details other than the two (broken) outstretched arms. The lower part of the body is broken but the curve at the bottom of the back hints that the figurine may have been attached to some object.

Stylistically, this figurine resembles the Iron II 'pillar figurines' with pinched faces. As more remote *comparanda* one may cite the following: a handmade clay figurine with a pinched face from Be'er Sheva', in Stratum II of the end of the eighth century BCE (Aharoni 1973: Pls. 27:2, 71:1) and a similar one that was found near the mound (Aharoni 1973: Pl. 79:2). Pillar figurines with pinched faces were uncovered in Tomb 106 at Lachish, dated to the seventh–sixth centuries BCE (Tufnell 1953: Pl. 27:1, 3); and cf. another Iron II pillar figurine from Tell Jemmeh (Van Beek 1993:669, upper right). Pillar figurines with pinched faces are also known from the City of David, dating to the eighth–seventh centuries BCE (Gilbert-Peretz 1996: Fig. 10:1–10).

Head of Horse Figurine No. 9 (Fig. 13.1:9; Pl. 13.1:9)
The fragment is 3 cm high and 4 cm wide. It comprises the front part of a long and round face with short ears pointed at their ends. The neck is wide.

For other Iron II horse figurines in Judah, cf., for example, Tell Beit Mirsim A (Albright 1943: Pl. 58:6–11, 14, 15) and Lachish (above, figurine No. 5). Cf. also horse heads at Tel 'Ira, in Strata 7–6 of the seventh century BCE (Beit-Arieh 1999: Fig. 24.2:1) and horse figurines from Jerusalem (Holland 1975: Figs. 21:5, 8–10; 22:8, 10–12; 25:4, 5; 43:11–15 and more).

OTHER CLAY OBJECTS

Clay objects comprise a variety of items—lids, stoppers, game pieces(?) and a burnishing tool, as well as altars.

Table 13.2. Catalogue of Various Clay Objects

Cat. No.	Object	Reg. No.	Locus	Locus Description	Area	Stratum	Plate
1	Lid	4007	2005	Pit	E	4b	Pl. 13.2:1
2	Stopper	8251/1	6120	Floor	C	4b	
3	Stopper	574/6	291	Above floor	A1	4b	Pl. 13.2:3
4	Stopper	457/2	223	Burnt layer	E	4a	Pl. 13.2:4
5	Stopper	8586/4	6294	Floor, installation	C	4	Pl. 13.2:5
6	Stopper	8594/2	6298	Fills	C	3c	Pl. 13.2:6
7	Lid	2765	1079	Fills	D	3c	Pl. 13.2:7
8	Stopper	2495/1	796	Floor	B	3b	Pl. 13.2:8
9	Stopper	5141	3059	Floor	B	3b	Pl. 13.2:9
10	Stopper/button	5154	3079	Fill	B	3b	Pl. 13.2:10
11	Stopper	374/6	181	Floor	E	3a-b	Pl. 13.2:11
12	Stopper	2239/5	675	Silo	C	3a-b	Pl. 13.2:12
13	Stopper	2282/3	1102	Fill of granary	C	3, 2	Pl. 13.2:13
14	Stopper	2251/1	666	Fill	C	3a-b	Pl. 13.2:14
15	Stopper	8020/6	6010	Fill of granary	C	3, 2	Pl. 13.2:15
16	Stopper	1390/2	634	Fill of granary	C	3, 2	Pl. 13.2:16
17	Stopper	2653/35	854	Silo	F	3a-b	Pl. 13.2:17
18	Cone	2653/34	854	Silo	F	3a-b	Pl. 13.2:18
19	Cone	2646/10	854	Silo	F	3a-b	Pl. 13.2:19
20	Stopper(?) seal(?)	876/2	491	Floor	A2	2	Pl. 13.2:20
21	Stopper	776/11	402	Debris and floor	A2	2	Pl. 13.2:21
22	Stopper	962/2	501	Floor	A2	2	Pl. 13.2:22
23	Stopper	2623/3	852	Fill of glacis	F	2	Pl. 13.2:23
24	Stopper	729/8	420	Floor makeup	A2	2	Pl. 13.2:24
25	Stopper	2609/7	851	Fill of glacis	F	2	Pl. 13.2:25
26	Stopper	879/6	492	Floor	B	2	Pl. 13.2:26
27	Stopper (fragment)	937/4	486	Debris to floor	B	2	Pl. 13.2:27
28	Stopper	7227/7	412	Above floor	A2	2	Pl. 13.2:28
29	Miniature altar	977	486	Debris and floor	B	2	Pl. 11.105:9
30	Miniature altar	1594	702	Fill	B	2, 1	Pl. 11.110:19
31	Burnishing tool	162/4	98	Floor	A2	1	Pl. 13.2:31
32	Stopper	9061	7026	Fill of moat	F	2, 1	Pl. 13.2:32
33	Stopper	721	410	Pit	A2	1	Pl. 13.2:33

Substrata 3a-b

Stopper/Button No. 10 (Fig. 13.2:10; Pl. 13.2:10)
This is a rounded potsherd in secondary use; it has two holes pierced through it (another such object was found in Substratum 3b, but was not catalogued). Such objects are customarily identified as buttons (see Macalister 1912 III:90), though other suggestions have also been offered, such as children's toys (Petrie 1928:18).

Similarly, according to Albright and Kelso (1968:58) these were toys (of the 'bull-roarer' type according to their terminology), and Van Beek suggested that they were 'buzz' toys, such as are still used today (a string is looped through the two holes and the players hold it at either end and pass the object back and forth). But he also allowed for the possibility that such objects could have been used as game pieces and perhaps even as pendants (Van Beek 1989:53–58; 1991:62–63). It is,

Fig. 13.2. Various clay objects (Cat. Nos. 10, 18–20, 29–31).

however, also possible that this object was used as a (perforated) stopper.

Clay Cones Nos. 18 and 19 (Fig. 13.2:18, 19; Pl. 13.2: 18, 19)
These are two small, handmade conical objects (2.5 cm and 2.0 cm high, respectively). They were both found in Silo 854 in Area F. Their shape, size and the fact that they come from the same context indicate that they were apparently used as game pieces.

Stratum 2

Stopper (Seal?) No. 20 (Fig. 13.2:20; Pl. 13.2:20)
This is a fired lump of clay, carelessly handmade, 3 cm in diameter, pinched in its upper part. The lower part is round and flat and incised with a circle and two crossing lines. This object may have been used as a stopper or, alternatively, it is a very crude seal.

Miniature Altars Nos. 29 and 30 (Fig. 13.2:29, 30; see Pls. 11.105:9, 11.110:19)
Though altar No. 30 was found in a mixed locus, it seems highly likely that it should be attributed, like No. 29, to Stratum 2.

Stratum 1

Burnishing Tool No. 31 (Fig. 13.2:31; Pl. 13.2:31)
This oval object is 5 cm long, 2.5 cm wide and 1 cm thick. It was made of a potsherd in secondary use, whose edges were rounded and smoothed. It was probably used to burnish pottery.

SIMPLE GROUNDSTONE VESSELS AND TOOLS

This category contains a range of tools, such as grinding stones, mortars and pestles, as well as vessels, such as bowls and lids.

Table 13.3. Catalogue of Simple Groundstone Vessels and Tools

Cat. No.	Object	Material	Reg. No.	Locus	Locus Description	Area	Stratum	Plate
1	Upper grinding stone	Limestone	5209	3097	Floor	B	Pre-4	
2	Lower grinding stone	Basalt	8477/2	6236	Floor	C	4b	
3	Lower grinding stone	Limestone	1770/2	819	Fill	E	4b	
4	Lower grinding stone	Basalt	872	472	Above floor	E	4b	
5	Lower grinding stone)	Limestone	2024/7	938	Floor	E	4b	
6	Lower grinding stone	Limestone	1830	823	Floor	E	4b	
7	Upper grinding stone	Limestone	574/7	291	Above floor	A1	4b	
8	Upper grinding stone	Limestone	5357/2	3199	Above floor	B	4b	
9	Upper grinding stone	Limestone	8239	6109	Floor	C	4b	
10	Upper grinding stone	Limestone	8533/2	6235	Floor	C	4b	
11	Upper grinding stone	Limestone	1703	820	Floor	E	4b	
12	Upper grinding stone	Limestone	3044	954	Fill	E	4b	
13	Upper grinding stone	Basalt	2041	954	Fill	E	4b	
14	Upper Grinding stone	Limestone	1763/2	816	Floor	E	4b	
15	Upper grinding stone	Basalt	2024/6	938	Floor	E	4b	
16	Mortar	Limestone	7089	5052	Fill	E	4b	Pl. 13.3:16
17	Mortar	Limestone	2046	954	Fill	E	4b	
18	Lid	Limestone	5369	3207	Floor	B	4b	
19	Lid	Limestone	8593/12	6300	Above floor	C	4	
20	Lid	Limestone	7090	5055	Floor	E	4b	
21	Lid	Limestone	2024/1	938	Floor	E	4b	
22	Lid	Limestone	2024/2	938	Floor	E	4b	
23	Lid	Limestone	2024/3	938	Floor	E	4b	
24	Lid	Limestone	2024/4	938	Floor	E	4b	
25	Lid	Limestone	2024/5	938	Floor	E	4b	
26	Lid	Limestone	1993/16	938	Floor	E	4b	
27	Lid	Limestone	2043/5	953	Floor	E	4b	
28	Lid	Limestone	1742	811	Above floor	E	4b	Pl. 13.3:28
29	Stopper/plug	Limestone	2028	947	Fill	E	4b	Pl. 13.3:29
30	Grinding slab	Sandstone	530	271	Burnt layer	A1	4a	
31	Lower grinding stone	Limestone	5368	3204	Floor	B	4a	

Fig. 13.3. Simple groundstone vessels and tools (Cat. Nos. 5, 7, 11, 12, 15, 16, 18–21).

Table 13.3 (cont.). **Catalogue of Simple Groundstone Vessels and Tools**

Cat. No.	Object	Material	Reg. No.	Locus	Locus Description	Area	Stratum	Plate
32	Upper grinding stone	Limestone	981	487	Brick debris	E	4a	
33	Mortar	Limestone	5128	268	-	A1	4a	
34	Mortar	Limestone	543/11	265	Above floor	A1	4a	
35	Lower grinding stone	Limestone	5273/1	3164	Floor	B	4	
36	Lower grinding stone	Limestone	5273/2	3164	Floor	B	4	
37	Lower grinding stone	Limestone	8589	6294	Installation, floor	C	4	
38	Upper grinding stone	Limestone	8503	6304	Above floor	C	4	
39	Upper grinding stone	Limestone	8586/5	6294	Installation, floor	C	4	
40	Upper grinding stone	Limestone	3024	939	Fill	E	4a, b	
41	Mortar	Limestone	584/2	283	Fill	A1	4a, b	
42	Mortar	Limestone	8593/11	6294	Installation, floor	C	4	
43	Lid	Limestone	5279/1	3165	Floor	B	4	
44	Lid	Limestone	5279/2	3165	Floor	B	4	
45	Lid	Limestone	5279/3	3165	Floor	B	4	
46	Lid	Limestone	8590	6292	Floor	C	4	
47	Lid	Limestone	8586/6	6294	Installation, floor	C	4	
48	Weight(?)	Limestone	2587	1231	Fill	B	3c	
49	Grinding slab fragment (cosmetic?)	Limestone	8415/2	6208	Fills	C	3c	Pl. 13.3:49
50	Grinding slab (cosmetic?)	Greenish, unidentified stone	1751	812	Fills	E	3c	Pl. 13.3:50
51	Lower grinding stone	Limestone	1388	127	Fills	A1	3c	
52	Lower grinding stone	Limestone	318	238	Fills	A1	3c	
53	Lower grinding stone	Limestone	3032	1302	Fills	D	3c	
54	Lower grinding stone	Limestone (?)	2875	1097	Fills	D	3c	
55	Lower grinding stone	Limestone	9002	7000	Fills	F	3c	
56	Upper grinding stone	Limestone	513	242	Fills	A	3c	
57	Upper grinding stone	Limestone	5101	3056	Fills	B	3c	
58	Upper grinding stone	Limestone	5347/1	3198	Fills	B	3c	Pl. 13.3:58

Fig. 13.3 (cont.). Simple groundstone vessels and tools (Cat. Nos. 22, 23, 26, 28, 29, 33, 40, 46, 48–50, 54).

Table 13.3 (cont.). **Catalogue of Simple Groundstone Vessels and Tools**

Cat. No.	Object	Material	Reg. No.	Locus	Locus Description	Area	Stratum	Plate
59	Upper grinding stone	Sandstone	8427	6217	Fills	C	3c	
60	Upper grinding stone	Limestone	949	498	Fills	C	3c	
61	Upper grinding stone	Limestone	1749	812	Fills	E	3c	
62	Upper grinding stone	Limestone	1751	812	Fills	E	3c	
63	Upper grinding stone	Basalt	815	471	Fill	E	3c	
64	Upper grinding stone	Limestone	871	471	Fill	E	3c	
65	Upper grinding stone	Limestone	1956	916	Fill	H	3c	
66	Mortar	Limestone	345	196	Fills	A1	3c	
67	Bowl (rectangular)	Basalt	2522	800	Fills	B	3c	Pl. 13.3:67
68	Lid	Limestone	2489	781	Fills	B	3c	
69	Lid	Limestone	8562	6274	Fills	C	3c	
70	Lower grinding stone	Limestone	8479	6233	Fill	A1	3b	
71	Lower(?) grinding stone	Limestone	2982	1243	-	B	3b	Pl. 13.3:71
72	Upper grinding stone	Limestone	8145	6233	Fill	A1	3b	
73	Upper grinding stone	Limestone	1363	609	-	C	3b	
74	Upper grinding stone	Limestone	1391	635	Floor	C	3b	
75	Lid	Limestone	2598	1243	-	B	3b	
76	Lid	Limestone	2445	779	Floor	B	3b	Pl. 13.3:76
77	Lower grinding stone	Limestone	1327	605	-	C	3a	
78	Bowl fragment	Basalt	1609	1204	Floor (disturbed?)	B	3a	
79	Upper grinding stone	Limestone	1304	684	-	C	3a-b	
80	Upper grinding stone	Limestone	2298	659	Fill	C	3a-b	
81	Upper grinding stone	Limestone	2281	1101	Fill	C	3a-b	
82	Upper grinding stone	Limestone	2691	853	Floor	F	3a-b	
83	Upper grinding stone	Limestone	1920	908	-	D	3a-b	
84	Lower grinding stone	Limestone	8114	6079	Fill	G	3a-b	
85	Stopper	Limestone	791/1	464	Floor	C	3a-b	Pl. 13.3:85

Table 13.3 (cont.). **Catalogue of Simple Groundstone Vessels and Tools**

Cat. No.	Object	Material	Reg. No.	Locus	Locus Description	Area	Stratum	Plate
86	Lid(?)	Limestone	1927	908	-	D	3a-b	
87	Lower grinding stone	Limestone	2205	634	Fill of granary	C	3, 2	
88	Upper grinding stone	Limestone	1390/3	634	Fill of granary	C	3, 2	
89	Upper grinding stone	Limestone	8503/5	6257	Fill of granary	C	3, 2	
90	Upper grinding stone	Limestone	8503/6	6257	Fill of granary	C	3, 2	
91	Upper grinding stone	Limestone	1069	528	Floor	C	2	
92	Lower grinding stone	Limestone	3275	1514	Floor of cistern	D	2	

Fig. 13.3. (cont.). Simple groundstone vessels and tools (Cat. Nos. 58, 59, 67, 71, 76, 84, 87).

Table 13.3 (cont.). **Catalogue of Simple Groundstone Vessels and Tools**

Cat. No.	Object	Material	Reg. No.	Locus	Locus Description	Area	Stratum	Plate
93	Lower grinding stone	Limestone	1907	905	-	D	2	
94	Upper grinding stone	Limestone	52	27	Fill	A1	2	
95	Upper grinding stone	Limestone	316/8	157	Floor	A2	2	
96	Upper grinding stone	Basalt	43	157	Floor	A2	2	
97	Upper grinding stone	Limestone	786/2	419	Floor makeup	A2	2	
98	Upper grinding stone	Limestone	395	186	Floor	A2	2	
99	Upper grinding stone	Limestone	876/3	491	Floor	A2	2	
100	Upper grinding stone	Basalt	58/2	46	Fill	A2	2	
101	Upper grinding stone	Basalt	790	401	Above floor	A2	2	
102	Upper grinding stone	Limestone	729/9	420	Floor makeup	A2	2	
103	Upper grinding stone	Limestone	1917/3	903	Above floor	A2	2	
104	Upper grinding stone	Limestone	1420	637	Floor	A2	2	
105	Upper grinding stone	Limestone	791/3	461	Above floor	B	2	
106	Upper grinding stone	Limestone	2430	770	Fill	B	2	
107	Upper grinding stone	Sandstone	1027/6	532	Wall removal	B	2	
108	Upper grinding stone	Sandstone	959/9	492	Floor	B	2	
109	Upper grinding stone	Sandstone	919	492	Floor	B	2	
110	Upper grinding stone	Limestone	1915	905	-	D	2	
111	Bowl fragment	Basalt	8401	6201	Fill	A1	2	Pl. 13.3:111
112	Bowl fragment	Basalt	45/1	39	Floor	A2	2	Pl. 13.3:112
113	Plug(?)	Limestone	73/3	58	Floor	A2	2	
114	Plug(?)	Limestone	1211	901	Above floor	A2	2	Pl. 13.3:114
115	Lower grinding stone	Limestone	4027	2003	Fill, debris	E	2, 1	
116	Upper grinding stone	Limestone	1018	500	Debris	C	2, 1	
117	Upper grinding stone	Limestone	4057	2014	Floor of moat	E	2	
118	Upper grinding stone	Limestone	4108/1	2150	Fill of moat	E	2	
119	Pestle	Limestone	3210	1512	Fill of cistern	D	2, 1	

Table 13.3 (cont.). **Catalogue of Simple Groundstone Vessels and Tools**

Cat. No.	Object	Material	Reg. No.	Locus	Locus Description	Area	Stratum	Plate
120	Upper grinding stone	Limestone	4057	2014	Floor of moat	E	2	
121	Upper grinding stone	Limestone	3210	2150	Fill of moat	E	2	
122	Mortar	Sandstone	9080	7037	Fill of moat	F	2, 1	
123	Polished stone (burnishing tool?)	Limestone	9098	7038	Floor of moat	F	2, 1	Pl. 13.3:123
124	Lid	Limestone	76	26	Pit	A1	1	
125	Upper grinding stone	Limestone	8578	6290	Balk removal	A1	4–2	
126	Lower grinding stone	Basalt	2299	1108	Floor and pit	C	3, 1	
127	Lower grinding stone	Limestone	327	160	Balk cleaning	A	-	
128	Lower grinding stone	Limestone	5285	3176	Fill	B	-	
129	Upper grinding stone	Limestone	7196	5088	Wall cleaning	H	-	

Fig. 13.3 (cont.). Simple groundstone vessels and tools (Cat. Nos. 103–105, 108, 114, 122, 125).

OTHER STONE OBJECTS

Under this heading are grouped a few stone objects that were separated from the previous category due to their being of more 'special' character than the tools/vessels enumerated above.

Table 13.4. Catalogue of Other Stone Objects

Cat. No.	Object	Material	Reg. No.	Locus	Locus Description	Area	Stratum	Plate
1	Cosmetic bowl	Reddish stone	8183/1	6096	Floor makeup	C	3c	Pl. 13.4:1
2	Cosmetic bowl	White limestone	2278/1	694	Fill of granary	C	3, 2	Pl. 13.4:2
3	Bowl	Basalt	5182/74	1204	Floor (disturbed)	B	3a	Pl. 13.4:3
4	Small altar	Soft white limestone	8131	6059	Fills	C	3c	Pl. 13.4:4
5	Small altar	White limestone	2660	861	Fill of silo	F	3a-b	Pl. 13.4:5
6	Game piece(?)	Soft limestone and traces of metal	2635/1	853	Floor	F	3a-b	Pl. 13.4:6
7	Rounded weight(?) (44 g)	Hematite	702/2	402	Fill to floor	A2	2	

Substratum 3c

Cosmetic Bowl No. 1 (Fig. 13.4:1; Pl. 13.4:1)
The rim of the bowl bears a meticulous incised guilloche, apparently executed with a compass, in the spaces of which are small perforations. The base is decorated with an incised rosette with pointed leaves.

Altar No. 4 (Fig. 13.4:4; Pl. 13.4:4)
This small altar is 15 cm high, composed of a pillar that widens at its top to form the square container. Both the pillar and the container were irregularly chiselled. The object was found in the Substratum 3c constructional fill, and thus its original use context cannot be determined. However, its size indicates its probable use a domestic altar.

Small stone altars in Iron II contexts were found, for example, at Tell Beit Mirsim, in Stratum A (Albright 1943: Pl. 65:1) and in the cult room in Stratum V at Lachish (the tenth century BCE, Aharoni 1975: Pls. 27:3, 43:7). The latter is similar to our altar, but significantly larger (45 cm high).

Substrata 3a-b

Basalt Bowl No. 3 (Fig. 13.4:3; Pl. 13.4:3)
The rounded bowl has a ring base; below the rim is a rounded ridge, perhaps a version of a bar handle. The rim is rounded and curves in. The bowl is well made and polished.

Complete basalt bowls of this type are known mainly in the late Iron Age, for example at Ashdod in a late eighth–late seventh century BCE context (Dothan 1971: Fig. 66:11), and at Ḥorbat 'Uza Stratum 4, of the seventh–early sixth centuries BCE (Beit-Arieh, forthcoming: Fig. 11:1). Later examples were published, for example, from the 'Solar Shrine' in Lachish Stratum I, of the fifth century BCE (Tufnell 1953: Pl. 65:7).

Small Altar No. 5 (Fig. 13.4:5; Pl. 13.4:5)
This oblong object is 4 cm high and 8 cm long on its nearly complete side. It is made of white limestone and has signs of burning inside. No meaningfull parallels are known for this object.

Fig. 13.4. Other stone objects (Cat. Nos. 1–6).

Game Piece(?) No. 6 (Fig. 13.4:6; Pl. 13.4:6)
In each of the corners of two of its faces (apparently the upper and lower faces) a small circle was incised. On a third side there are three incised circles and on a fourth, two incised circles. Bits of metal adhere to at least one face of the object.

Strata 3–2

Cosmetic Bowl No. 2 (Fig. 13.4:2; Pl. 13.4:2)
The rim of this bowl is undecorated, but in the center there is a delicately incised rosette with rounded leaves.

BONE OBJECTS

A wide variety of items, made from animal bones, was found. One worked fish vertebra was also recovered.

General Comments on Spatulae

Bone spatulae are ubiquitous at Kadesh Barnea, attested from Substratum 3c through Stratum 1. A plethora of opinions exist as to the the use of these objects. Macalister, for instance, believed that they were instruments for writing on wax or clay (1912 II: 274). Reisner, Fisher and Lyon (1924:372) suggested that they were used in household activities; Petrie (1928:17), that they were tools for preparing fish nets; Lamon and Shipton (1939: Pls. 95, 96) and Harrison (1947:265), that they were cosmetic utensils; Tufnell (1953:397), that they were used to separate threads while working the loom; and Van Beek and Van Beek (1990:208), that they were medical instruments, employed for removing intrusive items from the eyes. In light of the ubiquity of these objects at Kadesh Barnea and elsewehre (Van Beek 1990:205–206), it appears that this was a multi-purpose tool for various domestic and possibly also medical purposes.

Substrata 3a-b

Perforated Object No. 26 (Fig. 13.5:26; Pl. 13.5:26)
The object is triangular in shape, 12 cm long and 13 cm wide. It was made from a scapula of a large animal, and polished and perforated at one end. It may have been used as a pendant.

Table 13.5. Catalogue of Bone Objects

Cat. No.	Object	Reg. No.	Locus	Locus Description	Area	Stratum	Plate
1	Awl	8477/1	6236	Floor	C	4b	
2	Handle	4011	2005	Pit	E	4b	Pl. 13.5:2
3	Worked bone	8579/2	6288	Above floor	C	4	Fig. 19.8:2
4	Worked rib	2281	674	Fill	C	4	
5	Handle	8583/6	6294	Floor and installation	C	4	Fig. 19.8:7
6	Spatula	8419	6213	Cleaning	C	3c	Pl. 13.5:6
7	Spatula	787	471	Fill	E	3c	
8	Handle	1406/2	638	Fills	C	3c	
9	Awl	8057	6023	Fills	C	3c	
10	Worked fish vertebra	59	47	Fills	A1	3c	
11	Worked rib	8535	6266	Fills	A1	3c	
12	Worked bone	1414	641	Fills	C	3c	
13	Handle(?) fragment	5323	3187	Fills	B	3c	Pl. 13.5:13
14	Handle(?) fragment	5184	3085	Fills	B	3c	Pl. 13.5:14
15	Handle(?) fragment	1406/1	638	Fills	C	3c	Pl. 13.5:15
16	Handle(?) fragment	2825	1088	Fills	D	3c	Pl. 13.5:16
17	Handle(?) fragment	594	225	Fills	A1	3c	

Table 13.5 (cont). **Catalogue of Bone Objects**

Cat. No.	Object	Reg. No.	Locus	Locus Description	Area	Stratum	Plate
18	Worked bone (fragment)	1582	720	Floor	B	3b	
19	Spatula fragment	376/5	182	Above floor	A1	3a	Pl. 13.5:19
20	Spatula fragment	1352/5	613	-	C	3a-b	
21	Spatula fragment	1352/5	613	-	C	3a-b	
22	Spatula	5050	3024	Floor	C	3a-b	Pl. 13.5:22
23	Spatula fragment	1334/7	612	-	C	3a-b	
24	Pin	559	780	Floor makeup	B	3b	Pl. 13.5:24
25	Pin	8030	6008	Cleaning	C	3a-b	Pl. 13.5:25
26	Perforated object	5053	3024	Floor	C	3a-b	Pl. 13.5:26
27	Handle	3053	1407	Balk (mixed?)	D	-	Pl. 13.5:27
28	Worked rib	1334/8	612	-	C	3a-b	
29	Worked rib	309	150	-	A1	3a-b	Pl. 19.8:4
30	Spatula	8496	6246	Fill of granary	C	3, 2	Pl. 13.5:30
31	Spatula	8031/7	6016	Fill of granary	C	3, 2	Pl. 13.5:31
32	Spatula	1330	615	Fill of granary	C	3, 2	
33	Spatula	2671	694	Fill of granary	C	3, 2	
34	Spatula	8497	6252	Fill of granary	C	3, 2	
35	Decorated disc	1401	634	Fill of granary	C	3, 2	Pl. 13.5:35
36	Worked bone	2261/4	689	Fill of granary	C	3, 2	Pl. 13.5:36
37	Spatula	1914	903	Above floor	A2	2	Pl. 13.5:37
38	Spatula	801	424	Above floor	A2	2	Pl. 13.5:38
39	Spatula	904	501	Floor	A2	2	
40	Spatula	1413/5	637	Floor	A2	2	
41	Spatula	804	424	Above floor	A2	2	
42	Spatula	761	421	Above floor	C	2	
43	Worked bone	2469	774	Floor	B	2	
44	Handle	994/5	523	Above floor	A2	2	Pl. 13.5:44
45	Handle	8291	6128	Fill (balk)	C	2	Pl. 13.5:45
46	Pinhead	8177	6083	-	A2	2, 1	
47	Pin	3214	1500	Fill of cistern	D	2, 1	Pl. 13.5:47
48	Spatula fragment	3219	1500	Fill of cistern	D	2, 1	Pl. 13.5:48
49	Spatula	3074	1304	Fill of channel	D	3–1	Pl. 13.5:49
50	Spatula	4053	2014	Floor of moat	E	2	
51	Worked bone	3044	1404	Fill of cistern	D	2, 1	Pl. 13.5:51
52	Spatula	799	466	-	B	1	Pl. 13.5:52
53	Pin fragment	9073/2	7026	Debris in moat	F	2, 1	Pl. 13.5:53
54	Spatula	2300/4	1108	Floor and pit	C	3, 1	
55	Handle	8570	6283	Wall removal	C	-	Pl. 13.5:55

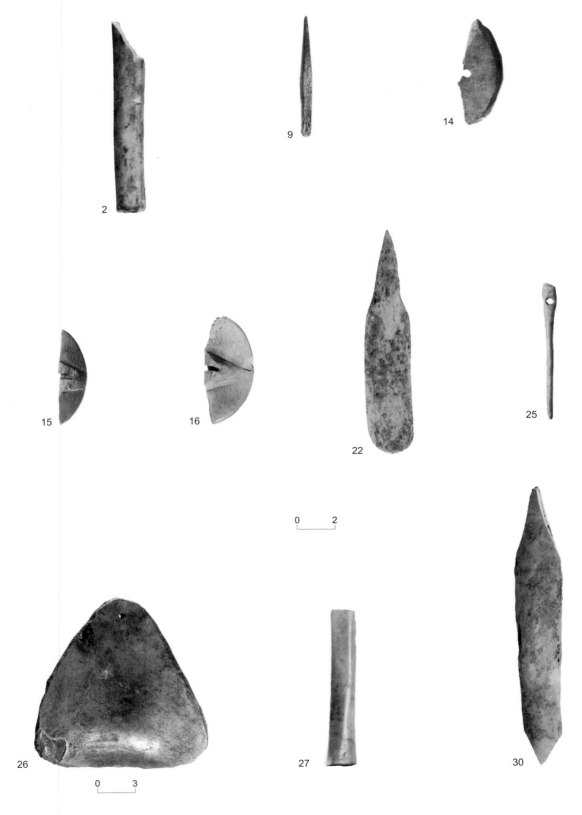

Fig. 13.5. Bone objects (Cat. Nos. 2, 9, 14–16, 22, 25–27, 30).

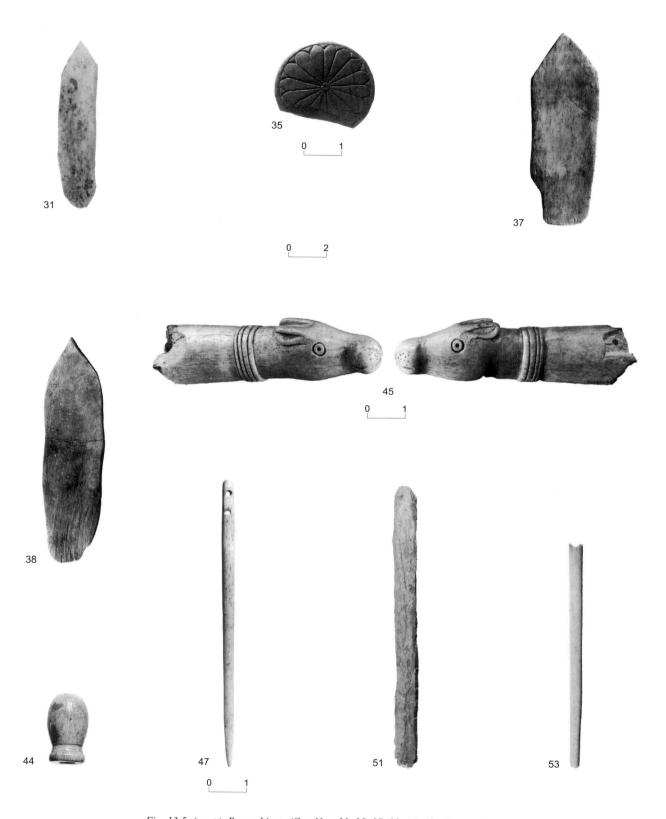

Fig. 13.5. (cont.). Bone objects (Cat. Nos. 31, 35, 37, 38, 44, 45, 47, 51, 53).

STRATUM 3–2

Decorated Disc No. 35 (Fig. 13.5:35; Pl. 13.5:35)
This fragmentary object is 2 cm in diameter, with one flat and one convex side. It is polished and decorated with an incised rosette. It probably served as an inlay, perhaps of a piece of furniture or a wooden box. A similar bone object was uncovered in an Iron Age context at Tell Beit Mirsim, Stratum B (Albright 1943: Pl. 60:13). Similar objects, but made of of ivory, were unearthed in Cemetery A at Tell el-Mazar (dated to the late Iron Age; Yassine 1984: Fig. 61:5), in Tomb 5 at Gezer (Macalister 1912 III: Pl. CXCV:61), and at Tawilan (dated to the seventh century BCE; Bennett and Bienkowski 1995: Fig. 9.12:11).

Stratum 2

Handle No. 44 (Fig. 13.5:44; Pl. 13.5:44)
This object is carefully made. It is adorned with incised rings. The socket indicates that this was probably a handle of an object, possibly of metal.

Carved Handle No. 45 (Fig. 13.5:45; Pl. 13.5:45)
This (broken) handle is 7 cm long. It, too, is carefully made and exhibits technological skill. It is shaped as the elongated head of a deer. The muzzle is rounded and bulbous, and details are incised. The eyes are represented by pairs of concentric circles. The carved ears are pulled backward. At the base of the animal's neck are four carved rings. This handle was apparently used for cosmetics, ointments and the like, as such tools were usually of higher technical quality and more attention was paid to their aesthetic qualities.

Strata 2–1

Pin No. 47 (Fig. 13.47; Pl. 13.5:47)
This 10 cm long pin is distinguished by the two 5 mm wide holes pierced in its wider end, an unusual feature.

METAL OBJECTS

This category also includes jewelry items made of metal; all objects are of bronze.

Table 13.6. Catalogue of Metal Objects

Cat. No.	Object	Reg. No.	Locus	Locus Description	Area	Stratum	Plate
1	Arrowhead	1815	821	Below floor	E	4c	Pl. 13.6:1
2	Arrowhead	8588	6294	Floor and installation	C	4	Pl. 13.6:2
3	Pin	1115	487	Brick collapse	E	4a	Pl. 13.6:3
4	Spearhead	1756	810	Fills	E	3c	Pl. 13.6:4
5	Arrowhead	8101	6041	Fills	C	3c	Pl. 13.6:5
6	Arrowhead	8070	6044	Mixed + granary	C	3c	Pl. 13.6:6
7	Arrowhead	1754	812	Fills	E	3c	Pl. 13.6:7
8	Arrowhead	1717	805	Fills	E	3c	Pl. 13.6:8
9	Ring	5158	3076	Burial + fills	B	3c	Pl. 13.6:9
10	Arrowhead	1615	726	Floor	B	3b	Pl. 13.6:10
11	Arrowhead	1387	629	Floor	C	3b	Pl. 13.6:11
12	Arrowhead	8042	6020	Fill	C	3a-b	
13	Arrowhead	8144/3	6079	Cleaning	G	3a-b	Pl. 13.6:13
14	Kohl stick	8075	6050	Floor makeup	C	3a-b	Pl. 13.6:14
15	Kohl stick	796	464	Floor	C	3a-b	Pl. 13.6:15
16	Pincers	2981	787	Above floor	B	3b	Pl. 13.6:16
17	'Horseshoe'	9510	8009	Stone pavement	G	3a-b	Pl. 13.6:17

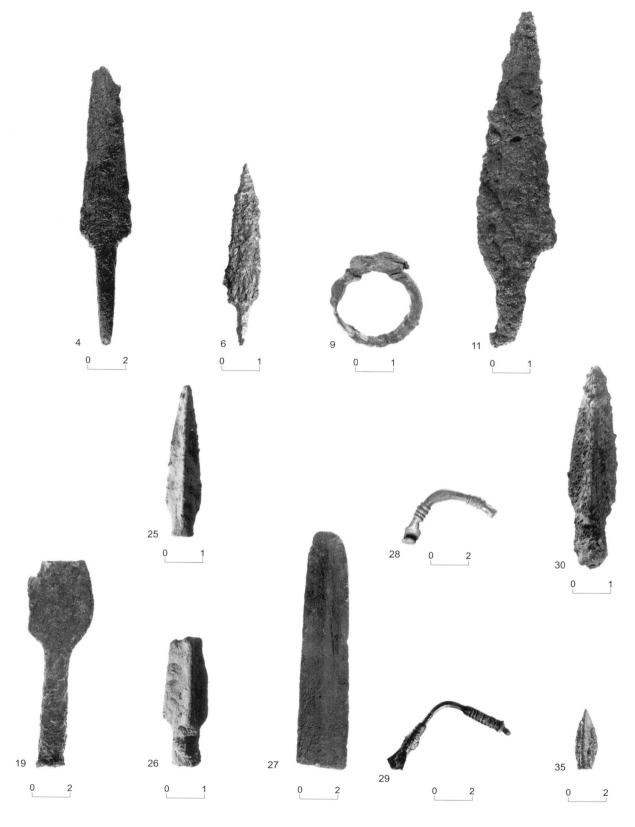

Fig. 13.6. Metal objects (Cat. Nos. 4, 6, 9, 11, 19, 25–30, 35).

Table 13.6 (cont.). **Catalogue of Metal Objects**

Cat. No.	Object	Reg. No.	Locus	Locus Description	Area	Stratum	Plate
18	Bracelet	8023	6002	Floor	C	3a-b	Pl. 13.6:18
19	Spearhead fragment	8444	6223	Fill of granary	C	3, 2	Pl. 13.6:19
20	Arrowhead	8500	6254	Fill of granary	C	3, 2	Pl. 13.6:20
21	Arrowhead	8044	6019	Fill of granary	C	3, 2	
22	Arrowhead	1904/3	904	Collapsed debris	D	3, 2	Pl. 13.6:22
23	Arrowhead	1913	903	Above floor	A2	2	Pl. 13.6:23
24	Arrowhead	1626	409	Fill	A2	2	Pl. 13.6:24
25	Arrowhead	483	186	Floor	A2	2	Pl. 13.6:25
26	Arrowhead	515	236	Fill	E	3, 2	
27	Blade	5040/1	3012	Floor	A2	2	
28	Fibula	755	414	Floor makeup	A2	2	Pl. 13.6:28
29	Fibula	800	424	Above floor	A2	2	
30	Arrowhead	1385	628	-	C	1	Pl. 13.6:30
31	Arrowhead	745	429	-	G	2, 1	Pl. 13.6:31
32	Pin	5150	3063	Fill of cistern	B	2, 1	Pl. 13.6:32
33	Cosmetic spoon	3220	1500	Fill of cistern	D	2, 1	Pl. 13.6:33
34	Arrowhead	8152	6085	Fill [?+pit]	C	3c[+1]	Pl. 13.6:34
35	Arrowhead	8040	6014	Fill	C	3c, 1	Pl. 13.6:35
36	Fibula	401	191	Disturbed	A1	3a, 1	Pl. 13.6:36

JEWELRY

Grouped here are jewelry items made from many types of raw material, except for metal. Those appear above in 'Metal Objects'.

Stratum 4

Faience Horus-Eye Pendants Nos. 1, 2 (Fig. 13.7:1, 2; Pl. 13.7:1, 2)

Two near-complete Egyptian Udjat ('Horus')-eye pendants were found in the same Stratum 4 locus (6300), an accumulation in one of the fortress' casemates. Along with pendant No. 3, found in the same context, they were probably strung on one neckace or bracelet. (An additional, fragmentary example, No. 19, was found in a mixed Strata 3 + 2 locus.)

Number 1 is unusual in shape; the eyeball, except for the pupil, is hollowed out. On No. 2 most of the eyeball is missing, but it seems that it was rendered similarly to that of No. 1.

Ivory Pendant No. 3 (Pl. 13.7:3)

This fragmentary object, found in the same context as pendants Nos. 1 and 2, is 2.5 cm long and 1.3 cm wide. The surviving part consists of a rectangular slab on which two feet are seen, the left one in front. This seems to be a fragment of an Egyptian amulet depicting the lioness-shaped goddess Sekhmet. In Iron Age Judah, faience Sekhmet amulets are known for example from Lachish Tomb 28, Room C, dated 804–750 BCE (Tufnell 1958: Pl. 34:18, 21).

Stratum 2

Faience Pendant No. 22 (Fig. 13.7:22; Pl. 13.7:22)

This Egyptian (Bes?) pendant/amulet has a hole pierced in its upper part. In Iron Age Judah, faience Bes-shaped amulets were found, e.g., in Lachish Tombs 120 and 1002 of the ninth–eighth centuries BCE (Tufnell 1958: Pls. 34:12, 13, 14; 36:48).

Table 13.7. Catalogue of Jewelry

Cat. No.	Object	Material	Reg. No.	Locus	Locus Description	Area	Stratum	Plate
1	Horus-eye pendant	Faience	8598	6300	Above floor	C	4	Pl. 13.7:1
2	Horus-eye pendant	Faience	8599	6300	Above floor	C	4	Pl. 13.7:2
3	Pendant fragment	Ivory	8595	6300	Above floor	C	4	Pl. 13.7:3
4	Bead	Carnelian	8581	6288	Above floor	C	4	Pl. 13.7:4
5	Bead	Carnelian	6000	4000	Cleaning	E	4	Pl. 13.7:5
6	Bead	Stone or clay	9040	7022	Above floor	F	4	Pl. 13.7:6
7	Bead	Carnelian	1974	929	Fills	E	3c	Pl. 13.7:7
8	Bead	Carnelian	8425/3	6216	Fills	C	3c	Pl. 13.7:8
9	Bead	Carnelian	8425/1	6216	Fills	C	3c	Pl. 13.7:9
10	Bead	Ostrich eggshell	8425/2	6216	Fills	C	3c	Pl. 13.7:10
11	Pendant	Limestone	8022	6001	Fills	C	3c	
12	Pendant(?)	Echinus spike	8143/2	6082	Floor? [+pit]	C	3c, 1	Pl. 13.7:12
13	Bead	Limestone	2247/4	666	-	C	3a-b	Pl. 13.7:13
14	Bead	Faience	1582	720	Floor	B	3b	Pl. 13.7:14
15	Bead	Ostrich eggshell	2627/1	853	Floor	F	3a-b	Pl. 13.7:15
16	Bead	Ostrich eggshell	2627/2	853	Floor	F	3a-b	Pl. 13.7:16
17	Pendant	Shell	2670	856	Ṭabun	F	3a-b	Pl. 13.7:17
18	Horus-eye pendant	Faience	398/1	189	Disturbance	A1	3a, 2	Pl. 13.7:18
19	Bead	Carnelian	8020/7	6010	Fill of granary	C	3, 2	Pl. 13.7:19
20	Bead	Glass	1904/1	904	Debris	D	3, 2	Pl. 13.7:20
21	Bead	Glass	1904/2	904	Debris	D	3, 2	Pl. 13.7:21
22	Pendant	Faience	1304/1	600	Fill	A2	2	Pl. 13.7:22
23	Bead	Carnelian	5040/2	3012	Floor	A2	2	Pl. 13.7:23
24	Bead	Steatite	705/3	405	Above floor	A2	2	Pl. 13.7:24
25	Bead	Faience	1903	903	Above floor	A2	2	Pl. 13.7:25
26	Bead	Glass	1078/4	542	Floor of tower	A2	2	Pl. 13.7:26
27	Bead	Dentalium	2604	850	Fill, debris	F	2	Pl. 13.7:27
28	Bead	Ostrich eggshell	385/13	186	Floor	A2	2	Pl. 13.7:28
29	Bead	Bone	964	501	Floor	A2	2	Pl. 13.7:29
30	Ring	Shell	802	461	Above floor	B	2	Pl. 13.7:30
31	Pendant	Limestone	1304/2	600	Fill	A2	2	Pl. 13.7:31
32	Pendant	Shell	705/1	405	Above floor	A2	2	Pl. 13.7:32
33	Pendant	Shell	705/2	405	Above floor	A2	2	Pl. 13.7:33
34	Bead	Steatite	493	229	Floor and fill	A2	2, 1	Pl. 13.7:34
35	Bead	Faience	3203	1500	Fill of cistern	D	2, 1	Pl. 13.7:35
36	Bead	Carnelian	5198	3086	Fill of cistern	B	2, 1	Pl. 13.7:36
37	Bead	Limestone	2968	1226	Disturbed fill	B	3c, 1	Pl. 13.7:37
38	Bead	Faience	-	-	Surface	-	-	Pl. 13.7:38
39	Bead	Shell (conch)	4018	2002	Fill	E	-	Pl. 13.7:39

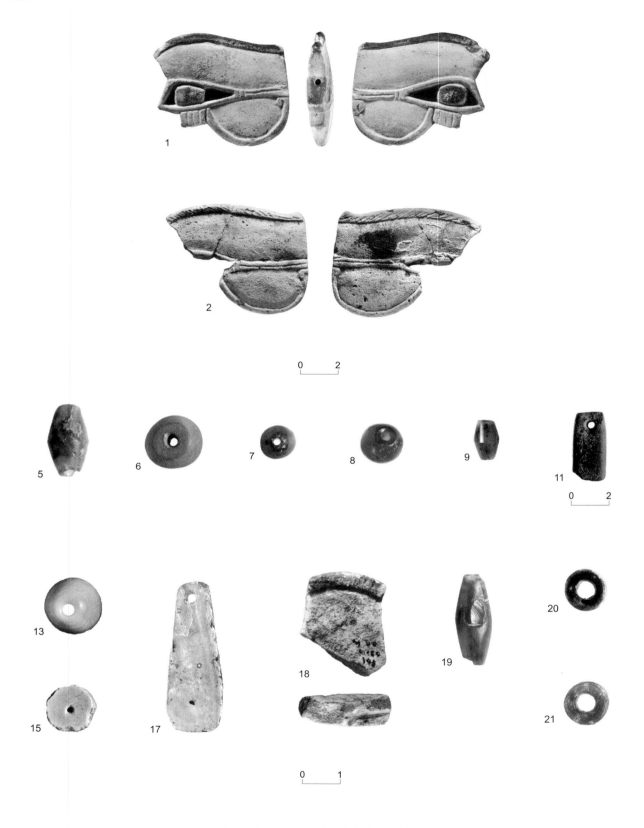

Fig. 13.7. Jewelry (Cat. Nos. 1, 2, 5–9, 11, 13, 15, 17–21).

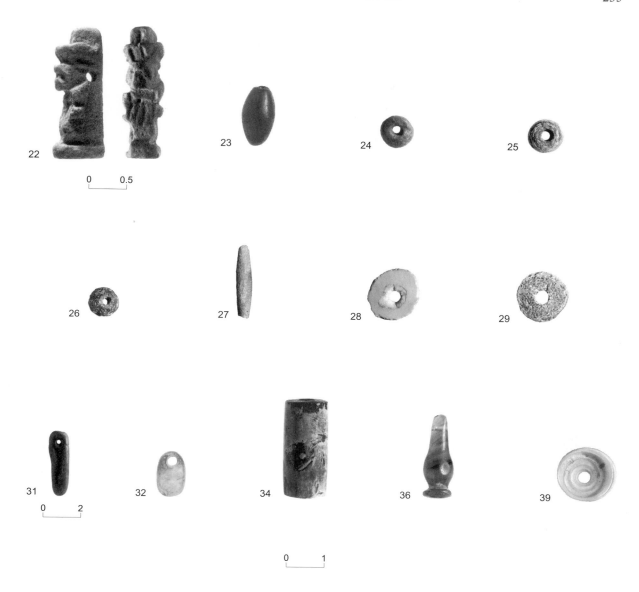

Fig. 13.7 (cont.). Jewelry (Cat. Nos. 22–29, 31, 32, 34, 36, 39).

NOTE

[1] Not all the existing illustrations of the 'small finds' have been included here. Additional photographs, especially of groundstone tools, are filed in the IAA archives.

CHAPTER 14

STAMP SEALS AND SEAL IMPRESSIONS

STEFAN MÜNGER

INTRODUCTION

This report presents three seals and three sealings uncovered in Strata 4–2. As the report was compiled after the artifacts were handed over to the Egyptian authorities, it is based on the photographs and line-drawings produced at the IAA and not on an examination of the objects themselves; measurements are taken from these photographs. Additional, simpler stamps, appearing on Negebite pottery, are presented in Chapter 12, and two *yhd* stamps are discussed in Chapter 15.

Analogous objects, in the 'Parallels' section for each item, are referred to only if they originate in authorized excavations. Parallels from museums or private collections are only cited when they are essential to the discussion.

A capital letter followed by a number (e.g., H6) refers to the List of Hieroglyphic Signs in Gardiner 1957:438–548.

Parallels marked * are of unknown stratigraphic attribution, or altogether have none; (*) indicates an uncertain stratigraphic attribution or find context.

This report follows the traditional ('high') chronology of the Iron Age in the Southern Levant, according to *NEAEHL* 4:1529. For the dates of the Egyptian dynasties, cf. von Beckerath 1997.

SEALS

No. 1. Bifacial Rectangular Plaque (Fig. 14.1)

Registration Details and Context: Reg. No. 8470, L6230, Area C, Stratum 4b (Iron IIA, tenth century BCE).

Object
Bifacial rectangular plaque, Type II (Keel 1995: §216–228; esp. §§220–224), perforated lengthwise, slightly chipped; hollowed-out engraving with hatching (Keel

1995: §§333, 334); faience/composition (Keel 1995: §§394, 395); color unknown; dimensions about 31.1 × 24.6 mm (according to Keel [1995: §221] such seals have an average length of 16.5 mm).

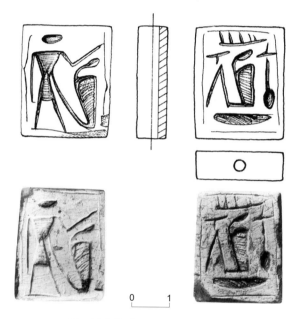

Fig. 14.1. Seal No. 1, Substratum 3b.

Side A
Description. Side A shows an anthropoid figure pacing to the right. The head is disconnected from the torso. The right arm hangs down along the body and the left arm is raised in a greeting/venerating gesture. A prancing uraeus (Keel 1995: §522) is in front of the figure, its tail touching the figure's waist. The scene seems to be bordered on the left, on the right and at the bottom by a thin line.

Discussion. This is an inept rendering of a motif common in the glyptic art of the New Kingdom, which originally showed a winged, falcon-headed deity with a sun-disk above its head,[1] spreading protectively its wing(s) over a uraeus (e.g., Tell el-Farʿah South, Tomb 222: Petrie 1930: Pl. 33:366 [oval piece with sheaf-shaped handle]; Tel Gerisa [Iron Ib context]: Shuval 1990:123–124, No. 2 [pyramidal seal]; el-Aḥwat: un-published; see also Tell Keisan, Stratum 9a: Keel 1980b:278–279, No. 22, with further references. This motif later developed into a variant where the uraeus is replaced by a flowering reed [M17] or a feather [H6] and the figure is not winged any longer; e.g., Megiddo Stratum VIA: Münger 2003: Fig. 1:3).[2]

Side B

Description. Upraised uraeus (Keel 1995: §529) with a long and bent tail (cf., e.g., (*)Tell Jemmeh, ʿStratum EFʾ: Petrie 1928: Pl. 19:18) facing a *nfr* (F35; Keel 1995: §459) to its right. Above the uraeus' head is a rake-shaped element (as, for example, *ʿAcco: Keel 1997: Akko No. 214). Above its tail is an unidentifiable T-shaped sign. A *nb* (V30; Keel 1995: §458) serves as an exergue. Four thin lines frame the scene.

Discussion. The combination ʿuraeus + nfr + nbʾ occurs in different arrangements on scarabs dated from MB II until Iron III (see, among others, Achziv: Brandl in Keel 1997: Achsib No. 141 [Phoenician, ninth–eighth centuries BCE]; Achsib No. 155 [XXVIth Dynasty]; Tell el-ʿAjjul: Keel 1997: Tell el-Aǧul No. 688 [XVth Dynasty or later]; Tell Beit Mirsim: Albright 1932:38, Fig. 7:2 [early XVIIIth Dynasty; cowroid]; Lachish: Tufnell 1953: Pl. 43:37 = 43A:37 [XXVIth Dynasty?]. Specimens outside the Southern Levant are Luxor: Newberry 1908: Pl. 41:36; Medinet Habu: Teeter 2003: Pl. 49c [frog scaraboid]; Arban: Giveon 1985:158–159, No. 7 [New Kingdom]; Kerkouan: Vercoutter 1945: Nos. 112, 113 [XXVIth Dynasty] and Tharros: Mendleson 1987: Pl. 49:14 [XXVIth Dynasty]).

It is not clear whether the rake above the uraeus' head is meant to be a *mn* (Y5; Keel 1995: §457) or is a misunderstood double feather crown. The latter is more likely, since in other iconographic compositions the *mn* is usually placed in different positions.[3]

Single uraei with a double feather crown are depicted, e.g., at Tell el-ʿAjjul: Keel 1997: Tell el-Aǧul No. 268 (Tomb 1117); *No. 369 (with the throne name of Ramesses II, 1279–1213 BCE; see also No. 288 [Tomb 1166C]); and at Megiddo, Stratum VII: Loud 1948: Pls. 152:190 = 158:190. In addition, there are scarab bases that show three crowned uraei in a row; e.g., at (*)Ashkelon: Keel 1997: Aschkelon No. 64; (*)Tel

Batash (mixed locus with LB II and Iron I material): Kelm and Mazar 1995:71, Fig. 4.38; Tell el-Farʿah South: Petrie 1930: Pl. 22:204 (Tomb 532; see also Pl. 22:200); Macdonald, Starkey and Harding 1932: Pls. 50:67 (Tomb 926b); 55:318 (Tomb 960j; degenerated); 50:95 (Tomb 961); and *Gezer: Macalister 1912 III: Pl. 202b:3.

Crowned uraei in combination with *nfr*- and *nb*-signs are nearly absent from the Palestinian corpus of glyptic finds from legal excavations. An exception—and an iconographically fine parallel—is a scarab dated to the XXth Dynasty from Lachish, Tomb 4002: Tufnell 1958:125, Pls. 39:369 = 40:369 (with an additional rope border). This motif is also known from Egypt and is found on collection items as well (cf. Hornung and Staehelin 1976: No. 494 with further parallels, and Nos. 687, 688). Hornung and Staehelin (1976:175) suggested that the combination ʿuraeus + nfr + nbʾ can be cryptographically read as an Amun-trigram (for a short overview on the principles of cryptography, see Keel 1995: §472–481). Conversely, however, it should be noted that the cryptographic reading of Amun trigrams on scarab bases is not unequivocally accepted (for a critical review of cryptography see now Coleman 2004).

Parallels

Side A is best paralleled by a bifacial rectangular plaque from *ʿAcco (Keel 1997: Akko No. 274, Side B). This item features on its other side the name of Amun-Rʿ with complementary elements. Given the possibility that the Kadesh Barnea item too displays on its Side B the name of Amun-(Rʿ) (though cryptographically written), the seal from ʿAcco and the one from Kadesh Barnea closely correspond—by the shape of the object, the iconographic style and the symbolic content.

Date

According to the seal type[4] and the iconographic parallels, the seal should be dated to the later XIXth or to the XXth Dynasty (c. 1250–1070 BCE). The occurrence of a seal of Late Bronze/Early Iron Age date in an Iron IIA context may be explained in two ways. First, seals were often deposited in later contexts because they were used as heirlooms (Keel 1995: §692). Second, the transfer of Egyptian ʿantiquitiesʾ to the Southern Levant during Iron IIA was extensive, when compared to other periods. This can, for example, be observed in Cemetery 200 at Tell el-Farʿah South.

No. 2. Scaraboid (Fig. 14.2)

Registration Details and Context. Reg. No. 1360, W162, Area C, Stratum 2 (Iron IIB, seventh–early sixth centuries BCE). The seal was found while dismantling W162 and its date must therefore be viewed as a *terminus ante quem non* for this wall.

Object
Scaraboid, Type II (Keel 1995: §§132–138; esp. §135); perforated lengthwise; *c.* 1/8 of the seal has broken off; linear and hollowed out engraving, partly with hatching (Keel 1995: §§331–334); unspecified stone of unknown color; 15.1 × 11.9 × 6.2 mm.

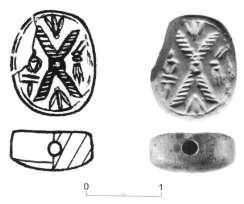

Fig. 14.2. Seal No. 2, Stratum 2.

Base
Description. The base is divided by an X-shaped element into four sectors. The four hatched 'wings' of this element radiate from a small circle. A floral motif facing outside is depicted in the upper sector, and another in the lower sector. The left sector is occupied by an ankh-shaped sign (S34; Keel 1995: §449). Its 'head' is triangular in shape and disconnected from the 'stem' by two parallel horizontal lines/bars (due to the partial damage to the seal, further iconographic elements cannot be traced in this sector). In the sector on the right is a fourth element consisting of two dots of slightly different size in the center, from which three strokes fan downward. Two more parallel strokes emanate obliquely from the upper dot. The base is bordered by a frame line.

Discussion. Seal bases with such a dominant divider are rather scarce among the glyptic material of the Southern Levant. A quite close parallel can, for example, be found on the base of the Hebrew name seal *lmnšh mlkyhw* (Avigad and Sass 1997: No. 244),[5] which is unfortunately of dubious provenance (but see also No. 233 there and possibly No. 602). It is dated on paleographic grounds around 700 BCE (Bordreuil and Lemaire 1982: No. 5).[6]

Uehlinger discussed 'rectangular-stylized,' (double-) barred, ankh-like iconographic elements in depth (1990; updated in Keel and Uehlinger 1998: §178). He cites, *inter alia*, parallels dating to late eighth and seventh centuries BCE from *'Acco, *Tell el-'Ajjul, Tell Keisan and *Lachish and concludes that this symbol is a Levantine adaptation of the Egyptian ankh-sign.[7] In addition to the material presented by Uehlinger, one can also cite an example from *Deve Hüyük, with a less pronounced triangularly shaped, double-barred ankh-like sign (Buchanan and Moorey 1988: Pl. 3:90). This latter seal also features the floral elements visible in the upper and lower sectors of the Kadesh Barnea seal.

The floral motif in question has been described by Porada (1947:151) as "cactus-like" (see also Collon 1987:83; Sass 1993:210), but it could also be interpreted as originally an Egyptian lotus flower (e.g., Hübner 1993:146; Keel 1997: Arad No. 15).

The fourth and last iconographic element to be mentioned most likely represents a bird, such as can be seen, for example, on a scaraboid from *Tell el-'Umeiri: Eggler, Herr and Root 2002: No. 4 (dated to the seventh–sixth centuries BCE) and on a scaraboid from Tell el-Kheleifeh, Period III: Pratico 1993: Pl. 79. See also the unprovenanced epigraphic seals of *ḥmlk* (Avigad and Sass 1997: No. 159, dated on paleographic grounds to the eighth–seventh centuries BCE; Timm 1989:199); of *'l'r bn 'lzkr* (Avigad and Sass 1997: No. 888, dated on palaeographic grounds to the mid-sixth century BCE; cf. Hübner 1992:58, No. 25), and of *bt'l* (Avigad and Sass 1997: No. 927, dated on paleographic grounds to the seventh century BCE; cf., e.g., Hübner 1992:77–78, No. 70).

Date
Scaraboids of Keel's Type II are attested from Iron IIA till Iron IIC (Keel 1995:290). However, the iconography on the seal's base allows its date to be narrowed down, according to the parallels, to the late eighth and seventh centuries BCE.

No. 3. Rectangular Piece with Convex Back (Fig. 14.3)

Registration Details and Context. Reg. No. 205, L117, Area A1, Stratum 2 (Iron IIB, seventh–early sixth centuries BCE).

Object

Rectangular piece with a convex back (loosely related to Keel's Type 'rectangular piece with bow-shaped handle', cf. Keel 1995: §§233–235); perforated lengthwise; bold linear engraving (Keel 1995: §§333, 334); unspecified stone of unknown color (possibly polished limestone); 17.2 × 11.9 × 6.8 mm.

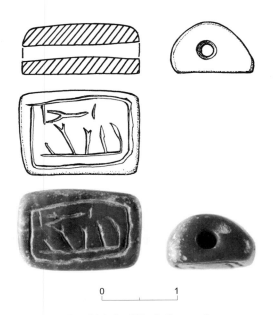

Fig. 14.3. Seal No. 3, Stratum 2.

Base

Description. The base is engraved with an indistinct, clumsily executed scribble: At the top is a horizontal line from which five strokes descend in more or less random directions. Below is a horizontally lying sign in the shape of a forked element, which is flanked by two short vertical strokes. A continuous line serves as a frame.

Discussion. The poorly exercised engraving allows for a variety of speculative interpretations. Most likely, the engraver intended a quadruped above a scorpion, cf., for example, (*)Bet Shemesh, Strata IV–III: Grant 1932: Pl. 48:1108. This motif became popular at the turn of the second millennium BCE and possibly refers to the sphere of a goddess (Keel and Uehlinger 1998: §93). However, due to the poor graphic rendering other interpretations are viable as well.

Date

Keel assembled a catalogue of limestone seals with comparable 'iconography' (Keel, Shuval and Uehlinger 1990:379–396). He dates such seals mainly to the late second millennium BCE (though without stating that they should be viewed as a distinct group; cf. also Keel 1995: §233). Nevertheless, similarly shaped rectangular pieces with a convex back and comparable engravings have been found, for example, in late Iron II contexts at Tell el-'Umeiri (Eggler, Herr and Root 2002: Nos. 41, 45). In light of those recent finds one wonders whether such seals were not produced until much later times. Therefore, an Iron IIC date for the seal under discussion should not be ruled out.[8]

SEALINGS

No. 4. Seal Impression on Krater Handle (Fig. 14.4)

Registration Details and Context. Reg. No. 1051, L533, Area B, Substratum 3c (constructional fill of Stratum 3; Iron IIA–IB; mixed tenth–eighth centuries BCE).

Object

Ovoid stamp-seal impression on a handle of a krater (Keel 1995: §§299–313), possibly executed by a conoid or a scaraboid (Keel 1995:132–138, §§246–260). The handle is broken off right alongside the left margin of the sealing, which is nevertheless almost fully preserved. Bold hollowed-out engraving with linear elements and drillings (Keel 1995: §§333, 334, 336); clay; 14.6 × 13.5 mm.

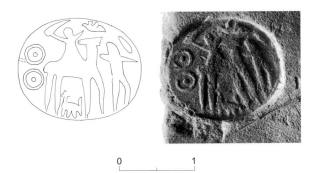

Fig. 14.4. Sealing No. 4, Substratum 3c.

Base

Description. The horizontally arranged scene is densely filled with various iconographic elements. In the center is a long-legged quadruped—most probably a horse (for representations of horses in the glyptic repertoire of the Southern Levant, see Schroer 1987:293–300, Figs. 107–121); its head is turned backwards.

On the horse's back sits a rider facing to the right. Depictions of horseback riding are rather rare in the Ancient Near East in the second and early part of the first millennia BCE (see the overview in Cornelius 1994:79–87 with bibliographical updates on p. 40). The rider's contours seamlessly merge with the contours of the horse, creating the (wrong?) impression that the figure is sitting on some sort of hump.[9] The arms of the rider are widely extended. In its left hand he holds a dagger or a sword.

In front of the horse stands an anthropoid figure—seemingly leading it—and to its right is an indistinct dash. Above the horse's head is a bird—according to parallels most probably a dove (Keel 1992:143–168)—flying toward the rider, to its left. Between the legs of the horse is a much smaller quadruped craning its neck, its tail raised. Two circles with a central dot fill the space between the seal impression's left margin and the rest of the scene.

Discussion. The iconography of No. 4 is an idiosyncratic blend of various motifs. A horse and rider[10] and an anthropoid figure leading the horse are attested, *inter alia*, on a scaraboid from *Ta'anach (Schroer 1987: Fig. 116), probably dating to the ninth–eighth centuries BCE;[11] the style of engraving on that seal is very similar to that of the seal impression discussed here.

The dove almost certainly determines the rider as a goddess (Winter in Keel 1977:37–78; Keel 1992:143–168). This is most likely the warlike goddess Astarte, who, according to Egyptian evidence (Leclant 1960) and that of Ugaritic texts (Wyatt 1999), is associated with horses (see also Cornelius 2004:93–94, Figs. 4.19, 4.20 showing the goddess in a similar pose holding a weapon in one hand). This is true even though in the present item the characteristic *atef*-crown of the goddess is missing.[12] A possible iconographic master to the composition on the Kadesh Barnea sealing (with the combination of the riding Astarte, the dove and an anthropoid figure leading the horse) is a human-face

scaraboid found in the vicinity of *Acco, dated to Iron I–IIA (Keel 1997: Akko No. 4, with further parallels).

It is not unlikely, however, that the horse's backwards-turned head and the small (young?) animal facing the opposite direction derive from a different spin-off—from the famous cow-and-calf motif (Keel 1980a: passim), though equids are hardly ever depicted in this posture (but see at *Acco, Keel 1997: Akko No. 192, attributed to Iron IIC). If this is valid, the goddess comes again into the play since this motif is within her realm (e.g., Keel and Uehlinger 1998:§§91–93).

The circles with a central dot seemingly function as space fillers. Such circles are attested as from the Middle Bronze Age (Keel 1995: §§491), but they also occur in later times, such as on 'oval pieces with sheaf-shaped handle' found in early Iron Age contexts at Tell el-'Ajjul, Bet She'an and Tell Qasile (Keel 1990: Figs. 59–61) and on scarabs, for example from Tell el-*Far'ah South[13] (Petrie 1930: Pl. 33:376; this item is possibly related to the so-called mass-produced stamp-seal amulets of Iron IB and early Iron IIA; cf. Münger 2003; 2005).

Date

Whereas the motifs on the seal's base are rooted in the Late Bronze and early Iron Age periods, the engraving style points to an Iron IIA(?)–B date of the original seal (see the above-mentioned scaraboid from Ta'anach). The assumed seal type also fits such a dating (Keel 1995:288–290).

No. 5. Seal Impression on Krater Handle (Fig. 14.5)

Registration Details and Context. Reg. No. 2962/3, L1242, Area B, Stratum 3b (Iron IIB, around the mid-eighth century BCE).

Fig. 14.5. Sealing No. 5, Substratum 3b.

Object

Oval stamp-seal impression on a handle of a (Negebite) krater (cf. Keel 1995: §§299–313), possibly produced by a scarab or a scaraboid; very faint impression, possibly hollowed out engraving (Keel 1995: §§333, 334); clay; 12.9 × 9.6 mm.

Base

The impression is very unclear. According to Bernick-Greenberg, the base engraving appeared to be divided into four with schematic cobras(?) in each quarter, which cannot be verified on the basis of the photograph. Should the identification of the iconography be correct, the following parallels may be cited: *Tell el-'Ajjul (Keel 1997: Tell el-Aǧul No. 874) and Ashdod, Stratum XII (Keel 1997: Aschdod No. 63, and see there additional parallels cited by Keel). This motif and variants thereof date mainly to the New Kingdom, i.e., the XVIIIth–XXth Dynasties (1550–1070/1069 BCE).

Due to the uncertainties regarding the base engraving, the seal is not datable.

No. 6. Seal Impression on Jar Handle (Fig. 14.6)

Registration Details and Context. Reg. No. 8494/6, L6249, Area C (Iron IIB mixed context: the pottery in Granary 6291 is attributable to Stratum 3 and early Stratum 2, but possibly also has some admixture of Substratum 3c material; see Chapter 11).

0   1

Fig. 14.6. Sealing No. 6, Stratum 3, mixed context.

Object

Oval stamp-seal impression on a jar handle (Keel 1995: §§299–313), possibly produced by a scarab or a scaraboid; incomplete impression; possibly hollowed out engraving (Keel 1995: §§333, 334); clay; 13.0 × 9.6 mm.

The design is indistinct, with a frame line. The iconography is unclear and the seal not datable.

ACKNOWLEDGEMENTS

I thank Hannah Bernick-Greenberg for preparatory work on the material. I am indebted to Othmar Keel and Jürg Eggler (Fribourg) for discussing with me the objects presented here. Sara Kipfer (Bern) made valuable suggestions regarding the manuscript.

NOTES

[1] Note that the disconnected head on the Kadesh Barnea seal could actually derive from a misunderstood sun disk above a falcon-headed figure, which in some cases has only an allusively drawn head with virtually no neck; see the examples cited below.

[2] Alternatively, the origin of the present scene might be sought in a cognate motif related to the above-mentioned motif, showing a falcon-headed deity with a sun disk above its head and a uraeus protruding from its left arm (e.g., Tell el-'Ajjul Tomb 1166: Keel 1997: Tell el-Aǧul No. 299 [rectangular plaque; + *nb tꜣwj*, 'lord of the two lands']; Tell el-Far'ah South: Petrie 1930: Pls. 12:164, 165 [Tomb 902]; Macdonald, Starkey and Harding 1932: Pls. 50:47 [Tomb 921; rectangular plaque]; 53:231 [Tomb 935; + additional uraeus]; 55:280 [Tomb 936; rectangular plaque]; 57:337 [Tomb 981; + debased *nb tꜣwj*, 'lord of the two lands']; 57:357 [Tomb 982; rectangular plaque]; Lachish: Tufnell 1958: Pls. 39:385 = 40:385 [Tomb 570; + additional uraeus];

36:241 = 137:241 [Tomb 4004; + additional uraeus]). Yet this motif is also known with an anthropoid figure instead of the falcon-headed deity (cf. Tell el-Far'ah South: Petrie 1930: Pl. 12:166 [Tomb 902; + *nb tꜣwj*, 'lord of the two lands']).

[3] A motif with a winged uraeus that is accompanied by a *mn* below it is found on faience scarabs, e.g., from Bet She'an, Level Upper V: James 1966: Fig. 113:7; (*)Tell el-Far'ah South: Macdonald, Starkey and Harding 1932: Pls. 73:17 (EF386'); 73:29 (C393'); Megiddo, Stratum VIIB: Loud 1948: Pls. 152:171 = 158:171; see also the *Udjat*-eye scaraboid made of faience in Lachish, Tomb 223: Tufnell 1953: Pls. 44A:134 = 45:134. An additional motif with two uraei flanking a vertical *mn* can be seen, for example, on an item kept at the *Cagliari Museum, see Hölbl 1986: Pl. 99:3 (with further parallels). Note, however, that there is a base of a cowroid that clearly shows a *mn* above a uraeus with a long and bent tail confronting a *nfr*, cf. London: British Museum Inv. No. EA3772 = Petrie 1889: Pl. 66 bottom right.

Furthermore, a singular XIXth–XXth Dynasty scarab with a winged sun disk, a mn and a *dd*-pillar flanked by two uraei (from top to bottom) was discovered at *Shiloh, see Brandl 1993:215, Fig. 8.13.

4 Rectangular plaques of Type II are uncovered most typically in Late Bronze Age contexts, with only few occurrences in later periods (Keel 1995: §224). This date is confirmed by three recently published finds from Tell Beit Mirsim: Brandl 2004: Nos. 14 (Tomb 100; LB II), 40 (Tomb 1; late LB I to Iron II, but LB II is dominant); and 49 (LB II).

5 But contrary to the seal discussed here, the floral elements are turned inward.

6 For a critical discussion of paleographic dating see now Schniedewind 2005.

7 Another possible adaptation of the Egyptian ankh-sign on a different medium is attested, for example, on a potsherd found at et-Tell/Bethsaida in Chamber 4 of the Iron II gate, see Arav 1999:84; for a different view see Wimmer 2000.

8 Cf. also the limestone seals with similar engravings from ʿArad (Keel 1997: Arad Nos. 28–35; and the comment by Keel for No. 28) and from Tel Shevaʿ (Keel and Münger, forthcoming)—all found in Iron IIA–C contexts.

9 In view of the scarce (but palpable) representations of camels in the miniature art of the Bronze and Iron Ages of the Ancient Near East (cf. Staubli 1991: Figs. 23, 49, 50, 61–77 and passim), it is not very likely that the animal here is a camel. The assumption that this animal is a horse, conflicts, however, with the fact that the characteristic horsetail is missing.

10 Depictions of riders on horses occur infrequently before the Persian period (e.g., *Acco: Keel 1997: Akko No. 93, with parallels).

11 This style of engraving can also be found on scaraboids decorated with the motif of 'the lord of the ostriches', found in Iron IIA–B contexts (Keel and Uehlinger 1998: §85). A seal impression from Tell el-Farʿah North, Stratum VIIb (Amiet 1996: Pl. 2:14) shows how this style of engraving is reflected in imprints into leather-hard clay.

12 This headgear is attested, for example, on a stele from Bet Sheʾan, Level VII (Rowe 1940:164, No. 475) and on a cylinder seal from *Beitin (XVIII–XIXth Dynasties; Rowe 1936:251–252 and cover page)—to cite examples from Israel/Palestine.

13 Petrie published it as originating from Tomb 211, whereas according to the inventory list at the Institute of Archaeology in London the item seems to come from the undatable pit grave, 128.

CHAPTER 15

INSCRIPTIONS

RUDOLPH COHEN

INTRODUCTION

Kadesh Barnea produced sixteen inscriptions, of which fourteen are ostraca and two are *yhd* stamps. Among the ostraca only one (No. 14) may possibly belong to Stratum 4, but this crucial stratigraphical attribution could not be ascertained. One ostracon (No. 9) possibly belongs to Substratum 3c, nine (Nos. 1, 3–8, 10, 11) belong, with various degrees of certainty, to Stratum 2, and three (Nos. 2, 12, 13) are unstratified or from mixed loci. In addition, a delicate engraving on a potsherd from Stratum 1, presented in Chapter 11 (Fig. 11.98; Pl. 11.135:13) might be part of an inscription. As, however, we could not attribute it to any script known to us, it is not included here.

Some of the inscriptions were previously discussed in Lemaire and Vernus 1980, 1983 and Cohen 1983b: 34–38. Since these publications, the stratigraphical attributions of some of the inscription have been re-evaluated and thus the stratigraphical determinations in the present text are the ones to be preferred.

In Cohen 1983b, five of the inscriptions (here Nos. 1–5) were defined as hieratic inscriptions. Following J. Naveh's observations (pers. comm.) we no longer hold this position. These inscriptions in fact combine Hebrew characters with numerals rendered in hieratic signs. It seems that these inscriptions were written in the Hebrew language. The incorporation of hieratic numerals was common practice in the First Temple period. The fact that on some ostraca there are repeated lists of ascending numbers, arranged in columns, indicates that these are writing exercises.

OSTRACA

Ostracon No. 1 (Fig. 15.1)

Registration Details and Context. Reg. No. 78, Area A2, L52, Stratum 2.

Previous Publication: Lemaire and Vernus 1980: Ostracon 5.

This small ostracon, a body sherd of a jar, retains part of a Hebrew inscription with hieratic numerals in black ink. The inscription is very unclear and difficult to read. Lemaire and Vernus (1980) identified here two columns with four lines and suggested that in the first two lines the number '100' might possibly be discerned.

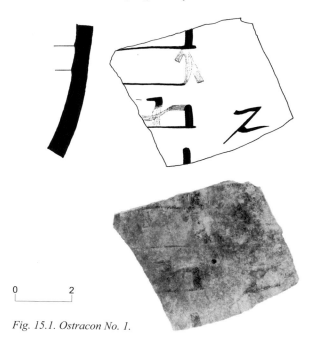

0   2

Fig. 15.1. Ostracon No. 1.

Ostracon No. 2 (Fig. 15.2)

Registration Details and Context. Reg. No. 2723, Area D, L1055, mixed context.
Previous Publication: Cohen 1983b: Fig. 36.

The locus in which this item was found belongs to the upper layer of debris above the water channel, which was mixed with dumps from previous seasons.

Fig. 15.2. Ostracon No. 2.

This inscription (alongside No. 4) was found in the collapsed material above the floor of Casemate 186 and can clearly be attributed to Stratum 2.

The inscription was written in black ink on the body sherd of a jar, below the shoulder. As mentioned, the fabric of the jar is similar to that of the jar of which ostracon No. 2 was made. Three columns survive here, comprising Hebrew characters with hieratic numerals. The left column is very clear and includes an ascending

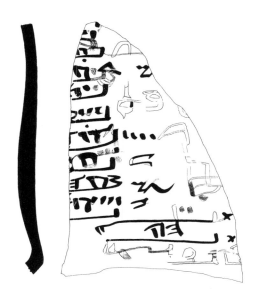

Here too, on a body sherd of a jar, there is part of an Hebrew inscription with hieratic numerals in black ink. Clearly this is part of some list comprising an unknown number of columns (this is especially visible on the right hand side, where there are two incomplete numerals). In the preserved column the numbers are in hundreds, from 100 to 500, arranged in ascending order; to their right are *sheqel* symbols. The fabric of the jar is very similar to that of the jar of which Ostracon No. 3 was made, which may hint that the two are parts of a single inscription.

Ostracon No. 3 (Fig. 15.3)

Registration Details and Context. Reg. No. 207, Area A2, L157, Stratum 2.
Previous Publication: Lemaire and Vernus 1980: Ostracon 3; Cohen 1983b: Fig. 35.

Fig. 15.3. Ostracon No. 3.

list of numbers, from 100 to 800, and next to each numeral is the Hebrew word גרה (*gerah*), the smallest unit of weight known, roughly equivalent to 0.5 g. The word *gerah* is also repeated thrice in the right-hand column, once, as suggested by Lemaire and Vernus (1980:343), with a spelling mistake.

Ostracon No. 4 (Fig. 15.4)

Registration Details and Context. Reg. No. 331, Area A2, L157, Stratum 2.
Previous Publication: Lemaire and Vernus 1980: Ostracon 4.

This inscription (alongside No. 3) was found in the collapsed material above the floor of Casemate 186 and can clearly be attributed to Stratum 2. Written in black ink, it was inscribed on a body sherd of a jar, mended from five fragments. It includes two columns of hieratic numerals.

Ostracon No. 5 (Fig. 15.5)

Registration Details and Context. Reg. No. 1306/2, Area C, L601, Strata 3a, 2.
Previous Publication: Cohen 1983b: Figs. 32–34: Lemaire and Vernus 1983: Ostracon 6.

Although the locus that produced this ostracon has been defined as the makeup of a Stratum 2 floor, it also included fill from below the floor. Two inscriptions are preserved here, written in black ink on both sides of a large body sherd of a jar (several mending sherds).

On the external (convex) side of the sherd (Fig. 15.5a) the inscription comprises six columns with numbers in ascending order: from 1 to 10, from 10 to 100 in tens, from 100 to 1000 in hundreds and from 1000 to 10000 in thousands. The number 10000 is composed of the numeral 10 and the word אלפמ (thousands) in Hebrew characters. This formula is repeated at least twice and indicates that this is a scribal exercise. *Sheqel* symbols appear alongside columns 4 and 5 adjacent to numbers 1 to 900.

On the inner (concave) side of the potsherd (Fig. 15.5b) the inscription is less clear. On the lower left three numbers can be discerned—4000, 5000 and 6000. To the right of these numbers are additional numerals that are difficult to identify, perhaps the numbers 100 to 400. Above these the number 1000 is quite clear. In the upper right hand side of the ostracon the number 3000 can be discerned, and again, the word אלפמ (thousands) in Hebrew characters (for a more detailed consideration, see Lemaire and Vernus 1983).

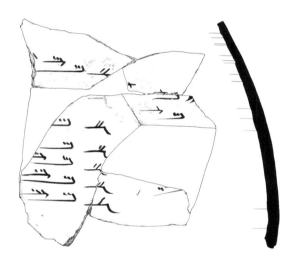

0   3

Fig. 15.4. Ostracon No. 4.

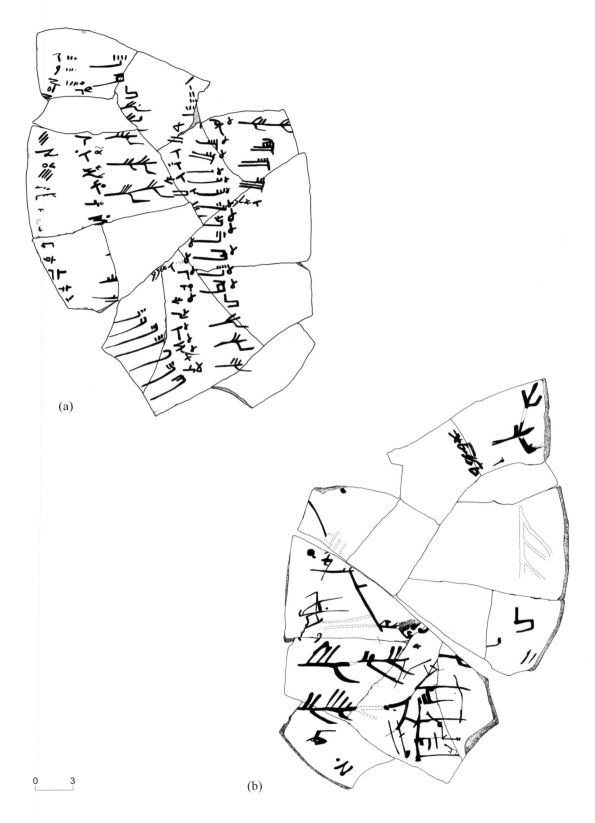

(a)

(b)

0   3

Fig. 15.5. Ostracon No. 5. (a) Outer face; (b) inner face.

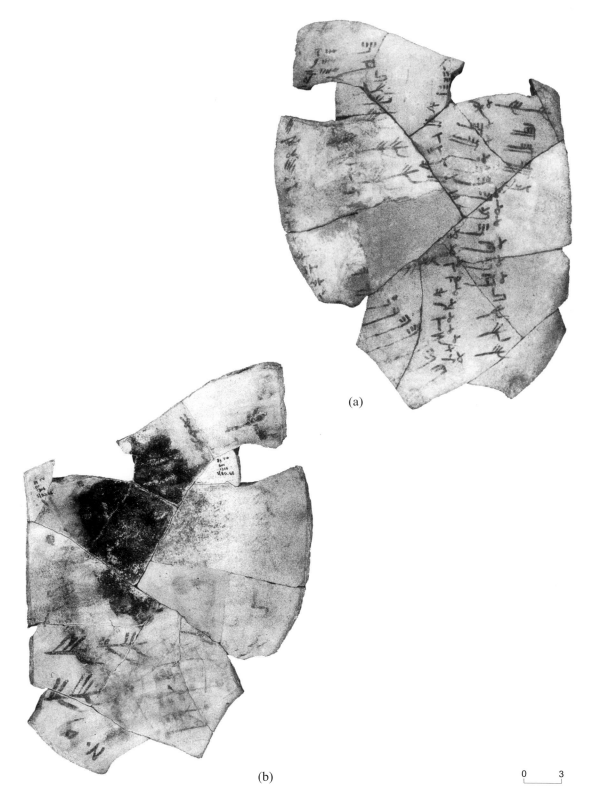

(a)

(b)

Fig. 15.5 (cont.). Ostracon No. 5. (a) Outer face; (b) inner face.

Ostracon No. 6 (Fig. 15.6)

Registration Details and Context. Reg. No. 2468/1,
Area B, L774, Stratum 2(?).
Previously unpublished.

This is an inscription in black ink on a horizontally
burnished body sherd (shoulder) of a jar or jug. It
was found following the removal of a balk, but it may
belong to a floor deposit of the the Stratum 2 fortress.

Two letters are clearly visible and to the right of
them there are traces of a third. The script is unclear.

Fig. 15.6. Ostracon No. 6.

Ostracon No. 7

Registration Details and Context. Reg. No. 47/1, Area
A1, L33, Stratum 2 (Fig. 15.7).
Previous Publications: Lemaire and Vernus 1980: No. 1;
Cohen 1983b: Fig. 31.

This ostracon was discovered above a Stratum 2 floor.
It is a small potsherd, on which three Hebrew letters

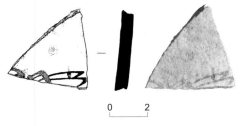

Fig. 15.7. Ostracon No. 7.

in black ink were preserved: ‏ט ח ז‎. This, apparently, is
part of an *abecedarium*, datable to the seventh century
BCE.

Ostracon No. 8 (Fig. 15.8)

Registration Details and Context. Reg. No. 860/2, Area
A2, L459, Stratum 2.
Previously unpublished.

The ostracon was recovered from destruction debris
above the floor of Casemate 459. It comprises a
Hebrew inscription in black ink on a body sherd of a
jar (a shoulder fragment), which is broken on the right
hand side. Originally the inscription may have been
longer. The three letters, ‏א ב ת‎, indicate a date in the
late seventh or early sixth century BCE.

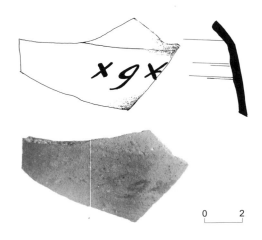

Fig. 15.8. Ostracon No. 8.

Ostracon No. 9 (Fig. 15.9)

Registration Details and Context. Reg. No. 8138/1,
Area C, L6080, Substratum 3c, 1.
Previous Publication: Cohen 1983b: Fig. 37.

Although part of the Strata 3c construction fill, this
area was disturbed by Stratum 1 pits and thus the
stratigraphical attribution of this ostracon is not secure
(as indeed borne out by the script).

The inscription includes two words inscribed in
black ink on a body sherd (shoulder) of a jar. It is written
in Aramaic and may be dated to the sixth century
BCE. The inscription is incomplete, and it appears that

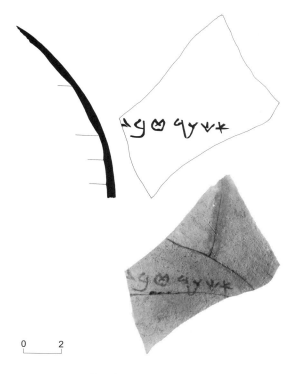

Fig. 15.9. Ostracon No. 9.

Fig. 15.10. Ostracon No. 10.

the second word had a continuation. The reading is
[   ] אשכר טבי, which may be completed as [הו]טבי.

Ostracon No. 10 (Fig. 15.10)

Registration Details and Context. Reg. No. 57/3, Area
A1, L45, Stratum 2.
Previous Publication: Lemaire and Vernus 1980:
Ostracon 2.

This unclear inscription has been written in black ink on
a body sherd of a jar found above a Stratum 2 floor.

In spite of the blurred condition of the inscription,
Lemaire attempted to decipher it and identified here
three lines containing two words repeated twice:
מלא מל[א] ותחסר ותחסר.

Ostracon No. 11 (Fig. 15.11)

Registration Details and Context. Reg. No. (2621/6),
Area F, L851, Stratum 2.
Previously unpublished.

The ostracon was retrieved from the fills of the
Stratum 2 glacis. A shallow incision was scratched,
after firing, on the outer wall of a carinated bowl.
The inscription is unclear and difficult to read. It
appears to be an unsuccessful attempt at writing.

Fig. 15.11. Ostracon No. 11.

Ostracon No. 12 (Fig. 15.12)

Registration Details and Context. Reg. No. 539/6, Area A1, L261, unstratified.
Previously unpublished.

The locus that produced this fragment has no stratigraphical value and is chronologically mixed. This inscription consist of two signs, incised after firing on the rim of a bowl, probably the letters: ל ש. For other *shin*-shaped incisions on pottery, see Pl. 11.139:1–9.

Ostracon No. 13 (Fig. 15.13)

Registration Details and Context. Reg. No. 2758/1, Area D, L1075, Substratum 3c.
Previous Publication: Cohen 1983b: Fig. 30.

This ostracon was found in the constructional fills southeast of the cistern, below Substratum 3b floors. The ostracon is very unusual as it comprises Hebrew letters incised on a Negebite bowl before firing (on its external face). Three letters, which may be read ד מ י, survived, but as the fragment is broken on the right, perhaps this can be reconstructed as [א] ד מ י.

Ostracon No. 14 (Fig. 15.14)

Registration Details and Context. Reg. No. (2957/1), Area B, L1231, Substratum 3c.
Previous Publication: Cohen 1983b: Fig. 29.

The lamp base on which this inscription is rendered was recovered above a Stratum 4 floor, in the Substratum 3c construction fills. It is a shallow incision, made before firing.

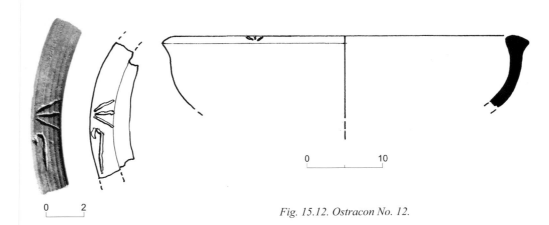

Fig. 15.12. Ostracon No. 12.

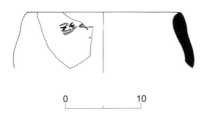

Fig. 15.13. Ostracon No. 13.

Fig. 15.14. Ostracon No. 15.

Impression No. 2 (Fig. 15.16)

Registration Details and Context. Reg. No. 1303/5, Area C, L603, Strata 2 [+1].
Previously unpublished.

The stamped jar handle was discovered on a Stratum 2 floor that was probably disturbed by a Stratum 1 pit. No letters can be clearly discerned here; possibly they were smudged when the handle was stamped. This may be one of the variants of the *yhd* stamp, or perhaps a one-line *mṣh* stamp (e.g., Stern 1983:207–209).

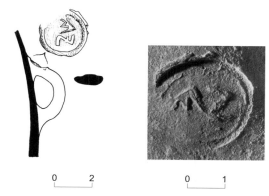

Fig. 15.15. Stamped handle No. 1.

The inscription comprises a word in Hebrew script. It is broken on the left and thus its end must be reconstructed. The reading is [ ] י נ ד א ל, possibly to be read [ו ה] י נ ד א ל. The letter *yod* seems to be a typical eighth-century BCE shape.

YHD IMPRESSIONS

Kadesh Barnea is the southernmost site at which *yhd* impressions are attested.

Impression No. 1 (Fig. 15.15)

Registration Details and Context. Reg. No. 8215/1, Area C, L6093, Stratum 1.
Previous Publication: Cohen 1983b: Fig. 22.

This stamped handle of a jar was found in a Stratum 1 pit that penetrated a Substrata 3a-b floor. The two letters in the impression can be clearly identified as two Aramaic letters י ה, short for יהוד/יהד, the province of Judea (see Stern 1982:202–205, Fig. 337, Type E).

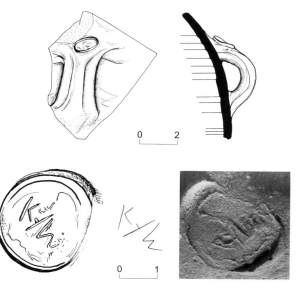

Fig. 15.16. Stamped handle No. 2.

CHAPTER 16

TEXTILES, LOOM WEIGHTS AND SPINDLE WHORLS

ORIT SHAMIR

INTRODUCTION

Fifty textile fragments were uncovered at Kadesh Barnea, a very rare discovery for the Iron Age in the Southern Levant. In addition, a single textile impression was preserved on a fragment of a wheel-made ceramic vessel. (In contrast, many impressions of both textiles and basketry were encountered on the Negebite handmade ware, and are discussed in Chapter 12.) This chapter also presents other artifacts unequivocally associated with spinning and weaving: twenty-four loom weights and 31 spindle whorls.[1]

TEXTILES

Of the 50 textile fragments (Table 16.1), six comprise two different textiles sewn together laterally, or patched one over the other (Cat. Nos. 10+11; 12+13; 14+15, 26+27, 29+30, 55+56), and thus we are actually dealing with 56 textiles. A few additional textiles were not catalogued due to their poor state of preservation.

All the fragments were found together within the fill of the Stratum 2 glacis in Area G (L6501). However, this fill overlay a Stratum 3 floor (L6504) and thus it cannot be determined with certainty whether the textiles belong to Stratum 3 or 2.

The fragments are very small and with few exceptions borders or selvedges did not survive. The largest textile fragment (Cat. Nos. 14, 15; Fig. 16.1) measures 8 × 10 cm.

The textiles were carbonized and their original colors were not discernible. Most of them are wrinkled and tend to crumble, and therefore they could not be cleaned.

Although no textile was preserved in its entirety, the fragments provide significant data regarding the raw material employed, spinning and weaving techniques, and the uses of the cloth.

Raw Materials

All the textiles are linen. For some of the fragments this was determined (by W.D. Cooke) by examination under a scanning electron microscope at a magnification of ×8500 (Cat. Nos. 15, 21; Figs. 16.2, 16.3). For the other fragments, identification of the fabric was performed with a regular microscope.

Spinning

The threads were S-spun, according to the natural twist of the linen. There is however, some variability in the tightness of the spinning (Table 16.2).

As is the rule cross-culturally, thin threads, tightly spun, were used as warp threads, and the weft threads are thicker (Sheffer and Tidhar 1991:3). The spinning is of high quality and the threads are usually of uniform thickness.

Weaving

The most common weaving technique attested at Kadesh Barnea is plain weave or tabby, with a few variations: tabby weave, balanced tabby and warp-faced tabby.

Fig. 16.1. Textile Nos. 14 + 15.

Table 16.1. Textiles from L6501, Stratum 2

Cat. No.	Reg. No	Length (cm) Warp	Length (cm) Weft	Spinning Direction Warp	Spinning Direction Weft	Spinning Tightness Warp	Spinning Tightness Weft	Threads per cm Warp	Threads per cm Weft	Weave	Density	Edge	Sewing	Weaving Faults	Comments	Figure
1	8501/1	5	0.6	S	S	T	T	16	8	W.F.	T	S*	-		*Crowded	16.13
2	8501/2	1.2	2.6	S	S	T	T	20	14	T	M	-	-			16.4
3	8501/3	3.5	3.5	S	S	M	M	12	10	T	T	-	+			16.15
4	8501/4	3	13.8	S	S	M	M	12	8	T	M	-	-			16.5
5	8501/5	3	2	S	S	M	M	20	20	Bal.	M	-	-	+		
6	8501/6	2.5	2	S	S	M	M	20	20	Bal.	T	-	-			16.12
7	8501/7	5.3	4.5	S	S	T	M	15	8	T	M	-	-			
8	8501/8	5	0.5	S	S	M	L	-	-	T	T	-	+			16.6
9	8501/9	6	2	S	S	T	T	24	16	T	T	-	+			16.16
10	8501/10a	6	7	S	S	T	M	13	8	T	T	-	+			16.14
11	8501/10b	4	5	S	S	T	M	21	13	T	T	-	+			16.14
12	8501/11a	4.6	8	S	S	T	T	13	9	T	L	-	+			16.18
13	8501/11b	1.5	1.3	S	S	M	M	24	20	T	M	-	+	+		16.18
14	8501/12a	10	8	S	S	T	M	14	9	T	M	-	+			16.1
15	8501/12b	2.8	3.5	S	S	M	M	20	14	T	M	-	+	+		16.1, 16.2
16	8501/13	4.5	4.2	S	S	T	M	24	17	T	M	-	-			
17	8501/14	2.4	2.5	S	S	M	L	14	7	W.F.	M	-	-			
18	8501/15	1.2	2.6	S	S	T	T	18	11	T	M	-	+			
19	8501/16	2.5	2.5	S	S	M	M	20	16	T	M	-	+	+		
20	8501/17	3.8	1.8	S	S	T	M	16	8	W.F.	M	-	-			
21	8501/18	2.4	2.3	S	S	T	M	13	9	T	M	-	-			16.3
22	8501/19	3.3	3	S	S	T	M	18	7	W.F.	M	S*	-		*Plain	
23	8501/20	4	2	S	S	M	M	14	7	W.F.	M	-	-			
24	8501/21	1.2	1.3	S	S	M	M	22	16	T	M	-	-			16.7
25	8501/22	3.7	2.9	S	S	T	T	24	14	T	M	-	-			
26	8501/23a	4.7	1.7	S	S	T	M	16	8	W.F.	M	-	+			
27	8501/23b	2	3.5	S	S	M	M	28	13	W.F.	T	-	+			
28	8501/24	2	0.6	S	S	T	T	20	8	W.F.	T	-	-			
29	8501/25a	3.6	1.5	S	S	T	T	24	13	T	M	-	+			
30	8501/25b	3	1.6	S	S	T	M	26	14	T	M	-	+			

Table 16.1 (cont.)

Cat. No.	Reg. No	Length (cm)		Spinning Direction		Spinning Tightness		Threads per cm		Weave	Density	Edge	Sewing	Weaving Faults	Comments	Figure
		Warp	Weft	Warp	Weft	Warp	Weft	Warp	Weft							
31	8501/26	4	4.3	S	S	M	M	20	20	Bal.	T	-	+			
32	8501/27	6	2	S	S	M	M	30	7	W. F.	T	S*	-		*Plain	
33	8501/28	2.7	1	S	S	M	M	15	10	T	M	-	+			
34	8501/29	3.5	2.5	S	S	M	M	18	18	Bal.	M	-	-			
35	8501/30	1.5	1.5	S	S	M	M	14	9	T	M	-	-			
36	8501/31	4	0.7	S	S	M	M	18	4	W. F.	M	-	+			
37	8501/32	2.3	0.7	S	S	M	M	30	13	W. F.	M	-	-			
38	8501/33	1	0.8	S	S	M	M	26	16	T	M	-	-			
39	8501/34	2.7	2	S	S	T	M	21	14	T	M	-	-			
40	8501/35	2.2	2.2	S	S	M	L	18	18	Bal.	M	-	-			16.10
41	8501/36	2.2	1.7	S	S	M	L	26	15	T	M	-	-			
42	8501/37	2	2	S	S	M	M	13	8	T	M	-	-			
43	8501/38	8	2	S	S	T	T	26	14	T	T	-	+			
44	8501/39	4.2	2.5	S	S	M	M	25	15	T	T	-	+			
45	8501/40	5	2.5	S	S	M	M	26	13	W. F.	M	-	+	+		
46	8501/41	3	1	S	S	M	M	26	14	T	M	-	-			
47	8501/42	3	1	S	S	M	M	26	16	T	M	-	-			
48	8501/43	2	2	S	S	M	M	20	14	T	M	-	-			
49	8501/44	3	3.5	S	S	L	L	18	18	Bal.	M	-	-			
50	8501/45	2	1.5	S	S	L	L	28	20	T	M	-	-			
51	8501/46	2.5	1.7	S	S	M	M	12	10	Bal.	T	-	-			16.11
52	8501/47	2	2	S	S	M	M	16	4	W. F.	T	-	-			
53	8501/48	3.5	1.5	S	S	M	M	14	8	T	T	-	-			
54	8501/49	1.5	1.5	S	S	M	M	20	20	Bal.	T	-	-			16.9
55	8501/50a	6	6	S	S	M	L	16	8	W. F.	T	-	+			16.8, 16.17
56	8501/50b	5	2.5	S	S	M	L	26	14	T	T	-	+			16.8, 16.17

Spinning Tightness: L = Loose; M = Medium; T = Tight; Weave: T = Tabby; W. F. = Warp-faced tabby; Bal. = Balanced tabby; S* = Selvedge

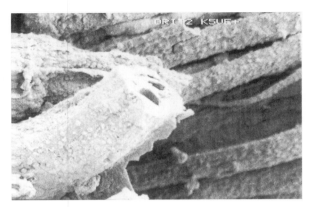
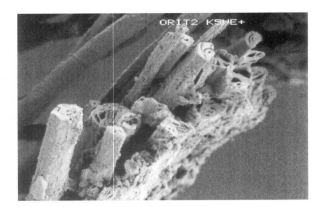

Fig. 16.2. Textile No. 15, fibers in weft threads; magnified ×8500.

Fig. 16.3. Textile No. 21, fibers in weft threads; magnified ×8500.

Table 16.2. Spinning Tightness

Warp	Weft	N
Medium	Medium	28
Tight	Tight	8
Loose	Loose	2
Tight	Medium	12
Medium	Loose	6

Most of the textiles (34) are tabby weave (e.g., Cat. Nos. 2, 4, 8, 24, 55; Figs. 16.4–16.8), with a slight tendency to a higher number of warp threads than weft threads per cm. Warp threads range between 12 and 24 per cm and weft threads between 8 and 20.

In eight textiles the technique is balanced tabby (e.g., Cat. Nos. 54, 40, 51, 6; Figs. 16.9–16.12), in which the warp and weft threads are equal in density per cm, and equal in thickness. The number of threads in both directions is 10–20 per cm.

Fourteen of the textiles are warp faced (e.g., Cat. No. 1; Fig. 16.13), meaning that the number of warp threads is larger than that of the weft (at least double) and the weft threads are hidden or almost hidden. The number of warp threads per cm in these cases is 14–30 and of the weft threads, 4–13.

The density of the textiles is usually medium and there are spaces between the threads. Very few weaving mistakes were discerned, such as skipping over two warp threads or more.

Selvedges

In a few examples the selvedge of the textile was preserved. In two cases (Cat. Nos. 22, 32) there is a plain selvedge, and in another (Cat. No. 1; Fig. 16.13) there is a crowded selvedge, where the warp threads are very dense.

Fig. 16.4. Textile No. 2.

Fig. 16.5. Textile No. 4.

Fig. 16.6. Textile No. 8.

Fig. 16.7. Textile No. 24.

Fig. 16.8. Textiles Nos. 55 + 56.

Fig. 16.10. Textile No. 40.

Fig. 16.11. Textile No. 51.

Fig. 16.9. Textile No. 54.

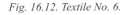

Fig. 16.12. Textile No. 6.

Fig. 16.13. Textile No. 1.

Sewing

Stitches could be clearly discerned on 15 textiles (Table 16.3) and scant traces of stitches were preserved on eight additional specimens. All sewing threads were made of two S-spun linen threads plied together into Z (S2Z) to create a strong thick thread.

In some of the textiles (e.g., Figs. 16.6, 16.8, 16.14, 16.15, 16.16, 16.17, 16.18; respectively Cat. Nos. 8, 55, 10, 3, 9, 55+56, 12+13; also Cat. Nos. 14, 43) the stitches are small and uniform in size (3–4 mm), evenly spaced (*c.* 4 mm apart), stitched in one direction only and carefully executed. In other examples (e.g., Fig. 16.14, Cat. No. 10, where both 'types'of stitches appear; also Cat. Nos. 29, 33, 45), the stitches are irregular, crude and inconsistent in size and direction. The intervals

Table 16.3. Sewing Stitches

Cat. No.	Purpose	Uniform Size of Stitches	Sewing Length (cm)	Figure
3	Rolled hem	+	2.5	16.15
8	Rolled hem	+	5	16.6
9	Rolled hem	+	4.5	16.16
10+11	Repair	-	3.5	16.14
10+11	Patch	+	2	16.14
12+13	Patch	+	7	16.18
14+15	Patch	+	6	16.1, 16.2
19	?	?	?	
26+27	Seam	?	Traces	
29+30	Seam	-	3.5	
33	Rolled hem	-	1.7	
36	Rolled hem	+	4.2	
43	Rolled hem	+	3	
45	Rolled hem	-	?	
55+56	Seam	+	4, 4.5	16.8, 16.17

Fig. 16.14. Textiles Nos. 10 + 11.

Fig. 16.15. Textile No. 3.

Fig. 16.16. Textile No. 9.

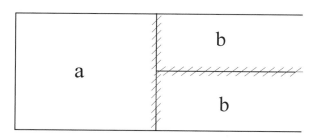
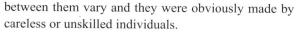

*Fig. 16.17. Textile Nos. 55 + 56; schematic
illustration of stitches (not to scale).*

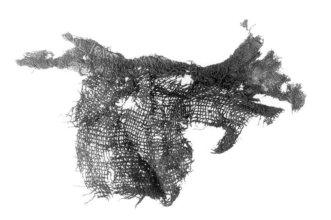

Fig. 16.18. Textiles Nos. 12 + 13.

between them vary and they were obviously made by careless or unskilled individuals.

Because the surviving textiles are small, it is impossible to assess the function of the stitches. Possible purposes are patching or mending, hemming to prevent unravelling of the threads, and seaming.

Patching or Mending
One textile was patched over another (Cat. No. 15 over No. 14; Fig. 16.1). The edges of No. 15 were folded and sewn to the other textile, apparently a square patch of which two sides have survived.

Another textile (Cat. No. 11) is folded and sewn, apparently as a patch, over No. 10 (Fig. 16.14); No. 11 also exhibits mending. Textile No. 12 (Fig. 16.18) is very worn and torn and No. 13 was patched over it. Their edges were joined with diagonal stitches.

Care was not always taken that the direction of the warp threads of the patches match those of the textile to which they were added. On some of the patches the edges were folded inward. In all cases mentioned above the torn areas of the textiles were not cut. It is probable that the patches were made from garments and the like that had gone out of use.

Hemming to Prevent Unravelling

In eight examples (e.g., Cat. Nos. 10+11, 3, 9; Figs. 16.14, 16.15, 16.16) hems were rolled and then sewn to prevent unravelling.

Seaming

In two cases (Cat. Nos. 26+27, 29+30), pairs of textiles were each folded separately, and then sewn to each other. Textile No. 56 is composed of two segments that were folded into two, sewn to each other and then joined to No. 55 (Figs. 16.8, 16.17).

A Textile Impression on Pottery

The impression (Fig. 16.19) survived on a fragment of a base of a well-fired wheel-made bowl from Stratum 2 (Reg. No. 1721, L708). It covers the entire surface of the potsherd (6 × 7 cm). The density of the threads is 9 × 34 per cm, weft faced.

The weft is S-spun. It is unclear what the direction of the warp spin was, as it is completely concealed.

The fabric that left its imprint on this potsherd was dense and delicate, compared to those attested by textile impressions on the Negebite pottery of Kadesh Barnea (Chapter 12) and those from Timna' (dating to the Late Bronze Age; Sheffer and Tidhar 1988:229–230), and relative to other ancient textiles found in Israel. This was probably a sheep (as opposed to camel, for example) woolen fabric (see Sheffer and Tidhar 1988:230).

Fig. 16.19. Textile impression on fragment of wheel-made bowl; Reg. No. 1721, L708, Stratum 2.

Discussion

Very few Iron Age textiles have been found in the Land of Israel. They are mostly known from Kuntillet 'Ajrud, dating to the end of the ninth century BCE (Sheffer and Tidhar 1991). A spindle with linen threads still wrapped around it was uncovered in a tenth-century BCE context at Tell el-Hama in the Jordan Valley (Shamir 1996a:142).

The textiles from Kadesh Barnea are very similar to those from Kuntillet 'Ajrud, where most of the textiles were linen (103 of 115).

Spinning, Weaving and Stitching Techniques

Both at Kadesh Barnea and at Kuntillet 'Ajrud the threads were S-spun. The quality of the spinning is high and the threads are uniform in thickness, attesting to the skill of the spinners. Likewise, the weaving technique at Kadesh Barnea is identical to that of the Kuntillet 'Ajrud textiles (Sheffer and Tidhar 1991:3) and the sewing at Kadesh Barnea also resembles that of this latter site: the threads are made of linen and the spinning is in the S2Z direction.

Differences, however, may be discerned in the patchwork. In the patched textiles at Kadesh Barnea the torn parts were not cut, while at Kuntillat 'Ajrud they were. Also, at Kuntillet 'Ajrud care was taken to match the warp and weft directions of the textiles that were patched to each other, while at Kadesh Barnea this was not always the case. In sum, the mending of textiles at Kadesh Barnea was not always careful, as opposed to the practice at Kuntillet 'Ajrud (Sheffer and Tidhar 1991:8).

Though the selvedges of the textiles at Kadesh Barnea are similar to those at Kuntillet 'Ajrud, at Kadesh Barnea no wedges were made, which is also in contrast to the practice at Kuntillet 'Ajrud (Sheffer and Tidhar 1991:4). (Wedges are weft threads thrown from the edges of the textiles only part of the way across the cloth, in order to reinforce uneven margins; see Crowfoot 1974:61–62.)

Decorations

As mentioned above, the textiles at Kadesh Barnea were carbonized and it was impossible to discern colors. Self-band decoration, typical of the linen fabrics at Kuntillet 'Ajrud (Sheffer and Tidhar 1991:6) was not discerned here.

The Sources of the Textiles

Flax could not be cultivated in the arid climate of the Sinai desert. One possible source for the textiles could thus be Egypt, but the textiles in Egypt are usually characterized by splicing (i.e., the act of joining the ends of two linen fibers so that they form one continuous piece; Barber 1991:47–49). This was not encountered at Kadesh Barnea (nor at Kuntillet 'Ajrud). In addition, in Egyptian textiles the threads are thinner and denser (Sheffer and Tidhar 1991:4).

Another possible source is the Jordan Valley, especially the Bet She'an region, which is known from various sources to have been a center of linen production in the Iron Age (see below, Tell el-Hama), while wool was probably produced in the Shephelah (Shamir 1992, 1996a:142; Browning 2001).

The loom weights and spindle whorls uncovered at Kadesh Barnea (see below) indicate that spinning and weaving took place on site, but judging by the scarcity of these finds, they were apparently not practiced on a large scale.

Function

All the textiles at Kadesh Barnea are very delicate and woven of relatively thin threads (diameters of threads were not measured as they were carbonized). It is reasonable to assume that they are remains of garments (Sheffer and Tidhar 1991:3, 12). No coarse fabrics were found here that could have been parts of sacks, as those uncovered at Kuntillet 'Ajrud (Sheffer and Tidhar 1991:3).

LOOM WEIGHTS

Twenty-four loom weights were found at the site (Table 16.4; Fig. 16.20). All of them are 'doughnut-shaped', their diameter being larger than their height, and they are perforated vertically. Most of them were manufactured of local yellow to brown-colored clay of various shades, occasionally with mineral inclusions up to 6 mm in diameter. As a rule they were not fired. Eighteen examples, e.g., Cat. Nos. 1, 11, 12, were fired secondarily, in some cases because the contexts in which they were found underwent destruction by fire.

The loom weights weigh between 24.5 and 272.7 g. Most of them cluster into two weight groups: 64.2–96.0 g and 110.0–155.3 g.

Find Spots

In all, very few loom weights were uncovered at Kadesh Barnea and never in large clusters, as opposed to the situation at other Iron Age sites (cf. Sheffer 1981; Browning 1988). Small clusters of weights were discovered in three places only. In L36, which comprises Substratum 3a debris in Area A1, a cluster of three loom weights (Cat. Nos. 6–8) was exposed, of which two could be weighed: 72.1 and 78.1 g. In L1108, a Stratum 3 floor and deposit in Area C (disturbed by

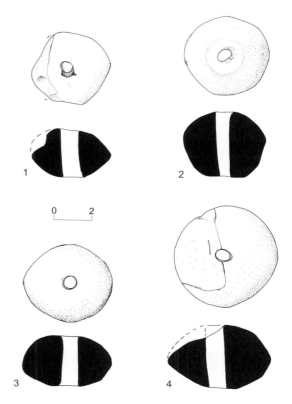

Fig. 16.20. Clay loom weights.

No.	Cat. No.	Stratum
1	9	2
2	11	1
3	12	1
4	18	3, 1

a Stratum 1 pit), there were three weights (Cat. Nos. 18–20), of which two could be weighed: 88.6 and 94.0 g. In L22, a Stratum 1 fill and floor, a cluster of six loom weights (Cat. Nos. 10–15), weighing between 64.2 and 78.3 g (average 71.3 ± 6.9 g), was recovered.

The rest of the weights were isolated finds scattered throughout the various strata, usually above floors.

Discussion

The objects under discussion here are commonly known in the literature as loom weights, but as at Kadesh Barnea, most of them were not encountered in clusters and it cannot be excluded that some of them were used for other purposes (Sheffer 1981). Indeed, Gal (1989; Gal and Alexandre 2000:125) suggested that such 'clay balls' are actually jar stoppers. This was based on the

Table 16.4. Loom Weights

Cat. No.	Reg. No.	Locus/ Square	Stratum	Locus Type	Material	Weight (g)	Diameter (cm)	Height (cm)	Hole Diameter 1 (cm)	Hole Diameter II (cm)	Hole Type	Comments	Figure
1	1825	823	4b	Floor	Clay	24.5	4.0	1.9	0.6		Plain	Groove inside	
2	1018	800	3c	Fill	Clay	68.7	3.8	4.0				Broken	
3	8021/1	6099	3, 2	Fill of granary	Poorly fired pottery	113.1	6.3	3.9	1.8		Plain		
4	8021/2	6099	3, 2	Fill of granary	Poorly fired pottery	110.0	6.2	3.8	2.0		Plain		
5	8494	6249	3, 2	Fill of granary	Clay	122.4	5.8	3.5	1.6	2.0	Chambered		
6	2	36	3a	Debris	Clay							Broken	
7	38	36	3a	Debris	Clay	78.1	4.8	3.1	1.0		Chambered		
8	39	36	3a	Debris	Clay	72.1	5.0	3.2	0.8		Plain	Groove inside	
9	754	424	2	Above floor	Poorly fired pottery	39.6	4.1	2.8	0.9		Plain	Groove inside	16.20:1
10	6	22	1	Floor	Clay	64.2	4.2	3.8	0.7		Plain		
11	122/1	22	1	Floor	Clay	78.3	4.6	3.6	0.7		Plain	Groove inside	16.20:2
12	122/2	22	1	Floor	Clay	64.3	4.4	3.0	0.7	2.0	Chambered	Groove inside	16.20:3
13	122/3	22	1	Floor	Clay	71.4	4.5	3.1	0.7		Plain	Groove inside	
14	122/4	22	1	Floor	Clay								
15	125	22	1	Floor	Clay	78.1	5.1	4.1	0.9		Plain		
16	9061	7025	2, 1	Fill of moat	Chalk	52.2	4.0	3.8	0.7		Plain		
17	2300/1	1108	3, 1	Floor + pit	Poorly fired pottery			4.3				Broken	
18	2300/2	1108	3, 1	Floor + pit	Clay	94.0	5.6	3.5	1.0	0.7	Chambered	Groove inside	16.20:4
19	2300/3	1108	3, 1	Floor + pit	Clay	88.6	5.6	3.2	0.8		Plain		
20	2285	K/7	-	Cleaning	Clay	131.5	6.1	4.0	1.0		Chambered		
21	1	-	-		Clay	272.7	9.0	3.7	2.7	1.7	Single cone		
22	2	-	-		Clay	152.1	6.8	3.7	1.5		Plain		
23	3	-	-		Clay	155.3	7.8	3.1	1.8		Plain		
24	-	-	-		Poorly fired pottery	126.3	6.2	3.9	1.9		Plain	Groove inside	

discovery of such artifacts *in situ*, sealing openings of storage jars in Iron II contexts at Ḥ. Rosh Zayit and Tell el-Hama, and also (in the Rosh Zayit case) on the correspondence between their size and the diameters of the storage-jar necks/rims. At Tell el-Hama, however, these are certainly loom weights in secondary use: in one case a loomweight was broken and only half of it was used as a stopper. Furthermore, at Tell el-Hama, spindles (one with linen threads still wrapped around it), whorls and 161 loom weights provided unequivocal evidence of extensive spinning and weaving activities at the site (Shamir 1996a:142). At Kadesh Barnea, at least in the three cases where clusters of weights were encountered, we may assume that they were associated with looms. In each cluster the weights were of similar weight.

On eight loom weights from Kadesh Barnea (Cat. Nos. 1, 8, 9, 11, 12, 13, 18, 24) a vertical groove, created by the rubbing of a single thread, is clearly discernible inside the perforation. This phenomenon is paralleled by a single example at late Iron Age Vered Jeriḥo (Shamir 1996b:155–162) and by MB II examples at Jericho (Wheeler 1982:623). Loom weights with similar marks, were also noticed at the site of Wusturg Dalem in Germany, dating to the early Middle Ages (Zimmerman 1982:132). This phenomenon corroborates the hypothesis that the Kadesh Barnea objects were used as loom weights.

These grooves also prove that the cluster of warp threads that was tied to the loom weight did not pass directly through the middle of its perforation, but was connected to the weight by a single loop. It was this loop that rubbed the walls of the perforation and created the single groove (Shamir 1996b:160). As mentioned, this practice is known from warp-weighted looms in the Southern Levant and is unknown, for example, in Egypt and Assyria, where altogether different types of looms were used. Thus, irrespective of the question of political dominance over the fortresses (see Chapter 1), the weavers seem to have been of southern Levantine stock.

SPINDLE WHORLS

Twenty-seven spindle whorls, made of clay, bone and chalk, were found at the site (Table 16.5; Fig. 16.21). They are discussed below according to material and morphology.

Highly Fired Clay Spindle Whorls

Disc-Shaped
Twenty-three flat disc-shaped spindles whorls were found in various loci (Cat. Nos. 1–14, 16–20, 23–25; Fig. 16.21:1–4, 6, 7, 9). They range between 2.9 and 9.2 cm in diameter, between 0.5 and 1.7 cm in height, and beween 12.5 and 106.7 g in weight. All were made of re-worked potsherds, in secondary use. E. Nodet (1980:320) suggested that the original use of these discs was as pivots for drills used for boring holes in ceramic or stone artifacts (in order to enable the application of the necessary vertical pressure). The drill head would have been fitted into a 'conical cavity' hollowed out in the disc. When, eventually, these pivots became pierced through prolonged use, they could have been employed secondarily as whorls. One object (Cat. No. 27) indeed corroborates this hypothesis: on both its surfaces there is evidence that drilling had begun, but the hole does not penetrate completely through (clearly, then, this object could not have been used as a weight).

Generally, the diameter of the perforations range between 0.4 and 1.5 cm. They were usually drilled in the center. In seven examples (Cat. Nos. 4, 5, 13, 14, 17, 18, 24; Fig. 16.21:3, 6, 10) the holes were drilled from both sufaces. This is evidenced by the fact that they are narrower in the center than at the surfaces—a chambered perforation. In eleven spindle whorls (e.g., Cat. Nos. 1, 3, 7, 15; Fig. 16.21:1, 2, 4, 5), the holes was drilled from one side only and they are thus cylindrical in shape. This shape is optimal for attaching the whorl to a spindle (Nodet 1980:316). In four whorls (Cat. Nos. 6, 8–10), the perforation is conical in section.

Other Shapes
There was one dome-shaped whorl (Cat. No. 15; Fig. 16.21:5), as well as one very small and light biconical whorl (Cat. No. 26). On the latter, the diameter of the perforation is somewhat too small (2 mm) for attachment to a spindle. Perhaps this was not a spindle whorl, but a bead or button.

Chalk Spindle Whorl

One cylindrical spindle whorl of chalk (Cat. No. 21; Fig. 16.21:8) had a hole created by drilling from both sides. This is evident from its chamfered perforation.

Table 16.5. Spindle Whorls

Cat. No.	Reg. No.	Locus/ Square	Stratum	Locus Type	Material	Shape	Weight (g)	Diameter (cm)	Height (cm)	Hole Diameter I (cm)	Hole Diameter II (cm)	Hole Type	Figure
1	1825	823	4b	Floor	Fired clay	Disc-shaped	106.7	9.2	1.2	1.0		Plain	16.21:1
2	1993	938	4b	Floor	Fired clay	Disc-shaped	29.2	5.2	1.0	1.0		Plain	
3	2001	938	4b	Floor	Fired clay	Disc-shaped	43.5	5.7	1.0	1.0		Plain	16.21:2
4	543	265	4a	Above floor	Fired clay	Disc-shaped	27.7	4.9	1.0	0.5		Chambered	16.21:3
5	1620	3162	4a	Floor	Fired clay	Disc-shaped	16.5	4.0	1.0	0.4		Chambered	
6	2276	674	4	Fill	Fired clay	Disc-shaped	56.0	7.0	0.8	0.4	0.7	Single cone	
7	2959	1231	3c	Fill	Fired clay	Disc-shaped	18.3	5.0	0.6	1.0		Plain	16.21:4
8	55	43	3c	Fill	Fired clay	Disc-shaped	30.0	4.2	1.2	0.6	0.8	Single cone	
9	85	66	3c	Fill	Fired clay	Disc-shaped	29.4	4.5	1.1	0.7	0.9	Single cone	
10	2885	1099	3c	Fill	Fired clay	Disc-shaped	98.0	7.5	1.7	1.4	2.0	Single cone	
11	2598	1238	3c	Fill	Fired clay	Disc-shaped	62.9	6.0	1.7	1.0		Plain	
12	1342	615	3, 2	Fill of granary	Fired clay	Disc-shaped	-	-	1.6	1.5		Plain	
13	2659	861	3a-b	Silo	Fired clay	Disc-shaped	12.5	3.7	0.7	0.5		Chambered	
14	8276	6133	3a-b	Above floor	Fired clay	Disc-shaped	35.0	5.2	1.0	0.8		Chambered	
15	8508	6259	3, 2	Floor of granary	Fired clay	Dome-shaped	31.4	3.8	2.3	0.8		Plain	16.21:5
16	491	235	3a-b	-	Fired clay	Disc-shaped	28.7	5.0	1.0	1.2		Plain	
17	977	526	3a-b	Above floor	Fired clay	Disc-shaped	26.7	5.4	0.7	1.0		Chambered	16.21:6
18	1352	613	3a-b	-	Fired clay	Disc-shaped	70.3	7.6	1.1	0.9		Chambered	
19	2280	700	3, 2	Mixed	Fired clay	Disc-shaped	44.0	5.6	1.3	1.3		Plain	16.21:7
20	2280	700	3, 2	Mixed	Fired clay	Disc-shaped	47.0	5.5	1.4	0.8		Plain	
21	59	37	2	Above floor	Chalk	Cylindrical	26.7	3.6	2.0	1.2		Chambered	16.21:8
22	784	402	2	Above floor	Bone	Dome-shaped	38.8	5.3	2.9	1.2		Plain	16.21:9
23	1331	616	2	Floor	Fired clay	Disc-shaped	20.0	4.3	0.8	1.0		Plain	
24	1303	603	2 [+1]	Floor(?)	Fired clay	Disc-shaped	6.3	2.9	0.5	0.5		Chambered	16.21:10
25	5136	3074	-	Fill in balk	Fired clay	Disc-shaped	54.5	5.7	1.3	1.4		Plain	
26	113	C/7	-	-	Fired clay	Biconical	2.5	1.8	1.1	0.2		Plain	
27	2035	P/9	-	Cleaning	Fired clay	Disc-shaped	23.2	4.5	0.8	1.0		None	

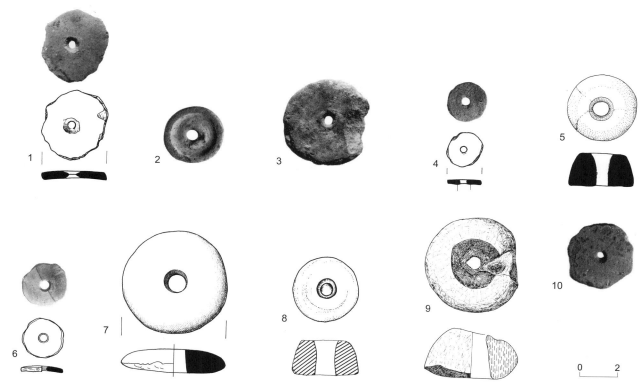

Fig. 16.21. Spindle whorls.

No.	Cat. No.	Material	Stratum
1	1	Clay	4b
2	3	Clay	4b
3	4	Clay	4b
4	7	Clay	3c
5	15	Clay	3, 2

No.	Cat. No.	Material	Stratum
6	17	Clay	3a-b
7	19	Clay	3, 2
8	21	Chalk	2
9	22	Bone	2
10	24	Clay	2 (+1)

Bone Spindle Whorl

One such dome-shaped spindle whorl was found (Cat. No. 22; Fig. 16.21:9).

Discussion

There is nothing unique about the Kadesh Barnea spindle whorls. Similar objects, especially whorls manufactured of potsherds in secondary use, are known in the Levant from the Neolithic period onward (Perrot 1966: Fig. 6:17; Wheeler 1982:626) and are most common in the Iron Age (Israeli 1962:1000–1001). This shape is known cross-culturally, for example, in Mesoamerica (present-day Mexico), from 1025 BCE to 700 CE (Smith and Hirth 1988:353–354).

ACKNOWLEDGEMENTS

I sincerely thank Rudolph Cohen and Hannah Bernick-Greenberg for their support and encouragement, Aliza Baginski and Tamar Schick for their helpful comments and William D. Cooke for his help in examining and photographing the textiles under the SEM.

NOTE

[1] In addition to the illustrations of textiles, loom weights and spindle whorls presented in this chapter, those of other objects can be found in the IAA archives.

CHAPTER 17

THE FLINT ASSEMBLAGE

MICHAL DRUK

INTRODUCTION

Analysis of the flints collected during the Kadesh Barnea excavations revealed the existence of material from three periods—Middle Paleolithic, Early Bronze Age and Iron Age. This report will concentrate on the latest assemblage, as it is the only one that corresponds with the date of the occupation periods at the site. Earlier finds will only be discussed based on their provenance and possibility of having been reused in the Iron Age. The remainder of the finds, although from periods known in the area, are probably simply components of the constructional fills of the fortresses, along with similarly sized pebbles and stones.

THE ASSEMBLAGE

The Iron Age

The material attributed to this period has been assigned on the basis of morphology and provenance. In the latter case, only those non-diagnostic artifacts found on floors (and not in fills) are included. Therefore, as most of the debitage and cores are from fills and appear to have been washed-in, and the frequencies of debitage, debris, core and tool categories (Table 17.1) support a hypothesis of unsystematic retrieval or off-site flint knapping activities, the issue of production will not be addressed here. The counts of the entire assemblage, however, are presented in Table 17.1.

The primary tool type comprises sixteen sickle elements that can be identified as large geometric sickles, typical of the Middle Bronze through Iron Ages, but more frequent in the latter period (Rosen 1997). These sickle elements could appear in two diverse variants. The first variant comprises geometric elements that are parallelogram in shape (Rosen 1983: 108–115; 1997:55) and were manufactured from wide blanks, usually wide and thick flakes (Fig. 17.1:1, 2). However, some were shaped on wide blade segments

Table 17.1. The Flint Assemblage

	N	%
Debitage		
Primary elements	34	14.6
Flakes	142	60.9
Blades	36	15.5
Bladelets	6	2.6
CTE	2	0.8
Burnt material	13	5.6
Total	233	100.0
Debris		
Chips	3	5.9
Chunks	48	94.1
Total	51	100.0
Debitage	233	59.6
Debris	51	13.0
Cores	18	4.6
Tools	89	22.8
Total	391	100.0

(Fig. 17.1:3). These blanks were further modified and their sides were shaped by semi-abrupt retouch, while the working edges, which are located on the wide distal end, were shaped by fine denticulation. The pronounced bulbs were thinned, probably for hafting.

The second variant comprises specimens that are rectangular in shape (Fig. 17.1:4–6), formed mainly on wide blade blanks. The wide blanks were backed and truncated, while the working edges exhibit fine denticulation. A few sickles of this variant have an arched back (Fig. 17.1:7, 8), indicating that they were mounted in an arched sickle; the triangular segment (Fig. 17.1:9) would have been placed at the end of the sickle.

All sickle elements display pronounced gloss on their working edges. The distribution of the gloss clearly indicates that these elements were in use over a

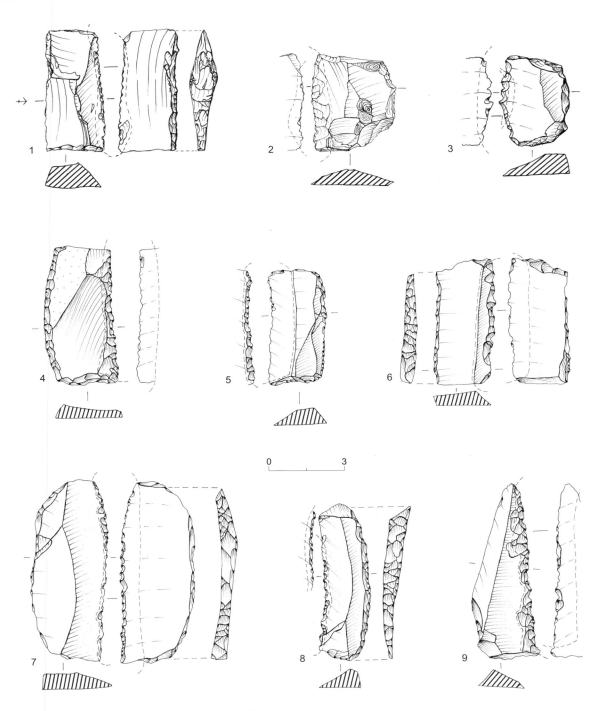

Fig. 17.1. Iron Age tools.

long period of time. It is also evident that some of the elements were retooled during maintenance.

Other tool types are ad hoc and include retouched flakes and blades, endscrapers, burins, and notches and denticulates. Unfortunately, none is diagnostic of any period; nonetheless, they are known in the Iron Age.

Other Periods

The flint collection includes several tools originating from earlier periods. Eight items are sickle blades shaped on elongated blades resembling Canaanean blades (Fig. 17.2:1–5). Based on their shaping technique, as

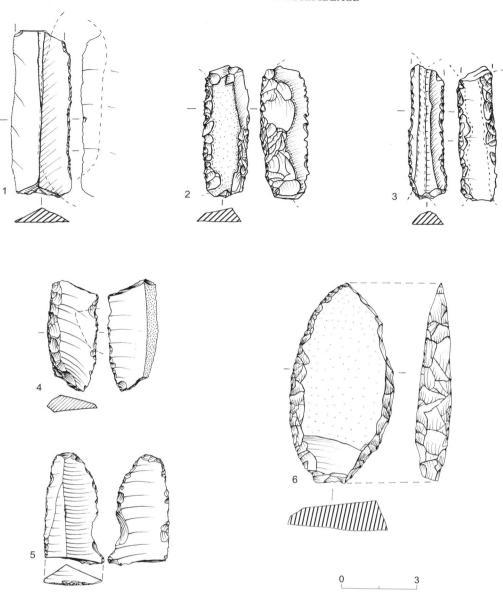

Fig. 17.2. Early Bronze Age tools.

well as raw material preference, they can be identified as belonging to the Early Bronze Age. An additional item of this period is a fanscraper (Fig. 17.2:6), which was manufactured from high quality Eocene tabular flint. This fan scraper could be attributed to the Early Bronze Age, despite the fact that it has no patterns incised into the cortex. This artifact was found on a floor, presumably in secondary use.

The flint collection also includes a large number of Mousterian artifacts that came from fills. It seems that they originated in the vicinity of the fortress. These artifacts were produced from dark flint but exhibit a double white patina, indicating that the artifacts were exposed over a long period of time. Most of the Mousterian artifacts are flakes, but a few Levallois tools are present and include one retouched point (Fig. 17.3:1), one convergent double sidescraper (Fig. 17.3:2) and one retouched blade (Fig. 17.3:3).

In addition, a large number of hammerstones (152) were found. Five display one smooth, flat face, and were perhaps used as grinding implements.

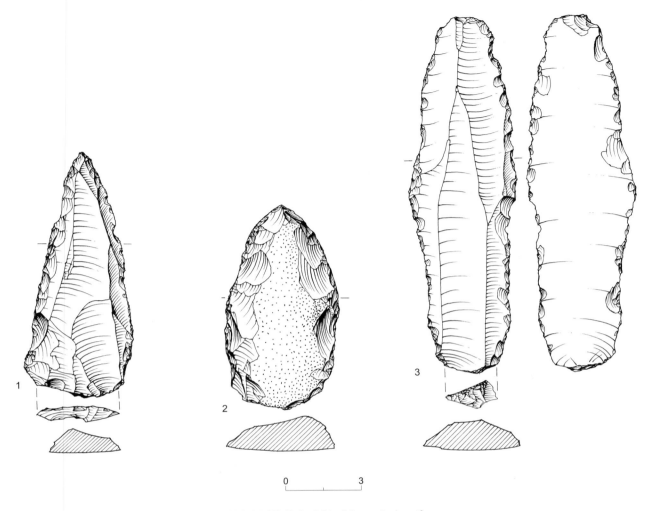

Fig. 17.3. Middle Paleolithic (Mousterian) artifacts.

CONCLUSIONS

Few conclusions can be drawn from the flint collection of Kadesh Barnea. The quantity of typical sickle elements indicates that the inhabitants of the fortressess practiced agriculture. The earlier finds indicate an intensive occupational sequence in this area, from the prehistoric periods until recent times. Middle Paleolithic sites have been reported by Wiegand (1920), Buzy (e.g., 1927; 1929), Neuville (1952), Anati (1958) and Haiman (see Chapter 21). Upper Paleolithic materials have been found by Neuville (1952) and Bar-Yosef (1980), and Early Bronze Age material by Beit-Arieh (1977), Beit-Arieh and Gophna (1976; 1981), Cohen (1983a) and by Haiman (1990b; see also Chapter 21).

ACKNOWLEDGEMENTS

I wish to thank Dr. Rudolph Cohen who made it possible to write this report. The flint figures were drawn by the author and Michael Smilanski. Hamoudi Khalaily offered advice and proofread the final version.

CHAPTER 18

SHELL TRADE AT KADESH BARNEA

DANIELLA E. BAR-YOSEF MAYER

INTRODUCTION

This report discusses 405 malacological and related finds excavated at Kadesh Barnea in the years 1976–1982. Most of them where retrieved by manual collection, as only a few assemblages were sifted. Some additional artifacts made of shell (Chapter 13) have not been included here, as I did not examine them. The assemblage (Tables 18.1, 18.2) comprises 389 mollusk shells and 16 fossil mollusks. In addition 12 other items of biological origin are also discussed. A total of 385 (99%) of the mollusk shells could be positively identified at the genus or species level. About 311 (80%) of the mollusks could be assigned to a specific stratigraphic unit.

Following is a description of the shells according to their stratigraphic assignment as determined by the excavators, including Strata 4, 3 and 2, representing

Table 18.1. Distribution of Mollusks Used as Artifacts

Class	Genus/Species	Origin	Stratum 4	Substratum 3c	Substrata 3a,b	Stratum 2	Stratum 1	Mixed	Total
Gastropods	Clanculus	RS			1	2		1	4
	Tectus	RS	1						1
	Nerita	RS	1	1	1			1	4
	Vermetus	?		1					1
	Lambis	RS		2	2	2	2	5	13
	Cypraea annulus	RS	17	18	24	30	9	30	128
	Cypraea spp.	RS/M			3	3		4	10
	Tonna	RS				1			1
	Phalium	M	1	1					2
	Charonia	?				2	5	3	10
	Muricidae	M			1	1		2	4
	Mitra	RS	1						1
	Conus spp.	RS	1		2	2	2	4	11
Bivalves	Glycymeris	M	13	11	12	14	1	13	64
	Pinctada	RS		11	4	1	2	1	19
	Ostrea	?						1	1
	Spondylus	RS	1		2				3
	Chambardia	N	2	5	5	1	1	2	16
	Cardiidae	M	4	15	2	2	1	6	30
	Tridacna	RS	3	3	8	5	2	5	26
	Donax	M	1	1					2
	Periglypta	RS				1			1
Scaphopods	Worked bivalve	?						1	1
	Dentalium	RS						2	2
Total			46	69	67	67	25	81	355

M = Mediterranean; N = Nile; RS = Red Sea

Table 18.2. Distribution of Mollusks and Other Biological Finds
(excluding items in Table 18.1)

	Stratum 4	Substratum 3c	Substrata 3a-b	Stratum 2	Stratum 1	Mixed	Total
Melanoides		1	1			1	3
Melanopsis	4	7	3	2	1	1	18
Sphincterochila	1	1	1	1			4
Unidentified land snail		1	2		2		5
Unidentified gastropod		1	1	1			3
Fossil bivalve	1	1		1	1		4
Sepia		1		1			2
Unidentified fossils			3				3
Coral	1	1				1	3
Crab claw			1				1
Sea urchin spine			1				1
Fish operculum			1				1
Ostrich egg shell						1	1
Total	7	14	14	6	4	4	49

Iron II, and Stratum 1, containing remains of the Persian-period occupation.

Within each stratigraphic unit, the shells are presented in taxonomic order. The description includes the origin of the shells (F = freshwater; L = land snail; M = Mediterranean ; N = Nile; RS = Red Sea). The shells are described as either complete shells, worked shells, broken shells (when more than half the shell is present) or fragments (when less than half the shell is present).

Table 18.1 presents only marine and freshwater shells considered artifacts (i.e., not including land snails, freshwater gastropods, and unidentifiable specimens). Therefore it includes only 355 out of the total mentioned above. Table 18.2 summarizes all the other finds, including those that are not mollusks. In the absence of a systematic study of other invertebrates, those that reached my attention are also included here. In addition, a fish operculum and an ostrich eggshell fragment (that are vertebrate remains) are recorded here (as they were included in the material handed over to me, having been misidentified in the field). For another ostrich eggshell, see Chapter 20.

DESCRIPTION

Stratum 4 (Iron IIA)

Gastropods

Tectus dentatus (RS). A broken shell, only the base of which is present.

Nerita sanguinolenta (RS). One complete shell.

Melanopsis sp. (F). Three complete and one broken shell. These could have originated in the nearby 'Ein el-Qudeirat.

Cypraea annulus (RS). Seventeen shells, mostly from floor deposits (twelve are complete, one is broken and four had their dorsa removed).

Phalium granulatum (M). One polished 'cassid lip' (Reese 1989a).

Mitra sp. (RS). One broken shell with a hole in the body whorl (Fig. 18.1).

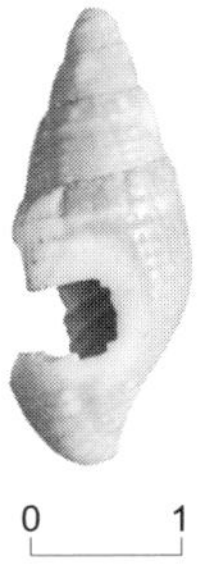

Fig. 18.1. Broken Mitra sp. shell with a hole in the body whorl, Substratum 4b.

0   1

Conus sp. One fragment of the base of the shell, unidentifiable at species level, and its origin unknown.
Sphincterochila zonata (L). One shell.

Bivalves
Glycymeris insubrica (M). Thirteen shells: four complete, one naturally abraded all around (the umbo is eroded) and eight have a natural hole worn in their umbones (Fig. 18.2).
Spondylus sp. This large fossil is of unknown origin.
Chambardia rubens (N). Two fragments of this freshwater bivalve.
Cerastoderma glaucum (M). Four shells: one complete, two broken and one with a natural hole in the umbo (Fig. 18.3; *Cardiidae* in Table 18.1).
Tridacna cf. *squamosa* (RS). There is one complete valve where the scales have been removed. There is slight evidence of porosity of the shell, indicating it lay dead in the ocean for a time before being picked up (Fig. 18.4).
Tridacna sp. (RS). One complete and one broken valve, both are porous.
Donax trunculus (M). One complete shell; it has a stripe of decalcification along its center, and seems fresh on the two sides of this stripe. The reason for this phenomenon is unknown.

Other
One fossil bivalve and one coral, both unidentified.

Substratum 3c (Iron IIB)

This is the constructional fill of the Stratum 3 fortress, comprising, according to the excavators, primarily Stratum 4 artifacts, but also some that may belong to the period of use of Stratum 3.

Gastropods
Nerita sanguinolenta (RS). One complete shell.
Melanoides tuberculata (F). One shell.
Melanopsis sp. (F). Seven shells.
Vermetus sp. One shell of unknown origin. This shell is rare in the archaeological record (Fig. 18.5).
Lambis truncata sebae (RS). Two items: one body whorl fragment, and one 'dish' made of the body whorl, found in conjunction with a stone surface (Fig. 18.6).
Cypraea annulus (RS). A total of eighteen shells were found; twelve are complete, five are 'cowrie beads'

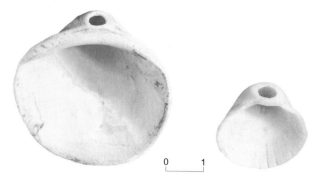

Fig. 18.2. Glycymeris insubrica with a natural hole in its umbo, Substratum 4b.

Fig. 18.3. Cerastoderma glaucum with a natural hole in the umbo, Stratum 4.

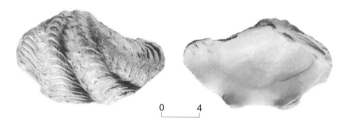

Fig. 18.4. Tridacna cf. squamosa, Substratum 4b.

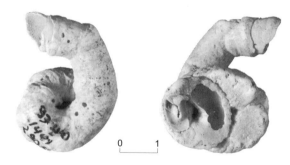

Fig. 18.5. Vermetus sp., Substratum 3c.

Fig. 18.6. Lambis truncata sebae 'dish', Substratum 3c.

(where the dorsum of the shell has been removed), and one is a shell missing its outer lip.

Phalium granulatum (M). A naturally-polished 'cassid lip'.

Sphincterochila sp. (L). One item was found.

In addition there was an unidentified land snail, as well as an unidentified gastropod.

Bivalves

Glycymeris insubrica (M). A total of eleven valves were retrieved: three complete valves, one broken, five valves with a naturally abraded hole in the umbo (one of those is broken) and one valve with a hole artificially perforated at the umbo (Fig. 18.7).

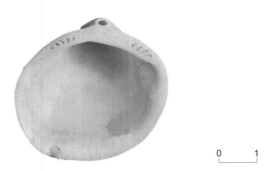

Fig. 18.7. Glycymeris insubrica with hole in the umbo, Substratum 3c.

Pinctada margaritifera (RS). A total of eleven fragments were found; six of them are from the same basket and could be of the same shell (Reg. No. 8127, L6076). Of the remaining five fragments, two are from Reg. No. 5063, L3020 and two from Reg. No. 3091, L1406, again indicating that the large number is biased due to breakage of this relatively fragile shell. All are from fills.

Chambardia rubens (N). Three broken valves and two smaller fragments.

Cerastoderma glaucum (M). A total of fifteen items: seven complete valves, seven broken ones, and one valve with an artificial hole at the umbo, as well as a hole created by a boring gastropod (Fig. 18.8; *Cardiidae* in Table 18.1).

Fig. 18.8. Cerastoderma glaucum valve with an artificial hole at the umbo, Substratum 3c.

Tridacna cf. *squamosa* (RS). One complete valve; the scales have been removed and there are signs of marine worms as well as very slight porosity, indicating that the valve was collected as a dead specimen.

Tridacna sp. (RS). Two valve fragments.

Donax trunculus (M). One complete valve.

Cephalopods

Sepia sp. (RS?). One internal shell of a cuttlefish, apparently from the Red Sea.

Other

One fossil bivalve and one coral, both unidentified.

Substrata 3a–b (Iron IIB)

Gastropods

Clanculus pharaonis (RS). One complete shell that was made into a bead by piercing a hole opposite the body whorl.

Nerita sanguinolenta (RS). One fragment with a hole in it.

Lambis truncata sebae (RS). Two items: one base fragment and a broken 'dish' made of the body whorl.

Cypraea annulus (RS). A total of twenty-four shells were found: seventeen complete (two of them are of juvenile specimens, i.e., relatively small); six are 'cowrie beads' (where the dorsum of the shell has been removed; of those one is burned), and one is a shell missing its outer lips.

Cypraea erosa nebrites (RS). One complete juvenile specimen.

Cypraea pantherina (RS). One fragment of the outer lip.

Cypraea turdus (RS). The outer lip of one shell.

Hexaplex trunculus (M). One complete shell, naturally abraded (*Muricidae* in Table 18.1).

Conus sp. Two beads made of the spire of the *Conus* by drilling the apex and removing most of the body whorl, thus leaving only the top part of the shell. One of them is broken (Fig. 18.9). Because the species is unknown, its origin is indeterminable.

Melanoides tuberculatum (F). One complete shell.

Fig. 18.9. Top part of Conus sp., Substratum 3a.

Melanopsis sp. (F). Two complete and one broken shell.

Sphincterochila zonata (L). One complete shell.

In addition, two unidentified local land snails were recovered, and one unidentifiable marine gastropod fragment.

Bivalves

Glycymeris insubrica (M). A total of twelve shells: four complete, two broken, five shells with a naturally abraded hole in the umbo, and one shell with an artificial hole perforated at the umbo.

Pinctada margaritifera (RS). Four fragments of mother-of-pearl.

Spondylus sp. (RS/M?). One complete shell from the Red Sea which could not be identified at species level, and another broken shell that could be either of Red Sea or Mediterranean origin.

Chambardia rubens (N). Four shells were found in Substrata 3a-b: one is a complete valve and comes from a floor deposit (Reg. No. 2630, L853) and the other four are fragments.

Cerastoderma glaucum (M). Two complete valves (*Cardiidae* in Table 18.1).

Tridacna sp. (RS). One complete, very eroded and porous specimen, as well as five fragments (two of them conjoin). There were also two broken shells, one of which is of special interest: the inner side of the valve shows striation marks and a part which is smooth, indicating that it might have been used for grinding (Reg. No. 8472, L6231).

Other

Three unidentified fossils, as well as one crab claw, one spine of a sea urchin, and one fish operculum.

Stratum 2 (Iron IIC)

Gastropods

Clanculus pharaonis (RS). Two shells with a hole in the body whorl, from the floor of Casemate L186.

Lambis truncata sebae (RS). A broken artifact in the shape of a 'dish', made of the body whorl, was found on a casemate floor (L420). In addition there was one fragment of the *columella*.

Cypraea annulus (RS). A total of thirty shells were found, of which twenty-four are complete (seven of them with traces of burning), and six were made into 'cowrie beads'. Most are from the casemates, in particular L186, L419 and L402, where several were found together.

Cypraea erosa nebrites (RS). One complete shell from a casemate (L186).

Cypraea pantherina (RS). The outer lip of one shell is present.

Ovula ovum (RS). This species is related to the cowries (and appears as such in Table 18.1). It is represented by a complete shell from a casemate floor (L157).

Tonna galea (RS). A fragment.

Charonia tritonis (RS or M). Two fragments were found, one of the body whorl and the other of the outer lip.

Bolinus brandaris (M). One shell, broken and burnt (*Muricidae* in Table 18.1).

Conus generalis maldivus (RS). A complete and naturally abraded shell.

Conus sanguinolentus (RS). A complete and naturally abraded shell.

Melanopsis sp. (F). Two shells.

Sphincterochila zonata (L). One complete shell.

Bivalves

Glycymeris insubrica (M). A total of fourteen shells: four complete, one fragment, six shells with a natural hole in the umbo (three of them are broken), and three shells with a perforated hole at the umbo.

Pinctada margaritifera (RS). One near-complete valve of mother-of-pearl.

Chambardia rubens (F). One broken valve.

Cerastoderma glaucum (M). Two shells, one complete and one with an artificial hole at the umbo and burnt (*Cardiidae* in Table 18.1).

Tridacna sp. (RS). Three broken valves; one of them bears evidence that the scales were removed. In addition there were two fragments, one of which might have been worked.

Periglypta puerpera (RS). A broken and burnt shell, from the floor of Casemate 553.

Cephalopods

Sepia sp. A fragment of the internal skeleton of a squid was found.

Other

In addition to the above there was one fossil bivalve, as well as another fragment of a mollusk which could not be determined.

Stratum 1 (Babylonian[?]/Persian Period)

Gastropods

Lambis truncata sebae (RS). One body fragment is possibly worked and another is a fragment of the outer lip.

Cypraea annulus (RS). There were nine shells: six of them complete, two broken, and one is a fragment of the dorsum of the cowrie. Five of the shells are from L6062, one of the Stratum 1 pits.

Charonia tritonis (RS or M). One complete shell (L495), as well as four fragments. A very large fragment includes the spire, and the others represent different body parts (a base, a body fragment, and one from the siphonal canal; see Fig. 18.11); they could thus belong to the same specimen, which is certainly true for the two fragments that were found in the same locus (L7025).

Conus arenatus (RS). A fragment of the base of the shell. It was possible to identify it due to the preservation of the pattern on the shell.

Conus flavidus (RS). A complete shell, naturally abraded.

Melanopsis sp. (F). One specimen.

In addition, two land snails were uncovered.

Bivalves

Glycymeris insubrica (M). One valve with a naturally abraded hole in the umbo.

Pinctada margaritifera (RS). One near-complete valve of mother-of-pearl, and one fragment.

Chambardia rubens (F). One fragment.

Cerastoderma glaucum (M). One complete valve (*Cardiidae* in Table 18.1).

Tridacna cf. *maxima* (RS). A broken valve; the scales have been removed and the shell is slightly porous, which means that it was collected as an empty shell after the mollusk died.

Other

There was one unidentified bivalve fossil.

Shells from Mixed Contexts or Unknown Stratigraphy

Gastropods

Clanculus pharaonis (RS). One complete and naturally abraded shell.

Nerita sanguinolenta (RS). One shell with a hole opposite the aperture.

Lambis truncata sebae (RS). Five fragments: two of the body whorl, one of the spire, and two of the outer lip (that conjoin). Four of the fragments come from the same basket (Reg. No. 65, L52) and might belong to the same specimen.

Cypraea annulus (RS). A total of thirty shells: twenty-four complete and six cowrie beads.

Cypraea arabica grayana (RS). A complete shell. It has one small hole which does not seem to have been produced artificially (Fig. 18.10).

Cypraea erosa nebrites (RS). One complete shell.

Cypraea lurida (M). One complete shell with a small natural hole in the body whorl.

Cypraea pantherina (RS). One outer lip.

Charonia tritonis (RS or M). Of the three specimens, two are large, retaining the spire, and one is the fragment of the outer lip (Fig. 18.11; the find spots of the specimens in the photograph are unknown).

Hexaplex trunculus (M). Two shells, both may have been worked. One had a perfectly round hole drilled in the body whorl, possibly with a metal tool. The other had two square holes in its body whorl (*Murcidae* in Table 18.1).

Conus flavidus (RS). One complete, naturally abraded shell (Fig. 18.12).

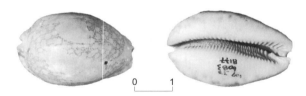

Fig. 18.10. Cypraea arabica grayana with small hole (apparently natural), Stratum 2 or 1.

Fig. 18.11. Charonia tritonis from unknown findspots.

Fig. 18.12. Naturally-abraded
Conus flavidus, Stratum 2 or 1.

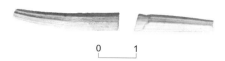

Fig. 18.13. Dentalium sp. from Strata 2–1
mixed context (left) and surface (right).

Conus sp. Three additional cones were found that were not identified at species level. One is a fragment of the base. Another is a Red Sea specimen, but although there are some faded remains of the original pattern of the shell, the species could not be determined. Most of the body whorl was removed, and only the top part is present and is about 10 mm high; its diameter is 20–25 mm. On the top of the shell there seems to be an area that was ground down and is smoother than the rest of the shell. On the other side there are some perforations that could be a result of natural pores that had formed as an outcome of the shell having been naturally eroded in the sea prior to collection. The third specimen is a large and broken perforated apex.

Melanoides tuberculatum (F). One broken shell.

Melanopsis sp. (F). One complete shell.

Bivalves

Glycymeris insubrica (M). A total of twelve valves: five complete, five with a natural hole in the umbo (three of which are broken), one broken valve, and one valve that is abraded all around (so there is no trace of the hinge area).

Glycymeris sp. (RS). One complete valve.

Pinctada margaritifera (RS). One fragment of mother-of-pearl.

Ostrea sp. A broken valve, its origin unknown.

Chambardia rubens (N). Two fragments of Nilotic mother-of-pearl.

Cerastoderma glaucum (M). There were five valves: two complete, two broken and one fragment (*Cardiidae* in Table 18.1).

Cardiidae. One fragment of an unidentifiable species of this family.

Tridacna sp. (RS). Five valves were uncovered: two complete, two fragments and one broken and porous.

In addition, there was one broken unidentifiable bivalve.

Scaphopods

Dentalium sp. (RS). Two specimens (Fig. 18.13).

Other

One fragment of a coral and one fragment of an ostrich eggshell.

DISCUSSION

Figure 18.14 presents the distribution of the major malacological finds from the Iron Age strata (4–2), presumed to have served as artifacts (the Stratum 1 shells were precluded due to their paucity, only 25 specimens). A comparison of the shells to those of other contemporaneous Iron II sites illustrates how mollusks were being exploited in the Southern Levant in this period. It is interesting to note that while the ceramic analysis links Stratum 3c to Stratum 4 (see Chapter 11), this is not apparent in the shell assemblage. This, however, may be a biased impression due to the relatively small quantity of shells in Stratum 4 (n = 46).

Gastropods

Lambis truncata sebae

This is the largest gastropod to be found in the Gulf of Eilat and a very common species, which served for producing various shell artifacts since the Ḥarifian (Mienis 1977; Cohen and Dever 1980; Bar-Yosef Mayer 1997, 2002). Of the 13 specimens recovered from the site, there are three 'dishes' (see Fig. 18.6), i.e., a large portion of the body whorl, which was cut to make a rounded concave artifact, measuring approximately 9 cm across. These may have been used as small bowls. They seem to be larger than the engraved discs described by Brandl (1984), which are also made of *Lambis* (Mienis 1988).

The rest of the specimens at Kadesh Barnea are fragments (including fragments of dishes), present throughout the stratigraphical sequence other than in Stratum 4, which is noteworthy. The fact that each of the three dishes came from a different Stratum (3c, 3b and 2; the latter two from floors) may indicate a continuation of the use of *Lambis* to produce these artifacts (but there is no telling, of course, which of the examples may have been re-deposited).

The only other published *Lambis* dish is from Be'er Resisim (Cohen and Dever 1980), a single occupation Intermediate Bronze Age site in the Negev. This prohibits us from determining the *Lambis* dish as an Iron Age artifact, until more specimens are found.

Lambis sp. are sometimes known to have been used as trumpets, as is the case in Tawilan (there, it was also found as an engraved disc, see Reese 1995a). (At Kadesh Barnea, in Strata 2 and 1, *Charonia* might have been used as trumpets, see below.) Being large, *Lambis* shells were multi-purpose and could have been used as trumpets and dishes, as well as for the production of many other artifacts. One should not rule out the possibility that the dishes, like trumpets, had a ritual use (they may have served, for example, as libation vessels).

While *Lambis truncata* is present in all strata from Stratum 3c onwards, *Charonia tritonis* is present only in Strata 2 and 1. Of the ten specimens at the site, one was a complete shell (found in a debris context of Stratum 1, L495), and three were spire fragments (one from Stratum 1 and 2 from mixed contexts), which are indicative of the actual number of complete shells (see Fig. 18.11).

The use of this shell as a trumpet is well known in the Aegean world (Åström and Reese 1990; Reese 1995b) and is well attested in the ethnographic record, oftentimes in ritual contexts (e.g., Safer and McLaughlin Gill 1982). The presence of *Charonia* at Kadesh Barnea, as well as at a few other Iron Age sites in Israel, such as Hazor, Tell Qasile and Yoqne'am (Yadin et al. 1960:35; Bayer 1963; Mazar 1980; Horwitz et al. 2005) might be related to Greek influences along the coast towards the end of the Iron Age (Stern 1989).

It should be noted that *Charonia* was also found at Late Bronze Age Tel Nami, under strong Mycenean influence (Baruch 2000), as well as at later sites such as Hellenistic Ḥorbat 'Eleq (Bar-Yosef Mayer 2000c). *Charonia tritonis* is known also from sites as far north and inland as Tell Rifa'at in Syria, where it may have had a connection with a temple of Neptune (Biggs 1967; the exact context of the shell is not mentioned in the report).

Cypraea annulus

The 128 specimens of *Cypraea annulus* form about one third of the total number of shells at Kadesh Barnea and are the dominant group of shells in every stratum. Twenty-seven of these shells are 'cowrie beads' (shells whose dorsum has been removed), four are broken shells and one represents solely the dorsum of the shell without the lips. The rest (96 shells, or 75%) are complete.

This species is known from the literature to have been used cross-culturally for centuries as 'shell money'. This is documented, for example, in China during the seventh century BCE (attested by written documents), Egypt during the Middle Ages, seventeenth-century India and in some parts of Africa, especially during the sixteenth–nineteenth centuries CE (Hogendorn and Johnson 1986:12–19).

Cypraea annulus appears consistently in most Iron Age sites in the Southern Levant (Table 18.3). Tell el-Kheleifeh (Glueck's excavation) is of special interest because of the overall resemblance of the site to Kadesh Barnea, and its location by the Gulf of Eilat, the closest source of these shells. There, this species forms almost half of the shell assemblage (pers. obs.). At Umm el-Biyara in Jordan and Ḥorbat Qiṭmit in the eastern Negev, *C. annulus* forms 87% and 100% of the

Table 18.3. *Cypraea annulus* in Selected Iron Age Sites

Site	*Publication*
Tell el-Kheleifeh	Personal observation
Tawilan	Reese 1995a
Buṣeirah	Reese 1995a
Umm el-Biyara	Reese 1995a
Ḥorbat Qiṭmit	Mienis 1995a
Tel Masos	Reese 1983
Aro'er	Personal observation
Tel Miqne-'Eqron	Golani 1996
Lachish	Bar-Yosef Mayer 2004
Tel Baṭash	Bar-Yosef Mayer 2006b
City of David	Mienis 1992
Megiddo	Bar-Yosef Mayer 2000c
Bet She'an	Bar-Yosef Mayer 2006
Tel Dan	Personal observation
Tall Sheh Hamad	Reese 1991
Hasanlu	Reese 1989b

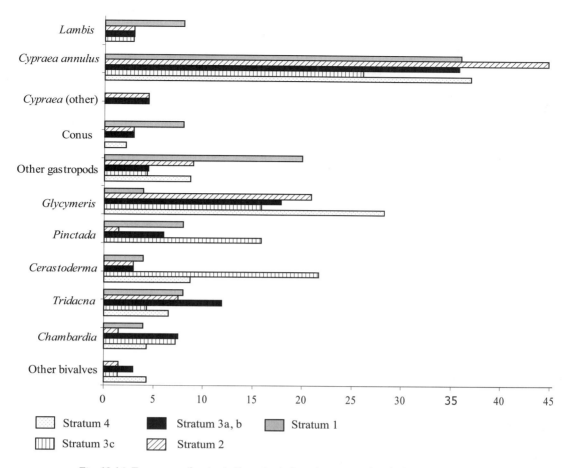

Fig. 18.14. Frequency of main shell species in Iron Age strata of Kadesh Barnea (N=249).

assemblages respectively and many of them are not worked (Reese 1995a; Mienis 1995a). Ninth-century BCE Hasanlu, in Iran, is another site of interest, where *C. annulus* makes up a large component of the shell assemblage (Reese 1989b). The cowries there could have originated in the Persian Gulf (today they are only known to be present in the southeastern part of the Gulf; see Bosch et al. 1995).

Mienis (1995a) raised the question of the specific function or use of *C. annulus* at Ḥorbat Qiṭmit, especially in view of the fact that the species is quite rare in the Red Sea. The dominance of this species throughout the Levant, as well as the fact that it is most often found as complete shells rather than beads, may suggest its use as currency. Its rarity in the Gulf of Eilat, the most plausible source, may account for the value attached to it (yet it is also possible that the species is rare nowadays due to over exploitation by humans over the past three millennia).

All this, however, does not contradict the possible use of cowries as decorations and/or fertility amulets (for further discussion see Bar-Yosef Mayer 2000a).

Other than *Cypraea annulus*, six other cowrie species were found at Kadesh Barnea. One is *Ovula ovum* (in Stratum 2), which is related to the cowrie family (super family: *Cypraeacea*) and is uncommon in the archaeological record. The other is *Cypraea lurida* (one example in a mixed context), which is the only Mediterranean cowrie at the site. The three *Cypraea erosa nebrites* (one from Stratum 3/2, L663 in the fill of the granary; one from Stratum 2, Casemate 186; and one from an unknown context) are complete. In addition, there were fragments of three *Cypraea pantherina*: one from a Stratum 3 fill, one from Casemate 501 of Stratum 2 and one from an unclear context. One *Cypraea arabica* was found in a mixed Strata 2–1 locus) and one *Cypraea turdus* originated in the fill of the granary.

None of the above were made into beads, and the use of these cowries, whether as currency and/or decoration, is not clear. In many of the Iron Age sites in Table 18.3 there are also other *Cypraea* species, but they are usually less common than *Cypraea annulus*.

Conus sp.

One worked *Conus* top from L274 is assigned to either Stratum 2 or 1 and appears in Table 18.1 in the 'mixed' category. However, it is reminiscent of the 'rectangular conus whorl beads' found at Hasanlu IVB, which are dated to the ninth century BCE (Reese 1989b; but it is not as elaborate as the Hasanlu specimens). Although I am not suggesting a direct connection between the two sites, the worked *Conus* from Hasanlu might suggest the reason for the collection and partial working of *Conus* tops. The fact that the *Conus* group at Kadesh Barnea consists of four complete shells, three base fragments and four spires might indicate that they were worked at the site, although the sample size is not large enough for any definite conclusion.

Other contemporaneous sites in which *Conus* sp. were found include the nearby fortress of Quseimeh (Meshel 1994: Figs. 17, 18), as well as the City of David in Jerusalem, Tel Miqne-'Eqron in the Shephelah, Buṣeirah and Umm el-Biyara in Jordan (Mienis 1992; Golani 1996; Reese 1995a and see further discussion of this species in Brandl 1985).

Bivalves

Pinctada margaritifera and Chambardia rubens

These two are mother-of-pearl shells, the former originating in the Red Sea and the latter in the Nile. Most of the shells of both species were found as fragments, since both are very fragile in comparison to other mollusks, and thus distinguishing between them is sometimes difficult. This causes a certain bias, clearly demonstrated in Fig. 18.14: The large number of *Pinctada* in Substratum 3c is a result of multiple fragments, often found together, which may in fact reflect fewer specimens. Both species, however, were also present as complete or almost complete valves, which enabled their identification.

Whereas at least one of these two species are present in all strata at Kadesh Barnea (when fragmentary, they cannot always be differentiated), it is interesting to note that only one complete valve of *Chambardia*

rubens was found on a floor of Stratum 3 (L853) and one almost complete valve of *Pinctada margaritifera* was on the floor of one of the Stratum 2 casemates (L501).

Unfortunately, no clear artifacts made of these species were found at Kadesh Barnea (but the fragments could represent such artifacts). Most of the fragments are from fills. Both species are present in other major Iron Age sites such as the City of David, Megiddo, Lachish and Bet She'an (and see Reese, Mienis and Woodward 1986).

Tridacna sp.

This species was present in all strata, comprising 4–12% of the shell assemblages. The complete or almost complete valves might have had a functional use such as cosmetic palettes, but there was no evidence for this. Similar shells are known to have been engraved during the Iron Age (Stucky 1974; Brandl 1984, 2001; Reese and Sease 1993; Mienis 1994).

Tridacna sp. was also used for making beads. Two unique examples of such artifacts, possibly in different stages of manufacture, were retrieved in Glueck's excavation at Tell el-Kheleifeh (pers. obs.).

Glycymeris insubrica and Cerastoderma glaucum

These two species, totaling together 94 shells, about 25% of the shell assemblage of Kadesh Barnea, seem to go hand in hand in many archaeological sites of the Levant. *Glycymeris* is nowadays the most common shell on the Levantine Mediterranean beaches, apparently a population on the verge of extinction (Sivan et al. 2006). They are usually collected naturally abraded and often with holes in their umbones, as is the case with the finds from all Iron Age strata at Kadesh Barnea. However, their relative frequency, no more than 28% of the marine shells in Stratum 4 (and down to 4% in Stratum 1) is low in comparison to sites that are closer to the Mediterranean. This prevents us from suggesting that they were used in construction, as is the case elsewhere (Bar-Yosef Mayer 2005a).

Freshwater Gastropods and Land Snails

All land snails seem to be of local species, and they could belong to any period before, during or after the occupation at the site. Land snails often aestivate in the ground, and fall easily into cracks. All land snails gathered at Kadesh Barnea derived from fill contexts.

One exception is a *Sphincterochila zonata* specimen that seems to have been made into a bead (although, it, too, was found in the Substratum 3c fill). Despite shell beads made of land snails being rare in the archaeological record, some examples are known, for example, from North Africa (Camps-Fabrer 1960:99).

The freshwater gastropods, *Melanoides tuberculatum* and *Melanopsis* sp., could both have originated in the nearby 'Ein el-Qudeirat, and might have been brought into the site accidentally, e.g., with mud for the construction of mud bricks (Bar-Yosef and Heller 1987) or even with drinking water. Therefore, they cannot be considered as artifacts or trade items.

Miscellaneous Shells Occurring in Small Quantities

Marine shells not discussed here are *Nerita sangui-nolenta, Clanculus pharaonis, Tectus* sp., *Vermetus* sp., *Tonna galea, Phalium granulatum, Hexaplex* and *Bolinus* spp. (see Table 18.1, *Muricidae*), *Dentalium* sp., *Ostrea* sp., *Donax trunculus, Spondylus* sp., *Periglypta puerpera* and *Sepia* sp. All of them appear at the site in very small numbers, and in Fig. 18.14 are referred to as 'other gastropods' and 'other bivalves'. The variability of shell species at the site is thus similar to that encountered in any shell assemblage in the Levant. These minor groups may have been collected by the inhabitants of the site on various trips and brought as 'souvenirs.' Some of them, being more typically species preferred during the Neolithic period (Bar-Yosef Mayer 1997; 2005b), were not necessarily brought from the Red Sea, but could have been collected at nearby Neolithic sites (Mienis 1995b). Some of the latter were obviously made into beads (apparently during the Neolithic period). Some of the *Cypraea* sp. (in particular *Cypraea erosa nebrites, Cypraea turdus* and *Cypraea pantherina*), as well as the cones (*Conus generalis maldivus* and *Conus sanguinolentus*) that are rare in the archaeological record, could also originate in Neolithic sites.

SUMMARY

The most conspicuous group of shells at Kadesh Barnea is that of *Cypraea annulus*, ranging between 26% and 45% in the different strata. They are followed by *Glycymeris insubrica*, ranging in frequency from 4% to 28%. The former were brought from the Red Sea, about 130 km away (as the crow flies) and the latter from the Mediterranean, over 80 km away as the crow flies. While the possible use of the cowries may have been 'shell money', the use of *Glycymeris*, mostly not manipulated, is unknown. Yet the demonstrable connection of Kadesh Barnea, throughout its occupation, to the Mediterranean and the Red Sea, as well as to the Nile, is of importance.

Herzog (1983:48) suggested that the Iron IIA fortresses of the Negev "…were in connection with Solomon's trade operations in the Red Sea". Whether the fortresses were operated by King Solomon and/ or by his descendants, the presence of Red Sea shells at Kadesh Barnea clearly testifies to a connection between the site and the Red Sea. The shells were traded into the site as beads, souvenirs, game pieces, charms, dishes, trumpets, raw material or currency, and some were probably traded out of it, in any one of these forms.

ACKNOWLEDGMENTS

I am grateful to Rudolph Cohen for entrusting me with the shells of Kadesh Barnea, to Gary Pratico of the Gordon Conwell Seminary for his advice on the material from Tell el-Kheleifeh, and to Joseph Greene of the Semitic Museum, Harvard University for allowing me to study the Tell el-Kheleifeh shells. My thanks also to Hannah Bernick-Greenberg, Anna Belfer-Cohen and Ze'ev Herzog for their useful comments on previous drafts. This study was supported by the American School of Prehistoric Research at the Peabody Museum, Harvard University.

CHAPTER 19

THE FAUNAL REMAINS

DALIA HAKKER-ORION

INTRODUCTION

The different occupations at Kadesh Barnea produced rich faunal assemblages. Most of the bones were collected manually (only selected contexts were sifted) and thus micromammalia, fish and other small animals are surely under represented. The assemblages consist mainly of livestock species, in addition to some wild ones, comprising herbivores, carnivores, fish and fowl.

The following report should be regarded as preliminary. Part of the original data base compiled in the early 1980s, which is the basis for the data presented in Tables 19.1–19.5 and Figs. 19.1 and 19.2, has been lost and could not be reworked.

The appendices include data retrieved from the original (handwritten) lists compiled after the first analysis of the bones. Appendix 1 is a list of species by locus; Appendix 2 lists body part representation of sheep/goats in Stratum 4; Appendix 3 lists body part representation of cattle in Strata 4–2. An electronic version of these lists is available from the IAA archives.

Additional, original (handwritten) records, listing species, body parts, age determinations of young ruminants, and various treatments of bones are kept in the IAA archives and are available for examination and re-manipulation.

Despite all these shortcomings, however (and other lacunae in the data), we still consider this report worthy of publication, because of the uniqueness of the site; general patterns and trends are definitely discernible.

Due to the fragmentary condition of the bones, only those which were clearly identifiable to species (and for some animals, only to families) were classified and quantified. Also, the bones considered here are only those that originated in 'clean' loci, the stratigraphic attribution of which was clear.

About 14% of the bones were burnt; about 3% bore gnawing marks. About 80 bones were fashioned into tools and/or bore cut marks.

FAMILIES AND SPECIES

The distribution of species (including only the main identified species; Table 19.1, Fig. 19.1) was calculated based on a total of 580 loci containing bones. These loci represent only part of the assemblage—138 from Stratum 4, 235 from Stratum 3 (Substrata 3c and 3a-b combined), 182 from Stratum 2 and 15 from Stratum 1. The extremely small Stratum 1 assemblage should be borne in mind when drawing conclusions based on it.

Identification of species was based on comparison with the collections of the zoological departments at Tel Aviv University and the Hebrew University, Jerusalem. General studies used were Chaplin 1971, Hakker-Orion 1972 and von den Driesch 1976. Sheep and goats were differentiated, when possible, based on the criteria mentioned in Boessneck 1969. For the identification of different species of gazelles, see Hakker-Orion 1987.

Table 19.1. Distribution of the Number of Loci containing the Main Families/Taxa in Strata 4–1

	Sheep/ Goat	Goat	Sheep	Gazelle	Ibex	Cattle	Equid	Camel	Bird	Pig/ Boar	Dog	Hare	Total
Stratum 4	51	18	15	10	2	5	6	18	7	-	4	2	138
Stratum 3	61	25	27	17	7	16	18	42	15	2	3	3	236
Stratum 2	40	24	22	14	8	10	15	30	12	1	4	2	182
Stratum 1	8	4	1	1	1	-	4	5	-	-	-	1	25
Total	160	71	65	42	18	31	43	95	34	3	11	8	580

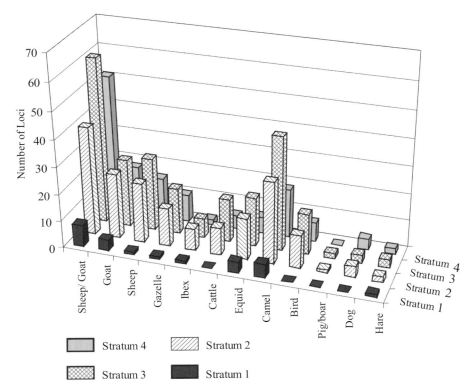

Fig. 19.1. Distribution of the number of loci containing the main families/taxa in Strata 4–1.

Sheep and Goats (*Ovis aries, Capra hircus*)

This category of small ruminants comprises most of the faunal remains in all four strata. Generally, other than in Stratum 3, goats are better represented than sheep.

Most of the goat horns attested are twisted horns (Fig. 19.2:1, 2), while some are straight (Fig. 19.2: 3–5). The dimensions of adult horns indicate that goat and sheep were of two size categories: a large-sized category and a more delicate one. This can be partly due to sexual dimorphism. Compare, for example the horn cores in Fig. 19.2:3–5 with measurements of a horn core from L292 (a mixed, Strata 2–1 context), whose dimensions are: width of base, 3.8 cm; length of base, 2.8 cm; total length, 11.7 cm. The variety in sizes can also be demonstrated, for example, by measurements of the proximal width of 38 metacarpal bones ranging from 2.10 to 2.70 cm and of the same measurement of 23 metatarsal bones ranging from 1.72 to 2.30 cm. For a discussion of the smaller body size of animals in southern Israel in comparison to the same species in northern Israel, see Hakker-Orion 1975:297–298, 1999b:331).

Sheep and goats were used for meat, milk, wool, skin, organic waste (sheep/goat manure is more suitable to serve as fertilizer than that of cattle, for example) and fuel. Goats in particular have the ability to adapt to the environment, can survive with little water, and the amount of milk produced in relation to body weight is the most bountiful.

Most of the small domestic ruminants were slaughtered in adulthood, which indicates their importance as a source of secondary products.

Cattle (*Bos taurus*)

Cattle is present in Strata 4–2 in small percentages, but is absent from the small assemblage of Stratum 1. Most of the bones belong to adult animals (Fig. 19.3), with younger ones represented mainly in the relatively large assemblage of Stratum 3 (two animals aged 2.5 years and two aged 3.5 years). Most of the skeletal parts of cattle are represented in the assemblage.

Some examples of bone dimensions are: A third phalanx from L816 (Stratum 4) has a distal width of 5.72 cm (similar measurements at 'Arad in the eastern Negev were 5.6 cm, 5.8 cm, 6.0 cm; Lernau 1978). In L3194 (Stratum 4) the proximal part of a right radius has proximal widths of 5.5 and 5.2 cm and a proximal length

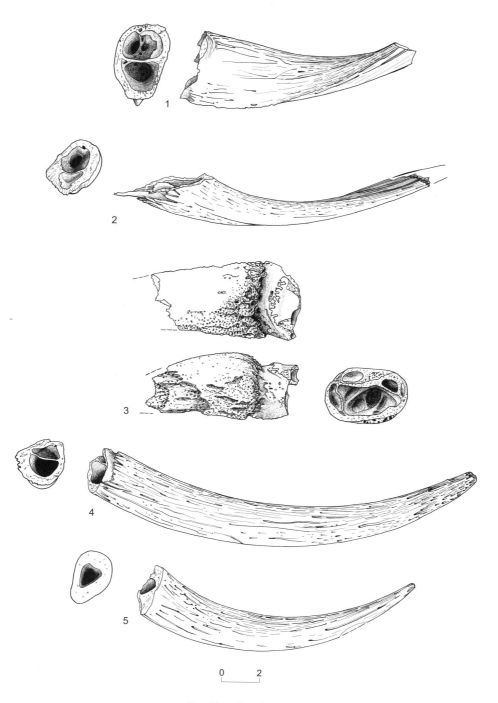

Fig. 19.2. Goat horns.

No.	Reg. No.	Locus	Stratum	Comments
1	8453/7	6223	Fill of the Stratum 3 granary	Twisted
2	8446/9	6223	Fill of the Stratum 3 granary	Twisted
3	8453/8	6223	Fill of the Stratum 3 granary	Straight
4	223/5	125	2	Straight
5	565	294	2	Straight

of 2.8 cm. In L3199 (Stratum 4) a distal left humerus has a distal width of 6.2 cm (cf. cattle from Tel Dan in the north, 6.25 cm; Wapnish, Hesse and Ogilvy 1977). In L94 and L657 (Stratum 3) proximal metatarsal bones have proximal widths of 4.3 and 4.2 cm, and

proximal lengths of 4.1 and 4.0 cm. In L1512 (the fill of the cistern) a metatarsal bone belonging to a larger animal was found, with a proximal width of 5.1 cm and a proximal length of 5.0 cm.

In the Iron Age, cattle in the northerly Negev regions (such as at ʿArad) were medium-sized, larger than those found in the Early Bronze Age (Lernau 1978). On the other hand, at Iron Age Taʿanach, for example (in the Jezreel Valley), identified Iron Age cattle remains were of a small breed, and only one part of one hindlimb was of the medium-sized type (Hakker-Orion 1975:297). The cattle at Kadesh Barnea belong to the same breed as at ʿArad; the larger metatarsal bone from L1512 may be attributed to sexual dimorphism. The restricted number of cattle bones does not enable a more detailed analysis.

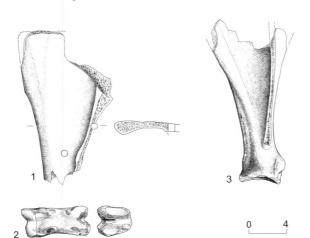

Fig. 19.3. Bovine bones and a tooth.

No.	Reg. No.	Locus	Stratum	Bone	Comments
1	5295	3180	3c	Scapula	Perforated
2	425/20	210	3c	Scapula	
3	2653/40	854	3a-b	First phalanx	

Equidae: Donkeys and Horses (*Equus asinus* and *Equus caballus*)

Bones of donkeys and horses (Fig. 19.4) could not always be differentiated (cf., for example, Hakker-Orion 1975:299; Buitenhuis 1991). Donkeys were probably a common beast of burden at Kadesh Barrnea, though apparently less so than camels (for which see

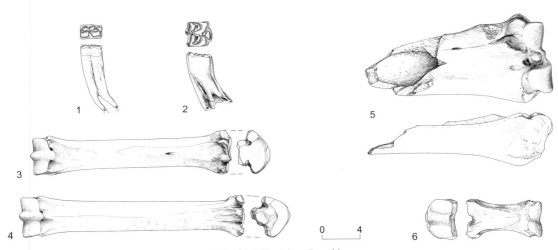

Fig. 19.4. Equid teeth and bones.

No.	Reg. No.	Locus	Stratum	Bone	Comments
1	3235	1500	Fill of cistern (Strata 2, 1)	Mandibular molar	Horse
2	571	288	4a	Maxillar molar	Horse
3	3102/1	1411	Fill of cistern (Strata 2, 1)	Metacarpal	
4	3102/2	1411	Fill of cistern (Strata 2, 1)	Metatarsal	
5	2653/41	854	3a-b	Radius (lower part)	Horse
6	3102/3	1411	Fill of cistern (Strata 2, 1)	First phalanx	Horse

below). Most of the animals identified were adults, but there were, for instance, three young animals (aged 1, 1.5 and 2.5 years) in Stratum 3 and an equid aged 10 months in Stratum 2 (the large assemblage of bones from this stratum, as mentioned, also produced larger amounts of young animals).

Bones that could be positively assigned to horses were very few (most of the identified equids are donkeys). In Stratum 4 there were mainly horse teeth (e.g., Fig. 19.4:2), metacarpal and metatarsal bones. In Stratum 3 were found teeth, scapulae, a humerus, a first phalanx and the lower part of a radius (Fig. 19.4:5).

Recovered from fill within the cistern was a concentration of horse, donkey and equid bones, consisting of a pelvis, metacarpal bones (two right and two left), metatarsal bones, various phalanx bones, a femur and teeth (e.g., Fig. 19.4:1, 3, 4, 6). For frequencies of equids at other Negev sites in the Iron Age and in other periods, see Hakker-Orion 1975; 1993; 2004b.

Camels (*Camelus dromedarius*)

Bones of camels, mostly of adult animals, were recovered from all strata at the site (Fig. 19.5). It seems that at Kadesh Barnea these were the main animals of burden (for frequencies of transport animals at other sites in the Negev and Aravah Valley, cf., for example Hakker-Orion 1991; 1993).

The overwhelming majority were adult animals (with at least two young animals in Stratum 3 and

two in Stratum 2). All parts of the skeleton were found. Measurements of metatarsal bones of camels indicate lower widths ranging between 4.90 and 5.32 cm and lengths of the distal side of the condyle between 4.4 and 4.7 cm. One especially large radius bone was uncovered in L473 of Stratum 3. Its lower width is 8.9 cm and lower length 6.3 cm (cf. Hakker-Orion 1984). Some of the camel scapulae (such as in L921 of Stratum 4; and see more below), were artificially pierced, but the purpose of this perforation is unclear.

Dogs (*Canis familiaris*)

Remains of dogs were found in Strata 4–2 (in Stratum 4—L3194, L5051, L5054, L5063; in Stratum 3—L200, L709; in Stratum 2—L45, L87). Most of them belong to adult animals.

The largest concentration, of at least 13 young and adult animals, is that from L5051 of Stratum 4 (Fig. 19.6:1–5), including maxillae and mandibulae, vertebrae, scapulae, ribs, radius and tibia bones, metacarpus, metatarsus, astragali and nineteen phalanx bones.

Locus 200 of Substrata 3a-b yielded six dog bones, among them a humerus (width of throchlea 3.5 cm) with many cut marks and a point at the upper end.

Additional dog remains came from loci whose stratigraphic attribution was unclear. The measurements were insufficient to determine which breeds of dogs are represented (cf. Hakker-Orion 1975:297).

Ibex (*Capra Ibex*)

Ibex remains were recovered from all strata at Kadesh Barnea. They are represented by horns (Fig. 19.6:6) and other body parts, some of them bearing cut marks.

Wild Carnivores and Wild Boar (*Sus scrofa*)

As these were represented by a few examples only, they are discussed here under one heading (note the carnivores were not included in Table 19.1 and Fig. 19.1).

Tibiae of wild boars were retrieved from L785 of Stratum 3 (a large specimen) and L616 of Stratum 2. The tibia in L616 is relatively narrow in its upper part. The lower joint is 17.4 cm long and 2.1 cm wide.

Locus 616 also produced an astragalus of a leopard, *Pantera pardus*. It is 4.7 cm long and its maximum

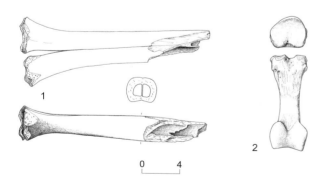

Fig. 19.5. Camel bones.

No.	Reg. No.	Locus	Stratum	Bone	Comments
1	13	26	1	Metacarpal	Young animal; joints of bone missing
2	2653/42	854	3a-b	First phalanx	

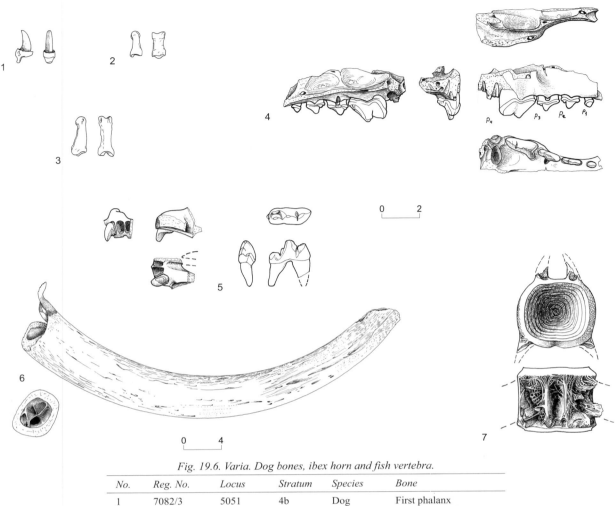

Fig. 19.6. Varia. Dog bones, ibex horn and fish vertebra.

No.	Reg. No.	Locus	Stratum	Species	Bone
1	7082/3	5051	4b	Dog	First phalanx
2	7082/4	5051	4b	Dog	Second phalanx
3	7082/5	5051	4b	Dog	Third phalanx
4	7082/6	5051	4b	Dog	Left and right maxilla
5	7082/7	5051	4b	Dog	Carnassial tooth
6	523/2	248	2	Ibex	Horn
7	310	150	3a-b	Tuna or Nile perch	Vertebra

width is 2.05 cm. The shape of the bone is typical of carnivores. It matches that of a leopard in the collection of the Department of Zoology at Tel Aviv University. In addition, a tibia in this locus apparently also belongs to a leopard. It was worked at its lower end and part of the body of the bone was removed, forming a sharp point. This apparent tool was 14.7 cm long and 3.8 cm wide at its lower part. Generally speaking, L616 was especially rich in faunal remains, including also small ruminants, a gazelle, an ibex and birds.

Locus 785 (Substratum 3b) yielded a tibia, probably belonging to a lion (*Panthera leo*). The proximal epiphysis is 4.4 cm long and 3.85 cm wide and the distal epiphysis is 2.2 cm long and 2.9 cm wide. The dimensions at the middle of the diaphysis are: length 2.7 cm and width 2.2 cm. The proximal epiphysis is only half fused, indicating a young animal. In the distal epiphyses, a hole was drilled, 1.2 cm in diameter.

Wild boars can still be found today in more northerly parts of the Negev (Hakker-Orion 1977). Leopards survive nowadays in the easternmost region of the Negev, and in certain parts of the Judean desert. In the past this desert species was common in southern Israel and Sinai. Lions survived in Israel until the Crusader period (Mendelssohn and Yom-Tov 1999).

Micromammalia

Of the wild micromammalia, only the hares (*Lepus capensis*), found in all strata, have been included in Table 19.1. The skull of a jerboa (*Jaculus jaculus*) and a femur of a mole rat (*Spalax* sp.) were recovered from L721 of Stratum 2. Other species represented (in L720, Substratum 3b) are marbeled polecat (*Vormela peregusna*) and Negev jird (*Meriones* sp).

Tortoises, Fish and Sea Urchins

Remains of tortoise (*Testudo* sp.) were discovered in L675 and L1106 of Substrata 3a-b and L1105 of Stratum 2. (The fragments from L1106 and L675 had regularly shaped, drilled holes and may have been used as pendants.)

Fish remains were found mainly in Stratum 3, in Areas C and F. They include a large vertebra (Fig. 19.6:7), mandibulae and back fins. The Stratum 3 fish comprise specimens of the Serranidae family, common in the Mediterranean Sea and the Red Sea, e.g., an operculum of a white grouper (*Epinephelus aeneus*) from L612 (Substrata 3a-b). The large vertebra in Fig. 19.6:7 (L150, Substrata 3a-b) belongs either to a tuna (*Thuunus* sp.) or to a Nile perch (*Lates niloticus*). A possible dusky grouper (*Epinephelus marginatus*) bone was retrieved from L6216 of Substratum 3c. In general, fish were not abundant, but as most of the sediments had not been sifted, small skeletal elements of fish were surely lost. It is interesting to note that in L1108 (a mixed Strata 3, 1 context) fish bones were accompanied by metal fish hooks (unpublished).

In L694 (Strata 3, 2) and L853 (Substrata 3a-b) were remains of sea urchins (*Eucidaris metularia*), originating in the Red Sea.

Aves (Birds)

Birds comprised about 5% of the faunal remains in the three Iron Age strata of Kadesh Barnea (see Fig.

19.1), which is a significant number. Among the specimens identified are the large beak of a cormorant (*Phalacrocorax carbo*) from L637, Stratum 2; the radius of a very large heron (*Ardea cinerea*) from L6249, Strata 3, 2; and the humerus of a young ostrich (*Struthio camellus*) from L1500, the fill of the cistern, as well as broken egg shells from L820 of Stratum 4, and L45 and Installation 721, both from Stratum 2; pigeon bones (*Columba livia*) from L52, L404, L616, L702, mostly Stratum 2; a carpometacarpus of a stork (*Ciconia ciconia*) from L1408, Substratum 3c; remains of quails (*Coturnix coturnix*) from L816 of Stratum 4 and L506, L612, L1051 of Stratum 3; a tarsometatarsus of a rock partridge (*Alectoris gracea*) from L183 of Stratum 2; and many other bird bones that could not be identified (cf. Hakker-Orion 1993:83–84).

It is unclear, however, how many of these species actually formed part of the inhabitants' diet, and if they did, whether they were hunted or scavenged. Some of the bones bore cut marks, for example a distal part of a tarsometatarsus from L816 and a humerus from L938, both of Stratum 4. It should be borne in mind that major migration routes of birds pass through Sinai from central Europe to east Africa and back. In northern Sinai, mainly in the autumn, quails appear along the coast and even today are trapped by local inhabitants in nets. In the same season, hundreds of thousands of water fowl pass through Sinai. They include storks and other species, e.g., dunlins (*Calidris alpina* and other Calidris species) and gulls (*Larus* sp., *Sterna* sp).

Herons, quails, pigeons and gulls may be found in the Kadesh Barnea area even today, alongside other species such as osprey (*Pandion haliaetus*) and spoonbill (*Platalea leucordia*).

MORTALITY PROFILES OF SHEEP/GOATS

Mortality profiles for sheep/goat were determined according to accepted criteria, based on the rate of bone fusion and the stage of dental eruption (see Habermehl 1961; Silver 1969; Hakker-Orion 1972 and references therein). (See Tables 19.2–19.5, Fig. 19.7.)

Analysis of the data from all the strata reveals that only about 15% of the animals were slaughtered before the age of 25 months and most of the animals survived to adulthood. This indicates that their main exploitation was for milk and other secondary products.

**Table 19.2. Age Distribution of
Young Ruminants less than
25 Months Old in Stratum 4**

Months	N	%
<3	45	31.9
3	42	29.8
6	13	9.2
12	3	2.1
17	27	19.1
25	11	7.8
	141	99.9

**Table 19.3. Age Distribution of
Young Ruminants less than
25 Months Old in Stratum 3**

Months	N	%
<3	24	11.6
3	53	25.6
6	14	6.8
12	15	7.2
17	60	29.0
25	41	19.8
	207	100.0

**Table 19.4. Age Distribution of
Young Ruminants less than
25 Months Old in Stratum 2**

Months	N	%
3	30	46.9
6	2	3.1
12	2	3.1
17	16	25.0
25	14	21.9
	64	100.0

**Table 19.5. Age Distribution of
Young Ruminants less than
25 Months Old in Stratum 1**

Months	N	%
3	3	20.0
6	4	26.7
12	5	33.3
17	1	6.7
25	2	13.3
	15	100.0

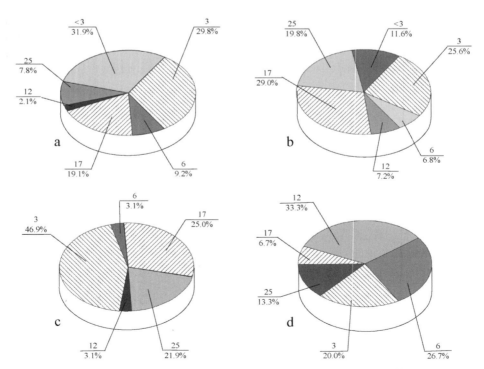

*Fig. 19.7. Age distribution of young ruminants less than 25 months old:
(a) Stratum 4; (b) Stratum 3; (c) Stratum 2; (d) Stratum 1.*

The discussion below pertains only to the young animals, less than two years old. These were divided into six age groups: fetuses and newborns less than 3 months old; animals about 3 months old; animals about 6 months old; animals about 12 months old; animals about 17 months old; animals about 25 months old.

The age profile of young small ruminants in Stratum 4 indicates a significant percentage (31.9%) of fetuses and newborns, a phenomenon not encountered in the later strata (the relatively good representation of this age group in Stratum 3 may be an artifact of the relatively large size of this assemblage).

The age profile of young small ruminants in Stratum 2 is different from those in the earlier occupations. The predominant difference vs. Stratum 3 is the high percentage (46.9%) of animals slaughtered at the age of around 3 months, and on the other hand, the absence of fetuses and newborns, which were well represented in Strata 4 and 3.

Notes on the Fauna of Installation 721

This large rounded brick installation is attributed to Stratum 2 but has clear Stratum 1 intrusions (see Chapter 3). As it included numerous bones, the excavators pondered whether it could have served a cultic function. Examination of the bones has demonstrated that *c.* 95% of them are fragments of vertebrae and ribs These parts do not carry much meat and are usually considered waste. The bones thus indicate the (probably secondary) use of the installation for waste disposal. Animals repesented in this assemblage were mainly camels, donkeys, small ruminants, hares and fowl.

Notes on Cut Marks

Cut marks were observed on 25 bones only (of which 12 were from Stratum 2), belonging mostly to sheep, goats, sheep/goats, cattle and ibex. Some of the the cuts are shallow, while others were deeper, made during dismemberment of the carcass and removal of the meat and/or tendons.

The cut marks appear most frequently on the the upper part of ulnae, on the upper part of radii, on the lower part, mainly the trochlea of humeri (e.g., Fig. 19.8:1), and on the lower part of femura. Cut marks, however, were also found on scapulae (on the glenoid fossa), on a spinous process of a vertebra, on pelves, on astragali and on a first phalanx. The locations of the cut marks indicate a consistent method of butchery (for cut marks, see, for example, Sadek-Kooros 1972).

Also found were items with holes (e.g., a hole above the trochlea of a humerus; pairs of holes in the bone shafts of young goats) and bones with damage to the periostium, mainly on the lower parts of forelimbs of small ruminants (for example, an oval injury above the trochlea of a sheep metacarpus; irregular damage above the trochlea of a metacarpus of a small ruminant, which penetrated the periostium but did not create a hole; and similar damage in the right metatarsus of a sheep). It is difficult to decide whether some of these holes are natural or deliberate (for the latter, see more below).

Notes on Secondary Use of Bones

In addition to the morphologically well-defined bone tools presented in Chapter 13, many bones were modified, probably to be used as tools (for worked bones cf., for example, Hakker-Orion 1999a). Naturally, these are primarily bones of sheep and goats.

A few bones seem to have been purposefully drilled, exhibiting regular holes, for example on the body of a tibia; in the medial part of the metacarpal trochlea of a sheep/goat (Fig. 19.8:2); on the shaft of a long bone of a sheep/goat (Fig. 19.8:3); two or three holes in a rib of a sheep/goat (Fig. 19.8:4); and holes in a bovine scapula (Fig. 19.3:1). (For holes in a bone of a lion and in a tortoise shell, see above.)

Additional examples of modifications of bones follow. (1) An astragalus of a goat was smoothed on one side. (2) A shoulder blade (of an ibex) had its tuber scapula and acromion removed, and the entire surface was polished. (3) Tibiae of sheep/goats were worked into sharp points (Fig. 19.8:5, 6). (4) A metapodial (of a gazelle) was smoothed, its ends removed and smoothed, and turned into a meticulously carved tool, possibly a handle, 12.20 cm long (Fig. 19.8:7). (5) The condyle of a sheep/goat metatarsus was sawed off at one end (Fig. 19.8:8). Additional worked bones were probably used as points, scrapers, spatulae, knives, drills, burins, chopping tools and discs (Table 19.6).

In Stratum 4, for example, the assemblage of modified bones includes mainly humeri, but also three radial bones, femuri and tibiae. The most common tool type there seems to be a point of sorts. On seven items signs of retouch were observed and eight seem to have been polished (gloss, however, may be either the result

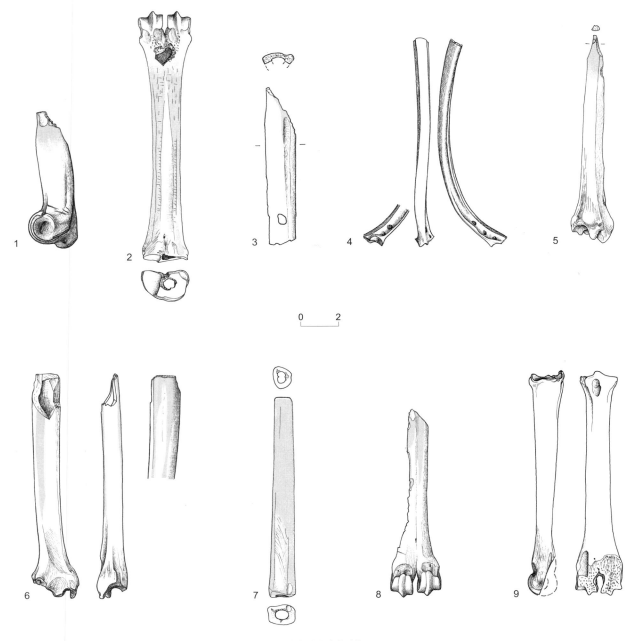

Fig. 19.8. Modified bones.

of deliberate burnishing or of use; in a few cases, gloss was apparently caused by burning).

In Stratum 3 the tools were made of bones of sheep, goats, gazelles, camels and wild boars. Locus 220 (Substratum 3c) produced a femur of a cow that was made into a chopper (the fossa above the distal epiphysis forms a handy holding point). Both sides of the bone were smoothed and polished and there are several signs of retouch on the the upper end. The total length of the tool is 11.30 cm. A hole (1.2 × 1.1 cm) was drilled into a pelvis of a camel from L473 (a silo). The upper part of a point made from a radius of a sheep was smoothed and polished; the lower part formed a suitable handle.

◄ Fig. 19.8

No.	Reg. No.	Locus	Stratum	Species	Bone	Modification	Comments
1	518	245	3c	Sheep/goat	Humerus (lower part)	Cut marks and retouch	
2	8579/2	6288	4	Sheep/goat	Metacarpal (upper part)	Hole drilled in trochlea	See Table 13.5:3
3	414	201	3a-b	Sheep/goat	Shaft of long bone	Hole	
4	309	150	3a-b	Sheep/goat	Rib	Perforated	See Table 13.5:29
5	1993/17	938	4b	Sheep/goat	Tibia	Pointed	
6	410/3	197	3b	Sheep/goat	Tibia	Proximal end cut	
7	8583/6	6294	4	Gazelle	Metapod	Cut and smoothed ends; handle?	See Table 13.5:5
8	208	130	2	Sheep/goat	Metatarsal	Distal joint sawn	130
9	40/5	33	2	Sheep/goat	Metacarpal (lower part)	Retouched	

Table 19.6. Distribution of Bones Used As Tools

No.	Stratum 4	Stratum 3	Stratum 2	Stratum 1	Total
Point	11	15	7	4	37
Scrapers	2	8	15	3	28
Spatulae	2	4			6
Knives	2				2
Drills	2				2
Burins	1				1
Chopping tools		1			1
Total	20	28	22	7	77

In Stratum 2, twelve of the bones from which tools were made belong to sheep, goats, an ibex, two gazelles and an equid. Body parts represented include a mandible, a scapula, two femura, a humerus, two radii, five femura, a tibia, and an astragalus. Some of them exhibit retouch and others were sawn or polished (Fig. 19.8:8, 9). Three tools could be clearly defined as scrapers, seven as points, two as knives, and one as a disc. One of the interesting speciments (in Installation 721) is a tibia of a wild boar A hole was drilled in its distal epiphysis, penetrating the bone.

SUMMARY

As expected, about 95% of the identified faunal remains were of domesticated species, indicating their central role in the economy. Sheep and goats comprise the bulk of the domesticated animals; cattle is found in low percentages throughout the sequence (and is entirely missing from the small Stratum 1 assemblage); and the number of pig/boar bones is negligible. This is typical of other Negev sites both in the Iron Age and in other historical periods (e.g., Hellwing 1984; Hakker-Orion 1986, 1993, 1999b, 2004a, 2004b; Horowitz 1995:298; Horwitz et al. 2002).

No significant differences were observed in dietary habits between the various occupations at Kadesh Barnea, but there are, on the other hand, some differences in the mortality profiles of young ruminants. Most of the small ruminants (about 85%) were slaughtered as adults. This means that they were primarily exploited for the production of secondary products, such as milk, milk products, wool, manure, etc. It is quite possible that both meat and secondary products created surpluses, which could be used in trade.

Camels and donkeys, and to a much lesser extent horses, are represented as from Stratum 4. They were probably used mainly for transportation and labor. Dogs (in Strata 4–2) were probably used for herding, but alternatively may have been no more than pariah dogs.

Non-domesticated animals, both carnivores and herbivores (a lion, leopards, wild boars, deer, gazelles, hares and ibex) were found in insignificant numbers, indicating that hunting was negligible.

Remains of birds, such as quails, partridges, ostriches, storks, pigeon and herons, represent the natural habitat of the oasis and there is some evidence for the use of ostrich eggs. Fish bones indicate that fish supplemented the diet. In all this, the assemblage is typical of arid regions, including oases like Kadesh Barnea.

Appendix 19.1. List of Species by Stratum and Locus

	Locus	Goat/Sheep	Goat	Sheep	Cattle	Pig/Boar	Equid	Donkey	Horse	Camel	Gazelle	Ibex	Canine	Bird	Other
Stratum 4	265	+										+		+	
Stratum 4	276	+													
Stratum 4	279	+	+							+					
Stratum 4	280	+	+												
Stratum 4	283	+													
Stratum 4	284	+	+								+				
Stratum 4	288	+	+		+				+						
Stratum 4	291	+	+		+						+				
Stratum 4	297	+	+												
Stratum 4	298	+													
Stratum 4	782	+	+	+			+			+					
Stratum 4	811	+								+	+				Hare
Stratum 4	816	+	+	+	+									+	Rodent
Stratum 4	819	+	+	+						+					Hare
Stratum 4	820	+	+							+				+	Ostrich eggshell
Stratum 4	821	+						+			+	+		+	
Stratum 4	921									+					
Stratum 4	930	+	+	+						+			+	+	
Stratum 4	938	+	+	+			+			+	+			+	Human
Stratum 4	3159	+		+											
Stratum 4	3162	+	+	+											
Stratum 4	3185	+	+	+						+					
Stratum 4	3194	+	+		+					+			+	+	
Stratum 4	3195	+					+								
Stratum 4	3199	+		+	+										
Stratum 4	3200	+		+											
Stratum 4	3209	+		+						+	+				
Stratum 4	3212	+	+												
Stratum 4	5050	+									+				Human
Stratum 4	5051												+	+	
Stratum 4	5053	+						+							
Stratum 4	5054	+											+		Human
Stratum 4	5058	+													
Stratum 4	5063												+		
Stratum 4	6104						+								
Stratum 4	6109	+	+							+					
Stratum 4	6117	+		+											
Stratum 4	6118						+								

Appendix 19.1 (cont.)

	Locus	Goat/Sheep	Goat	Sheep	Cattle	Pig/Boar	Equid	Donkey	Horse	Camel	Gazelle	Ibex	Canine	Bird	Other
Stratum 4	6120	+													
Stratum 4	6230	+													
Stratum 4	6235	+		+											
Stratum 4	6236	+													Ostrich eggshell
Stratum 4	6288	+	+	+						+	+				
Stratum 4	6289	+			+										
Stratum 4	6292	+	+	+											
Stratum 4	6294	+		+											
Stratum 4	6297				+							+			
Stratum 4	6300	+													
Stratum 4	6301	+	+	+							+				
Stratum 4	6302	+									+				
Stratum 4	7002	+								+					
Stratum 4	7006	+													
Stratum 4	7007	+								+					
Stratum 4	7023	+	+				+			+	+				
Stratum 4	7024	+	+												
Stratum 4	8011	+			+										
Substratum 3c	127	+		+	+						+			+	
Substratum 3c	178	+								+					
Substratum 3c	210				+										
Substratum 3c	220	+			+										
Substratum 3c	266	+		+											
Substratum 3c	676				+					+					
Substratum 3c	699	+							+		+	+			
Substratum 3c	1408	+	+	+	+					+				+	Bird
Substratum 3c	3044		+	+	+										Fish
Substratum 3c	3175	+					+			+	+				
Substratum 3c	3180				+					+					
Substratum 3c	3196	+	+							+					
Substratum 3c	6059	+													Human
Substratum 3c	6216	+	+	+	+					+					Fish
Substratum 3c	6273	+								+					
Substrata 3c, b	671		+	+	+					+		+			
Substratum 3a	36	+	+	+	+			+			+				
Substratum 3a	70			+											
Substratum 3a	84	+													
Substratum 3a	92	+					+	+							
Substratum 3a	94	+			+										

Appendix 19.1 (cont.)

	Locus	Goat/ Sheep	Goat	Sheep	Cattle	Pig/Boar	Equid	Donkey	Horse	Camel	Gazelle	Ibex	Canine	Bird	Other
Substratum 3b	96	+								+					
Substratum 3a	107	+										+			
Substrata 3a-b	109	+								+					
Substratum 3b	110	+													
Substratum 3b	119	+	+		+					+			+		
Substratum 3b	120	+		+						+					
Substrata 3a-b	150	+			+					+	+				Fish
Substratum 3a	165	+						+						+	
Substratum 3a	182	+													
Substratum 3b	187														
Substratum 3b	193	+													
Substratum 3b	197	+			+					+		+			
Substratum 3b	198	+													
Substrata 3a-b	200	+			+							+	+		
Substrata 3a-b	201	+									+	+			
Substratum 3b	206	+												+	
Substratum 3b	211	+								+					
Substratum 3b	212	+													
Substrata 3a-b	263		+	+								+			
Substrata 3a-b	289	+	+							+					
Substrata 3a-b	473	+					+			+					
Substratum 3a	503						+								
Substratum 3a	517	+						+		+				+	
Substrata 3a-b	526	+			+					+		+		+	
Substrata 3a-b	531	+		+						+	+				
Substrata 3a-b	612	+												+	Hare, fish
Substrata 3a-b	613	+	+	+											
Substratum 3b	629														
Substrata 3a-b	672	+		+	+									+	
Substrata 3a-b	675		+	+	+					+		+	+	+	Tortoise
Substratum 3b	720														Marbeled polecat, Negev jird
Substratum 3b	727														
Substratum 3a	731														
Substratum 3b	785	+				+								+	Wild boar, lion
Substrata 3a-b	853														Sea urchin
Substrata 3a-b	854	+	+	+	+			+	+	+					Fish, sea urchin
Substrata 3a-b	856	+		+						+					

Appendix 19.1 (cont.)

	Locus	Goat/Sheep	Goat	Sheep	Cattle	Pig/Boar	Equid	Donkey	Horse	Camel	Gazelle	Ibex	Canine	Bird	Other
Substrata 3a-b	858	+								+	+				Fish
Substrata 3a-b	861	+	+	+						+					
Substratum 3a	1051	+													Human
Substratum 3b	1052	+													Hare
Substrata 3a-b	1056	+				+								+	
Substratum 3a	1216		+	+	+					+	+				
Substratum 3b	1229	+								+	+				
Substratum 3b	3004	+	+		+					+	+				
Substratum 3b	3014	+			+					+					Fish
Substratum 3b	3021	+		+						+					
Substrata 3a-b	3027	+	+	+				+		+	+			+	
Substrata 3a-b	6002		+	+						+				+	
Substrata 3a-b	6259		+	+						+	+				
Substrata 3a-b	6277	+								+					
Substrata 3a-b	6278	+	+	+						+					
Substrata 3, 2	617	+	+							+	+				
Strata 3a, 2	62	+	+	+						+	+			+	Bird
Strata 3a, 2	524	+													
Strata 3, 2	673	+	+							+					
Strata 3, 2	689		+	+						+	+			+	
Strata 3, 2	694	+						+	+	+		+			Sea urchin
Strata 3, 2	700	+													
Strata 3, 2	1514		+	+	+										
Strata 3, 2	6000	+	+	+				+	?	+		+			
Strata 3, 2	6010	+	+	+				+		+	+			+	
Strata 3, 2	6223	+	+	+	+					+		+			
Strata 3, 2	6249	+	+	+	+						+	+		+	Bird
Strata 3, 2	6255	+	+	+	+										
Strata 3, 2	6257				+										
Strata 3, 2	6258	+	+												
Stratum 2	27	+	+	+						+					
Stratum 2	28	+		+								+			
Stratum 2	33	+		+		+				+					
Stratum 2	34	+		+						+					
Stratum 2	37		+												
Stratum 2	39	+								+				+	
Stratum 2	40	+								+					
Stratum 2	45	+	+	+				+					+	+	Ostrich eggshell
Strata 2 (+1)	52	+	+	+	+					+				+	Hare

Appendix 19.1 (cont.)

	Locus	Goat/ Sheep	Goat	Sheep	Cattle	Pig/Boar	Equid	Donkey	Horse	Camel	Gazelle	Ibex	Canine	Bird	Other
Stratum 2	53	+	+	+							+				
Stratum 2	57		+	+	+									+	
Stratum 2	69	+						+							
Stratum 2	71	+	+	+											
Stratum 2	72	+						+							
Stratum 2	76									+					
Stratum 2	87	+											+	+	
Stratum 2	125		+								+				
Stratum 2	157	+	+	+											
Stratum 2	164	+								+					
Stratum 2	175	+	+	+	+					+				+	
Stratum 2	177	+			+										
Stratum 2	183														Bird
Stratum 2	248											+			
Stratum 2	294		+												
Stratum 2	401	+		+						+	+				
Stratum 2	402	+													Human
Stratum 2	404	+		+						+	+			+	
Stratum 2	413		+	+						+					
Stratum 2	414	+													
Stratum 2	419		+	+				+							
Stratum 2	421	+					+				+	+			
Stratum 2	425	+									+			+	Human (child)
Stratum 2	427	+	+					+							Human
Stratum 2	459	+			+			+		+		+			
Stratum 2	460	+	+							+					
Stratum 2	461	+	+	+			+								
Stratum 2	467	+			+							+			
Stratum 2	482										+				
Stratum 2	485	+								+					
Stratum 2	491											+			
Stratum 2	501	+	+								+				
Stratum 2	508	+													

Appendix 19.1 (cont.)

	Locus	Goat/Sheep	Goat	Sheep	Cattle	Pig/Boar	Equid	Donkey	Horse	Camel	Gazelle	Ibex	Canine	Bird	Other
Stratum 2	520	+													
Stratum 2	523	+													
Stratum 2	528	+								+					
Stratum 2	532	+	+	+							+	+			
Stratum 2	542	+	+	+											
Stratum 2	616	+	+	+		+				+	+	+		+	Leopard, wild boar, bird, fish, ostrich eggshell
Stratum 2	721						+			+					Jerboa, mole cat
Stratum 2	746		+	+	+		+			+	+				Human, tortoise
Stratum 2	1105	+								+					Tortoise
Stratum 2	2157	+	+		+		+			+					
Stratum 2	2159						+								
Strata 2, 1	229										+				
Strata 2, 1	274	+													
Strata 2, 1	299	+	+							+					
Strata 2, 1	702														Bird
Strata 2, 1	1411, 1500				+		+	+	+	+				+	Bird
Strata 2, 1	1512	+	+		+		+	+		+					
Strata 2, 1	7025	+	+					+		+					
Strata 2, 1	7026	+	+	+				+		+		+			Hare
Stratum 1	21	+	+							+					
Stratum 1	26	+								+	+			+	
Stratum 1	253	+								+					
Stratum 1	457	+													
Stratum 1	628	+	+							+			+		
Stratum 3 (disturbed)	1106														Tortoise
Strata 3, 1	191	+								+					
Strata 3, 1	1108				+		+			+	+	+		+	Hare, fish
Unstratified	636				+										
Unstratified	5059	+	+												

Appendix 19.2. Body Part Representation of Sheep/Goats in Stratum 4

Skeletal Element	N	Skeletal Element	N
Horn	8	Metacarpal	35
Tooth	17	Femur	36
Vertebra	154	Tibia	36
Rib	311	Metatarsal	21
Cranium (fragment)	27	Carpal	1
Maxilla	12	First phalanx	27
Mandibula	32	Second phalanx	61
Scapula	57	Third phalanx	2
Pelvis	37	Astragalus	10
Humerus	38	Calcaneus	28
Patella	12	Large unidentified fragments	112
Radius	39		
Ulna	17	Total	1130

Appendix 19.3. Body Part Representation of Cattle in Strata 4–2 by Find Spots

Locus	Body Part	Total
Stratum 4		
816	Third phalanx	1
3194	Proximal part of right radius	1
3199	Rib, distal part of left humerus	2
6289	Epiphysis and polished part of diaphysis	2
6297	Mandibula	
Stratum 3		
94 (3a)	Proximal part of metatarsal	1
119 (3b)	Horn	1
150 (3a-b)	Scapula, horn, teeth	3+
200 (3a-b)	Mandibula	1
657 (3a-b)	Proximal part of metatarsal	1
854 (3a-b)	First phalanx	1 (Fig. 19.3:3)
3004 (3b)	Humerus, tibia, tibia of a calf, phalanx	4
6216 (3c)	Metacarpal of young animal, humerus (trochlea), tibia	3
Granary, L6223 (3, 2)	Horn, skull (fragment)	2
Granary, L6255 (3, 2)	Mandibula, humerus, tibia, phalanx	4
Granary, L6257 (3, 2)	Tooth	1
Stratum 2		
25	Second phalanx	1
52	Horn, third phalanx	2
175	Femur (sawed)	1
Fill of cistern, L1512 (2, 1).	Horn, mandibula, metatarsal, third phalanx	4

CHAPTER 20

RADIOCARBON DATES

ISRAEL CARMI AND DROR SEGAL

INTRODUCTION

Eighteen samples from Kadesh Barnea were submitted for radiocarbon dating in the Radiocarbon Dating Laboratory at the Weizmann Institute of Science, Rehovot; fourteen are presented here.[1] Two of them (RT-898 and RT-933) were processed in the 1980s; the rest were submitted and measured in 1992 (Table 20.1; Segal 1998).

The samples were mostly charcoal and wood and only three were short-lived (seasonal plants). One sample (RT-1708) was an ostrich eggshell fragment. The samples were large and of high quality and most of them allowed high sensitivity measurement.

Due to the excellent quality and state of preservation of most of the samples, no special difficulties were encountered during cleaning and preparation, which were carried out in the laboratory according to standard procedures. The samples were treated with HCl and NaOH, oxidized to CO_2, converted to ethane and measured in proportional counters. The efficiency of the chemistry in the second stage of the measurements was over 95% (see n. 1). Sample RT-1708, the ostrich eggshell, was problematic in that H_2S was released during its preparation, which required additional cleaning. The presence of H_2S may indicate that the egg did not mature.

COMMENTARY

STRATUM 4

RT-1652 and RT-1653, two charcoal samples, produced dates that are significantly higher than the archaeological date of the stratum, a phenomenon discussed below. Likewise, RT-1708, the ostrich eggshell fragment, produced a very high age determination. This may indicate that the chemical procedure applied in cleaning the fragment sample was inefficient, because H_2S is detrimental for the counters used for the measurements.

Charcoal samples RT-1702 and RT-1709 gave dates that are too young for the archaeological date of this stratum. RT-1709 falls entirely within the Halstatt plateau (and its stratigraphical attribution is not secure). RT-1702, by its context, may actually already belong to the Substratum 3c fill and not to Stratum 4. However, even considering this possibility, most of its distribution is too young.

Substratum 3c

All the samples (RT-1646, RT-1650, RT-1705, RT-1707) are apparently from constructional wood. RT-1650 and and RT-1705 are very high (see below). RT-1646 and RT-1707 are much closer to the supposed date of the construction of the Stratum 3 fortress (eighth century BCE), but still too early to provide a meaningful *terminus post quem*.

Stratum 2

The main distribution of the short-lived RT-898 falls within the Halstatt plateau, which should be expected from a context dated on archaeological considerations to the late seventh/early sixth centuries BCE.

Two of the charcoal samples (RT-1648 and RT-1703) produced dates that are very high relative to the archaeological date of this stratum (see further below). On the other hand, RT-1704 and RT-1706 fall within the Halsttat plateau, which, as mentioned, fits the archaeological context.

Old Wood

The most conspicuous phenomenon in Table 20.1 is that many dates are significantly older than the archaeologically plausible dates of the occupation layers in which they were found. Most of them are from long-living trees (in stratigraphic order—RT-1652, RT-1653, RT-1708, RT-1646, RT-1650, RT-1705, RT-1707, RT-1648, RT-1703).

Table 20.1. Kadesh Barnea Radiometric Dates*

Sample No.	Material and Stratigraphy	Registration Details	$\delta 13C$ ‰	Years BP	Calibrated Age ± 1σ	Probability %
RT-1652	Charcoal below Substratum 4c floor	Area C, L6302, B8600/3	-21.9	3345 ± 60	1730–1720 1700–1530	3 97
RT-1653	Charcoal (*Acacia raddiana*) from Stratum 4 floor makeup	Area C, L6301, B8597/7	-21.7	3140 ± 60	1500–1370 1340–1320	90 10
RT-1708	Ostrich eggshell fragment on Substratum 4b floor	Area E, L820, B1798/2	-7.2	3350 ± 55	1730–1710 1700–1580	5 95
RT-1709	Charcoal (*Pistacia atlantica*) possibly from Substratum 4b floor	Area A1, L114, B192/3	-23.7	2310 ± 50	410–350 290–230	66 34
RT-1702	Charcoal (*Phoenix dactylifera*) from fill above Substratum 4b earthen floor	Area A1, L291, B574/8	-21.5	2520 ± 50	790–730 690–540	28 72
RT-1646	Wooden beam among stones of Stratum 3 (3c) fortification wall	Area F, W200, B2614	-19.8	2775 ± 50	980–890 880–840	75 25
RT-1650	Wooden beam bonded in Stratum 3 (3c) fortification wall	Area D, W273, W202, B3036	-20.6	2960 ± 40	1260–1120	100
RT-1705	Wooden beam (*Acacia pachyceras*) bonded in Stratum 3 (3c) fortification wall	Area G, W203, B839/8	-20.4	3035 ± 50	1390–1250 1240–1210	92 8
RT-1707	Wooden beam (*Ziziphus Spina-Christi*) in Substratum 3c constructional fill	Area B, L3070, B5132	-20.7	2830 ± 30	1020–925	100
RT-898	Carbonized grains inside storage jar on Stratum 2 floor	Area A2, L523, B994/6	-21.2	2600 ± 45	830–760 690–670	91 9
RT-1648	Charcoal (*Phoenix dactylifera*) from collapsed debris above Stratum 2 floor	Area B, L486, B1019/2	(-21)	2740 ± 50	930–820	100
RT-1703	Wooden beam (*Pistacia atlantica*) in Stratum 2 tower	Area A2, L479, B849/3	-21.5	3335 ± 55	1690–1600 1590–1530	61 39
RT-1704	Charcoal (*Retama roetam*) on Stratum 2 casemate floor	Area A2, L637, B1397/12	-21.5	2470 ± 95	760–500 460–410	90 10
RT-1706	Charcoal (*Haloxylon persicum*) Stratum 2 casemate floor	Area A2, L186, B385/14	-20.7	2520 ± 50	790–730 690–540	28 72

* The samples are listed in stratigraphical order, from early to late. Botanical identification was performed by Nili Liphschitz of Tel Aviv University. Dendrochronological calibration was performed with the latest version of OxCal 3.10 (Bronk Ramsey 1995).

These high dates can be accounted for not only by the longevity of the trees, but also by the location and nature of the site. In such a multi-layered site, in a region where wood is scarce, wood was not only 'naturally' re-deposited, but certainly reused again and again.

These phenomena, alongside undetected disturbances (by pits, foundation trenches, etc.), may construct a very misleading chronological picture, especially when there are no significant chronological gaps between occupation levels.

This, of course, does not account for the fact that six dates (in stratigraphic order—RT-1652, RT-1653, RT-1708, RT-1650, RT-1705, RT-1703) are earlier than the (known) beginning of the site by hundreds of years, falling in the seventeenth–eleventh-century BCE range. Not all of them can be explained solely by the longevity of trees.

It thus seems reasonable to assume that some of these dates indicate secondary use of wood that was brought to the site from elsewhere. The scarcity of good construction wood probably led the builders of the fortresses to seek out wood at distant, more northerly sites, which had existed in the Middle and Late Bronze Ages. The dry desert climate would have preserved the wood for ages. This is a well-known phenomenon in remote arid regions, occasionally also in regard to building materials other than wood. For example, to this day the Beduin transport, from distant areas via camels, construction materials such as stone, which is, of course, much heavier than wood (David Alon, pers. comm.). Considering the probability that the builders of the fortresses were officials of the kingdom that ruled the area to the north (see discussion in Chapter 1), this indeed seems very reasonable.

NOTE

[1] Four samples (RT-933, RT-1647, RT-1649 and RT-1651) presented very low efficiency during preparation, which could produce serious fractionation of the carbon isotopes, affecting the radiocarbon content. These samples, thus, should be regarded with suspicion and have been rejected for consideration in this report.

CHAPTER 21

ARCHAEOLOGICAL SURVEY OF THE KADESH BARNEA VICINITY: 'EIN EL-QUDEIRAT AND 'EIN QADIS

MORDECHAI HAIMAN

INTRODUCTION

The survey of the area of 'Ein el-Qudeirat and 'Ein Qadis was conducted in the framework of the Kadesh Barnea Excavation project during October 1981 and from February to April 1982. The survey, which covered an area of approximately 30 sq km, documented 123 sites, of which about 50 had been surveyed in the past (M. Dothan 1963; Y. Aharoni 1967; Rothenberg 1961; Bar-Yosef 1980; Beit-Arieh and Gophna 1976, 1981).

The objective was to define settlement patterns around 'Ein el-Qudeirat and 'Ein Qadis in conjunction with the already surveyed areas of the Negev Highlands, to the east (Haiman 1986). This region was of particular interest due to the presence of perennial water sources, as opposed to other areas surveyed in the Negev Highlands that lacked a permanent water supply, thereby enabling a study of the influence of water sources on settlement patterns in different periods. It became evident that only seldom was there a connection between the location of water sources and settlement distribution, in spite of the arid nature of the region (Tables 21.1, 21.2; p. 346).

In the Early Bronze Age, a clear relationship was found between perennial water sources and the location of large settlements. A very dense concentration of sites was recorded in the areas around 'Ein el-Qudeirat and 'Ein Qadis. In contrast, these springs did not particularly influence site distribution in most of the other periods, and site density is equal or even less than that of areas in which natural water sources are far away.

It seems that the distribution of sites of the types found in desert regions such as the Negev Highlands was more likely to be influenced by the proximity of fortresses or way stations. Such proximity, revealing a strong association with the sedentary population, enabled the inhabitants of desert settlements to subsist in areas poor in resources where the traditional semi-nomadic economy of pastoralism/dry agriculture was insufficient without the addition of external input. This preference—proximity to sedentary settlements rather than perennial water sources—is best illustrated in MB I and in the Nabatean period, when more sites were found in Mishor Ha-Ruḥot, 10–15 km away from the closest water source, than in the areas near the springs of 'Ein el-Qudeirat and 'Ein Qadis.

ARCHEOLOGICAL OVERVIEW (Table 21.2)

Prehistoric Periods

Flint tools and flakes are scattered about the plains to the north and south of Wadi el-Qudeirat. They range from the Middle Paleolithic to the Neolithic period (Map 1, p. 347). However, very few *in situ* sites have been discovered in this region (cf. Bar-Yosef 1980: 11–12). One site, of the Middle Paleolithic (Site 28), is reminiscent of sites surveyed in neighboring areas (Bar-Yosef 1980:15). Three surveyed Pre-Pottery Neolithic B sites featured an abundance of arrowheads. Two of these sites were found in the streambed of Wadi el-Qudeirat, to the east of contemporaneous sites previously surveyed by Bar-Yosef (1980:35–36), and the third, discovered near 'Ein Qadis, was subsequently excavated (Rosen, Goring-Morris and Gopher 1983).

The Early Bronze Age

Sites dating to the Early Bronze Age were first identified in the region by Cohen (1983a:2–3). In a subsequent survey conducted by Beit-Arieh and Gophna (1976; 1981), approximately 20 sites were surveyed and excavated in the area of 'Ein el-Qudeirat. The survey presented here reveals that most of the sites in the region attributed previously to MB I should actually be ascribed to the Early Bronze Age.

In the present survey 47 Early Bronze Age sites were registered (Map 2, p. 347), including those surveyed by Beit-Arieh and Gophna. It is clear that during this period settlement was most intensive in the areas of

'Ein el-Qudeirat and 'Ein Qadis, comprising some 40% of all the surveyed sites. Settlement density is further emphasized by the fact that the area of the present survey is only one third a standard 'survey map' (100 sq km) as defined by the Archaeological Survey of Israel.

Many of the Early Bronze Age sites are among the largest in the Negev Highlands. They feature one to five clustered structures, as well as a varying number of single-room structures. The typical clustered structure contains as many as 20 rooms and courtyards. Most of the structures are circular, although rectilinear ''Arad-type' rooms are also found, which may evidence some influences from southern Canaan. In the Negev Highlands rectilinear rooms comprise c. 5% of all the rooms, which is less than their relative occurrence at sites in southern Sinai. The sites in the 'Ein el-Qudeirat region are characterized by a large dwelling area, occasionally comprising half of the entire site. Presumably, most of the sites in the region were permanent settlements; large sites of this type are found mainly in proximity to perennial water sources that enable year-round habitation. They differ from the sites located further away from water sources, where sheep and goat pens occupy most of the site, reflecting transitory settlement (Haiman 1991:14*–15*).

While it is possible to define most of the sites in the area of 'Ein el-Qudeirat as permanent settlements, the actual length of time they were occupied is unknown. It can be assumed that not all were occupied contemporaneously, and the remains observed today are the result of an accumulation of sites built one alongside the other over a long time span. Thus, it is possible that the abundance of sites in the area reflects a dynamic of settlement abandonment and reconstruction in another place, a pattern recalling certain desert societies that change the location of their habitation sites every year (Briggs 1967).

Although many potsherds were collected by the surveyors, the variety of types was extremely poor, and no significant chronological discussion is possible. In light of the resemblance of these sites to those of southern Sinai (Beit-Arieh 1977), they appear to date, based on a correlation with 'Arad, to EB II (Amiran, Beit-Arieh and Glass 1973). The holemouth jar with the thickened rim dominates; it is tempered with large amounts of granitic sand, a temper that was in use for centuries. The frequency of this type of holemouth jar is a characteristic—even a *fossil directeur*—of sites of the type described here (Beit-Arieh 1977:92), but, on the other hand, uncharacteristic of earlier Early Bronze Age sites in the southern Negev; the latter are typified by small round structures, a very small number of holemouth jars and by transversal arrowheads (Beit-Arieh 1977:72–73; Goren 1980:253–256).

At a few sites in the 'Ein Qudeirat region, fragments of Egyptian jars, similar to those from southern Sinai and which postdate the beginning of the third millennium BCE, were found (Beit-Arieh 1977).

The Early Bronze Age sites in the western Negev Highlands and those in southern Sinai thus form a sphere of uniform material culture. Throughout the Early Bronze Age, additional cultures may be defined in those regions, each one featuring distinct chronological, cultural and regional characteristics. These are, for example the northern Sinai sites, characterized by a predominance of Egyptian finds (Oren 1980:104–108); 'Arad and its satellites (Amiran et al. 1980); the 'Nawamis' culture of southern Sinai (Goren 1980); and the Biq'at 'Uvda sites, where transversal arrowheads were found (Rosen 1983), and were probably seasonal camps of short duration were associated with the 'Nawamis' culture.

It should be mentioned that scholars who advocate a later chronological horizon than that presented above for the Negev and Sinai sites also attribute the phenomenon of clustered structures, containing 'Arad-type' broadrooms such as those known from 'Ein el-Qudeirat, to a period postdating the beginning of the third millennium BCE (Avner 1990; Rothenberg and Glass 1992). Some scholars date the end of the Early Bronze Age settlements to EB III, based on the long life span of the holemouth jar. Others believe that at the end of EB II or the beginning of EB III a change took place in the settlement patterns of the Negev and Sinai deserts: the inhabitants retreated to the regions on either side of the Dead Sea, where sites yielded pottery clearly belonging to EB III (Rast and Schaub 1974; Amiran and Gophna 1989; Beit-Arieh 1990; Richard 1990).

In the author's opinion, the sites of the Negev spread from southern Sinai northward, as a result of economic and cultural contacts with southern Canaan (Beit-Arieh 1977). The contact between 'Arad and the desert hinterlands apparently supplied an external economic safety net, independent of the subsistence economy dictated by the scarce natural resources of the region. This enabled the semi-nomadic inhabitants, whose traditional economy was pastoral-agricultural, to spread into inhospitable areas such as central Sinai and the southern Negev. The economic system of the Beduin who occupy these areas today is similar: it includes pasturage and agriculture, but as these are insufficient, the mainstay of their livelihood is based on external sources of livelihood.

The assumption that the settlements spread northward from southern Sinai raises the question of the origin of these EB II inhabitants. The most reasonable candidate is the 'Nawamis' culture population, centered in southern Sinai. The economy of the southern Sinai settlements was based on hunting, as evidenced by the arrowheads, as well as on agriculture, including husbandry of small flocks of sheep and goats, attested by the small pens found at the occupation sites (Goren 1980). It appears that in a late phase of the Early Bronze Age, following contacts with the sedentary entity to the north, the local population grew and the settlements expanded to the more northerly desert regions. This expansion, in addition to some elements in their material culture, points to extensive contacts with southern Canaan. Moreover, a significant change in the subsistence economy took place, involving larger flocks and the disappearance of hunting.

Settlement in the most arid regions of Sinai and the Negev prospered as long as the conditions that enabled its growth continued to exist. The decline of 'Arad and the retreat of the sedentary/permanent settlements in southern Canaan at the end of EB II (Beit-Arieh 1977; Amiran and Gophna 1989) eliminated the main economic basis of these sites. Left with only local resources, which were insufficient to support the entire population, the inhabitants were forced to abandon these areas and 'follow' the sedentary/permanent settlements into more hospitable lands.

Middle Bronze Age I

Potsherds from this period were found at 15 sites (Map 3, p. 348). At ten sites Early Bronze Age pottery was also found, apparently an indication of later settlements superimposed on earlier ruins (the extent of which can only be determined by excavation). The remaining five sites, those that yielded only MB I finds, are small and they do not reach the size of major contemporaneous sites of the northern Negev Highlands such as 'En Ziq, Har Yeruham and Be'er Resisim (Cohen 1992:107–116; 1999). The sites comprise only one to eleven structures, most of them one-room structures and animal pens.

The paucity of MB I settlements, despite the springs 'Ein el-Qudeirat and 'Ein Qadis, is surprising. For the sake of comparison, 45 sites from this period were surveyed at Mishor Ha-Ruhot, some 10–15 km from a water source.

Following the general trend of site distribution in this region, the sparse settlement characterizing this period decreases even further the farther south the site is from the main settlement areas (Haiman 1991: 16*–19*). The small group of large settlements of the northern Negev Highlands (located in a confined area) perhaps served as a link in the network that transported copper from Feinan through northern Sinai to Egypt. Hundreds of small transient sites of the type surveyed at 'Ein el-Qudeirat are distributed to the south of these large sites. Their economy, while including pasturage and agriculture, was apparently based chiefly on the contact with the inhabitants of the large sites and thus the main factor in the location of the transient sites was proximity to the large settlements and not the location of water sources. This is evidenced by the small number of sites in the vicinity of 'Ein el-Qudeirat, the relatively large number of sites in central Sinai, and the complete absence of sites in southern Sinai, which is rich in water sources (Rothenberg 1979).

It seems that following the abandonment of the large sites, the inhabitants of the temporary sites could no longer survive, and they too were forced to abandon the area.

Iron Age II

Iron II sherds were found at 22 sites (Map 4, p. 348). Five of these are fortresses, mostly on the cliffs around 'Ein el-Qudeirat, such as the fortress near Wadi Umm Hashim (Site 44), overlooking an extensive area that includes the fortress of 'Ein Qadis, some 10 km to the southeast. Another site (Site 54), apparently a fortress whose construction was not completed, includes a segment of a massive wall c. 2.5 m wide, built of cyclopean stones preserved one to two courses high, which runs for a length of approximately 10 m. To its south, a segment of a casemate wall was found, which was built along the cliff above Wadi el-Qudeirat. The long stone fence surrounding 'Ein el-Qudeirat, attributed to the Byzantine or Early Islamic period (see below), traverses the wall. In the course of the survey, two long casemate rooms and fragments of additional walls, stretching to a total of *c.* 15 m, were recorded at Site 54 (the two casemate rooms were excavated by Y. Porath, unpublished). In the site's center a square building (*c.* 8 × 8 m) was traced, whose south-facing entrance was built of monolithic stones. In shape this building resembles a tower (Haiman 1986:17*) rather than a dwelling. The site was enclosed by a thin line of small stones inserted into the ground, ending at the edge of the cliff above Wadi el-Qudeirat, which separates the site from the plain to the south. The significance of this stone line is unclear and it may have been intended as a marker, indicating the outline of a wall to be constructed around the square tower, which was, however, never constructed.

Most of these Iron II sites are distributed along Wadi el-Qudeirat and represent the western margin of a dense concentration of *c.* 200 sites arrayed along the Ramat Matred–Ramat Barnea' line. A small group of sites was surveyed along Wadi Umm Hashim, between the 'Ein Qadis and Wadi Umm Hashim (Site 44) fortresses. Dwellings, mainly curvilinear, consist of a single room. Only a few structures have a rectilinear plan, e.g., Site 48, which consists of a rectangular room built of monoliths. It should be noted that many of the round structures, although of simple plan, were built of especially large stones, for example Site 53, which includes some 20 such buildings. Some of the sites included pens and threshing floors and thus reflect exploitation of the region for pasturage and seasonal agriculture. A simply built cistern was found at one site only. It seems that the short distance from the springs (4–6 km) rendered the hewing of cisterns superfluous.

The picture revealed by Iron II site distribution in the Negev Highlands (Cohen and Cohen-Amin 2004) indicates the centrality of 'Ein el-Qudeirat in this period, although there were no especially large dwellings at the site. To the south of the network of sites extending between the Be'er Sheva' Valley and 'Ein el-Qudeirat a decline in the number of structures in each settlement and a transition from rectilinear to curvilinear architecture can be discerned. This architectural transition is a function of their distance from the impact of the settled lands and has no connection with environmental factors. No changes are noted in the quality of construction of the fortresses and they are all well-built. It appears that the area of 'Ein el-Qudeirat fell within the range of Iron II settlement, as evidenced by the location of five fortresses in the limited area near the spring and on the surrounding cliffs.

The Persian Period

A single campsite related to the Persian period (Map 5, p. 349) was surveyed near 'Ein Qadis (Site 122). As no campsites from this period were surveyed in the Negev Highlands, this site may represent the southeast margins of a concentration of ephemeral sites that were distributed chiefly along the coast of northern Sinai, some 70 km to the northwest (Oren 1980). In addition, the nearby fortress at Tell el-Qudeirat, one of the few fortresses that existed in the Negev Highlands in the Persian period, continued to exist (Cohen and Cohen-Amin 2004:159–202).

The Hellenistic Period

Six campsites from this period were surveyed (Map 5, p. 349), most of them consisting of stone circles (diam. 2–10 m). Four sites were clustered south of 'Ein el-Qudeirat, forming an almost continuous area scattered with potsherds (*c.* 1 km). In the Negev Highlands, only a few Hellenistic sites are known, presumably representing the beginning of the Nabatean presence there. As in the Persian period, it can be assumed that these campsites comprised the outer limit of the well-documented concentration of similar sites along the northern Sinai coast (Oren 1980).

The Nabatean Period

A single campsite from this period (Site 118; Map 5, p. 349) was surveyed near 'Ein Qadis, consisting of a scattering of low stone circles surrounded by potsherds. The site is reminiscent of contemporaneous campsites surveyed in the Negev Highlands and apparently was a tent encampment. Another site, not included in the present survey, was recorded in the past to the west of the spring and apparently contained sedentary/permanent structures (Rothenberg 1967:143; Aharoni 1967; Porath 1985:144–155). The scarcity of settlement near the spring is not surprising, since the distribution of campsites in the Negev Highlands basically corresponds with the Nabatean trade routes, and is not necessarily related to water sources. In comparison, dozens of campsites were surveyed on Mishor Ha-Ruḥot, 10–15 km distant from any natural water source but closer to the Sha'ar Ramon–'Avedat section of the Nabatean spice route. This is evidence of the importance of external resources as opposed to proximity to water sources as an influence on choice of sites (Haiman 1991:21*–22*).

The Roman Period

Potsherds that may be attributed to the third–fourth centuries CE were collected at seven sites (Map 5, p. 349). In the absence of finds allowing better chronological resolution, it is possible that some of the pottery is in fact Byzantine, of the fourth–fifth centuries CE. Four sites (1, 23, 39 and 40) are campsites, consisting of low wall outlines, low stone piles and pottery scatters, spread over a few dozen meters, apparently reflecting tent encampments. Two other sites, situated near 'Ein Qadis, are apparently related to seasonal activity and consist of simple, round structures: an animal pen (diam. 8 m) at Site 123, and three circular structures (diam. 4 m) and a pen (18 × 8 m), upon which a cairn was constructed, at Site 111.

The Byzantine and Early Islamic Periods

Thirty sites (Map 6, p. 349) were broadly dated to the sixth–eighth centuries CE. Some scholars prefer to date Negev Highlands sites containing 'transitional ceramic assemblages' of this sort to the sixth–seventh centuries (Avni 1992:18*–20*), while others favor a date in the Early Islamic period only—the seventh–eighth centuries CE (Nevo 1991:41).

Five of the sites (35, 70, 72, 73 and 74) are farmsteads of a type common in the Negev Highlands, which seems to date to the seventh–eighth centuries CE (Haiman 1990a). The walls of these structures were constructed of two rows of small hewn stones set upon a foundation of large fieldstones. This construction style dominates at well-preserved sites throughout the Negev Highlands.

Settlement density in this period was low compared to that of Ramat Barnea', to the east (Haiman 1990a), despite the spring. However, the farmsteads at Sites 72 and 73 are larger than most of the farmsteads in Ramat Barnea'. The lack of cisterns at these farmsteads (as opposed to those located elsewhere, which contain several cisterns per site), is of interest. It appears that 4–6 km was considered a reasonable distance for regular transportation of drinking water and the labor involved in hewing cisterns was not considered justifiable.

Also assignable to this period is the long stone fence (c. 2 km) encompassing 'Ein el-Qudeirat, which has attracted the attention of scholars from the beginning of modern research. The fence traverses two Iron Age sites (44, 54), and is clearly associated with the agricultural terraces in Wadi el-Qudeirat and not with Tell el-Qudeirat (Kadesh Barnea). The terraces end at the eastern end of the fence, where it descends to the wadi. Geomorphologic analyses of the soil in the terraces indicate that it accumulated mainly in the Byzantine and Early Islamic periods (Bruins 1986:121–174) and no earlier than the Roman period (Goldberg 1984).

It appears that the spring and the terraced wadi enclosed by this fence, and perhaps also the small settlement at the western end of the fence (Aharoni 1967), represent an agricultural unit that was under special ownership, as opposed to other farmsteads in the Negev Highlands, which were smaller and representative of a local population (Haiman 1990a:117–118). The actual outlet of the spring, however, was not included in the area closed off by the fence. This may reflect the concept, still common among the Beduin to this day, that major water sources do not belong to any specific tribe, and may be accessed by all, for drinking and watering the herds. Most of the water, however was channeled into pools and irrigation channels (Porath 1985:144–155) enclosed by the fence.

The remaining sites of this period are campsites of the type found throughout the Negev Highlands and indicate, for the most part, seasonal activity of semi-nomadic shepherds.

THE SITES

1. 09–00/9–9/1   Jebel el-'Ain   09980 00960
Campsite (10 × 30 m) in a valley south of Jebel el-'Ain: stone piles and outlines of walls.
Ceramic finds: Iron II and Roman-Byzantine.

2. 09–00/6–8/1   Jebel el-Qudeirat   09680 00845
Structure in a wadi bed (a tributary of Wadi el-Qudeirat), comprised of four circular rooms (diam. *c.* 3 m). The walls, of medium-sized fieldstones, are preserved up to two courses high.
Ceramic finds: EB.

Fig. 21.1. Site 3. Structure—rooms adjoining a courtyard.

3. 09–00/6–8/2   Jebel el-Qudeirat   90695 00825
Twenty structures, spread over 150 m on a spur on Jebel el-Qudeirat. Most are one-room structures (diam. *c.* 3 m), others are pens (diam. up to *c.* 20 m). Five of the structures contain circular rooms (diam. 3–5 m) and adjoining courtyards (diam. 5–20 m; Fig. 21.1). The walls, of small stones, are preserved up to three courses high.
Ceramic finds: EB.

4. 09–00/7–8/1   Jebel el-Qudeirat   09700 00845
Campsite (*c.* 15 × 20 m) near the edge of a cliff on Jebel el-Qudeirat: remains of walls (one course of stone). Some 150 m to southeast—three stone circles (diam. *c.* 3 m).

5. 09–00/7–8/2   Jebel el-Qudeirat   09740 00850
Five structures near the edge of a cliff on Jebel el-Qudeirat. One structure consists of a courtyard (diam. 5 m) and three circular rooms (diam. *c.* 3 m). Two structures are rectangular and the remaining two are circular (2–3 × 5 m). Near the structure with the courtyard there is a semicircular structure with a black stone (*c.* 0.2 m high) in its center, bearing a carving of a pregnant donkey. The stone is encircled by a ring of small stones (Fig. 21.2).
Ceramic finds: EB.

Fig. 21.2. Site 5. Engraving of a pregnant donkey on a black stone in the center of the circular structure.

Fifty meters east of the structures—a cairn (diam. *c.* 6 m) and an adjoining pen. Some 150 m south of the structures—a square pen (*c.* 5 × 5 m).

6. 09–00/7–8/6   Jebel el-'Ain   09780 00860
Two circular pens (diam. *c.* 8 m) on the slope of Jebel el-'Ain. Nearby—two stone piles (diam. *c.* 3 m).
Ceramic finds: Iron II.

7. 09–00/7–8/7   Jebel el-'Ain   09790 00870
Two structures on shoulder of ridge, on Jebel el-'Ain. One structure consists of rooms (diam. 3 m) and courtyards (diam. 10 m; Fig. 21.3), the other is a pen (diam. 8 m). The walls, constructed of small stones, are preserved up to three courses high. This site apparently dates to the Early Bronze Age.

8. 09–00/7–8/9   Jebel el-'Ain   09725 00800
A structure (10 × 12 m), consisting of two circular rooms, a rectangular room and a courtyard, in a flat area south of Jebel el-'Ain. Nearby—remains of additional structures.
Ceramic finds: EB.
The site was surveyed in the past (Beit Arieh and Gophna 1981: Site 1208).

9. 09–00/7–8/8   Jebel el-'Ain   09770 00835
A structure on the slope of a spur south of Jebel el-'Ain, comprising circular rooms (diam. *c.* 2 m) around a circular courtyard (diam. *c.* 8 m).
Ceramic finds: EB.

10. 09–00/8–8/2   Jebel el-'Ain   09865 00865
Two structures on the shoulder of a spur on Jebel el-'Ain. One structure consists of a room (diam. *c.* 3 m) and a courtyard (diam. *c.* 6 m; Fig. 21.4). The other includes three rooms (diam. 2–4 m) and an oval courtyard (6 × 10 m; Fig. 21.5). One course of small fieldstones survives from the walls.
Lithic finds: EB (Fig. 21.6).

Fig. 21.3. Site 7. The first structure.

Fig. 21.4. Site 10. The first structure.

Fig. 21.5. Site 10. The second structure.

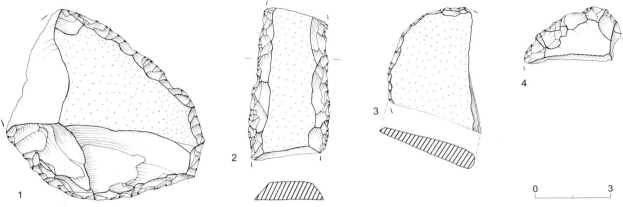

Fig. 21.6. Site 10. EB fanscrapers.

11. 09–00/8–8/1   Jebel el-'Ain   09895 00850
Pen (diam. *c.* 10 m) near a tributary of Wadi el-Qudeirat, south of Jebel el-'Ain; one course of small fieldstones survives. Abutting the pen—a stone pile (diam. *c.* 2 m, 0.5 m high).

12. 09–00/9–8/1   Jebel el-'Ain   09965 00895
Two cairns (diam. 3 m, 0.5 m high), constructed of a circle of upright fieldstones and a stone fill, in a flat area on Jebel el-'Ain. Some 100 m to the south—a pen (diam. *c.* 5 m). About 100 m south of the pen—three circular structures (diam. *c.* 4 m) and a pen (diam. *c.* 10 m).
Ceramic finds: Byzantine.

13. 09–00/9–8/4   Jebel el-'Ain   09975 00875
Circular structure (diam. *c.* 8 m) on the slope of a spur on Jebel el-'Ain. The walls are constructed of flat upright fieldstones inserted in the ground.
Ceramic finds: MB I.

14. 09–00/4–7/1   Jebel el-Qudeirat   09475 00740
Two pens constructed of small fieldstones (diam. 15, 20 m) on the shoulder of a spur on Jebel el-Qudeirat; two courses survive (Fig. 21.7). Near the pens—a circular structure (diam. *c.* 3 m), constructed of small fieldstones and preserved up to six courses high.

15. 09–00/5–7/2   Jebel el-Qudeirat   09520 00730
Campsite (*c.* 100 × 100 m) in a valley south of Jebel el-Qudeirat: 15 stone circles, 2–3 m in diameter, one course high.

16. 09–00/5–7/1   Jebel el-Qudeirat   09540 00715
Structure (*c.* 25 × 25 m), containing rooms (diam. 3 m) around a courtyard (diam. *c.* 20 m; Plan 21.1), in a valley south of Jebel el-Qudeirat. A cairn (diam. *c.* 3 m, 1 m high) is superposed on the courtyard wall. Near the structure—three additional cairns.
Ceramic finds: EB and Byzantine.

Fig. 21.7. Site 14. The first pen.

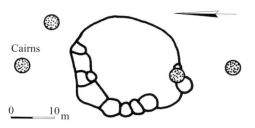

Cairns

Plan 21.1. Site 16.

17. 09–00/5–7/6   Jebel el-Qudeirat   09530 00705
Square fortress (*c.* 20 × 25 m; Plan 21.2; Fig. 21.8) on the edge of a cliff overlooking Wadi el-Qudeirat. The walls, constructed of two rows of flat fieldstones, are *c.* 1 m wide and preserved up to *c.* 2 m high. The entrance (*c.* 1 m wide) is located in the eastern wall.
Ceramic finds: Iron II.

Some 100 m south of the fortress, midway up the slope— two adjoining pens (diams. 6, 12 m) constructed of small fieldstones; one course survives.
Ceramic finds: Iron II.
The site was surveyed in the past (Dothan 1963).
Some 250 m west-southwest of the fortress—structures and cairns, extending over an area of *c.* 50 × 100 m (Plan 21.3).
Ceramic finds: EB.
The site was surveyed in the past (Beit-Arieh and Gophna 1976: Site 1205).

18. 09–00/5–7/3   Jebel el-Qudeirat   09570 00700
Eleven structures near the edge of a cliff overlooking Wadi el-Qudeirat, extending over an area of *c.* 30 × 100 m (Plan 21.4).
Ceramic finds: EB.
The site was surveyed in the past (Beit-Arieh and Gophna 1976: Site 1204).

Fig. 21.8. Site 17. The fortress.

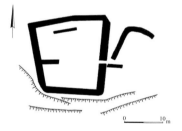

Plan 21.2. Site 17. The fortress.

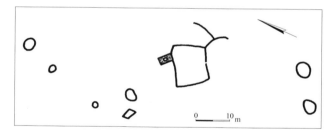

Plan 21.3. Site 17. The EB structures.

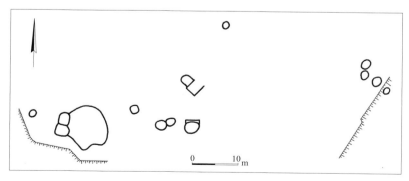

Plan 21.4. Site 18.

19. 09–00/5–7/4   Jebel el-Qudeirat   09590 00740
Structures spread over an area of *c.* 100 × 100 m near the
edge of a cliff overlooking Wadi el-Qudeirat. Some of the
structures have circular and rectangular rooms with adjoining
courtyards, others consist of a single circular room.
Ceramic finds: EB and Early Islamic (Fig. 21.9).

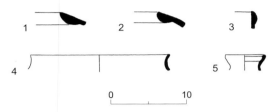

Fig. 21.9. Site 19. Pottery. EB: (1, 2) holemouth
jars; Early Islamic: (3) bowl; (4) jar; (5) juglet.

This site was surveyed in the past (Beit-Arieh and Gophna
1976: Site 1207).

20. 09–00/6–7/1   Jebel el-Qudeirat   09615 00760
Five stone circles (diam. 4–5 m, one course high) on the top
of a ridge north of Wadi el-Qudeirat.
Lithic finds: EB (Fig. 21.10).

21. 09–00/6–7/2   Jebel el-Qudeirat   09650 00780
Approximately 20 structures, spread over an area of *c.* 150 ×
200 m, in a valley north of Wadi el-Qudeirat. Six of the
structures (10–15 × 20–50 m) are circular rooms arranged
around courtyards (Plan 21.5). The other structures consist of
one or two circular rooms (diam. up to *c.* 10 m). The walls,
of small and medium-sized fieldstones, are preserved up to
three courses high.
Ceramic finds: EB and MB I.

22. 09–00/6–7/3   Jebel el-Qudeirat   09685 00785
Remains of structures, extending over an area of *c.* 20 × 30 m,
on a slope descending south to Wadi el-Qudeirat. At the top

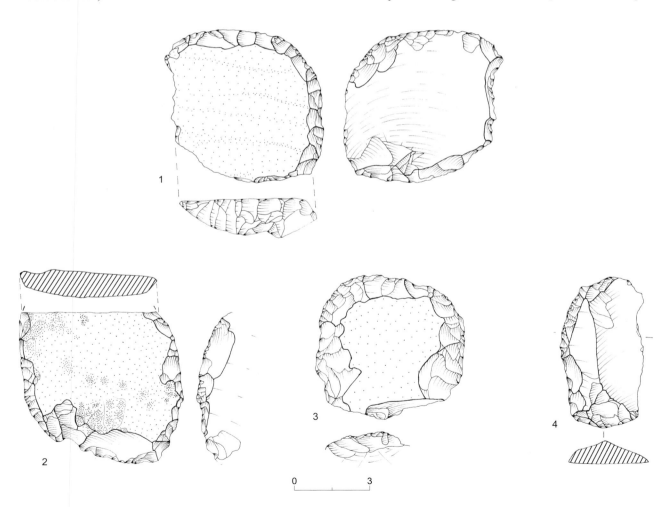

Fig. 21.10. Site 21. EB flints. (1–3) Fanscrapers; (4) backed blade.

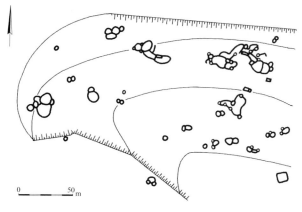

Plan 21.5. Site 21.

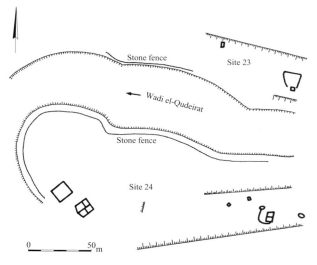

Plan 21.6. Sites 23 and 24.

of the hill, north of the structures—two cairns. To the south—two additional cairns.

Ceramic finds: EB.

23. 09–00/6–7/4   Wadi el-Qudeirat   09699 00750

Remains of a square structure (*c.* 10 × 10 m; Fig. 21.11) on a shoulder ending in a cliff (Plan 21.6), overlooking Wadi el-Qudeirat from the north. The walls are constructed of large fieldstones (up to 1 m long). About 70 m west of the structure, at the edge of the cliff—a rectangular structure (*c.* 2 × 4 m) whose walls are of large stones (up to 1 m long) and a low fence (120 m long) constructed of one course of large stones (up to 0.5 m high) on the wadi bank.

Lithic finds: EB.

Ceramic finds: Iron II.

East of the square structure is a dense concentration of flint tools and flakes, extending over an area of *c.* 40 × 150 m.

Lithic finds: PPNB.

Fifty meters east of the square structure is a campsite—a row of stone circles (diam. 2–3 m) extending along *c.* 70 m, constructed of one course of small stones.

Ceramic finds: Roman.

24. 09–00/6–7/7   Wadi el-Qudeirat   09685 00745

Six structures (each *c.* 3 × 6 m) on a shoulder, ending in a cliff overlooking Wadi el-Qudeirat from the north (Plan 21.6; Fig. 21.12). Structure 1 comprises two rectangular rooms (4 × 6 m) and a courtyard. Structures 2, 3 consist of a single rectangular room (2 × 3 m). Structure 4 is circular (diam. *c.* 3 m). Structures 5 and 6 are square (*c.* 10 × 10 m, 9 × 9 m). The structures' walls are constructed of medium-sized fieldstones and flat stones and preserved to a height of

Fig. 21.11. Site 23. Square structure.

Fig. 21.12. Site 24. Corner of the sixth structure.

Fig. 21.13. Site 24. Iron II Negbite kraters.

c. 1 m. Surrounding the site, along the wadi bank, are remains of a stone fence built of one row of large fieldstones (one course high).

Ceramic finds: Iron II (Fig. 21.13).

Near the structures—two flint scatters (c. 50 × 60 m, 10 × 20 m) c. 70 m apart.

Lithic finds: PPNB.

25. 09–00/6–7/10   Jebel el-'Ain   09650 00725
Three structures, extending over c. 100 m, on a slope south of Wadi el-Qudeirat (Plan 21.7). Structure 1 has 16 circular rooms (diam. 3–4 m) arranged in a circle (diam. c. 20 m). Structure 2 is an oval room (4 × 8 m). Structure 3 consists of five circular courtyards (diam. 6–8 m).

Ceramic finds: EB.

The site was surveyed in the past (Beit-Arieh and Gophna 1976: Site 1203).

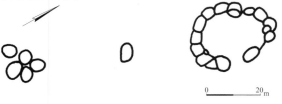

Plan 21.7. Site 25.

26. 09–00/6–7/9   Wadi el-Qudeirat   09699 00700
Three structures, each comprising rooms and a courtyard (Plan 21.8), on a slope south of Wadi el-Qudeirat. Two cairns are superposed on the walls of one of the structures.

Ceramic finds: EB and MB I.

The site was surveyed in the past (Beit-Arieh and Gophna 1981: Site 1210, Units A, B, C).

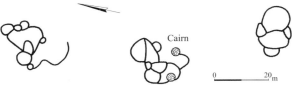

Plan 21.8. Site 26.

27. 09–00/7–7/8   Wadi el-Qudeirat   09705 00725
Four structures (Plan 21.9) in a flat area, south of Wadi el-Qudeirat. The largest, Structure 1 (c. 30 × 40 m) has c. 20 round rooms. A hunting scene is carved in the stone door jamb of one of the rooms (Figs. 21.14–21.16). Structure 2 includes a courtyard and two rooms; one of the rooms has a central pillar (Fig. 21.17). The walls of this structure are constructed of flat upright stones inserted into the ground. Structure 3 consists of a courtyard (diam. c. 20 m) and five rooms. Structure 4 contains two circular rooms (diam. 3 m). The walls of Structures 3 and 4, of medium-sized fieldstones, are preserved three courses high. Near the structures are four circular surfaces (diam. 5–20 m): circles of medium-sized fieldstones (one course), the interior paved with flat stones. On the east side of each surfaces is a stone pile (diam. 2 m, 1 m high).

Lithic finds: EB (Fig. 21.18).

Ceramic finds: EB and MB I.

The site was surveyed in the past (Beit-Arieh and Gophna 1981: Site 1210, Units A, B, C).

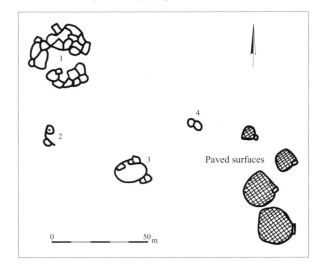

Plan 21.9. Site 27.

Fig. 21.14. Site 27. Circular room; in center, a stone doorjamb decorated with incisions.

Fig. 21.16. Site 27. Room in a large structure.

Fig. 21.15. Site 27. Incised decoration on stone doorjamb.

Fig. 21.17. Site 27. Room with a pillar in the second structure.

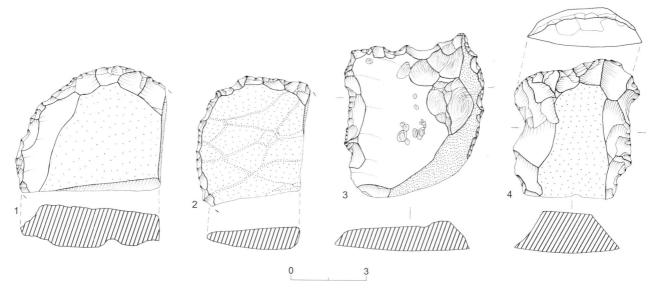

0 _____ 3

Fig. 21.18. Site 27. EB flints. (1–4) Fanscrapers.

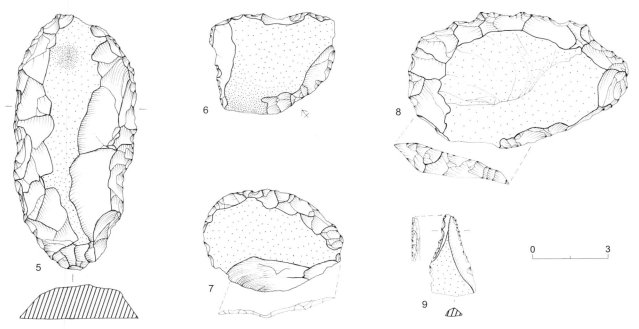

Fig. 21.18 (cont.). Site 27. EB flints. (5–8) Fanscrapers; (9) drill.

28. 09–00/7–7/6   Wadi el-Qudeirat   09740 00740
Twenty circular structures (diam. 2–4 m; Fig. 21.19), extending along *c.* 250 m, on a hill southeast of Wadi el-Qudeirat; one course survives.

Ceramic finds: EB and MB I.
Near the structures—a concentration of flint tools and flakes (area of *c.* 50 × 50 m).
Lithic finds: Middle Paleolithic.

29. 09–00/7–7/4   Wadi el-Qudeirat   09725 00740
Two structures in a valley south of Wadi el-Qudeirat. One structure is oval (3 × 4 m), the other is a round pen (diam. *c.* 20 m; Fig. 21.20). The walls, of small fieldstones, are preserved up to two courses high.
Ceramic finds: Iron II (Fig. 21.21).

◄ *Fig. 21.19. Site 28. Circular building.*

Fig. 21.20. Site 29. Pen.

Fig. 21.21. Site 29. Iron II Negebite kraters.

30. 09–00/7–7/2   Wadi el-Qudeirat   09780 00775
Three circular structures (diam. *c.* 3 m) on a ridge overlooking Wadi el-Qudeirat from the south.
Ceramic finds: EB.

31. 09–00/7–7/3   Wadi el-Qudeirat   09775 00785
Seven structures extending along *c.* 200 m (Plan 21.10), on a slope descending north to Wadi el-Qudeirat. One structure is rectangular (*c.* 10 × 12 m; Fig. 21.22), with two rooms and a courtyard in which a cairn was built (diam. *c.* 2 m, 0.7 m high). Four are one-room oval or rectangular structures

(*c.* 4 × 6 m). The sixth structure consists of two adjoining rooms (diam. *c.* 4 m). Nearby—a threshing floor (diam. *c.* 15 m) built of small fieldstones arranged in a circle around an earthen floor. On the other side of the wadi—a rectangular structure consisting of two courtyards (4 × 11 m). The walls of all the structures are constructed of large fieldstones preserved up to two courses high.
Ceramic finds: Iron II.

32. 09–00/7–7/1   Wadi el-Qudeirat   09765 00790
Circular pen (diam. *c.* 6 m) built of small fieldstones on a slope descending south to Wadi el-Qudeirat; one course survives.

33. 09–00/7–7/5   Wadi el-Qudeirat   09770 00790
A dam (1.5 m high, 1 m wide, 20 m long), spanning Wadi el-Qudeirat.

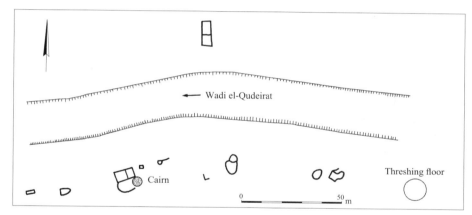

Plan 21.10. Site 31.

Fig. 21.22. Site 31. Rectangular structure.

34. 09–00/8–7/3   Wadi el-Ḥalufi   09870 00790
Rectangular structure (*c.* 15 × 30 m), containing five rooms
(each *c.* 3 m wide) and two courtyards (*c.* 10 m wide; Plan
21.11; Fig. 21.23), at the edge of a cliff north of Wadi el-
Ḥalufi. The walls, constructed of a two rows of small hewn
fieldstones (*c.* 0.7 m wide), are preserved up to 1 m high.
Three terraced wadis that meet near the structure are enclosed

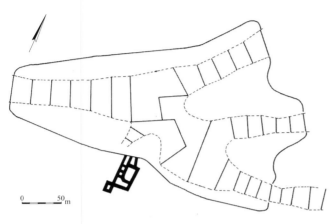

Plan 21.11. Site 34.

by a stone fence (area of *c.* 25 × 350 m), which functioned as
a dam at the point where it spans the wadis. The fence abuts
the walls of the structure. Five conduits channel water into
the terraced wadis from the slopes to the south. Sluices in the
fence wall regulated the flow of water from the conduits into
the terraced wadis.
Ceramic finds: Early Islamic.

35. 09–00/8–7/4   Wadi el-Ḥalufi   09870 00770
Nine structures on the top of a hill and at its foot, north of
Wadi el-Ḥalufi (Plan 21.12). Two structures (8–10 × 10–20 m)
include three to five square rooms with rounded corners and
two or three courtyards. Three structures are circular (diam.
c. 3 m). One structure is rectangular (3 × 8 m) and another
(*c.* 10 × 20 m) is partitioned into three rooms. The two latter
structures are pens (diam. *c.* 10 m). There are remains of
additional structures (2–3 × 4–6 m) and a threshing floor
(diam. *c.* 10 m) constructed of a circle of upright stones
around an earthen surface.
Lithic finds: Iron II (Fig. 21.24).
Ceramic finds: Iron II and Byzantine and a molded ceramic
incense burner (Fig. 21.25).

Fig. 21.23. Site 34. One of the structure's courtyards.

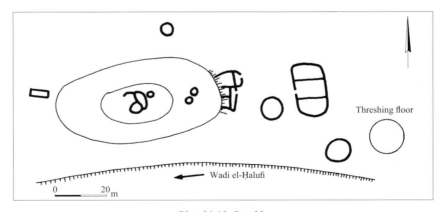

Plan 21.12. Site 35.

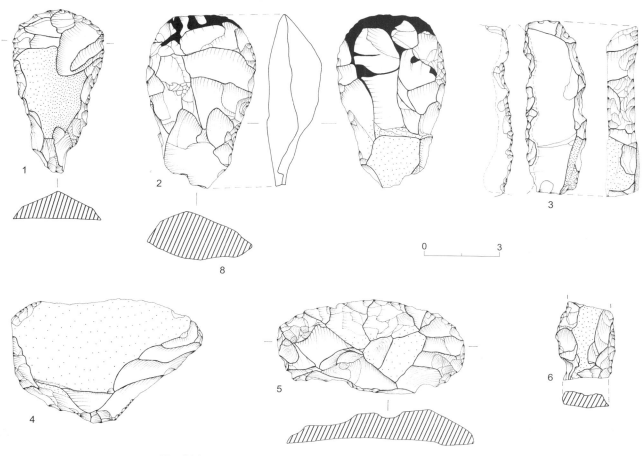

Fig. 21.24. Site 35. EB flints. (1, 4–6) Scrapers; (2) axe; (3) sickle blade.

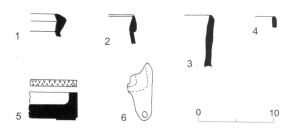

Fig. 21.25. Site 35. Iron II pottery and other finds.
(1) Krater; (2) jar; (3, 4) Negebite kraters;
(5) ceramic incense burner; (6) pierced stone tool.

Fig. 21.26. Site 36. General view.

36. 09–00/8–7/1   Wadi el-'Asli   09860 00760
Three structures spread over an area of 50 × 100 m (Fig.
21.26) close to the bank of Wadi el-'Asli. One structure is
rectangular (*c.* 1 × 3 m; Fig. 21.27), the other two are circular
(diam. 3–5 m). The walls, constructed of large fieldstones,
are preserved up to two courses high. Nearby, on the wadi
bank—a fence (*c.* 70 m long) built of one course of fieldstones
surrounding the settlement.
Ceramic finds: Iron II.

Fig. 21.27. Site 36. Rectangular structure.

Fig. 21.28. Site 37. The stone fence.

37. 09–00/8–7/5   Wadi el-Ḥalufi   09870 00740
Stone fence (*c.* 100 m long), built of one row of fieldstones, at the edge of a spur south of Wadi el-Ḥalufi (Fig. 21.28). No dams span the wadi bed.
Some 100 m north of the fence, on the wadi bank—a wall encloses a terraced agricultural plot (*c.* 10 × 30 m).
Ceramic finds: Iron II and Byzantine.

38. 09–00/8–7/2   Wadi el-'Asli   09890 00735
Campsite (*c.* 20 × 30 m) south of Wadi el-'Asli—remains of stone circles and low stone piles. On the slope near the site are ten terrace walls 20–30 m long, 10–50 m apart.
Ceramic finds: Byzantine.

39. 09–00/8–7/6   Wadi el-Furni   09860 00725
Campsite (*c.* 20 × 40 m) near Wadi el-Furni—low stone piles, stone circles and faint outlines of walls.
Ceramic finds: Roman.

40. 09–00/9–7/1   Wadi el-'Asli   00720 09915
Agricultural plot (*c.* 30 × 40 m) on a slope southwest of Wadi el-'Asli. At the edges of the site—low stone heaps. Signs of modern plowing are visible. Nearby—a circular installation (diam. *c.* 0.5 m) built of upright stones.
Ceramic finds: Roman.

41. 09–00/9–7/3   Wadi el-Ḥalufi   09905 00735
Structures at the edge of a spur, north of Wadi el-Ḥalufi (Fig. 21.29). The main structure has 15 rooms arranged around a courtyard (diam. *c.* 15 m).
Ceramic finds: EB and Hellenistic.

Fig. 21.29. Site 41. General view

42. 09–00/9–7/2   Wadi el-Ḥalufi   09940 00765
Six structures and remains of additional structures (*c.* 20 × 70 m; Plan 21.13) in a flat area north Wadi el-Ḥalufi. Most of the structures are circular (diam. 5–10 m). One structure has a courtyard (diam. *c.* 8 m) and a square room (*c.* 2 × 2 m). The structures' walls, built of large stones, are preserved up to two courses high. Nearby, a threshing floor (diam. *c.* 8 m)—a circle of small stones around an earthen surface. On the north slope, east of the structures—a cistern (*c.* 2 m deep) fed by a conduit (*c.* 100 m long).
Ceramic finds: Iron II (Fig. 21.30) and Byzantine.

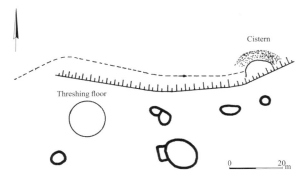

Plan 21.13. Site 42.

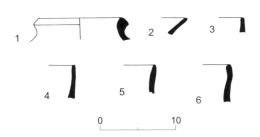

Fig. 21.30. Site 42. Iron II pottery.
(1) Jar; (2–6) Negebite kraters.

Fig. 21.31. Site 43. A circular structure.

43. 09–00/1–6/1   Jebel el-‘Ura   09130 00625
Circular structure (diam. 4 m) built of small fieldstones (Fig. 21.31) on a hilltop (spot height 477) on Jebel el-‘Ura.
Fifty meters southwest of the structure, further along the ridge—a stone circle (diam. *c.* 2 m).

44. 09–00/4–6/1   Wadi Umm Hashim   09430 00605
An oval casemate fortress (*c.* 20 × 40 m) on a hilltop surrounded by cliffs (Plan 21.14). Nearly the entire circumference of the outer fortress wall, built of large fieldstones (*c.* 1 m long), is preserved (1 m high, *c.* 0.6 m wide). The inner wall only partially survives. Casemate rooms (*c.* 2 m wide) are visible mainly in the north part of the fortress (Fig. 21.32); the gate was apparently located on the south. The fortress is traversed by the stone fence surrounding the area around ‘Ein el-Qudeirat (which postdates the fortress). This part of the fence, built of two rows of stones, is *c.* 0.8 m wide and *c.* 1.6 m high.

Ceramic finds: Iron II and Byzantine.
The site was partially excavated (Cohen and Cohen-Amin 2004:106–107).

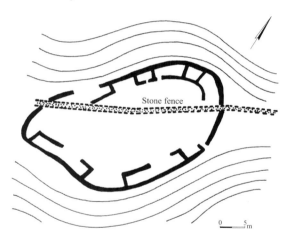

Plan 21.14. Site 44.

Fig. 21.32. Site 44. To the right, the fortress courtyard; to the left, the wall encircling ‘Ein el-Qudeirat.

45. 09–00/4–6/2   Jebel el-Qudeirat   09450 00630
Rectangular cairn (c. 1.8 × 8 m, c. 0.5 m high), constructed
of a frame of fieldstones laid lengthwise and filled with earth
and small stones, on a plateau on Jebel el-Qudeirat.

46. 09–00/4–6/3   Jebel el-Qudeirat   09465 00630
Three pens (diam. c. 8 m) built of medium-sized fieldstones
in an area of c. 50 × 100 m, on a plateau on Jebel el-Qudeirat;
four courses are preserved. Stone piles (diam. c. 3 m)
surmount the walls of two of the pens.
Fifty meters west of the pens are three circular cairns (diam.
c. 2 m)—circles of upright fieldstones filled with small stones.
Lithic finds: EB (Figs. 21.33).
Ceramic finds: EB (Fig. 21.34).

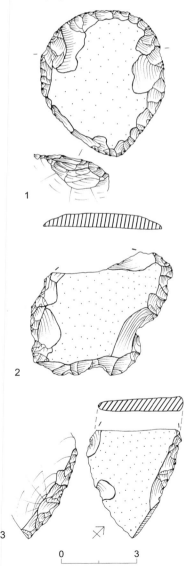

1

2

3

Fig. 21.33. Site 46. EB fanscrapers.

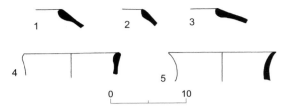

*Fig. 21.34. Site 46. EB II pottery.
(1–3) Holemouth jars; (4, 5) jars.*

47. 09–00/4–6/4   Jebel el-Qudeirat   09470 00640
Two structures on a spur on Jebel el-Qudeirat. One structure
comprises a courtyard (diam. c. 10 m) and three oval rooms.
The other structure is oval (2 × 6 m). Fifty meters south of
the structures is a cairn (diam. c. 3 m)—a circle of upright
fieldstones filled with stones.
Ceramic finds: EB and Hellenistic (Fig. 21.35).

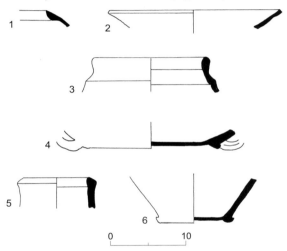

*Fig. 21.35. Site 47. Pottery. EB: (1) holemouth jar;
Hellenistic: (2) bowl; (3, 4) krater; (5, 6) jars.*

48. 09–00/4–6/5   Jebel el-Qudeirat   09495 00645
Rectangular structure (c. 3.5 × 12 m) consisting of three
rooms (Plan 21.15), on a hilltop on Jebel el-Qudeirat. The
structure's entrance, located in the center of the wall of the
central room, has two stone door posts (c. 0.8 m high). The
walls, of medium-sized fieldstones, are preserved up to

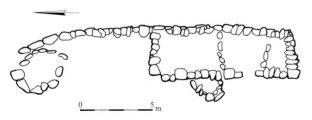

Plan 21.15. Site 48.

c. 1.2 m. The eastern wall, extending an additional *c.* 8 m, terminates in a square installation (3 × 3 m).

Ceramic finds: Iron II, Hellenistic and Roman (Fig. 21.36).

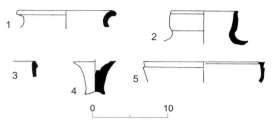

Fig. 21.36. Site 48. Pottery, Hellenistic: (1–4) jars; Roman: (5) bowl.

49. 09–00/4–6/7   Jebel el-Qudeirat   09490 00630

Remains of structures, extending over an area of *c.* 50 × 100 m, on a plateau on Jebel el-Qudeirat.

Lithic finds: check which period: EB, MB I? (Fig. 21.37).

Ceramic finds: EB, MB I, Iron II, Hellenistic, Roman and Byzantine (Fig. 21.38).

50. 09–00/4–6/8   Jebel el-Qudeirat   09470 00605

Campsite (*c.* 50 × 200 m) on a hilltop and its slopes on Jebel el-Qudeirat: outlines of walls and stone circles.

Ceramic finds: Hellenistic (Fig. 21.39).

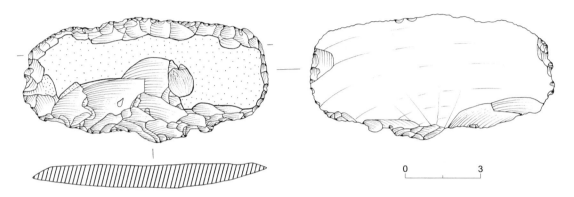

Fig. 21.37. Site 49. EB fanscraper.

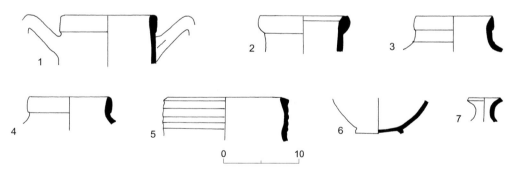

Fig. 21.38. Site 49. Hellenistic pottery. (1–5) Jars; (6) jug; (7) juglet.

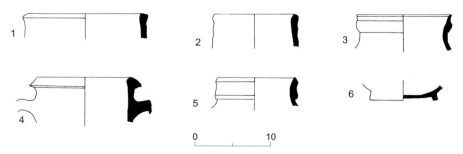

Fig. 21.39. Site 50. Hellenistic pottery. (1–5) Jars; (6) jug.

51. 09–00/4–6/9   Jebel el-Qudeirat   09485 00600
Campsite (*c.* 200 × 300 m) on a plateau on Jebel el-Qudeirat:
stone circles and low stone piles (Plan 21.16). In the south
part of the site—rock carvings and indecipherable Arabic
inscriptions.
Ceramic finds: Hellenistic (Fig. 21.40).

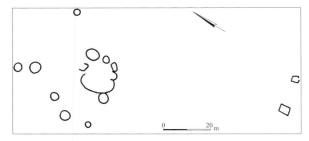

Plan 21.16. Site 51.

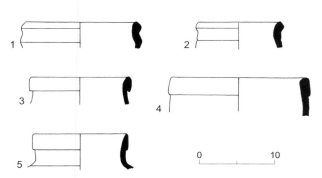

Fig. 21.40. Site 51. Hellenistic pottery. (1) Bowl; (2–5) jars.

52. 09–00/5–6/3   Jebel el-Qudeirat   09505 00600
Campsite (*c.* 100 × 200 m) on a plateau on Jebel el-Qudeirat:
dozens of stone circles (Plan 21.17; Fig. 21.41). In the
southwest portion of the site—rock engravings (Fig. 21.42).
Ceramic finds: Hellenistic.

Plan 21.17. Site 52.

Fig. 21.41. Site 52. Stone circles.

Fig. 21.42. Site 52. Rock engravings.

53. 09–00/5–6/4   Jebel el-Qudeirat   09520 00645
Twenty structures on a hilltop near the edge of a cliff that
plunges into Wadi el-Qudeirat (Plan 21.18; Fig. 21.43).
Most are rectangular one-room structures (2–3 × 4–5 m)
with entrances flanked by stone door posts (*c.* 0.80 m high).
The walls, built of large fieldstones (up to 1 m long), are
preserved up to two courses high.
Ceramic finds: Iron II.

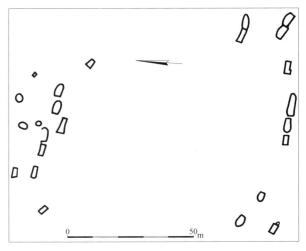

Plan 21.18. Site 53.

Fig. 21.43. Site 53. Remains of EB structures.

At the south end of the site—remains of a structure, comprising a courtyard (diam. 6 m) and several rooms. Nearby—four cairns (diam. 4 m).
Ceramic finds: EB.

54. 09–00/5–6/5   Jebel el-Qudeirat   09535 00660
Square tower and remains of a wall on a hilltop, near the edge of a cliff that plunges down to Wadi el-Qudeirat (Plan 21.19). The tower (*c.* 8 × 8 m), built of large fieldstones (up to 1 m long), is preserved up to three courses high (Fig. 21.44). The entrance (*c.* 0.50 m wide), in the west wall, is flanked by two large stone door posts (Fig. 21.45).
Near the tower—a ruined structure (*c.* 15 × 15 m).
Thirty meters west of the tower are two casemate rooms (*c.* 2 × 10 m; remains of a fortress), built at the cliff's edge.

The stone fence surrounding ‘Ein el-Qudeirat is superposed on the casemate walls.
Northwest of the square tower—a section of a thick wall (*c.* 2.5 × 10 m) built of two rows of cyclopean stones and a small stone fill. Two courses survive.
A semicircular line of small stones (*c.* 150 m long) embedded in the ground delimits the southern portion of the site. Both ends of the line reach the steep cliff, which plunges down to Wadi el-Qudeirat, separating the square tower from the plateau to its south. The purpose of this line is unclear; it may have defined the outline for construction of a wall around the tower.
Ceramic finds: Iron II (Fig. 21.46).

*Fig. 21.44. Site 54. Section of a massive
Iron Age fortification wall.*

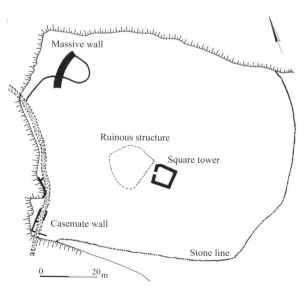

Massive wall

Ruinous structure

Square tower

Casemate wall

Stone line

0   20 m

Plan 21.19. Site 54.

Fig. 21.45. Site 54. Entrance to the square tower.

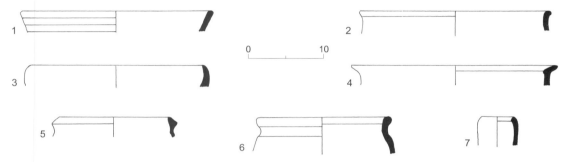

Fig. 21.46. Site 54. Iron II pottery. (1, 3) Bowls; (2, 4) kraters; (5–7) jars.

Fig. 21.47. Site 55. 'Arad-like' rectangular structure.

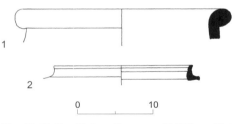

Fig. 21.48. Site 55. Iron II pottery. (1) Pithos; (2) jar.

flanked by stone door posts and benches, running along the walls.

Ceramic finds: EB and Iron II (Fig. 2.1.48).

56. 09–00/5–6/6–9   Jebel el-Qudeirat   09580 00640
Ten structures and remains of additional structures on a plateau, spread over an area of *c.* 500 × 500 m.
Ceramic finds: EB.
The site was surveyed in the past. See: Beit-Arieh and Gophna 1976: Site 1202, Units 1–11.

57. 09–00/6–6/1   Wadi Umm Hashim   09680 00620
Two groups of structures on both banks of a tributary of Wadi Umm Hashim. North of the wadi—nine circular one-room

55. 09–00/5–6/6   Jebel el-Qudeirat   09545 00650
Structure, comprising four rooms, some rectangular, arranged around a courtyard (diam. *c.* 10 m; Fig. 21.47) on a plateau.
Ceramic finds: EB.
This site was surveyed in the past. See: Beit-Arieh and Gophna 1976: Site 1201.
North of the structure—four additional structures (*c.* 2–4 × 4–5 m), one rectangular and three oval. Some have entrances

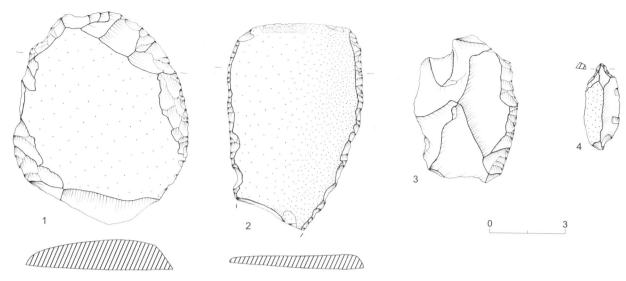

Fig. 21.49. Site 57. MB I flints. (1, 2) Fanscrapers; (3) scraper; (4) drill.

structures (diam. 3–5 m), spread over an area of *c*. 50 × 50 m. South of the wadi, *c*. 100 m from the nine structures—two circular structures (diam. *c*. 3 m). One to two courses survive of the walls, built of medium-sized fieldstones.
Lithic (Fig. 21.49) *and ceramic finds*: MB I.

58. 09–00/8–6/2   'Amrat el-Furni   09800 00690
Structures on a slope, extending over an area of *c*. 30 × 100 m (Plan 21.20), north of 'Amrat el-Furni. The main structure consists of three oval rooms (*c*. 3 × 5 m; Fig. 21.50) and an oval courtyard (*c*. 5 × 10 m). Near it are several circular, one-room structures (diam. 3–4 m), a square cairn (*c*. 2 × 2 m) built of cyclopean stones (Fig. 21.51), two circular cairns and a cupmark (Fig. 21.52).
Ceramic finds: EB.

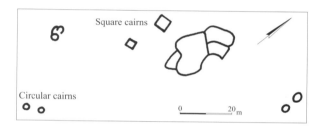

Plan 21.20. Site 58.

Fig. 21.51. Site 58. Square cairn.

Fig. 21.50. Site 58. Circular structures.

Fig. 21.52. Site 58. Cupmark.

59. 09–00/8–6/3   'Amrat el-Furni   09810 00655
Structure at the foot of a hill (spot height 530) northwest of
'Amrat el-Furni: a courtyard (diam. *c.* 25 m) surrounded by
several circular rooms (diam. *c.* 3 m; Plan 21.21). Nearby—a
square cairn (*c.* 4 × 4 m) built of cyclopean fieldstones (each
more than 1 m long; Fig. 21.53). The burial cist (*c.* 1.5 × 1.5 m,
1.5 m deep), built of small stones, was covered with heavy
stone slabs (*c.* 1.5 m long). Two heaps of bones, including
four skulls, were found inside the burial cist. Also found were
a mortar and pestle of limestone and two copper rings.
Lithic and ceramic finds: EB.

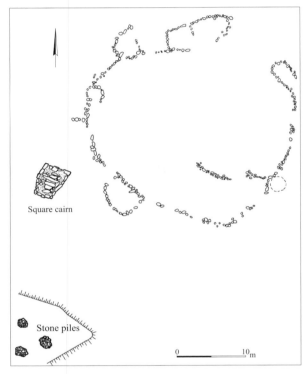

Plan 21.21. Site 59.

Fig. 21.53. Site 59. Square cairn.

The site was excavated by the author; see Haiman 1984:64.
On the summit of the hill, south of the site—three stone piles
(diam. *c.* 3 m).

60. 09–00/9–6/1   'Amrat el-Furni   09910 00635
Threshing floor (diam. *c.* 15 m) on a plateau on 'Amrat
el-Furni: upright fieldstones arranged in a circle around a
beaten-earth surface. The threshing floor is situated in the
heart of a flat area, which features deep loess appropriate
for agricultural exploitation, one of a few such locations in
the Negev Highlands. The loess surface near the threshing
floor (*c.* 500 × 2000 m) reveals traces of modern-day
plowing.

61. 09–00/9–6/2   Wadi el-'Asli   09970 00695
Five circular, one-room structures (diam. 2–4 m) extending
c. 100 m along the edge of an escarpment (Fig. 21.54) north
of Wadi el-'Asli. Two courses of medium-sized fieldstones
survive of the walls.
Ceramic finds: Iron II.

62. 09–00/9–6/1   Wadi el-'Asli   09990 00680
Two groups of structures in a valley north of Wadi el-'Asli.
One group consists of two pens (diam. 10 m, 15 m), one of
which has an adjoining room (diam. *c.* 3 m; Fig. 21.55). The
second group comprises a pen (diam. *c.* 20 m) and two cairns
(diam. *c.* 3 m).
Ceramic finds: EB, MB I, Byzantine.

63. 09–00/1–6/1   Jebel el-'Ura   09130 00625
Two circular structures (diam. 2 m, 4 m; Fig. 21.56) built of
flat upright stones inserted in the ground, on a slope on Jebel
el-'Ura.

64. 09–00/1–5/2   Jebel el-'Ura   09190 00540
Remains of structures spread over an area of *c.* 30 × 40 m, on
a ridge on Jebel el'Ura.

65. 09–00/1–5/3   Jebel el-'Ura   09185 00520
Five structures in a valley (Plan 21.22) on Jebel el-'Ura. One
structure has five rectangular rooms (2–3 × 4–5 m) adjoining
an oval courtyard (*c.* 5 × 10 m). Another structure is circular
(diam. *c.* 3 m). The remaining three structures are square
pens (5–10 × 15–20 m). The structures' walls are built of
medium-sized fieldstones, preserved up to four courses
high.
Ceramic finds: MB I.

Fig. 21.54. Site 61. General view.

Fig. 21.55. Site 62. Pens in the first group.

Fig. 21.56. Site 63. Circular structure.

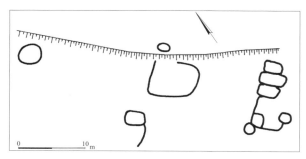

Plan 21.22. Site 65.

66. 09–00/2–5/6   Jebel el-'Ura   09210 00585

Five one-room structures arranged in a circle. Four of the structures are circular (diam. 2–5 m), the fifth is rectangular (*c.* 2 × 4 m). The walls are built of medium-sized fieldstones; one course survives.

Ceramic finds: EB.

67. 09–00/2–5/4   Jebel el-'Ura   09225 00585

Structure, consisting of seven circular rooms (diam. 3–4 m), and two circular courtyards (diam. 10 m, 20 m), on a ridge (Fig. 21.57) on Jebel el-'Ura. Nearby, to west—a stone pile (diam. *c.* 4 m, 1 m high).

Ceramic finds: EB, Byzantine and Early Islamic.

68. 09–00/2–5/5   Jebel el-'Ura   09210 00555

Six structures spread over an area of *c.* 20 × 50 m on a slope descending north, on Jebel el-'Ura. Three structures have one or two rooms (diam. 3 m) and courtyards (diam. 6–10 m). The other three consist of a single circular room (diam. *c.* 3 m). The structures' walls, built of medium-sized fieldstones, are preserved up to three courses high.

Ceramic finds: EB (including Egyptian wares).

69. 09–00/2–5/3   Jebel el-'Ura   09230 00535

Three cairns (diam. *c.* 3 m, *c.* 0.50 m high) on a ridge on Jebel el-'Ura. Nearby—a circular installation (diam. *c.* 1.5 m) and rock drawings.

70. 09–00/2–5/2   Wadi el-Qudeirat   09275 00575

Rectangular structure (*c.* 6 × 18 m), built of two rows of medium-sized fieldstones, near the south bank of Wadi el-Qudeirat.

North of the structure—remains of two additional structures.

Ceramic finds: Byzantine and Early Islamic.

71. 09–00/5–5/1   Jebel el-Qudeirat   09515 00575

Eight structures on a slope north of Wadi el-Qudeirat. Seven are circular (diam. 3–4 m), the eighth is rectangular (*c.* 2 × 5 m). The walls are built of small fieldstones. Monolithic stone door posts flank the entrances.

Ceramic finds: MB I.

72. 09–00/5–5/3   Wadi Umm Hashim   09570 00540

Nine structures near a terraced tributary draining into Wadi Umm Hashim (Plan 21.23). Each structure consists of one or more rooms (3–4 × 4–5 m) and a courtyard. The structures' walls (*c.* 0.70 m wide), built of two rows of small lightly drafted stones, are preserved up to 1 m high. Large lightly drafted stones are set at the entrances and corners (Fig. 21.58).

Near the structures—a stone fence (1000 m long), enclosing part of the terraced wadi bed (25 m wide).

Ceramic finds: Early Islamic (Fig. 21.59).

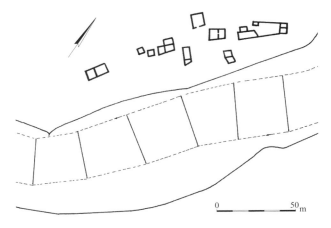

Plan 21.23. Site 72.

Fig. 21.57. Site 67. Structure.

Fig. 21.58. Site 72. Entrance to one of the structures.

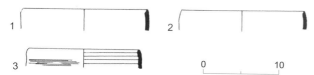

Fig. 21.59. Site 72. Early Islamic bowls.

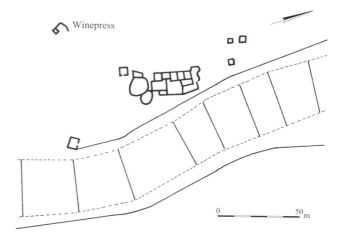

Plan 21.24. Site 73.

73. 09–00/5–5/2   Wadi Umm Hashim   09550 00520
Five structures on the bank of a terraced tributary draining
into Wadi Umm Hashim (Plan 21.24; Fig. 21.60). The main
structure (*c.* 20 × 50 m) contains eight rooms (3 × 4–5 m)
and three courtyards (*c.* 10 m long; Fig. 21.61). The walls
(*c.* 0.70 m wide), built of two rows of small lightly drafted
stones, are preserved up to 0.80 m high.
Thirty meters east of the structure, higher up the wadi slope—
a square installation and a poorly preserved winepress,
consisting of a treading floor (1 × 2 m) and a collecting vat
(1 × 1.5 m). The inner face of the winepress's walls (*c.* 0.20 m
wide), built of small lightly drafted stones, is coated with
thick white plaster.

Fig. 21.61. Site 73. One of the structures.

Fig. 21.60. Site 73. General view.

Near the structures is a stone fence (*c.* 500 m long), surrounding a segment of the terraced wadi (*c.* 30 m wide). *Ceramic finds*: Early Islamic.

74. 09–00/5–5/4   Wadi Umm Hashim   09550 00500
Rectangular structure (*c.* 6 × 12 m) near the confluence of Wadi Umm Hashim and a tributary. One course survives of the walls, built of two rows of large fieldstones. The entrance (*c.* 0.70 m wide) is located in the southern wall.

75. 09–00/6–5/1   Wadi Umm Hashim   09620 00575
Stone fence (*c.* 500 m long), enclosing a terraced wadi bed (*c.* 20 m wide; tributary of Wadi Umm Hashim).

76. 09–00/6–5/2   Wadi Umm-Hashim   09650 00520
Three circular structures (diam. *c.* 4 m) and two cairns (diam. *c.* 3 m) extending *c.* 50 m along the edge of a cliff, north of Wadi Umm Hashim.

77. 09–00/6–5/3   Wadi Umm Hashim   09660 00530
Structure (*c.* 20 × 40 m) in a valley north of Wadi Umm Hashim, comprising five circular rooms (diam. 3–4 m) and an oval courtyard (*c.* 10 × 20 m). In the center of the courtyard—a square cairn (*c.* 4 × 4 m, 0.80 m high). Some 50 m south—two circular cairns (diam. *c.* 4 m). *Ceramic finds*: EB.

78. 09–00/7–5/3   Wadi Umm Hashim   09710 00570
Rock-hewn cistern (*c.* 3 m deep, diam. of mouth *c.* 1 m) near the streambed of a tributary draining into Wadi Umm Hashim from the northwest.

79. 09–00/7–5/5   Wadi Umm Hashim   09715 00575
Structure (*c.* 15 × 20 m), consisting of rooms arranged around a central courtyard, on a slope descending south to a tributary

of Wadi Umm Hashim. The walls, built of medium-sized fieldstones, are poorly preserved.

80. 09–00/7–6/1   Wadi Umm Hashim   09750 00600
Four structures spread along *c.* 150 m on the slope of a hill, *c.* 1.5 km north of Wadi Umm Hashim. Structure 1 consists of three adjoining pens (diam. 5–7 m). Structure 2 comprises four circular rooms (diam. *c.* 3 m) and an oval courtyard (*c.* 10 × 20 m). Structure 3 is an oval pen (*c.* 10 × 15 m), and Structure 4 consists of eight circular rooms (diam. 3–5 m) and a circular courtyard (diam. *c.* 20 m). One course survives of the walls, built of medium-sized fieldstones.
Ceramic finds: EB.
Some 100 m north of the structures, on the hilltop—a cairn (diam. *c.* 3 m).

81. 09–00/7–5/2   Wadi Umm Hashim   09760 00535
Three structures on a slope, north of Wadi Umm Hashim. Structure 1 is rectangular (*c.* 8 × 30 m); its walls (*c.* 0.60 m wide), built of two rows of medium-sized fieldstones, are preserved up to 0.80 m high. Structure 2 is rectangular (*c.* 4 × 10 m); the entrance, facing west, is flanked by monolithic stone door posts. Structure 3 is oval.
Ceramic finds: Byzantine.

82. 09–00/7–5/1   Ḥawuz el-Ḥāshimiya   09780 00525
Structure, a rock-hewn cistern and a stone fence, south of a wadi to the north of Ḥawuz el-Ḥāshimiya. The structure is rectangular (*c.* 4 × 8 m; Fig. 21.62), consisting of two rooms built of medium-sized fieldstones. The adjacent cistern has two openings (diams *c.* 2 m), into which water flowed, and in the ceiling, supported by a pillar, are three drawing holes (diams. 1–1.5 m; Fig. 21.63). A conduit (*c.* 150 m long) leads to the cistern. A segment of the wadi is enclosed by a stone fence, which terminates facing the wadi bed and functions

Fig. 21.62. Site 82. Rectangular structure.

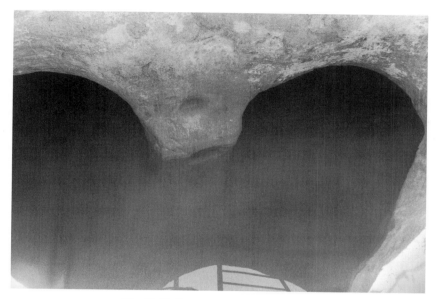

Fig. 21.63. Site 82. Interior of the cistern.

as a dam. The wadi bed is terraced (for a length of *c.* 150 m, width 20–50 m).
Ceramic finds: Early Islamic.

83. 09–00/7–5/4   Ḥawuz el-Ḥāshimiya   09795 00520
Pen (diam. 7 m), built of medium-sized fieldstones, on a slope descending east on Ḥawuz el-Ḥāshimiya.

84. 09–00/09–00/85/4 ʿAmrat el-Furni   09825 00570
Poorly preserved structure (*c.* 30 × 40 m; Plan 21.25) at the foot of a cliff south of ʿAmrat el-Furni—about 20 rooms and courtyards, around a central courtyard (diam. *c.* 30 m).
Ceramic finds: EB, MB I, Byzantine.
Some 200 m west of the structure, at the edge of the cliff—two circular structures (diam. 6 m, 10 m).
Some 250 m southeast of the first structure—three pens (diam. *c.* 10 m) and two cairns (diam. *c.* 4 m).

85. 09–00/8–5/6   ʿAmrat el-Furni   09870 00570
Two pens in a valley south of ʿAmrat el-Furni. One pen is oval (*c.* 6 × 10 m), the other is circular (diam. *c.* 10 m) and adjoined by a circular room (diam. *c.* 6 m).
Ceramic finds: Byzantine.

86. 09–00/8–5/1   ʿAmrat el-Furni   09880 00570
Two structures and cairns at the top of a hill and at its foot (Plan 21.26), northeast of ʿAmrat el-Furni. The eastern structure comprises about 12 circular rooms (diam. 3–4 m;

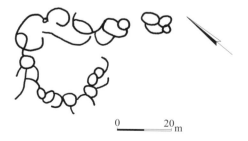

Plan 21.25. Site 84, the first structure.

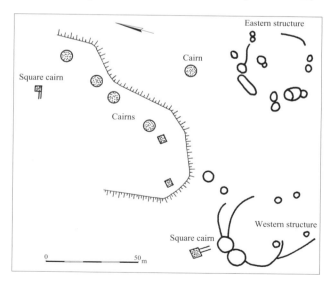

Plan 21.26. Site 86.

Fig. 21.64) arranged in a circle (diam. *c.* 40 m). The western structure includes seven circular rooms (diam. *c.* 3–5 m), two courtyards (diam. *c.* 10 m) and a pen (diam. *c.* 40 m). To its northwest is a square cairn (2 × 3 m, 0.80 m high; Fig. 21.65), with two parallel walls (*c.* 8 m in length; Fig. 21.66) issuing out from its base. On the hilltop, rising above the structures, are seven cairns. Five are circular (diam. 7–8 m), each consisting of a circle of upright stones and a small-stone fill. Two are square (each *c.* 4 × 4 m, 0.70 m high). The last cairn resembles the square cairn near the western structure.
Lithic and ceramic finds: EB.

87. 09–00/09–00/85/2 ‘Amrat el-Furni   09880 00525
Structure (*c.* 30 × 40 m) on a slope on ‘Amrat el-Furni: several circular rooms and two courtyards (diams. 10 m, 15 m).
Ceramic finds: EB.
Nearby, on the other side of the hill—remains of two structures.
Ceramic finds: Iron II.

88. 09–00/9–5/2   ‘Amrat el-Furni   09915 00510
Remains of *c.* ten structures, extending over an area of 50 × 100 m (Plan 21.27), on a slope on ‘Amrat el-Furni. The structures, circular and rectangular in shape, measure 2–3 × 3 m) and surround a courtyard (diam. *c.* 20 m). Some of the structures are built of flat upright stones. A number of entrances are flanked by monolithic stone doorjambs.
Ceramic finds: EB.

Fig. 21.64. Site 86. A circular room in the eastern structure.

Fig. 21.65. Site 86. Square cairn on the hilltop.

Plan 21.27. Site 88.

Fig. 21.66. Site 86. Two parallel walls at the base of a
square cairn, near the western structure.

89. 09–00/9–5/1 Wadi el-Furni 09990 00540
Structures and a cairn on a slope descending west to Wadi el-Furni. The main structure (*c.* 30 × 30 m) contains four rooms and three courtyards. Most of the other structures, poorly preserved, consist of one circular room. One course of medium-sized fieldstones survives of the structures' walls. Some 50 m south of the structures is a cairn (diam. 5 m): a circle of upright stones and a small-stone fill, with two central burial cists.
Ceramic finds: EB and MB I.

90. 09–00/2–4/1 Jebel el-'Ura 09215 00490
Oval structure (*c.* 4 × 6 m) on a ridge on Jebel el-'Ura, built of small fieldstones (one course survives).

91. 09–00/2–4/4 Jebel el-'Ura 09250 00490
Circular cairn (diam. *c.* 3 m, 0.60 m high) at the edge of a cliff on Jebel el-'Ura. Some 100 m to its north—a square cairn (*c.* 2.5 × 2.5 m, 1.50 m high; Fig. 21.67), built of flat

fieldstones laid lengthwise. In its center—a burial cist covered by stone slabs.

92. 09–00/2–4/2 Jebel el-'Ura 09250 00455
Two structures in a valley on Jebel el-'Ura. One structure is oval (*c.* 6 × 10 m), containing a few rooms and a courtyard. The other is circular (diam. *c.* 3 m). The walls, built of medium-sized fieldstones, are preserved up to two courses high.

93. 09–00/2–4/3 Jebel el-'Ura 09270 00450
Eight structures in a valley (Plan 21.28) on Jebel el-'Ura. Three structures consist of rooms adjoining one or two courtyards (10 × 15–25 m; Fig. 21.68). Five are circular one- or two-room structures (diam. 3–4 m). The walls, built of medium-sized fieldstones, are preserved up to three courses high.
Ceramic finds: EB.

Fig. 21.67. Site 91. Square cairn.

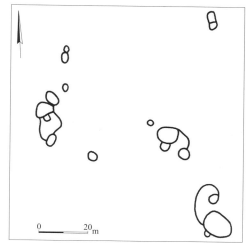
Plan 21.28. Site 93.

Fig. 21.68. Site 93. Structure—rooms adjoining a courtyard.

94. 09–00/6–4/4   Wadi Umm Hashim   09695 00450
Five circular one-room structures (diam. 3–4 m), arranged in
a semicircle (diam. *c.* 50 m) on a plateau east of Wadi Umm
Hashim. The walls are built of upright fieldstones.
Some 200 m northwest of the five structures—two circular
structures (diam. 5 m, 8 m).
Some 400 m west of the five structures—two circular
structures (diam. 5 m, 6 m) and additional structural
remains.

95. 09–00/6–4/3   Wadi Umm Hashim   09650 00470
Three structures on the south bank of Wadi Umm Hashim.
One structure (20 × 30 m) has three circular rooms (diam.
3–4 m) and an oval courtyard (5 × 10 m). The other two are
circular one-room structures (diam. *c.* 3 m).
Ceramic finds: MB I.

96. 09–00/7–4/2   Wadi Umm Hashim   09750 00445
Six structures spread over *c.* 200 m in a valley east of Wadi
Umm Hashim. In the north portion of the site are two circular

adjoining pens (diam. *c.* 10 m). In the south part of the site—
three circular structures (diam. 3–4 m).
Nearby—remains of two additional structures.

97. 09–00/7–4/1   Wadi Umm Hashim   09780 00425
Cairn (diam. *c.* 3 m, 1.5 m high; Fig. 21.69) on hilltop (spot
height 530).

98. 09–00/8–4/1   Wadi Umm Hashim   09825 00470
Remains of five circular structures (diam. 1–4 m) alongside a
dense scatter of flints (area of *c.* 50 × 100 m) on a slope north
of Wadi Umm Hashim.
Lithic finds: EB.

99. 09–00/8–4/3   Wadi Umm Hashim   09830 00435
Four structures at the edge of a cliff overlooking Wadi Umm
Hashim from the north. Three structures contain two or three
circular rooms (diam. *c.* 3 m). The fourth structure consists of
one room (diam. *c.* 4 m) and a courtyard (diam. *c.* 10 m; Fig.
21.70). The walls, built of large fieldstones, are preserved up

Fig. 21.69. Site 97. Cairn.

Fig. 21.70. Site 99. The fourth structure.

to three courses high. Monolithic stone door posts flank a few of the entrances.
Ceramic finds: EB.

100. 09–00/8–4/2   Wadi Umm Hashim   09820 00405
Three structures spread over an area of *c.* 30 × 50 m on a narrow saddle ending in a cliff, overlooking Wadi Umm Hashim from the north. Structure 1 consists of two circular rooms (diam. *c.* 3 m) and a circular courtyard (diam. *c.* 10 m). Structure 2 contains adjoining circular rooms (diam. *c.* 3 m). Structure 3 has a circular courtyard (diam. *c.* 8 m) and two circular rooms (diam. 2–4 m).
Ceramic finds: EB and Iron II.

101. 09–00/9–4/1   Wadi Umm Hashim   09970 00440
Ten circular structures (diam. 3 m) and two cairns (diam. 3 m; Fig. 21.71), extending over an area of *c.* 70 × 200 m, on a hilltop east of Wadi Umm Hashim.

102. 09–00/6–3/1   Wadi Umm Hashim   09690 00380
Scatter of flint tools (area of *c.* 50 × 100 m) near the south bank of Wadi Umm Hashim.

103. 09–00/7–3/1   Wadi Umm Hashim   09730 00360
Three structures near the streambed of Wadi Umm Hashim. One structure (*c.* 20 × 30 m) consists of rooms and courtyards. Two are circular one-room structures (diams. 5 m, 10 m; Fig. 21.72). Stone door posts flank the entrances.
Ceramic finds: EB, MB I, Iron II and Byzantine.

104. 09–00/9–3/1   Wadi Umm Hashim   09980 00370
Five structures, extending over an area of *c.* 100 × 100 m (Plan 21.29), in a valley north of Wadi Umm Hashim. Structures 1 and 2 consist of two rectangular rooms (4–5 × 2–3 m). Structure 3 is circular (diam. *c.* 3 m), Structure 4 is rectangular (4 × 10 m; Fig. 21.73) and Structure 5 is a circular pen (diam. 25 m; Fig. 21.74). The walls are built of

Fig. 21.71. Site 101. Cairn.

Fig. 21.72. Site 103. Circular structure.

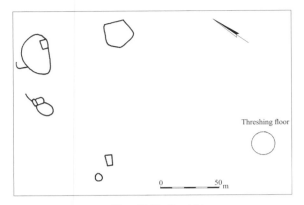

Plan 21.29. Site 104.

*Fig. 21.73. Site 104. Stone door posts flanking
the entrance to the fourth structure.*

Fig. 21.74. Site 104. Pen.

Fig. 21.75. Site 104. Threshing floor.

*Fig. 21.76. Site 104. Pottery. Iron II:
(1–3) Negebite cooking pots; Byzantine: (4, 5) jars.*

fieldstones (up to *c.* 1 m long), preserved up to three courses high. The entrances to the rooms are flanked by monolithic stone door posts (up to 0.80 m high). Nearby is a threshing floor (diam. *c.* 10 m; Fig. 21.75) built of small fieldstones arranged in a circle around a beaten-earth surface.
Ceramic finds: Iron II and Byzantine (Fig. 21.76).

105. 09–00/9–1/1   Wadi Umm Bali'an   09930 00100
Round rock-hewn cistern (diam. 4 m; diam. of mouth 2 m) in a valley, west of Wadi Umm Bali'an. The roof, about 2 m thick, is buttressed by a square pillar (0.40 × 0.40 m). A water conduit (*c.* 100 m long) leads to the cistern.

106. 09–00/9–1/2   Wadi Umm Bali'an   09940 00105
Four structures (area of 5 × 30 m) in a valley, west of Wadi Umm Bali'an. The walls, built of small fieldstones, are preserved up to four courses high.
Ceramic finds: Byzantine.

107. 09–00/9–1/3   Wadi Umm Bali'an   09945 00130
A chain of three stone fences, enclosing a terraced section of Wadi Umm Bali'an (*c.* 250 m long, streambed *c.* 35 m wide). A settlement associated with the terraces is located on the east bank, outside of the surveyed area.
Ceramic finds: Early Islamic.

108. 09–00/8–0/4   Wadi Qadis   09855 00050
A pen and two cairns near the edge of a cliff (Fig. 21.77) north of Wadi Qadis. The pen (diam. *c.* 20 m) is built of medium-sized fieldstones and preserved up to four courses high. The cairns (diam. *c.* 4 m) are circles of upright stones (*c.* 0.50 m high) with a fill of small stones.
Ceramic finds: EB.

Fig. 21.78. Site 109. Stone piles.

109. 09–00/8–0/3   Wadi Qadis   09860 00070
Five stone piles (diam. 4–5 m), spread over an area of *c.* 30 × 50 m (Fig. 21.78), at the foot of a cliff overlooking Wadi Qadis.

110. 09–00/8–0/2   Wadi Umm Bali'an   09880 00090
Structure (*c.* 50 × 50 m), consisting of circular rooms (diam. *c.* 3 m) and circular and rectangular courtyards (5–6 × 6–7 m; Plan 21.30; Fig. 21.79), in a valley west of Wadi Umm Bali'an. The walls, built of medium-sized fieldstones are preserved up to three courses high. Four cairns are superposed on the courtyards' walls. Near the structure—remains of one-room structures. On a flat rock surface near the structure—a hewn cupmark (diam. 0.20 m).
Lithic finds: EB (Fig. 21.80).
Ceramic finds: EB and MB I.

Fig. 21.77. Site 108. Pen and cairns.

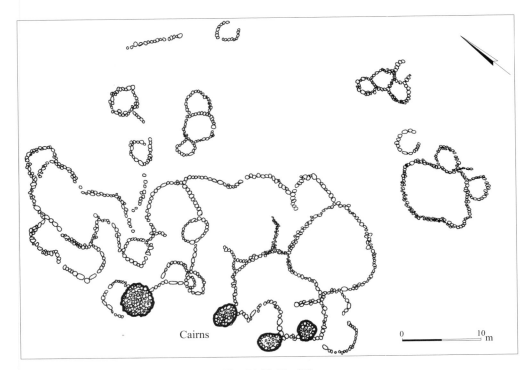

Plan 21.30. Site 110.

Fig. 21.79. Site 110. General view.

Some 100 m southwest, on a ridge—three cairns, spread along *c.* 200 m, each consisting of a circle of upright fieldstones and a small-stone fill.

111. 09–00/8–0/1 Wadi Umm Bali'an 09890 00080
Three structures, two circular and one square (3–10 × 6–15 m; Plan 21.31), in a valley west of Wadi Umm Bali'an. The walls are built of small fieldstones (Fig. 21.81). A cairn rests on the walls of one of the structures.
Ceramic finds: Roman.

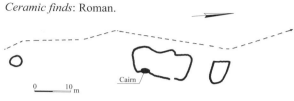

Plan 21.31. Site 111.

112. 09–00/9–0/4 Wadi Umm Bali'an 09935 00099
Four structures (area of *c.* 30 × 50 m) in a valley west of Wadi Umm Bali'an. One structure consists of a room (diam. 4 m) and an oval courtyard (10 × 20 m; Fig. 21.82). The second structure is circular (diam. *c.* 4 m). The other structures are circular pens (diam. 6–10 m).
Lithic finds: EB (Fig. 21.83).
Ceramic finds: EB.

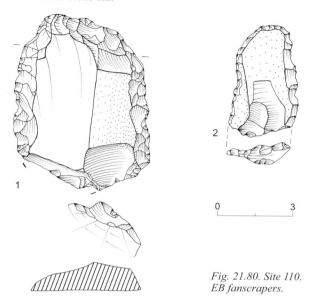

Fig. 21.80. Site 110. EB fanscrapers.

Fig. 21.81. Site 111. Structures.

Fig. 21.82. Site 112. The first structure.

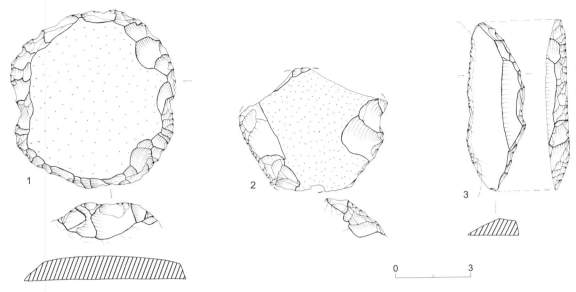

Fig. 21.83. Site 112. EB flints. (1, 2) Fanscrapers; (3) sickle blade.

113. 09–00/9–0/3   Wadi Qadis   09915 00060
Two cairns near the edge of a cliff (diam. 6 m, 8 m) north of
Wadi Qadis: circles of upright stones (*c.* 0.50 m high), filled
with small stones.

114. 09–00/9–0/5   Wadi Umm Baliʻan   09960 00075
Campsite in a valley (20 × 50 m) near the beginnings of Wadi
Umm Baliʻan: stone circles and low stone piles.
Ceramic finds: Byzantine.

115. 09–00/9–0/2   Wadi Qadis   09955 00040
Stone pile (diam. *c.* 2 m, 0.80 m high) on a hilltop north of
Wadi Qadis.

116. 09–00/9–0/1   Wadi Qadis   09975 00045
'Kite' installation (Plan 21.32; Fig. 21.84) north of Wadi
Qadis: two arms (each *c.* 100 m long) built of two courses of

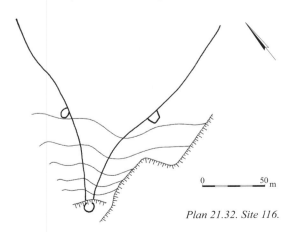

Plan 21.32. Site 116.

Fig. 21.84. Site 116. 'Kite'.

medium-sized fieldstones, which converge at the edge of a cliff (*c.* 5 m high); the kite's head (diam. *c.* 5 m) is below, at the foot of the cliff. A circular structure (diam. 5 m) adjoins the west arm midway. A straight-cornered structure adjoins the eastern arm of the installation.

Ceramic finds: Byzantine (Fig. 21.85).

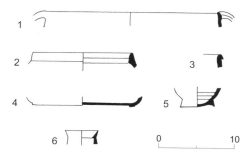

Fig. 21.85. Site 116. Byzantine pottery. (1) Bowl; (2) cooking pot; (3, 4) jars; (5, 6) juglets.

117. 10–99/0–9/2   'Ein Qadis   10015 99935
Cairn in a flat area (diam. *c.* 5 m, 0.30 m high), southwest of 'Ein Qadis.

Ceramic finds: Byzantine.

118. 10–99/0–9/1   'Ein Qadis   10000 99940
Campsite (30 × 150 m) west of 'Ein Qadis, close to the streambed of Wadi Qadis—25 stone circles (one course, diam. 1–10 m; Fig. 21.86).

Ceramic finds: Nabatean.

Nearby, on a hilltop—a Beduin cemetery.

119. 10–99/09/5   'Ein Qadis   10050 99935
Campsite (30 × 50 m) on a natural terrace in Wadi Qadis, south of 'Ein Qadis: mounds of stones (diam. 1–2 m, 0.50 m high).

120. 10–99/0–9/4   'Ein Qadis   10070 99930
Remains of a rectangular structure (*c.* 3 × 4 m) near Wadi Qadis, southeast of 'Ein Qadis: one course of medium-sized fieldstones.

121. 10–99/0–8/1   'Ein Qadis   10025 99890
Circular structure (diam. *c.* 4 m) in a valley, at the foot of a cliff southwest of 'Ein Qadis. The walls, built of medium-sized fieldstones, are preserved up to three courses high.

Ceramic finds: Byzantine.

122. 10–99/0–9/3   'Ein Qadis   10095 99905
Campsite (*c.* 50 × 100 m) on the shoulder of a hill southeast of 'Ein Qadis: stone circles (diam. *c.* 2 m; one course).

Ceramic finds: Persian.

Some 50 m northeast—a dense scatter of flint tools and flakes (area of *c.* 30 × 100 m).

Lithic finds: PPNB.

An excavation was conducted; see Rosen, Goring-Morris and Gopher 1983.

123. 10–99/0–8/2   'Ein Qadis   10070 99895
Campsite (*c.* 30 × 40 m) on the shoulder of a hill, south of 'Ein Qadis: a pen (diam. *c.* 8 m) and stone circles (one course) nearby.

Fig. 21.86. Site 118. A stone circle.

Table 21.1. Index of Site Names

Name	Site No.
'Amrat el-Furni	58–60 84–88
'Ein Qadis	117–123
Ḥawuz el-Ḥāshimiya	82 83
Jebel el-'Ain	1 6–13 25
Jebel el-Qudeirat	2–5 14–22 45–56 71
Jebel el-'Ura	43 63–69 90–93
Wadi el-'Asli	36 38 40 61 62
Wadi el-Furni	39 89
Wadi el-Ḥalufi	34 35 37 41 42
Wadi Qadis	108 109 113 115 116
Wadi el-Qudeirat	23 24 26–33 70
Wadi Umm Bali'an	105–107 110–112 114
Wadi Umm Hashim	44 57 72–81 94–104

Table 21.2. Index of Sites by Period

Period	Site No.	Total
Middle Paleolithic	28 102	2
Pre-Pottery Neolithic B	23 24 122	3
Early Bronze	2 3 5 7–10 16–19 21 22 25–28 30 41 46 47 49 53 55 56 58 59 62 66–68 76 77 80 84 86–89 93 98–100 103 108 110 112	47
Middle Bronze I	13 21 26–28 49 57 62 65 71 84 89 95 103 110	15
Iron II	1 6 17 23 24 29 31 35–37 42 44 48 49 53–55 61 87 100 103 104	22
Persian	122	1
Hellenistic	41 47–52	7
Nabatean	118	1
Roman	1 23 39 40 48 49 111 123	8
Byzantine and Early Islamic	1 12 16 34 35 37 38 42 44 49 62 67 70 72–75 78 81 82 84 85 103–107 114 117 121	30

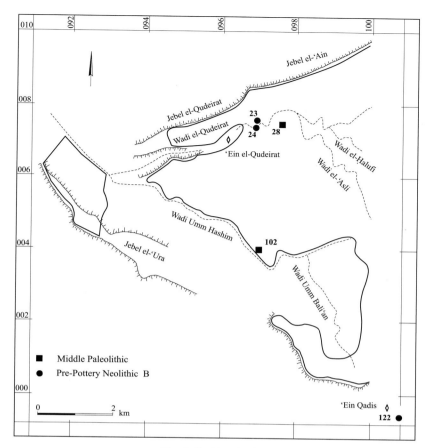

Map 1. Prehistoric sites.

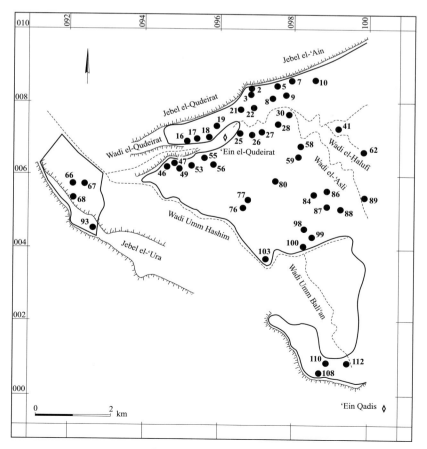

Map 2. Early Bronze sites.

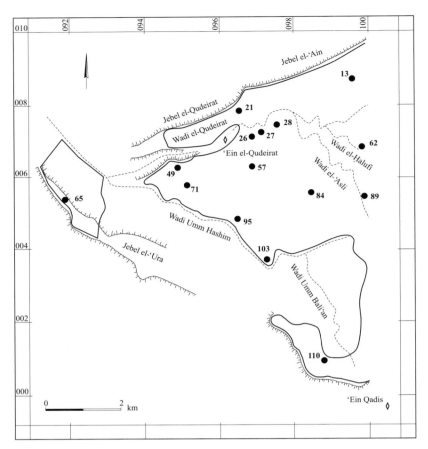

Map 3. Middle Bronze I sites.

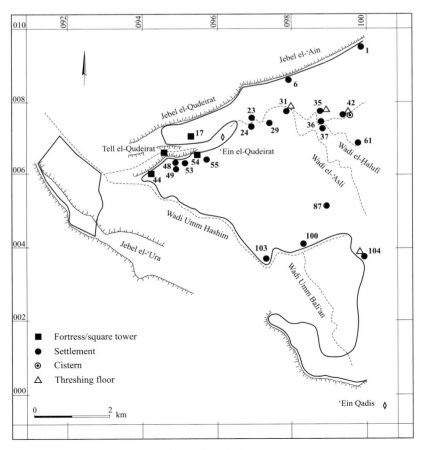

Map 4. Iron II sites.

351

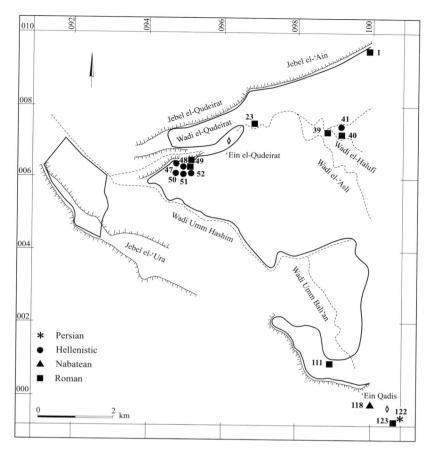

Map 5. Persian–Roman sites.

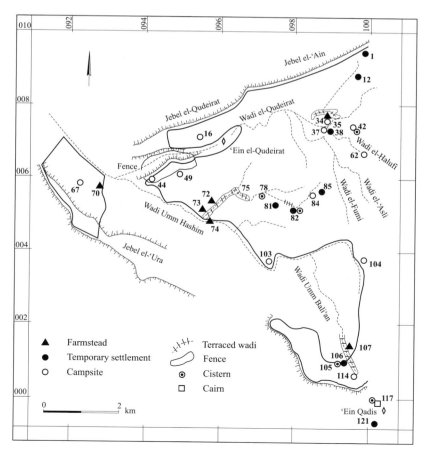

Map 6. Byzantine–Early Islamic sites.

References

Aharoni M. 1981. The Pottery of Strata 12–11 of the Iron Age Citadel at Arad. *Eretz Israel* 15:181–204.

Aharoni M. and Aharoni Y. 1976. The Stratification of Judahite Sites in the 8th and 7th Centuries B.C.E. *BASOR* 224:73–90.

Aharoni Y. 1958a. Kadesh Barnea and Har Sinai. In B. Rothenberg. *Discoveries at Sinai.* Tel Aviv. Pp. 101–119 (Hebrew).

Aharoni Y. 1958b. The Negev of Judah. *IEJ* 8:26–38.

Aharoni Y. 1961. Kadesh-Barnea and Mt. Sinai. In B. Rothenberg. *God's Wilderness: Discoveries in Sinai.* London. Pp. 117–146.

Aharoni Y. 1962. *Excavations at Ramat Raḥel I: Seasons 1959 and 1960.* Rome.

Aharoni Y. 1964. *Excavations at Ramat Raḥel II: Seasons 1961 and 1962.* Rome.

Aharoni Y. 1967. Kadesh Barnea and Har Sinai. In B. Rothenberg. *Tagliot Sinai.* Ramat Gan. Pp. 106–107 (Hebrew).

Aharoni Y. 1973. *Beer Sheba I: Excavations at Tel Beer Sheba, 1969–1971.* Tel Aviv.

Aharoni Y. 1975. *Lachish V: The Sanctuary and the Residency* (MSSMNIA 4). Tel Aviv.

Aharoni Y., Evenari M., Shanan L. and Tadmor N.H. 1960. The Ancient Desert Agriculture of the Negev, V: An Israelite Agricultural Settlement at Ramat Matred. *IEJ* 10:97–111.

Albright W.F. 1932. *The Excavation of Tell Beit Mirsim I: The Pottery of the First Three Campaigns* (AASOR 12). New Haven.

Albright W.F. 1943. *The Excavation of Tell Beit Mirsim III: The Iron Age* (AASOR 21–22). New Haven.

Albright W.F. and Kelso J.L. 1968. *The Excavation of Bethel (1934–1960)* (AASOR 39). Cambridge, Mass.

Amiet P. 1996. Les sceaux et empreintes de sceaux de Tell el-Far'ah. In P. Amiet, J. Briend, L. Courtois and J.-B. Dumortier. *Tell el Far'ah: histoire, glyptique et ceramologie* (OBO SA 14). Fribourg–Göttingen. Pp. 15–34.

Amiran R. 1969. *Ancient Pottery of the Holy Land: From Its Beginnings in the Neolithic Period to the End of the Iron Age.* New Brunswick, N.J.

Amiran R., Alon D., Arnon C., Gavish D. and Amiran D.H.K. 1980. The Arad Countryside. *Levant* 12:22–29.

Amiran R. and Gophna R. 1989. Urban Canaan in the Early Bronze II and III Periods: Emergence and Structure. In P. de Miroschedji ed. *L'urbanisation de la Palestine à l'âge du Bronze ancien* (BAR Int. S. 527). Oxford. Pp. 171–179.

Amiran R., Beit-Arieh I. and Glass Y. 1973. The Interrelationship between Arad and Sites in Southern Sinai in the Early Bronze Age II. *IEJ* 23:193–197.

Anati E. 1958. Recherches préhistoriqes au Sinai. *Bulletin de la Societé Préhistorique Francaise* 55:203–212.

Arav R. 1999. Bethsaida. *Qadmoniot* 32:78–91 (Hebrew).

Ariel D. and Shoham Y. 2000. *Local Stamped Handles and Associated Body Fragments of the Persian and Hellenistic Periods.* In D.T. Ariel ed. *City of David Excavations 1978–1985, Final Report VI* (Qedem 41). Jerusalem. Pp. 137–169.

Åström P. and Reese D.S. 1990. Triton Shells in East Mediterranean Cults. *Journal of Prehistoric Religion* 3–4:5–14.

Avigad N. and Sass B. 1997. *Corpus of West Semitic Stamp Seals.* Jerusalem.

Avner U. 1990. Ancient Agricultural Settlement and Religion in the Uvda Valley in Southern Israel. *BA* 53:125–141.

Avni G. 1992. *Map of Har Saggi (225)* (Archaeological Survey of Israel). Jerusalem.

Ayalon E. 1995. The Iron Age II Pottery Assemblage from Hurvat Teiman (Kuntillet 'Ajrud). *Tel Aviv* 22:144–205.

Barber E.J.W. 1991. *Prehistoric Textiles.* Princeton.

Baruch I. 2000. Triton Shells from the Eastern Mediterranean and Their Cultic Use during the Late Bronze Age. Paper Presented at the Annual ASOR Meeting. Nashville.

Bar-Yosef D.E. and Heller J. 1987. Mollusca from Yiftahel, Lower Galilee, Israel. *Paléorient* 13:131–135.

Bar-Yosef Mayer D.E. 1997. Neolithic Shell Bead Production in Sinai. *JAS* 24:97–111.

Bar-Yosef Mayer D.E. 2000a. The Economic Importance of Molluscs in the Levant. In M. Mashkour, A.M. Choyke, H. Buitenhuis and F. Poplin eds. *Archaeozoology of the Near East IVA: Proceedings of the Fourth International Symposium on the Archaeozoology of Southwestern Asia and Adjacent Areas.* Gröningen. Pp. 218–227.

Bar-Yosef Mayer D.E. 2000b. Mollusc Shells. In I. Finkelstein, D. Ussishkin and B. Halpern eds. *Megiddo III: The 1992–1996 Seasons* (MSSMNIA 18). Tel Aviv. Pp. 478–486.

Bar-Yosef Mayer D.E. 2000c. A Shell from Horvat 'Eleq. In Y. Hirschfeld. *Ramat Hanadiv Excavations. Final Report of the 1984–1998 Seasons.* Jerusalem. P. 749.

Bar-Yosef Mayer D.E. 2002. Egyptian–Canaanite Interaction during the Fourth and Third Millennia B.C.: The Shell Connection. In E.C.M. van den Brink and T.E. Levy eds. *Egypt and the Levant: Interrelations from the 4th through the Early 3rd Millennium B.C.E.* London. Pp. 129–135.

Bar-Yosef Mayer D.E. 2004. The Mollusc Shells. In D. Ussishkin ed. *The Renewed Archaeological Excavations at Lachish (1973–1994)* V (MSSMNIA 22). Tel Aviv. Pp. 2490–2503.

Bar-Yosef Mayer D.E. 2005a. The Exploitation of Shells as Beads in the Palaeolithic and Neolithic of the Levant. *Paléorient* 31:176–185.

Bar-Yosef Mayer D.E. 2005b. Pelecypod Beds Revisited: *Glycymeris* in Bronze Age Sites. *Mitekufat Haeven, Journal of the Israel Prehistoric Society* 35:45–52.

Bar-Yosef Mayer D.E. 2006a. Construction and Trade: The Shells from Tel Beth-Shean. In A. Mazar. *Excavations at Tel Beth-Shean 1989–1996* I: *From the Late Bronze Age IIB to the Medieval Period.* Jerusalem. Pp. 711–722.

Bar-Yosef Mayer D.E. 2006b. Mollusc Shells from Tel Batash. In N. Panitz-Cohen and A. Mazar eds. *Timnah (Tel Batash)* III: *The Finds from the Second Millennium B.C.E.* (Qedem 45). Jerusalem. Pp. 315–318.

Bar-Yosef O. 1980. The Stone Age in the Sinai Peninsula. In Z. Meshel and I. Finkelstein eds. *Qadmoniot Sinai.* Tel Aviv. Pp. 11–40 (Hebrew).

Bayer B. 1963. The Blowing Shell of Hazor. *Tatslil* 3:140–142 (Hebrew).

von Beckerath J. 1997. *Chronologie des pharaonischen Ägypten* (Münchener Ägyptologische Studien 46). Mainz am Rhein.

Beit-Arieh I. 1977. *Southern Sinai in the Early Bronze Period.* Ph.D. diss. Tel Aviv University. Tel Aviv (Hebrew).

Beit-Arieh I. 1990. The Early Bronze III Stratum at Tel ‘Ira in the Northern Negev. *Eretz Israel* 21:66–79 (Hebrew; English summary, p. 103).

Beit-Arieh I. ed. 1995. *Horvat Qitmit: An Edomite Shrine in the Biblical Negev* (MSSMNIA 11). Tel Aviv.

Beit-Arieh I. 1999. *Tel ‘Ira: A Stronghold in the Biblical Negev* (MSSMNIA 15). Tel Aviv.

Beit-Arieh I. Forthcoming. *Horvat ‘Uza and Horvat Radum: Two Fortresses in the Biblical Negev* (MSSMNIA 25). Tel Aviv.

Beit-Arieh I. and Gophna R. 1976. Early Bronze Age II Sites in Wadi el Qudeirat (Kadesh Barnea). *Tel Aviv* 3:142–150.

Beit-Arieh I. and Gophna R. 1981. The Early Bronze Age II Settlement at ‘Ain el Qudeirat. *Tel Aviv* 8:128–33.

Bennett C.M. 1966. Fouilles d’Umm el-Biyara: rapport préliminaire. *RB* 73:372–403.

Bennett C.M. 1974. Excavations at Buseirah, Southern Jordan, 1972: Preliminary Report. *Levant* 6:1–24.

Bennett C.M. 1975. Excavations at Buseirah, Southern Jordan, 1973: Third Preliminary Report. *Levant* 7:1–19.

Bennett C.M. 1977. Excavations at Buseirah, Southern Jordan, 1974: Fourth Preliminary Report. *Levant* 9:1–10.

Bennett C.M. and Bienkowski P. 1995. *Excavations at Tawilan in Southern Jordan.* Oxford.

Biggs H.E.J. 1967. Notes on Mollusca. In M.V. Seton-Williams. The Excavations at Tell Rifa‘at, 1964. Second Preliminary Report. *Iraq* 29:26–27.

Bikai P.M. 1978. *The Pottery of Tyre.* Warminster.

Biran A. 1987. Tel ‘Ira and ‘Aroer towards the End of the Judean Monarchy. *Cathedra* 42:26–33 (Hebrew).

Biran A. and Cohen R. 1981. Aro‘er in the Negev. *Eretz Israel* 15:250–273 (Hebrew; English summary, p. 84*).

Boessneck J. 1969. Osteological Differences between Sheep (*Ovis aries Linne*) and Goats (*Capra hircus Linne*). In D.R. Brothwell and S. Higgs eds. *Science in Archaeology.* New York. Pp. 331–338.

Bordreuil P. and Lemaire A. 1982. Nouveau sceaux hébreux et araméens. *Semitica* 2:45–63.

Bosch D., Dance S.P, Moolenbeek R.G and Oliver P.G. 1995. *Seashells of Eastern Arabia.* London.

Brandfon F.R. 1984. The Pottery. In Z. Herzog ed. *Beer Sheba* II: *The Early Iron Age Settlements* (Tel Aviv University Institute of Archaeology Publications 7). Tel Aviv. Pp. 37–69.

Brandl B. 1984. The Engraved *Tridacna*-Shell Discs. *Anatolian Studies* 34:15–41.

Brandl B. 1985. Scarab, Scaraboid and Beads Made of Shell from the Persian Period at Yafit. In I. Magen. Two Tumuli in the Jordan Valley (Yafit). *Eretz Israel* 18:290–292 (Hebrew; English summary, p.75*).

Brandl B. 1993. Scarabs and Other Glyptic Finds. In I. Finkelstein ed. *Shiloh: The Archaeology of a Biblical Site* (MSSMNIA 10). Tel Aviv. Pp. 203–222.

Brandl B. 2001. Two Engraved Tridacna Shells from Tel Miqne-Ekron. *BASOR* 323:49–62.

Brandl B. 2004. Scarabs, Seals, an Amulet and a Pendant. In S. Ben-Arieh. *Bronze and Iron Age Tombs at Tell Beit Mirsim* (IAA Reports 23). Jerusalem. Pp. 123–188.

Briend J. and Humbert J.B. 1980. *Tell Keisan (1971–1976): une cité Phénicienne en Galilée.* Paris.

Briggs L. 1967. *The Tribes of the Sahara.* Cambridge.

Bronk Ramsey C. 1995. Radiocarbon Calibration and Analysis of Stratigraphy: The OxCal Program. *Radiocarbon* 37:425–430.

Browning D.C. 1988. *The Textile Industry of Iron Age Timnah and its Regional and Socioeconomic Contexts: A Literary and Artifactual Analysis.* Ph.D. diss. Southwestern Baptist Theological Seminary. Fort Worth.

Browning D.C. 2001. Loomweights. In A. Mazar and N. Panitz-Cohen. *Timnah (Tel Batash)* II: *The Finds from the First Millennium BCE* (Qedem 42). Jerusalem. Pp. 248–258.

Bruins H.J. 1986. *Desert Environment and Agriculture in the Central Negev and Kadesh Barnea during Historical Times.* Ph.D. diss. The Agricultural University of Wageningen. Newkirk.

Buchanan B. and Moorey P.R.S. 1988. *Catalogue of Ancient Near Eastern Seals in the Ashmolean Museum* III: *The Iron Age Stamp Seals (c. 1200–350 B.C.).* Oxford.

Buitenhuis H. 1991. Some Equid Remains from South Turkey, North Syria and Jordan. In R.H. Meadow and H.P. Uerpmann eds. *Equids in the Ancient World.* Wiesbaden. Pp. 34–74.

Bunimovitz S. and Lederman Z. 2003. The Last Days of Beth Shemesh and the ‘Pax Assyriaca’ in the Shephelah of Judah. *Eretz Israel* 27:41–49.

Buzy D. 1927. Les stations lithiques d’el Qeseime. *RB* 36:90–92.

Buzy D. 1929. Une station de Magdalénienne dans le Negev (Ain el Qedeirat). *RB* 38:364–381.

Camps-Fabrer H. 1960. Parures des temps préhistoriques en Afrique du Nord. *Libyca* 8:9–221.

Carmi I. and Segal D. 1992. Rehovot Radiocarbon Measurements IV. *Radiocarbon* 4:115–132.

Chaplin R.E. 1971. *The Study of Animal Bones from Archaeological Sites*. London–New York.

Cohen R. 1970. Atar Haro'a. *'Atiqot (HS)* 6:6–24 (English summary, pp. 1*–3*).

Cohen R. 1976a. Excavations at Ḥorvat Ḥaluqim. *'Atiqot (ES)* 11:34–50.

Cohen R. 1976b. Qadesh Barnea, Survey. *HA* 57–58:43.

Cohen R. 1976c. Tel Qadesh Barnea. *HA* 57–58:41–42.

Cohen R. 1981a. The Excavations at Kadesh-Barnea, 1976–1978. *BA* 44:93–107.

Cohen R. 1981b. Kadesh Barnea, 1980–1981. *HA* 77:45–48.

Cohen R. 1983a. Excavations at Kadesh Barnea, 1976–1982. *Qadmoniot* 61:2–14 (Hebrew).

Cohen R. 1983b. *Kadesh-Barnea: A Fortress from the Time of the Judaean Kingdom* (Israel Museum Catalogue 233). Jerusalem.

Cohen R. 1984. Qadesh Barne'a—1981–1982. *ESI* 1:95–96.

Cohen R. 1985. Qadesh-Barnea et les forteresses du Negev Central. *Le Monde de le Bible* 39:9–48.

Cohen R. 1986. *The Settlement of the Central Negev*. Ph.D. diss. The Hebrew University. Jerusalem (Hebrew).

Cohen R. 1992. Nomadic or Semi-Nomadic Middle Bronze Age I Settlement in the Central Negev. In O. Bar-Yosef and K. Khazanov eds. *Pastoralism in the Levant*. Madison. Pp. 105–132.

Cohen R. 1999. *Ancient Settlement of the Central Negev* I (IAA Reports 6). Jerusalem (Hebrew; English summary, pp. 44*–57*).

Cohen R. and Cohen-Amin R. 2004. *Ancient Settlement of the Negev Highlands: The Iron Age and the Persian Period* (IAA Reports 20). Jerusalem (Hebrew; English summary, pp. 5*–15*).

Cohen R. and Dever W.G. 1980. Preliminary Report of the Second Season of the "Central Negev Highlands Project". *BASOR* 236:41–60.

Coleman J.D. 2004. *The Enigmatic Netherworld Books of the Solar-Osirian Unity: Cryptographic Compositions in the Tombs of Tutankhamun, Ramesses VI and Ramesses IX* (OBO 198). Fribourg–Göttingen.

Collon D. 1987. *First Impressions: Cylinder Seals in the Ancient Near East*. London.

Cornelius I. 1994. *The Iconography of the Canaanite Gods Reshef and Ba'al: Late Bronze and Iron Age I Periods (c. 1500–1000 BCE)* (OBO 140). Fribourg–Göttingen.

Cornelius I. 2004. *The Many Faces of the Goddess: The Iconography of the Syro-Palestinian Goddesses Anat, Astarte, Qedeshet, and Asherah c. 1500–1000 BCE* (OBO 204). Fribourg–Göttingen.

Crowfoot E. 1974. Textiles. In P.W Lapp and N.L. Lapp. *Discoveries in the Wâdi ed-Dâliyeh* (AASOR 41). New Haven. Pp. 60–77.

Crowfoot G. 1956. Textiles, Basketry and Mats. In C.J. Singer ed. *History of Technology* I. Oxford. Pp. 413–455.

Crowfoot G.M. 1957. The Israelite Pottery, General List. In J.W. Crowfoot, G.M. Crowfoot and K.M. Kenyon. *Samaria-Sebaste* III: *The Objects*. London. Pp. 134–198.

Crowfoot J.W., Crowfoot G.M. and Kenyon K.M. 1957. *Samaria-Sebaste* III: *The Objects*. London.

De Groot A. and Ariel D.T. 2000. Ceramic Report. In D.T. Ariel ed. *Excavations in the City of David 1978–1985* V: *Extramural Areas* (Qedem 40). Jerusalem. Pp. 91–154.

von den Driesch A. 1976. *A Guide to Measurements of Animal Bones from Archaeological Sites*. Cambridge, Mass.

Dothan M. 1963. The Fortress of Kadesh Barnea. In *Elath, the Eighteenth Archaeological Convention, October 1962*. Jerusalem. Pp. 100–117 (Hebrew).

Dothan M. 1965. The Fortress at Kadesh Barnea. *IEJ* 15:134–151.

Dothan M. 1971. *Ashdod* II–III: *The Second and Third Seasons of Excavations 1963, 1965: Sounding in 1967* (*'Atiqot [ES]* 9–10). Jerusalem.

Dothan M. and Freedman D.N. 1967. *Ashdod* I: *The First Season of Excavations, 1962* (*'Atiqot [ES]* 7). Jerusalem.

Dothan M. and Porath Y. 1982. *Ashdod* IV: *Excavation of Area M, the Fortifications of the Lower City*. (*'Atiqot [ES]* 15). Jerusalem.

Dothan M. and Porath Y. 1993. *Ashdod* V: *Excavation of Area G, the Fourth–Sixth Seasons of Excavations 1968–1970* (*'Atiqot [ES]* 23). Jerusalem.

Eggler J., Herr L.G. and Root R. 2002. Seals and Seal Impressions from Excavation Seasons 1984–2000. In L.G. Herr, D.R. Clark, L.T. Geraty, R.W. Younker and Ø.S. LaBianca eds. *Madaba Plains Project 5: The 1994 Season at Tall al-'Umayri and Subsequent Studies*. Berrien Springs.

Elgavish J. 1968. *Archaeological Excavations at Shikmona* I: *The Levels of the Persian Period, Seasons 1963–1965*. Haifa (Hebrew).

Evenari M., Aharoni Y., Shanan L. and Tadmor N.H. 1958. The Ancient Desert Agriculture of the Negev, III: Early Beginnings. *IEJ* 8:231–268.

Finkelstein I. 1985. The Iron Age "Fortresses" of the Negev—Sedentarization of Desert Nomads. *Eretz Israel* 18:366–379 (Hebrew; English summary, p. 78).

Finkelstein I. 1990. Excavations at Khirbet ed-Dawwara: An Iron Age Site Northeast of Jerusalem. *Tel Aviv* 17:163–208.

Finkelstein I. 1996. The Archaeology of the United Monarchy: An Alternative View. *Levant* 28:177–178.

Fritz V. 1994. Vorbericht über die Grabungen in Barqa el-Hetiye in Gebiet von Fenan, Wadi el-'Araba (Jordanien) 1990. *ZDPV* 110:125–150.

Fritz V. and Kempinski A. 1983. *Ergebnisse der Ausgrabungen auf der Hirbet el-Mšāš(Tēl Māśōś) 1972–1975*. Wiesbaden.

Gal Z. 1989. Loom Weights or Jar Stoppers? *IEJ* 39:281–283.

Gal Z. and Alexandre Y. 2000. *Horbat Rosh Zayit: An Iron Age Storage Fort and Village* (IAA Reports 8). Jerusalem.

Gardiner A. 1957. *Egyptian Grammar: Being an Introduction to the Study of Hieroglyphics* (3rd revised edition). Oxford.

Gilbert-Peretz D. 1996. Ceramic Figurines. In D.T. Ariel and A. De Groot eds. *Excavations at the City of David 1978–1985* IV: *Various Reports* (Qedem 35). Jerusalem. Pp. 29–84.

Gilboa A. 1996. Assyrian-Type Pottery at Dor and the Status of the Town during the Assyrian Occupation Period. *Eretz Israel* 25:122–135 (Hebrew, English summary, p. 92*).

Gitin S. 1989. Tel Miqne-Ekron: A Type Site for the Inner Coastal Plain in the Iron Age Period. In S. Gitin and W.G. Dever eds. *Recent Excavations in Israel: Studies in Iron Age Archaeology* (AASOR 49). Winona Lake. Pp. 23–58.

Gitin S. 1990. *Gezer* III: *A Ceramic Typology of the Late Iron II, Persian and Hellenistic Periods*. Jerusalem.

Giveon R. 1985. *Egyptian Scarabs from Western Asia from the Collections of the British Museum* (OBO SA 3). Fribourg–Göttingen.

Glueck N. 1935. *Explorations in Eastern Palestine* II (AASOR 15). New Haven.

Glueck N. 1938. The First Campaign at Tell el-Kheleifeh (Ezion-Geber). *BASOR* 71:3–18.

Glueck N 1967. Some Edomite Pottery from Tell el-Kheleifeh. Parts I and II. *BASOR* 188:8–38.

Glueck N. 1969. Some Ezion-Geber: Elath Iron II Pottery. *Eretz Israel* 9:51–59.

Golani A. 1996. *The Jewelry and the Jeweler's Craft at Tel Miqne-Ekron during the Iron Age*. M.A. thesis. The Hebrew University. Jerusalem.

Goldberg P. 1984. Late Quarternary History of Qadesh Barnea, Northern Sinai. *Z. Geomorph N.F.* 28:193–217.

Goren A. 1980. The Nawamis of Southern Sinai. In Z. Meshel and I. Finkelstein eds. *Qadmoniot Sinai*. Tel Aviv. Pp. 243–264 (Hebrew).

Grant E. 1932. *'Ain Shems Excavations* II. Haverford.

Habermehl K.H. 1961. *Die Altersbestimmungen bei Haustieren, Pelztieren und bein jagdbaren Wild*. Berlin–Hamburg.

Haiman [Heimann] M. 1984. Qadesh Barne'a, Survey. *ESI* 3:89–90.

Haiman M. 1986. *Archaeological Survey of Israel, Map of Har Ḥamran—Southwest (198)*. Jerusalem.

Haiman M. 1989. *Shepherds and Farmers in the Qadesh Barnea' Region*. Sede Boqer (Hebrew).

Haiman M. 1990a. Agricultural Settlement in Ramat Barnea' in the Seventh–Eighth Centuries CE. *'Atiqot (HS)* 10:111–124 (English summary, p. 20*).

Haiman M. 1990b. The Early Bronze Age in the Western Negev Highlands. *Eretz Israel* 21:152–166 (Hebrew; English summary, pp. 106–107).

Haiman M. 1991. *Archaeological Survey of Israel, Map of Mizpe Ramon—Southwest (200)*. Jerusalem.

Hakker-Orion D. 1972. *Osteology as an Auxiliary Science to Archaeology*. Tel Aviv (Hebrew).

Hakker-Orion D. 1975. Hunting and Stock Breeding in Israel. In A.T. Clason ed. *Archaeozoological Studies*. Amsterdam. Pp. 295–301.

Hakker-Orion D. 1977. Faunal Remains from the Naḥal Alexander Site. In S. Dar. *Ancient Sites in Emeq Hefer*. Ma'barot. Pp. 91–101 (Hebrew).

Hakker-Orion D. 1984. The Role of the Camel in Israel's Early History. In J. Clutton-Brock and Caroline Grigson eds. *Animals and Archaeology* (BAR Int. S. 202). Oxford. Pp. 207–213.

Hakker-Orion D. 1986. Faunal Remains from Iron Age Sites in the Negev. In R. Cohen. *The Settlements of the Central Negev*. Ph.D. diss. The Hebrew University. Jerusalem. Pp. 396–402, 459–462 (Hebrew).

Hakker-Orion D. 1987. The Determination of Sex and Species of Gazelles with the Use of Stepwise Discriminant Analysis. In L.H. Van Wijngaarden-Bakker ed. *International Workshop of Data Management in Archaeozoology*. Amsterdam. Pp. 173–184.

Hakker-Orion D. 1991. Animal Remains in Sites along the Spice Roads, Preliminary Report. In E. Orion and Y. Eini eds. 1991. *The Spice Roads*. Sede Boqer. Pp. 78–79 (Hebrew).

Hakker-Orion D. 1993. *Faunal Remains from the Sites along the Frankincense and Myrrh Route*. In A.T. Clason and H. Buitenhuis eds. *Archaeozoological Studies*. Gröningen. Pp. 77–86.

Hakker-Orion D. 1999a. Bone Characteristics, Types and Processing Methods. In E. Ayalon and H. Sorek eds. *Bare Bones: Ancient Artefacts from Animal Bones*. Tel Aviv. Pp. 8–12 (Hebrew; English summary).

Hakker-Orion D. 1999b. Faunal Remains from Middle Bronze Age Sites in the Negev Highlands. In R. Cohen. *Ancient Settlement of the Central Negev* I (IAA Reports 6). Jerusalem. Pp. 327–336 (Hebrew).

Hakker-Orion D. 2004a. Animal Bones from Sites of the Iron Age and Persian Period. In R. Cohen and R. Cohen-Amin. *Ancient Settlement of the Negev Highlands* II (IAA Reports 20). Jerusalem. Pp. 220–222 (Hebrew).

Hakker-Orion D. 2004b. Animal Remains from the Village at Upper Naḥal Besor. *'Atiqot* 48:123*–125* (Hebrew; English summary, p. 161).

Hamilton R.W. 1933. Excavations at Tell Abu-Hawam. *QDAP* 4:1–69.

Harding G.L. 1945. Two Iron Age Tombs from 'Amman. *QDAP* 11:67–74.

Harding G.L. 1948. An Iron Tomb at Sahab. *QDAP* 13:92–102.

Harding G.L. 1950. An Iron Age Tomb at Meqabelein. *QDAP* 14:44–48.

Harrison M. 1947. Toilet Articles, Jewelry and Other Artistic Products. In C.C. McCown ed. *Tell el Nasbeh* I: *Archaeological and Historical Results*. Berkeley–New Haven. Pp. 265–272.

Hart S. 1988. Excavations at Ghrareh, 1986. Preliminary Report. *Levant* 20:89–99.

Hellwing S. 1984. Human Exploitation of Animal Resources in the Early Iron Age Strata at Tel Beer-Sheva. In Y. Aharoni ed. *Beer-Sheva* I: *Excavations at Tel Beer Sheva, 1969–1971 Seasons*. Tel Aviv. Pp 105–115.

Herzog Z. 1983. Enclosed Settlements in the Negeb and the Wilderness of Beer-Sheba. *BASOR* 250:41–49.

Herzog Z. 1984. *Beer Sheba* II: *The Early Iron Age Settlements*. Tel Aviv.

Herzog Z. 1994. The Beer-Sheba Valley. In I. Finkelstein and N. Na'aman eds. *From Nomadism to Monarchy*. Jerusalem. Pp. 122–149.

Herzog Z. 1997. *The Arad Fortresses*. Tel Aviv.

Herzog Z. 2002. The Fortress Mound at Tel Arad: An Interim Report. *Tel Aviv* 29:3–109.

Herzog Z. and Singer-Avitz L. 2004. Redefining the Centre: The Emergence of State in Judah. *Tel Aviv* 31:209–244.

Herzog Z., Aharoni M., Rainey A.F. and Moshkovitz S. 1984. The Israelite Fortress at Arad. *BASOR* 254:1–34.

Herzog Z., Rapp G. and Negbi O. 1989. *Excavations at Tel Michal, Israel* (MSSMNIA 8). Minneapolis–Tel Aviv.

Hofner M. 2000. Remarks on Potsherds with Incised South Arabian Letters. In D.T. Ariel ed. *City of David Excavations 1978–1985, Final Report* VI: *Inscriptions* (Qedem 41). Jerusalem. Pp. 26–28.

Hogendorn J. and Johnson M. 1986. *The Shell Money of the Slave Trade* (African Studies Series 49). Cambridge.

Hölbl G. 1986. *Ägyptisches Kulturgut im phönikischen und punischen Sardinien* (Études préliminaires aux religions orientales dans l'empire romain 102). Leiden.

Holland T.A. 1975. *A Typological and Archaeological Study of Human and Animal Representations in the Plastic Art of Palestine during the Iron Age*. Ph.D. diss. Oxford University. Oxford.

Holland T.A. 1977. A Study of Palestinian Iron Age Backed Clay Figurines with Special Reference to Jerusalem Cave I. *Levant* 9:121–155.

Hornung E. and Staehelin E. 1976. *Skarabäen und andere Siegelamulette aus Basler Sammlungen* (Ägyptische Denkmäler in der Schweiz 1). Mainz am Rhein.

Horwitz L.K. 1995. The Faunal Remains. In I. Beit-Arieh ed. *Horvat Qitmit: An Edomite Shrine in the Biblical Negev* (MSSMNIA 11). Tel Aviv. Pp. 297–302.

Horwitz L.K., Bar Giora N., Mienis H.K. and Lernau O. 2005. Faunal and Malacological Remains from the Middle Bronze, Late Bronze and Iron Age Levels at Tel Yoqne'am. In A. Ben-Tor, D. Ben-Ami and A. Livneh. *Yoqne'am* III: *The Middle and Late Bronze Ages* (Qedem Reports 7). Jerusalem. Pp. 395–435.

Horwitz L.K., Tchernov E., Mienis H.K., Hakker-Orion D. and Bar-Yosef-Mayer D.E. 2002. The Archaeozoology of Three Bronze Age Sites in Nahal Besor, North Western Negev. In *Quest of Ancient Settlements and Landscapes*. Tel Aviv. Pp. 107–134.

Hübner U. 1992. *Die Ammoniter: Untersuchungen zur Geschichte, Kultur und Religion eines transjordanischen Volkes im 1. Jahrtausend v. Chr.* (Abhandlungen des Deutschen Palästinavereins 16). Wiesbaden.

Hübner U. 1993. Das ikonographische Repertoire der ammonitischen Siegel und seine Entwicklung. In B. Sass and C. Uehlinger eds. *Studies in the Iconography of Northwest Semitic Inscribed Seals* (OBO 125). Fribourg–Göttingen. Pp. 130–160.

Israeli Y. 1962. Crafts: Spinning, Weaving and Dyeing. In *Encyclopedia Biblica* 4:998–1010. Jerusalem (Hebrew).

James F.W. 1966. *The Iron Age at Beth Shan: A Study of Levels VI–IV* (University Museum Monograph). Philadelphia.

Jarvis C.S.. 1938. *Desert and Delta*. London.

Keel O. 1977. *Vögel als Boten. Studien zu Ps 68, 12-14, Gen 8, 6-12, Koh 10,20 und dem Aussenden von Botenvögeln in Ägypten. Mit einem Beitrag von Urs Winter zu Ps 56,1 und zur Ikonographie der Göttin mit der Taube* (OBO 14). Fribourg–Göttingen.

Keel O. 1980a. *Das Böcklein in der Milch seiner Mutter und Verwandtes in Lichte eines altorientalischen Bildmotivs* (OBO 33). Fribourg–Göttingen.

Keel O. 1980b. La glyptique. In J. Briend and J.B. Humbert eds. *Tell Keisan (1971– 1976): une cité phénicienne en Galilée* (OBO SA 1). Fribourg–Göttingen. Pp. 257–295.

Keel O. 1990. Früheisenzeitliche Glyptik in Palästina/Israel (mit einem Beitrag von H. Keel Leu). In O. Keel, M. Shuval and C. Uehlinger. *Studien zu den Stempelsiegeln aus Palästina/Israel* III: *Die frühe Eisenzeit. Ein Workshop* (OBO 100). Fribourg–Göttingen. Pp. 331–421.

Keel. O. 1992. *Das Recht der Bilder gesehen zu werden. Drei Fallstudien zur Methode der Interpretation altorientalischer Bilder* (OBO 122). Fribourg–Göttingen.

Keel O. 1995. *Corpus der Stempelsiegel-Amulette aus Palästina/Israel: Von den Anfängen bis zur Perserzeit. Einleitung* (OBO SA 10). Fribourg–Göttingen.

Keel O. 1997. *Corpus der Stempelsiegel-Amulette aus Palästina/Israel: Von den Anfängen bis zur Perserzeit* I: *Von Tell Abu Farağ bis 'Atlit* (OBO SA 13). Fribourg–Göttingen.

Keel O. and Münger S. Forthcoming. Stamp-Seal Amulets. In Z. Herzog ed. *Beer-Sheba* III. Tel Aviv.

Keel O. and Uehlinger C. 1998. *Göttinnen, Götter und Gottessymbole. Neue Erkenntnisse zur Religionsgeschichte Kanaans und Israels aufgrund bislang unerschlossener ikonographischer Quellen* (Quaestiones disputatae 134; fourth, expanded edition). Freiburg im Breisgau–Basel–Vienna.

Keel O., Shuval M. and Uehlinger C. 1990. *Studien zu den Stempelsiegeln aus Palästina/Israel* III: *Die frühe Eisenzeit. Ein Workshop* (OBO 100). Fribourg–Göttingen.

Kelm G.L. and Mazar A. 1985. Tel Batash (Timnah) Excavations. *BASOR Supplement* 23:93–120.

Kelm G.L. and Mazar A. 1995. *Timnah: A Biblical City in the Sorek Valley*. Winona Lake.

Kletter R. 1999. Iron Age Pithoi Bearing Potters Marks. In I. Beit-Arieh. *Tel 'Ira: A Stronghold in the Biblical Negev* (MSSMNIA II). Tel Aviv. Pp. 350–359.

Kochavi M. 1969. Excavations at Tel Esdar. *'Atiqot (ES)* 5:14–48.

Kühtreiber T. 1914. Bericht über meine Reisen im Palästina im Johre 1912. *ZDPV* 37:1–20, 113–123.

Lamon R. S. and Shipton G. M. 1939. *Megiddo I: Seasons of 1925–34, Strata I–V* (OIP 42). Chicago.

Leclant J. 1960. Astarté à cheval d'après les représentations égyptiennes. *Syria* 37:1–67.

Lemaire A. and Vernus P. 1980. Les ostraca paléo-hébreux de Qadesh-Barnéa. *Orientalia* 49:341–345.

Lemaire A. and Vernus P. 1983. L'ostracon paléo-hébreu N° 6 de Tell Qudeirat (Qadesh-Barnéa). In M. Görg ed. *Fontes atque pontes. Eine Festgabe für Hellmut Brunner* (Ägypten und Altes Testament 5). Wiesbaden. Pp. 302–326.

Lernau H. 1978. Faunal Remains; Strata 1–3. In R. Amiran, U. Paran and P. Beck. *Early Arad: The Chalcolithic Settlement and Early Bronze City* I: *First–Fifth Seasons of Excavations, 1962–1966.* Jerusalem. Pp. 83–113.

London G. 1991. Aspects of Early Bronze and Late Iron Age Ceramic Technology at Tell-el 'Umeiri. In L.G. Herr ed. *Madaba Plains Project* 2. Berrien Springs. Pp. 383–419.

Loud G. 1948. *Megiddo* II: *Seasons of 1935–1939* (OIP 62). Chicago.

Macalister R.A.S. 1912. *The Excavation of Gezer, 1902–1905 and 1907–1909* I–III. London.

Macdonald E., Starkey J.L. and Harding G.L. 1932. *Beth-Pelet* II: *Prehistoric Fara—Beth-Pelet Cemetery* (BSAE 52). London.

Mazar A. 1980. *Excavations at Tell Qasile* I: *The Philistine Sanctuary: Architecture and Cult Objects* (Qedem 12). Jerusalem.

Mazar A. 1985. *Excavations at Tell Qasile* II: *Various Objects, the Pottery, Conclusions* (Qedem 20). Jerusalem.

Mazar A. 1997. Iron Age Chronology: A Reply to Finkelstein. *Levant* 29:157–167.

Mazar A. and Panitz-Cohen N. 2001. *Timnah (Tel Batash)* II: *The Finds from the Millenium BCE* (Qedem 42). Jerusalem.

Mazar B., Dothan T. and Dunayevsky E. 1963. 'Ein-Gedi. Pottery in the Clark Collection. *Yediot* 27:31–55 (Hebrew).

Mazar B., Dothan T., and Dunayevsky. 1966. *'En Gedi: The First and Second Seasons of Excavations 1961–1962* (*'Atiqot [ES]* 5). Jerusalem.

Mazar E. 1985. Edomite Pottery at the End of the Iron Age. *IEJ* 35:254–269.

Mendelssohn H. and Yom-Tov Y. 1999. *Fauna Palestina: Mammalia of Israel.* Jerusalem.

Mendleson C. 1987. Scarabs and Seals. Egyptian and Egyptianizing. In R.D. Barnett and C. Mendleson eds. *Tharros: A Catalogue of Material in the British Museum from Phoenician and Other Tombs at Tharros.* London. Pp. 96–97.

Meshel Z. 1976. *Kuntillet 'Ajrud—A Religious Centre from the time of the Judean Monarchy on the Border of Sinai* (Israel Museum Catalog 175). Jerusalem.

Meshel Z. 1977. Horvat Ritma, an Iron Age Fortress in the Negev Highlands. *Tel Aviv* 4:110–135.

Meshel Z. 1994. The "Aharoni Fortress" near Quseima and the "Israelite Fortresses" in the Negev. *BASOR* 294:39–68.

Meshel Z. and Sass B. 1974. Notes and News: Yotvata. *IEJ* 24:273–274.

Mienis H.K. 1977. Marine Molluscs from the Epipaleolithic and Harifian of the Har Harif, Central Negev (Israel). In A.E. Marks. *Prehistory and Paleoenvironments in the Central Negev, Israel.* Dallas. Pp. 347–354.

Mienis H.K. 1988. Een gegraveerde Lambis-schijf uit de opgravingen van de "City of David" in het oude Jeruzalem, Israel. *Correspondentieblad van de Nederlandsche Malacologische Veneninging* 242:430–433.

Mienis H.K. 1992. Molluscs. In A. De Groot and D.T. Ariel eds. *Excavations in the City of David 1978–1985* III: *Stratigraphical, Environmental and Other Reports* (Qedem 33). Jerusalem. Pp. 122–130.

Mienis H.K. 1994. Early Use of Giant Clams in the Middle East. *Clamlines* 13:18.

Mienis H.K. 1995a. Molluscs. In I. Beit-Arieh ed. *Horvat Qitmit: An Edomite Shrine in the Biblical Negev* (MSSMNIA 11). Tel Aviv. Pp. 276–277.

Mienis H.K. 1995b. Molluscs from the Excavation of the Pre-Pottery Neolithic B Site of 'Ein Qadis I, Sinai. *'Atiqot* 28:35–36.

Münger S. 2003. Egyptian Stamp-Seal Amulets and Their Implications for the Chronology of the Early Iron Age. *Tel Aviv* 30:66–82.

Münger S. 2005. Stamp-Seal Amulets and Early Iron Age Chronology—An Update. In T.E. Levy and T. Higham eds. *The Bible and Radiocarbon Dating: Archaeology, Text and Science.* London–Oakville. Pp. 381–404.

Na'aman N. 1987. The Negev in the Last Century of the Kingdom of Judah. *Cathedra* 42:3–15 (Hebrew).

Nadelman Y. 1990. Chiseled Inscriptions and Markings on Pottery Vessels from the Iron Age II. *IEJ* 40:32–41.

Naveh J. 1962. The Excavations at Mesad Hashavyahu. *IEJ* 12:89–113.

Naveh J. 1982. *Early History of the Alphabet.* Jerusalem.

Neuville R. 1952. Station Acheuléenne du Siniai Septentrianal Djebel el Faleq. *Bulletin de la Societé Préhistorique Française* 49:77–80.

Nevo Y. 1991. *Pagans and Herders: A Re-Examination of the Negev Runoff Cultivation Systems in the Byzantine and Early Arab Periods.* Sede Boqer.

Newberry P.E. 1908. *Scarabs: An Introduction to the Study of Egyptian Seals and Signet Rings.* London.

Nodet E. 1980. Fusaïoles et Pesons. In J. Briend and J.B. Humbert. *Tell Keisan (1971–1976): une cité phénicienne en Galilée.* Paris. Pp. 315–321.

Oakeshott M.F. 1978. *A Study of the Iron Age II Pottery of the East Jordan, with Special Reference to Unpublished Material from Edom.* Ph.D. diss. University of London. London.

Oakeshott M.F. 1983. The Edomite Pottery. In J.F.A. Sawyer and D.J.A. Clines eds. *Midian, Edom and Moab.* Sheffield. Pp. 53–63.

Oren E. 1980. Survey of Northern Sinai 1972–1978. In Z. Meshel and I. Finkelstein eds. *Qadmoniot Sinai.* Tel Aviv. Pp. 101–158 (Hebrew).

Oren E. 1992. Ashlar Masonry in the Western Negev in the Iron Age. *Eretz Israel* 23:94–105 (Hebrew; English summary, pp. 149*–150*).

Oren E. 1993. Haror, Tel. *NEAEHL* 2. Pp. 580–584.

Oren E. and Morrison F. 1986. Land of Gerar Expedition. *BASOR Supplement* 24:57–87.

Perrot J. 1966. La troisiéme campagne de fouilles à Munhata (1964). *Syria* 43:49–63.

Petrie W.M.F. 1889. *Historical Scarabs: A Series of Drawings from the Principal Collections, Arranged Chronologically.* London.

Petrie W.M.F. 1928. *Gerar* (BSAE 43). London.

Petrie W.M.F. 1930. *Beth-Pelet* I: *Tell Fara* (BSAE 48). London.

Petrie W.F.M. and Ellis J.C. 1937. *Anthedon, Sinai.* London.

Porada E. 1947. Suggestions for the Classification of Neo-Babylonian Cylinder Seals. *Orientalia* 16:145–165.

Porath Y. 1974. A Fortress of the Persian Period. *'Atiqot (HS)* 7:43–55 (English summary, p. 6*).

Porath Y. 1985. *Ancient Irrigation Agriculture in the Arid Zones of Eretz Israel.* Ph.D. diss. Tel Aviv University. Tel Aviv (Hebrew).

Pratico G.D. 1985. Nelson Glueck's 1938–1940 Excavations at Tell el-Kheleifeh: A Reappraisal. *BASOR* 259:1–32.

Pratico G.D. 1993. *Nelson Glueck's 1938–1940 Excavations at Tell el-Kheleifeh: A Reappraisal* (ASOR Archaeological Reports 3). Atlanta.

Rainey F.A. 1987. Arad in the Latter Days of the Judean Monarchy. *Cathedra* 42:16–25 (Hebrew).

Rast W. and Schaub R.T. 1974. Survey of the Southern Plain of the Dead Sea, 1973. *ADAJ* 19:5–53.

Reese D.S. 1983. Marine Shells. In V. Fritz and A. Kempinski eds. *Ergebnisse der ausgrabungen auf der Ḥirbet el-Mšāš (Tēl Māśōś) 1972–1975.* Wiesbaden. Pp. 224–226.

Reese D.S. 1989a. On Cassid Lips and Helmet Shells. *BASOR* 275:33–39.

Reese D.S. 1989b. Treasures from the Sea: Shells and Shell Ornaments from Hasanlu IVB. *Expedition* 31/2–3:80–86.

Reese D.S. 1991. Marine and Fresh-Water Shells and an Ostrich Eggshell from Tall Seh Hamad, Syria. In H. Kuhne ed. *Die rezente umwelt von Tall Seh Hamad und daten zur umweltrekonstruktion der Assyrischen stadt dur-Katlimmu.* Berlin. Pp. 133–136.

Reese D.S. 1995a. Marine Invertebrates and Fossils. In C.M. Bennett and P. Bienkowski. *Excavations at Tawilan in Southern Jordan.* Oxford. Pp. 93–96.

Reese D.S. 1995b. The Triton Shell Vessel, Building AB. In P. Betancourt and C. Davaras. *Pseira* I: *The Minoan Buildings on the West Side of Area A* (University Museum Monograph 90). Philadelphia. P. 42.

Reese D.S. and Sease C. 1993. Some Previously Unpublished Engraved Tridacna Shells. *JNES* 52:109–128.

Reese D.S., Mienis H.K. and Woodward F.R. 1986. On the Trade of Shells and Fish from the Nile River. *BASOR* 264:79–84.

Reisner G.A., Fisher C.S. and Lyon D.G. 1924. *Harvard Excavations at Samaria, 1908–1910.* Cambridge, Mass.

Richard S. 1990. The 1987 Expedition to Khirbet Iskander and Its Vicinity: Fourth Preliminary Report. *BASOR Supplement* 26:33–58.

Robinson E. 1860. *Biblical Researches* 2 (2nd edition). Boston.

Rosen S. 1983. *Lithics in the Bronze and Iron Ages in Israel.* Ph.D. diss. University of Chicago. Chicago.

Rosen S.A. 1986. Note on the Gezer Flint Cache. In W.G. Dever. *Gezer* IV: *The 1969–1971 Seasons in Field VI, the 'Acropolis'.* Jerusalem. Pp. 259–263.

Rosen S.A. 1993. The Lithic Assemblages from Naḥal Mitnan. *'Atiqot* 22:62–69.

Rosen S.A. 1997. *Lithics after the Stone Age: A Handbook of Stone Tools from the Levant.* Walnut Creek.

Rosen S., Goring-Morris A.N. and Gopher A. 1984. 'Ein Qadis (Sinai). *ESI* 1:25.

Rothenberg B. 1961. *God's Wilderness: Discoveries in Sinai.* London.

Rothenberg B. ed. 1979. *Sinai.* Bern.

Rothenberg B. 1988. *The Egyptian Mining Temple at Timna* I. London.

Rothenberg B. and Glass J. 1981. Midianite Pottery. *Eretz Israel* 15:85–114 (Hebrew; English summary, pp. 80*–81*).

Rothenberg B. and Glass J. 1983. The Midianite Pottery. In J.F.A. Sawyer and D.J.A. Clines eds. *Midian, Edom and Moab.* Sheffield. Pp. 65–124.

Rothenberg B. and Glass J. 1992. The Beginnings and Development of Early Metallurgy and Settlement and Chronology of the Western Arabah from the Chalcolithic Period to Early Bronze Age IV. *Levant* 24:141–157.

Rowe A. 1936. *A Catalogue of Egyptian Scarabs, Scaraboids, Seals and Amulets in the Palestine Archaeological Museum.* Cairo.

Rowe A. 1940. *The Four Canaanite Temples of Beth-Shan* I: *The Temples and Cult Objects* (Publications of the Palestine Section of the Museum of the University of Pennsylvania 2). Philadelphia.

Sadek-Kooros H. 1972. Primitive Bone Fracturing: A Method of Research. *American Antiquity* 37:369–381.

Safer J.F. and McLaughlin Gill F. 1982. *Spirals from the Sea.* New York.

Sass B. 1993. The Pre-Exilic Hebrew Seals: Iconism vs. Aniconism. In B. Sass and C. Uehlinger eds. *Studies in the Iconography of Northwest Semitic Inscribed Seals* (OBO 125). Fribourg–Göttingen. Pp. 194–256.

Schmidt N. 1910. Kadesh Barnea. *JBL* 29:61–76.

Schniedewind W.M. 2005. Problems in the Paleographic Dating of Inscriptions. In T.E. Levy and T. Higham eds. *The Bible and Radiocarbon Dating: Archaeology, Text and Science.* London–Oakville. Pp. 405–412.

Schroer S. 1987. *In Israel gab es Bilder. Nachrichten von darstellender Kunst im Alten Testament* (OBO 74). Fribourg–Göttingen.

Segal D. 1998. *The Carbon-14 Dating Method and Its Uses in Chronological and Regional Archaeological Research.* MA thesis. Tel Aviv University. Tel Aviv (Hebrew; English abstract).

Shamir O. 1992. A Twelfth-Century BCE Linen Textile Fragment from Beth She'an. *Archaeological Textiles Newsletter* 14:4.

Shamir O. 1996a. Loomweights and Whorls. In D.T. Ariel ed. *Excavations at the City of David 1978–1985* IV: *Various Reports* (Qedem 35). Jerusalem. Pp. 135–170.

Shamir O. 1996b. *Textile Production in Eretz-Israel in the Iron Age in the Light of the Archaeological Finds*. M.A. thesis. The Hebrew University. Jerusalem (Hebrew).

Sheffer A. 1973. An Object of Palm Frond. In Y. Aharoni. *Beer Sheba* I. Tel Aviv. Pp. 47–51. amend

Sheffer A. 1976. Comparative Analysis of a 'Negev Ware' Textile Impressions? from Tel Masos. *Tel Aviv* 3:81–88.

Sheffer A. 1981. The Use of Perforated Clay Balls on the Warp-Weighted Loom. *Tel Aviv* 8:81–83.

Sheffer A. and Tidhar A. 1988. Textiles and Textile Impressions on Pottery. In B. Rothenberg. *The Egyptian Mining Temple at Timna* I. London. Pp. 224–232.

Sheffer A. and Tidhar A. 1991. Textiles and Basketry at Kuntillat 'Ajrud. *'Atiqot* 20:1–26.

Shiloh Y. 1985. A Hoard of Hebrew Bullae from the City of David. *Eretz Israel* 18:73–87.

Shoham Y. 2000. Inscribed Pottery. In D.T. Ariel ed. *Excavations at the City of David 1978–1985* VI: *Inscriptions* (Qedem 41). Jerusalem. Pp. 17–25.

Shuval M. 1990. A Catalogue of Early Iron Stamp Seals from Israel. In O. Keel, M. Shuval and C. Uehlinger. *Studien zu den Stempelsiegeln aus Palästina/Israel* III: *Die frühe Eisenzeit. Ein Workshop* (OBO 100). Fribourg–Göttingen. Pp. 67–161.

Silver I.A. 1969. The Ageing of Domestic Animals. In D. Brothwell and E.S. Higgs eds. *Science in Archaeology*. London. Pp. 283–302.

Singer-Avitz L. 1989. Iron Age Pottery. In Z. Herzog, G. Rapp and O. Negbi. *Excavations at Tel Michal, Israel* (MSSMNIA 8). Minneapolis–Tel Aviv. Pp. 76–87.

Sivan D., Potasman M., Almogi-Labin A., Bar-Yosef Mayer D.E., Spanier E. and Boaretto E. 2006. The *Glycymeris* Query along the Coasts and Shallow Shelf of Israel, Southeast Mediterranean. *Palaeogeography, Palaeoclimatology, Palaeoecology* 233:134–148.

Smith M.E. and Hirth K.G. 1988. The Development of Prehispanic Cotton-Spinning Technology in Western Morelos, Mexico. *JFA* 15:349–358.

Staubli T. 1991. *Das Image der Nomaden im Alten Israel und in der Ikonographie seiner sesshaften Nachbarn* (OBO 107). Fribourg–Göttingen.

Stern E. 1970. Excavations at Gil'am (Kh. er-Rujm). *'Atiqot (HS)* 6:31–55 (English summary, pp. 4*–5*).

Stern E. 1978. *Excavations at Tel Mevorakh (1973–1976)* I: *From the Iron Age to the Roman Period* (Qedem 9). Jerusalem.

Stern E. 1982. *The Material Culture of the Land of the Bible in the Persian Period 538–332 BCE*. Warminster.

Stern E. 1989. The Beginning of the Greek Settlement in Palestine in the Light of the Excavations at Tel Dor. In S. Gitin and W.G. Dever eds. *Recent Excavations in Israel: Studies in Iron Age Archaeology* (AASOR 49). Winona Lake. Pp. 107–124.

Stern E. and Magen I. 1982. A Persian Period Pottery Assemblage from Qadum in the Samaria Region. *Eretz Israel* 16:182–197 (Hebrew; English summary, p. 258*).

Stern E., Berg, J., Gilboa A., Guz-Zilberstein B., Raban A., Rosenthal-Heginbottom R. and Sharon I. 1995. *Excavations at Dor, Final Report* 1B: *Areas A and C: The Finds*. Jerusalem.

Stucky R.A. 1974. The Engraved Tridacna Shells. *Dédalo* 19:1–170.

Stuiver M. and Kra R.S eds. 1986. Calibration Issue. Proceedings of the 12th International 14C Conference. *Radiocarbon* 28:805–1030.

Teeter E. 2003. *Scarabs, Scaraboids, Seals, and Seal Impressions from Medinet Habu: Based on the Field Notes of Uvo Hölscher and Rudolf Anthes. With Post-Pharaonic Stamp Seals and Seal Impressions by T.G. Wilfog* (OIP 118). Chicago.

Timm S. 1989. *Moab zwischen den Mächten. Studien zu historischen Denkmälern und Texten* (Ägypten und Altes Testament 17). Wiesbaden.

Trumbull H.C. 1884. *Kadesh Barnea*. London.

Tufnell O. 1953. *Lachish (Tell ed-Duweir)* III: *The Iron Age*. London.

Tufnell O. 1958. *Lachish (Tell ed-Duweir)* IV: *The Bronze Age*. London.

Uehlinger C. 1990. Ein 'nh-ähnliches Astralkultsymbol auf Stempelsiegeln des 8./7. Jhs. In O. Keel, M. Shuval and C. Uehlinger. *Studien zu den Stempelsiegeln aus Palästina/ Israel* III: *Die frühe Eisenzeit. Ein Workshop* (OBO 100). Fribourg–Göttingen. Pp. 322–330.

Ussishkin D. 1983. *Excavations at Tel Lachish 1978–1983* (*Tel Aviv* 10). Tel Aviv.

Ussishkin D. 1995. The Rectangular Fortress at Kadesh Barnea. *IEJ* 45:118–127.

Van Beek G.W. 1989. The Buzz: A Simple Toy from Antiquity. *BASOR* 275:53–58.

Van Beek G.W. 1991. Buzz or Button? *BAR* 17:62–63.

Van Beek G.W. 1993. Jemmeh, Tell. *NEAEHL* 2. Pp. 667–674.

Van Beek G.W. and Van Beek O. 1990. The Function of the Bone Spatula. *BA* 53:205–209.

de Vaux R. and Savignac R. 1938. Chronique: nouvelles recherches dans la région de Cades. *RB* 47:89–98.

Vercoutter J. 1945. *Les objets égyptiens et égyptisants du mobilier funéraire carthaginois* (Bibliothèque archéologique et historique 40). Paris.

Von Raumer G. 1935. *Palastina*. Leipzig.

Wampler J.C. 1947. *Tell en Nasbeh* II: *The Pottery*. Berkeley.

Wapnish P., Hesse B. and Ogilvy A. 1977. The 1974 Collection of Faunal Remains from Tell Dan. *BASOR* 227:35–62.

Wheeler W. 1982. Loomweights and Spindle Whorls. In K.M. Kenyon and T.A. Holland. *Excavations at Jericho* IV: *The Pottery Type Series and Other Finds*. London. Pp. 623–637.

Wiegand T. 1920. *Sinai*. Berlin–Leipzig.

Wimmer S. 2000. Zu einer kurzen Ritzinschrift aus et-Tell/ Beth Saida. *BN* 102:33–34.

Woolley C.L. and Lawrence T.E. 1914–1915. *The Wilderness of Zin* III. London.

Wyatt N. 1999. Astarte. In K. van der Toorn, B. Becking and P.W. van der Horst eds. *Dictionary of Deities and Demons in the Bible*. Leiden–Boston–Köln. Pp. 109–114.

Yadin Y., Aharoni Y., Amiran R., Dothan T., Dothan M., Dunayevsky I. and Perrot J. 1961. *Hazor* III–IV: *The Third and Fourth Seasons of Excavations 1957–1958: Plates*. Jerusalem.

Yadin Y., Aharoni Y., Amiran R., Dothan T., Dunayevsky I. and Perrot J. 1958. *Hazor* I: *The First Season of Excavations 1955*. Jerusalem.

Yadin Y., Aharoni Y., Amiran R., Dothan T., Dunayevsky I. and Perrot J. 1960. *Hazor* II: *The Second Season of Excavations 1956*. Jerusalem.

Yassine K. 1984. *Tell el Mazar* I: *Cemetery A*. Amman.

Zertal A. 1989. The Wedge-Shaped Decorated Bowl and the Origin of the Samaritans. *BASOR* 276:77–84.

Zimhoni O. 1997. *Studies in the Iron Age Pottery of Israel* (Journal of the Institute of Archaeology of Tel Aviv University Occasional Publications 2). Tel Aviv.

Zimmermann W.H. 1982: Archäologische Befunde frühmittelalterlicher Webhäuser. Ein Beitrag zum Gewichtswebstuhl. *Jahrbuch der Männer vom Morgenstern* 61:111–144.

APPENDIX 1

BOTANICAL REMAINS

During or after the excavation, at least part of the Kadesh Barnea botanical remains were sent for analysis, but the results of this study were not available for publication in this volume. The following list of botanical materials was compiled during the processing of the finds for publication, but it is unclear whether it is complete (Table App. 1.1; Figs. App. 1.1, 1.2). In addition, the identifications provided here are preliminary and should be regarded with caution. Additional botanical remains (wood charcoal) that were sent for ^{14}C dating are listed in Chapter 20.

Fig. App. 1.1. Apple.

Fig. App. 1.2. Pomegranate.

Table App. 1.1. Botanical Remains

Registration No.	Locus	Area	Stratum	Comments	Preliminary Identification
1788	820	E	4b		Grain and other seeds
475	207	A1	3c	Probably modern	Plum pit
793	464	C	3a-b		Pomegranate peel
1121	860	F	3a-b		Almond peel
8299	6254	C	3, 2		Date stone
858/5	460	B	2	In same locus, remains of basket or textile	Apples
955	460	B	2	In same locus, remains of basket or textile	Apples and date stones
898	461	B	2		Pomegranate
938	486	B	2		Apples
979/3	486	B	2		Apples and date stones
918	508	A2	2	Under floor of casemate	Palm fibers
994	523	A2	2		Wheat and other grains

Appendix 2

Permits and Banks of Locus and Basket Numbers by Season

Season	Permit No.	Dates	Area	Loci	Baskets
1	Sinai 1	18.1–26.1.1976	All areas	20–60	1–83
2	Sinai 4	1.3–8.3.1976		65–132	84–229
3	Sinai 49	15.1–26.1.1978		150–303	300–597
4	Sinai 66	17.12–28.12.1978		400–560	700–1121
5	Sinai 89	16.12.1979–2.1.1980	B	701–753	1501–1657
			C	600–644	1300–1423
			E	801–823	1701–1830
				1001–1013	2101–2124
			D, H	901–1000	1901–1930
6	Sinai 93	10.12.1980–2.1.1981	B	760–800	2401–2600
				1201–1245	2950–2981
			C	650–700	2200–2301
				1350–1354 1101–1109	2901–2915
			D	1050–1100	2701–2900
				1301–1305	3001–3050
			E	910–957	1950–2062
			F	850–864	2601–2676
7	Sinai 99	17.5–22.5.1981	B	3000–3027	5000–5069
			C	6000–6031	8000–8061
			E	4000–4005	6000–6012
			F	7000–7007	9000–9015
8	Sinai 109	25.10–13.11.1981	B	3040–3097	5080–5211
			C	6040–6150	8070–8326
			D	1400–1424	3000–3147
			E	2000–2030	4000–4083
			F	7020–7039	9020–9096
			G	6500–6504	8500–8507
			H	5050–5092	7080–7142
9	Sinai 114	20.12–29.12.1981	B	3150–3166	5250–5280
			C	6200–6228	8400–8460
			D	1500–1503	3200–3237
			E	2150–2159	4100–4133
			F	7050–7053	9150–9154
			G	8000–8011	9501–9514
			H	5150–5151	7200–7202
10	Sinai 119	14.2–26.2.1982	B	3170–3212	5285–5377
			C	6230–6310	8470–8602
			D	1510–1523	3240–3299

LOCUS LIST

Locus	Area	Permit No.*	Square	Upper Level	Lower Level	Stratum	Description
20	A1	S.1	M10	26.47	26.35	1	Floor
21	A1	S.1	M9	26.07	25.93	1	Floor
22	A1	S.1	M8	26.87	25.85	1	Floor
23	A1	S.1	M8	-	25.55	1	Installation
24	A1	S.1	M7	25.85	25.75	1	Floor
25	A1	S.1	M9	25.93	25.76	2	Fill
26	A1	S.1	M8	25.85	25.59	1	Pit
27	A1	S.1	M7	25.64	25.60	2	Fill
28	A1	S.1	M9	25.76	25.57	2	Fill
29	A1	S.1	M10	26.35	25.74	2	Fill
30	A1	S.1	N8	26.20	25.80	2, 1	Debris
31	A2	S.1	N8	26.20	25.85	2, 1	Debris
32	A1	S.1	M9	25.57	25.40	2	Above floor
33	A1	S.1	M8	25.60	25.41	2	Above floor
34	A1	S.1	M9	25.40	25.03	2	Floor
35	A1	S.1	M10	25.74	25.45	2	Above floor
36	A1	S.1	M9	25.03	24.80	3a	Debris
37	A2	S.1	M10	-	25.50	2	Above floor
38	A1	S.1	M10	25.45	25.18	2	Floor
39	A2	S.1	N8	25.85	25.35	2	Floor
40	A1	S.1	M7	25.13	25.01	2	Floor
41	A1	S.1	M10	25.18	-	3a	Floor?
42	A1	S.1	M9	24.80	-	3b	Fill
43	A1	S.1	M10	-	-	3c	Fills
44	A1	S.1	M10	-	24.40	3c	Fills
45	A1	S.1	M8	25.44	24.30	2	Floor
46	A2	S.1	M10	25.50	25.30	2	Fill
47	A1	S.1	M9	-	23.86	3c	Fills
48	A1	S.1	M10	24.40	24.20	3c	Fills
50	A1	S.1	M9	23.86	-	3c	Fills
51	A1	S.1	N7	-	-	1	Debris
52	A2	S.1	N7	-	25.42	2	Floor
53	E	S.1	O7	-	-	2	Fill of glacis
54	A1	S.1	M8	25.30	-	2	Floor makeup
55	E	S.1	O6	-	-	2, 1	Cleaning
57	A1	S.1	N7	25.65	25.55	2	Above floor
58	A2	S.1	M10	25.30	-	2	Floor

* See Appendix 2

Locus	Area	Permit No.	Square	Upper Level	Lower Level	Stratum	Description
59	A2	S.1	M10	-	-	2	Below floor
60	A2	S.1	N7	-	25.82	2, 1	Fill
61	A1	S.1	M7	25.01	-	2	Floor (+76)
62	A1	S.1	M8	25.30	24.97	3a, 2	
63	A1	S.1	M10	24.20	-	3a-b	Fill
65	A2	S.4	O8	25.16	25.08	2	Floor
66	A1	S.4	M9	-	23.43	3c	Fills
67	A1	S.4	M8	25.03	24.96	3a, 2	Mixed
68	A1	S.4	M7	25.07	-	2	Floor (+76)
69	A1	S.4	M7	25.01	-	2	Floor (+40)
70	A1	S.4	M7	25.01	24.78	3a	Above floor
71	A1	S.1	N7	25.59	25.36	2	Floor
72	A1	S.1	N7	25.55	25.34	2	Floor
73	A1	S.4	M9	23.43	23.25	3c	Fills
74	A1	S.4	M10	-	23.62	3c	Fills
75	A2	S.4	O8	25.08	-	2	Tower
76	A1	S.4	M7	25.54	25.12	2	Floor
77	A1	S.4	M9	23.25	23.08	3c	Fills
78	A1	S.4	M7	25.00	24.55	3a	
79	A1	S.4	M7	24.80	24.48	3a	Floor
81	A1	S.4	M9	23.08	22.83	3c	Fills
82	A1	S.4	M8	24.97	24.85	3a	Fills
83	A1	S.4	M8	24.97	24.59	3a	Floor
84	A1	S.4	M8	24.97	24.73	3a	Floor
85	A1	S.4	M9	22.83	22.36	3c	Fills
86	A1	S.4	M7	24.87	24.50	3a, 2	
87	A1	S.4	N7	25.36	24.93	2	Floor makeup
88	A1	S.4	M9	21.98	21.89	4a	Burnt layer
89	A1	S.4	M7	25.12	24.54	3a, 2	
90	A1	S.4	M7	24.40	24.26	3b	Above floor
91	A1	S.4	M8	24.70	24.40	3b	Fill
92	A1	S.4	M8	24.85	24.70	3a	Installation
94	A1	S.4	N7	24.93	24.76	3a	Fill
95	A1	S.4	N7	25.34	24.99	2	Floor makeup
96	A1	S.4	M7	24.26	24.03	3b	
97	A1	S.4	N8	25.80	25.40	2	Floor
98	A2	S.4	N10	-	26.16	1	Floor
99	A1	S.4	N10	-	26.33	1	Floor
100	A1	S.4	M9	21.89	21.76	4b	Above floor
101	A1	S.4	N7	24.93	24.77	3a	Fill
102	A1	S.4	M7	24.54	24.38	3a, b	Fill
103	A1	S.4	M6	-	-	1	Debris
104	A1	S.4	M6	-	25.38	1	Debris
105	A1	S.4	M8	24.73	24.52	3b	Above floor
106	A1	S.4	N7	24.77	24.70	3a	Floor

Locus	Area	Permit No.	Square	Upper Level	Lower Level	Stratum	Description
107	A1	S.4	N7	24.99	24.71	3a	Floor
108	E	S.4	O7	-	24.53	2	Fill of glacis
109	E	S.4	O7	23.77	23.73	3a-b	Silo
110	A1	S.4	M8	24.60	24.33	3b	Above floor
111	A2	S.4	N10	26.16	25.81	1	Pit
112	A1	S.4	M6	-	25.35	2	Above floor
114	A1	S.4	M9	21.76	21.44	4b	Floor
115	A1	S.4	M7	24.03	23.93	3c	Fills
116	E	S.4	O7	24.53	24.13	3a-b	Paved floor
117	A1	S.4	N8	25.40	25.19	2	Paved floor
118	A1	S.4	N8	25.14	25.07	3a	Fill
119	A1	S.4	M8	24.52	24.39	3b	Floor
120	A1	S.4	N7	24.70	24.43	3b	Fill
121	A1	S.4	M7	23.93	23.60	3c	Fills
122	A2	S.4	N10	25.81	25.71	1	Pit
123	A1	S.4	M6	25.38	25.14	2	Above floor
124	A1	S.4	M6	-	25.60	1	Mixed
125	A1	S.4	M6	-	-	2	Floor
126	A1	S.4	M7	24.06	23.96	3b	Fill
127	A1	S.4	M8	24.39	24.13	3c	Fills
128	A1	S.4	N/7–8	-	24.78	3, 2	Balk
130	A1	S.4	M6	25.26	25.05	2	Installation
132	E	S.4	O6	-	-	-	Cleaning
150	A1	S.49	M7	24.06	23.83	3a-b	
151	A1	S.49	M–N/7	24.13	-	3a-b	Cleaning
152	A1	S.49	M7	24.58	24.33	3a	Floor
154	A1	S.49	M8	24.31	24.03	3c	Below floor
156	A1	S.49	N7	-	-		Section
157	A2	S.49	N10	25.25	25.19	2	Floor
158	A1	S.49	N7/8	24.78	-	3a	Balk
159	A1	S.49	M10	26.11	25.51	2, 1	
160	A1	S.49	M–N/8	-	24.33	-	Balk
161	A1	S.49	N7	24.36	24.05	3b	
162	A1	S.49	M–N/7	24.86	24.09	3a-b	
163	E	S.49	O6	-	24.38	1	Fill of glacis
164	A1	S.49	M6	25.48	25.30	2	Above floor
165	A1	S.49	M5	-	24.66	3a	
166	A1	S.49	N7	-	24.95	3a, 2	
167	A1	S.49	N8	-	25.53	2	Cleaning
168	A1	S.49	M–N/8	-	24.12	3a-b	Balk
169	A1	S.49	N7	24.70	24.30	3a-b	Fill
170	A1	S.49	N11	25.99	25.69	-	
171	A1	S.49	M10	25.58	25.44	2	Fill
172	A1	S.49	N7	24.08	23.73	3c	Fills
173	A1	S.49	N7	24.05	-	3c	Fills

Locus	Area	Permit No.	Square	Upper Level	Lower Level	Stratum	Description
174	A1	S.49	M8	24.80	24.24	3b	Floor
175	A1	S.49	M6	25.21	25.05	2	Floor
176	A1	S.49	N6	25.60	25.40	2, 1	Fill
177	A1	S.49	N8	25.53	24.73	2	Fill
178	A1	S.49	M8	24.40	24.31	3c	Fill
179	A1	S.49	M10	25.44	25.20	2	
180	E	S.49	O9	-	24.80	2	Fill of glacis
181	E	S.49	O6	24.38	24.23	3a-b	Paved floor
182	A1	S.49	N8	25.02	24.35	3a	Above floor
183	A1	S.49	N6	25.40	25.00	2	
184	A1	S.49	M5	-	24.66	3a	Fill
186	A2	S.49	N9	26.30	25.25	2	Floor
187	A1	S.49	M7	24.38	24.33	3b	Floor
188	E	S.49	O6	24.23	-	3c	Fill
189	A1	S.49	N7	24.96	24.49	3a, 2	Disturbance
190	E	S.49	O/9–10	24.80	24.45	3a-b	Floor? Backfill from Dothan excavation
191	A1	S.49	M6	25.00	24.47	3a, 1	Disturbed
192	A!	S.49	M6	25.05	24.60	3a	
193	A1	S.49	M7	25.15	25.03	3b	Installation
194	A1	S.49	M10	25.20	24.70	3a-b	Above floor
195	A1	S.49	M10	24.79	24.70	3a-b	Floor cleaning
196	A1	S.49	M9	-	21.95	3c	Fills
197	A1	S.49	M6	24.47	24.20	3b	Floor
198	A1	S.49	M6	24.50	24.20	3b	Floor
199	A1	S.49	N6	24.76	24.35	3a	Fill
200	A1	S.49	N6	25.00	24.19	3a-b	Fill
201	A1	S.49	N6	25.00	24.65	3a-b	Fill
202	A1	S.49	N5	24.66	24.20	3a-b	Fill
203	E	S.49	O7	23.73	23.27	3a-b	Silo
204	E	S.49	O7	23.27	21.80	3c	Fills
205	A1	S.49	M7	23.85	23.45	3c	Fills
206	A1	S.49	N7	24.40	24.16	3b	Floor
207	A1	S.49	N7	23.73	23.66	3c	Fill
208	A1	S.49	M8	-	-	-	Balk
209	A1	S.49	M8	24.35	24.05	3a-b	Balk
210	A1	S.49	M8	24.05	23.77	3c	Fills
211	A1	S.49	N8	24.30	23.73	3b	
212	A1	S.49	N8	24.38	24.04	3b	Floor?
213	A1	S.49	M–N/8	24.67	24.30	3b	
214	A1	S.49	N8	23.73	23.09	3c	Fills
215	A1	S.49	N8	24.04	24.00	3c	Fills
216	E	S.49	O6	22.61	22.08	3c	Fills
217	E	S.49	O6	22.08	21.96	4a	Burnt layer
218	A2	S.49	N11	25.69	25.15	2, 1	Tower

Locus	Area	Permit No.	Square	Upper Level	Lower Level	Stratum	Description
219	E	S.49	O6	21.96	21.30	4	
220	A1	S.49	N5	24.20	24.00	3c	Fills
221	E	S.49	O10	-	21.86	3c	Fills
222	E	S.49	O10	21.86	21.80	3c	Fills
223	E	S.49	O7	21.80	-	4a	Burnt layer
224	A2	S.49	M6	24.15	23.81	3c	
225	A1	S.49	N7	24.16	-	3c	Fills
226	A1	S.49	M7	23.45	22.96	3c	Fills
227	A1	S.49	N6	24.19	24.00	3c	Fills
228	A1	S.49	M8	23.76	23.68	3c	Fills
229a	A2	S.49	N9	26.20	25.66	1	Fill
229b	A2	S.49	N9	25.66	25.25	2	Floor
230	A1	S.49	M9	21.73	-	4	Fill
231	E	S.49	P/11–12	-	-	-	
232	E	S.49	P–O/10	-	-	2	Fill
233	A1	S.49	N8	23.09	23.00	3c	Fills
234	A1	S.49	M9	-	21.52	4	Above floor
235	A1	S.49	N6	24.65	24.27	3a-b	
236	E	S.49	P9/10	23.85	-	3, 2	Fill
237	A1	S.49	M8	23.68	23.42	3c	Fills
238	A1	S.49	M6	23.81	23.41	3c	Fills
239	.A1	S.49	M9	21.52	20.70	4	
240	E	S.49	O9	24.45	-	3c	Fill
241	A1	S.49	N8	24.32	24.03	3b	Floor makeup
242	A1	S.49	N8	24.03	23.33	3c	Fills
243	A1	S.49	M8	23.42	23.28	3c	Fills
244	A1	S.49	M7	22.96	22.76	3c	Fills
245	A1	S.49	M8	23.28	23.15	3c	Fill
246	A1	S.49	M6	23.44	23.06	3c	Fills
247	A1	S.49	N6	24.27	23.72	3c	Fills
248	A1	S.49	N/6–7	-	24.98	2	Balk
249	A1	S.49	M10	24.73	23.99	3c	Fills
250	A1	S.49	M8	23.15	22.96	3c	Fills
251	A1	S.49	N8	23.35	22.75	3c	Fills
252	F	S.49	M11	-	-	1	Fill
253	E	S.49	N12	-	-	1	Fill
254	E	S.49	O10	-	-	2, 1	Fill
255	A1	S.49	M9	21.00	20.70	4c	
257	A1	S.49	M6	23.06	22.72	3c	Fills
258	A1	S.49	M8	22.96	22.60	3c	Fills
259	A1	S.49	N8	22.75	22.40	3c	Fills
260	A1	S.49	M6	22.72	-	3c	
261	A1	S.49	N/6–7	-	-	-	Cleaning
262	A1	S.49	M10	23.99	22.76	3c	Fills
263	A1	S.49	N10	-	24.46	3a-b	Fill

Locus	Area	Permit No.	Square	Upper Level	Lower Level	Stratum	Description
265	A1	S.49	N8	22.40	21.85	4a	Above floor
266	A1	S.49	N10	24.46	-	3c	Fill
267	A1	S.49	M6	22.72	22.10	4a	Floor
268	A1	S.49	M6	22.72	-	4a	
269	A1	S.49	M7	22.76	22.20	3c	Fill (stones)
270	A1	S.49	N6	23.70	-	3c	Fills
271	A1	S.49	M8	-	22.30	4a	Burnt layer
272	A1	S.49	M8	22.60	21.72	4a	
273	C	S.49	J/5–6	26.00	24.50	3, 2, 1	Mixed
274	C	S.49	J6	26.00	25.01	2, 1	
275	A1	S.49	M10	22.76	22.60	3c	Fills
276	A1	S.49	M8	22.60	21.93	4a	Floor
277	A1	S.49	N6	-	23.12	3c	Fills
278	A1	S.49	M6	22.11	21.97	4a	Installation
279	A1	S.49	M6	21.97	21.57	4b	Above floor
280	A1	S.49	N8	21.85	21.45	4b	Floor
281	A1	S.49	M7	22.70	21.70	4a	Floor
283	A1	S.49	M8	22.36	21.84	4a, b	Fill
284	A1	S.49	M8	21.93	21.75	4b	Above floor
285	A1	S.49	M8	21.72	21.42	4b	Above floor
286	A1	S.49	M10	22.60	22.24	4b	Fill
287	A1	S.49	N8	21.53	21.29	4b	Floor makeup
288	A1	S.49	N6	23.21	22.00	4a	Above floor
289	C	S.49	J/5–6	24.50	24.41	3a-b	Fill
290	A1	S.49	M6	21.57	21.50	4b	Floor
291	A1	S.49	M10	22.24	21.55	4b	Above floor
292	B	S.49	J/9–10	25.70	25.51	2, 1	
293	A1	S.49	M7	21.70	21.60	4b	Above floor
294	B	S.49	J/9–10	25.51	-	2	
295	C	S.49	J6	25.01	-	3a-b	
296	A1	S.49	M8	21.42	21.24	4c	Fill
297	A1	S.49	M8	21.24	21.00	4c	Virgin soil
298	A1	S.49	M10	21.55	21.50	4b	Floor
299	B	S.49	H/9–10	-	-	2, 1	
300	E	S.49	O7	-	-	4	
301	G	S.49	C9	-	-	1	Debris
302	A1	S.49	M7	21.60	21.40	4b	Floor
303	A1	S.49	M7	21.40	-	4	Virgin soil
305	E	S.49	O6	-	-	4	
400	A2	S.66	L/10–11	26.02	-	2	Cleaning
401	A2	S.66	E/9–10	25.91	25.06	2	Above floor
402	A2	S.66	F–H/10	25.36	24.97	2	Fill + floor
403	E	S.66	O6	22/00	21.47	4a	
404	A2	S.66	J/4–5	25.92	25.02	2	Above floor
405	A2	S.66	D9	25.94	25.23	2	Above floor

Locus	Area	Permit No.	Square	Upper Level	Lower Level	Stratum	Description
406	E	S.66	O6	23.45	22.42	3a-b	Fill
407	E	S.66	O7	22.18	21.61	4a	Above floor
408	A2	S.66	D8	25.93	-	2	Above floor
409	A2	S.66	K10	25.93	-	2	Fill
410	A2	S.66	G10	25.71	25.53	1	Pit
411	H	S.66	H4	-	-	2(?)	Fill
412	A2	S.66	K/4–5	25.93	24.95	2	Above floor
413	A2	S.66	F10	-	25.60	2	Fill
414	A2	S.66	E10	25.45	24.45	2	Floor makeup
415	A2	S.66	F10	25.60	-	2	Floor
416	A2	S.66	G10	25.75	25.60	1	Pit
417	B	S.66	G9	26.00	25.34	2	Fill
418	B	S.66	F–G/10	25.80	25.00	2	Dismantling of wall
419	A2	S.66	J/4–5	25.02	24.80	2	Floor makeup
420	A2	S.66	K/4–5	24.95	-	2	Floor makeup
421	C	S.66	J5	25.00	24.80	2	Above floor
422	A2	S.66	J11	-	-	2	Tower
423	A2	S.66	J10	25.95	-	2	Above floor
424	A2	S.66	H–J/10	26.43	-	2	Above floor
425	A2	S.66	D9	-	25.23	2	Floor
426	B	S.66	E9	26.01	25.65	1	Floor & *tabun*
427	A2	S.66	D10	-	-	2	Floor
428	G	S.66	C9	25.30	24.35	2, 1	Fill
429	G	S.66	C9	24.35	23.27	2, 1	Fill
430	G	S.66	C9	24.35	23.19	2	Fill of glacis
451	E	S.66	O6	22.42	21.97	4a	
452	E	S.66	O6	-	24.01	3a-b	Dismantling of floor
453	E	S.66	O6	24.01	23.85	3a-b	Ash layer
454	B	S.66	J10	25.79	-	2, 1	
455	B	S.66	E9	-	25.88	1	Debris
456	A2	S.66	F10	25.60	25.31	2	Above floor
457	B	S.66	F9	26.47	25.62	1	Fill
458	B	S.66	F9	25.62	25.46	2	Above floor
459	A2	S.66	F10	25.40	25.07	2	Floor
460	B	S.66	F9	25.46	25.00	2	Floor
461	B	S.66	G9	25.58	25.37	2	Above floor
462	C	S.66	J5	-	24.80	2	Installation
463	C	S.66	J5	24.80	-	3a-b	Fill
464	C	S.66	J5	24.94	24.19	3a-b	Floor
465	C	S.66	J6	-	-	Mixed	Section
466	B	S.66	J9	25.94	25.65	1	
467	B	S.66	J9	25.65	25.35	2	Fill, debris
468	B	S.66	J9	25.35	25.21	2	Paved floor
469	B	S.66	J/9–10	25.35	25.06	2	Floor
470	B	S.66	J9	25.06	24.90	3, 2	Fill

Locus	Area	Permit No.	Square	Upper Level	Lower Level	Stratum	Description
471	E	S.66	O6	24.47	22.88	3c	Fill
472	E	S.66	O7	21.61	21.40	4b	Above floor
473	G	S.66	C9	23.16	22.03	3a-b	Silo
474	G	S.66	C9	23.19	22.65	3a-b	Above floor
475	G	S.66	C9	22.65	22.36	3a-b	Floor?
476	G	S.66	C9	22.70	22.43	3a-b	
477	B	S.66	E9	25.88	25.71	1	
478	B	S.66	E9	25.71	25.43	2	Above floor
479	A2	S.66	D7	-	24.79	2	Above floor
480	B	S.66	E8	26.02	24.79	2	
481	B	S.66	F9	25.46	24.90	2	Floor
482	A2	S.66	F10	25.02	24.57	2	Below floor
483	B	S.66	G9	25.00	24.90	3a	Fill
485	B	S.66	H9	25.79	25.04	2	Paved floor
486	B	S.66	G9	25.58	24.75	2	Floor, debris
487	E	S.66	O–P/6	22.55	21.81	4a	Brick debris
488	E	S.66	O6	22.02	21.92	4a	Ash layer
489	E	S.66	P6	22.66	21.74	2, 1	Fill
490	B	S.66	E9	25.43	25.02	2	Above floor
491	A2	S.66	D6	25.21	24.80	2	Floor
492	B	S.66	E9	25.43	24.63	2	Floor
493	B	S.66	G9	24.97	24.80	2	Floor
494	B	S.66	G9	24.80	24.17	3b	Above floor
495	B	S.66	H9	24.00	25.37	1	Debris
496	B	S.66	G9	24.80	24.50	3a	
497	B	S.66	H9	25.10	24.70	3a, 2	Fill
498	C	S.66	J5	24.19	23.54	3c	Fills
499	C	S.66	K5	-	-	1	Pit?
500	C	S.66	K5	-	25.13	2, 1	Debris
501	A2	S.66	H–J/10	-	-	2	Floor
502	B	S.66	J8	25.38	24.90	2 (+1)	Above floor
503	B	S.66	J8	24.90	24.77	3a	Below floor
504	B	S.66	J8	24.90	24.77	3a	
505	B	S.66	J9	24.90	24.77	3a	Fill
506	E	S.66	O6	21.92	21.50	4b	Fill
507	E	S.66	O7	21.40	20.88	4	
508	A2	S.66	D7	24.79	-	2	Below floor
509	G	S.66	C9	22.56	22.21	3, 2, 1	Mixed
510	G	S.66	C9	22.21	21.60	3c	Fill
511	G	S.66	C9	21.60	21.30	3c	Fills
512	B	S.66	E9	25.02	24.83	3a	Above floor
513	B	S.66	E8	24.79	24.38	3a	Above floor
514	B	S.66	E9	24.83	24.28	3a	Brick debris
515	B	S.66	E8	26.00	25.02	2	Above floor
516	A2	S.66	D7	25.03	24.80	2	Floor

Locus	Area	Permit No.	Square	Upper Level	Lower Level	Stratum	Description
517	B	S.66	F9	24.89	24.38	3a	Floor
518	B	S.66	F9	24.76	24.35	3a	Brick debris
520	B	S.66	E8	25.02	24.87	2	
521	B	S.66	E8	24.87	-	3a	
522	G	S.66	D8	-	-	1	Debris
523	A2	S.66	D6	26.00	25.20	2	Above floor
524	B	S.66	H9	25.10	24.73	3a, 2	Above floor
525	B	S.66	H9	24.70	24.30	3a-b	Above floor
526	B	S.66	H9	24.70	24.30	3a-b	Above floor
527	B	S.66	E9	24.63	-	3a-b	
528	C	S.66	K5	25.13	24.75	2	Floor
529	C	S.66	K5	25.50	25.00	2	Floor
530	B	S.66	G9	24.90	24.80	3a	Fill
531	B	S.66	G9	24.80	24.12	3a-b	Above floor
532	B	S.66	G9	24.90	24.80	2	Dismantling of wall
533	B	S.66	H9	24.30	22.20	3c	Fill
535	A2	S.66	D5	26.01	25.39	2	Floor
536	B	S.66	J9	24.77	-	3b	
537	B	S.66	J/9–10	24.77	-	3b	
538	B	S.66	J8	24.61	24.19	3b	
539	B	S.66	J9	24.19	23.98	3c	Fill
541	B	S.66	E9	24.28	24.10	3b	Floor
542	A2	S.66	D4	25.72	-	2	Floor
548	B	S.66	H9	25.35	24.80	2	Dismantling of wall
549	B	S.66	H9	22.20	22.00	3c	Fills
553	A2	S.66	D5	-	25.39	2	Floor
554	B	S.66	E9	25.45	25.00	1	Dismantling of wall
560	A2	S.66	D6	25.20	24.90	2	Floor makeup
600	A2	S.89	K/4–5	-	24.92	2	Fill
601	C	S.89	K5	25.09	24.63	3a, 2	Floor + fill
602	C	S.89	J–K/5	25.50	24.46	3a, 2	Dismantling of wall
603	C	S.89	J–K/6	25.67	25.11	2 (+1)	Floor?
604	A2	S.89	L/4–5	25.94	24.92	2	Fill
605	C	S.89	K5	24.63	24.41	3a	
606	C	S.89	J–K/5	24.46	24.00	3a-b	Above floor
607	C	S.89	J–K/6	25.11	24.87	2	Floor
608	C	S.89	K–L/6	26.23	25.37	2, 1	
609	C	S.89	J–K/5	24.00	23.89	3b	
610	H	S.89	K4	-	23.26	1	Debris
611	C	S.89	K6	25.46	24.84	2	Floor
612	C	S.89	K5	24.41	24.25	3a-b	
613	C	S.89	K5	24.41	24.24	3a-b	
615	C	S.89	K–J/5	24.86	24.11	3, 2	Fill of granary
616	C	S.89	K6	25.38	24.95	2	Floor
617	C	S.89	J5	23.76	23.42	3, 2	Fill of granary

Locus	Area	Permit No.	Square	Upper Level	Lower Level	Stratum	Description
618	H	S.89	K4	23.37	22.61	3a-b	Silo
619	C	S.89	K6	24.95	24.46	3a-b	
621	C	S.89	J–K/5	23.45	22.96	3c	Fills
622	C	S.89	K–L/6	24.46	24.11	3a	Fill
623	C	S.89	J6	24.11	-	3, 2	Fill of granary
624	C	S.89	L/5–6	26.00	25.26	2	Debris
625a	C	S.89	K6	24.48	24.16	3a-b	Above floor
625b	C	S.89	K6	24.41	24.16	3, 2	Fill of granary
626	C	S.89	K6	24.46	24.16	3a-b	
627	C	S.89	J5	23.16	22.95	3c	Fills
628	C	S.89	L6	26.06	25.49	1	
629	C	S.89	K6	24.16	23.87	3b	Floor
630	C	S.89	K5	24.08	23.64	3c	Fills
631	C	S.89	K5	24.07	23.64	3c	Fills
632	C	S.89	J5	22.96	22.78	3c	Fills
633	C	S.89	L5	25.93	25.45	2	Debris
634	C	S.89	K6	23.79	23.56	3, 2	Fill of granary
635	C	S.89	K6	24.15	23.83	3b	Floor
636	H	S.89	M–N/4	24.35	21.07	-	Section
637	A2	S.89	D–E/4–5	26.00	25.25	2	Floor
638	C	S.89	J5	22.78	21.36	3c	Fills
639	C	S.89	K6	23.65	23.41	3c	Fills
640	C	S.89	K6	23.83	23.70	3c	Fills
641	C	S.89	K5	23.95	23.28	3c	Fills
642	C	S.89	J5	21.36	21.20	3c	Fill
643	C	S.89	J5	21.20	20.71	4	Silo
644	C	S.89	J5	21.20	20.90	4	Floor
650	C	S.93	K7	25.37	25.19	1	Disturbed
651	C	S.93	J7	25.05	24.55	3, 2	Fill
652	C	S.93	K7	25.19	24.97	2	Floor
653	C	S.93	J7	24.93	24.83	3a-b	Ash
654	C	S.93	J7	24.97	24.83	3, 2	Debris + fill
655	C	S.93	K7	24.83	24.70	3a-b	Burnt layer
656	C	S.93	J7	24.55	24.48	3a-b	Fill
657	C	S.93	J7	24.48	24.36	3a-b	Floor
658	C	S.93	J7	24.48	24.36	3a-b	Above floor
659	C	S.93	K7	24.77	24.60	3a-b	Fill
660	C	S.93	J7	24.36	-	3a-b	Floor?
661	C	S.93	J7	24.36	24.24	3a-b	
662	C	S.93	K7	24.60	24.55	3a-b	Above floor
663	C	S.93	J6	24.91	24.28	3, 2	Fill of granary
664	C	S.93	J5	23.01	22.91	3c	Fills
665	C	S.93	K7	24.55	24.40	3a-b	
666	C	S.93	K7	24.55	24.40	3a-b	
667	C	S.93	J7	24.27	23.89	3c	Fills

Locus	Area	Permit No.	Square	Upper Level	Lower Level	Stratum	Description
668	C	S.93	J5	22.91	22.51	3c	Fills
669	C	S.93	K7	24.50	24.40	3a-b	
670	C	S.93	K7	24.55	24.30	3, 2	Pit in silo
671	C	S.93	J7	24.36	23.96	3b +3c	Floor + fill
672	C	S.93	K7	24.30	24.19	3a-b	
673	C	S.93	J6	24.28	24.25	3a-b	Fill of granary
674	C	S.93	J5	22.51	21.29	4	Fill
675	C	S.93	K7	24.42	23.34	3a-b	Silo
676	C	S.93	J7	23.89	23.79	3c	Fills
677	C	S.93	J7	24.36	23.96	3b, 3c	Floor + fill
678	C	S.93	J6	24.91	24.34	3, 2	Fill of granary
679	C	S.93	J7	23.92	23.66	3c	Fills
680	C	S.93	J7	23.80	23.66	3c	Fills
681	C	S.93	J7	23.96	23.66	3c	Fills
682	C	S.93	J7	23.96	23.58	3c	Fills
683	C	S.93	K7	24.24	24.00	3a-b	
684	C	S.93	K7	24.24	24.00	3a-b	
685	C	S.93	L6	25.44	25.27	2	Debris
686	C	S.93	L6	25.27	25.20	2	Above floor
687	C	S.93	J5	21.29	21.19	4	Above floor
688	C	S.93	L7	25.96	25.33	1	
689	C	S.92	J–K/6	23.47	23.15	3, 2	Fill of granary
690	C	S.93	L7	25.93	25.40	1	Installation
691	C	S.93	L6	25.08	24.81	3, 2	Mixed
692	C	S.93	K6	23.89	23.52	3c	Fills
693	C	S.93	K5	23.34	23.00	3c	Fills
694	C	S.93	J–K/6	23.15	22.89	3, 2	Fill of granary
695	C	S.93	K5	23.00	22.65	3c	Fills
696	C	S.93	L7	25.33	25.20	2	Floor
697	C	S.93	L6	24.81	24.45	3a-b	Fill
698	C	S.93	K6	23.52	23.30	3c	Fills
699	C	S.93	K5	22.65	22.16	3c	Fills
700	C	S.93	L7	25.20	24.86	3, 2	Mixed
701	B	S.89	F8	25.55	25.07	1	Fill
702	B	S.89	G8	24.85	24.50	2, 1	Fill
703	B	S.98	H8	25.30	25.03	2	Floor
704	B	S.89	G7	24.90	24.00	-	Fill
705	B	S.89	G9	25.62	24.64	1	Pit
706	B	S.89	G9	25.72	25.00	1	Pit
707	B	S.89	H8	24.60	24.45	3a-b	Fill
708	B	S.89	F8	25.30	25.00	2	Above floor
709	B	S.89	G7	24.34	23.26–23.11	3a-b	Floor
710	B	S.89	F9	24.54	24.15	3a	Above floor
711	B	S.89	F9	24.15	24.11	3a	Floor
712	B	S.89	F9	24.89	24.46	3a	Floor

Locus	Area	Permit No.	Square	Upper Level	Lower Level	Stratum	Description
713	B	S.89	F8	25.00	24.62	3a	Floor
714	B	S.89	F8	25.00	24.60	3a	Floor
715	B	S.89	G8	24.54	24.02	3b	Floor
716	B	S.89	G7	24.26	23.70	3c	Fills
717	B	S.89	H8	24.76	24.50	2	Installation
718	B	S.89	F7	24.12	-	3a	Floor
719	B	S.89	F7	25.00	24.45	3a	Paved floor
720	B	S.89	F9	24.40	24.15	3b	Paved floor
721	B	S.89	G8	24.84	24.28	2	Installation
722	B	S.89	H9	25.15	24.60	3a	Above floor
723	B	S.89	F7	24.28	24.11	3b	Floor
724	B	S.89	E7	25.50	24.60	3a, 2	
725	B	S.89	E7	25.50	24.40	3a, 2	
726	B	S.89	F9	24.15	23.90	3b	Floor
727	B	S.89	G9	24.10	23.90	3b	Floor
728	B	S.89	G9	24.23	23.98	3b	Floor
729	B	S.89	E7	24.80	24.50	3a-b	Fill + floor
730	B	S.89	F9	24.30	24.07	3b	Installation
731	B	S.89	E8	24.89	24.57	3a	Fill + burial
732	B	S.89	E8	25.82	25.24	2	Debris
733	B	S.89	G8	24.50	24.28	3b	Floor
734	B	S.89	G8	24.28	24.00	3c	Fills
735	B	S.89	G8	24.00	23.90	3c	Fills
736	B	S.89	F9	23.80	23.60	3c	Fills
737	B	S.89	E8	25.24	24.82	3a, 2	Fill
738	B	S.89	F8	24.45	24.35	3b	Floor
739	B	S.89	F8	24.44	24.35	3b	Ṭabun
740	B	S.89	E7	24.85	24.75	3a	Floor
741	B	S.89	E7	24.88	24.70	3a	Floor
742	B	S.89	E7	24.78	24.64	3a	Floor
743	B	S.89	E7	24.75	24.32	3b	Floor
744	B	S.89	J8	-	24.25	-	Cleaning
745	B	S.89	E9	26.00	25.59	1	Fill
746	B	S.89	E9	25.59	25.00	2	Floor
747	B	S.89	G9	24.50	24.27	3b	Above floor
748	B	S.89	G9	24.20	24.00	3b	Floor
749	B	S.89	G8	24.80	24.40	3b	Above floor
750	B	S.89	F8	24.57	24.38	3b	Floor
751	B	S.89	G9	24.30	24.08	3b	Floor
752	B	S.89	G7	23.70	23.50	3c	Fills
753	B	S.89	G7	23.50	22.83	3c	Fills
760	B	S.93	G7	22.73	22.24	3c	Fills
761	B	S.93	E–F/8–9	25.75	25.00	2	
762	B	S.93	E–F/9	25.75	25.20	2	
763	B	S.93	F/8–9	25.70	24.90	2	

Locus	Area	Permit No.	Square	Upper Level	Lower Level	Stratum	Description
764	B	S.89	F–G/9	25.80	25.00	2	
766	B	S.93	G–H/8–9	25.10	24.80	2	Fill
767	B	S.93	F–G/9	24.98	24.20	3b	Balk
768	B	S.93	G9	24.83	24.00	3b, 2	Balk
769	B	S.93	H9	26.40	25.35	2	Floor
770	B	S.93	J9	25.70	25.48	2	Fill
771	B	S.93	J9	25.48	25.00	2	Floor
772	B	S.93	F8	25.14	24.30	3a	Fill
773	B	S.93	H–J/9	25.37	24.68	3a	Floor
774	B	S.93	E5	25.47	24.75	2	Floor
775	B	S.93	E8	25.25	25.00	2	Floor
776	B	S.93	E9	25.00	24.55	3a	Floor
778	B	S.93	H9	24.68	24.30	3b	Floor
779	B	S.93	H9	24.60	24.28	3b	Floor
780	B	S.93	H9	24.20	24.00	3b	Floor makeup
781	B	S.93	G/6–7	22.25	22.00	3c	Fills
782	B	S.93	G7	22.00	21.00	4	Floor
784	B	S.93	G7	24.30	24.26	3b	Cleaning
785	B	S.93	F9	24.26	23.80	3b	Floor
786	B	S.93	H–J/8	24.92	24.66	3a	Above floor
787	B	S.93	H–J/8	24.66	24.33	3b	Above floor
789	B	S.93	H9	24.32	24.05	3c	Fill
790	B	S.93	G–H/8	24.89	24.69	3c	Fill
791	B	S.93	G8	24.70	24.07	3b	Floor
792	B	S.93	H8	24.41	24.01	3b	Floor
793	B	S.93	H9	23.97	22.80	3c	Fills
794	B	S.93	J8	24.10	23.81	3b	Floor
795	B	S.93	E6	24.79	24.45	3a	Above floor
796	B	S.93	F8	24.45	24.30	3b	Floor
797	B	S.93	E9	24.09	23.81	3b	Floor
798	B	S.93	E7	24.80	24.50	3a	Floor
799	B	S.93	J/8–9	25.18	24.80	3a	Fill
800	B	S.93	H8	23.80	23.30	3c	Fills
801	E	S.89	O/9–10	25.88	24.43	3, 2	Glacis fill down to floor
802	E	S.89	P9	24.22	22.26	2	Fill
803	E	S.89	P10	23.69	22.52	3c	Fills
804	E	S.89	O9	24.00	23.82	3a-b	Floor makeup
805	E	S.89	O10	24.43	22.68	3c	Fill
806	E	S.89	P10	22.52	21.99	3c	Fills
807	E	S.89	P9	22.26	21.72	4b	Above floor
808	E	S.89	P9	22.26	21.93	3c	Debris
809	E	S.89	P10	22.52	21.93	3c	Fills
810	E	S.89	O9	24.05	22.40	3c	Fills
811	E	S.89	P10	21.99	21.64	4b	Above floor
812	E	S.89	O10	22.68	22.09	3c	Fills

Locus	Area	Permit No.	Square	Upper Level	Lower Level	Stratum	Description
813	E	S.89	P10	21.64	21.15	4c	Below floor
814	E	S.89	P9	21.93	21.61	3c	Fills
815	E	S.89	P10	21.61	21.23	3c	Fills
816	E	S.89	O10	22.09	21.63	4b	Floor
817	E	S.89	O9	22.40	22.30	3c	Fill
818	E	S.89	P9	21.50	21.01	4c	Fill
819	E	S.89	O9	22.30	21.95	4b	Fill
820	E	S.89	O9	22.30	21.63	4b	Floor
821	E	S.89	O10	21.63	20.55	4c	Below floor
822	E	S.89	O9	21.63	21.23	4c	Fill
823	E	S.89	P9	21.93	21.64	4b	Floor
850	F	S.93	K–M/11	25.70	24.40	2	Fill, debris
851	F	S.93	K–L/11	24.40	23.40	2	Fill of glacis
852	F	S.93	M11	24.40	23.10	2	Fill of glacis
853	F	S.93	K11	23.61	23.00	3a-b	Floor
854	F	S.93	M11	23.10	22.37	3a-b	Silo
855	F	S.93	M11	23.18	22.84	3a-b	Fill
856	F	S.93	K11	23.43	23.10	3a-b	*Ṭabun*
857	F	S.93	K11	23.54	23.18	3a-b	Floor
858	F	S.93	L11	23.54	22.46	3a-b	Silo
859	F	S.93	K11	23.32	23.18	3a-b	*Ṭabun*
860	F	S.93	K11	23.54	23.13	3a-b	Fill
861	F	S.93	M11	22.17	21.53	3a-b	Hearth in silo
862	F	S.93	L11	23.13	21.97	3a-b	Silo
863	F	S.93	L11	23.50	22.89	3a-b	Above floor
864	F	S.93	L11	23.00	22.33	3a-b	Silo
865	F	S.93	H–J/11	-	23.76	3, 2, 1	Debris
901	A2	S.89	G–H/4	-	24.50	2	Above floor
902	H	S.89	H/3–4	-	22.90	3a-b	Crushed lime surface
903	A2	S.89	F–G/4	25.41	24.46	2	Above floor
904	D	S.89	H5	25.21	24.67	3, 2	Debris
905	D	S.89	H5	24.47	24.17	2	
906	D	S.89	H5	24.47	-	3, 2	Debris
907	H	S.89	H/3–4	22.90	-	3a-b	Fills
908	D	S.89	H5	24.42	23.96	3a-b	
909	D	S.89	H5	-	-	2	
910	H	S.93	G/3–4	22.94	-	3a-b	Fill of rampart
911	H	S.93	H/3–4	22.39	21.29	3a-b	Fill of rampart
912	G	S.93	B–C/3	-	-	1	Debris
913	G	S.93	C4	-	-	1	Debris
914	H	S.93	H/3–4	21.29	21.15	3c	Fill of rampart
915	H	S.93	H/3–4	21.15	20.70	3c	Fill of rampart
916	H	S.93	H/3–4	20.70	20.40	3c	Fill of rampart
917	H	S.93	H4	20.40	20.18	4	Living surface
918	H	S.93	H4	20.18	19.76	4?	Below floor

Locus	Area	Permit No.	Square	Upper Level	Lower Level	Stratum	Description
919	H	S.93	H3	20.18	19.76	Pre-4	Below floor
920a	H	S.93	H3	21.41	20.30	3c	Fill of rampart
920b	H	S.93	H3	20.30	19.76	4	
921	H	S.93	H3	19.93	19.49	4	Fill in silo
922	E	S.93	O7	-	-	4	Cleaning
923	E	S.93	O6	-	21.26	4	Cleaning
924	E	S.93	P6	23.17	22.50	3c	Fills
925	E	S.93	Q5	21.60	20.70	1	Debris
926	E	S.93	O6	21.90	21.41	4b	Above floor
927	E	S.93	O7	-	-	-	Cleaning
928	E	S.93	O6	21.26	20.95	4c	
929	E	S.93	P6	22.50	21.95	3c	Fills
930	E	S.93	O7	21.60	21.40	4b	Above floor
931	E	S.93	P7	-	-	-	Cleaning
932	E	S.93	P5	21.55	21.12	1	Debris
933	E	S.93	P7	21.60	21.40	4b	Floor
934	E	S.93	O7	21.80	21.60	4b	Above floor
935	E	S.93	O7	22.40	21.80	4a	Dismantling of wall
936	E	S.93	P6	21.95	21.77	4a	Fill
937	E	S.93	P6	21.46	21.40	4b	Floor
938	E	S.93	P6	21.60	21.42	4b	Floor
939	E	S.93	P6	22.80	21.96	4a, b	Fill
940	E	S.93	O7	21.48	21.33	4b	Floor makeup
941	E	S.93	P7	21.96	21.60	4b	Above floor
942	E	S.93	P7	22.23	21.60	4a	Fill
944	E	S.93	O7	21.24	20.98	4c	Floor
945	E	S.93	O9	21.51	21.32	4a	Fill
946	E	S.93	O7	21.79	21.00	4b	Added to 954
947	E	S.93	P7	21.91	-	4b	Fill
948	E	S.93	P7	22.00	21.67	4, 3, 2, 1	Mixed fill
949	E	S.93	P8	21.95	21.75	4b	Floor
950	E	S.93	P8	-	22.25	4, 3, 2, 1	Mixed debris
951	E	S.93	P8	22.25	21.75	4, 3, 2, 1	Mixed fill
952	E	S.93	O–P/8	21.95	21.57	4b	Floor
953	E	S.93	P7	21.70	21.40	4b	Floor
954	E	S.93	P7	21.79	21.00	4b	Fill
955	E	S.93	P8	21.91	21.68	4b	Floor
956	E	S.93	P8	21.90	21.68	4b	Floor
957	E	S.93	P8	-	-	4b	Fill
1001	H	S.89	N–M/4	-	-	1	Cleaning
1002	E	S.89	O6	22.84	22.64	3a-b	Dismantling of wall
1003	E	S.89	P7	23.89	-	1	Cleaning
1004	E	S.89	O7	24.02	22.38	3a-b	Dismantling of wall
1005	E	S.89	P6	22.50	-	4a	Fill
1006	E	S.89	O6	22.63	22.00	4a	Fill

Locus	Area	Permit No.	Square	Upper Level	Lower Level	Stratum	Description
1007a	E	S.89	O6	21.55	21.40	4b	Floor
1007b	E	S.89	O6	21.45	21.05	4c	Floor
1008	E	S.89	O7	22.40	22.20	3c	Fills
1009	E	S.89	O6	21.83	21.09	4b	Fill
1010	E	S.89	O6	21.85	21.30	4b	Burnt layer
1011	E	S.89	P7	21.69	21.46	4b	Fill
1012	E	S.89	O6	24.30	21.09	4c	Floor
1013	E	S.89	P7	21.46	-	4c	Fill
1050	D	S.93	H6	24.22	23.77	2, 1	Debris
1051	D	S.93	H5	24.00	23.92	3a	Fill
1052	D	S.93	H5	24.40	23.76	3a	Fill
1053	D	S.93	H5	24.40	23.84	3a	Fill
1054	D	S.93	G5	24.00	23.51	2, 1	Fill in cistern
1055	D	S.93	G5	23.98	23.44	-	Mixed
1056	D	S.93	H5	23.76	22.95	3c	Fill + debris
1057	D	S.93	H5	23.84	23.82	3b	Floor
1058	D	S.93	H5	23.92	23.83	3b	Above floor
1059	D	S.93	H5	23.84	22.67	3c	Fills
1060	D	S.93	H5	23.82	23.50	3c	Fills
1061	D	S.93	H6	23.91	23.80	3, 2	Debris
1062	D	S.93	H5	23.83	23.80	3a	Fill
1063	D	S.93	H5	23.80	23.40	3b	Above floor
1064	D	S.93	H6	23.77	23.64	3a	Debris
1065	D	S.93	H6	23.81	23.64	3b	Floor
1066	D	S.93	H6	23.73	23.49	3b	Debris
1067	D	S.93	H6	24.39	23.94	3a	Debris
1068	D	S.93	H5	23.80	23.62	3b	Floor
1069	D	S.93	H6	24.39	24.04	-	Pit
1070	D	S.93	H6	23.62	23.45	3c	Fills
1071	D	S.93	H5	23.45	23.03	3c	Fills
1072	D	S.93	G5	23.43	23.06	3c	Fills
1073	D	S.93	G5	23.43	21.08	2, 1	Fill in cistern
1075	D	S.93	H5	23.40	22.93	3c	Fills
1076	D	S.93	H6	23.96	23.86	3b	Floor
1077	D	S.93	H6	23.49	23.02	3c	Fills
1078	D	S.93	H6	23.64	23.00	3c	Fills
1079	D	S.93	H6	23.81	23.24	3c	Fills
1080	D	S.93	G5	23.55	23.34	-	Debris, fill
1082	D	S.93	H6	23.86	23.46	3c	Fills
1083	D	S.93	H5	23.50	23.19	3c	Fills
1085	D	S.93	H6	23.46	23.39	3c	Fills
1086	D	S.93	G5	23.06	22.73	3c	Fills
1088	D	S.93	G5	22.98	22.18	3c	Fills
1089	D	S.93	H5	24.40	24.26	3a	Fill
1090	D	S.93	G6	24.20	22.85	2, 1	Fill in cistern

Locus	Area	Permit No.	Square	Upper Level	Lower Level	Stratum	Description
1091	D	S.93	H6	23.80	23.75	3b	Floor
1092	D	S.93	H5	22.93	22.25	3c	Fills
1093	D	S.93	H5	23.03	22.59	3c	Fills
1094	D	S.93	G5	23.52	23.46	3a, b	Floor
1095	D	S.93	H6	23.10	22.09	3c	Fill
1096	D	S.93	H6	23.10	22.86	3c	Fill
1097	D	S.93	G5	23.46	22.06	3c	Fill
1099	D	S.93	H6	22.86	22.70	3c	Fills
1100	D	S.93	G5	22.18	21.60	3c	Stone surface
1101	C	S.93	L6	24.45	24.25	3a-b	Fill
1102	C	S.93	J–K/6	22.89	22.82	3, 2	Fill of granary
1103	C	S.93	K5	22.16	-	3c	Fills
1104	C	S.93	L6	24.25	-	3a-b	Floor (disturbed)
1105	C	S.93	L7	25.46	25.04	2	Floor
1106	C	S.93	L7	24.86	24.49	3a-b	Fill (disturbed)
1107	C	S.93	L7	25.34	25.10	2	Floor makeup
1108	C	S.93	L7	24.49	24.36	3, 1	Floor + pit
1109	C	S.93	L7	25.11	-	3a-b	Fill
1201	B	S.93	F8	24.40	23.96	3c	Fills
1202	B	S.93	E9	24.00	23.70	3b	Floor
1203	B	S.93	E/7–8	25.50	25.00	2	Floor (balk)
1204	B	S.93	E8	25.09	24.68	3a	Floor (disturbed?)
1205	B	S.93	F7	24.35	22.84	3c	Fills
1206	B	S.93	E7	24.69	24.16	3a	
1207	B	S.93	E5	24.75	24.21	3a	Floor
1208	B	S.93	E8	24.60	24.30	3a	Floor
1209	B	S.93	E7	24.53	24.38	3a	Floor makeup
1210	B	S.93	E9	24.55	24.30	3b	Above floor
1211	B	S.93	E9	24.68	24.37	3a	Floor
1212	B	S.93	E9	24.37	24.10	3b	Floor
1213	B	S.93	E8	24.68	24.05	3b	Floor
1214	B	S.93	F9	24.16	23.91	3b	Floor
1215	B	S.93	F9	25.00	24.59	3a	Debris
1216	B	S.93	E6	24.37	23.98	3a	Floor
1217	B	S.93	H8	25.00	24.50	3a	Floor
1218	B	S.93	H8	24.70	24.20	3b	Fill
1219	B	S.93	G7	23.25	22.68	3c	Fills
1220	B	S.93	F5	25.06	24.74	2	Fill
1221	B	S.93	F5	24.65	24.26	3b	Floor
1222	B	S.93	G8	24.29	24.18	3b	Fill
1223	B	S.93	G8	24.18	23.98	3b	Floor
1224	B	S.93	J8	23.30	22.78	3c	Fills
1225	B	S.93	E8	24.48	24.29	3b	Fill
1226	B	S.93	F5	24.37	23.28	3c, 1	Fill (disturbed)
1227	B	S.93	G7	22.70	22.13	3c	Fills

Locus	Area	Permit No.	Square	Upper Level	Lower Level	Stratum	Description
1228	B	S.93	E/8–9	24.25	23.90	3b	Floor
1229	B	S.93	J8	24.33	23.88	3b	Floor
1230	B	S.93	J8	23.85	22.70	3c	Fills
1231	B	S.93	G7	21.90	21.00	3c	Fills
1232	B	S.93	E7	24.75	24.42	4a	Fill
1233	B	S.93	E5	24.62	24.22	3a	Fill
1234	B	S.93	G8	-	-	-	Mixed (balk)
1235	B	S.93	J8	22.78	22.00	3c	Fills
1236	B	S.93	J8	22.00	21.40	3c	Fills
1237	B	S.93	G7	21.90	21.00	4	Floor
1238	B	S.93	J8	22.70	22.00	3c	Fills
1239	B	S.93	J8	22.00	21.50	3c	Fills
1240	B	S.93	E6	23.90	23.04	3c	Fills
1241	B	S.93	E7	24.63	24.48	3a	Floor
1242	B	S.93	E5	24.25	23.97	3b	
1243	B	S.93	F5	24.11	23.78	3b	
1244	B	S.93	F8–9	24.78	24.17	3a-b	Balk
1245	B	S.93	J8	21.50	21.00	4	Above floor
1301	D	S.93	G6	22.85	20.85	1, 2	Fill in cistern
1302	D	S.93	H6	23.45	22.54	3c	Fills
1303	D	S.93	H6	23.94	22.27	3c	Fill, debris
1304	D	S.93	G5	21.60	20.60	3, 2, 1	Fill in channel
1305	D	S.93	G5	22.06	21.81	3c	Fill, debris
1350	C	S.93	L9	25.75	25.42	2	Fill
1351	C	S.93	K9	25.73	25.32	2	
1352	A2	S.93	K10	-	-	2	Fill
1400	D	S.109	G6	24.22	20.89	2, 1	Fill in cistern
1401	D	S.109	H6	23.30	22.31	3c	Fills
1402	D	S.109	H6	23.10	22.57	3c	Fills
1403	D	S.109	G5	22.55	21.99	3c	Fill
1404	D	S.109	G5	22.19	20.95	1, 2	Fill in cistern
1405	D	S.109	G5	21.91	20.57	4, 3c	Fill
1406	D	S.109	H5	23.58	21.50	3c	Fills
1407	D	S.109	G–H/5	24.00	22.32	-	Mixed
1408	D	S.109	H5	22.32	21.44	3c	Fill
1409	D	S.109	H5	22.21	21.28	3c	Fill
1410	D	S.109	G5	21.25	19.12	2, 1	Fill in cistern
1411	D	S.109	G6	20.07	19.07	2, 1	Fill in cistern
1412	D	S.109	H5	21.44	21.14	4	Floor
1413	D	S.109	H5	21.50	21.18	3c	Fill
1414	D	S.109	H6	22.35	21.65	3c	Fill
1415	D	S.109	H6	22.85	21.59	3c	Fill
1416	D	S.109	H5	21.18	20.68	3c	Debris in silo
1417	D	S.109	H5	21.18	19.90	4	Silo
1419	D	S.109	H5	21.18	20.73	4	Fill

Locus	Area	Permit No.	Square	Upper Level	Lower Level	Stratum	Description
1420	D	S.109	H5	21.14	21.10	4	Floor makeup
1421	D	S.109	H5	21.10	21.03	4	
1422	D	S.109	H6	22.73	22.33	-	Fill
1423	D	S.109	G5	20.57	19.91	-	Fill
1424	D	S.109	H5	21.03	20.14	4c	Fill
1500	D	S.114	G/5–6	24.15	18.60	2, 1	Fill in cistern
1501	D	S.114	H6	21.74	21.29	3c	Fill
1502	D	S.114	H6	21.42	21.23	4	Floor
1503	D	S.114	H6	21.23	21.17	4	Floor makeup
1510	D	S.119	G–H/6	24.20	22.73	2, 1	Fill in cistern
1511	D	S.119	H6	21.17	20.81	4	Section
1512	D	S.119	G6	22.73	17.33	2, 1	Fill in cistern
1513	D	S.119	G6	17.77	17.30	2, 1	Fill in cistern
1514	D	S.119	G6	17.36	17.10	3–2	Floor of cistern
1515	D	S.119	F6	21.20	20.54	2, 1	Fill in cistern
1516	D	S.119	G6	17.18	16.79	3	Section—cistern
1517	H	S.119	G3	20.59	20.56	3	Section—channel
1518	H	S.119	G3	20.55	20.51	3	Section—channel
1519	H	S.119	G3	20.60	19.82	3	Section—channel
1520	H	S.119	G3	20.46	20.37	3	Section—channel
1521	D	S.119	G5	20.60	20.59	3	Section—cistern
1522	H	S.119	G3	20.35	20.21	3c	
1523	H	S.119	H/1–2	19.47	16.41	-	Section—geological
2000	E	S.109	P10	21.26	20.97	-	Cleaning
2001	E	S.109	P7/8	21.24	20.26	4c	
2002	E	S.109	P8	21.07	20.88	-	Fill
2003	E	S.109	P11	20.92	19.85	2, 1	Fill, debris
2004	E	S.109	O9	21.29	21.00	4c	Fill
2005	E	S.109	O7	21.18	21.00	4b	Pit
2006	E	S.109	Q10	20.19	19.27	2	Fill in moat
2007	E	S.109	O10	21.00	20.91	4	Fill
2008	E	S.109	p8	20.88	20.14	-	Fill
2009	E	S.109	Q9	20.06	19.08	2	Moat
2010	E	S.109	Q8	20.06	19.50	2	Debris in moat
2011	E	S.109	Q6	20.06	19.26	2	Fill in moat
2012	E	S.109	Q9	18.89	18.62	2	Floor in moat
2013	E	S.109	Q8	18.89	18.39	2	Floor in moat
2014	E	S.109	Q6	19.38	18.77	2	Floor in moat
2015	E	S.109	Q5	20.06	19.83	2	Fill in moat
2016	E	S.109	Q5	19.89	19.45	2	Floor in moat
2018	E	S.109	Q11	20.25	19.47	2	Fill in moat
2019	E	S.109	Q13	19.38	18.58	2	Fill in moat
2020	E	S.109	Q12	19.11	18.59	2	Fill in moat
2021	E	S.109	Q10	19.27	19.27	2	Floor in moat
2022	E	S.109	Q9	18.84	-	2	Fill in moat

Locus	Area	Permit No.	Square	Upper Level	Lower Level	Stratum	Description
2023	E	S.109	Q8	18.70	18.53	2	Floor in moat
2024	E	S.109	Q9	18.61	-	2	Fill in moat
2025	E	S.109	Q9	19.73	19.02	2	Fill in moat
2026	E	S.109	Q11	19.03	-	2	Floor(?) in moat
2027	E	S.109	Q12	18.44	-	2	Fill
2028	E	S.109	Q9	18.85	-	2	Floor + fill, moat
2029	E	S.109	Q9	18.42	-	2	Fill in moat
2030	E	S.109	Q11	18.22	-	2	Fill in moat
2150	E	S.114	Q9	18.43	18.11	2	Fill in moat
2151	F	S.114	P/12–13	18.70	18.15	2	Fill in moat
2152	E	S.114	Q9	18.07	-	2	Cleaning
2153	E	S.114	O13	18.47	18.40	2	Fill in moat
2154	F	S.114	L–M/13	18.19	18.14	2	Fill in moat
2155	F	S.114	P13	18.91	-	2	Fill in moat
2156	F	S.114	P13	18.40	17.67	2	Fill in moat
2157	E	S.114	Q9	19.50	18.97	2	Fill in moat
2158	F	S.114	P13	18.91	18.61	2	Fill
2159	E	S.114	Q9	18.97	18.08	2	Floor in moat
3000	B	S.99	H8	25.00	24.47	3a	Fill
3001	B	S.99	J9	25.10	24.64	3a	Fill
3002	B	S.99	H9	25.10	24.91	3a	Fill
3003	B	S.99	F8	24.60	24.44	3a	Fill above floor
3004	B	S.99	F8	24.44	24.16	3b	Floor
3005	B	S.99	H9	24.91	24.57	3a	Floor
3006	B	S.99	H9	24.90	24.60	3a	Floor
3007	B	S.99	H8	24.50	24.16	3b	Floor
3008	B	S.99	F8	24.16	23.68	3c	Fills
3009	B	S.99	H8	24.47	24.24	3b	Floor
3010	B	S.99	H9	24.47	24.05	-	Section
3011	B	S.99	J9	24.57	24.31	3a	Floor
3012	A2	S.99	J10	25.60	25.11	2	Floor
3013	B	S.99	H9	24.60	24.37	3b	Floor
3014	B	S.99	H9	24.60	24.09	3b	Floor
3015	C	S.99	L9	25.60	25.28	2	Fill
3016	B	S.99	G–H/8	24.90	24.77	2	Installation
3017	B	S.99	G–H/8	24.77	24.40	3a	Fill
3018	B	S.99	H8	24.40	24.03	3b	Floor
3019	C	S.99	L9	25.28	24.90	3a-b	Fill
3020	B	S.99	H9	24.37	23.80	3c	Fill
3021	B	S.99	J9	24.31	24.10	3b	Floor
3022	B	S.99	F8	23.68	23.31	3c	Fills
3023	C	S.99	L9	25.90	24.75	1	Pit
3024	C	S.99	L9	24.90	24.77	3a-b	Floor
3025	B	S.99	J9	24.35	24.19	3b	Floor
3026	B	S.99	J9	24.40	24.18	3b	Floor

Locus	Area	Permit No.	Square	Upper Level	Lower Level	Stratum	Description
3027	C	S.99	L9	24.90	24.65	3a-b	Floor
3040	B	S.109	E5	24.57	24.14	3b	Fill
3041	B	S.109	E5	24.14	23.76	3b	Fill
3042	B	S.109	E5	23.99	23.72	3b	Floor
3043	B	S.109	H9	24.98	24.45	4b	
3044	B	S.109	J8	24.00	21.38	3c	Fills
3045	B	S.109	J9	24.50	24.14	3a-b	Cleaning
3046	B	S.109	J9	25.03	24.80	3a	Fill (balk)
3047	B	S.109	J9	24.80	24.51	3a	Floor
3048	B	S.109	H9	24.45	24.14	3b	Floor
3049	B	S.109	H8	24.86	24.59	3a	Floor
3050	B	S.109	G8	24.05	23.65	3c	
3051	B	S.109	G8	24.39	23.97	3b	Fill
3052	B	S.109	F9	24.11	23.79	3b	Fill
3053	B	S.109	F5	23.72	23.14	3b	Floor
3054	B	S.109	F8	24.68	24.44	3b	Floor
3055	B	S.109	G9	24.08	23.81	3c	Fill
3056	B	S.109	G9	23.94	23.50	3c	Fill
3057	B	S.109	G9	24.11	23.58	3c	Fills
3058	B	S.109	G8	24.03	23.79	3c	Fills
3059	B	S.109	H8	24.59	23.99	3b	Floor
3060	B	S.109	J/8–9	24.39	24.09	3b	Floor
3061	B	S.109	J9	24.51	24.13	3b	Floor
3062	B	S.109	F5	23.10	22.98	3c	Fill
3063	B	S.109	F5	22.98	20.98	2, 1	Fill in cistern
3064	B	S.109	J8	21.38	21.18	4	Above floor
3065	B	S.109	F5	22.98	22.00	3c	Fills
3066	B	S.109	E8	24.46	24.34	3b	Above floor
3067	B	S.109	G9	23.89	23.72	3c	Fills
3068	B	S.109	J8	21.18	20.97	4	Floor
3069	B	S.109	F8	24.49	24.20	3b	Floor
3070	B	S.109	G9	23.82	23.52	3c	Fills
3071	B	S.109	J8	21.05	20.93	4	Floor
3072	B	S.109	J8	20.92	19.69	4	Silo
3073	B	S.109	E5	24.70	24.44	-	Mixed (balk)
3074	B	S.109	E5	24.44	23.97	-	Fill (balk)
3075	B	S.109	H/8–9	24.50	24.21	3a	Installation
3076	B	S.109	F5	23.75	22.85	3c	Fills + burial
3077	B	S.109	J8	20.96	20.52	Pre-4	Virgin soil
3078	B	S.109	F5	24.80	23.58	1	Fill (balk)
3079	B	S.109	H7	24.50	24.27	3b	Fill
3080	B	S.109	F5	22.67	21.99	3c	Fills
3081	B	S.109	F8	24.00	23.50	3c	Fills
3082	B	S.109	G8	24.14	-	3b	Floor
3083	B	S.109	H7	24.25	23.74	3b	Floor

Locus	Area	Permit No.	Square	Upper Level	Lower Level	Stratum	Description
3084	B	S.109	H7	24.30	23.98	1	Pit
3085	B	S.109	F8	23.50	21.70	3c	Fills
3086	B	S.109	F6	22.80	22.18	2, 1	Fill in cistern
3087	B	S.109	F6	22.18	21.60	2, 1	Fill in cistern
3088	B	S.109	F5	21.50	19.98	3c	Fills
3089	B	S.109	F8	22.03	21.73	3c	Fills
3090	B	S.109	H7	24.27	24.00	3b	
3092	B	S.109	F8	21.73	21.55	4	Above floor
3093	B	S.109	F8	21.73	21.56	4	Above floor
3094	B	S.109	F8	21.75	21.45	4	Above floor
3095	B	S.109	F8	21.47	21.11	4a	Floor
3096	B	S.109	F8	21.11	21.00	4b	Floor
3097	B	S.109	F8	21.00	20.80	4c	
3150	B	S.114	F/8–9	24.24	23.78	3c	Fills
3151	B	S.114	F/8–9	24.24	23.78	3c	Fills
3152	B	S.114	F/5–6	23.61	22.72	2, 1	Fill in cistern
3153	B	S.114	F/8–9	23.00	22.00	3c	Fills
3154	B	S.114	G9	23.68	23.07	3c	Fills
3155	B	S.114	G9	23.68	22.84	3c	Fills
3156	B	S.114	E6	24.00	23.17	3c	Fills
3157	B	S.114	E6	23.17	22.70	3c	Fills
3158	B	S.114	E6	22.70	21.20	4 (?3c)	Above floor
3159	B	S.114	F8	22.00	21.03	4	Floor
3160	B	S.114	E8	22.00	21.05	4	Floor
3161	B	S.114	G9	23.68	23.11	3c	Fills
3162	B	S.114	F8	22.00	21.60	4a	Floor
3163	B	S.114	F8	22.00	21.29	4	Above floor
3164	B	S.114	F9	22.00	21.02	4	Floor
3165	B	S.114	E6	21.20	20.67	4	Floor
3166	B	S.114	F8	21.03	19.87	4c	
3170	B	S.119	F9	-	23.35	-	Dump
3171	B	S.119	E9	25.10	24.30	3	Mixed (balk)
3172	B	S.119	E9	24.30	24.00	3b	Floor
3173	B	S.119	E8	24.30	24.00	3b	Floor
3174	B	S.119	G8	23.50	23.21	3c	Fills
3175	B	S.119	G8	23.21	21.99	3c	Fills
3176	B	S.119	E6	24.70	24.00	-	Fill
3177	B	S.119	E6	24.00	22.49	3c	Fill
3178	B	S.119	F9	23.35	22.83	3c	Fills
3179	B	S.119	E/8–9	24.25	23.50	3b	Floor
3180	B	S.119	E8	24.00	23.00	3c	Fills
3181	B	S.119	F9	22.80	22.50	3c	Fills
3182	B	S.119	E6	22.49	22.25	3c	Fills
3183	B	S.119	H8	24.01	23.83	3c	Fills
3184	B	S.119	E8	23.50	23.40	3c	Fills

Locus	Area	Permit No.	Square	Upper Level	Lower Level	Stratum	Description
3185	B	S.119	G8	21.99	21.20	4a	Floor
3186	B	S.119	F9	22.50	22.00	3c	Fills
3187	B	S.119	E–F/8–9	23.00	22.10	3c	Fills
3188	B	S.119	E8	24.20	23.00	3c	Fills (balk)
3189	B	S.119	E6	22.25	22.09	3c	Fills
3190	B	S.119	E6	22.09	21.96	3c	Fill
3191	B	S.119	E/5–6	21.18	20.70	4	Floor
3192	B	S.119	E/5–6	20.70	-	Pre-4	
3193	B	S.119	E6	21.96	21.63	3c	Fill
3194	B	S.119	E6	21.63	20.70	4	Floor
3195	B	S.119	G8	21.20	20.70	4b	Floor
3196	B	S.119	F9	21.80	21.41	3c	Fill
3197	B	S.119	E8	24.70	21.90	3c	Fill
3198	B	S.119	E/8–9	22.20	22.00	3c	Fills
3199	B	S.119	F9	22.00	21.00	4b	Above floor
3200	B	S.119	F8	21.70	21.25	4	Floor
3201	B	S.119	G8	20.70	20.00	4b	Silo
3202	B	S.119	E9	22.00	21.70	3c	Fills
3203	B	S.119	E–F/8–9	22.00	21.70	3c	Fills
3204	B	S.119	E/8–9	21.70	21.06	4a	Floor
3205	B	S.119	F/8–9	21.80	21.20	4a	Floor
3206	B	S.119	E8	21.70	20.97	4	Floor
3207	B	S.119	E/8–9	21.06	20.84	4c?	Floor
3208	B	S.119	F/8–9	21.20	20.65	4c?	Floor
3209	B	S.119	E8	21.70	20.93	4	Floor
3210	B	S.119	F8	21.70	20.92	4b	Floor
3211	B	S.119	F8	21.60	20.92	4	Floor
3212	B	S.119	F9	21.70	20.80	4	Floor
3213	B	S.119	F8	20.95	20.28	4	Silo
4000	E	S.99	P8	-	-	4	Cleaning
4001	E	S.99	P7	21.89	-	Pre-4	Fill
4002	E	S.99	P7	21.24	21.00	-	Cleaning
4003	E	S.99	P–Q/8	21.24	-	-	Cleaning
4004	E	S.99	Q8	21.45	20.46	-	Debris in moat
4005	E	S.99	Q9	21.69	20.83	-	Fill in moat
5050	E	S.109	P6	21.40	21.30	4b	Floor makeup
5051	E	s/109	P7	21.50	21.44	4b	Floor
5052	E	S.109	P7	21.10	21.03	4b	Fill
5053	E	S.109	O7	21.60	21.14	4b	
5054	E	S.109	P6	21.31	21.21	4c	Fill
5055	E	S.109	P7	21.49	21.30	4b	Floor
5056	E	S.109	O7	21.14	21.06	4c	Fill
5057	E	S.109	P6	21.06	20.60	4c	Fill
5058	E	S.109	P6	21.16	21.03	4c	Floor
5059	E	S.109	-	21.19	21.07	-	Fill

Locus	Area	Permit No.	Square	Upper Level	Lower Level	Stratum	Description
5061	E	S.109	P7	21.03	20.00	4c	Fill
5062	E	S.109	P6	21.16	20.59	4c	Fill
5063	E	S.109	P7	21.27	20.48	4c	Fill
5064	E	S.109	P6	21.03	20.90	Pre-4	Fill
5066	H	S.109	L/N–4	21.00	20.88	-	Cleaning
5067	H	S.109	L4	20.88	20.82–20.55	-	Fill
5068	H	S.109	M4	20.88	20.61	-	Fill—cleaning
5069	H	S.109	N4	20.88	20.65	-	Fill—cleaning
5070	H	S.109	G/3–4	22.45	21.83	3a-b	Fill
5071	H	S.109	F/3–4	22.05	21.84	3a-b	Fill
5072	H	S.109	J3	-	-	-	Cleaning
5073	H	S.109	G/3–4	21.83	20.58	3a-b	Fill
5074	H	S.109	G/3–4	21.83	20.58	3a-b	Fill in channel
5075	H	S.109	G/3–4	21.83	20.60	3a-b	Fill
5076	H	S.109	F/3–4	21.21	20.42	3a-b	Fill
5077	G	S.109	C–D/5–6	-	-	-	Cleaning
5078	H	S.109	H/3–4	-	-	-	Cleaning
5079	H	S.109	F/3–4	20.43	20.09	4?	Fill
5080	H	S.109	F/3–4	20.24	19.43	4	Fill in silo
5081	H	S.109	F/3–4	20.09	19.45	4	Fill in silo
5082	H	S.109	F/3–4	20.09	-	4	Floor
5083	H	S.109	H/3–4	19.93	19.59	-	Cleaning
5084	H	S.109	H/3–4	19.91	19.51	Pre-4	Fill
5085	H	S.109	F/3–5	19.94	19.10	4	Silo
5086	H	S.109	F3	-	-	2	Cleaning
5087	H	S.109	H/3–4	19.91	19.28	Pre-4	Fill
5088	H	S.109	F3	-	-	-	Cleaning of wall
5089	H	S.109	H/3–4	19.28	18.25	Pre-4	Fill
5090	H	S.109	H/3–4	20.24	19.43	4	Silo
5091	H	S.109	G2	19.81	19.50	-	Cleaning of wall
5092	H	S.109	G2	20.10	19.71	-	Fill
6000	C	S.99	J6	-	22.71	3, 2	Fill of granary
6001	C	S.99	K7	24.16	23.73	3c	Fills
6002	C	S.99	K7	24.30	23.92	3a-b	Floor
6003	C	S.99	K7	23.99	23.95	3c	Fills—cleaning
6004	C	S.99	J7	23.88	23.53	3c	Fills
6005	C	S.99	J7	23.59	23.53	3c	Fills—cleaning
6006	C	S.99	J7	24.16	23.96	3c	Fill
6007	C	S.99	J7	-	-	-	Section
6008	C	S.99	L7	24.78	24.65	3a-b	Cleaning
6009	C	S.99	J6	23.53	23.42	3c	Fills
6010	C	S.99	J6	22.71	22.61	3, 2	Fill of granary
6011	C	S.99	J7	23.96	23.61	3c	Fills
6012	C	S.99	K7	23.92	23.74	3c	Fills
6013	C	S.99	K7	23.73	23.64	3c	Fills

Locus	Area	Permit No.	Square	Upper Level	Lower Level	Stratum	Description
6014	C	S.99	K7	23.95	23.72	3c (+1)	Fill
6015	C	S.99	L7	24.36	24.26	3a-b	Above floor
6016	C	S.99	J6	22.60	22.35	3, 2	Fill of granary
6017	C	S.99	L7	24.26	24.14	3a-b	Floor makeup
6018	C	S.99	L7	24.65	24.47	3a-b	Fill—cleaning
6019	C	S.99	J6	22.35	22.10	3, 2	Fill of granary
6020	C	S.99	L7	24.47	24.39	3a-b	Fill
6021	C	S.99	K7	23.72	23.61	3c	Fills
6022	C	S.99	K7	23.64	23.63	3c	Fills (balk)
6023	C	S.99	K7	23.74	23.60	3c	Fills
6024	C	S.99	L7	24.39	-	3a-b	Floor
6025	C	S.99	K6	22.45	22.31	3c	Fill
6026	C	S.99	J6	22.10	21.92	3, 2	Fill of granary
6027	C	S.99	J6	22.10	21.92	3, 2	Fill of granary
6028	C	S.99	L7	22.31	-	3c	Add to 6088
6029	C	S.99	L7	24.39	24.05	3a-b	Pit
6030	C	S.99	K6	22.31	-	3c	
6031	C	S.99	L7	23.99	23.93	3c	Fills
6040	C	S.109	K7	23.65	23.57	3c	Fills
6041	C	S.109	K7	23.64	23.57	3c	Fills
6042	C	S.109	K7	23.51	23.50	3c	Fill + dismantling of wall
6043	C	S.109	J7	23.58	23.50	3c	Fill–cleaning
6044	C	S.109	J6	22.10	21.95	3c	Mixed + granary
6045	C	S.109	K6	23.33	-	3c	Fills
6046	C	S.109	L6	24.26	23.94	3a-b	Cleaning
6047	C	S.109	L6	23.90	23.77	3c	Cleaning
6048	C	S.109	L7	24.21	-	3a-b	Pit—cleaning
6049	C	S.109	K7	22.45	22.37	3c	Mixed
6050	C	S.109	K7	24.55	24.60	3a-b	Dismantling of floor
6051	C	S.109	J/6–7	-	-	-	Balk
6052	C	S.109	K7	24.70	24.00	3a-b	Dismantling of wall
6053	C	S.109	L6	23.94	23.64	3c	Fills
6054	C	S.109	J7	-	24.21	3a-b	Mixed, fill
6055	C	S.109	L7	23.77	23.65	3c	Mixed, fill
6056	C	S.109	L7	25.10	24.21	-	Dismantling of wall
6057	C	S.109	L6	23.64	23.19	3c	Fills
6058	C	S.109	K6	23.30	23.14	3c	Fills
6059	C	S.109	J7	23.50	23.02	3c	Fills
6060	C	S.109	K7	23.57	23.44	3c	Fills
6061	C	S.109	K6	23.14	23.37	3c	Fills
6062	C	S.109	K7	23.98	23.44	1	Pit
6063	C	S.109	L7	24.29	-	1	Balk
6064	C	S.109	J7	-	-	1	Pit (balk)
6065	C	S.109	L6	23.19	-	3c	Fills
6066	C	S.109	L6	23.19	22.53	3c	Fills

Locus	Area	Permit No.	Square	Upper Level	Lower Level	Stratum	Description
6067	C	S.109	J6	-	-	-	Balk
6068	C	S.109	K7	23.44	22.97	3c	Fills
6069	C	S.109	K6	23.14	22.37	3c	Fills
6070	H	S.109	K4	-	-	3(?)	Silo
6071	C	S.109	L7	23.65	23.41	3c	Fills
6072	C	S.109	K7	22.97	22.45	3c	Fills
6073	C	S.109	L7	24.29	24.04	3a-b	Floor
6074	C	S.109	K7	23.37	22.84	3c	Fills (balk)
6075	H	S.109	E–F/3	-	-	-	Cleaning
6076	C	S.109	L7	24.10	23.92	3c	Fills
6077	C	S.109	J7	23.02	22.71	3c	Fills
6078	C	S.109	K7	22.84	22.37	3c	Fills
6079	G	S.109	C8	-	-	-	Cleaning
6080	C	S.109	L7	23.41	23.32	3c	Fills
6081	C	S.109	J6	21.92	21.69	3, 2	Fill of granary
6082	C	S.109	K/6–7	22.57	22.46	3c + 1	Floor? (+ pit)
6083	A2	S.109	L10	-	-	2, 1	
6084	C	S.109	L6	22.53	22.22	3c	Floor
6085	C	S.109	L7	23.92	23.32	3c, 1	Fill (?+ pit)
6086	C	S.109	J7	22.71	22.21	3c	Fills
6087	C	S.109	J7	22.21	22.05	3c	Fills
6088	C	S.109	K/6–7	22.34	22.27	3c	Ṭabun
6089	C	S.109	J7	22.05	21.75	3c	Fills
6090	C	S.109	J7	21.75	21.21	4a	Fill
6091	C	S.109	L9	-	24.68	3a-b	Cleaning
6092	C	S.109	K9	25.32	25.31	1	Cleaning
6093	C	S.109	K9	24.72	24.52	1	Pit
6094	C	S.109	L9	24.80	24.77	3a-b	Above floor
6095	C	S.109	L9	24.77	24.64	3a-b	Fill
6096	C	S.109	K/6–7	22.38	22.14	3c	Floor makeup
6098	C	S.109	L9	24.68	24.33	3c, 1	Fills (disturbed)
6099	C	S.109	J6	21.71	21.39	3, 2	Fill of granary
6100	C	S.109	L9	24.90	24.45	3a-b	Fill
6101	C	S.109	K9	24.52	-	3a-b	Fill
6102	C	S.109	K/6–7	22.03	21.85	3c	Fills
6103	C	S.109	K/6–7	22.14	21.91	3c	Fills
6104	C	S.109	K/6–7	21.91	21.46	4a	Floor
6105	C	S.109	K9	24.50	24.30	3a-b	Above floor
6106	C	S.109	K9	24.52	24.05	3a-b	Above floor
6107	C	S.109	K/6–7	21.91	21.66	4a	Above floor
6108	C	S.109	J7	21.67	21.30	4a	Above floor
6109	C	S.109	J7	21.19	21.04	4b	Floor
6110	C	S.109	K/6–7	21.66	21.55	4a	Floor
6111	C	S.109	K/6–7	21.55	21.48	4	Section
6112	C	S.109	K/6–7	21.55	21.31	4b	Floor

Locus	Area	Permit No.	Square	Upper Level	Lower Level	Stratum	Description
6113	C	S.109	K10	26.13	24.98	2	Fill (balk)
6114	C	S.109	L10	26.13	25.71	2	Cleaning
6116	A1	S.109	M/9–10	-	-	-	Cleaning
6117	C	S.109	J7	21.30	21.13	4b	Floor
6118	C	S.109	K/6–7	21.48	21.19	4b	Sections
6119	C	S.109	L10	25.71	25.40	2	Fill
6120	C	S.10-9	K/6–7	21.46	21.40	4b	Floor
6121	C	S.109	J–K/10	24.80	24.42	3a-b	Floor?
6122	C	S.109	L10	25.40	25.35	2	Living surface
6123	A1	S.109	M10	-	-	-	Cleaning
6124	A1	S.109	M10	-	-	-	Cleaning
6125	A1	S.109	M/9–10	26.38	25.95	1	Cleaning
6126	C	S.109	K/6–7	21.46	21.35	4b	Floor
6127	C	S.109	J9	-	-	-	Balk
6128	C	S.109	L/6–7	-	25.05	2	Fill
6129	C	S.109	J10	-	-	-	Fill
6130	C	S.109	K10	-	-	3a-b	Fill (balk)
6131	C	S.109	J10	-	-	3a-b	Fill
6132	C	S.109	L9	-	-	-	Cleaning
6133	C	S.109	L10	25.35	24.67	3a-b	Above floor
6134	C	S.109	L10	25.35	24.80	3a-b	Above floor
6135	C	S.109	K10	24.44	24.23	3a-b	Floor
6136	C	S.109	K10	24.61	24.16	3a-b	Floor
6137	C	S.109	K–L/9–10	-	24.38	3, 2	Fill (balk)
6138	C	S.109	K/9–10	24.30	24.23	3a-b	Floor makeup
6139	C	S.109	L6/7	25.05	24.61	3a-b	Balk
6140	C	S.109	L7	24.61	24.10	3a-b	Floor
6141	A1	S.109	M–N/9	25.95	25.77	1	
6142	C	S.109	L/6–7	24.45	24.17	3a-b	Fill
6143	A1	S.109	M/9–10	25.77	25.44	2	Burnt layer
6144	C	S.109	K/9–10	24.23	24.09	3a-b	Fill
6145	A1	S.109	M9	26.77	25.94	1	Dismantling of wall
6146	C	S.109	L9	24.74	24.50	3a-b	Floor makeup
6147	C	S.109	L7	23.34	22.05	3c	Fills
6148	C	S.109	M9	25.78	-	2	Fill
6149	A1	S.109	M9	25.44	25.08	2	Fill
6150	A1	S.109	M9	25.10	24.05	3a	Fill
6200	C	S.114	K7	21.58	21.10	3a	Dismantling of wall
6201	A1	S.114	M9	25.60	25.00	2	Fill
6202	C	S.114	K/6–7	-	-	1	Pit (= 6062)
6204	C	S.114	K7	21.20	-	-	Cleaning
6205	C	S.114	K7	21.17	-	-	Cleaning
6206	C	S.114	L7	23.33	-	3c	Mixed
6207	A1	S.114	M9	24.98	23.90	3a, 2	Fill
6208	C	S.114	L7	23.33	22.18	3c	Fills

Locus	Area	Permit No.	Square	Upper Level	Lower Level	Stratum	Description
6209	C	S.114	K6	22.02	-	3c	
6211	C	S.114	K/6–7	21.58	21.50	4a	Dismantling of wall
6212	C	S.114	K6	23.46	22.20	3c	Fills
6213	C	S.114	J6	22.32	-	3c	Cleaning
6214	C	S.114	K/6–7	21.50	-	3b	Fill
6215	C	S.114	L7	22.30	22.05	3c	Fills
6216	C	S.114	J6	22.45	22.00	3c	Fills
6217	C	S.114	K7	22.20	21.68	3c	Fills
6218	A2	S.114	J11	25.23	-	-	Trench—tower
6219	C	S.114	L7	22.41	21.68	4a, 3c	Fills
6220	C	S.114	L7	22.11	21.72	3c	Fills
6221	C	S.114	K6/7	21.50	21.08	4	
6222	C	S.114	L7	23.00	21.82	3c	Fills
6223	C	S.114	J6	21.67	21.37	3, 2	Fill of granary
6224	C	S.114	J7	24.43	23.51	3c	Fills
6225	A1	S.114	M9	-	-	3a	Cleaning
6226	C	S.114	L7	21.89	21.77	4a	Above floor
6227	C	S.114	L7	21.68	21.55	4a	Above floor
6228	C	S.114	L7	-	-	4a	Fill
6230	C	S.119	L7	-	21.21	4b	Above floor
6231	C	S.119	M9	24.65	24.18	3a-b	Fill
6232	A1	S.119	M9	26.15	24.75	3, 2	Balk
6233	A1	S.119	M9	24.75	-	3b	Fill
6234	A1	S.119	M9	-	24.41	3b	Cleaning
6235	C	S.119	L7	21.17	21.12	4b	Floor
6236	C	S.119	L7	21.37	20.95	4b	Floor
6237	C	S.119	J6	24.39	-	3, 2	Fill of granary
6243	C	S.119	J6	24.75	24.39	3a-b	Dismantling of wall
6244	C	S.119	J6	24.39	24.33	3, 2	Fill of granary
6245	C	S.119	J6	24.33	24.20	3, 2	Fill of granary
6246	C	S.119	J6	24.20	24.03	3, 2	Fill of granary
6247	C	S.119	J6	24.03	23.56	3, 2	Fill of granary
6248	C	S.119	J6	23.56	23.41	3, 2	Fill of granary
6249	C	S.119	J6	23.41	23.00	3, 2	Fill of granary
6250	C	S.119	J6	23.00	22.78	3, 2	Fill of granary
6251	C	S.119	J6	22.78	22.62	3, 2	Fill of granary
6252	C	S.119	J6	22.62	22.46	3, 2	Fill of granary
6253	C	S.119	J6	22.46	22.34	3, 2	Fill of granary
6254	C	S.119	J6	22.34	22.17	3, 2	Fill of granary
6255	C	S.119	J6	22.17	22.07	3, 2	Fill of granary
6256	C	S.119	J6	22.07	21.87	3, 2	Fill of granary
6257	C	S.119	J6	21.87	21.60	3, 2	Fill of granary
6258	C	S.119	J6	-	-	3, 2	Sections—granary
6259	C	S.119	J6	21.60	21.50	3, 2	Floor of granary
6261	C	S.119	K9	23.99	23.34	3c	Fill, dismantling of wall

Locus	Area	Permit No.	Square	Upper Level	Lower Level	Stratum	Description
6262	A1	S.119	M9	24.65	24.15	3b	Fill
6263	A1	S.119	M9	24.20	24.15	3b	Fill
6264	A1	S.119	M9	24.63	24.20	3b	Fill
6265	A1	S.119	M9	23.66	23.48	3c	Fills
6266	A1	S.119	M9	23.95–23.52	23.48	3c	Fills
6267	C	S.119	K9	23.76–23.34	23.16	3c	Fills
6268	C	S.119	L7	-	-	-	Balk
6269	C	S.119	K9	-	-	-	Cleaning—section
6270	A1	S.119	M9	-	-	-	Cleaning—section
6271	C	S.119	L9	25.30	24.40	3a-b	Dismantling of wall
6272	C	S.119	K9	23.34	22.83	3c	Fills
6273	C	S.119	K9	23.34	22.83	3c	Fills
6274	C	S.119	L9	24.44	24.03	3c	Fills
6275	C	S.119	L9	24.46	23.85	3c	Fills
6276	C	S.119	L9	23.48	23.14	3c	Fills
6277	C	S.119	K9	24.69	24.55	3a-b	Above floor
6278	C	S.119	K9	24.55	24.44	3a-b	Floor
6279	C	S.119	K9	22.83	22.46	3c	Fills
6280	C	S.119	K9	-	-	2	Fill (balk)
6281	C	S.119	L/9–10	23.75	23.29	3c	Fills
6282	C	S.119	L9	23.86	23.34	3c	Fills
6283	C	S.119	K9	-	-	-	Dismantling of wall
6284	C	S.119	K–L/9–10	23.30	22.47	3c	Fills
6285	C	S.119	K–L/9	23.07	22.29	4	Above wall
6287	C	S.119	L9	22.87	22.10	4	Fill
6288	C	S.119	L9	23.03	21.91	4	Above floor
6289	C	S.119	L9	22.10	21.59	4	Above floor
6290	A1	S.119	M10	-	-	4, 3, 2	Balk
6291	C	S.119	J6	21.50	21.40	3a-b	Floor of granary
6292	C	S.119	L9	21.59	-	4	Floor
6293	C	S.119	K–L/9	22.93	21.60	4	Test trench
6294	C	S.119	L9	21.60	21.17	4	Floor and installation
6295	C	S.119	K/6–7	-	-	4–1	Balk
6296	C	S.119	K/6–7	-	-	-	Balk
6297	C	S.119	K9	21.40	-	-	Add to 6293
6298	C	S.119	L–M/10	-	-	3c	Fills
6299	C	S.119	L9	22.70	22.11	4	Above floor
6300	C	S.119	L9	22.11	21.81	4	Above floor
6301	C	S.119	L9	21.81	21.61	4	Floor makeup
6302	C	S.119	L9	21.61	21.49	4c	Below floor
6303	C	S.119	L9	21.49	21.15	Pre-4	Virgin soil
6304	C	S.119	L10	22.40	21.50	4	Above floor
6310	C	S.119	J6	21.40	21.03	Pre-4	Below silo
6500	G	S.109	C/8–9	21.72	21.42	3c	Fill
6501	G	S.109	C–D/6	24.13	23.03	2	Fill of glacis
6502	G	S.109	D6	23.03	22.86	3a-b	*Ṭabun on* floor

Locus	Area	Permit No.	Square	Upper Level	Lower Level	Stratum	Description
6503	F	S.109	C11	19.22	19.02	2	Fill in moat
6504	G	S.109	C–D/6	23.03	22.86	3a-b	Floor
7000	F	S.99	L11	23.34	22.14	3c	Fills
7001	F	S.99	L11	22.14	21.98	3c	Fills
7002	F	S.99	L11	21.98	21.53	4b	Above floor
7003	F	S.99	L11	21.98	21.32	4b, c	Debris
7004	F	S.99	M11	21.98	21.76	4b	Above floor
7005	F	S.99	M12	21.89	21.59	4b	Debris
7006	F	S.99	L11	21.98	21.41	4b, c	Test trench
7007	F	S.99	M11	21.76	21.48	4c	Fill
7021	F	S.109	L11	-	21.46	4	Cleaning
7022	F	S.109	K11	22.08	21.40	4	Above floor
7023	F	S.109	M/11–12	21.46	21.14	4c	
7024	F	S.109	M/11–12	21.46	21.14	4c	
7025	F	S.109	L–M/12	21.43	18.96	2, 1	Fill in moat
7026	F	S.109	K12	22.00	18.40	2, 1	Debris
7027	F	S.109	L11	21.07	21.04	Pre-4	Cleaning
7028	F	S.109	K11	21.22	20.41	Pre-4	Fill
7029	F	S.109	M/11–12	21.14	21.00	Pre-4	Fill
7030	F	S.109	M/11–12	21.14	20.96	Pre-4	Fill
7031	F	S.109	K11	21.40	20.40	Pre-4	Fill
7032	E	S.109	P/11–12	23.54	21.37	2, 1	Cleaning
7033	F	S.109	K–M/13	-	21.66	2, 1	Cleaning
7034	F	S.109	K11	20.41	19.67	-	Virgin soil
7035	F	S.109	J12	21.98	20.15	-	Moat
7036	F	S.109	M13	18.96	18.64	2, 1	Fill in moat
7037	F	S.109	O13	19.54	18.68	2, 1	Fill in moat
7038	F	S.109	K12	18.40	17.92	2, 1	Floor in moat
7039	F	S.109	K13	17.92	17.34	2, 1	Fill in moat
7050	F	S.114	K13	17.85	17.78	2, 1	Installation
7051	F	S.114	K13	17.85	17.83	2, 1	Fill in moat
7052	F	S.114	K13	17.96	17.26	2, 1	Fill in moat
7053	F	S.114	K13	18.98	18.86	-	Virgin soil
8000	G	S.114	C–D/6	22.82	22.58	3a-b	Paved floor
8001	G	S.114	C/8–9	20.38	20.03	Pre-4(?)	Fill
8002	G	S.114	B3	19.40	18.56	2, 1	Fill in moat
8003	G	S.114	C4	-	20.83	3a-b	Paved floor
8004	G	S.114	C3	21.89	21.00	3a-b	Paved floor
8005	G	S.114	C3	19.70	18.85	2, 1	Fill in moat
8006	G	S.114	C5	-	22.58	3a-b	Paved floor
8007	G	S.114	C–D/6	22.79	21.79	3c	Fill
8008	G	S.114	C/D6	21.79	21.00	3c	Fill
8009	G	S.114	C4	-	22.20	3a-b	Paved floor
8010	G	S.114	B3	-	-	4	Above floor
8011	G	S.114	D6	20.71	20.57	4	Floor
8012	G	S.114	C/D6	20.55	20.40	4	Floor

IAA Reports

No. 1 G. Avni and Z. Greenhut, *The Akeldama Tombs: Three Burial Caves in the Kidron Valley, Jerusalem*, 1996, 129 pp.

No. 2 E. Braun, *Yiftaḥ'el: Salvage and Rescue Excavations at a Prehistoric Village in Lower Galilee, Israel*, 1997, 249 pp.

No. 3 G. Edelstein, I. Milevski and S. Aurant, *Villages, Terraces and Stone Mounds: Excavations at Manaḥat, Jerusalem, 1987–1989*, 1998, 149 pp.

No. 4 C. Epstein, *The Chalcolithic Culture of the Golan*, 1998, 352 pp. + plans. Hardcover.

No. 5 T. Schick, *The Cave of the Warrior: A Fourth Millennium Burial in the Judean Desert*, 1998, 137 pp.

No. 6 R. Cohen, *Ancient Settlement of the Central Negev: The Chalcolithic Period, the Early Bronze Age and the Middle Bronze Age* I (Hebrew, English Summary), 1999, 396 pp.

No. 7 R. Hachlili and A. Killebrew, *Jericho: The Jewish Cemetery of the Second Temple Period*, 1999, 202 pp.

No. 8 Z. Gal and Y. Alexandre, *Ḥorbat Rosh Zayit: An Iron Age Storage Fort and Village*, 2000, 247 pp.

No. 9 U. Dahari, *Monastic Settlements in South Sinai in the Byzantine Period: The Archaeological Remains*, 2000, 250 pp. + map.

No. 10 Z. Yeivin, *The Synagogue at Korazim: The 1962–1964, 1980–1987 Excavations* (Hebrew, English Summary), 2000, 216 pp.

No. 11 M. Hartal, *The al-Ṣubayba (Nimrod) Fortress: Towers 11 and 9*, 2001, 129 pp.

No. 12 R. Gonen, *Excavations at Efrata: A Burial Ground from the Intermediate and Middle Bronze Ages*, 2001, 153 pp.

No. 13 E. Eisenberg, A. Gopher and R. Greenberg, *Tel Te'o: A Neolithic, Chalcolithic and Early Bronze Age Site in the Ḥula Valley*, 2001, 227 pp.

No. 14 R. Frankel, N. Getzov, M. Aviam and A. Degani, *Settlement Dynamics and Regional Diversity in Ancient Upper Galilee: Archaeological Survey of Upper Galilee*, 2001, 175 pp. + color distribution maps and foldout map.

No. 15 M. Dayagi-Mendels, *The Akhziv Cemeteries: The Ben-Dor Excavations, 1941–1944*, 2002, 176 pp.

No. 16 Y. Goren and P. Fabian, *Kissufim Road: A Chalcolithic Mortuary Site*, 2002, 97 pp.

No. 17 A. Kloner, *Maresha Excavations Final Report* I: *Subterranean Complexes 21, 44, 70*, 2003, 183 pp.

No. 18 A. Golani, *Salvage Excavations at the Early Bronze Age Site of Qiryat 'Ata*, 2003, 261 pp.

No. 19 H. Khalaily and O. Marder, *The Neolithic Site of Abu Ghosh: The 1995 Excavations*, 2003, 146 pp.

No. 20 R. Cohen and R. Cohen-Amin, *Ancient Settlement of the Negev Highlands* II (Hebrew, English Summary), 2004, 258 pp.

No. 21 D. Stacey, *Exavations at Tiberias, 1973–1974*: *The Early Islamic Periods*, 2004, 259 pp.

No. 22 Y. Hirschfeld, *Excavations at Tiberias, 1989–1994*, 2004, 234 pp.

No. 23 S. Ben-Arieh, *Bronze and Iron Age Tombs at Tell Beit Mirsim*, 2004, 212 pp.

No. 24 M. Dothan and D. Ben-Shlomo, *Ashdod VI: The Excavations of Areas H and K (1968–1969)*, 2005, 320 pp.

No. 25 M. Avissar, *Tel Yoqne'am: Excavations on the Acropolis*, 2005, 142 pp.

No. 26 M. Avissar and E.J. Stern, *Pottery of the Crusader, Ayyubid, and Mamluk Periods in Israel*, 2005, 187 pp., 53 figs., 34 color plates.

No. 27 E.C.M. van den Brink and Ram Gophna, *Shoham (North), Late Chalcolithic Burial Caves in the Lod Valley, Israel*, 2005, 214 pp.

No. 28 N. Getzov, *The Tel Bet Yeraḥ Excavations, 1994–1995*, 2006, 204 pp.

No. 29 A.M. Berlin, *Gamla* I: *The Pottery of the Second Temple Period, the Shmarya Gutmann Excavations, 1976–1989*, 2006, 181 pp.

No. 30 R. Greenberg, E. Eisenberg, S. Paz and Y. Paz, *Bet Yeraḥ: The Early Bronze Age Mound* I: *Excavation Reports, 1933–1986*, 2006, 500 pp.

No. 31 E. Yannai, *'En Esur ('Ein Asawir)* I: *Excavations at a Protohistoric Site in the Coastal Plain of Israel*, 2006, 308 pp.

No. 32 T.J. Barako, *Tel Mor: The Moshe Dothan Excavations, 1959–1960*, 2007, 276 pp.

No. 33 G. Mazor and A. Najjar, *Bet She'an* I: *Nysa-Scythopolis: The Caesareum and the Odeum*, 2007, 316 pp.

No. 34 R. Cohen and H. Bernick-Greenberg, *Kadesh Barnea (Tell el-Qudeirat) 1976–1982*, 2007. In 2 parts. Part 1: Text, 410 pp.; Part 2: Plates, Plans and Sections, 332 pp.